MARRIAGE AND FAMILY

SOCIOLOGY SERIES
John F. Cuber, Editor
Alfred C. Clarke, Associate Editor

MARRIAGE AND FAMILY
A DEVELOPMENTAL APPROACH

Atlee L. Stroup
The College of Wooster

New York
APPLETON-CENTURY-CROFTS
Division of Meredith Publishing Company

This book is dedicated to
TWYLA SCHMUCKER STROUP

Foreword

This is a time when newspapers herald a new revolution almost every day of the year, when research findings pour from the universities in staggering profusion, when the ink is hardly dry on a research study dealing with sex, marriage, or family before its results are—sometimes shrilly—reported in the press.

Seen in perspective, the so-called "sexual renaissance" or "sexual revolution" of midcentury takes on the aspect of an accelerating social movement rather than of a sudden or apocalyptic change. There was the first restless stirring in the early years of the century; an avant garde under the leadership of Freud probing deeply into the psyche produced by the Victorian family; new and unaccustomed demands being made on women by the new industrialism, by wars, by depressions; questioning and uncertainty about the relations between the sexes; the long process of de-tabooing sex as each generation of writers went farther and farther in an almost compulsive apotheosis of sex; an increasingly open preoccupation with homosexuality, with sadism, with masochism, with the sexually bizarre. And, along with this insistence on the offbeat, an equally strident insistence that sex could, should, even must conform to certain ideal canons of perfection . . . By the middle and late 1960's, sex had become the subject of satire. A magazine originally addressed to men only found the oppressive emphasis on female orgasm fair game for its malicious barbs. An early rebel against the Victorian sexual ethos now himself protested against the excesses of the movement . . .

In such a time it is important to have this sober, scholarly book assemble a whole generation of research and present it in reassuring perspective. This book does more. It evaluates the great mass of research and shows how the parts dovetail, thus adding greatly to its contribution. History, we are told, must be rewritten every generation. So, too, must research be reinterpreted by every generation. The author is not afraid to let his own values show in the process. Students will be especially appreciative of this, whether they agree with him on every issue or not. They will recognize a sincere and honest man wrestling with some of the most puzzling issues of our time, convinced by the evidence in favor of his point of view, but as far from removed from dogmatism as from indifference.

The author addresses himself to middle-class readers without apologies or excuses. He does not fall into the fallacy of implying that "middle class" values are capricious or quaint. He does not quail before the sometimes pejorative implications of the term. By the late 1960's research on culturally deprived children had made us aware of the really complex curriculum most middle-class children had been through by the time they entered school; the importance of child-rearing practices was newly appreciated. It was something we learned from "middle-class" values.

This book, finally, hews to no doctrinaire line. It is in the tradition of the so-called functional approach. But it by no means scants attention to the institutional aspects of the subject. Its historical data enrich our understanding of the current scene. Social psychological data have been mined for their contribution. The author, in brief, is interested in presenting relevant information whatever its source, whatever its "brand name." Still the book never becomes merely encyclopedic. The result is a well-rounded book that both student and teacher, I am sure, will find useful and enlightening.

Jessie Bernard
Research Scholar Honoris Causa
Pennsylvania State University

Preface

The author of a textbook in the marriage and family field has many difficult choices to make. Materials are available from a wide variety of sources. These can be collated and presented in any number of ways. The mere collection and presentation of information from diverse sources however do not necessarily lead to wisdom on the part of the reader. If care is not exercised, the use of such materials may instead simply encourage dilettantism and superficiality.

Coming from their individual backgrounds of experience and interest, students have their own expectations which they bring to a marriage and family course. Their interests are often primarily practical. Many want reliable advice on mate selection, marital relationships, and child rearing. These concerns are perfectly reasonable, and student questions must somehow be answered. But educators must challenge students to probe deeply, to find sound bases from which to make practical decisions. Superficial advice has no place in the collegiate program.

With this in mind, an attempt has been made to write an integrated, substantial book which will provide both a theoretical understanding of the American marriage and family system and a foundation for practical decision-making. It is hoped that the book will be "functional" in the truest sense of the term.

The subject field is approached first by reference to historical materials and institutional aspects of the American family system. Building on this base, a developmental approach is used starting with mate selection and continuing through the life cycle. More stress is placed on parent-child relationships than is common in marriage and family text books. While the focus is on the interaction within the marriage and family system, attention is always given to the larger society within which this interaction takes place. In Chapter 1 a detailed discussion of the frame of reference of the book is presented.

The orientation of the author is essentially that of the family sociologist. Practical experience and training in marriage counseling will be reflected in certain portions of the book. The bulk of the materials have been developed in the author's own teaching experience. Some central ideas reflect seminar participation under Dr. Reuben Hill, now with the Family Study Center of the University of Minnesota.

I owe a special debt to Professors John F. Cuber, editor of the Sociology Series, and Raymond Sletto, of the Ohio State University, who encouraged me to pursue advanced study in the marriage and family field. A debt of gratitude is owed Dr. Emily Mudd who arranged for and supervised my marriage counseling in-service training at the Marriage Council of Philadelphia, Department of Psychiatry, University of Pennsylvania.

While it is impossible to acknowledge all the individuals to whom I am indebted for material used, I wish to thank the various authors who gave permission to quote from their respective works.

In addition to the above mentioned the following individuals have been of direct help in one way or another: Charles Bowerman, Ernest Q. Campbell, Charles Erasmus, Paul Glasser, Donald Irish, Hallowell Pope, Daniel Price and Richard Simpson.

I wish to express my appreciation to President Howard F. Lowry and Dean J. Garber Drushal of The College of Wooster for their sustained interest in and support of this project. Miss Maudie Nesbitt and her efficient library staff have been very helpful in many ways. Mrs. Edna Comin offered important assistance at crucial periods.

Paul K. Jentes, M.D. is listed as collaborator for Chapter 19. This does not do justice to his contributions, which were substantial in providing medical information for Chapter 18 as well.

My wife, Twyla, has offered constant encouragement and has contributed directly to the project through typing various drafts of the manuscript and handling of various editorial chores.

Our children Rick, Carrie, Glenda, and Will deserve credit for their willingness to await the return of their father to the ranks of regular people.

A. L. S.

Contents

one

Orientation and Introduction

1

The Study of Marriage and Family

Even Adam and Eve did not escape some of the difficulties of marriage, as any student of the Old Testament knows. In fact, certain learned Patriarchs claim that most of our marriage and family troubles started with Eve's tempting Adam. While this theory may be disputed, that early man and woman had no easy task getting marriage and family life started on a harmonious basis is suggested by an Indian story of man's first reaction to woman:

(And the Lord made woman and gave her to man.) But after one week, man came to him and said: 'Lord, this creature that you have given me makes my life miserable. She chatters incessantly and teases me beyond endurance, never leaving me alone; and she requires incessant attention, and takes all my time up, and cries about nothing, and is always idle; and so I have come to give her back again, as I cannot live with her.' So the Lord said: 'Very well;' and he took her back. Then after another week, man came again to him and said; 'Lord, I find that my life is very lonely, since I gave you back that creature. I remember how she used to dance and sing to me, and look at me out of the corner of her eye, and play with me, and cling to me; and her laughter was music, and she was beautiful to look at, and soft to touch; so give her back to me again.' So the Lord said: 'Very well;' and gave her back again. Then after only three days, man came back to him again and said: 'Lord, I know now how it is; but after all I have come to the conclusion that she is more of a trouble than a pleasure to me; so please take her back again.' But the Lord said: 'Out on you! Be off! I will have no more of this. You must manage how you can.' Then man said: 'But I cannot live with her.' And the Lord replied: 'Neither could you live without her.' And he turned his back on man, and went on with his work. Then man said: 'What is to be done? For I cannot live either with her or without her.' [1]

[1] Reprinted by permission of G. P. Putnam's Sons from *A Digit of the Moon* by F. W. Bain. Copyright, 1905.

3

Dilemmas regarding marriage and family are, then, not just modern phenomena. Solomon wondered about "the way of a man with a maid," basing his observations on considerable experience. The great Count Keyserling spoke of marriage as "a tragic state of tension." [2] He asked why man should enter this estate. "Is not the risk too great? Is it worth the effort?" he questioned.

Many modern young people are interested in preparation for marriage and family living. They know that problems arise and that many marriages are not ideal. If they are realistic, they sense that marriage will not be just one long honeymoon and that family living will present many challenges. Most people apparently reason, as did Count Keyserling after his queries, that life including marriage "is not a tragedy in the last resort, and for this reason, in spite of its drawbacks, it is beautiful and consequently, where conjugal happiness is achieved, it outweighs all possible suffering." [3]

Many young adults appreciate the fact that the veil has been partially lifted from marriage and family and that it can now be studied. It is to such that this book is dedicated. A little knowledge is a dangerous thing. We must, therefore, probe deeply into our subject in order to achieve understanding. To develop a background for such probing, we turn, in this chapter to a consideration of the American system of marriage and family. This will be followed by a brief discussion of its relationship to other social systems. After a description of some basic concepts which will be used in the book, and some alternative approaches to the study of marriage and family, the point of view of this book will be delineated.

THE AMERICAN SYSTEM OF MARRIAGE AND FAMILY

In the various studies of marriage and family in America a number of major features stand out as preponderant characteristics. Monogamy is the accepted legal form of marriage. Young people select their mates with a relatively free hand, with parents exercising limited control. There is a tendency for mates to be chosen from within a circle of eligibles from relatively similar class or ethnic backgrounds, although with the exception of the prohibition of interracial marriage in certain states, such practice is not required by law. Once the couple are married they establish a residence apart from both sets of relatives, keeping some contact with them socially and emotionally. The prevailing ethos suggests that the young couple will rise above the social level of the parental families if possible, or at least attain a higher level of living. To do this it may be necessary to move about both geographically and socially, following opportunity as it beckons.

[2] Count Hermann Keyserling, *The Book of Marriage* (New York, Harcourt, Brace & World, 1926), pp. 47–48.
[3] *Ibid.*

Romantic considerations rather than prudential motivations are presumed to lead young people to choose partners and to marry. Once they are married, their romance is not expected to die.[4] A plethora of advice as to how it can be retained or enhanced continues to pour in from various sources. It is not considered proper that the husband have romantic liaisons outside the home, although this, as a subrosa venture, is by no means uncommon. Marriages in which love has waned are often but by no means always considered poor marriages, and while divorce is considered to be unfortunate, it is accepted as a method of escape for those who cannot continue with their marriages.

It is understood that within marriage certain tasks must be performed in order that the couple and their children can receive personal satisfaction. There is not, however, a general feeling of responsibility to community, church, or state with respect to the social functions performed. Rather the functions are performed within the family circle to satisfy the needs of the persons involved. From the point of view of the family members, marriage and family exist to fulfill the personalities of husband and wife and to develop the personalities of children. This is in sharp contrast to cultures where the individual is considered to be perpetuating a family line to which he owes duty and obedience. Marriage and family life tends then to become individuated and there is minimum recourse to the larger family when strain develops.

The basic structure of the American family is not secure. Given the high expectations with which people enter marriage, it is inevitable that often their hopes are not achieved. Roles are not clearly defined and an equalitarian ethos prevails. This means that the wife-mother may challenge the husband-father for the leadership role that in traditional societies would have been his by right. In general, however, the male is expected to take the lead in decision-making of great importance to family welfare.[5]

Children are desired as extensions of the parents. There is an emphasis on the quality rather than quantity of children. This has sometimes been called the "century of the child" because children are given both greater attention and greater freedom than in former generations. The wife of a visiting professor from Pakistan remarked that the situation in America is certainly a contrast to that in Pakistan, for "In America children are the masters."

By way of summary we can use Sirjamaki's identification of family configurations in America:

1. Marriage is a dominating life-goal for men as well as for women.
2. The giving and taking in marriage should be based on personal affection and choice.

[4] Clark Ellzey, *Romance in Christian Marriage* (New York, Association Press, 1958).
[5] John Sirjamaki, "Culture Configurations in the American Family," *American Journal of Sociology,* Vol. 53 (May, 1948), pp. 464–470.

3. The criterion of successful marriage is the personal happiness of husband and wife.
4. The best years of life are those of youth, and its qualities are the most desirable.
5. Children should be reared in a child's world and shielded from too early participation in adult woes and tribulations.
6. The exercise of sex should be contained within wedlock.
7. Family roles of husband and wife should be based on a sexual division of labor, but with the male status being superior.
8. Individual, not familial, values are to be sought in family living.[6]

These are covert sentiments rather than overt behavior patterns. They are "moral standards to secure some degree of conformance." These configurations are basic to the value system of this particular country. Regarding marriage and family, ". . . they furnish the meanings and determine right and wrong behavior in courting, in husband-wife and parent-child relationships, in heterosexual social activity and in ideas about sex," says Sirjamaki.[7]

Some may doubt that these configurations will hold for certain segments of the American population. Just how seriously they are taken by all is indeed a moot question. There are regional, class, and other variations. In spite of this they may still in the words of the author, ". . . express the dominant values which are thought to be necessary for the continued functioning of the society."

RELATIONS WITH OTHER SOCIAL SYSTEMS

The marital or family group does not live in isolation. Its members go back and forth between the outside world and the home. As we shall describe in more detail later, outside systems have a tremendous impact upon the family. Formerly the American family was a productive unit characterized by something approximating self-sufficiency. Now the *family* is far from this. Where would the average family be today without the organized school, the factory system and networks of business organization, the police, fire, and other protective services, the specialized governmental services, or the organized church? Reflections on the depression of the thirties will remind any adult of the consequences for families when the economic machine grinds to a halt. The forties demonstrated convincingly that the military machine can rend many a family structure asunder.

This relationship with the outside world is a two-way street. For example, the family is expected to give at least elementary training to the child so that he can enter the larger community after being finally "proc-

[6] *Ibid.,* pp. 465–470. Reprinted by permission.
[7] *Ibid.,* p. 465.

essed" in the school. When it is thought that the family is not meeting general community expectations, people accuse it of neglecting its duty. At times in a dynamic society disagreements will arise as to a proper balance of functions and relationships between two or three systems. The question of character education of children involving home, church, and school is a case in point. The community is of course dependent on the various appropriate families for backing and support. Voluntary community agencies must have families who give of time, services, finances, and general moral support if they are to function.

The family and the industrial systems are functionally interdependent. From the home come workers for the industrial machine. The home consumes many of the goods turned out for distribution in the market place. The industrial worker must first of all have been trained in minimum skills and attitudes which will motivate him toward achievement in work or other arenas. It is in the family that this training and orientation first takes place.[8] Further, the worker usually is concerned with producing in order to benefit, in money wages, members of a family unit or a potential family unit rather than himself alone.

In various types of societies, including capitalistic ones, the economic system makes some adjustment to the family system. Special conditions obtain for women workers as against men, young people as against adults, etc. In a number of modern countries it is mandatory that the pregnant mother's job be held for her return after the birth of the child.

Modernization in the economic realm usually spells doom to the traditional large family system, according to various authorities. The old-fashioned, large, extended family was better suited to an agricultural economy than to an industrialized one. Even the modern nuclear family must adapt to the large, industrial complexes. It is suggested that often the wives of men in management are made to feel that their husbands are "owned" by the company.

At times in a dynamic society disagreements will arise as to a proper balance of functions and relations between two or three subsystems. An example would be that of character or moral development of the child in America. At present there is some confusion regarding the appropriate roles of the family, the school, and the church.

SOME CONCEPTS AND DEFINITIONS

In this book, as a general rule, technical terms will be defined as they appear. It is necessary to clarify a few basic concepts at this point, however, since they are not consistently used in the literature.

[8] Ernest Burgess, Harvey Locke, and Mary Thomes, *The Family: From Institution to Companionship,* 3rd ed. (New York, American Book, 1963), p. 7.

First, marriage is a special kind of relationship between two people. It may be defined in our society as a socially sanctioned union of a man and woman as husband and wife. Burgess and Locke distinguish marriage and mating—animals mate but man marries. This indicates that marriage is more than a sexual relationship. It involves a complex of role relationships which are allowed or expected in a culture. In other words, society systematizes or institutionalizes the relations between the sexes. In some societies plural marriages are allowed. This may involve either *polygyny,* with one man having several wives, or *polyandry,* the marriage of one woman to a number of husbands. In the great majority of societies where plural unions are allowed most marriages are monogamous. To what extent this is due to sentiment and exclusive affection and to what extent it is due to economic considerations is not known.

The *family* is a term upon which there is not full agreement. Just which persons are to be included, what purposes must be served, whether all members must have a common residence, and other such questions are under debate. A standard definition specifies that "the family is a group of two or more persons related by blood, marriage, or adoption, who reside in a common household, interact and communicate with each other in their respective family roles, and create and maintain a common culture." [9] Various types of families will be discussed later in the book. The family unit of parents and children which Americans regard as typical is spoken of as the *nuclear* or *conjugal* family. In many societies an extended or large family system is common. In such cases relatives of a number of degrees and generations live together, and function more or less as a unit.

Culture is not used by social scientists to mean refinement of taste. It refers to the way of life or the social heritage of the particular society under discussion. Specifically, it refers to the "patterns of learned behavior and the products of this behavior, typically exhibited by the members of a society." [10] All groups of men have been forced to come to grips with a number of basic problems to insure survival. Culture represents the patterned ways men in a particular group have developed to meet these problems and make adjustments and adaptations. The concept of culture is highly important since man is not a creature well supplied with instincts. No instinct is available to teach one how to read a book, arrange a spray of flowers, boil a lobster, catch a pass, use a finger bowl, solve a riddle, grill a steak or conduct a romance. This lack of fixed, inborn behavior patterns gives man a great measure of freedom, but also demands that adaptations be made in order that basic needs be met. A *subculture* or subcultural group refers to a segment within a larger culture which is distinct enough in its ways and ideas to be separately identified.

[9] *Ibid.*
[10] A. L. Kroeber and Clyde Kluckhohn, *Culture: A Critical Review of Concepts and Definitions, Peabody Museum Papers,* Vol. 1, No. 1 (Harvard University, 1952).

Society is used ordinarily to refer to a group of persons large enough to be organized and to have its own culture. Sometimes the terms society and culture are used synonymously, although this does not make for conceptual clarity. In most if not all societies differences in status exist. That is, some individuals outrank others on the basis of a certain criterion. Valuations used to rank people differ from one culture to another, but family background, wealth, occupation, amount of education, area of residence, and the like are often used. If a segment or particular level stands out, it may become known as a *social class*. The land-owning gentry of Prussia, the Junkers, were an example of an *upper class*. In our society disagreement exists as to whether or not we have a clear-cut system of social classes or simply a continuum of social status. There is, however, a definite tendency to speak of upper, middle, or lower classes in the United States. One school of thought insists that subdivisions are found within each of these categories.[11]

FRAMES OF REFERENCE

A number of theoretical approaches are possible as bases for the study of marriage and the family. A few generations ago the approach generally used was historical. There was great concern with the origins of marriage and the family, and much time was spent trying to determine what the "natural" family was like. Attention was also given to the possibility of evolutionary stages through which the family must, according to some authorities, inevitably have passed. The search for social origins came at a time when anthropology was becoming established, and this led some scholars to studies of marriage and family practices among preliterates of the Nonwestern World.

Both of these approaches essentially involved the study of the family as an institution. The first focused on the family and social change over time. The second tended to compare marriage and family forms and practices in various societies, with some attention usually given to the relation of the family to the larger institutional structure. Both were essentially descriptive approaches. Over the years new developments in social science, especially in sociology, led to what may be termed an analytical approach. The family as a social institution was analyzed, both in terms of its inner workings and its relation to other institutions.

Two recent, compatible developments have occurred which have an important bearing on marriage and family study. One is the development in sociology and anthropology of the structure-function approach. The family is conceived as a social system which interacts with other systems in society

---

[11] See W. Lloyd Warner and Paul Lunt, *The Status System of a Modern Community* (New Haven, Yale, 1942), and other works by the Warner group.

to form a social network. Concern is or can be given either to the inner workings of the family or its functions as performed for the total society. A second development which merits attention is the impact of social psychology on the marriage and family field. The family with this approach is considered in its interpersonal relationships, as a "unity of interacting personalities."

All of these approaches to marriage and the family have their demerits as well as merits. For example, an appreciation of family life in the past can help give added perspective to the student who is all too often the captive of his own period. But the problems of the present persist, and esoteric and ancient solutions to them are not necessarily appropriate. Further, an historical approach must cover vast territories and eons of time in a very generalized fashion. Particular familial situations and problems tend to be overlooked. Therefore, it is difficult to bridge the gap between historical treatment and family issues of our present day.

Since we are concerned with a solid underpinning of theory and research as a basis for understanding present-day marriage and family life, we need an outline for the selection and interpretation of information and data which will provide a maximum breadth. We have chosen therefore one particular social psychological orientation called the "developmental." As Hill and Hansen say, this represents "an attempt to transcend the boundaries of several approaches through incorporation of their compatible sections into one unified scheme." [12] Parts of the system come from different disciplines. The concept of a family life cycle has been borrowed from rural sociology, and developmental tasks and needs from child development. From the structure-function theory has been taken the concept of functional prerequisites as basic to family stability.

This approach will be explained in detail in Chapter 4. Here we need only point out that its merit is that it provides a framework around which a wide variety of information and reflective effort can be organized. Using this approach, we begin in Part Two with an analysis of the American mate-selection system. This is the stage of development at which the individual leaves his parental family to move out toward bisexual association and sooner or later toward marriage. Once marriage takes place, a new group is started which has a life history that can be projected from its beginning to its disintegration, within a fairly uniform series of stages. The couple is seen moving through the early years of marriage into parenthood. Considerable discussion is involved with the preschool family and the family with school-age children. Chapter 25 gives a telescoped treatment of the later stages of the family cycle through the stage of eventual, complete contraction.

[12] Reuben Hill and Donald Hansen, "The Identification of Conceptual Frameworks Utilized in Family Study," *Marriage and Family Living,* Vol. 22 (November, 1960), p. 307.

This developmental approach seems particularly appropriate for at least three reasons: (1) It focuses on the typical form of an isolated nuclear family, which is emerging in American society; (2) Regardless of the background from which the student may come, he has ordinarily been a member of a family that has been going through a developmental cycle, and he will probably move into a new one of his own; and (3) The model provides a better framework in which to consider so-called "practical" questions than do the other approaches.

It must again be made clear that we have borrowed materials from various disciplines when this seemed appropriate for pedagogical purposes. Chapters 12 and 19 are sections which include medical and biological materials. Information from other sources will be noted from time to time in the book. The point is that some frame of reference will and should predominate in a book for integrative purposes. Otherwise, the student may end up with an encyclopedic mass of facts which are not as meaningful as they might be.

It must be granted that while an eclectic approach has the advantage of being broader in its coverage, the treatment may become such a hodgepodge that only confusion and fatigue result. The developmental approach seems to be a good compromise because it draws freely from divergent sources and yet integrates materials into a reasonably logical framework. This is perhaps the best that can be accomplished at this time, given the present stage of developments in research, theory, and clinical work in marriage and family life.

MIDDLE-CLASS FOCUS

As is true of most textbooks on marriage, this book has as its major focus marriage and family in the middle class of American society. This emphasis is easy to justify. Most readers of this book will probably be from this class or at least will be oriented to marriage and family life at this social level. Further, most of our research studies have used middle-class people as research sources.

This is not to suggest that the emerging American marriage and family system is the only valid model available. It is not. The systems of former eras have many advantages, especially in terms of stability. Some of our sectarian groups such as the Amish have a type of family life that is possibly more healthful and fulfilling to their members than is family life to the average middle-class American. We are not suggesting then that it is necessarily desirable that middle-class values prevail at all times for all people. Simpson seems on solid ground when he suggests that if certain norms are held up by society as models and then those beneath them are blocked in their striving towards the models, serious strain results.[13] It is a moot question whether it is fair that the habits, language, and perspective of the lower-class child be judged by the standards which prevail in the middle-class home. On the other hand, it is hard to deny that the urban, middle-class values do have a tremendous impact throughout our total institutional structure; therefore, it seems appropriate that a book have as its focus that system which has the greatest probability of being the type in which the student will live.

Even the divergent subcultures are coming to embody middle-class standards. The Negro is a case in point. As is well known, the Negro under slavery did not have a standard family system. From this weak base Negroes moved along under a severe handicap in both rural and urban areas. Migration to both northern and southern cities has brought thousands of them in contact with unfamiliar and often demoralizing conditions. Slowly under various pressures, a Negro middle class has been emerging in these urban areas.[14] Among these families, standards regarding health, respectability, divorce, birth control, education, childrearing, and the like are not different in substance from those of other middle-class groups. However, some of the strains that often result when groups and individuals undergo changes in status or in normative standards are evident in the Negro middle class. So great is the desire to become acceptable that some families overadjust to the point that deleterious results are forthcoming, especially with respect to emotional well-being.[15]

Negroes are not the only group thus affected. The Catholic sociologist, Thomas, believes that many Catholic families have been influenced by our general middle-class values to the point that they are losing their traditional ideas regarding birth control and other practices.[16] The social scientist, Eby, writing to his own religious group, the Brethren, laments that they, in becoming part of the respectable middle class, are giving up many of the old values.[17] Campisi has documented changes in the Italian family as it feels the impact of the dominant American culture.[18] The Irish in Boston who have moved from the "shanty" level to the "lace-curtain" level look rather askance at those a rung below them on the shamrock path.[19]

---

[13] George Simpson, *People in Families* (New York, Crowell, 1960), p. 8.

[14] E. F. Frazier, "Ethnic Family Patterns: The Negro Family in the United States," *American Journal of Sociology,* Vol. 53 (May, 1948), p. 438.

[15] Simpson, *op. cit.,* p. 12.

[16] John Thomas, "The Urban Impact on the American Catholic Family," *American Catholic Sociological Review* (December, 1949), pp. 264–266. See also by the same author, *The American Catholic Family* (Englewood Cliffs, N.J., Prentice-Hall, 1956).

[17] Kermit Eby, *The God in You* (Chicago, The University of Chicago Press, 1954).

[18] Paul Campisi, "Ethnic Family Patterns: The Italian Family in the United States," *American Journal of Sociology,* Vol. 53 (May, 1948), pp. 443–449.

[19] Sister Frances Woods, *The American Family System* (New York, Harper & Row, 1959), p. 205.

The Old Order Amish, the Ozark Highlanders, and certain other groups whose family patterns do not conform to the general norms form subcultures in the country. The upper classes of Boston and various other areas are also a "poor fit" to the model. The existence of these in no way denies, however, the presence of a general family system in America, nor its impact on groups who do not conform in all ways. Whatever the reader's background, it is doubtful that he can escape the influence of the dominant system of marriage and family in America, even if he so desires.

THE GENERAL VS. THE CASE APPROACH

Since this book makes some claim to be functional as well as reliably academic, something should be said regarding methodology: the question of the general vs. the specific. A common reaction of the student in a marriage and family course is to exclaim, "But this doesn't fit my case." He is probably partially right but also probably partially wrong. Generalizations or principles that do not seem to apply to himself or his family may be nonetheless true; he may soon come to see that he is not really unique, as he likes to think he is.

It must be appreciated that a scientific approach requires an attempt to discover uniformities and commonalities, whether the focus is physical or behavioral. Through studies of many cases, generalizations are obtained which apply in the majority (often vast majority) of instances, but not admittedly to all cases. In the social realm, moreover, uniformities are difficult to discover. Furthermore, their meaning in an individual case is not always clear. Sometimes, in order to understand a particular person more fully, a so-called case approach is used. Here all the factors bearing on the individual are ascertained. If there is a problem, premarital or postmarital, the case approach is typically used by the counselor. Even so, he must not lose sight of the general in concentrating on the specific. For example, suppose a young couple, the boy nineteen and the girl seventeen, is being counseled regarding a possible forthcoming marriage. Their families are of different religious backgrounds. The young people report that they are much in love, believe they can solve their financial problems, and feel they are ready for marriage. They have appeared for counseling because both sets of parents prefer delay of the marriage. The counselor will turn both to materials derived from statistical and other sources dealing with early marriage and mixed marriage, and to his own experience in dealing with such marriages. He will also attempt to ascertain and help the couple assess all the strengths and weaknesses of their relationship. From the strict point of view of scientific prediction, it is known that early marriages and mixed marriages are more prone to divorce or marital difficulty than those not falling into these categories. However, a great many of them are successful. The question of *their particular risk* becomes a most important one for this couple. At least for the counselor, the general information he has drawn from sources other than the couple is needed as a base from which he can proceed to work with them.

Both the general and the individual approaches are useful in studying marriage and family, depending upon the problem at hand. As far as a text treatment is concerned, generalizations confirmed on great numbers of cases should form the core of the book. Well worth reading as studies of families are Hess and Handel's *Family Worlds* dealing intensively with five families in America, and Lewis' *Five Families* reporting on Mexican urban family life among the poor. These can be used to challenge general principles, as illustrative material, and as bases from which to examine one's own family life.

WHY MARRIAGE AND FAMILY STUDY?

Unfortunately, the subject of marriage and family life has seldom received the systematic, academic attention it has deserved. Of all institutions, in many ways the family is the most basic. Compared to political or economic institutions, the family has lost power. In the case of depression or war it is the family that has to give and not the reverse. In times past, if hog cholera or some such problem became rampant, action was taken, and ordinarily under political auspices. Family problems were a different story. It is only recently that monies of any size have been made available to serious researchers who are concerned with marriage and family problems. However, the tide seems to be turning. Most "respectable" colleges and universities have at least one course in the curriculum, and many high schools are giving, or considering the possibility of giving some instruction in the subject.

Increasingly serious attention to the study of marriage and family would seem to be imperative. Such problems as childrearing, divorce, marriage and family tensions, and care of the aged are to be found in most communities. Attempts to grapple with them will not get far if they are based on popular clichés, useful as these may be for speech-making purposes. Sound, solid analyses of our marriage and family system, its weaknesses and potentialities, are greatly needed if any lasting results are to be forthcoming. At the personal level each individual will have his own particular set of marriage and family issues or problems with which he is grappling. Again, pious platitudes will usually be an inadequate method to operate systematically and to bring order out of confusion. Vigorous, persistent attention, sometimes over long periods, is necessary for growth and adequate problem-solving in marriage as well as in other areas of endeavor. It is hoped that the pages which follow will stimulate thought and provide bases from which individuals can move realistically.

This is not to suggest that collective or individual attention should be given to a subject only when problems arise. Such a negative approach to life has often been criticized. We see it appearing in various forms such as "fox-hole religion" or the seeking of medical attention only when illness prevails. A more positive point of view is represented by modern preventive medicine. Here the person is encouraged to assess his potentialities in order to achieve the greatest satisfaction possible in life through maximum use of his physical abilities. An analogy can be drawn in the marriage field. One studies the marriage and family system in our society and his own relationship to it and to his own particular family, in order to provide a basis for a more satisfactory life. If there are problems, individual or social, they are seen in proper perspective. The book is written with such an ideal in mind and is not directly or primarily problem-centered. Topics normally considered problematic are not evaded, but they are included in a broad, non-problem oriented framework.

We begin with an historical perspective in the following two chapters. Despite their essential brevity, they may serve as a corrective to those of us who tend to be locked into the present era or who tend to be "temprocentered" as Bierstedt puts it. Old-fashioned though the approaches of our forefathers may seem, a reminder that some of the issues faced by them may still be with us, although in different form, is helpful.

SELECTED READINGS

Becker, Howard, and Hill, Reuben (Eds.), *Family, Marriage, and Parenthood* (Boston, Heath, 1955), Chapter 1.

Bell, Norman, and Vogel, Ezra (Eds.), *A Modern Introduction to the Family* (New York, Free Press, 1960), Chapter 1, Introductory essay.

Blitsten, Dorothy, *The World of the Family* (New York, Random House, 1963).

Blood, Robert, *Marriage* (New York, Free Press, 1962), Introduction.

Bowman, Henry, *et. al.*, "Teaching Ethical Values in the Marriage Course: A Debate," *Marriage and Family Living*, Vol. 19 (November, 1957), pp. 325–339.

Burgess, Ernest, and Locke, Harvey, *The Family: From Institution to Companionship* (New York, American Book, 1953), Preface.

Cavan, Ruth (Ed.), *Marriage and Family in the Modern World* (New York, Crowell, 1960), Chapter 1.

Christensen, Harold (Ed.), *Handbook of Marriage and the Family* (Chicago, Rand McNally, 1964), Part I.

Duvall, Evelyn, *Family Development* (Philadelphia, Lippincott, 1964), Part 1.

Farber, Bernard, *Family: Organization and Interaction* (San Francisco, Chandler Publishing Company, 1964), Chapter 1.

Gorer, Geoffrey, *The American People: A Study in National Character* (New York, Norton, 1948).

Kenkel, William, *The Family in Perspective* (New York, Appleton-Century-Crofts, 1960).

Kephart, William, *The Family, Society and the Individual* (Boston, Houghton Mifflin, 1961), Chapter 1.

Kirkpatrick, Clifford, *The Family* (New York, Ronald, 1955), Chapter 1.

Kolb, William, "Family Sociology, Marriage Education, and the Romantic Complex: A Critique," *Social Forces,* Vol. 29 (October, 1950), pp. 65–72.

Lantz, Herman and Snyder, Eloise, *Marriage* (New York, Wiley, 1962), Chapter 1.

Lee, Alfred, and Lee, Elizabeth B., *Marriage and the Family* (New York, Barnes and Noble, 1961), Chapter 1.

Le Masters, E. E., *Modern Courtship and Marriage* (New York, Macmillan, 1957), Chapter 2.

Martinson, Floyd, *Marriage and the American Ideal* (New York, Dodd, Mead, 1960), Chapter 1.

Nimkoff, Meyer, *Marriage and the Family* (Boston, Houghton Mifflin, 1947), Part I.

Mead, Margaret, "The Contemporary American Family as an Anthropologist Sees It," *American Journal of Sociology,* Vol. 53 (May, 1948), pp. 453–459.

Waller, Willard, and Hill, Reuben, *The Family,* rev. ed. (New York, Holt, Rinehart and Winston, 1951), Chapter 1.

Winch, Robert, *The Modern Family* (New York, Holt, Rinehart and Winston, 1963), Chapter 1.

Woods, Sister Francis, *The American Family System* (New York, Harper & Row, 1959), Chapter 1.

DISCUSSION QUESTIONS AND EXERCISES

1. Why is it difficult to generalize about the American family? Discuss.
2. How do lower-class families in the United States differ from middle-class families?
3. What motivates students to take marriage and family courses? Do you differ from the average? If so, how and why?
4. What should the student be expected to learn from a study of marriage and family living? Should his values and behavior change after such study? Why or why not?
5. Do animals have families? Why or why not? Discuss.
6. Some say that stressing the importance of marriage and family life can be overdone. On the other hand, Montagu makes the following statement: "The fundamentally social nature of all living things has its origin in the

reproductive relationship between parent and offspring; in the fact that the life of either one or the other is at some time dependent upon the potential or actual being of the other." Is this too strong a statement? Discuss.

7. Make a study of an ethnic or racial subgroup in the United States, comparing its family patterns with those of the dominant majority.

8. Read Chapter 1 in Cavan. On the basis of your reading and thinking write a paper on "The Significance of Marriage and Family Life for America."

9. Read Martinson's Chapter 1 and Bowman (cited in readings) in which they discuss the problem of values for the marriage educator. Write a paper indicating your position on the matter of the teacher's handling of values in a marriage course.

2

The Historical Perspective

Some historical perspective is necessary for understanding any major institution in modern society. A comprehensive understanding of modern marriage and family life would demand a thorough study of the social history of the Middle East and the West from the dawn of civilization to our own day. Such a study is impossible in a book of this sort, but it is possible to outline briefly some of the main features of the traditional forms from which our present family system has emerged. To do this, we turn first to the early Hebraic-Christian family, from which later modifications were to come.

THE EARLY HEBREW FAMILY

The early Hebrew family was originally a nomadic, patriarchal, and extended family unit.[1] It was basically religious, dominated by the concept of *Yahweh,* or God, who was ruler of the universe. The patriarch was the recognized leader of the family and discharged social, economic, political, and religious roles. Polygyny was the privilege of the leaders, but monogamy was the common practice. Children, especially sons, were very much desired. Barrenness was considered a curse. Concubinage, the practice of having second-class wives in the household, was practiced partly in order to insure progeny as successors for future generations.

With the development of towns and cities the Hebrew home became a center of industry and education where children were strictly trained and disciplined, and taught to respect their elders. Family life involved many

[1] Our treatment of this material is based primarily on the Old Testament. See also the references cited at the end of the chapter.

sacred practices which eventually became ritualized. All except the handicapped were expected to marry and help establish a home. In case of death
of one of the partners, provisions were made to care for the remaining
partner in some household. The Hebrews were family-centered to a great
degree. The home or household originally contained not only the small
nuclear unit but also more than one generation plus assorted relatives and
servants.

Mate selection among early Hebrews was a serious affair. Ordinarily
the parents assumed the initiative in seeking out a proper prospective
spouse. However, over the years the young couple exercised more and more
control over their marital choice. The initial stage of marriage involved
the betrothal or agreement to marry. The actual marriage ceremony itself
came after some time had passed.

Sex was viewed by the Hebrews as a natural urge, and was especially a
male prerogative. Fornication was frowned upon; adultery was condemned.
Since betrothal was considered by some of the poorer elements of the population to be the same as marriage, complete sex relations between those
betrothed were not uncommon. Since commitment to marry was the most
important basis of marriage to the Hebrews, such behavior was tolerated
more freely than was adultery, as is shown in Deuteronomy. Evidently in
the early days divorce for desertion was sometimes allowed for women, as
evidenced by the familiar story of Michal and David. When David, fearing
Saul, fled from the court, his wife, Michal, was given by her father Saul to
another man. A parallel story is told of Samson and his wife.

The marital relationship was to be taken seriously. However, provision
was made for divorce, and in line with male superiority the husband had a
special right to divorce. In the early days the husband could simply issue a
bill of divorcement to his wife. Public opinion being as strong as it was,
however, it is doubtful that Hebrew husbands had quite the authority to
dismiss their wives that seems to be implied. Sending a wife home without
cause might bring down the wrath of her relatives upon a man's household,
which was no small thing in a day when family alliances were customary.
Further, if a man made a girl pregnant previous to marriage, he forfeited
any right to divorce.[2] With the development of towns and cities and an
organized church it was necessary for a man to write a formal bill of
divorcement and have it approved by the Rabbi before it became final. Although such procedures seem simple compared to our formal practices of
today, it must be remembered that local social control served to prevent
many men from acting in haste for trivial reasons.

It should be stressed that the Hebrew family in the early days did not
focus on the marital pair and children, or the small nuclear group. The
household represented a large group of people of a number of generations,
some of whom were not related by blood or marriage. The daughter of a

[2] Deuteronomy, Chapter 22.

large family too poor to support her might end up as a servant in a more wealthy household, and possibly as a concubine, if she found favor in her master's eyes. Relatives who could not provide for themselves were often temporary residents of a household. The early Hebrew household was thus quite radically different from the small nuclear home that we envision when the term "family" is used.

Town and city life was to bring a decline in the size of the Hebrew household, although contact with kin remained a strong tradition. One is impressed by the Hebrew heritage for strong family traditions which have survived to the modern era in spite of the diversity of cultural conditions to which Jewish people have been exposed over the years in various parts of the world.

THE EARLY GREEKS

The Greek family was similar in many respects to the Hebrew family. It was patriarchal in form, with the husband having almost absolute power over wife and children. As in the case of the Hebrews, heirs to the male line were desired. If a man's wife produced no heirs, the husband had recourse to a concubine if he so wished. The husband had greater power over his wife and children than did the Hebrew father.[3] The children could be rejected by him at birth if they were deformed, especially in the case of girls. If so, they might be left to die from exposure.

Within the household the regular round of duties in connection with developing the children was carried on. Until the age of seven, boys and girls were given moral and religious training on an equal basis. At that age boys were sent off to school to be trained in the humanities, political and business arts followed eventually by military instruction. Girls were not permitted training outside the home and were not given intellectual or social education within the home to any degree.[4] They were trained in the domestic arts.

As a result it is small wonder that the sexes were not considered equal. Wives were restricted in rigid fashion in the early days, except in Sparta where their status was higher. The early Greek stress on learning, and excellence in the pursuit of education, government, or business was confined to men. A statement, attributed to Demosthenes, serves to indicate the status of the wife in the Greek household: "Mistresses we keep for pleasure, concubines for daily attendance upon our person, wives to bear us legitimate children, and be our faithful housekeepers." But apparently upper-class men

---

[3] Arnold Nash, "Ancient Past and Living Present," in Howard Becker and Reuben Hill (Eds.), *Family, Marriage, and Parenthood* (Boston, Heath, 1955), p. 96.

[4] Willystine Goodsell, *A History of Marriage and the Family* (New York, Macmillan, 1934), p. 109.

felt the need for some companionship with women who were cultivated. There existed a class of such women who were trained entertainers of men. They were known as the *hetairae*. Many of these were the intellectual and social superiors of the average wife. They were popular with men of learning and reputation who were bored with their ill-trained, naive wives. Perhaps the call girl who caters to the wealthier classes is the modern equivalent of the *hetairae,* although there is some disagreement as to the stress on wit and intellectuality in the call girl as against sex appeal in the context of class.

Regarding divorce, the husband had rights similar to those of the Hebrew male. Since marriage did not involve the state or church, the husband did not have to appeal to authorities if he found fault with his wife. However, he had to return the dowry to her father or male kin. Given this obligation and the pressure of public opinion against divorce for mere whim, it is not surprising that the Greek divorce rate was relatively low.[5] Adultery was severely frowned upon, and the husband who caught his wife *in flagrante delicto* was expected to divorce her.

Zimmerman suggests that the Greek family moved from a "trustee" extended type during the days of Homer through the "domestic" type, from 700 B.C. to the age of Pericles.[6] The former period involved kinship control; in the latter period the nuclear family came into its own, although the wife was still subject to her husband.

The age of Pericles was a period of rampant individualism and declining interest in family life. Divorce, homosexuality, prostitution, and general licentiousness became common. The state of public and private morality weakened, and many couples were childless. The traditional structure of family life was rent asunder. Public leaders kept mistresses openly. "Along with this was the rise of unscrupulous women, hasty and nonfamily controlled marriages, and the use of marriage by them to get money out of weak-minded and unattached old men, and easy divorce." [7] Conditions became so disorganized that Demosthenes and others began to call for reform. As is well known, Greek society finally crumbled and decayed. According to Zimmerman, family disorganization preceded and caused the general social deterioration. The development of extreme individualism in family life signaled the downfall of the nation.

It may be instructive to examine the theories of Plato and Aristotle as they pertain to marriage and family life. Plato was the more radical of the two. In his *Republic* he suggests ideas that we ascribe to totalitarian societies of our modern era and to those forecasted, such as the society predicted in Orwell's *1984*. On a eugenic basis a select group of elite men and women

---

[5] Nash, *op. cit.*

[6] Carle Zimmerman, *Family and Civilization* (New York, Harper & Row, 1947), Chapters 11–13.

[7] *Ibid.,* p. 280.

were to be the governing or guardian class. Matings of the superior men and women were to be by lot, on great connubial holidays. Children born of these matings would be separated immediately from their natural parents and taken to state nurseries where they would be reared by nurses and attendants. No parent was to be allowed to know his own child, and no child was to know who his parents were. The parents were expected to develop paternal emotions towards all children born at a certain period among whom would be their own offspring.[8] Being realistic, Plato knew that the common people would also produce children. These children were to be exposed if malformed; otherwise they were to be kept out of the forefront of public life and prevented from reproducing their kind if possible. Plato was thus among the first to suggest a eugenics program based on social class.

Aristotle criticized Plato's ideas on marriage and family, considering them impractical. He did, however, strongly believe in state regulation of family life. Legislators should regulate carefully such things as the timing of marriage, and the education of children. Women were to marry at eighteen and men at thirty-seven, the ages at which both were entering their prime of life, especially intellectually. Early marriage would have dysgenic effects. Population should be strictly controlled by state officials. "Extra" children or those deformed or otherwise incapacitated should be exposed quickly. The family should be regulated for the benefit of the state.[9]

Aristotle believed that relationships within the family circle should parallel those in the political sphere. The father should be in authority over his wife and children as a lord is over his subjects. The idea that women are inferior to men was not challenged by Aristotle. In fact, he felt that the women of Sparta were given too much authority and that this led to some disorganization.[10]

It must be said that the common people in the days of Plato and Aristotle went about their business, married, and reared their families in ingorance of what the great men were saying. However, the writings of these men were to pervasively affect the thinking of Augustine, Aquinas, and other church fathers, and in an indirect way they were to make an impact on the family system that was to emerge in the Western world.

THE FAMILY OF ANCIENT ROME

In the early days of Rome the patriarchal family as a type reached its greatest height. The Roman father had the power, *patria potestas,* even to the extent of requiring death over all in his household. As was true for the

[8] *Ibid.,* pp. 298–301.

[9] See especially Aristotle, *Politics* (Book II), Jowett Translation (Fair Lawn, N.J., Oxford, 1923).

[10] Rollin Chambliss, *Social Thought* (New York, Holt, Rinehart and Winston, 1954), p. 204.

Greek father, he could decide whether a child should be taken into the household or exposed to die. A daughter was under his power until she married, at which time she came under the control of her husband. During the periods when the Romans were taking slaves, the slave was under the authority of the patriarch who was, without question, the master of his household by law and custom.[11]

Within the household the patriarch had religious, economic, and educational leadership. Rituals involving worship at an altar were a very important part of family life, with the father officiating. It was he who trained or supervised the training of the sons although the socialization of the daughters was the responsibility of the mother. Elementary training in what we would call the "three R's" was given to all children, plus training in domestic duties and regular labor. Upper-class boys were given training in business or the law in preparation for future roles of leadership in the Forum or public life, including the military establishment.

Marriages among the early Romans did not involve the state or community to the degree true in many societies. It was considered a private contract. In the earlier days this meant an arrangement had to be made between the fathers of the prospective bride and groom, the latter having the power to refuse consent. Over the years the authority of the parents gave way to a degree to individual mate selection.

There were three types or degrees of marriage ceremonies.[12] *Confarreatio,* frequently used by early patricians, involved considerable ritual. This included a procession in which the bride was escorted through the streets to the home of her future husband. Once there, in front of ten witnesses, she repeated the statement "Wherever you are master, I am mistress." With further ceremony, including the eating of a sacred cake, the two were made man and wife. A second type of ceremony was called *coemptio.* In this a mock sale of the girl was carried on in the presence of five witnesses. Ceremonial aspects were not as elaborate as in the confarreatic form, and forms symbolizing union and requiring the giving of consent were minimal. A third form, *usus,* required little if any ceremony. Supposedly the giving of consent was necessary. In actuality the couple began to cohabit in the same household. If the wife did not absent herself from the household for more than two consecutive nights over a period of a year the marriage became legal.

The type of marriage entered into by the parties concerned depended partially upon social status. If both the parties were of equal rank, the man received the power of *patria potestas cum manus.* This meant that the wife left the authority of her father and came under the authority of her husband. She became a member of her husband's family and this was an advantage

---

[11] Sir Henry Maine, *Ancient Law* (New York, Holt, Rinehart and Winston, 1894), pp. 123–139.
[12] Goodsell, *op. cit.,* p. 123.

to the wife in case of the husband's departure for military service or other purposes. If the two parties were of unequal social status, marriage without *patria potestas* or *manus* was possible. Children who were born of such a marriage did not have full rights of citizenship or inheritance, although the marriage was legal.

From the very early days divorce was allowed by the Romans, it being referred to in the *Laws of the Twelve Tables.* Since marriage was a private, nonstate matter it followed that divorce was the same. This did not mean that the husband could divorce his wife at will, however. Actually, a ceremony of *diffarreatio* or *confarreatio* in reverse was necessary if the marriage had been performed at that level. This included ceremonial red tape and the presence of the original witnesses. At the lesser levels of marriage, a minimum of formality was necessary to obtain a divorce. In the earlier years it is doubtful that divorce was very common.

The Upper-Class Roman Family After the Punic Wars

The Punic War period of the second and third centuries B.C. was to bring considerable change in family structure in Rome, and the results were to be far-reaching, especially in regard to the upper classes. Women were required to discharge many obligations and assume roles formerly taken by men. The long periods of absence from home and association with women of easy virtue during their military service resulted in a weakening of sex codes. As a consequence of these two factors and others, relations between spouses were often strained. After achieving a bit of hard-won freedom the woman was reluctant to return to the strict authority of the husband, or to accept sexual freedom outside of marriage without complaint or demand for similar privilege. In many cases widows were left to support the family when men did not return from the field of battle.

It must be noted that the republic of Rome underwent considerable transformation during this period and the eventual effect was the well-known Roman Empire. Military conquest resulted in dominance over far-flung provinces from which wealth and booty were obtained. This resulted in the development of a very wealthy upper class, along with a large group of slaves and a very poor class at the bottom of the status pyramid. The system demanded supervision on the part of the Romans and the absence of many husbands from home for extended periods.

While considerable wealth and power came to Rome during this period, some of the social concomitants helped disorganize the older order. Gross materialism became a dominant motif, according to some writers.[13] Stable family life became, so we are told, a relic of the past. Many men and

[13] Ludwig Friedländer, *Roman Life and Manners Under the Early Empire,* Vol. I, 7th ed. (New York, Dutton), pp. 212–215.

women began to marry, seeking monetary or social gain. If such marriages could not be arranged, the possibility of not marrying but living without moral restrictions was freely considered. Among the wealthy, marriage without *manus* became common. Some writers interpret this as an attempt by fathers to prevent the loss of wealth to fortune hunters through their daughters.[14] This created a tendency for a wife to feel free to act independently, since she was not a member of her husband's family. Once married, many couples were not interested in the responsibilities of parenthood. Abortion was frequently resorted to and abandonment of offspring was common. When children were kept, their supervision was turned over to slaves and nurses when possible.

Divorce became a problem during the last years of the Roman Republic.[15] Seneca's cynical comment to the effect that women counted the years not by the calendar but by husbands was no doubt an exaggeration of the true state of affairs, but it indicates the problem as seen by some of the leaders of the time. Divorce by mutual consent was common. Also troublesome were cases where one party was able to divorce the partner, even though the latter wished to preserve the marriage. Many who were divorced did not remarry, but instead engaged in illicit affairs which had no legal or social standing. Marriage and family life as they had previously been known, at least for the upper classes, became severely disorganized.

Various Roman leaders tried to stem the tide. Metellus Macedonicus made public addresses encouraging men and women to marry for the good of society. Julius Caesar attempted to increase the marriage rate by introducing an incentive system. Augustus Caesar, after much haggling with the Senate, was able to obtain legislation which rewarded those who married and penalized those who remained single or refused to rear children. Inheritance rights, eligibility for public office, and other privileges were effected by these legal measures.[16] All went for naught, however. As Nash states:

. . . the canker had eaten too far into the fabric of Roman society. The sickness was too deep for financial inducement, direct or indirect, to have a profound effect. Augustus Caesar soon realized that Rome faced a crisis not only in her attitude towards marriage but also in her economic life and in her political ideals. The empire had lost its nerve, for the crisis was one of faith. Whether his attempt, to use his own words, "to establish the republic safe and sound on its foundations" was doomed to failure from the very outset is a problem of speculation to be left to the philosophically minded political historian. What we do know is where his efforts failed Christianity succeeded.[17]

[14] E. S. Turner, *A History of Courting* (New York, Dutton, 1955), pp. 22–26.

[15] William Fowler, *Social Life at Rome in the Age of Cicero* (New York, Macmillan, 1915), pp. 149–155.

[16] William Davis, *The Influence of Wealth in Imperial Rome* (New York, Macmillan, 1910), pp. 300–310.

[17] Nash, *op. cit.,* p. 100.

Many causal factors were involved in the decay of Roman civilization. As Chambliss puts it, "Many factors—military, political, biological, economic and religious contributed to the decline and fall of Rome." [18] Historians will speculate for years as to which factors were most crucial. Certainly decay and disorganization left the society wide open to challenge from some new and vigorous system. The system or ideology which was to provide the challenge and to institute a new order was Christianity.

THE IMPACT OF EARLY CHRISTIANITY

It must be stressed that the early Christians were a polyglot group in terms of customs and traditions. Therefore, there was not full consistency of position regarding marriage and family life, or other phases of life, for that matter. In effect, the early Christians were Hebrews, Greeks, Romans, or members of some mid-eastern group, who were converted to the new religious ideas pertaining to man's relations to man and to God. This meant that over the years disagreements were to arise as to the legitimacy of certain customs. These are reflected in the minutes of church council sessions. It is important also to note that Jesus did not issue many specific commands regarding sex and family life, whereas Paul did.[19] Further, as many western missionaries and anthropologists have noted in Africa and elsewhere, ideological conversion may lead people to break with older standards and customs, but not to have consistent replacements for them. This happened in some of the early Christian communities, as, for example at Corinth.

Space limitations prevent us from attempting to delineate Christ's general position on marriage, sex, and family at any great length. It would seem reasonable to suggest that he essentially accepted the basic Hebrew family system of his time. A strong case can be made for the proposition that he wanted to raise the status of women and children. He set high standards but put great stress on inner attitudes or motivations as against institutionalized or pharisaical form. Paul was more conservative. As a Roman citizen who was exposed to Hellenistic learning and culture, he reflected the Roman's legalistic approach to life and the Greek dualism regarding the flesh and the spirit. One cannot make sense of Paul's statements on sex, marriage, or the position of women without noting at least these minimal factors.[20]

The early Christians were a pacifistic, radical element in the body politic of Roman civilization. In the beginning most of them were from the lower social classes. At times, under inward and outward pressure, they

[18] Rollin Chambliss, *Social Thought* (New York, Holt, Rinehart and Winston, 1954), p. 231.
[19] I Corinthians.
[20] William Cole, *Sex and Love in the Bible* (New York, Association Press, 1959).

were disorganized and given to moral and physical excess, if we dare make any inferences from Paul's letter to the group at Corinth. But they were tenacious and full of missionary zeal. In spite of trial and persecution they persisted, until finally in the beginning of the fourth century, status as a legal religion came. Eventually Christian philosophy as interpreted by the early church leaders became embedded in Roman culture, and a synthesis emerged that was to form a major part of the base of western civilization.

On both class and moral grounds the early Christians were critical of the licentiousness and decadence of the Roman upper classes. Carrying the utterances of Paul to their logical extremes, the church leaders of the fourth and fifth centuries adopted the dualistic position and preached against sex and even marriage.[21] The doctrine was espoused that sex was the great temptation and that woman was the temptress. The doctrine of original sin couched in sexual terms was popular. The first-class Christians must therefore take the vow of celibacy, according to some of the leaders.[22] They prevailed on the council in 402 A.D. to order the bishops, priests, and deacons to remain unmarried. Many of the priests fought this ruling openly. Their arguments were numerous. Paul had suggested that the relation between man and wife was symbolic of that between Christ and the church. Christ had blessed marriage. They further pointed out that the church needed new offspring to perpetuate itself. The final decision, a compromise, stated that the clergy must be celibate but the common people could marry.

The early church took a strong stand against abortion, infanticide, and divorce by mutual consent.[23] Monogamy was also stressed. And while women were put on the defensive by the criticisms of their sensual nature, Christian leaders insisted that women were on an equal spiritual plane with men. This in some ways was the most radical of the Christian doctrines, for it is difficult long to deny social equality if spiritual equality is granted.

It must be noted again that the common people married, raised their families, and went about their regular life tasks while these religious debates were going on. Only slowly is a new doctrine incorporated into a culture to the point where it has a strong impact on the common people. Mate selection and marriage were private, family affairs during the period. As the Roman church became more powerful, it tried to bring marriage and divorce under its control. The Teutonic invasions of Europe were to curtail this for a time, however. In the meantime attempts were made to convert the new groups. Eventually Western civilization developed as a synthesis of Roman and Germanic culture with the church and state united in a powerful alliance. By the twelfth century, the church had gained control over marriage

[21] F. A. Wright (Ed.), *Select Letters of Saint Jerome,* Letter No. XXII (New York, Putnam, 1933), pp. 99–103.

[22] Goodsell, *op. cit.,* Chapter 5.

[23] Rockwell Smith, "Hebrew, Greco-Roman, and Early Christian Family Patterns," in Howard Becker and Reuben Hill (Eds.), *Marriage and the Family* (Boston, Heath, 1942), pp. 67–71.

and divorce, and by then most of the clergy were celibate. Marriage became a sacrament and divorce was severely limited.

THE GERMANIC FAMILY

The Germanic tribes had a family system similar to that of the Hebrews in their early days.[24] They were a vigorous people who did not look kindly on Roman control, religious or political. Slowly but surely the wandering tribes settled into particular territories, and tribal and military chieftains were replaced by lords. The manorial system developed with two main social classes, the nobility and the peasants with freemen, the clergy, and others having marginal statuses. Feudalism as a social system was to provide a bridge between the old Roman Empire and the development of the respective modern nation-states.[25]

For our purposes, mention must be made of the rise of romanticism and the industrial and religious revolutions. During the Dark Ages any romanticism that might have carried over from the Near East was pretty well stamped out. The life of the common people was coarse and difficult, and little time could be granted to lighter affairs of the heart. Marriage among the nobility was often arranged for economic and political advantage. Quite typically a girl of thirteen or fourteen married a noble in his twenties or thirties. Untutored and lonesome in her large castle, the lady was highly vulnerable to the attentions of a wandering knight on a white charger who seemed much more attractive than her cold, distant husband. The wandering troubadours developed songs describing the love that developed between various legendary knights and ladies. Being legally unavailable to each other, the romantic partners could not consummate their love, although at times they apparently did. This was considered a threat to regular, legitimate marriage.[26] Like a bastard baby, it had either to be "put away" or "taken in." We need not stress the point with the American reader that romanticism was not thrown out, although its relation to marital stability remains controversial to this time and age.

THE INDUSTRIAL AND RELIGIOUS
REVOLUTIONS

Broadly conceived, the industrial revolution obtained its start with the development of trade and the rise of towns. Great social forces shook the

[24] Stuart Queen, et al., The Family in Various Cultures (Philadelphia, Lippincott, 1951), Chapter 10.

[25] Richard Schermerhorn, "Family Carry-overs of Western Christendom," in Howard Becker and Reuben Hill (Eds.), Family, Marriage, and Parenthood (Boston, Heath, 1955), Chapter 4.

[26] Turner, op. cit., Chapter 2.

very foundations of the old feudal system, and we are still feeling their effect today. *"Stadtluft macht frei"*—especially for the poor man. More precisely, the small family could be free from the control of the noble landlord, of the trustee or extended family, if it wished to be. Furthermore the town furnished an avenue of social mobility. Division of labor and specialization demanded the skilled artisan and the trader, forerunner of the small businessman. Life for the great majority of the families of the West, and their descendants, was to be greatly affected by the revolutionary processes at work.

Scholars have debated and will continue to debate the relationship between the religious and industrial revolutions. Weber takes the position that Puritan Protestantism was especially adaptable to the rise of business and industry, since it stressed hard work and duty at whatever station one found oneself. Others suggest that the industrial revolution brought about the religious revolution. Very possibly there were basic causal factors at work which brought about concomitant changes in both.

The religious revolution was to revive some of the controversies in the realms of sex, marriage, and family which had subsided during the Middle Ages. Luther declared that marriage was not a sacrament, and he married Katherine Von Bora to make clear his attitude on the celibate clergy. He held that marriage was both a spiritual and a civil matter, with the state setting the regulations and keeping the books on marriage in view of inheritance and social control. Luther did expect the actual ceremony to be performed under religious auspices.

Calvin, and especially his Puritan and Independent followers in the British Isles and in Holland went further than Luther on the issues of civil control of marriage.[27] Marriage was to them a civil contract. It could be broken by state authority. They bitterly opposed the Anglican church controls on marriage and divorce, considering them little better than the Roman patterns which they replaced. During this period seeds of ferment were sown which were to culminate in some of the modern patterns which we have with us today. Basically, however, family forms were left intact during this period, especially in regard to the structure of the family and the statuses of husband, wife, and child.

THE FAMILY IN THE AMERICAN COLONIES

The colonists coming to America brought with them their particular traditions and laws based on their Old World background. Many of the original groups had a sense of urgency which led them to stress certain values. When they began to dig into the wilderness, if not before, they

[27] Una B. Sait, *New Horizons for the Family* (New York, Macmillan, 1938), Chapter 4.

sensed that their society had a precarious base. This realistic appraisal of conditions, coupled with a strong sense of religious and economic duty, made marriage, family, and life in general a rather serious business.

While all the early colonists came from Western Europe, differences in family life developed to the degree that an examination of family life in New England, the Middle Colonies, and the Southern Colonies is legitimate, even though the general structure and function of the colonial family system was essentially the same.

The New England Family

The early New Englanders focused their interests on the family and small communities, in contrast to the situation in the southern colonies, where many originally settled as single individuals. Colonization involved multiple family projects from the start. Calhoun suggests that this emphasis on the family unit accounts for the success of English colonization as contrasted with the brilliant but nonfamilial settlements of the Spanish and French.[28]

The family was father-centered and father-dominated, with wives being expected to defer to their husbands. Many women married in their teens, and the rigors of wilderness life and frequent pregnancies made them appear to be old women by their late thirties or early forties. The requirements of child bearing and rearing, household and farm duties made the wife and mother a most important person. This no doubt served to increase her status, although the husband quite clearly was legally in charge of the household.

Home life in New England was strict. The Puritan ethic demanded that individuals labor to show themselves pleasing in the sight of the Lord. Idleness was akin to sin. A businesslike efficiency was encouraged. The household was really a small establishment which was devoted to the varied activities of weaving, spinning, baking, sewing, and cooking. Idle hands were considered the devil's tools.

Courtship was not the romantic transaction that it is today. Parents exercised considerable control over the process. The oft-cited diary of Judge Sewall indicates some of the anxieties fathers had in those days, waiting until their daughters were suitably married off. That the mercenary motive sometimes entered the picture is suggested by a number of authors. Calhoun refers to one Emanual Downing, who writes of his matrimonial projections for his own children and his niece.[29] For the latter the good Puritan was able to secure a "varie good match," a young man of fine reputation and an estate of four or five hundred pounds. Especially did financial considera-

---

[28] Arthur Calhoun, *A Social History of the American Family* (New York, Barnes and Noble, 1945), Vol. 1, Chapter 3, p. 51.

[29] *Ibid.,* p. 57.

tions enter the picture in second marriages. Courageous Judge Sewall, who not atypically outlived several wives, shopped prudently and arduously among the widows of means in order to repair his empty life.[30] The little widows were not all taken in by his guile. A number of them asked pointed questions regarding his own property holdings and his provisions for his children. One gets the impression that when the Judge finally married again it was partly because he was worn out by the "waiting game."

The Puritan code was rigid on sex matters, with ministers like Jonathan Edwards implying that sex was the basis of all sin.[31] It is easy to understand then that some supervision would be exercised over young, unattached persons. In New Haven a law was passed which stated "that in order to suppress inconvenience and disorders inconsistent with the mind of God in the fifth commandment, single persons not in service or dwelling with their relatives are forbidden to diet or lodge alone; but they are required to live in "licensed families"; and the governors of such families are "ordered to observe (their) course, carriage and behavior." [32]

In spite of the stern attitude of the elders, young people at times stole away to stroll hand in hand. In fact, "strolling on the green" in the center of town became customary even though there were attempts to stamp it out. Further, "bundling" was allowed at least in the lower classes. By this practice a young man and woman could carry on their courtship in bed, fully clothed, after the lights were put out and the fire had diminished. This curious custom must be put in proper context, however. In the poorer

[30] Samuel Sewall, *Diary of Samuel Sewall* (Judge), (Massachusetts Historical Society Collections, Series 5, Volumes 5–7, 1878–1882), pp. 204–205.

[31] It is perhaps impossible to treat the influence of Puritan attitudes and practices on marriage and family life without engaging in the use of stereotypes. Scholarly research, especially by Perry Miller and Thomas Johnson, has indicated that the image we have had of the Puritan is not completely correct. It appears that restrictive practices were typical of the eighteenth rather than the seventeenth-century community. In the former century as evidenced by the poetry of Anne Bradstreet for example, a certain robustness is indicated which does not seem "Puritan." [See Perry Miller (Ed.), *The American Puritans: Their Prose and Poetry* (Garden City, Doubleday, 1956), Chapter 5.] As Miller and Johnson [Perry Miller and Thomas Johnson, *The Puritans* (New York, American Book, 1938), p. 3] point out, certain types of "Fundamentalist" doctrine (American brand) and Unitarianism developed from a common Puritan source. It is entirely possible that the conservative ethic on sex matters which we have come to associate with the term "puritanism" does not fairly represent the ideals or practices of the average man or woman in New England, of either the seventeenth or eighteenth century but represents instead an offshoot of only one aspect of Puritan life. Nevertheless that an ethic of restrictiveness developed can hardly be denied. It was stressed in fiery sermons by men like Jonathan Edwards. Too, Kirkpatrick [Clifford Kirkpatrick, *The Family* (New York, Ronald, 1955), p. 166] suggests, "It is difficult to know whether the attempt was made to bring about a high degree of conformity to the norm or whether frequent indiscretion called for a severe approach on the part of the leaders." At any rate a restrictive ethic known as Puritanism was introduced into our culture, traces of which remain with us to the present time.

[32] Trumball, James, *True Blue Laws of Connecticut and New Haven* (Hartford, American Publishing Company, 1876), p. 258.

homes where this was customary the family "retired" in the same room with the courting couple. The Puritan mores were formally strict, but some outlets were permitted to soften their impact to a degree.

Children were wanted and needed to populate the virgin territory. The birth rate was high, but a fantastic number of children died before reaching their maturity. Since they "inherited the sins of Adam" the ones who survived were given serious attention. It was held that their spirits must be broken in order to make them pliable enough to assimilate sound teaching. In spite of this ideology and in view of the fact that the children were to perpetuate the family, in actual practice many parents were not as cruel to their children as we have been led to believe.[33] Parents were certainly strict in their discipline by our present standards, however.

Since the Puritans objected strongly to ecclesiastical control of marriage and divorce it was natural that this feeling would be reflected in the New World. Accordingly, in the early days, New England clergymen were forbidden to solemnize marriage. Because marriage was a contractual relationship with strong property implications, the state was empowered to grant a marriage or, for due cause, to allow its dissolution. It was only after considerable time had elapsed that the various New England colonies relented and allowed ministers to act as representatives of both state and church in officiating at marriage ceremonies.

The Family in the South

As in New England, the monogamous, semipatriarchal family system was to prevail in the early southern colonies. A few of the major differences in the background of the two areas must be stressed in order to further an understanding of our present family system.

The South was the most stratified of the early territories. With slavery taking hold, there developed three levels of society: the planters or aristocrats, the white families of more modest means, and the Negro slaves. Somewhat divergent patterns of family life prevailed in these different classes. The plantation family involved numerous people in the administration of a system that reminds one of a feudal manor. It was in many ways a domestic factory in which raw materials were processed into consumable products. Outside activities involved the growing and processing of cotton and the care of animals. Related to these were spinning, weaving, soap making, basket weaving, and countless other similar productive activities. The plantation system allowed the Old South a degree of specialization that was not found in rural areas in other parts of the country. The owner families became essentially administrators. Included in the administrative hierarchy were the wives, who were in charge of the many activities carried on within

---

[33] Manford Kuhn, "American Families Today: Development and Differentiation of Types," in Howard Becker and Reuben Hill (Eds.), *Family, Marriage, and Parenthood* (Boston, Heath, 1955), p. 136.

the households.[34] Patterning their way of life after the model of the British countryside, planter families attempted to assure some continuity through the use of such customs as entail and primogeniture, both of which were ruled out by the Revolution.

Since the upper classes in the South favored the Anglican church there was not the fear of church board control of marriage that prevailed in New England.[35] Consequently, in many of the colonies during the earlier periods only Episcopal ministers could perform marriage ceremonies. Later the laws were liberalized to include marriages under other religious auspices, and in the majority of areas civil marriages were also authorized. The possibility of divorce usually accompanied these changes in the law. Roman Catholic influence in the border state of Maryland should not be overlooked.

Something approaching an earlier European conception of romanticism arose among the upper classes of the Plantation South, according to some authorities. Women "were put on a pedestal," and were objects of romantic affection. Social life was stressed, as the well-known plantation-style party indicated. Actually the women occupied a twofold position. On the one hand they were held high as examples of purity and objects of devotion; on the other hand, they were considered to have inferior minds and to be in great need of protection. This dual concept was by no means confined to the Plantation South, but it seems to have been accentuated there.

A corollary of this dualism was a double standard of sex morality.[36] Men were allowed access to female slaves who were available in quantity. Most of the relationships that developed were casual but patterns approaching concubinage occasionally developed. From the children of such unions were chosen the house servants, who were to form the base for the middle and upper-class Negro families of today.

While the plantation families were to receive extensive coverage in history books and actually to dominate much early political and economic life, the majority of white families were in the more modest classes. The latter families were predominantly English and Scotch-Irish, but a sizable German strain was added, especially in Virginia and North Carolina. These groups carried their peasant and small farm traditions from the old country to the southern lowlands and mountain areas. A rugged, vigorous people, they tended to develop or perhaps redevelop an extended or trustee family system in some of the isolated mountain areas as a substitute for more formal government.[37] The present Ozark family represents a carry-over of this family type to the present day.

Negro family life was virtually nonexistent among the field Negroes who lived in the cabins and performed the menial work on the plantations.[38]

[34] Ruth Cavan, *The American Family* (New York, Crowell, 1953), Chapter 2.

[35] Calhoun, *op. cit.,* Vol. 1, Chapter 15, p. 259.

[36] *Ibid.,* Vol. 1, Chapter 19.

[37] Zimmerman, *op. cit.,* pp. 708–717.

[38] E. F. Frazier, *The Negro Family* (New York, Holt, Rinehart and Winston, 1951).

There were no functions that belonged to a nuclear family per se which had to be performed. A casual attitude of males toward the women and children was allowed, if not encouraged. Further, stable relationships even among mothers and children were always subject to arbitrary interference by way of the slave market. Old family patterns known in the mother country were broken and not replaced by any consistent new ones that were perpetuated in the slave group. If we even wish to use the concept, Negro slave family system, it must be in terms of a quasi-family that was structurally weak with few well-defined functions.

The Family in the Middle Colonies

Both geographically and socially, the Middle Colonies fall between the other two major systems about which we have been speaking. In regard to ethnic background they were the most heterogeneous, but the English Quakers, Pennsylvania Germans, and Scotch-Irish predominated. Slavery never flourished in the Middle Colonies and stratification was not so pronounced as in the South. Since transportation was easier, business and small industry developed rather rapidly. Families therefore were never quite so self-sufficient as their counterparts in other regions, although they were more so than present-day families.

Family ideology lacked the harshness of the Puritan doctrines. The Quakers did not believe in original sin and while the other groups in some cases did, they were not as extreme about it as the Puritans. Children, in consequence, were given more leeway than they were in New England, but they were still strictly trained and disciplined. Those from the poorer families were bound out in order to alleviate their own families' situations and to allow them to learn a trade.

Ostentation was frowned upon by most groups in the Middle Colonies. Antagonism to the English Royalists or German upper classes had been a major motive in migration for many and unlike the southern colonists they were not inclined to emulate these groups in forging a new way of life in this country. Hard-working, and thrifty, the Middle Colony families were to contribute much to the development of the farm and town and to what was to become known as the "traditional" family of the United States.[39]

Marriage could be solemnized by religious or civil ceremony, although the former was favored. Provision for divorce eventually came in most of the colonies, but sentiment was more conservative than in New England. Most of the religious groups stressed endogamous marriage. Parents usually attempted to exercise some control over mate selection, but the possibility of moving westward via elopement led to the diminution of parental control.

[39] Calhoun, *op. cit.*, Vol. 1, Chapter 11.

The Influence of the Frontier

As life became relatively settled in the seaboard colonies, some showed signs of clinging to traditional European family patterns. This was not true on the frontier. Patriarchal rule, marriage along clan lines, and subordination of children, for example, were practices which were difficult to maintain in the fluid, rough-and-ready climate of the frontier. The frontier was a great leveler of men and of traditions of men. Pragmatic adjustments to situational demands replaced reliance on the "old ways." Indians and other neighbors of a family in the woods knew little about the origins and status of a particular Jones family from an obscure New England small town and cared less. Further, many a family included an alleged horsethief, pauper, or member who for some reason was *persona non grata* back East. A norm developed that it was improper if not downright foolhardy to make pointed inquiry about a person's origin. Under such circumstances it was to be expected that a certain freedom of action and spirit would invade such traditional institutions as family and church, and encourage the development of the concept of extreme individual freedom as we know it.

On the frontier, practices which would ordinarily have been considered irregularities could be construed as necessary adjustments. If two young people wished to marry and the circuit minister was not due for another six months, they might simply live together until a visiting parson or magistrate appeared, at which time the marriage was solemnized. It must be noted that small religious sects often migrated westward as colonizing groups taking their ministers and other functionaries with them. In such cases less irregularity prevailed. Nevertheless, the free and unsettled conditions of the frontier tended to liberalize the traditional patterns of even the most conservative groups.

If the frontier leveled men, it also elevated women and children. The wife became a true helpmate in the wilderness, being spared only the most heavy and dangerous work. Life circumstances were so compelling that each individual was required to assume an important role if the group was to survive. Old concepts of the frail, inhibited lady who had to be protected from the world were forced to give way. The frontier was a killer. Incessant childbearing coupled with other exigencies made the life span of the average pioneer woman exceedingly short. Calhoun writes, "The elevation that came in the status of woman was earned by devotion, labor, courage, self-control, and heroism. Never was the adaptability of female character more strikingly displayed than in the opening of the West. Reciprocity in the marriage relation was the logical consequence where woman bore a man's share in the struggle for existence." [40]

Children came into their own on the frontier. Hired hands were impos-

[40] *Ibid.,* Vol. 2, Chapter 5, pp. 106–107.

sible to obtain and parents literally raised their own. Children were a great asset in helping to clear the forest, raise new buildings, till the soil, and care for the animals. Age-graded tasks were easy to come by and much more was expected of children as economic contributors than could possibly be true today. The father was clearly the functional leader of the family unit, but the child had a clear-cut status in the group and he knew it. Danger was always present and childhood diseases took their toll. Those who survived to adulthood were a sturdy lot who were not hesitant or timid about taking mates and carving out homes of their own.

So basic was the frontier in the development of American institutions that the historian Turner, after his studies of the frontier period, was moved to become a frontier determinist.[41] According to Turner, Old World practices gave way and new patterns were formed by the frontier experience. This thesis seems overdrawn in that cultural traditions are seldom completely forgotten. That the frontier made an important impact on our institutions, however, cannot be doubted.

The Settling-in Period

One frontier after another was conquered in America until finally the country was colonized from the Atlantic to the Pacific. Families settled in to consolidate and develop what they had acquired. The Civil War brought considerable disruption to the country as did industrial developments in the cities. As a whole, however, the tendency in the rural area and small town was to develop a rather consistent type of family life, deeply embedded in a local community network of institutions. While many European traditions were lost under the impact of the frontier, the conservative influence of the settled and small town and rural culture tended to revise some of the more traditional patterns and to solidify indigenous ones. The family developed closer ties to the church than were typical during the colonial frontier period. Home life developed a patterned rhythm about which men like Canby and others have spoken with nostalgia. Victorian values made their impact. Family rituals were typical, and were integrated into the total pattern of activities.[42] Let Canby speak on the meaning of home at the end of the century as he understood it to be:

Home life in the nineties could be very sweet, and often profoundly dull, and sometimes an oppressive weight of routine inescapable; security was bought at a ruinous price; yet what conditioned reflexes it set up! The peace movement of the early nineteen-hundreds . . . was an attempt to make the world

[41] Fredrick J. Turner, *The Frontier in American History* (New York, Holt, Rinehart and Winston, 1921).

[42] James Bossard, *The Sociology of Child Development* (New York, Harper & Row, 1954), Chapter 4.

our home, our American home. Nor was heaven exempt from the home-making activities of the American family. We sang lustily in church—

> There we shall rest
> There we shall rest
> In our Father's House
> In our Father's House.

The age of confidence got the habit of security in its homes.[43]

Actually revolutionary processes were already underway in the nineties which were eventually to shake the very foundations of the type of family life about which Canby speaks so eloquently. The home was not as secure as people thought it to be at the turn of the century. Many could not perceive the processes already at work around them nor could they foresee the great social changes which were forthcoming in the new century. It is to some of these changes and their impact on American marriage and family that we now turn our attention.

SELECTED READINGS

Andrews, Charles, *Colonial Folkways* (New Haven, Yale, 1919).

Baber, Ray, *Marriage and the Family* (New York, McGraw-Hill, 1953), Chapter 2.

Bainton, Roland, *What Christianity Says About Sex, Love, and Marriage* (New York, Association Press, 1957).

Bardis, Panis, "Family Forms and Variations Historically Considered," Chapter 11 in Harold Christensen (Ed.), *Handbook of Marriage and the Family* (Chicago, Rand McNally, 1964).

Beard, Mary R., *Woman As a Force in History* (New York, Macmillan, 1945).

Calhoun, Arthur, *A Social History of the American Family*, 3 vols. (New York, Barnes and Noble, 1945).

Carcopino, Jerôme, *Daily Life in Ancient Rome* (New Haven, Yale, 1940).

Chambliss, Rollin, *Social Thought* (New York, Holt, Rinehart and Winston, 1954).

Colacci, Mario, *Christian Marriage Today* (Minneapolis, Augsburg, 1958).

Cole, William, *Sex and Love in the Bible* (New York, Association Press, 1959).

Cole, William, *Sex in Christianity and Psychoanalysis* (New York, Oxford University, 1955).

Couch, Herbert, "Women in Early Roman Law," *Harvard Law Review,* Vol. 8 (April, 1894), pp. 39–50.

Cross, Earl, *The Hebrew Family* (Chicago, The University of Chicago Press, 1927).

Doroghi, Ervin, *Grounds for Divorce in European Countries* (New York, The New School for Social Research, 1955).

Earle, Alice M., *Child Life in Colonial Times* (New York, Macmillan, 1937).

[43] Henry S. Canby, *American Memoirs* (Houghton Mifflin, 1955), p. 35.

Friedländer, Ludwig, *Roman Life and Manners Under the Early Empire,* 4 vols. (New York, Dutton, 1908–1913).

Goodsell, Willystine, *A History of Marriage and the Family* (New York, Macmillan, 1937).

Howard, George, *A History of Matrimonial Institutions,* 3 vols. (Chicago, The University of Chicago Press, 1904).

Kuhn, Manford, "American Families Today: Development and Differentiation of Types," in Howard Becker and Reuben Hill (Eds.), *Family, Marriage, and Parenthood* (Boston, Heath, 1955), pp. 131–147.

Lawrence, Henry W., *The Not-Quite Puritans* (Boston, Little, Brown, 1928).

Maine, Sir Henry, *Ancient Law* (New York, Holt, Rinehart and Winston, 1894).

Mace, David, *Hebrew Marriage* (New York, Philosophical Library, 1953).

Nash, Arnold, "Ancient Past and Living Present," in Howard Becker and Reuben Hill (Eds.), *Family, Marriage and Parenthood* (Boston, Heath, 1955), pp. 84–103.

Nimkoff, Meyer, *Marriage and the Family* (Boston, Houghton Mifflin, 1947), Chapter 3.

Queen, Stuart, and Adams, John B., *The Family in Various Cultures* (Philadelphia, Lippincott, 1952), Chapters 6, 7, and 8.

Schermerhorn, Richard, "Family Carry-overs of Western Christendom," in Howard Becker and Reuben Hill (Eds.), *Family, Marriage and Parenthood* (Boston, Heath, 1955), Chapter 4.

Sirjamaki, John, *The American Family in the Twentieth Century* (Cambridge, Harvard, 1953).

Spruill, Julia, *Woman's Life and Work in the Southern Colonies* (Chapel Hill, The University of North Carolina Press, 1938).

Stern, Bernhard, *The Family, Past and Present* (New York, Appleton-Century-Crofts, 1938), Parts 2 and 3.

Stiles, Henry, *Bundling, Its Origin, Progress, and Decline in America* (Knickerbocker Publishing Company, Reprinted by the Book Collectors Association, New York, 1928).

Turner, E. S., *A History of Courting* (New York, Dutton, 1955).

Zimmerman, Carle, *The Family of Tomorrow* (New York, Harper & Row, 1949).

Wright, F. A. (Ed.), *Selected Letters of Saint Jerome* (New York, Putnam, 1933).

DISCUSSION QUESTIONS AND EXERCISES

1. Can we reconstruct a picture of the family life of Ancient Greece by studying the writings of Plato and Aristotle? Why or why not? Discuss.

2. How do you account for the extreme position taken by some of the third and fourth century church leaders on such matters as the legitimacy of marriage, sex, the status of women, etc.?

3. Read the account of Amish family life in Kollmorgen, *The Old Order Am-*

ish of Lancaster County, Pennsylvania, U.S. Dept. of Agriculture, Bureau of Agricultural Economics, 1942. Do you agree that the Amish family system more closely represents that of previous centuries than any other in the United States? Discuss.

4. Discuss the strengths and weaknesses of Roman marriage and family from your point of view.

5. What value do you see in the study of the history of marriage and family? Discuss.

6. Write an essay on the effects of the frontier on the development of American marriage and family life. Is Turner's thesis overdrawn? Include references to Turner in your essay.

7. Debate continues on the question of Christ's position on birth control, divorce, the status of women, etc. What accounts for this persistent disagreement?

8. Calhoun insists that the mercenary element was strong in courtship and marriage in the early colonial period. Evaluate his position after reading Volume I and parallel materials in Goodsell, Baber, Turner, and others cited.

9. Compare and contrast the New England, Middle, and Southern Colonies on patterns of marriage and family life. How do you account for these differences?

10. Write an essay comparing divorce in the Middle Ages with divorce today in the United States.

11. What elements of early Hebrew, Greek, and Roman marriage and family traditions do you find preserved intact in our culture?

12. Read the famous diary of Judge Sewall. How adequate a picture of colonial marriage and family life do you think you can get from it?

3

The American Family in Transition

What is to happen to us in the time we have left on this planet? Great grandmother, who lives in our house, has a memory that spans the period from the Gay Nineties down on the farm (minus all modern conveniences) to the small town, then the bustling city and finally to the quiet suburb which is geographically only a few miles from the old homestead. I need not stress the fact that she has seen the introduction of electric power, the automobile, radio and television, not to mention new fangled contraceptives, plastics, space ships, and Freudian psychiatry. Until a few years ago I thought that most of the frontiers and new inventions were behind us. Now I sense that the society in which I live out my life will probably change faster than it did for my parents and for grandmother. What this will mean to our marriage and family life is an open question. I must confess the possibilities overwhelm me at times.[1]

What will happen to the American family in the space age? Will basic changes take place in the system, or are American family patterns so fundamental that only slight adaptations will be necessary? Perhaps it would be wise to explore briefly some of the changes that have taken place in the American family. After such exploration we should have a better base from which to answer the questions posed above. Necessary to the understanding and recognition of changes in the family structure is the consideration of those forces which have influenced the modern-day family pattern.

THE SCIENTIFIC-TECHNOLOGICAL REVOLUTION

The search for causes in the realm of human affairs is a most complicated problem, as Ogburn and Nimkoff and others have shown.[2] Often a

[1] From a student report in the author's files.
[2] William Ogburn and Meyer Nimkoff, *Technology and the Changing Family* (Boston, Houghton Mifflin, 1955), Chapter 2.

configuration of variables can be identified which appears to be related causally to a given outcome. These factors may at times converge, or at least
seem to converge, to the point that it is difficult to separate them except in
the abstract. Such seems to be the case regarding the agents which have
been causally involved in bringing about marriage and family changes. A
causal sequence may be involved in a chain reaction form. Further, it is
sometimes difficult to separate effect from its antecedents.

Given all the difficulties of causal analysis, there is a high degree of
agreement existing among social scientists regarding the factors which have
had great impact on the present American family. Basically the scientific-
industrial revolution and its corollaries would seem to be most essentially
responsible for the changes that have shaken the traditional systems.[3]

The development of new methods of power usage led to the organization of the factory method of production. Through the use of the "put out"
system in the early cities in England, household productions were temporarily encouraged. Factory production accentuated, or better, demanded
urban concentration and sounded the final bell on production in the family
circle.

Closely allied to the industrializing forces mentioned above are the
factors of transportation and communication. Scientific and technical developments have provided the means whereby factory production and com-
merce can have masses of men and materials moved rapidly. Closely related
to transportation is communication. It is now possible to pick up a telephone in the college dormitory, dial an area code number and a telephone
number and tap the family coffers for extra cash. Perfecting of Bell's and
Marconi's inventions makes it an everyday occurrence to talk directly with
ships at sea, astronauts orbiting the earth, or call direct to the taxi one
needs to get to the airport. Dick Tracy's wrist radio is no longer a fiction of
the writer's imagination.

Another important element in the cause of family change is the accumulation of scientific medical knowledge and allied techniques. Medical
discoveries have helped tremendously to increase the average life span by
lowering the death rate. Contraceptive devices allow the size of the family
to be essentially controlled, and also circumvent biological processes for
the unmarried. New developments forecast the possibility of greater eugenic
control if it is desired.[4] The evolution of medical science has tremendous
implications.

NON-SCIENTIFIC REVOLUTIONARY CHANGES

Impinging on the more traditional family systems have been changing
ideas and theories regarding social institutions other than the family. We

[3] Clifford Kirkpatrick, *The Family* (New York, Ronald, 1955), p. 119.
[4] Meyer Nimkoff, "Technology, Biology, and the Changing Family," *American
Journal of Sociology,* Vol. 58 (July, 1951), pp. 20–26.

limit the Reformation Period to an overly narrow framework. Concomitant to changes in religious ideas were changes in the political realm as well. Ideas of freedom, equality, and democracy which were originally applied to religious, political, and economic systems, were also to have an impact on the family.[5] It is no secret that democratic notions in the political fields have seeped over into the family to influence the status of women and children. The extension of the "general welfare" clause of the U.S. Constitution to embrace general social services has taken place during the time the family was giving up many of its protective functions. These shifts in values or ideologies have not been brought about necessarily by scientific and technological developments. They have all been, however, outside impinging forces which have disturbed older family patterns.

Size of the Family Group

One major fact that stands out regarding the American family is its decreasing size. As is shown in Table 1 the average household size was 5.28 persons in 1860. By 1960 it was 3.29. This means a decrease in size of 36 percent in one century.

TABLE 1

Average Number of Persons per Family Household, 1860–1960

Year	Persons per Household
1860	5.28
1870	5.09
1880	5.04
1890	4.93
1900	4.76
1910	4.54
1920	4.34
1930	4.11
1940	3.77
1950	3.51
1960	3.29

SOURCE: U.S. Bureau of Census Reports, *A Century of Population, Growth from the First Census of the United States to the Twelfth.* 1790–1900; pp. 95–97; and U.S. Bureau of Census Reports General Population Characteristics, Pc (1) 1B, p. 175.

Actually two processes are at work here.[6] The census figures involve both the birth rate and the size of the household. It is quite clear that the overall trend of both has been downward for the century under question.

[5] See also William Goode, *World Revolution and Family Patterns* (New York, Free Press, 1963).

[6] Paul Glick, *American Families* (New York, Wiley, 1957), Chapter 2.

To an extent this reflects a changing type of household. The modern family unit is typically composed of mother, father, and children, without the extra relatives who more often in former years were attached to the nuclear family.

Getting the full picture of the birth rate is not a simple matter because one can choose between crude birth rate, proportion of children to mothers in the childbearing ages, and other statistical conventions for measuring change. Nevertheless, certain trends are reasonably clear. Our birth rate dropped sharply during the depression years, then shot upward during the forties and fifties, and has declined since. What is to happen in the future is still a matter hazardous to predict. It does appear that, given both affluence and perpetual cold war, plus early marriage, our birth rate will remain higher than it was in the thirties. As Kenkel points out, this does not mean that we are going to a model of six or more children per family.[7] Rather it means that compared to depression days, significantly more parents are having the third or fourth child than the depression norm of two. Present indications are that the moderate sized family will be rather typical for the period immediately ahead.

The age at which marriage is typically entered is important in a number of ways. It provides an indication of the degree of popularity of marriage and of general economic and social conditions. It can tell us something about the birth rate, since the chances of having children are greater for those who marry young. It is also obviously correlated with questions of higher education, age of entrance into the job market, and many other problems and issues.

Marriage data for the United States is available from the year 1890. Looking at Table 2 we see that the typical man married at 26.1 years of age and his bride would be 22.0 years of age. By 1960 the median age at first marriage was 22.8 and 20.3 for the male and female respectively. What accounts for this decline? What are some of the implications of this trend? Although we are not able to fully explain the downward trend, some hypotheses can be advanced. Marriage is an important life-goal in our society. Sex and romance are stressed to a greater degree than in former periods. Dating patterns are being extended downward into the grade school years. Many children and young people are not being trained in families who stress the virtues of hard work and conservatism in decision-making. The increasing emergence of a "sex is fun" morality does not encourage planning and waiting before moving into marriage. The idea of parental financial aid to the young couple is no longer considered shocking in many circles. College marriages are increasing in number. Many a coed is now expecting and expected to help finance her husband through graduate school.

A comparison of our typical patterns of marriage with those of the

[7] William Kenkel, *The Family in Perspective* (New York, Appleton-Century-Crofts, 1960), p. 203.

TABLE 2

Median Age at First Marriage, by Sex, for the United States, 1890–1960

Year	Male	Female
1890	26.1	22.0
1900	25.9	21.9
1910	25.1	21.6
1920	24.6	21.2
1930	24.3	21.3
1940	24.3	21.5
1950	22.8	20.3
1960	22.8	20.3

SOURCE: U.S. Bureau of the Census, "Population Characteristics," *Current Population Reports,* Series P-20, No. 72, December 21, 1956, Table C, p. 3; and Statistical Abstract of the United States, 1961, Table 71, p. 67. 1950 and 1960 figures are from the latter source.

Irish countryside is revealing. There land-hungry farm families have developed a system whereby young people must delay marriage until they can take over management of the farm after the parental generation retires from active work. Many a young man is in his thirties or forties before he has any real possibility of marriage.

Our society places no such restrictions on its young people. However, one could reason that a complex society such as ours demands a certain level of maturity, if marriage is to be successful. Raising a family under modern conditions would seem to require more background and preparation than would have been needed during previous periods. Many authorities believe that a significant proportion of our citizens who marry early are not prepared socially, economically, or emotionally for the requirements of marriage and parenthood.[8] Nevertheless the trend toward lower age at marriage has been with us for over a half century. A careful study of the year to year trends for the last decade leads one to believe that a leveling off is in process. It stands to reason that our society will not officially encourage marriages below the late teens, in the immediate future although thousands occur annually.[9]

Mobility has been a basic characteristic of American society. The wide open spaces were settled in the eighteenth and nineteenth centuries, and a slight but steady movement westward has continued to this day. More important than the specific geographic direction of our movement has been the rural to urban shift. In 1790 one out of every twenty persons was an urban-

[8] Paul Glick, and Herman Miller, "Educational Level and Potential Income," *American Sociological Review,* Vol. 21 (June, 1956), p. 310.

[9] Emmanuel Landau, "The Coming Marriage and Housing Boom," Chapter XVII in Donald Bogue (Ed.), *Application of Demography,* Scripps Foundations for Research in Population Problems, Miami, Ohio, Study Number 13.

ite. By 1860 this ratio had changed to one in five. The 1920 census showed that the flow of humanity to the city had reached the point that more than half of our people lived in urban areas. By 1960 about seven out of every ten Americans were urban residents.[10] This shift from the rural, farm home to the city or its environs is highly significant in terms of the new pressures and expectations which ordinarily accompany city life.

In the modern nuclear system marriage means the beginning of a new household as against the addition to the larger family which would be characteristic in some societies. Our concepts suggest that the newly married couple should seek occupational success for the husband. This means a willingness to be geographically mobile. The old homestead becomes just a fading memory as the young couple get on wheels and on the American super highways. Census reports show that since 1950 about one family in five moves its residence in any given year.[11] Families in which the parents are in the younger age brackets are more inclined to move than those in the older categories, as might be expected.

The "American Dream" has held the possibility that persons of modest means might climb the social and economic ladder to a more affluent way of life. Debate continues as to whether or not the actual possibilities of moving up on the social scale have increased, decreased, or remained substantially the same. Whatever the overall trend, some individuals or families do change their status over time. In general such movement makes for strain rather than for stability.

Popularity of Marriage

If a Martian anthropologist were to visit many of our nightclubs and listen to the typical run of jokes, or if he were to engage in conversation with some of our Bohemians or Beatniks he might gather that formal marriage is not a popular estate. As a matter of fact, if he were to live briefly in a fraternity house or college men's dormitory he might emerge in a similar frame of mind. Facts, however, indicate otherwise. If we can in any way gauge the interest in an institution by the number of people who enter it, marriage is not the waning state it might appear.[12] Americans presently are a very marriage-prone people. Nine out of ten Americans marry sometime in their lifetime.[13] The remarriage rates for those who are divorced or widowed is high, especially for those whose marriages are broken in the early years. Marriage seems to be a dominant goal in the United States.

[10] U.S. Bureau of the Census, *U.S. Census of Population: 1960, Characteristics of the Population,* Part A (U.S. Government Printing Office, 1961), Table B.P. XI.

[11] Glick, *op. cit.,* p. 90.

[12] Paul Jacobson, *American Marriage and Divorce* (New York, Holt, Rinehart and Winston), pp. 33–36.

[13] *Ibid.,* Chapter 1.

Many of our married couples have serious difficulty but this does not seem to reduce the popularity of marriage.

Divorce

It is generally known that the American divorce rate is higher than it was in previous generations. Focusing on the crude rate, we can note the following. (See Figure 1 and Table 3). In 1867 the divorce rate per thousand

TABLE 3

Marriage and Divorce Rates per 1000 Female Population Fifteen Years of Age and Over, United States, 1920–1960

Year	Marriage Rate	Divorce Rate
1920	92.0	8.0
1925	79.0	
1930	67.6	7.5
1935	72.5	7.8
1940	82.8	8.8
1945	83.6	14.4
1950	90.2	10.3
1955	80.9	9.3
1960	73.5	9.2

Source: U.S. Department of Health, Education and Welfare, National Office of Vital Statistics, "Marriage and Divorces," *Vital Statistics–Special Reports,* April 9, 1958, Table B, p. 53, and Statistical Abstracts of the United States, Annual Editions.

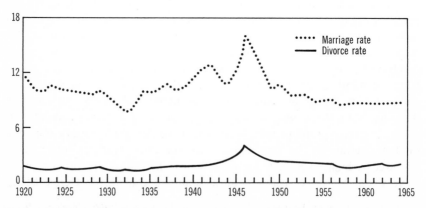

Figure 1. *Crude Marriage and Divorce Rates: United States, 1920–1964 (Rates per 1,000 population).* source: U.S. Department of Health, Education, and Welfare, National Office of Vital Statistics, "Marriages and Divorces," *Vital Statistics' Special Reports* (April 9, 1958), Vol. 48, No. 51 and Statistical Abstracts of the United States, Annual Editions.

population was 0.3. By 1920 it had risen to 1.6. The period of the twenties and thirties showed a general leveling off of the rates although a new low was reached during the depths of the depression. The decade of the forties revealed a great upsurge especially in the immediate postwar period, followed by a decline. Since the Korean war a plateau seems to have been reached, which is slightly higher than in any decade previous to 1940. Some of the suggested causal factors involved in divorce and the implications of such will be discussed in detail in Chapter 26.

The Changing Status of Women

Slowly but surely the status of the woman in society has arisen in the Western World since the days of the extended family. Comparatively speaking, modern women are not held in subjection, legally, socially, educationally, and economically as they were in more traditional societies. Compared to Blackstone's day in England women now have a much freer legal status than they had. They make up approximately one-third of our labor force outside the household. Many of the occupations formerly closed to them have been opened. In the public services in general, women receive equal pay for equal work and in private industry the tendency is in that direction. In the educational realm, girls are allowed to enter curricula at all levels, although they are not particularly encouraged in some. In general they do work slightly above the output of boys at given ability levels as measured by our present tests. Women are teachers at all levels of our educational system and they tend to predominate in the grade and high schools.

Where women go from here is at present highly controversial. Mead, along with some of our leaders concerned with adding women to our scientific pool in greater numbers, thinks that women are heading "back to the cave." [14] She feels now that the battle against older inequalities has been virtually won, women are not following up their opportunities outside the home. She feels that they are not making use of their personal potentials in the general community to the degree that society would presently allow. Many are restricting their lives to their own boring existences, mainly focusing on mate selection, the rearing of children, and the maintenance of a household.

Betty Friedan goes much further. In her provocative book, *The Feminine Mystique,* she criticizes social scientists, advertisers, men, and society for a generally conservative attitude regarding women's role. The feminine mystique denies the woman her identity. She is forced to achieve an identity through husband or children, not in her own right. It is impossible

[14] Margaret Mead, "Return of the Cave Woman," *Saturday Evening Post,* Vol. 235 (March 3, 1962).

for her to achieve identity in this fashion, or through housework. In Mrs. Friedan's own words:

If women do not put forth, finally, that effort to become all that they have it in them to become, they will forfeit their own humanity. A woman today who has no goal, no purpose, no ambition patterning her days into the future, making her stretch and grow beyond that small score of years in which her body can fill its biological function, is committing a kind of suicide. For that future half a century after the child-bearing years are over is a fact that an American woman cannot deny. Nor can she deny that as a housewife, the world is indeed rushing past her door while she just sits and watches. The terror she feels is real, if she has no place in that world.

The feminine mystique has succeeded in burying millions of American women alive. There is no way for these women to break out of their comfortable concentration camps except by finally putting forth an effort—that human effort which reaches beyond biology, beyond the narrow walls of home, to help shape the future. Only by such a personal commitment to the future can American women break out of the housewife trap and truly find fulfillment as wives and mothers—by fulfilling their own unique possibilities as separate human beings.[15]

Many questions remain. While Mrs. Friedan's thesis seems overdrawn, she probably reflects an uneasiness that is common in certain groups of educated women. The basic problem is probably that of coordinating outside-the-home roles for women with those in the home.

Economic Functions

As we previously described it, the early American family was basically a cooperative, self-sufficient, productive-consumptive unit. The early settlers with the help of their neighbors raised their own barns and houses, planted and harvested their own food, and processed raw materials into clothing for their own use. They made most of their tools and used them to grow and develop products, most of which they consumed. Slowly but surely this picture was to change to the point that the family can no longer be said to be a productive unit. New machine technology on the farm has increasingly meant that the farm family produces more than it can consume. The town and city family now buys mostly products that have been manufactured by others. Presently it can be said that in many rural areas factory methods of production and labor are rapidly displacing even the modern type of farm family as we have known it in this generation. The tendency toward the use of processed staples is especially pronounced.

This is not to say that no work is done in the home. Final preparation of foods for serving takes place in the home. Even this has been taken over

[15] Betty Friedan, *The Feminine Mystique* (New York, Dell, 1963), pp. 324–325.

in the form of TV dinners for emergency occasions! Mechanical and other inventions have been tremendous aids to the housewife as labor-saving devices. While the growth of service institutions such as restaurants, beauty shops, and laundries has been steady there remains a division of labor between the home and outside organizations. In spite of the above exceptions, the overall trend has certainly been away from the older type of productive-consumptive unit toward one oriented toward consumption.

It must not be inferred that the family which is a productive unit is the only source of all that is good and noble. When the family, especially the large one, has full control over production and consumes most of its goods, productive efficiency is limited.[16] A high level of living as we know it demands specialization, marketing organization, and the accumulation of surpluses beyond their own needs by those involved in production. How many families would have automobiles, refrigerators, and radios if they were forced to produce their own?

The modern system demands its price. The factory and office pull the father and, to an increasing extent, the mother away from the children. Children become expensive liabilities rather than home-grown helping hands. Older and marginal persons are not as readily utilized as they were in a more simplified system of production. Even marriage itself is no longer the economic necessity that it once was. The integrative outcomes of sharing in an on-going productive venture are lost. We are speaking of a major revolutionary process at work here.

Religious Activity

For a number of years social scientists have suggested that in the Western World, at least, a general movement from a sacred to secular orientation is taking place. While this thesis is now subjected to some challenge, it seems clear that there has been a tendency for the home to be less of a religious institution than it once was. If we may be permitted to go back to the European and Near Eastern origins of our family system, the first religious practices were held within the home with the father or patriarch as priest. Eventually in Europe the institutional church replaced the family functions to some extent. In colonial America and especially on the frontier the family was again inclined to operate as a religious unit. Grace at the table, oral reading of the Bible, and family prayer were common practices. For those who took their religion seriously the family was a religious institution, blessed by God and engaged in carrying on His work. Children were taught religious precepts and otherwise socialized within a religious framework.

It must again be emphasized that the early colonists represented diverse

---

[16] Ogburn and Nimkoff, *op. cit.,* Chapter 12.

religious groups. In initial settlements church buildings often did not exist. Further, many immigrants coming to this country were attempting to escape from the state or established church in Europe. With this background in mind we can understand the fact that formal church affiliation in early America was low, comprising in many communities less than 10 percent of the population. In 1963 more than 64 percent of our peoples were affiliated with the organized church.[17] Does this mean that families are more religious than they previously were? [18]

There has been a recent flurry of interest in organized religion, especially since World War II. Its significance is difficult to interpret. It is doubtful that it signifies a return to family religion in the traditional sense. It is perhaps rather in upper and middle-class circles partly a matter of conformity and status. Further, the gap between religious activity in the church as a family, and religious affiliation is great. Many children are deposited at the church door to attend Sunday School and to be called for after the parents have had a delayed breakfast in peace with the Sunday newspaper. The traditional family more typically worshiped as a unit in either the home or church house.

The change that has come about involves a change in conception of the family. Many families are no longer clear as to what values they wish to stress or embody. They do, as attitude studies indicate, wish their children to be exposed to some kind of religious instruction.[19] Not being sure of themselves as qualified teachers they defer to the church and wish it or perhaps the public school to impart the desired training. This seems to be especially true in Protestant but to some degree also in Catholic circles.[20]

Educational Functions

Using the formal language of the anthropologist we can say that the primitive society had no differentiated or specialized institution responsible for the education of the young. The function was that of the family. As we move from the older traditional society to the modern, urban society there is a tendency for the school to assume more and more educational tasks. The situation is complicated by the fact that enlarged and divergent conceptions of the ends as well as the means of education are involved. In our own country training in work skills, morals (character), and manners (social

[17] Benson Landis (Ed.), *Yearbook of American Churches,* National Council of Churches of Christ in U.S.A., 1965, p. 280.

[18] This has been a matter of considerable controversy. Most religious journals, such as *Christian Century,* carry articles and editorials on the subject from time to time. See also any standard text in the Sociology of Religion.

[19] John Seeley, *et al., Crestwood Heights* (New York, Basic Books, 1956), Chapter 8.

[20] John Thomas, "Religion and the Child," *Social Order* (May, 1951), pp. 205–210.

skills), was originally carried on within the family. In general children were expected to follow the occupations of their parents, and the farm home certainly provided a general vocational training. The aristocrats often hired private tutors to give training in the arts to their children; however, the tutoring was done in the household. Eventually it was held that families could not provide the reading, writing, and simple mathematical training needed for Bible reading and home engineering. The one-room school with its three R curriculum was developed as a supplement to the home to meet a need which was strongly felt in many communities. Obviously this school was a far cry from our present system. In many cases students were in attendance only when they were not needed at home.

Slowly the complicated, multipurpose school system has emerged as a dominant force in American society. New conceptions of human nature and of the role of the school have resulted in the development of instructional programs involving far more than elementary skills. Not only has the school become involved in the teaching of social skills, but it also gives some attention to physical and mental health, recreational pursuits, and food intake. The entrance of the school into areas other than the three R's has involved considerable controversy. Such matters as responsibility for religious and moral training are not resolved. Nevertheless, it is logical to assume that formal education outside the home will remain a part of our society in the future.[21]

Further Functions

A number of other functions formerly carried by the family have been lost or transferred to other institutions. Recreation was formerly centered in the home and small community. With the coming of new transportation facilities and the development of cities, commercial entertainment was to become an important business. While developments such as television and radio represent to a degree countertrends, the overall tendency has been toward a breakup of many of the older family patterns of recreation. Older so-called protective and welfare functions have increasingly been adopted by local, state, and national governmental agencies. In general, what were formerly family and kinship, or perhaps local church or community responsibilities have been transferred to the larger community represented by the state or nation. Developments which bring to mind the concept "welfare state" represent especially the transfer of the so-called protective functions, most of which once resided in the family, to the larger, secular governmental bodies. Whether this is a matter of Parkinson's law of bureaucratic development or because of other social forces at work, it is doubtful that this trend will be appreciably reversed.

[21] Nimkoff, *op. cit.,* Part III.

ARE MARRIAGE AND THE FAMILY ABOUT TO DISAPPEAR?

We have examined some of the major changes of structure and function which have been underway in the American marriage and family system. Noting the variations that still exist in various subgroups it is true that some of the traditional functions are no longer being performed by the family, at least in the manner that they previously were. Marriage and family life are "not what they used to be." One can legitimately ask: "Do we have before us a system which is in its dotage? Is the family an example of cultural lag, an outmoded institution which is dead but not yet buried?" A number of writers have given attention to such questions. For convenience they can be labeled as liberal and conservative critics, it being granted that each group is concerned with movement toward a more satisfying life as it sees it.

Two Harvard sociologists have been outstanding critics of the modern family from a position which is to the right of center. Sorokin takes the stand that western society has been in transition from a sacred, stable type of culture (ideational) to a contract-sensate style of life.[22] This latter type of society emphasizes values that are essentially false and weak. Materialism, happiness, security, comfort, and indulgence are substituted for the more basic values developed in Greece of the eighth to fifth centuries B.C. or the medieval period of Europe. Basic causal factors involved in this transition to a sensate culture have been Protestantism, paganism, capitalism, and utilitarianism.

The possibilities for a family life worthy of the name in a sensate culture are not good. Writing in 1937, Sorokin declared:

The family as a sacred union of husband and wife, of parents and children, will continue to disintegrate. Divorces and separations will increase until any profound difference between socially sanctioned marriages and illicit sex-relationships disappears. Children will be separated earlier and earlier from parents. The main sociocultural functions of the family will further decrease until the family becomes a mere incidental cohabitation of male and female while the home will become a mere overnight parking place mainly for sex-relationship.[23]

Zimmerman, a colleague of Sorokin for a number of years, holds that the family has been in transition from the large extended *trustee* type through the *domestic* to the *atomistic*. He believes that the old trustee type had to give way in the West under the revolutionary pressures at work in the religious and economic realms of society. However, the domestic

---

[22] Pitrim Sorokin, *The Crisis of Our Age* (New York, Dutton, 1941), pp. 130–140.

[23] Pitrim Sorokin, *Social and Cultural Dynamics,* Vol. 4 (New York, Harper & Row, 1937), p. 776.

type family is most favorable for society. It is a solid, stable, patriarchal unit performing many functions. It produces many children. The roles within the family are clear-cut. Duty and fidelity as against love and freedom are stressed.

The atomistic family is weak and cannot last as a system according to Zimmerman. It is nihilistic and carries within it the seeds of its own destruction. Divorce, adultery, homosexuality, and other such aberrations, are correlates of the atomistic family, and symptoms of the decay which has set into the domestic system. The real cause of the trouble is that the general populace is giving up its faith in the values of familism. Zimmerman is a family determinist, holding that family change is the "final decisive force" in historical change. As he notes in reference to Greece and Rome, if the family becomes atomistic the whole country is eventually doomed to decay.[24]

Zimmerman and Sorokin must be given credit for their willingness to deal with masses of material and for their attempts to bring order into it. Their work really falls under the category of "philosophy of history," and it suffers from the same shortcomings that other works in this field have evidenced. The idea that individualism can be pushed to the point that structural strains are induced in an institution is accepted by many social scientists, this writer among them. Suggesting that we are in a stage similar to that of the declining days of Rome or Greece is another matter. Certainly there are many factors of life present in our culture today which were not present in previous periods. These theories seem to oversimplify phenomena in the pursuit of order.

On the liberal side, strong criticisms of monogamous marriage and family life as we know it came in the twenties. Writers such as Key, Russell, Calverton, Lindsey, and others stirred up a storm of controversy by their writings which called into question many beliefs about monogamous marriage.[25] A number of themes were common to the writers cited above, especially the first three. Marriage is an outmoded institution. Signs of decay are everywhere in abundance. Conventional marriage and family patterns represent bourgeois carry-overs which have no meaning in our present world. A new moral system is needed which will separate love in marriage and the childbearing function.

As university teacher of mathematics and as a lay philosopher, Russell observed the behavior of youth around him.[26] Many seemed to be possessed by sex to the point that their studies were affected. He proposed that trial marriages should be allowed, to be followed by more regular marriages at later periods. Russell was more conservative than some writers regarding children born of such trial marriages. He insisted that they be cared for

[24] Carle Zimmerman, *Family and Civilization* (New York, Harper & Row, 1947).
[25] See Una Sait, *New Horizons for the Family* (New York, Macmillan, 1938), Chapter 20, for a thorough discussion of the radical marriage theories of the twenties.
[26] Bertrand Russell, *Marriage and Morals* (New York, Liveright, 1929).

adequately. Actually what he proposed in essence was trial marriage with liberal divorce for the childless who did not wish to continue the marriage.

Russell's most radical proposal involved extramarital sex relations. Where marriage is successfully established, "The expectation ought to be that it will be lifelong, but that it will not exclude other sex relations." [27] Temporary alliances should be accepted by both parties. The problem is to develop a high level of control lest "orgies of jealousy" ensue.

Lindsey, for many years a nationally known divorce court judge in Denver, proposed the concept of "companionate marriage." [28] Noting the kinds of problems that came before him and, especially, the sexual pressures on the unmarried, Judge Lindsey favored youthful marriage and the use of contraceptives so that parenthood could be delayed. If the partners were satisfied with each other, well and good. The couple would move along normally and children would come. But the system "would also afford a line of retreat in case the marriage failed." With no children to consider, the divorce would be by mutual consent with no provision for alimony.

A modern critic, Moore, takes a more moderate point of view, but he writes in the intellectual tradition of Russell, as he acknowledges. Moore feels that the family is not making up for its lost functions of the past by an emphasis on social-psychological functions. The duty of affection to relatives and family members is to him a barbaric relic. Parents are increasingly unable to exert authority over their children. Motherhood really is frequently a degrading experience and it is useless to try to raise the social value of the role of housewife and mother. Moore feels that parents will have to assert authority much more vigorously if the family structure is to regain any semblance of solidarity. He doubts that this more conservative approach will offer any real solution. The task of child care and supervision could be handled by specialized institutions with the help of machinery such as the Skinner box. We need not worry about the absence of fondling, the giving of affection, and the early socialization. "A nurse can perform these tasks . . . just as well as the parents, often better." [29] Certain adaptations to shore up the middle-class family are also considered by Moore but he believes that like the old soldier, the family may not die but will just fade away.

The Efficacy of Marriage and Family

What can be said regarding the value of our present system of marriage and family? It should be clear to the reader that this is a complicated question and that where one stands is to a considerable degree determined by his

[27] *Ibid.*, p. 315.

[28] Benjamin Lindsey and Wainwright Evans, *The Companionate Marriage* (New York, Liveright, 1927).

[29] Barrington Moore, *Political Power and Social Theory* (Cambridge, Harvard, 1958), Chapter 5.

orientation as he approaches the question. For example, Marxists will view certain aspects of the American system as decayed relics. Those of a conservative bent are inclined to be disturbed by changes they consider pathological while others might simply consider them as signs of adaptive adjustments. All of us "see through a glass darkly" and what we see we interpret by use of our particular frame of reference. Given this condition certain observations may be in order.

First of all attention may be given to the matter of the loss of functions. As Parsons points out, there is no agreement as to the number of functions the family must perform in a culture in order for it to be important and useful. In assessing the literature one finds listed with regularity the following family functions: (a) channeling of sex and affection, (b) reproduction, (c) socialization and education of children, (d) economic, (e) protection, (f) recreation, and (g) religion. We will discuss these briefly in reverse order. We have already mentioned that great changes have taken place in the religious, recreational, and protective functions formerly borne by the family. However, some values, religious or otherwise, are transmitted within the family in the socialization process over which the family has more control than the church. Some recreation is carried on in the home, family vacations are common, and devices such as television and such practices as cookouts represent possible countertrends. While the family does not perform the functions of the police force, the fire department and the like, it certainly provides the major protective force for the very young child. The productive functions of the family, however, are largely obsolete.

As Kuhn points out, the family is a major consuming organization.[30] Mother may insist on shopping alone when buying a new hat, but she is very much concerned with the opinions of father and the children. Right on through the college level the children are dependent on the *family* checking account. Further, families furnish the manpower for the industrial machines, and according to some authorities they must learn to adapt to our businesses and military institutions to a greater degree than they already do. The narrow focus of some of our past economics on production has blinded us to certain family realities.

The multiplication of educational facilities outside the home is really a significant revolution and it will continue. However, scholars of various fields agree that what may be called *primary* socialization is extremely important if not critical. The family gets the first chance to train the child at a period when he is most susceptible to influence. Further and ideally, the teaching can be done in an atmosphere of warmth and affection through use of informal methods. Social scientists, educators, clinicians, religious leaders, and others may disagree on how adequately the family is perform-

[30] Manford Kuhn, "American Families Today," in Howard Becker and Reuben Hill (Eds.), *Family, Marriage and Parenthood* (Boston, Heath, 1955), p. 165.

ing this function, but it is generally agreed that no substitutes are available for the family at this time. Whether such substitutes will be found in the future is an open question. Further learning takes place in the family circle throughout an individual's lifetime. Reinforcement of basic attitudes consistently takes place within the family environment, as any person engaged in social action well knows.

The first two categories mentioned are closely associated. Although there are predictions of test tube societies, so far we have found it necessary to institutionalize carefully the reproduction of new members. Nowhere in the world is this a casual matter for a total society. Certain experiments have been made in regard to precisely how the process is to be patterned, of course, but reproduction is never left to chance. It is highly doubtful that it could be.

Finally we come to the function of channeling of sexual and affectional relations. While the Kinsey and other studies show considerable premarital and some extramarital sexual experimentation the fact remains that within marriage and the family circle, love can be and is expressed in a fashion not matched outside. As a matter of fact, our expectations in this regard are very high, relatively speaking. With the breakup of the large family and the old style community the family circle is now for some the main arena in which intimate affection, sexual and nonsexual, can be freely expressed. If the average human has a great need for this type of interaction the family to which he regularly returns provides for this important relationship.

A reasonable appraisal of the functions formerly performed by the family will indicate then, that at least a minimum number are being performed to a reasonable degree. It would appear that the critics to both the left and the right suffer from overemphasis. Regarding the right, it is doubtful that as a total society we can ever turn back the years. It is questionable whether the old style traditional family could exist in a modern industrial complex. The Amish, perhaps our strongest proponents of the traditional western family system believe that it cannot. The family is embedded in our larger institutional complex and in many ways is at the mercy of stronger systems. These must be returned to their old-fashioned forms if marriage and the family are to be also. Unfortunately, many proponents of a sharp reversal of social change lean toward fascist programs which if followed would represent psuedosystems bereft of many of the basic values of former periods. This is not meant as a criticism of all attempts to induce some stability in our present system, however.

Critics on the left have tended to be critical of the restrictions marriage and family systems bring on individual freedom regarding sex, divorce, and the freedom of women. Outside the U.S. the totalitarian left has also been concerned about the tendency of the family to resist the political regime, as have leaders of the totalitarian right, for that matter. There is no question that some of these criticisms are based on sound observations. Actually many of the restrictions that previously obtained in the family no longer exist. The person who feels unduly bound by present-day marriage and family patterns has, relatively speaking, an extreme point of view on individualism. The old problem of freedom versus order is in evidence. A minimum of order would seem necessary for group survival.

As to the suggestion that marriage and family are dead but not yet buried it must be pointed out that the corpse is a rather lively one. Marriage is very popular and children are appearing in numbers which are disturbing the complacency of school boards. Our family system is not what it used to be, and its organization in many individual families is none too strong, but it is still very much with us.

What we face is the problem of distinguishing elements of reorganization and adaptation from those of disorganization. A substantial block of social scientists of which the schools of Burgess, Locke, and Parsons would be representative, takes the position that modern marriage and family represent essential adjustments to the emerging milieu. The writer would tend to agree with the following summary position:

The development of this sort of family system is not the result of chance. The family system is closely integrated with the occupational system, and the values and requirements of the latter apparently determine the family's rules and structure . . . occupational roles are organized around standards of accomplishment, and upward movement economically or in terms of power and prestige requires freedom from ties of all sorts—geographical, sentimental, what-you-will. It is only by being regarded as a unit, and by being a small unit with children too young to compete or otherwise interfere, that the family is saved from destruction by the occupational system. To maintain this unity, however, the family must be free to follow the husband-father in his job quest; it must not make demands on him that are inconsistent with his performance in the occupational sphere; its values and ambitions must be those that promote his advance. In addition, it must be a buffer between him and the impersonal, emotionally neutral world of work, where he is valued not so much for what he is as for what he can accomplish. Hence, the high value put on personal relationships within this little family, the emphasis on being "in love," the insistence on the right to dissolve the marriage if emotional needs are not met.

This kind of family, then, would seem to be the kind that the American system, with its emphasis on individual achievement and success requires. It is a family that has only slight ties to former generations, that imposes few lineal responsibilities on its children, that sets the children free to leave home, choose their marital partners, and follow job opportunities as they see fit.[31]

This is not to suggest that all is well. Our system of marriage and family is under severe strains, some of which will be delineated in later

[31] Helen Witmer and Ruth Kotinsky (Eds.), *Personality in the Making* (New York, Harper & Row, 1952), pp. 183–184.

chapters. The reader may want to make his own assessments, and he is encouraged to do so. The point is that our family system is embedded in our total social structure; it is as strong as that structure. Some authorities feel that our family cannot stand much more external pressure without being seriously weakened. If this does happen the blame, if one wishes to use this moralistic terminology, will have to be laid at the source of the pressure.

SELECTED READINGS

Allen, Fredrick L., *The Big Change* (New York, Harper & Row, 1952).

Abrams, Ray, "The Concept of Family Stability," *Annals American Academy of Political and Social Science,* Vol. 272 (November, 1950), pp. 1–8.

Burgess, Ernest, and Locke, Harvey, *The Family: From Institution to Companionship* (New York, American Book, 1953), Chapter 22.

Cavan, Ruth, *The American Family* (New York, Crowell, 1953), Chapter 1.

Duvall, Evelyn, *Family Development* (Philadelphia, Lippincott, 1957), Chapter 2.

Kenkel, William, *The Family in Perspective* (New York, Appleton-Century-Crofts, 1960), Part II.

Kephart, William, *The Family, Society and the Individual* (Boston, Houghton Mifflin, 1961), Part 3.

Farber, Seymour, Mustacchi, Piero, and Wilson, Roger (Eds.), *Man and Civilization: The Family's Search for Survival* (New York, McGraw-Hill, 1965).

Kirkpatrick, Clifford, *The Family* (New York, Ronald, 1955), Part II.

Landis, Judson, and Landis, Mary, *Readings in Marriage and the Family* (Englewood Cliffs, N.J., Prentice-Hall, 1952), Part I.

Lundberg, Ferdinand and Farnham, Maryina, *Modern Woman, The Lost Sex* (New York, Harper & Row, 1947).

Miller, Daniel, and Swanson, Guy, *The Changing American Parent* (New York, Wiley, 1958), Chapter 2.

Nimkoff, Meyer, "The Family in the United States," *Marriage and Family Living,* Vol. 16 (November, 1954), pp. 390–396.

Ogburn, William, and Nimkoff, Meyer, *Technology and the Changing Family* (Boston, Houghton Mifflin, 1955).

Parsons, Talcott, and Bales, Robert F., *Family, Socialization, and Interaction Process* (New York, Free Press, 1955), Chapter 1.

Peterson, James, *Education for Marriage* (New York, Scribner, 1964), Chapter 1.

Winch, Robert, and McGinnis, Robert, and Barringer, H. R. (Eds.), *Selected Studies in Marriage and the Family* (New York, Holt, Rinehart and Winston, 1962), Part I.

Winch, Robert, *The Modern Family* (New York, Holt, Rinehart and Winston, 1963), Part 2.

Zimmerman, Carle, and Cervantes, Lucius, *Marriage and the Family* (Chicago, Regnery, 1956), Chapter 4.

QUESTIONS AND EXERCISES

1. Write an essay entitled "The Probable Impact of Science and Technology on Marriage and the Family in the Next Twenty Years."
2. Ask one of your grandparents to compare from memory the marriage and family patterns in the "old days" with present practices.
3. Ogburn and Nimkoff refer to the suggestion that steam was the enemy of family life (see the cited reference). Is this true or untrue? Defend your answer.
4. Is there a minimum number of functions the family must perform for society in order for both the family and society to be healthy? Discuss.
5. Do you agree with Zimmerman's position to the effect that a society with an atomistic family system will eventually decay? Discuss.
6. Governmental services for the family seem to have been on the increase in Western Europe and the United States in the last two or three decades. How would you explain this trend? Is it inevitable? Is it undesirable?
7. The subtitle of the well-known book by Burgess and Locke (see cited reference)is "From Institution to Companionship." Are you willing to accept the thesis that the family has withered away to the extent that it is only a companionship and not an institution?
8. Is it necessary, in order to have political and economic democracy, that the home be democratic? Discuss.
9. Ask your parents to discuss the impact of the depression of the thirties on their marriage and family life. Do you have any advice to share on the basis of their experience?
10. Is it possible to turn the clock back and return to marriage and family life of the "good old days"? Why or why not?
11. Seeley, *et. al.* have written *Crestwood Heights* describing life in an upper middle-class suburb. Write a critique of this book based on your own experience.
12. Church membership is at an all-time high in the United States. Do you believe that the average family is more religious than it was a generation or two ago? What is the basis for your answer?

4

The Developmental and Life Cycle Approach in Marriage and Family

All the world's a stage,
And all the men and women merely players.
They have their exits and their entrances;
And one man in his time plays many parts,
His acts being seven ages. At first the infant,
Mewling and puking in the nurse's arms.
And then the whining school-boy, with his satchel
And shining morning face, creeping like snail
Unwillingly to school. And then the lover,
Sighing like furnace, with a woeful ballad
Made to his mistress' eyebrow. Then a soldier,
Full of strange oaths and bearded like the pard;
Jealous in honour, sudden and quick in quarrel,
Seeking the bubble reputation
Even in the cannon's mouth. And then the justice,
In fair round belly with good capon lined,
With eyes severe and beard of formal cut,
Full of wise saws and modern instances;
And so he plays his part. The sixth age shifts
Into the lean and slipper'd pantaloon,
With spectacles on nose and pouch on side;
His youthful hose, well saved, a world too wide
For his shrunk shank; and his big manly voice,
Turning again toward childish treble, pipes
And whistles in his sound. Last scene of all,
That ends this strange eventful history,
Is second childishness, and mere oblivion,
Sans teeth, sans eyes, sans taste, sans everything.
—SHAKESPEARE, *As You Like It*—

Change is an inherent aspect of life. To live is to grow and to develop. The person changes from the small cell starting at conception to the adult measuring five or six feet in height. Accompanying these changes in gross physical size of the individual are a multitude of physical, psychological, and social changes as well. The organs grow, the basic body functions develop, and the mind matures.

While the growth processes are not absolutely predictable, a certain order in the change can be readily observed. This has motivated many students of human behavior to attempt to divide the individual life cycle into a series of stages.

INDIVIDUAL STAGES

One of the more detailed and interesting attempts to delineate a series of life stages and correlated characteristic activities is provided by Feldman:

Stage	Characteristic
1. First prenatal, embryonic period:	Acquisition of human form
2. Second prenatal, fetal period:	Beginnings of motility
3. First period of infancy:	Head and eye practice
4. Second period of infancy:	Reaching
5. Third period of infancy:	Dual orientation
6. First period of childhood:	Domestication
First period of socialization:	Central point of reference adult, parents
7. Second period of childhood:	Parting of the generations
Second period of socialization:	Activity beyond home: child with own generation. Two zones of child's world, outdoor and domestic
8. First period of adolescence:	Quasi adulthood
Third period of socialization:	Acts and regards self as grown up. Own generation as model. Others "old "
9. Second period of adolescence:	Beginnings of individualization
10. First period of maturity:	Self-realization. Sustained application to responsibility
11. Second period of maturity:	Self-appraisal, the beginning of retrospection of one's life-career
12. First period of senescence:	Retirement, Period of contraction, Outside interests and employment given up. A new period of domestication
13. Second period of senescence:	Farewell, l'envoi. Farewell said in variety of ways; carrying on, calm preparations, hurry, panic, resignation, flight to retrospection. . .[1]

[1] Adapted from S. Feldman, "Origins of Behavior and Man's Life-Career," *American Journal of Psychology,* Vol. 54 (January, 1941), p. 54.

Feldman's thirteen stages are instructive but unwieldy. A more work-able sequence identifies eight stages:

1. Pre-natal
2. Babyhood
3. Early childhood
4. Late childhood

5. Adolescence
6. Young adulthood
7. Middle adulthood
8. Later maturity [2]

It is clear that individual differences must be taken into consideration. One infant begins to reach out for objects well before the neighbor child of similar age and sex. A particular seventh grade boy achieves the height of 5'10" (to the delight of the basketball coach) while the average boy in the class is 5'5". College advisors and parents often wonder if "that boy will ever outgrow his sophomoric approach" to academic and nonacademic life problems.

It must be recognized that in addition to individual differences in rates of development, there is the further problem that the stages overlap; they are not clear-cut. For these two reasons, at least, the identified stages may not fit the realities of life for every individual. Nevertheless the delineation of a series of stages has been found helpful as a conceptual teaching and learning device in many areas of science, pure and applied. For purposes of pedagogy, of planning and visualization of a future lifetime development, it would appear that the use of a series of stages would be extremely worth-while. We will operate on this assumption.

FAMILY STAGES

The individual, then, goes through a series of developments which have been described as involving a life cycle. So it is in the family—it also has a developmental cycle which can be identified.

The family life cycle is generated by a number of interacting processes which we can separately name and discuss but cannot disassociate in actual living. The individual man and woman, as husband and wife, begin with the birth of the first child. As successive children are born they must enlarge their roles to encompass the second, third, and additional children as individuals and as members of the growing family group. Each addition to the family brings not merely an enlargement of the family group, but a significant reorganization of family living, compelling sometimes far-reaching changes in the patterns of living and of interpersonal relationships, as well as reflecting the increasing age and maturation of all those within the family circle. The family therefore is never static, but always changing and no two children are ever born into the "same" family any more than any two people can bathe a year or two apart in the same river.

[2] See Elizabeth Hurlock, *Developmental Psychology* (New York, McGraw-Hill, 1953) for a parallel series of individual developmental stages.

Thus as the children grow older, the parents are also growing older, changing their needs and desires, their hopes and expectations as well as their responses to the alteration in the demands and pressures of the growing children. Likewise the children are progressively changing in their relationship to their parents and their brothers and sisters.[3]

Depending partially on the factors emphasized, the family may be directed into a large or a small number of stages. The logical minimum would be two stages, with terms such as expanding and contracting used to designate the two. This seems too undifferentiated. If, on the other hand, we could find some characteristic that changed slightly every two or three years we could delineate some fifteen or twenty stages of development. This would prove too cumbersome to be handled analytically. A moderate number of stages would seem to be more desirable. At least such a view corresponds with the thinking of several professional students of the family.

Two groups of sociologists in the early thirties made use of a four-stage cycle. Kirkpatrick and associates, focusing on the family in relation to the school level of the children, delineated these stages: (1) the preschool family, (2) the grade school family, (3) the high school family, and (4) the all adult family.[4] Sorokin and associates also made use of four stages, but focused on the constellation of family members: (1) married couples just starting pair living, (2) couples with one or more children, (3) couples with one or more self-supporting (adult) children, and (4) couples growing old.[5] Bigelow, interested in family consumptive and expenditure patterns in relation to the family cycle, describes seven periods as follows: (1) family establishment, (2) childbearing and preschool period, (3) elementary school period, (4) high school period, (5) college period, (6) recovery period, and (7) retirement period.[6]

It must be clear that various factors enter the picture to complicate the problem of slicing the family cycle into a particular number of stages. Such factors as the number of children born, their spacing, the time of the arrival of the first child, and the amount of education are immediately apparent. Other complicating items such as permanent or temporary absences or addition of family members due to death, desertion, or military service are apparent.

The family life cycle schema is more complicated than the individual life cycle profile because of the greater possibility of overlapping. Actually

[3] Lawrence Frank, in foreword to Evelyn Duvall and Reuben Hill, co-chairmen, report of committee on *Dynamics of Family Interaction,* National Conference on Family Life (February, 1948), mimeographed, p. 1.

[4] E. L. Kirkpatrick, *et. al.,* "The Life Cycle of the Farm Family in Relation to Its Standard of Living," *Research Bulletin 121,* University of Wisconsin, Agricultural Experiment Station, (1934).

[5] Pitrim Sorokin, *et al., A Systematic Sourcebook in Rural Sociology,* Vol. II (Minneapolis, The University of Minnesota Press, 1931).

[6] Howard Bigelow, "Financing the Marriage," in Howard Becker and Reuben Hill (Eds.), *Family, Marriage and Parenthood* (Boston, Heath, 1955), pp. 411–414.

when more than one child is involved the family will in a sense be in two stages simultaneously. For example, a couple who has a child when they are in their early forties might easily be a family with teenagers and a family with a preschool child at one and the same time. Other possibilities will come to mind.

One reasonable solution to the problem of overlapping of stages is to focus on the first child.[7] Using this approach it is reasoned that the family enters each new stage with the maturation of the oldest child, because in such sequence it learns to adapt to the requirements of the new stage.

The following series of family stages, thus, seem logical: (1) childless couple, (2) expectant pair, (3) preschool family, (4) school-age family, (5) teen-age family, (6) family in middle years, and (7) family in later years.

Brief attention to the marriage and family cycle in terms of number of years spent in each stage and so on should prove initially instructive. Through the use of census projection for 1980 the typical family cycle may be outlined based on median ages in all cases. (See Table 4). The young couple will marry at age twenty for the girl and twenty-three for the boy. The first child will be born about two years later. Two more babies will be born four or five years after the marriage. The interval between birth of the third and second will be greater than between the first and second. This means that the mother will be approaching thirty and the father will be in his early thirties when the last child is born.

Projection for the school period and teen period follow the preschool years. Note that we are focusing on the oldest child in each case to estimate the number of years which are spent in a stage. When the last child leaves the home to marry, the mother will be about forty-nine or fifty and the father will be in his early fifties. After this the couple will be alone again for a period of about thirteen years until the husband reaches retirement age (set here at sixty-five). The couple then enters the later years with the strong possibility of widowhood for one of the parties.

---

[7] Seminar groups under Dr. Reuben Hill have been attempting to develop a conceptual scheme which will be manageable and yet take into account overlapping and other problems of the family life cycle. One outcome of this has been a publication by Roy Rodgers entitled *Improvements in the Construction and Analysis of Family Life Cycle Categories* (Kalamazoo, The Western Michigan University Press, 1962), pp. 1–65. Rodgers argues that for research purposes greater account must be taken of "plurality patterns." He does not believe that the first child sets the tone for the family and that stages of development should be delineated on the basis of the first child's development. Instead he proposes that, tentatively, the stages of the family life cycle be defined both in terms of the oldest and youngest child. It must be noted that taking other than the first child into account greatly complicates the task of delineating stages. By focusing on a sample of families and using both older and younger children, Rodgers found it necessary to use twenty-four stages. This is just one of the complexities introduced, although there is considerable merit to the Rodgers' proposal as far as research is concerned. For the purpose of this book where the stress is on pedagogy rather than research as such, a less complicated scheme would seem to be more useful.

TABLE 4

*Median Age of Husband and Wife at Selected Stages
of the Life Cycle of the Family, for the
United States: 1890–1980*

Stage	1890	1940	1950	1960	1980[b]
MEDIAN AGE OF WIFE AT—					
First marriage	22.0	21.5	20.1	20.2	19.5–20.4
Birth of last child	31.9	27.1	26.1	25.8	27–28
Marriage of last child ...	55.3	50.0	47.6	47.1	48–49
Death of husband[a]	53.3	60.9	61.4	63.6	65–66
MEDIAN AGE OF HUSBAND AT—					
First marriage	26.1	24.3	22.8	22.3	22–23
Birth of last child	36.0	29.9	28.8	27.9	29–30
Marriage of last child ...	59.4	52.8	50.3	49.2	51–52
Death of wife[a]	57.4	63.6	64.1	65.7	68–69

[a] This refers to the death of one spouse only. There is a gap of some years between the figure cited and the expected age of death of the spouse. The chances are very high that the wife will outlive the husband. Women have a longer life expectancy and also tend to marry men several years older than themselves.
[b] Projected
SOURCE: 1890, 1940, and 1950 data are from Paul Glick, "The Life Cycle of the Family," *Marriage and Family Living,* Vol. 20 (February, 1955). Those for 1960 and 1980 are from Paul Glick, David Meer, and John Beresford, "Family Foundation and Family Composition: Trends and Prospects," unpublished paper, kindly supplied by Dr. Glick.

The projected series of stages by the age when the spouses enter each period is essentially as follows:

	Husband's Age	Wife's Age
1. Childless couple	23.0	20.4
2. Expectant pair	24.7	22.01
3. Preschool family	25.4	22.8
4. School-age family	31.4	26.8
5. Teen-age family	38.4	33.8
6. Family in middle years	52.0	49.0
7. Family in later years	65.0	62.0

DEVELOPMENTAL TASKS

Individual

The life of the individual proceeds by stages or cycles. The concept of developmental stages has also an important corollary in the concept of *developmental task.* Theorists in the human development field have concluded that certain tasks must be mastered by the individual if he is to have satisfactory growth and development in his society. These are tasks which must be learned and accomplished if the person is to consider himself successful and to be so considered by his associates around him.

So viewed, a developmental task is ". . . a task which arises at or about a certain period in the life of an individual, successful achievement of which leads to his happiness and to success with later tasks, while failure leads to unhappiness in the individual, disapproval by the society, and difficulty with later tasks." [8]

Havighurst suggests that developmental tasks have an origin which is threefold. First, some developmental tasks arise because of physical developments and growth which we speak of as maturation. The infant must learn to balance himself at a certain age, the child to dress himself, and the female adolescent to adjust to the menses. In later years the individual must learn to cope with sex needs, pregnancy, illnesses, declining physical powers, and so on. Societal standards form a second source of individual developmental tasks. The child learns to cover his genitals, to defer to his elders, and to use the King's English or a reasonable facsimile thereof. The adolescent finds that he is pressured to prepare for an occupational role so that he may earn his bread. The woman who has taken certain vows finds that she is expected to be loyal to her husband, even if her personal inclinations tempt her to stray. Between the biological and the cultural is a third basis of individual developmental tasks—that of the individual himself.[9] Even in the most rigid and authoritarian society imaginable, the individual has some leeway in fashioning a life for himself. In the primitive band one man tries to become the best hunter in the group while his cousin is willing to lag behind on everything. One wife in our society attempts to be a glamour girl even though she lacks the physical wherewithal to do so gracefully. A college student runs for a political office, even though his grade average may be endangered in the process. Society presents as it were a general role script for an individual who is at a particular level. The given individual is permitted to "ad lib" to a certain degree.

Parsons and others have stressed the idea that there are certain "functional prerequisites" which exist as conditions which must be met if the group is going to thrive and have continuity over time.[10] A group which wishes to survive must grapple with problems of solidarity, morale, and allocation of responsibility, authority, and resources. The following tasks are in this context basic to the family in America:

1. Maintenance of Order and Intra-family Stability

    a. Providing mechanisms to facilitate channeling of emotional ties among family members

[8] Robert Havighurst, *Human Development and Education* (New York, McKay, 1953), p. 2.

[9] *Op. cit.,* p. 4.

[10] See Talcott Parsons, *Essays in Sociological Theory, Pure and Applied* (New York, Free Press, 1949).

    b. Controlling sex expression

    c. Establishing channels of communication in the family

2. Establishing a Working Relationship with the Larger Family Network and the Community

    a. Developing a balanced relationship between intrafamily living and relations with the outside world

3. Providing a Physical Base for Family Members

    a. Providing clothing, food, and housing

    b. Providing an economic undergirding for the family

4. Dividing and Allotting Responsibility and Authority

    a. Providing means of determining who does what, when, and why

    b. Organizing and dividing the work of the home

    c. Developing habitual roles (reciprocal) so that tasks are performed on reasonable schedule

5. Developing a Family Value System and Pattern of Socialization

    a. Developing a system of values and goals on which there is basic agreement among adult members

    b. Developing a philosophy and method of child rearing

    c. Socialization of children into increasingly more mature roles

6. Maintenance of Morale and Incentive

    a. Developing patterns to give recognition and reward to family members achieving family goals

    b. Developing emotional release mechanisms that are reintegrative for family structure

    c. Providing a systematic method of assuring support to family members needing aid and encouragement

7. Regulating the Reproductive Processes

    a. Mastering negative and positive control of conception

8. Development of Techniques of Incorporating New Members into the Family and Releasing the Young at the Appropriate Time

    a. Assimilating new members (by adoption or from the wider family circle) into the family group and home

    b. Releasing members at young adulthood to marriage and the larger social and economic world [11]

Focusing on the family as an interacting group existing over time, we see then, that particular tasks appear which usually must be achieved if the family is to progress "normally." At the beginning of the family developmental cycle the married pair will have the special problems involved

---

[11] Adapted from Reuben Hill, "Basic Tasks of the Family as a Social System Particularized for Specific Developmental Stages of the Family Life Cycle," mimeographed and wall chart. I am indebted to Dr. Hill and to members of the National Conference on Family Life, *op. cit.,* for some of the basic ideas expressed in this chapter. My first introduction to the developmental approach came in one of Dr. Hill's seminars in family development theory.

in establishing a home base. Economic and other pressures will normally not be as great as when growing children are in the home. However, important tasks have to be met and handled by the young couple during the early months of marriage, if a family structure strong enough for the rigors of childbearing and child rearing is to be built.

The following are basic developmental tasks which may be delineated for the early married couple:

1. Giving full expression to love and affection held toward each other.
2. Developing what will hopefully become a sound system of communication between the pair.
3. Establishing a relationship with the respective in-laws, neighbors, and with organizations in the community.
4. Locating and establishing housing facilities.
5. Securing and maintaining an occupational pursuit which will provide for the economic necessities.
6. Developing an initial set of reciprocal role relationships which will allow individual initiative but will suggest spheres of authority.
7. Development of a procedure for organizing and allotting work tasks.
8. Establishing a minimum time schedule and routine correlated with outside work activities.
9. Developing a *modus operandi* of decision-making.
10. Establishing and developing a mutually acceptable philosophy of life and set of family goals.
11. Developing methods of maintaining morale as a couple.
12. Establishing a relationship that will allow the incorporation of future children into the home.

These basic tasks are hypothesized as being necessary for the married couple to secure minimum adjustment during the initial months of marriage. When pregnancy occurs, usually during the second half of the first year of marriage, new adjustments are necessary. Some new tasks appear, such as facing the inconveniences of pregnancy, childbirth, and parenthood. On the other hand, some previously established tasks remain and must be adapted and modified to the new conditions. A good example of this involves adapting sex relations to pregnancy. Once the child is born, the configuration of the family changes and the developmental task "picture" becomes much more complicated.

With a new child in the family a triad with a unique type of structure emerges. The married couple must develop a new network of love and emotional attachments which include the developing child. Financial adjustment will be called for, to take into account not only the predictable pressures on the household physical quarters and equipment but also contingencies that will arise from time to time. From alternatives which are presented a method and philosophy of child rearing must be instituted.

By the time the first child is ready for school another child will have been born. The family must be adaptable enough to carry the tasks that come with a child in school and yet proceed with the care and nurture of the younger sibling. Having a child in school means the development of new patterns of relating to and communicating with groups and individuals outside the home. At the same time new patterns of work and decision-making that include the children must be developed. Methods of meeting financial, space, and various physical pressures must of course be devised.

Having one or more children in the teens brings the family to its peak in terms of financial pressures, if not others. The teenager will have many contacts with and be greatly influenced by his peers. This may strain the relationships between the generations in the home. This is the period when youth will strive for identity and when initial occupational and career choices must be made. New adjustments in getting household tasks performed, and decisions made within a framework which keeps a high level of morale will be necessary.

In the late teens the children must be "launched" into new school environments, careers, or new families of their own making. This is essentially a transitory period although it will last a number of years for the model American family. During this period the problem arises of maintaining an equilibrium within the family circle and yet relating to more people in the larger community, including potential in-laws.

As the children move out of the home it is necessary that the family regroup and that the mother and father re-emphasize the marital pair relationship. This means that certain functions in the home are given greater stress than they could possibly have received when young children were there. Some couples will develop new or reactivate old patterns of relationships with the larger family network and the community. In some cases their married children will need assistance in establishing successful homes of their own.

Finally the family will enter the stage of late maturity. The husband typically retires from his active occupational role. Post-occupational adjustments and adaptations to declining physical prowess, income, and health are problems normally involved. New emotional, physical, and social tasks present themselves as hurdles if life is to be lived successfully and gracefully.

CONCLUSION

It must be stressed then that the individual has a development cycle in his own right and that the family has a cycle as well. At each "stage" in the cycle of each developmental tasks occur. They may be coordinated or in conflict. For example, a man's sexual needs do not atrophy during the late stages of pregnancy and postpartum weeks when the family cycle precludes free sex expression. A demanding career devours great slices of a man's time during the period when his wife and children need his presence and help desperately. Moreover, it must be admitted that each individual and family is also unique and that some differences are to be expected in the cycles and tasks when individuals or families are compared with each other. In spite of the differences an approach utilizing the concepts of developmental cycle and developmental stages is useful as a standard backdrop for any realistic study of mate selection, marriage, and parenthood.

The remainder of this book is organized in terms of the life cycle scheme which the present chapter has introduced. Part Two focuses mainly on the individual at the post high school level, when he is breaking away from his family of orientation and typically preparing to marry and start a home. A major task of the individual at this stage is to select a mate, and the theme of mate selection as a task dominates Part Two.

Part Three focuses on the new marital pair in the first two stages of the family cycle. Chapters 12 through 19 all deal with basic developmental tasks facing the pair at these two periods (see pages 219–389). Part Four continues the study of the emerging family by focusing on the developmental tasks typical with young children in the home. Part Five gives a synopsis of the rest of the stages in the cycle and disjunctive points that may appear.

The reader is urged to familiarize himself thoroughly with the developmental cycle and developmental task concepts. Theoretically they should be helpful in analyzing his own individual and family life, especially in regard to projections into the future.[12]

SELECTED READINGS

Bigelow, Howard, "Financing the Marriage," in Howard Becker and Reuben Hill (Eds.), *Family, Marriage and Parenthood* (Boston, Heath, 1955), Chapter 13.

Blackwell, Gordon, "Correlates of the State of Family Development Among Farm Families on Relief," *Rural Sociology,* Vol. 7 (June, 1942), pp. 161–174.

Blalock, Ann, "Introduction to a Study of the Theory of Family Development," M.A. thesis, University of North Carolina, 1955.

Blood, Robert, "Contributions from Structure-Function Sociology to a Conceptual Framework for Family Analysis," November, 1950, unpublished paper.

Bowerman, Charles, and Kinch, J. W., "Changes in Family and Peer Orientation of Children Between the Fourth and Tenth Grades," *Social Forces,* Vol. 37 (March, 1959), pp. 206–211.

[12] See Reuben Hill and Roy Rodgers, "The Developmental Approach," in Harold T. Christensen (Ed.), *Handbook of Marriage and Family* (Chicago, Rand McNally, Chicago, 1964), Chapter 5 for a thorough discussion of the technical and theoretical aspects of the developmental approach in the family field. See also Evelyn Duvall, *Family Development* (Philadelphia, Lippincott, 1962).

Cavan, Ruth, *Marriage and Family in the Modern World* (New York, Crowell, 1960), Chapter 2.

Clark, L. H. (Ed.), *Consumer Behavior,* Vol. 2, *The Life Cycle and Consumer* (New York, New York University Press, 1955).

Duncan, O. D., *Analysis of Farm Family Organization in Oklahoma,* Ph.D. thesis, Louisiana State University, 1941.

Duvall, Evelyn, *Family Development* (Philadelphia, Lippincott, 1962), Part I.

Duvall, Evelyn, and Hill, Reuben (Eds.), *Report of Committee of the Dynamics of Family Interaction,* National Conference on Family Life, 1948, mimeographed.

Erikson, Erik, *Childhood and Society* (New York, Norton, 1950), Chapter 7.

Glick, Paul, "The Family Cycle," *American Sociological Review,* Vol. 12 (April, 1947), pp. 164–174.

Glick, Paul, "The Life Cycle of the Family," *Marriage and Family Living,* Vol. 17 (February, 1955), pp. 3–9.

Haimowitz, Morris, *Human Development: Selected Readings* (New York, Crowell, 1960).

Havighurst, Robert, *Human Development and Education* (New York, McKay, 1953).

Hill, Reuben, and Rodgers, Roy, "The Developmental Approach," in Christensen, Harold (Ed.), *Handbook of Marriage and the Family* (Chicago, Rand McNally, 1964), Chapter 5.

Johannis, T. B. and Rollins, J. M., "Attitudes of Teenagers Toward Family Relationships and Homogamy of Social Characteristics of Their Parents," *Sociology and Social Research,* Vol. 43 (July–August, 1959), pp. 415–420.

Kirkpatrick, Clifford, *The Family* (New York, Ronald, 1955), Part III.

Kirkpatrick, E. L. *et. al.,* "The Life Cycle of the Farm Family," University of Wisconsin, *Experiment Station Bulletin 121,* 1934.

Lansing, John, and Kish, Leslie, "Family Life Cycle as an Independent Variable," *American Sociological Review,* Vol. 22 (October, 1957), pp. 512–519.

Pineo, P. C. "Disenchantment in the Late Years of Marriage," *Marriage and Family Living,* Vol. 23 (February, 1961), pp. 3–11.

Rodgers, Roy, *Improvements in the Construction and Analysis of Family Life Cycle Categories* (Kalamazoo, Western Michigan University, 1962).

Stott, Leland, "The Longitudinal Approach to the Study of Family Life," *Journal of Home Economics,* Vol. 46 (February, 1954), pp. 79–81.

Woods, Sister Francis, *The American Family System* (New York, Harper & Row, 1959), Part III.

QUESTIONS AND EXERCISES

1. Is it going too far to say that one can predict his family's future? Discuss.
2. Do you agree that there are certain bases or prerequisites necessary for family survival in any type of society? If so, what are they? Discuss.

3. What effect if any will social class position have on the developmental tasks which present themselves to a given family at a particular stage in life? Discuss.

4. Show by illustration how the individual tasks of one particular marital partner might conflict with those of the spouse.

5. How far into the family cycle do you believe the average college student should be asked to project himself ahead, if he is enrolled in a marriage and family course? Give the reasons for your answer.

6. In what ways do individual developmental cycles parallel and in what ways do they diverge from family developmental cycles? Discuss.

7. What are some of the implications of the lower median age of marriage in the United States for the typical young person, in relation to the individual and family developmental cycle?

8. What are the advantages for the student, in terms of functional preparation for marriage, of a developmental cycle approach as against a broad historical or institutional approach to the materials?

9. The book by Jan De Hartog, *The Fourposter,* has been successfully produced in play form. After reading the book, indicate the major family stages and essential developmental tasks suggested by the author.

10. Analyze the major developmental tasks which your family is facing as a family. Which ones are the most difficult? Why?

two

Mate Selection:
Moving Out of the Family of Orientation

5

Early Dating:
Preliminaries to Serious Mate Selection

In this chapter we are beginning our analysis of the American system of mate selection and some of its implications both for the individuals involved and for the society. In our historical treatment we have already indicated that the frontier and the accompanying pressure of the values of freedom and individualism had broken down some of the old traditions of mate selection. But in the settled communities in America up to this present century, or perhaps up to World War I, traditional courtship patterns retained considerable influence. People "courted" in the old days or "kept company" as they sometimes put it.

By long practice courtship is a social term involving obligation, a kind of chain process which, once initiated, one is under social pressure to carry through to completion in marriage. In Colonial times when a boy asked for permission to call on a man's daughter, he in effect asked for permission to marry her if she would consent. Much more recently a first call by a man on a young woman was a public indication of interest in marriage, and repeated calling was the near equivalent of announcement of an engagement and forthcoming marriage. From its initiation to its end courtship is a public avowal of intent to marry. Back of that avowal, there has long been in America social pressure upon the individual to carry out his commitment.

In contrast, dating is a relationship expressing freedom, lack of commitment or public obligation for any sort of future action. In truth, up to the time of announcement of engagement dating participants have a minimum of accepted responsibility to continue the relationship. Continuation is largely a matter between the two concerned. That is to say, the rise of the term dating is a reflection of the freedom of the young to associate in pairs without others —parents or the community—assuming or insisting that merely because they are dating they have further responsibilities to each other or to the community. Such freedom is what distinguishes dating from courtship.[1]

[1] Samuel Lowrie, "Dating Theories and Student Responses," *American Sociological Review* (June, 1951), p. 337.

Dating as we know it is a modern phenomenon. It may be casual in intent or it may be serious. More often the frivolous and the serious intentions and consequences are intertwined. Waller was one of the first to discuss the modern system of mate selection analytically and to assess its functions.[2] Since that time a number of scholars have been involved in similar work and they still are. In spite of many disagreements among observers certain features of the present system of mate selection stand out. LeMasters describes some of them as follows:

1. The system is competitive.
2. The system is youth centered rather than parent controlled.
3. The system is an elaborate process.
4. The system has a double standard of behavior.
5. Our mate selection system is very romantic.
6. The system is flexible.
7. The system is democratic.
8. The system involves the progressive commitment of the individual.[3]

We have before us then a system which is controlled by the young people themselves, which leads eventually to marriage for each of the pair but not, as a rule, to each other, through progressive and sequential involvement. A series of stages or steps appears fairly clear in most communities. These may be delineated as follows:

1. Group dating
2. Random dating
3. Casual going steady
4. Serious going steady
5. Informal engagement
6. Formal engagement

Further explanation is in order. The system is somewhat flexible, since not all couples or individuals move systematically through these stages. The process reminds one of the Indianapolis or Daytona Beach Speedway racers. Certain ones drop out of the competition quickly in discouragement. Others drop out temporarily to regroup their forces and get cooled off before reentering the competition. Most persist over the long run until they have won something, although perhaps not always the prize originally sought.

Again, there are revolutionary changes involved in the system. Central is dating for its own sake. Group dating, random dating, and casual or nonmarriage oriented going steady involve association between members of the opposite sex with no conscious movement toward marriage. The young people associate together simply because they enjoy each other's company. The specific purpose of the date for the particular individual involved may be recreation, prestige, fun, or sex excitement. In the "old

[2] Willard Waller, "The Rating and Dating Complex," *American Sociological Review,* Vol. 2 (October, 1937), pp. 727–734.

[3] Ersel LeMasters, *Modern Courtship and Marriage* (New York, Macmillan, 1957), Chapter IV.

days," courtship was serious in its direct focus on marriage. The first three stages as delineated above are *casual*. Intent to marry is not a consideration. As Cuber suggests, the relationship "is its one excuse for being." [4] However, none of these stages is unrelated to marriage *in the long run*. In fact there is often little correlation between success in dating and in marriage; many a good date is an impossible mate. This is understood at least vaguely by the participants, their parents, and others around them.

Starting in one of the early stages eventually involves the young person in a process that leads toward marriage. In a sense what we have is redefinition of the mate selection process which culminates in marriage oriented activity known as "courtship" in previous generations. Even though most college students are still close in time to nonmarriage oriented dating, a perspective on courtship is provided by taking a somewhat professional look at one's recent past.

PRE-HIGH SCHOOL DATING

Group dating is a pattern which seems to be spreading over the country in the junior high school and in some cases the upper elementary grades. Under this system dances, parties, and other functions are arranged for groups but the students are encouraged to pair off. Since girls apparently mature more quickly than boys, the former often take the initiative in making the arrangements. Dancing teachers and eager mothers are frequently working behind the scenes to get Johnny out of his baseball togs and into a mood in which he will take a proper interest in Susie. Once a pattern develops to the point that everyone must date in order to belong, the pressure is on. Mead believes that early dating under pressure arouses resentments especially on the part of the boys who are not ready to take the initiative and yet who are not happy if the girls do so.[5] A number of mothers have voiced similar complaints in print.[6] Without present pressures young adolescent boys and girls grow out of their one-sex groups into mixed groups a bit more slowly. Heterosexual activity in which roughhouse play is sometimes used to ease strain is fairly typical. Eventually and cautiously pairings take place for temporary periods. Crist's findings, while focused on high school dating, suggest the importance of smooth, satisfactory cross-sex relationships preceding dating.[7] Wholesome contacts in heterosexual

[4] John F. Cuber, "Changing Courtship and Marriage Customs," *The Annals of the American Academy of Political and Social Science,* Vol. 229 (September, 1943), pp. 30–38.

[5] Margaret Mead, *Male and Female* (New York, Morrow, 1948), p. 280.

[6] See for example Phyllis McGinley, "The Fearful Aspect of Too-Early Dating," *Catholic Digest,* Vol. 20 (August, 1956), pp. 46–51, pp. 287–288.

[7] John Crist, "High School Dating as a Behavior System," *Marriage and Family Living,* Vol. 15 (February, 1953), pp. 23–28.

groups enables the adolescent to move by degrees into group dating and finally into random dating. Those who have not had successful predating group experience with the opposite sex tend to exhibit difficulties in adapting to later dating. Hollingshead's data on Elmtown confirm this need for satisfactory predating experience.[8]

Group dating seems to serve an important function for some young people and perhaps for their parents as well. Bolstered by their peers, the young people are able to develop habits which will enable them to proceed into random dating.

Adequate studies are not available to indicate the extent of group dating over the country. LeMasters reports from a study of 120 middle-class parents that 84 percent of their children had engaged in group dating.[9] It is probable that such a figure is fairly typical for middle- and upper-class areas at least. Some individuals go immediately into random dating or going steady, as is well known. The age at which they enter the mate selection process, the attitudes of their parents, peer group expectations, and other factors are involved when it comes to the practice of particular individuals.

JUNIOR AND SENIOR HIGH SCHOOL DATING

In the average junior high school today some random dating will be taking place. It is difficult to get a reliable estimate on how much full-fledged dating, with parental approval, actually exists at that period. Cavan reports that 19 percent of the boys and 16 percent of the girls in her sample had begun to date in the seventh grade.[10] In Elmtown according to Hollingshead, 58 percent of the girls and 43 percent of the boys will have been on at least one date during grade school. It seems clear that in spite of regional and subcultural variations a fairly clear-cut pattern is emerging. A minority of students begin random dating in grade school or junior high. More enter the field each year during the high school period. By the senior year in high school 80 to 90 percent will have dated, at least occasionally.

In Cavan's study of a sample of students in a small private college, Alpha, 8 percent did not date while in high school. Burgess and Wallin, studying a sample of similar background, found that 17.8 percent of their men and 9.9 percent of their women had not started dating until they were 18 or older.[11] However, the latter were dating in the prewar period while the Alpha college students were in high school in the fifties. Group pressure

[8] August Hollingshead, *Elmtown's Youth* (New York, Wiley, 1949), Chapter 9.
[9] LeMasters, *op. cit.,* p. 96.
[10] Ruth Cavan, *The American Family* (New York, Crowell, 1963), Chapter 12.
[11] Ernest Burgess and Paul Wallin, *Engagement and Marriage* (Philadelphia, Lippincott, 1953), p. 119.

to date is now so common that most students will try to date at least occasionally.[12]

The pattern of dating will vary by region, circumstances, age of participants, and class level. The following description by Gorer, a British observer, is presumably meant to refer to dating during the upper high school or college years.

The "date" starts as an invitation from a young man to a girl for an evening's public entertainment, typically at his expense. . . . The entertainment offered depends on the young man's means and aspirations, and the locality; but it is in a public place always, and nearly always includes eating food together, the food being anything from an ice-cream soda at the local drugstore to the most elaborate and expensive meal that the locality can provide. Besides the food, the most usual entertainment is dancing—the place of the dance ranging anywhere from the cheap roadside café with a jukebox to the most expensive cabaret or country club. The male (the "escort") should call for the girl in a car (unless he be particularly young or poor) and should take her back in the car. If the entertainment proposed is of a formal or expensive nature, the man should provide a corsage—flowers for the girl to wear on her dress or in her hair. . . .

"Showing the girl a good time" is the essential background for a "date," but it is not its object, as far as the man is concerned; its object is to get the girl to prove that he is worthy of love, and therefore a success. In some cases superior efficiency in dancing will elicit the necessary signs of approval; but typically, and not unexpectedly, they are elicited by talk. Once again, the importance of words is paramount.

Since, on first "dates" the pair are normally comparative strangers to one another, a certain amount of autobiography is necessary in the hopes of establishing some common interest or experience, at the least to prove that one is worthy of the other's attention. These autobiographies, however, differ at most in emphasis, in tone of voice, from those which should accompany any American meeting between strangers. What distinguishes the "date" from other conversation is a mixture of persiflage, flattery, wit, and lovemaking which was formerly called a "line" but which each generation dubs with a new name.

The "line" is an individual variation of a commonly accepted pattern which is considered to be representative of a facet of a man's personality. Most men are articulately self-conscious about their "lines" and can describe them with ease; they are constantly practiced and improved with ever differing part-

---

[12] See James Coleman, *The Adolescent Society* (New York, Free Press, 1961), for a discussion of the pressure of the peer group on the individual in high school. Some subgroups and high schools put more emphasis on social activity, dating and rating than others. See also Sussman, Marvin and Vincent, Clark (Co-Ed's.), Special Issue, "American Adolescents in the Mid-Sixties," *Journal of Marriage and the Family,* Vol. 27 (May, 1965) for a number of articles dealing with teen-agers in home and school.

ners. The object of the "line" is to entertain, amuse, and captivate the girl, but there is no deep emotional involvement; it is a game of skill.

The girl's skill consists in parrying the "line" without discouraging her partner or becoming emotionally involved herself. To the extent that she falls for the "line" she is a loser in this intricate game; but if she discourages her partner so much that he does not request a subsequent date in the near future she is equally a loser. To remain the winner, she must make the nicest discriminations between yielding and rigidity.

The man scores to the extent that he is able to get more favors from the girl than his rivals, real or supposed, would be able to do. The proving time is the return journey from the place of public entertainment to the girl's home. A good-night kiss is almost the minimum repayment for an evening's entertainment; but how much more depends on the enterprise of the man, the self-assurance of the woman, and the number of "dates" the pair have had together. This love-making is still emotionally uninvolved; it is still part of the game, though the gestures and intimacies and language are identical with true love-making; it is not, save most rarely, an attempt at seduction; and the satisfactions sought are not, in the first instance, sensual but self-regarding. The man should demonstrate his enterprise and prove that he is worthy to be loved by pressing for ever further favors; but the girl who yields too much, or too easily, may well be a disappointment, in exactly the same way as too easy a victory in tennis or chess may be a disappointment.[13]

Gorer probably means to exaggerate in order to stress specific points. In some areas, certain of the patterns described would not be typical of the majority of the dating couples. The reference to the corsage would not apply to young people of modest means, other than for events such as the Prom. It must be stressed that class differences exist in dating patterns in the United States. Note the contrasts which follow below. The first describes certain aspects of dating in an eastern upper-class suburban community, as related to the author by a parent in the community.

It seems to me that high-school dating as you have described it is not common here. For one thing most of the fellows and girls go to private preparatory schools, non-coed. The few students from our group who go to public schools do not take too active a part in school-sponsored social activities. Private or country club parties or social events sponsored by the prep schools are popular. These days of course young people insist on running their own affairs. But by selecting the type of school they will go to, by making sure responsible adults are around at parties, and in other somewhat subtle ways parents in this neighborhood really are able to exercise considerable control over their children.[14]

[13] Reprinted from *The American People,* Revised Edition, 1964 by Geoffrey Gorer. By permission of W. W. Norton & Company, Inc. Copyright 1948 by Geoffrey Gorer. Revised Edition Copyright © 1964 by Geoffrey Gorer.

[14] The author has lived for brief periods adjacent to the community from whence the informant came. For the second conversation we draw on personal experience in research in an industrial area of northeastern Ohio. Compare this with the

The second is from a conversation between two lower-class teenagers in an urban area.

Jack, if you could just get your brother's car it would be a cinch. If those girls don't show up at the skating rink I'm sure they'll be at Joe's place. If that East-end crowd gives us any more trouble we'll have to do something about it. I don't see why those girls hang around them anyway. Say did you hear about the blonde we picked up last Saturday night over in Milltown? She was really something.

The reader will see a number of important differences in class patterns of dating as exemplified in the two samples. As Cavan and others have shown, upper-class young people do not find it necessary to use dating itself as a status device.[15] They have status by virtue of family origin. They do associate with members of the opposite sex on a casual, noncommittal precourtship level. Adults seem to exercise more control over the young people by indirect methods than they do in other classes, especially the lower classes.

In contrast to the upper- and middle-class youth many lower-class youths tend to drop out of high school early and accept low-paying employment. They tend to resist parental control and insist on their own control of premarital behavior. Many "dates" are not prearranged; couples pair off at centers where the youth congregate. These centers (skating rinks, taverns, eating places) take no real responsibility in supervising the activities of the young people. Sexual intimacy seems to be rather typical on dates which develop in this fashion. In more stable working-class families parents exercise more control over the dating process especially regarding hours to be kept, places to be visited, and other limitations.

CASUAL GOING STEADY

In some quarters, there is a tendency to overlook a major shift in premarriage behavior which has come about in the last generation.[16] This is the phenomenon of "going steady" but with a nonmarriage if not quite casual approach. Waller described casual dating as essentially a revolutionary courtship practice. Perhaps casual going steady should be considered in the same light.

description of lower-class dating behavior described in Hollingshead, *op. cit.,* Chapters 9 and 16. It should be noted that class differences can be carried only so far. Whyte in his book *Street Corner Society* indicated that lower-class Italian-American boys defined two groups of girls, namely "good girls" and "bad girls." The approaches of the boys to the two types of girls were distinctly different.

[15] Cavan, *op. cit.,* Chapters 12, 13.

[16] Robert Herman, "The Going Steady Complex: A Reexamination," *Marriage and Family Living,* Vol. 17 (February, 1955), pp. 36–40.

Herman studied a group of college students, mainly freshmen and sophomores, at the University of Wisconsin regarding their high school dating experiences. Seventy-seven percent reported having gone steady with at least one person. While relative inactivity or random dating was reported to be characteristic of the ninth and tenth grades, going steady was the dating norm of the junior and senior high school years.

There is evidence of two types of going steady in high school. The one group is college oriented and the going steady is a *dalliance relationship* and is not expected to eventuate in marriage. In the noncollege oriented group the relationship may be more serious.

Ranking high among the benefits of going steady in high school are the following, as reported by the students:

1. Status and peer group recognition.
2. Guarantee of a partner for school co-ed social affairs.
3. Alleviation of the competitive struggle for dates.

Herman raises two important questions regarding the functions of going steady. He asks whether it is possible that the going steady relationship is less exploitative than random dating. In the latter the individual has the chance to "use" the partner, since the relationship is casual, fleeting, and not exceedingly personal. Going steady may diminish some of the possibilities for exploitation. Further, steady dating may allow more learning regarding interpersonal adjustment to take place in that the relationship is less superficial than it is in casual dating.[17]

On the negative side there are those, this author included, who are suspicious of the tendency for going steady so early. In some areas the practice is now appearing in the upper grade and junior high levels where it should probably be considered as evidence of immaturity and insecurity in many cases. While we need more careful studies on the subject, it appears that many grade and junior high pupils are pushed too quickly into relationships they are unable to handle adequately. In some cases the children are apparently encouraged by their parents who may have frustrated romantic goals or status ambitions that they are trying to attain vicariously through their children.

CRITIQUES OF CASUAL DATING IN COLLEGE

Social scientists and others have been critical of certain features of dating since Waller's provocative critique.[18] Waller, studying dating on X State University campus, in the mid-thirties, was impressed with its competitive, superficial, and exploitative aspects. Each girl wanted to date the Big Man on Campus and each fellow hoped to increase his campus prestige

---

[17] *Ibid.*
[18] Waller, *op. cit.*

by dating a campus queen. Each person tried to satisfy his own desires for thrills and adventure. The object was to receive satisfaction of one's own ego-needs without commitment or emotional involvement. To achieve this the male developed his "line" and the co-ed her fencing skill.

Students were rated on a campus prestige system emphasizing materialistic values. Fraternity membership, a "smooth" personality, access to a car, and other such attributes were the prerequisites for high rank in the case of men. For women popularity involved dancing skill, good clothes, and especially a record of dating success. Since the aims of dating were ego-centered rather than pair-centered, Waller held that dating was often dysfunctional in relation to successful marriage.

Various studies of campus dating have been made in the last two decades. Some sustain the Waller hypothesis; others tend to qualify it. In the early 1950's Smith did a restudy of the campus which was originally the focus of Waller's work, using the questionnaire approach.[19] Tables five

TABLE 5

Percentage Distribution of Replies to What a Fellow Must Do To Be Popular on X Campus

Characteristic	344 Men		258 Women		Total 602	
	Agree	Disagree	Agree	Disagree	Agree	Disagree
Be smooth in manners	82	7	85	4	83	6
Know how to dance well	62	22	72	14	66	19
Be prominent in activities	43	38	39	28	41	38
Have good clothes	40	32	36	33	38	33
Be good looking, attractive	31	46	41	36	35	41
Avoid exploitation (by opposite sex)	29	46	35	41	32	44
Neck	38	35	13	66	27	48
Have a car or access to car	32	54	13	72	24	61
Belong to a fraternity	17	70	30	60	21	65
Have a good line	27	55	11	77	20	64
Enjoy liquor in groups	19	62	17	68	18	65
Date with friends' approval	11	70	25	49	17	61
Pet	22	54	3	87	14	68
Come from "right" family	10	72	16	57	13	65
Have plenty of money	19	63	4	81	12	71
Smoke	9	76	7	74	8	75
Date popular students only	10	75	4	86	7	79
Invite imports for special occasions	11	73	1	90	7	80
Belong to honor societies	8	80	3	80	6	80
Have sex relations	7	77	1	95	4	84
Be on football squad	4	87	1	90	3	88

SOURCE: William Smith, Jr., "Rating and Dating: A Restudy," *Marriage and Family Living,* Vol. 14 (November, 1952), pp. 312–317.

[19] William Smith, Jr., "Rating and Dating: A Restudy," *Marriage and Family Living,* Vol. 14 (November, 1952), pp. 312–317.

and six give the responses of the men and the women respectively to the question: What must a fellow (girl) do to be popular on X campus? As can be seen, the students in general *rejected* the more materialistic items in favor of personality items. For example, the students *rejected* the idea that a boy must be a football player, have sex relations, have a "copious supply of spending money, belong to a fraternity, or have access to a car" in order to rank at the top of the dating hierarchy. In the case of both sexes, smoothness in manners and appearance, and ability to dance well were considered most important. For both sexes being of attractive appearance and having good clothes to aid the appearance were ranked high. For boys prominence in activities was more important than looks, appearance, and the like.

Results of studies in this realm are still somewhat contradictory. Blood,

TABLE 6

Percentage Distribution of Replies to What a Girl Must Do to Be Popular on X Campus

Characteristic	344 Men		258 Women		Total 602	
	Agree	Disagree	Agree	Disagree	Agree	Disagree
Be smooth in manners, appearance	80	8	85	5	82	7
Know how to dance well	69	17	83	7	75	12
Be good looking, attractive	52	28	53	24	52	26
Have good clothes	46	30	48	23	47	27
Go to popular places	50	33	43	39	47	36
Be in demand as a date	61	37	46	34	46	36
Accept last minute dates	40	33	45	25	42	30
Avoid exploitation by opposite sex	35	42	52	24	42	34
Be prominent in activities	33	49	33	42	33	46
Neck	44	33	15	62	31	45
Use secrecy, discretion when violating conventions	28	47	23	56	28	51
Date with friends' approval	17	64	29	46	22	56
Be seen often with same boys	21	57	22	51	21	54
Go to beer parlors	24	61	16	67	21	63
Have many partners at a dance	16	64	15	68	16	66
Have a good line	14	72	13	72	14	72
Come from the "right" family	11	73	16	59	13	67
Pet	21	54	4	87	13	68
Enjoy liquor in groups	14	69	12	74	13	71
Date popular students only	14	69	6	84	11	76
Belong to a sorority	8	82	8	76	8	79
Belong to honorary societies	6	82	4	81	5	81
Be seen in expensive places	6	80	4	85	5	81
Have sex relations	8	77	1	95	5	84
Smoke	3	84	5	80	4	82

SOURCE: William Smith, Jr., "Rating and Dating: A Restudy," *Marriage and Family Living,* Vol. 14 (November, 1952), pp. 312–317.

in a study at Michigan, obtained results more in line with Smith's findings than with Waller's.[20] At Iowa State College Rogers and Havens found considerable evidence of prestige-ranking influencing student motivations.[21] Interestingly enough in contradiction to Waller, the authors found that such considerations operated to influence all stages of mate selection, from casual dating on. Waller's interpretations may have been affected by his focus on fraternity and sorority practices. Smith concentrated on the general campus. It is possible that the discrepancies reflect differences in the methodological approach to the problem.[22] Time differences should not be overlooked. However, it does appear that at least verbally many students are less materialistic and status conscious than were students a generation ago. Status-oriented, highly competitive dating is probably most typical among strong national fraternity and sorority groups on college campuses.

It appears that Ray,[23] and Burgess and Wallin,[24] tend to support Waller, while Blood, and Leslie and Richardson do not.[25] Perhaps of interest is the fact that except for Waller's study and Smith's replication, all the other studies cited have used midwestern samples. We do not know what we might find were eastern, southern, or western colleges and university groups studied.[26]

Dating Desirability

What type of date do you prefer? Must he be "tall, dark, and handsome?" It may be of interest to compare the sexes on response patterns. It would seem fair to say that men are slightly more romantic in expectations than are women. Perhaps girls are more interested in possible

[20] Robert Blood, "Uniformities and Diversity in Campus Dating Preferences," *Marriage and Family Living* (February, 1956), pp. 37–45; see also Robert Blood, "A Retest of Waller's Rating Complex," *Marriage and Family Living,* Vol. 17 (February, 1955), pp. 41–47.

[21] Everett Rogers and A. Eugene Havens, "Prestige Rating and Mate Selection on a College Campus," *Marriage and Family Living,* Vol. 22 (February, 1960), pp. 55–59.

[22] It must be noted that some controversy presently exists in social science regarding the best research to be used in probing attitudes and values which are ego-involving. The divergent results appearing may be reflecting simply the difference in approaches being used by the various researchers. However, there may be real differences either between school populations or in the same school at different periods.

[23] J. D. Ray, "Dating Behavior as Related to Organizational Prestige," unpublished thesis, cited in Robert Winch, *The Modern Family* (Holt, Rinehart and Winston, 1952), appendix.

[24] Burgess and Wallin, *op. cit.,* Chapters 3 and 4.

[25] Gerald Leslie, and Arthur Richardson, "Family Versus Campus Influence in Relation to Mate Selection," *Social Problems,* Vol. 4 (October, 1965), pp. 117–121.

[26] Research of a comparative and longitudinal nature is sorely needed in this area of marriage and family.

marriage and therefore in characteristics reputedly associated with marital success and stability. At any rate the above differences between the sexes appear in a number of studies although they tend to be slight in magnitude. Research of a more refined nature will enable us to distinguish more sharply between casual dating interests and the more long-term courtship interests that might lead to further involvement or marriage.

The reader may wish to compare his own expectations and characteristics with those reported here. If he is a student he should bear in mind that each person cannot expect his personality and dating expectations to fit campus norms in all respects nor should he be discouraged if they do not. An individual must make some kind of adjustment to the various groups around him but still live his own life. This means that each person must take cognizance of his own needs and values, being always aware of group pressures and standards. If his own codes and tastes clash with those prevailing generally on the campus he may be able to find a congenial group. For example, a serious-minded, religiously-oriented young man who does not believe in social drinking might find himself out of place in a social fraternity. He may feel more comfortable at the Wesley Foundation or a similar organization of his own religious group. In spite of some of the educational and other problems which arise when the campus is split into many small and different groups, their existence provides certain possibilities for the satisfaction of divergent student needs.

PROBLEMS OF CASUAL DATING

A major problem of modern dating seems to be the degree of physical intimacy which is to be maintained. The tendency in American culture to glorify sex, the great freedom of association given to the sexes, the diversity of standards, and other factors are involved in this area of tension.

In grandmother's day the problem was not acute. In most communities there were standards which were fairly well agreed upon by the majority of people concerned. Caressing previous to engagement was frowned upon. Kissing was reserved for the engagement period. The reader need not be told that "times have changed." But he may, upon recalling stories of well-mannered Dobbin who could be driven with one or no hand, question whether the change has been so great.

Of significance is the fact that young people today are thrown together under conditions of intimacy without the controls formerly exercised by adults and peers. This means that individual standards of control are the only ones which can be enforced. Those who work with them report they find the great majority of young people with whom they come in contact to be searching for satisfactory standards of behavior. Glover of California had over 1200 college students list for him their chief problems. Values, ethics, and morals were the chief concerns.[27]

It has been alleged that some young people themselves are beginning to develop restrictive codes for behavior, but it remains to be seen what kinds of standards will emerge. In the meantime the individual who has personal problems may be well advised to seek counsel from those in whom he puts trust. The relation of day-to-day behavior to long-run plans and goals should constantly be borne in mind.

Differential Involvement

One problem that deserves special attention is that of differential involvement. Random dating is not supposed to be serious in its intent toward marriage. No commitments are to be made or inferred—no strings are attached. If this is fully understood by all parties concerned, well and good. This is based on the rather dangerous presumption that the feelings and emotions of both parties concerned will be under rational control. Actually in a considerable number of cases one partner becomes more emotionally involved in the relationship than the other. This leads to the "principle of least interest." [28]

In a situation where two parties are unequally involved or interested in maintaining a relationship, control over the relationship goes to the one least interested in perpetuating the relationship. Advantage can be taken by the least interested person in various ways. In the case of the fellow, sex exploitation is often involved. The girl may use the boy to gain material goods, or to acquire a convenient escort to social affairs. An individual of either sex with sadistic tendencies may receive pleasure in carrying the partner along, only to drop him or her without warning or in a particularly cruel fashion.

The advantage of the old-fashioned courtship system was in the degree of correlation which could be assumed between outward appearances and inward motivations. Group patterns were clear-cut and well understood locally, and it was in this context that courtship took place. Negative sanctions were provided against those who tried to take advantage. The young man who wished to toy with a girl's affections was either foolhardy or lacking in good judgment or both. Even so, our elders can supply us with plenty of cases from any community in any previous period where hurt feelings, misunderstandings, and traumatic experiences were the outcome of courtship involvement. If such were the case under a more restricted system in more traditional society, the probabilities for trauma are considerably

---

[27] As reported in James Peterson, *Education for Marriage* (New York, Scribner, 1964), p. 157.
[28] Waller and Hill, *op. cit.*, pp. 190–192.

increased under our extended system of mate selection in a more complicated social context.[29]

Getting Dates

Another major problem seems to be that of getting dates. Since the
girl must usually wait until the boy asks her, getting an acceptable date may
be a real problem. This is especially so where the getting of dates is itself
a mark of prestige. Student counselors in most colleges and universities find
that a considerable number of students complain about the dating situation.
Especially crucial is the plight of the junior or senior girl who has been
"passed by." Since there is usually a norm to the effect that the girl dates
fellows from her own class or classes above her, the senior girl who is unattached finds herself in a difficult position. Unless she is deeply career-
minded, she may experience great frustration as the year slips by. One
student reported to the author as follows:

You never saw such a sickly looking group of girls in your life as the girls
in the senior dorm who do not date. They call themselves the X group. When
a new ring appears in the dorm or an engagement is announced they go into a
panic. They spend their evenings sitting around together griping about the
boys, the college, and life in general. They get on the nerves of the rest of us
and give the counselors fits, but none of them can seem to do anything about
the situation.

General solutions to problems of this sort are difficult to suggest. Certain approaches will be discussed under the section entitled "Modification of
Dating Practices." The individual caught in a situation where he or she is
dateless in or out of school, has various avenues of action open. Bowman
suggests the following possibilities as being of help in gaining friends and
possible dates:

1. You must get to where members of the opposite sex congregate if you
   wish to meet them.
2. Have a wide circle of friends of your own sex.
3. Cultivate and develop a variety of skills and interests.
4. Avoid being overanxious, lest you repel others.
5. Maintain cleanliness.
6. Learn the details of etiquette, the principles of courtesy, and the niceties of
   associating with others.
7. Avoid undue dependence on wealth or social position.
8. Insofar as possible, eliminate manners which are distasteful to others.[30]

[29] Burgess and Wallin, *op. cit.,* Chapter 3.
[30] Adapted from Henry Bowman, *Marriage for Moderns* (New York, McGraw-
Hill, 1954), pp. 159–161.

It is difficult to deal with datelessness adequately without knowing the circumstances involved in a given local situation or in regard to the particular persons involved. Bowman's suggestions will be inadequate for those with other than mild personality problems. Premarriage counseling or psychotherapy may be in order for some. It should be noted that such a factor as the sex ratio obtaining in a given locale cannot be overlooked. On many American campuses where the two sexes are roughly equal in numbers, a substantial proportion of the girls will not be able to date in what to them is a satisfactory manner. Presumably the boys will defer dating more often than girls lest it lead to involvement and threaten projected career patterns.

POSSIBILITIES OF RANDOM DATING

What are the potentials in dating for the individual if he uses some degree of rational judgment and control? A major possibility is personality development. Association with a member of the opposite sex gives the person an opportunity to "try his personality for size." Through a long process the individual by dating age has developed a cluster of attitudes and attributes of various kinds, which configuration we label "personality." Dating gives one a chance to see this personality mirrored in the reactions of various members of the opposite sex. This process can take place in any kind of interpersonal relationship, but dating provides a special kind of learning situation for those who are perceptive. Some people for the first time gain the ability through dating to empathize and communicate with members of the opposite sex. Personal adequacy, poise, ability to communicate, emotional control, adaptability, sociability, and various other attributes and competencies can be developed through dating.

In addition to the opportunity to develop and test one's personality, dating provides the opportunity to know and test others. One finds that it "takes all kinds" to make a world, but since he marries only one (at a time, at least) he needs to know not only that one man's meat is another's poison, but which is which *for him*. Even within a fairly narrow group circumscribed by race, ethnic origin, socioeconomic position, and other factors, individuals vary considerably. We speak much today of the "uniqueness" of the individual personality, but do not always fully recognize all the implications of our assertions. If through dating one can learn to appreciate individuals for themselves one has developed an appreciation which should be valuable for later marriage and family life, and social life in general.

Along with the development of an appreciation of individual personalities, judgment in relation to members of the opposite sex is allowed to function in dating. Judgment as a skill or competency will be discussed in the next chapter. Since young people often arrive at dating age with prejudices and stereotypes against members of the opposite sex, dating has definite possibilities for the development of this skill. Through dating one may learn to predict the behavior of members of the opposite sex, within limits.

In a sense random dating involves the first steps in compatibility testing, which are carried further in serious going steady and engagement. The individual finds that dating is pleasing for both parties with some people and not with others. Compatibility testing requires more than the ability to recognize personality differences. Through this process along with additional ones the individual may explore his dating motives, the characteristics of the ideal mate he desires, and finally his own "marriageability." This latter concept will be explored in Chapter 6.

Finally, another feature of dating involves a psychological weaning from the parents. In effect, the fumbling overture toward members of the opposite sex is a first step in breaking away from the parental family and establishing a new family. While the break is a small one, it is a crack in the closed wall of the family circle. Whether the process is a maturing one depends on the circumstances.

It must be emphasized that the above functions can obtain only under "ideal" conditions. If the person has such a great need for intimate response that he becomes infatuated during the early dating period some of the possibilities for personal and social development may well be lessened. (The relation of love to mate selection and marriage is considered so important that Chapter 7 will be devoted to it.) Or if the person is motivated to seek ego-satisfaction only, with no thought for the partner, it may de difficult for him to make rational judgments of his own personality or that of others.

POSSIBLE MODIFICATION OF DATING PRACTICES

Many believe that dating in some form is here to stay. This is hardly startling. Being inclined to agree, we raise the question: What can be done to modify the system constructively? Proposals vary. The following might be suggested for consideration.

Materialistic attitudes and practices involve fundamental human values. The boy who has real respect for human beings cannot knowingly exploit a dating partner. The girl who is willing to date a Big Man On Campus for the prestige it gives her, knowing she could never be serious about him, might well reconsider her general social and moral attitudes. Her problem isn't dating and men—it is her own character. Perhaps the young person is reflecting family conditioning. The individual brought up in a family devoted to passing the Joneses in all respects may well carry over these same attitudes into dating, engagement, and marriage. Fair play, respect, dignity, and other human values will be characteristic of dating behavior only when buttressed by emphasis on them in other areas of our social life especially in the family, church, and school.

Buber in his various writings distinguishes between relating to an individual as a person and using him as a thing.[31] He proposes an ethic for interpersonal relations which might well apply to dating. If a partner is simply "used" to gain prestige, sexual satisfaction or the like, his fundamental integrity is being violated. From a slightly different frame of reference Waller was making the same point a generation ago. He thought that such practices, if persistent, were not good preparation for the shared relationship of marriage. His point was well taken. It is only when a partner is treated as a person, with the full consideration due him, that his general welfare is protected and preserved.

Lowrie suggests that we are in transition regarding our dating behavior and that new codes will eventually be developed by the young people themselves. It may be, however, that adults will wish to find methods whereby the dating system is not regulated solely by the young peer group but is subjected to the more general societal controls. As Cavan shows, ". . . adolescents have been permitted—in fact given an open field—to create a little exclusive social world of their own that tends to separate them from, rather than integrate them into, the adult world and mature social activities." [32]

Writing with a focus on adolescent behavior in the school system, Coleman demonstrates that the youth group often works at cross-purposes with the adult community.[33] The existence of a large gap between the adolescent and the adult world can be dysfunctional to both groups. This is not to say that the influence of the peer group is always negative for the adolescent. As Parsons points out, it is necessary for the child to move away by degrees from the parental home if he is to be able to establish a home and occupational role of his own.[34] This necessity does not nullify the possibility of exploitation and hardship in the absence of reasonable dating standards, at least for certain individuals.

One area in which adults and young people may be able to cooperate for the mutual benefit of all is in the extension of opportunities for social relationships under approved auspices. This will take ingenuity on the part of both young people and adults alike. More emphasis could be given to organized activities where individuals work and play together, not necessarily on a pair basis. The outcome may be twofold: (1) cutting down somewhat the emphasis on dating, and (2) providing wholesome companionships

[31] Martin Buber, *I and Thou* (Edinburgh, T. Clark, 1937).

[32] Cavan, *The American Family, op. cit.,* p. 328.

[33] Coleman, *op. cit.*

[34] Talcott Parsons, *et al., Family, Socialization and Interaction Process* (New York, Free Press, 1955), Chapter 2.

across sex lines which may lead to dating. A persistent complaint is heard from young people that they do not have sufficient opportunities to meet members of the opposite sex who would make suitable marriage partners. There are two sides to this issue. On the one hand, many will be sympathetic with proposals to provide opportunities for young people to meet members of the opposite sex under optimal conditions. In contrast, some writers believe we presently have too much organization. The latter would prefer to stress the development of autonomy, initiative, and judgment on the part of our young persons of dating age.

Casual dating is here to stay. Much more research might well be done regarding the effects of certain of its patterns such as early going steady. Disruptive and inconsistent aspects of the system may well be corrected by the combined efforts of young people and adults, if enough interest is shown. As a whole, casual dating is consistent with a social structure stressing freedom, individualism, social mobility, and similar values. To effect major changes in our system of mate selection would require alteration of much of our basic social structure. This seems highly unlikely, at least in the short run.

SELECTED READINGS

Bell, Robert R., and Blumberg, Leonard, "Courtship Intimacy and Religious Background," *Marriage and Family Living,* Vol. 21 (November, 1959), pp. 356–360.

Bernard, Jessie, Buchanan, Helen, and Smith, William Jr., *Dating, Mating and Marriage* (Cleveland, Howard Allen, 1958), Chapter 3.

Blood, Robert O., "Uniformities and Diversities in Campus Dating Preferences," *Marriage and Family Living,* Vol. 18 (February, 1956), pp. 37–45.

Blood, Robert O., *Marriage* (New York, Free Press, 1962), Part I.

Broderick, Carlfred B., and Fowler, Stanley E., "New Patterns of Relationships Between the Sexes Among Pre-Adolescents," *Marriage and Family Living,* Vol. 23 (February, 1961), pp. 27–30.

Burgess, Ernest, and Wallin, Paul, *Engagement and Marriage* (Philadelphia, Lippincott, 1953), Chapters 3 and 4.

Cavan, Ruth, *Marriage and Family in the Modern World* (New York, Crowell, 1960), Chapter 6.

Crist, John, "High School Dating As a Behavior System," *Marriage and Family Living,* Vol. 15 (February, 1953), pp. 23–28.

Delora, Jack, "Social Systems of Dating on a College Campus," *Marriage and Family Living,* Vol. 25 (February, 1963), pp. 81–84.

Duvall, Evelyn, and Hill, Reuben, *Being Married* (Boston, Heath, 1960), Chapter 1.

Ehrmann, Winston, *Premarital Dating Behavior* (New York, Holt, Rinehart and Winston, 1959).

Hewitt, Lester, "Student Perception of Traits Desired in Themselves as Dating and Married Partners," *Marriage and Family Living,* Vol. 20 (November, 1958), pp. 344–349.

Hollingshead, August, *Elmtown's Youth* (New York, Wiley, 1949).

Koller, Marvin, "Some Changes in the Courtship Behavior in Three Generations of Ohio Women," *American Sociological Review,* Vol. 16 (June, 1951), pp. 366–370.

LeMasters, Ersel, *Modern Courtship and Marriage* (New York, Macmillan, 1957), Chapter 5.

Lowrie, Samuel, "Early and Late Dating: Some Conditions Associated with Time," *Marriage and Family Living,* Vol. 23 (August, 1961), pp. 284–291.

McGinnis, Robert, "Campus Values in Mate Selection: A Repeat Study," *Social Forces,* Vol. 36 (May, 1958), pp. 368–373.

Sussman, Marvin and Vincent, Clark (Co-Ed's.), Special Issue, "American Adolescents in the Mid-Sixties," *Journal of Marriage and the Family,* Vol. 27 (May, 1965).

Taylor, Donald, rev. of Norman Himes, *Your Marriage* (New York, Holt, Rinehart and Winston, 1955), Chapter 2.

Wallace, Gerald, "High Schools and Married Students—Are They Compatible?" *Marriage and Family Living,* Vol. 24 (August, 1962), pp. 295–297.

Waller, Willard, and Hill, Reuben, *The Family: A Dynamic Interpretation* (New York, Holt, Rinehart and Winston, 1951), Chapter 9.

QUESTIONS AND EXERCISES

1. What to you are the implications of the extension of dating into the grade school level? Discuss.

2. What are the advantages and disadvantages of the new going steady complex? Discuss.

3. Write a paper comparing dating patterns of the middle class with those of the lower-class young people in your hometown.

4. Read Waller, Smith, Blood, Lowrie, Burgess and Locke, Rogers and Havens, Leslie and Richardson, etc. all of whom deal with the question of materialistic emphasis in American dating patterns. Which author best describes conditions on your campus?

5. Write a critique of American dating patterns. Include suggested improvements and the rationale of your proposals for change.

6. It has been suggested by Waller and others that dating is poor preparation for marriage. Indicate your position on this matter and defend it.

7. What is the main dating problem on your campus or in your group, as you view the situation? What constructive solutions do you have to help remedy the situation?

8. Comment on Hewitt's article (cited) especially regarding mistaken impressions men have of women's interests and women of men's interests.

9. In spite of the fact that dating is a new and modern invention, many

traditional emphases are retained. For example, the boy must still take the initiative in making the date, must pay ·the expenses, etc. How far would you go in changing these patterns? Discuss.

10. What are possible alternative methods of cutting down the amount of exploitation which presently takes place in dating relationships? Can it ever be completely eliminated? Why or why not?

11. Ask a grandparent or older person to describe patterns of "keeping company" which prevailed in former eras, and then compare them with our own.

12. Read the Blood and Nicholson article dealing with international dating attitudes and practices. (Robert O. Blood and S. O. Nicholson, "The Attitudes of American Men and Women Students Toward International Dating," *Marriage and Family Living,* Vol. 24, 1962, p. 35). After a study of the situation write a paper describing dating attitudes and practices on your own campus, and compare them to those of other countries.

6

Marriageability

What is a marriageable personality? [1] Am I a marriageable person? Will my personality clash with Joe's if we marry? While not phrased in precisely this terminology, such questions as these are and ought to be in the minds of young people, and they are often posed by them to marriage educators and counselors. This chapter will attempt to provide some general answers to the first questions and indicate how the individual person may get help with his more specific questions. The analysis will involve four main factors: general personality, interpersonal competence, adaptability and maturity in relation to marriage, and methods of assessing the individual's potentialities.

PERSONALITY FACTORS

Many nonscientists believe that personality factors are the major causes of marital failure or success. Such characteristics as stubbornness, jealousy, selfishness, irritability, meanness, and uncontrollable temper have been reported as marital disrupters for generations. Almost everyone has at one time or another heard a friend exclaim "I could never live with her. That temper would drive me crazy." In reference to the other end of the continuum, marital success, a friend stated recently that "Mrs. Z has such an adaptable personality I believe that she could get along (in marriage) with anybody."

Psychiatrists often emphasize neuroticism as being the major cause of marital discord. Bergler has been especially forthright in this position,

---

[1] As we are using the terms in this chapter, marriageable personality and marriageability are synonomous. By this usage we mean that the person who falls into this category has the potentialities for successful marriage, with a suitable partner.

95

insisting that extreme marital difficulty is an inevitable index of neurosis.[2] Stokes, while not in agreement with Bergler on many issues, does refer to the "true causes of disharmony (mostly infantile personality defects)" in similar fashion.[3]

The psychologist Terman was one of the first researchers to put some of our insights from common sense and clinical experience to test. Comparing happily and unhappily married couples through the use of items from the Bernreuter and Strong personality inventories, he came to the conclusion that personality factors predispose persons for happiness or unhappiness in marriage.

Happily married women in Terman's sample tended to have the following characteristics:

Happily married women as a group, are characterized by kindly attitudes toward others and by the expectations of kindly attitudes in return. They do not easily take offense and are not unduly concerned about the impressions they make upon others. They do not look upon social relationships as rivalry situations. They are cooperative, do not object to subordinate roles, and are not annoyed by advice from others. Missionary and ministering attitudes are frequently evidenced in their responses. They enjoy activities that bring educational or pleasurable opportunities to others and like to do things for the dependent and underprivileged. They are methodical and painstaking in their work, attentive to details, and careful in regard to money. In religion, morals, and politics they tend to be conservative and conventional. Their expressed attitudes imply a quiet self-assurance and a decidedly optimistic outlook on life.

Unhappily married women are described as follows:

Unhappily married women, on the other hand, are characterized by emotional tenseness and by ups and downs of moods. They give evidence of deep-seated inferiority feelings to which they react by aggressive attitudes rather than timidity. They are inclined to be irritable and dictatorial. Compensatory mechanisms resulting in restive striving are common. These are seen in the tendency of the unhappy wives to be active "joiners," aggressive in business, and over anxious in social life. They strive for wide circles of acquaintances but are more concerned with being important than with being liked. They are egocentric and little interested in benevolent or welfare activities, except insofar as these offer opportunities for personal recognition. They also like activities which are fraught with opportunities for romance. They are more inclined to be conciliatory in their attitudes toward men than toward women and show little of the sex antagonism that unhappily married men exhibit. They are impatient and fitful workers, dislike cautious or methodical and painstaking effort. In politics, religion, and social ethics they are more often radical than happily married women.[4]

[2] Edmund Bergler, *Divorce Won't Help* (New York, Harper & Row, 1948).
[3] Walter Stokes, *Modern Pattern for Marriage* (New York, Holt, Rinehart and Winston, 1948), p. 108.
[4] From Lewis Terman, *Psychological Factors in Marital Happiness.* Copyright 1938. McGraw-Hill Book Company, Inc., pp. 145–146. Used by permission.

Happy and unhappy men showed the following characteristics:

Happily married men show evidence of an even and stable emotional tone. Their most characteristic reaction to others is that of cooperation. This is reflected in their attitudes toward business superiors, with whom they work well; in their attitude toward women, which reflects equalitarian ideals; and in their benevolent attitudes toward inferiors and underprivileged. In a gathering of people they tend to be unselfconscious and somewhat extroverted. As compared with unhappy husbands, they show superior initiative, a greater tendency to take responsibilities, and greater willingness to give close attention to detail in their daily work. They like methodical procedures and methodical people. In money matters they are saving and cautious. Conservative attitudes are strongly characteristic of them. They usually have a favorable attitude toward religion and strongly uphold the sex mores and other social conventions.

Unhappy husbands, on the other hand, are inclined to be moody and somewhat neurotic. They are prone to feelings of social inferiority, dislike being conspicuous in public, and are highly reactive to social opinion. This sense of social insecurity is often compensated by domineering attitudes in relationships where they feel superior. They take pleasure in the commanding roles over business dependents and women, but they withdraw from a situation which would require them to play an inferior role or to compete with superiors. They often compensate this withdrawal by daydreams and power fantasies. More often than happy husbands, they are sporadic and irregular in their habits of work, dislike detail and the methodical attitude, dislike saving money, and like to wager. They more often express irreligious attitudes and are more inclined to radicalism in sex morals and politics.[5]

Terman's study was made over a quarter of a century ago. To what extent his conclusions, even if wholly true for that time, would be true in today's social, moral, and intellectual climate one can only guess.

Burgess and Wallin also made a study in which the relationship between personality characteristics and marital success was investigated. They reported that the happily married and unhappily married tend to exhibit the following differences.

Happily Married	Unhappily Married
Emotionally stable	Emotionally unstable
Considerate of others	Crtiical of others
Yielding	Dominating
Companionable	Isolated
Self confident	Lacking self confidence
Emotionally dependent	Emotionally self sufficient [6]

[5] *Ibid.,* pp. 153–155.
[6] Ernest Burgess and Paul Wallin, *Engagement and Marriage* (Philadelphia, Lippincott, 1953), p. 529.

The reader will probably be impressed with the fact that these characteristics emerging in the two studies contrast those individuals who are sociable, stable, happy, and generally well-adjusted with those who are not. This is not to say that one can predict accurately from personality factors alone what a person's marital success will be. There are inherent difficulties in attempting to analyze personality factors in relation to marital success.[7] "Cause" and "effect" may be difficult to disentangle. Marital difficulties may be caused by a preexisting personality trait of emotional instability but an unhappy marriage may drive a stable person toward emotional instability. Inferential logic from marriage studies and clinical evidence does tell us that other things being equal, the person with a generally healthy personality will have a better than even chance of marital success. The person on the opposite end of the personality continuum is called upon to make greater adaptations to achieve success.

It seems clear, and fortunate for all concerned, that there is no one, narrow personality "type" that can be guaranteed success in marriage. Most individuals have the personality potentials for at least moderate success in marriage as in other areas of life. By young adulthood the "basic personality" has been formed and major aspects of it can be modified only with difficulty. To be successful it is imperative that the individual make the best use that he can of his potentials for development and select a mate whose characteristics bring out the best in himself.

It must be stressed at this point that a particular type of marital success is being referred to here. The scales used tend to measure what is usually spoken of as "marital adjustment." Those who are interested in pursuing this should turn to Burgess and Locke for a detailed description of these measures and their strengths and weaknesses.[8] Kolb,[9] Hill, and others have criticized studies of this type rather sharply. A major charge is that they stress a narrow type of adjustment and conformity to middle-class values. While these critiques are at times overdone they cannot be dismissed lightly. It must be made clear that the scales give high rank in general to persons who have *conventional marriages* as we have known them in this country. We do not as yet have adequate scales to measure the creative, nonconformist type of marriage which can also be quite successful.

[7] Clifford Kirkpatrick, *The Family: As Process and Institution* (New York, Ronald, 1955), Chapter 15.

[8] Ernest Burgess and Harvey Locke, *The Family* (New York, American Book, 1963), Chapter 14.

[9] William Kolb, "Sociologically Established Family Norms and Democratic Values," *Social Forces,* Vol. 26 (May, 1948), pp. 541–546; Willard Waller and Reuben Hill, *The Family* (New York, Holt, Rinehart and Winston, 1951), Chapter 17. For the more technically oriented student the following two articles suggest pros and cons of marital adjustment tests and marriage prediction scales: Lewis Terman and Paul Wallin, "The Value of Marriage Prediction and Marital Adjustment Tests," *American Sociological Review,* Vol. 14 (August, 1949), pp. 497–505; Charles Bowerman, "Prediction Studies," in Christensen, Harold (Ed.), *Handbook of Marriage and the Family* (Chicago, Rand-McNally, 1964), Chapter 6.

A new conceptual approach has been suggested by Cuber and Harroff which deserves consideration here. A fivefold typology of marriages is defined as follows:

Conflict-Habituated Relationships—This configuration of husband-wife interaction can be characterized briefly as controlled conflict and tension. There is some private quarreling, nagging and "throwing up the past." The over-riding life force of this relationship is handling of the tension and conflict and keeping it concealed.

"Devitalized" Relationships—Here the relationship is essentially meaningless and empty and lacking in zest. There is no serious tension or conflict. There may be some satisfying aspects of the relationship such as mutual interest in children, property, or family tradition. These marriages remain intact, reinforced by the legal and ecclesiastical requirements.

Passive-Congenial Relationships—This is a comfortably adequate situation. There is little conflict. They stress their community of interests which seldom where itemized appear vital or involve participation and sharing which could not be achieved with comparative strangers or persons of the same sex. This type of relationship shows little vitality and little evidence that the spouse is essential.

Vital Relationships—These couples are sharing an exciting life experience be it work, association in a creative enterprise, child rearing, or even hobby participation. The importance of their enterprise is consuming their efforts and interest and the person who shares it is indispensable.

Total Relationships—The total relationship is the vital relationship encompassing many facets of existence. This is a relationship in which all important aspects of existence are fully shared and enthusiastically participated in. One might conclude that neither existed without the other. The total relationship is reported to be particularly precarious. By reason of its multifacets it is multivulnerable as conditions change.[10]

The above model is meant at this time to be appropriate only in the subculture of the upper middle class in America. Until we have completed more research on other class strata and also upon successful, unconventional marriages we cannot assume that these findings are general to the society.

Interpersonal Competence

Nelson Foote and Leonard Cottrell have reported on their work at the Family Study Center at Chicago and this report merits attention here.[11]

[10] Adapted from John F. Cuber and Peggy Harroff, "The More Total View: Relationships Among Men and Women of the Upper Middle Class," *Marriage and Family Living,* Vol. 25 (May, 1963), pp. 141–143.

[11] We are heavily indebted to the following sources for the interpersonal competency materials: Nelson Foote and Leonard Cottrell, Jr., *Identity and Interpersonal Competence* (Chicago, The University of Chicago Press, 1955); Thomas Gillette, "Interpersonal Competency," (unpublished paper); and Leonard Cottrell, Jr., "New Directions for Research on the American Family," *Social Casework,* Vol. 34 (February, 1953), p. 54.

They stress new ideas involving the personality in the social environment, especially in a family environment. Their key concept is interpersonal competence. By this term the authors mean skill in getting along with one's fellows in intimate, face-to-face relationships. Bearing heavily on their pioneer work we shall analyze interpersonal competency in six major areas and consider it as another aspect of marriageability.

Health.   Good health, the first component, is used here in the broad sense. It implies more than the negative freedom from disease. Rather it refers to the optimum use of one's potentialities in such respects as energy, dexterity, strength, and organ function.

In the absence of good health one's relationships with a fiance, spouse, or child will almost inevitably suffer. The husband whose wife is always "poorly" is to be pitied quite as much as she is. Even the person with a basically healthy, friendly personality may be difficult to live with when his physical resources are at a low ebb. Good physical condition in the positive sense of the term is invaluable. The individual wishing to prepare for the demands and opportunities of married living will be well advised to maintain a maximum level of health within his own physiological limits.

Intelligence.   The concept is used here with the same meaning that it is given in educational circles, except that special emphasis is put on application. Some of the more specific capacities emphasized are the capacity to communicate well and be articulate, skill in mobilizing and making use of available resources, and skill in abstracting experience and manipulating symbols of experience. Emphasis would be placed especially on the individual's skill in developing his latent capacities and utilizing them to their fullest. The former concept of intelligence—the ability to do abstract thinking—is too narrow, at least for our present purposes, although such competency is by no means unrelated to interpersonal competency.

Empathy.   Empathy is a type of subtle interpersonal sensitivity which involves the ability to step into another person's being and think and feel as he does. Sometimes known as "taking the role of the other", this ability is essential to effective communication and in a minimal degree to social interaction. One has a high degree of empathy when he can correctly perceive and interpret another's overt behavior in terms of the covert thoughts and feelings behind it. The college co-ed who moans "my boy friend doesn't understand me" really means "my boy friend just can't share my perceptions, my rationales, my emotional needs and states." He can't empathize with her, and perhaps she can't with him.

Empathy is extremely important in the intimate interaction of courtship, marriage, and parenthood. It is often necessary in marriage that one spouse perceive the other's mood without necessarily getting many obvious cues such as the spoken word. Unfortunately empathic thermostats are not as reliable as those attached to gas heating systems.

Autonomy.   The concept of autonomy brings to mind independence, self-confidence, self-control, and self-direction. Many writers have recently commented on the tendency of Americans to have no clear-cut identity as individuals.[12] While some of the writings may appear exaggerated, it also seems true that many people in this era of mass organization are finding it difficult to maintain a sense of their own integrity and identity. Feelings of self-respect and self-worth are related to this, but autonomy is not thought of as a state or trait. Rather it is seen as an ability or skill. The person with a high degree of autonomy can act as he chooses with confidence in his ability to comfortably handle situations that normally arise. He is not afraid of people's reactions to him.

Judgment.   The capacity to judge, to make decisions, to evaluate various alternatives in a given situation involves the competency of judgment. It refers to the ability to make correct decisions. The person with good judgment is able to discriminate and differentiate between values. He can come to a reasonable decision when faced with a number of alternatives and incomplete evidence. Also involved is the ability to distinguish between long and short run consequences of a given act of behavior. The person with poor judgment tends to make decisions which he later regrets.

An obvious place where judgment is called for is in serious mate selection.

When we were going together I was so madly in love that I guess I was blind. Good common sense should have told me we were not meant for each other. We seldom quarreled but I realize now that we dodged the real issues that should have been settled before marriage. Had I known her religion meant so much to her, how difficult her parents would be as in-laws, and certain other things, I believe I wouldn't have wanted to marry her. I guess you can't put an old head on young shoulders, as the old saying goes.

In the above case the married man seems to be saying that better judgment on his part would have made a crucial difference in his life circumstances.

Creativity.   Perhaps the most difficult to define of all the competency components is creativity. It is used here not in its more general meaning, but in relation to interpersonal situations. In essence it refers to the individual's ingenuity in developing new and fresh perspectives from which to evaluate established patterns and relationships, as well as his ingenuity in attaining new goals and objectives. Some of the characteristics commonly attributed to the inventor and to the artist are called for, although the

[12] David Riesman, *The Lonely Crowd* (New Haven, Yale, 1950).

emphasis is obviously on social inventiveness. This requires attitudes of self-confidence, adventuresomeness, and flexibility and adaptability. The person who is uncreative is often "at the end of his wits" when facing a new situation for which old experiences do not suffice. The creative person is able to adopt new ways of action more easily.

Creativity is called for in many aspects of mate selection, marriage, and parenthood. Creativity on the part of the boy will often make the difference between a date being an enjoyable or just a routine affair. Both members of a newly engaged couple are called upon to handle creatively situations which they have not previously experienced. And no matter what the preparation may be, creativity on the part of both parents is helpful when the first, (or the fifth!) newly born baby disrupts the preexisting relationship. Ability to develop new and fresh perspectives may also be crucial in renewing a marriage which has reached a dead level.[13]

Adaptability

The characteristic of adaptability should also be added here. Burgess and Wallin found adaptability to be important in their study of marital success.[14] Adopting their conception of adaptability we find four subcomponents involved: empathy, flexibility, motivation to adapt, and command of appropriate responses. Empathy has already been discussed as a component of interpersonal competence. There may be other overlappings with other interpersonal competency concepts as well. Flexibility is used as the "ability to vary one's responses in interpersonal relations." We may be able to empathize with another person but unable to make any real functional adaptations unless we have flexibility. The inflexible person is trapped in rigid, compulsive reactions to situations. In one sense the psychotic or neurotic falls in the extreme of this category. So does the rigid moralist, along with the authoritarian or the person with the "closed mind." [15]

Motivation to adapt seems to be an important variable in successful interaction in school, marriage, and many other realms. Very difficult to measure, it often seems to be involved in cases where individuals with a poor prognosis make greater achievements than were expected or predicted. When it is coupled with command of appropriate responses, difficult obstacles can often be overcome.

An individual may understand or perceive certain difficulties and be highly motivated to adapt his behavior but be unable to command the

[13] It must be stated that research regarding the specific relationship between interpersonal competency items and marital success is still in progress. Our analysis is based on inference and logic rather than empirical research.

[14] Burgess and Wallin, op. cit., Chapter 19.

[15] Theodore Adorno, et al., The Authoritarian Personality (New York, Harper & Row, 1950).

appropriate responses. Fortunately this condition of adaptability can be developed, probably more easily than the others mentioned, according to Burgess and Wallin. They suggest that, given moderate judgment and intelligence, the individual can acquire knowledge before marriage by formal courses. The individual can also learn through trial and error and if necessary, private counseling both before and after marriage, and eventually acquire more appropriate responses.

There is some overlapping in the subcategories or conditions of adaptability as used here, and the concept is closely related to some of the interpersonal competence items. It could be considered as a seventh component of interpersonal competency.

Maturity for Marriage

Although no research study has been able to isolate maturity as a specific factor and relate it to marital success, common sense and clinical evidence suggest an association. Psychiatrists make many references to such evidences of immaturity as parental fixations, various infantilisms common in adult personalities, narcism, and the like as being important causes of marital discord.

Dean has attempted to measure maturity, especially as it relates to something he calls "romanticism." He has been developing a maturity scale which is still in process of refinement. At present this maturity scale has not been shown to relate directly to marital success, but the possibility of such a relationship may be worth exploring. An abridged version of this test follows.

I. Stress Tolerance

The Mature Person:

A. Doesn't worry needlessly; tries to react imaginatively.
B. Remains cheerful even when things aren't going his way.
C. Lives calmly, rather than frequently having the "jitters."
D. Relieves tension by well-placed humor.

II. Handling Anger

The Mature Person:

A. When disappointed, refuses to give in to sulking.
B. When frustrated, reacts constructively rather than harboring resentment.
C. Works off anger by walking, in sports, or other physical activity.
D. When angered by superiors, does not "take it out on" relatively helpless individuals.

III. Reactions to Authority

The Mature Person:

A. Doesn't resent reasonable rules and regulations.

B. Obeys rules only after satisfying himself that they are justified.

C. Complies with reasonable requests cheerfully.

D. Doesn't avoid unpleasant but necessary tasks.

IV. Integration

The Mature Person:

A. Has a clearly defined "philosophy of life."

B. Has a clearly defined sense of purpose.

C. Seems emotionally secure; seldom exhibits anxiety.

D. Tries to live by his own principles, even if they are unpopular.

V. Self-Control

The Mature Person:

A. Doesn't make unreasonable demands for special privileges.

B. Is never presumptuous with others.

C. Doesn't blame others for undesirable consequences of his own actions.

D. Tells the truth, rather than lying in order to defend himself.

VI. Judgment

The Mature Person:

A. Seeks facts before making decisions.

B. Faces the inevitabilities of life such as illness, and loss of job with calmness.

C. Is able to reason logically.

D. Postpones immediate gratifications in favor of long-range goals.

VII. Man-Woman Relationships

The Mature Person:

A. Has many friends of both sexes.

B. Views sex as a natural and respected aspect of the whole person's life.

C. Does not talk excessively about sex matters.

D. Has friendships with the opposite sex not mainly based on physical attraction.

VIII. Attitude toward Learning

The Mature Person:

A. Listens respectfully to those of differing opinion.

B. Disciplines self when necessary to spend more time on difficult subjects.

C. Shows initiative and conscientiousness in learning endeavors.

D. Enjoys investigating challenging new fields of interest.

IX. Intellectual Maturity:

The Mature Person:

A. Attempts to synthesize and integrate knowledge gained from various fields into a usable whole.

B. Is humble in the knowledge which he has.

C. Enjoys reading and learning.

D. Listens to both sides of an issue before taking a stand.

X. Responsibility

The Mature Person:

A. Willingly assumes the normal chores required in day-to-day living.
B. Can be counted on to do what he promises.
C. Plans his time, adapting if necessary.
D. Does his fair share of the work in the organization to which he belongs.

XI. Egocenteredness-Sociocenteredness

The Mature Person:

A. Can enter imaginatively into the problems and joys of others.
B. Stands by his principles, even though they are unpopular.
C. Tries to fulfill others' reasonable expectations.
D. Respects and accepts people who hold ideas different from his own.

XII. Communication

The Mature Person:

A. Enjoys and can maintain conversation of a profound, serious nature.
B. Is able to communicate adequately with logical background or tell why he feels a certain way.
C. Is a good listener.
D. Shares ideas with others, rather than monopolizing conversation.

XIII. Security—Insecurity

The Mature Person:

A. Is tolerant of others, yet stands up for his own beliefs.
B. Does not find it difficult to accept those not sharing his ideas.
C. Can admit mistakes to others readily.
D. Never gossips about others.

XIV. Social Poise

The Mature Person:

A. Is adept at conversing with people for the first time.
B. Can speak or read before a large group without stumbling or faltering.
C. Feels at ease with people of any age.
D. Makes social introductions easily.[16]

SELF-ANALYSIS

We have discussed four factors relative to the personality of the marriageable person as indicated by our present state of knowledge based on research, clinical findings, and logical deduction from both. This is not

[16] See Dwight Dean, "Romanticism and Emotional Maturity, A Preliminary Study," *Marriage and Family Living,* Vol. 23 (February, 1961), pp. 44–45. Other papers will be forthcoming. The scale has considerable face validity, since it draws heavily on the works of Overstreet, Eilbert, Bowman, Ellzey, and Abrahamsen. However, the concept of maturity itself will probably always be open to controversy. The material we include is by permission of the author.

meant to include a discussion of all aspects of personality. The application of knowledge to one's own circumstances is a part of personality assessment as is rational self-appraisal. A rational man or woman should be concerned about whether or not he or she is a marriageable person. If he is interested only in his chances of marrying as against not marrying, the former are very high. In fact the chances are roughly nine to one that any person will marry, since slightly over 90 percent of those who live to marriageable age do so.

The question refers, of course, to one's chances for a *successful* marriage. Self-analysis, often with the aid of counseling, is one way of finding a reasonable answer. But it does not come easily or quickly. The person will attempt first to assess his general personality. Objective self-insight is a characteristic that not all people have, but it can be cultivated and in time prove helpful. Careful reflection on the items discussed in this chapter alone should give a person at least an initial understanding of his own strengths and weaknesses.

What are legitimate motives for marriage? What motives provide an inadequate basis for moving into marriage? Need they be the same for all people? The reasons for entering marriage are often complicated and varied. According to some authorities only an analysis probing the depths of the personality would reveal the real motives behind a given action, particularly marriage. Without considering the depth level however, it is possible to discuss some of the more apparent and important reasons for marriage.

Sexual Interest

Given the attention this factor receives in public communication, one might conclude that sex desire is the strongest motivating factor behind marriage for most individuals. Many writers doubt this assertion. Nevertheless the possibility of having a socially approved consistent source of sexual expression and gratification appears basic, and psychologically and physically healthy according to present scientific criteria, and is a prominent developmental task for both sexes.

Companionship

A second motive for marriage (not clearly separable from sex, of course) is to find companionship. Close intimate response to a partner may be the most important motivation for marriage. In a good mating, companionship deepens and grows. At the younger age level most persons have only a very hazy idea of what the future is to bring. However, they usually foresee themselves moving through the various stages of later life as a marital pair rather than merely as individuals. The wish for this type of intimate emotional response is strong in most people of all ages.

Romantic Love or Infatuation

Often difficult to disassociate from sex and companionship is a desire "to live happily ever after" with a beloved partner. Such sentiments have been termed infatuations, and those who marry on such thin grounds are usually said to be doomed to frustration. Just why such brave hopes should be inimical to happiness is not clear. Perhaps it is that the disillusioned who did not find lasting fulfillment and enduring love, think therefore that others cannot either. A minority does in fact live most happily ever after. These fortunate people remain actively in love throughout their lives and put the lie to the more dyspeptic cynical view. It is, of course, also true that some who dream such dreams may be disappointed by reality.

Security

It has often been said that women are especially prone to marry for reasons of security. But security may be only a mirage. Marriage entails inevitable and soul-rending risks, including a fairly high probability of divorce. Further, it is by no means clear from a strictly economic point of view that marriage is in the best interests of every man or woman. Nevertheless marriage still seems to many to offer such security. To those who wish psychological security, to have an enduring relationship with a loved one, and to build a home and family, the invitation to marry is strong. The very concept "home" implies a type of security and stability which is unique.

Children

It is doubtful that most young people in our society marry with the specific intent of having children. Yet, in general, children are expected to be a normal outcome of the marital relationship. It is probable that the wish to have children is deep-seated, but that it does not readily come to the surface of consciousness until after marriage.

In the final analysis young people have been trained for marriage from the time they were small children. Our society is organized with the expectation that most people will marry during adulthood. Individual motives will differ to a degree, but many societal pressures and expectations are available in the community to help young adults "see the light." Unmarried adults to be sure, are not stigmatized as they would be in some cultures, but the fact that most of our institutional and informal community practices are arranged on a pair basis amounts to a persistent if subtle pressure to "be normal and get married."

From the personal point of view the question as to whether one's motives for marriage are realistic or unrealistic, healthy or unhealthy, adequate or inadequate, rational or neurotic, is important. Each individual is well advised to analyze as best he can his motives, attitudes, and needs in regard to marriage. Materials in this book and similar books should prove helpful in this endeavor. Yet we all perceive dimly and are prone to err. Assistance from books and counselors can be helpful, but it is no panacea.

The world is made up of many types of individuals with various types and shadings of personality. Granted this wide range of divergence in personality and personal and social adjustment, there will always be those who have severe problems and difficulties in relation to potential marriage. Major personality changes can ordinarily be achieved only with the help and counsel of a psychiatrist or professional in a closely related field.

The personal counselor or marriage counselor can be of some help to the individual in the ascertaining of general personality structure, personal and social adjustment, maturity for marriage, and general marriageability ranking. It must be stressed at this point however, that marriage involves a combination of unique personalities. Marriage is a *relationship*. One person regardless of his high capacity for success in marriage cannot guarantee a successful marriage for himself and certainly not for the spouse he may love. Nor can he know in advance how his traits or those of his spouse will actually affect the relationship as it moves through time. He can only vaguely anticipate the effects of aging, success or failure in career, the demands of children, and possible ill health upon his earlier traits of personality or character. The same is true for his spouse. The surprising fact is not that so many are unsuccessfully or unhappily married, but that so many actually attain even the modest successes they do.

SELECTED READINGS

Burgess, Ernest and Wallin, Paul, *Engagement and Marriage* (Philadelphia, Lippincott, 1953), Chapter 4.

Cavan, Ruth, *Marriage and Family in the Modern World: A Book of Readings* (New York, Crowell, 1960), Chapter 11.

Christensen, Harold, "Why All These Young Marriages?" *National Parent-Teacher,* Vol. 52 (April, 1958), pp. 4–5.

Dean, Dwight, "Romanticism and Emotional Maturity: A Preliminary Study," *Marriage and Family Living,* Vol. 23 (February, 1961), pp. 44–45.

Ellis, Evelyn, "Social Psychological Correlates of Upward Sociological Mobility Among Unmarried Career Women," *American Sociological Review,* Vol. 17 (October, 1952), pp. 558–563.

Foote, Nelson, and Cottrell, Leonard, Jr., *Identity and Interpersonal Competency* (Chicago, The University of Chicago Press, 1955).

Hillman, Christine, "An Advice Column's Challenge to Family Life Education," *Marriage and Family Living,* Vol. 16 (February, 1954), pp. 51–54.

Klemer, Richard, "Factors of Personality and Experience Which Differentiate Single from Married Women," *Marriage and Family Living,* Vol. 16 (February, 1954), pp. 41–44.

Klemer, Richard, *A Man for Every Woman* (New York, Macmillan, 1959).

Landis, Judson, and Landis, Mary, *Building A Successful Marriage* (Englewood Cliffs, N.J., Prentice-Hall, 1953), Chapter 6.

Landis, Judson, "Attitudes and Policies Concerning Marriages Among High School Students," *Marriage and Family Living,* Vol. 18 (May, 1956), pp. 128–136.

Le Masters, Ersel, *Modern Courtship and Marriage* (New York, Macmillan, 1957), Chapter 10.

Martinson, Floyd, "Ego Deficiency as a Factor in Marriage," *American Sociological Review,* Vol. 20 (April, 1955), pp. 161–164.

Moss, Joel, and Gingles, Ruby, "The Relationship of Personality to the Incidence of Early Marriage," *Marriage and Family Living,* Vol. 21 (November, 1959), pp. 373–377.

Nimkoff, Meyer, and Wood, Arthur, "Courtship and Personality," *American Journal of Sociology,* Vol. 53 (January, 1948), pp. 263–269.

Overstreet, H. A., *The Mature Mind* (New York, Norton, 1949).

Peterson, James, *Education for Marriage* (New York, Scribner, 1964), Part 3.

Simpson, George, *People in Families* (New York, Crowell, 1960), Chapter 12.

Vernon, Glenn, and Stewart, Robert, "Empathy as a Process in the Dating Situation," *American Sociological Review,* Vol. 22 (February, 1957), pp. 48–52.

QUESTIONS AND EXERCISES

1. What would the concept *marriageability* mean in traditional China or Japan? Discuss.
2. In your estimation, what kind of parental environment is needed to produce marriageable personalities?
3. What to you are the major problems facing the young person who attempts a self-analysis and evaluation regarding his preparation for marriage?
4. Make a study of college marriages on your campus, including percentage married, housing facilities, number of husbands and wives working, etc. Then have two or three couples meet with your group to discuss the pros and cons of marrying while in college.
5. Read Christensen's cited article in which he analyzes some of the major reasons and motivations for early marriage. Do you agree with his general interpretation? Discuss.
6. Why from your point of view would it be difficult to devise tests to measure maturity for marriage? Explain.
7. Write a critique of Bergler's book (footnote 2). Indicate whether or not you agree that persons who get into marital difficulty are basically neurotic.
8. If you have an interest in this area, apply to your college guidance bureau for a series of personality and occupational tests. (This is not to imply

that you are neurotic or potentially so.) Ask that the tests be interpreted for you. Remember that at present, problems of validity and reliability of the various diagnostic scales have not been fully solved. The results may be helpful to you in assessing your marriageability, however. Why is it that such an approach has limitations in the prediction of marital success? Discuss.

9. The tendency toward early marriage, while confined largely to noncollege people, will eventually be affecting more of the college-bound group. Under what circumstances, if any, would you favor early marriage?

10. Many high schools do not allow married students to continue in class attendance, especially if they are pregnant. What is your position on this policy matter? Defend it.

7

Love

It is with justified trepidation that a social scientist attempts a chapter on love. As both Maslow [1] and Foote have pointed out, members of the academic and scientific community tend to have doubts about one's respectability if he entertains serious thoughts on this topic. When Foote wrote a short paper with the same title he received a number of comments. [2] They fell into the following categories: cynical, joking, sentimental, and matter-of-fact, with the first three being the most common. Many so-called tough-minded persons feel themselves "above" such a topic as love, while others doubt that such a subject is even amenable to objective analysis. The implication is that such matters should be left to literary people or perhaps to writers of "advice to the lovelorn" columns. Fortunately such attitudes are not universal. Goode has written a recent article stressing both the importance of love in the family structure and as a topic for study. [3] Other researchers and writers have been giving the subject attention and their work will be referred to in the chapter.

A central problem is that of arriving at a clear, well-defined concept of love. In spite of the fact that most Americans use the word "love" daily, it has no consistent meaning. One "loves" limburger cheese, Verdi's operas, golf, his dachshund puppy, as well as his sister, father, and sweetheart. In this connection it would probably be well to use the term "like" in referring to nonhuman things or animals and to confine the term love to feelings involving persons. Even this leaves differentiated feelings lumped together:

[1] A. H. Maslow, *Motivation and Personality* (New York, Harper & Row, 1954), Chapter 13.

[2] Nelson Foote, "Love," *Psychiatry; Journal for the Study of Interpersonal Processes,* Vol. 16 (August, 1953), pp. 245–251.

[3] William Goode, "The Theoretical Importance of Love," *American Sociological Review,* Vol. 24 (February, 1959), pp. 38–47.

one's love for a sweetheart has little in common with one's love for an aged grandmother! Social scientists themselves show little consistency in the use of the word.

For introductory purposes love may be considered as a complex of strong and positive sentiments and attitudes toward another person.[4] Since love is object-directed this means that a reciprocal process is often but not necessarily involved. When there is reciprocity we may speak of a love *relationship* existing between the people concerned.

DEVELOPMENT OF LOVE (AFFECTION) IN THE PERSON

The individual child is at first interested in neither himself nor others but only in objects relevant to certain needs; later, persons become the objects of his responses. The newly born infant is incapable even of distinguishing himself from the surrounding environment. Through an elementary conditioning process he learns rather quickly to associate some adult, normally the mother or nurse, with physical and emotional comforts. As time passes he becomes accustomed to mother's feeding or nursing, to her changing his clothing, and also to her caressing and fondling contacts. These experiences produce pleasurable feelings in him, but the infant is not for a time aware that his mother or others are persons. He simply enjoys having mother or nurse care for him and he comes to associate pleasant emotions with them.

Fairly early, however, the infant learns to distinguish his mother or nurse from the general environment of things and persons and to become attached to or feel dependent upon her. The first out-reaching phase is a very important part of affectional development. Until the individual can give and receive affection he may be said to be, in effect, only in "love with himself." "Autoerotic" and "narcissistic" are terms used especially by Freudians to describe this level of affection. There are those adult individuals who never seem to be able to love persons other than themselves. Hence, the emphasis of child development specialists on the early affectional relationships have a certain rationale.

Orthodox Freudians have long held that the child "falls in love" with his parent of the opposite sex and that incest taboos soon make him repress his feelings and desires with consequent emotional maladjustments. It now appears that the child usually develops strong attachments (elementary love, if you wish) to one of the parents, not necessarily of the opposite sex. There may be an erotic element involved, but if so it is most surely of a very elementary nature.[5]

[4] Ernest Burgess, Harvey Locke, and Mary Thomes, *The Family: From Institution to Companionship,* 3rd ed. (New York, American Book, 1963), p. 322.
[5] *Ibid.,* p. 367.

Eventually the child develops affection for other family members and then his circle is widened to include individuals outside the family. Typically this involves playmates of both sexes. During the so-called latency period affection usually centers on members of his own sex. During the adolescent period heterosexual interests begin to predominate and eventually, during the dating and courtship period, affectional interests become less diffused and tend to center on a possible mate. Heterosexual love is considered in this framework as a mature form of love.

Affectional or love development as described above might be considered typical, but in many individuals the process is not even at all points. At any level in the process from self-love to other-love the individual may become fixated, or more rarely regress to an earlier level. A host of writers have recently used overattachment between son and mother to explain many of our current mental health problems.[6] While this theme is probably exaggerated, there is always the danger that the affectional development of the person will become fixed short of full heterosexual maturity. A major task of parents involves establishing close emotional relationships with the child in the early years and then helping and allowing him to move toward mature heterosexual love relationships in the teen and young adult years.

LOVE IN THE AMERICAN CULTURAL CONTEXT

A visitor from Mars might say that Americans are preoccupied with love. By reading our literature, going to our movies, noticing our advertising, and listening to our radio and TV serials, he might easily arrive at this conclusion. As David Cohn says,

Few peoples talk about love as much as Americans. This is only natural perhaps in a land where love is regarded as a secret infirmity; hedonism and puritanism are at war in the breasts of multitudes; flirtation (petting) is a widely practiced form of amusement and an end in itself; seminude drum-major waitresses serve hot dogs to cavaliers in Chevrolets; artificial bosoms create artificial horizons; girls in crowded sweaters give the landscape an appearance of lush opulence; sex-appeal photographers' models feature the advertising of trucks and flypaper; Freud is a handmaiden of love along with Dorothy Dix and Helena Rubenstein; the automobile has given rise to our sole contribution to the art of amour—the love-death clinch at sixty miles an hour—while the car that takes a feed salesman to his work by day becomes a perambulating Florida beach by night.[7]

[6] See Philip Wylie, *Generation of Vipers* (New York, Holt, Rinehart and Winston, 1942), and Edward Strecker, *Their Mother's Sons* (Philadelphia, Lippincott, 1946).

[7] David Cohn, *Love in America* (New York, Simon and Schuster, 1943), p. 7.

Thinking of love as a cultural trait or complex or traits, what can be said about the rise and spread of the love accent in America? Outstanding is the stress on romanticism and romantic love. Central concepts in romanticism are (1) exclusive concentration of affection on one love partner; (2) individual freedom in choice of the partner; (3) idealization and almost worship of the woman by the man; (4) marriage for love rather than for more practical considerations; (5) aesthetic and dramatic settings for dating and courtships; (6) emphasis on an intense love relationship in and of itself.[8]

Authorities disagree as to the precise origins of romantic love in the western world. It probably goes back at least to Roman and Greek civilizations. There something akin to a modern romantic relationship existed between the few educated women in the society and some of the upper-class men. Usually these relationships were extramarital. During the so-called Dark Ages in Europe romance as we know it did not exist. In the twelfth and thirteenth centuries romantic love became a favorite theme of the troubadours. It typically involved a wandering knight doing deeds of bravery for his lady. The lady usually was married to a noble much her senior with whom she was not in love. Both the troubadours and the clergy disapproved of love within marriage.

Apparently the romantic love similar to that of today and associated with marriage received a great impetus in the courtly circles from the seventeenth through the nineteenth centuries. Courtly affairs served to attract women of charm and grace from the upper classes, and occasionally even those of more humble birth were attracted to the outer courtly circles. While many alliances developed on an extramarital level, others led to more permanent arrangements. Important philosophical, economic, political, and social changes during this period were associated with the development of romanticism, although not necessarily caused by it. Among them were individualism, the rise of capitalism, the Protestant revolution, and laissez faire. The break up of feudal society involved proposals of freedom of choice in both the affairs of the market place and the affairs of the heart.[9]

In America the frontier environment tended to break down class and family considerations in mate selection. Geographic and social mobility have served to accentuate this process. Accompanying the development of concepts of individual freedom and democracy, opportunities of social mobility and the impersonal, secular atmosphere of the urban environment have emerged.

Compared to other societies love is stressed in America. To fall in

[8] Francis Merrill, *Courtship and Marriage* (New York, Holt, Rinehart and Winston, 1949), Chapter 2.

[9] Willystine Goodsell, *A History of Marriage and the Family* (New York, MacMillan, 1934), Chapter 7.

love is the expected, "normal" thing to do. Everybody "falls" in love. If one isn't in love or hasn't been in love "something is amiss."

ELEMENTS OF LOVE FEELING

Folsom delineates three elements of "love feelings": erotic feeling, tenderness, and joy.[10] *Erotic feeling* or sexual feeling begins with the physical attractiveness of a partner. The feeling can vary from lust to a more diffused and sentimentalized type of sexual feeling and interest. The conscious center of the feeling seems to be in the genital areas. The range of intensity is great.

Tenderness seems to be a pleasant feeling associated with motives of protection and care. Feelings similar to those obtaining when one performs nursing activities are typical. Emotions involved in nonerotic cuddling and kissing also come under this category. Pleasures associated with sensations of warmth, light, and restful contact seem to be central. The sensations of tenderness seem to arise from caressing of the skin especially that of the chest, face, and inner surface of the arms.

Joy, a very broad concept, involves a number of sensations and experiences. It may come as a result of reaching emotional heights in positive fashion, or as a negative sense of relief from burden, doubt, or fear. There is the joyous rapture that comes in the excitement of the newly found love as well as the deeper, more profound joy which one feels when he is in the presence of a loved one. The nostalgic feelings associated with remembrances and the gay, playful feelings stimulated by the presence of an attractive love object are all included under this category. Deep, rapid breathing and muscular pleasure are characteristic of this element of love feeling. Folsom believes that joy is the keystone of the three love feelings.

Wish for Response

Burgess and Locke believe that the sentiment of love is associated mainly with the wish for response. They suggest that many components may be associated with this wish for intimacy including the following:

1. Sexual desire: The strictly physical component of love
2. Physical attraction: Sex-appeal in terms of personal and physical qualities
3. Attachment: Mutual affection and rapport
4. Emotional interdependence: Mutual complementation of basic personality needs
5. Idealization: Construction of a distorted mental image of the partner

[10] Joseph Folsom, *The Family and Democratic Society* (New York, Wiley, 1943), Chapter 11.

6. Companionship: Association of the partners based on common interest, mental stimulation, and response rather than sex
7. Stimulation: Fulfillment in the desire for new experience in pursuit of and living with a mate
8. Freedom of communication and action: Liberty to act freely in the loved one's presence and to exchange confidence
9. Emotional reassurance: Feeling of assurance in the affectional relationship
10. Status: Feeling of self-esteem in meeting one's own expectations and those of others in possessing the love partner [11]

LOVE AND NEEDS

Winch and others stress the theory that love, like all behavior, is based on needs. The needs may be conscious or unconscious. Love needs are social in that they arise from interpersonal association. In the middle-class environment in America a great need is created for security and acceptance, "and this need in turn is experienced as a generalized need to love and be loved." [12]

There seems to be no doubt but that people seek love partners to fulfill a need or needs, conscious or unconscious. In former eras in America a person received intimate response from many people in the primary group environment. One's emotional relationship with any one particular person in those days was therefore as intense as it would tend to be today, because he had supportive relationships with a number of people. Today we live in a more competitive, impersonal group atmosphere. It is doubtful that our basic cravings for ego-satisfaction have diminished. As a matter of fact one can well hypothesize that they have increased.

Romantic love, although taken for granted by most of us, is a comparatively recent trend in the Western hemisphere. Whereas in the past, mates were thrown together out of economic advantage, today couples are mutually attracted by the emotional complex we know as romantic love. A study by Anselm Strauss indicates the emphasis placed upon love as the criterion for courtship, engagement, and marriage.[13]

As can be seen from Table 7, all the needs mentioned seem to be constituents of the complex, romantic love; needs such as economic support are not listed. As direct evidence of the importance attached to love, the need for someone to "love me" was chosen most frequently by both sexes. It appears that women's needs were generally more intense, especially regarding the need for love and affection, security, and intimate response than

[11] Adapted from Burgess and Locke, *op. cit.*, Chapter 12.

[12] Robert Winch, *The Modern Family* (New York, Holt, Rinehart and Winston, 1952), pp. 323–324.

[13] Anselm Strauss, unpublished Ph.D. thesis, University of Chicago, as cited in Burgess and Locke, *op. cit.*, p. 368.

TABLE 7

Expressed Needs To Be Satisfied in Marriage, by Percentage

Need Someone To:	Men	Women
Love me	36	54
Confide in me	31	42
Show me affection	21	38
Respect my ideals	26	26
Appreciate my goals of achievement	28	24
Understand my moods	23	28
Help me make important decisions	15	33
Stimulate my ambition	27	21
Look up to	16	29
Give me self-confidence	20	24
Stand back of me in difficulty	16	26
Appreciate me just as I am	20	21
Admire my ability	19	20
Make me feel I count for something	21	17
Relieve my loneliness	19	19

SOURCE: Anselm Strauss, unpublished doctoral thesis, University of Chicago, as cited in Ernest Burgess, Harvey Locke, and Mary Thomes, *The Family: From Institution to Companionship*, 3rd ed. (New York, American Book, 1963), p. 368.

men's. Perhaps this is the result of the female's inclination to be concerned with the complex emotional manifestations of romantic love, as against a male viewpoint which is allegedly more narrowly focused.

Perhaps it can be said that romantic love in the Western world receives so much emphasis because the complexity of life presents one with barriers to the direct expression of sexual needs. Furthermore, since marriage must be postponed far beyond sexual maturity, many romantic love affairs must necessarily be inconclusive. Therefore, it would be interesting to discover whether such relationships follow a significant pattern of development and termination.

PATTERN OF THE ROMANTIC LOVE AFFAIR

Some interesting evidence is revealed by a study of the love affairs of students at the University of Minnesota by Kirkpatrick and Caplow. In order to discover any significant pattern, Kirkpatrick and Caplow presented students with three graphs which represented possible courses of love experience.[14] Each graph presented the possible movements through four degrees of intensity: "Love," "Attraction," "Indifference," and "Dislike."

[14] Clifford Kirkpatrick, and Theodore Caplow, "Emotional Trends in the Courtship Experience of College Students as Expressed by Graphs with Some Observations on Methodological Implications," *American Sociological Review*, Vol. 10 (October, 1945), pp. 619–626.

The graphs represented the emotional trend from the beginning of an affair to its close; they were classified as *regular, cyclical,* and *irregular.* The *regular* love affair began in indifference, rose to love, and closed within a range between love and indifference. The *cyclical* pattern involved sudden shifts from love to dislike and the reverse. The *irregular* trend fell intermediate between the other two; changes in feeling fell between the gradual

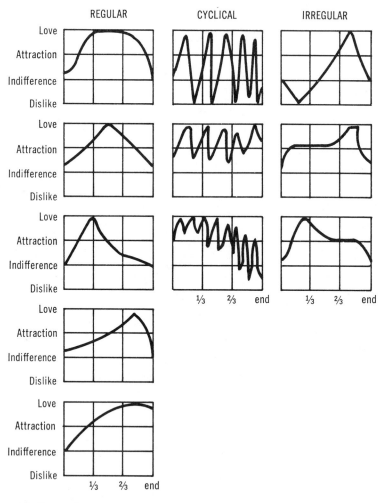

FIGURE 2. *Examples of Curves Drawn by Students to Indicate Emotional Experience in Courtship.* SOURCE: Clifford Kirkpatrick and Theodore Caplow, "Courtship in a Group of Minnesota Students," *American Journal of Sociology,* Vol. 51 (September, 1945), pp. 114–125.

rise and fall of the regular pattern and the sudden shifts of the cyclical trend. In addition to these three, a blank graph was provided so that students could draw the trends of their affairs which did not fit the three provided.

The graphs presented are shown above in Figure 2 under "For Duration of Affair."

Students were asked to choose the graph which best represented their personal experiences. The results were significant. Over 60 percent of both sexes chose the regular curve. About 15 percent indicated the cyclical pattern, and less than 20 percent chose the irregular trend. Thus, it can be said that for most couples, love follows a normal development and termination pattern without significant shifts in emotions.

Figure 3 indicates the "Extension to Readjustment Experience." This would indicate the level of emotion at the termination of the affair and at the beginning of the readjustment period. It was found that most students'

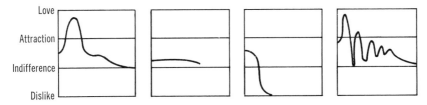

FIGURE 3. *Example of Curves Drawn by Students to Indicate Readjustment Following Breakup of Relationship.* SOURCE: Clifford Kirkpatrick and Theodore Caplow, "Courtship in a Group of Minnesota Students," *American Journal of Sociology,* Vol. 51 (September, 1945), pp. 114–125.

affairs ended in indifference, with very few ending in love, or dislike. This finding again suggests the pattern of a normal affair involves no serious traumas.

Kirkpatrick and Caplow also investigated the trend in emotion after the break up of an affair.[15] For this criterion, they presented students with four graphs indicating again the possible developments through "Love," "Attraction," "Indifference," and "Dislike." Type I represented a rise to a height of idealized love followed by a steady decline. Type II is a consistent feeling at the indifference level. Type III involves a progression from indifference to dislike. Type IV indicates a series of fluctuations above and below the indifference level; these become less extreme, indicating a gradual decline in the intensity of such emotional shifts. Such fluctuations indicate a feeling of confusion. Once again, the findings were significant in discerning trends of emotional readjustment. Approximately 60 percent of the students chose Type II; most experienced consistent indifference.

[15] *Ibid.*

About 15 percent chose Type I, 15 percent chose Type IV, and only a few chose Type III. The findings seem to refute the common belief that mixed emotions of love and dislike are present after breakup. They instead reinforce the idea that most affairs proceed naturally and present no extreme emotional upset during readjustment.

Kirkpatrick and Caplow provided the students with a check list of emotional states from which they were to choose the one they experienced after breakup. Table 8 indicates the emotional states and student responses.

TABLE 8
Emotional States After Breakup

Reaction Pattern	Male N-230	Female N-414
Bitter	5.9	4.4
Hurt	10.0	14.3
Angry	3.3	3.5
Remorseful	6.6	6.7
Crushed	1.8	5.0
Indifferent	19.4	16.2
Relieved	15.2	16.8
Satisfied	11.5	8.5
Happy	4.4	3.5
Mixed regret and relief	21.9	21.1
Total	100.0	100.0

SOURCE: Adapted from Clifford Kirkpatrick and Theodore Caplow, "Courtship in a Group of Minnesota Students," *American Journal of Sociology,* Vol. 51 (September, 1945), p. 124. Reprinted by permission of the authors.

Only about 20 percent experienced bitterness, hurt, or anger. About the same proportion of students felt mixed emotions of regret and relief. Most significant, however, was the most common reaction of indifference. Those findings may indicate that students today view love affairs realistically; perhaps this is because they can accept the fact that love affairs are a natural part of one's life experiences and that many must be inconclusive in the complex society of today.

TYPES OF LOVE

Three separable types or phases of love have been differentiated: infatuation, romantic love, and mature or conjugal love.

Infatuation

Infatuation, as in the case of "puppy love," is said to be typical among teenagers in our society, although it is not necessarily confined to that age level. As has been stressed, the American cultural context provides a milieu where to fall in love is the expected thing. An evening of dancing to sweet music followed by the midnight drive and lovemaking in the soft moonlight prepares John and Susan for infatuation much better than it prepares them psychologically for Monday's algebra class. Attachments of a short-term nature which are narrowly and sexually focused tend to involve strong emotions but do not often have lasting satisfaction. It is not unusual to find the young teenager infatuated with a favorite teacher or an older unavailable person. Usually someone more available becomes the next love object.

Physical attraction is dominant in infatuation although the emotions are often diffused on the part of the girl. Receiving thrills from a particularly romantic experience, the person comes to associate the thrills with the stimulus and to idealize the partner. Thus the image of the partner may become artificial and unrealistic. Since the focus is restricted it may prove impossible to maintain the high level of initial interest, and feelings of frustration tend to accrue. Rapidly, sequential and even coexistent infatuations come into existence and individuals move freely from partner to partner when passions cool and interests wane.[16]

An unrequited infatuation is virtually impossible to maintain. Even when the attachment is reciprocal the chances of permanent equilibrium are poor. Genuine interest in the total personality of the partner may of course develop, which is another way of saying that infatuation has been superceded by more total, lasting love. Infatuation may thus give way to a more mature type of affection and attachment bringing new emotions and attitudes, and usually motivations of more serious dating or possibly of marriage.

Infatuation seems to be especially related to particular wishes for response as listed by Burgess and Locke. Prominent would be motives for sex, physical satisfaction, attachment (intense but short-lived) and idealization. Spending a lot of time away from his family, propelled by inward drives, and finding himself thrown into heterosexual groups, the adolescent in America is prepared to "fall" for a member of the opposite sex. The wish for new experience may help turn the attention to greener pastures. Actually, in spite of the fact that the person seems to direct all of his attention to his partner, the major motive in pure infatuation is probably self-gratification.

Romantic Love

Romantic love falls between infatuation and companionship or conjugal love. It has some common elements with infatuation but there are important differences. Physical attraction and idealization are both present but as Cavan says, romantic love is "more inclusive of the whole personality

[16] Ruth Cavan, *The American Family* (New York, Crowell, 1963), p. 372.

and more readily adjusted to the realities of marriage." [17] While infatuation involves "being in love with love" romantic love focuses on the partner to a greater extent. It is less ego-centered, more relationship-centered. More of a "we feeling" or unity develops in romantic love than in infatuation. In fact a pair-centered exclusiveness is very characteristic of a romantic relationship. A song of a generation ago puts it thus:

> With someone like you, a pal so good and true,
> I'd like to leave it all behind, and go and find,
> Some place that's known to God alone,
> Just a spot to call our own.

Family and social prerogatives count for little in romantic love. The characteristics of the individual personality are stressed. In this respect romantic love is the epitome of mating democracy.

Family students are divided on the function of romantic love in relation to marriage. De Rougemont is on the extreme side with those who believe that romantic love is incompatible with successful marriage.[18] He believes that romance thrives on obstacles and that in marriage with nothing to keep them apart, the feelings of the partners wane and disillusionment sets in.

Most family writers criticize romantic love as a base for a solid, integrated marriage. This congruence of opinion was probably bound to produce defenders of romantic love. Among those who have appeared are Beigel,[19] Kolb,[20] and others. Kolb believes that most of the above writers in effect are tacitly giving support to sterile concepts of adjustment, integration, and stability in their critiques of romanticism. He thinks that actually they are biased against core American values such as personal development, individualism, and personal freedom. Beigel says that romantic love helps ease the pain of living in an impersonal society and furnishes the main bond between the marital pair.

Johnson believes that romantic love serves to promote mutual loyalty between the spouses and hence makes for stability.[21] He also makes the point that romantic love enables the young person to resist parental pressure in regard to mate choice. This is regarded as a positive function in that the young person is the one who will have to live with the partner, not the parents.

It is difficult to assess romantic love objectively. Very probably it has

[17] Ruth Cavan, *The American Family* (New York, Crowell Co., 1953), p. 406.

[18] Dennis de Rougemont, *Love in the Western World* (New York, Harcourt, Brace & World, 1940).

[19] Hugo Beigel, "Romantic Love," *American Sociological Review,* Vol. 16 (June, 1951), pp. 326–334.

[20] William Kolb, "Sociologically Established Family Norms and Democratic Values," *Social Forces* (May, 1948), pp. 451–456.

[21] Harry Johnson, *Sociology,* Vol. 26 (New York, Harcourt, Brace & World, 1960), pp. 67–68.

both functions and dysfunctions for lasting, monogamous marriage. As an ideology romanticism contains irrational elements, as do many ideologies. Some Hollywood varieties hardly seem appropriate as models for successful marriage as most Americans seem to want it. Overidealization may prevent the person from coming to grips with personal reality during the premarriage period only "to set him up for a fall" during marriage. However, those who insist that romantically inclined persons are always immature, selfish, and neurotic must come forth with research findings to sustain their position. Dean, in a study of freshmen women at a midwestern college, found no substantial relationship between romanticism and emotional maturity.[22] Since there is not full agreement as to how to measure either of these characteristics it may be that future research will also show inconclusive results. Further, research needs to deal with people in the noncollege groups.

Arguments as to whether romantic love is "real love" or not seem fruitless. It now appears that a romantic love relationship is a model for most of our young people. It would also appear that romance in and of itself is not an adequate, total base upon which to build a successful marriage. And while we do not have the research to prove it, it seems reasonable that those who rely only or chiefly on romantic ideals as a basis for lasting marriage are headed for trouble. However, many young people are apparently able to take some of the extremes of romanticism with a grain of the salt of realism.

Beigel thinks that romantic love seen in proper perspective has "saved monogamous marriage from complete disorganization."[23] To attribute to the single factor of romantic love the survival of a basic cultural institution such as monogamous marriage seems overdrawn and extreme, although in individual cases it is demonstrably true. Nevertheless under our system it is now probably necessary that couples think and feel that they are romantically in love before they turn to more prudential considerations in mate selection.

Conjugal Love

What are some of the characteristics of companionship or conjugal love? In the first place, it seems to partake of more reality than does romantic love, and of less idealization. In popular language we speak of "settling down" to marriage. There are unfortunate negative connotations to the words, but if they imply a respect for reality, considerable truth may be stored in them. Marriage entails swallowing the bitter with the sweet. A type of resilient love is needed that can stand considerable strain. The wife must be able to love the man who emerges from the basement workshop with a streak of grease across his forehead and his hair in Bushman

[22] Dwight Dean, "Romanticism and Emotional Maturity: A Preliminary Study," *Marriage and Family Living,* Vol. 23 (February, 1961), pp. 44, 45.
[23] Beigel, *op. cit.,* p. 334.

style. The man who forgets to mail an important letter and who is sulky after a round with the boss at the office is still "that loving husband." The husband who feels strongly affectionate toward his wife, decked out in pin curls, or bristly rollers, who still can't cook like his mother, has the makings of conjugal love. Not that idealization need be sacrificed. Each partner will feel that none else could quite measure up to his spouse. Undesirable traits are pushed out of the consciousness of the perceptor and qualities which are approved are stressed and recognized. But the partner in marriage can hardly remain on some unattainable pedestal.

Sex feelings in conjugal love reach different forms through recurring lovemaking and intercourse. While the thrill of anticipation may not be as consistently high as in romantic love, the joy, security, and erotic pleasure of recurrent mutual possession may more than make up for this loss.

Mutuality is a key concept of conjugal love, placing stress on the factors of companionship, status, and freedom of communication and action, as used in our previous list on page 116. Sentiments and attitudes stressing this are pertinent. Sullivan [24] and Fromm [25] suggest attitudes of mutual responsibility in their approaches. Mutual responsiveness, the willingness to share, empathy, feelings of "togetherness" and unity, all are involved. [26]

Maslow's work with so-called self-actualizing persons is of interest here. On the basis of his sampling of mature, psychologically healthy people he offers a description of the characteristics of love between the sexes which may be considered ideal.

1. There is a special sexual attraction between the partners. The beloved has more power than anyone else of arousing specific, conscious sex desire.
2. There is a desire for psychological as well as physical intimacy, expressed often in terms of a secret language, special gestures understandable only to themselves, etc.
3. Quite characteristic is the feeling of generosity, of wanting to give and to please. The lover gets special pleasure from doing things for and making gifts for the loved one.
4. There is a tendency to more and more complete spontaneity, the dropping of defenses, the dropping of roles, and of trying and striving in the relationship. There is less maintenance of distance, mystery, glamour, and secrecy.
5. Self-actualizing people have the power to love and the ability to be loved. They know how to love, and can do so freely, easily, and naturally without getting wound up in conflicts, threats, or inhibitions.
6. Sex and love tend to be fused together for these people. Sex is not sought for its own sake. Without affection there would be little interest in it.

[24] Harry Stack Sullivan, *Conceptions of Modern Psychiatry* (New York, Norton, 1953).

[25] Erich Fromm, *Man for Himself* (New York, Holt, Rinehart and Winston, 1947), pp. 120–135.

[26] Foote, *op. cit.,* p. 247.

7. Orgastic experience and sex in general are both very important and yet the absence of sexuality is tolerated. Sex is something to be enjoyed, something to build on, and is important like water or food. At the same time it does not play a central role in the philosophy of life.

8. Sex is accepted as a fact of life which, going along with a more intense, profound, and satisfying love relationship, makes it less necessary for compensation or neurotic sex affairs to be sought outside marriage. The easier acceptance of the facts of sexuality seems to make it easier rather than harder to be relatively monogamous.

9. When love is felt for the partner there is the effect that one feels the other's needs as if they were his own and feels his own needs to some extent as if they belonged to the other. To some extent the unit has become for psychological purposes a single person, a single ego. The loving spouse gets as much pleasure from his partner's achievements as from his own. In case of illness it is an illness of the couple rather than of the individual.

10. There is a basic acceptance of the partner's individuality. He is acknowledged as an independent entity and as a separate and autonomous individual. The partner is allowed a fundamental, irreducible dignity, and he will not unnecessarily humiliate the partner.

11. Ideally love is regarded as an end in itself, and often approached in wonder, admiration, and awe. The persons involved are attracted into it rather than driven into it by neurotic, aim-inhibited motives. The love-deprived person falls in love because he needs and craves love, which he lacks. The healthy person needs to make up no deficiency, and is free to express love and receive it.

12. In healthy individuals love is not blind. Even when in love partners are essentially perceived for what they are. The partner may have faults or shortcomings, but these are either not regarded as shortcomings or are accepted.[27]

Technical problems cannot be overlooked by the serious student at this point. Many research oriented scholars and others will remain somewhat skeptical as to the validity of these generalizations, until more of their bases can be demonstrated. How many people presently exhibit these characteristics in total? Would they hold for people at all levels of society? Are they ideal regardless of region, race, or religion? Many will desire more definite findings before they will be satisfied. Nevertheless Maslow and others are to be encouraged in their attempts to study this phenomenon of love between the sexes, no matter how difficult the study may be. To Montagu, the anthropologist, "love is the form of behavior having the highest survival value." [28] Now that Foote, Goode, Maslow, Harlow, Winch, and others are making the study of love scientifically respectable we may hope for some important breakthroughs in the future.

[27] Adapted from sections of A. H. Maslow, *Motivation and Personality* (New York, Harper & Row, 1954), Chapter 13.
[28] M. F. Ashley Montagu, *The Direction of Human Development* (New York, Harper & Row, 1955), Chapter 9.

Another type of problem is raised for the average couple. There is sometimes the tendency to feel that such descriptions of love as we have from Maslow and others are so far above them as to be discouraging. From a pedagogical point of view this is an important point. If expectations cannot realistically be met they in themselves can be very frustrating. However, ideal models will always exist around one in various forms. The Hollywood ideal of marriage, for example, can hardly be escaped, given our media of communication. Other models of love of a more realistic nature might well be considered as ideals toward which to strive, even though it be fully understood that not everyone will approach such ideals.

SELECTED READINGS

Bailey, Derrick, *The Mystery of Love and Marriage* (New York, Harper & Row, 1952).

Bertocci, Peter, *The Human Venture in Sex, Love and Marriage* (New York, Association Press, 1951).

Beigel, Hugo, "Romantic Love," *American Sociological Review,* Vol. 16 (June, 1951), pp. 326–334.

Blanton, Smiley, *Love or Perish* (New York, Simon and Schuster, 1955).

Blood, Robert, *Marriage* (New York, Free Press, 1962), Chapter 4.

Burgess, Ernest, Locke, Harvey, and Thomes, Mary, *The Family: From Institution to Companionship,* 3rd ed. (New York, American Book, 1963), Chapter 12.

Bowman, Henry, "The Diagnosis of Love," in Fishbein, Morris and Kennedy, Ruby Jo (Eds.), *Modern Marriage and Family Living* (Fairlawn, N.J., Oxford University Press, 1957), Chapter 9.

Cavan, Ruth, *Marriage and Family in the Modern World* (New York, Crowell, 1960), Chapter 8.

Foote, Nelson, "Love," *Psychiatry, Journal for the Study of Interpersonal Processes,* Vol. 16 (August, 1953), pp. 245–251.

Fromm, Erich, *The Art of Loving* (New York, Harper & Row, 1956).

Flügel, J. C., *The Psycho-analytic Study of the Family* (London, Hogarth, 1939), Chapter 11.

Goode, William, "The Theoretical Importance of Love," *American Sociological Review,* Vol. 24 (February, 1959), pp. 38–47.

Harlow, Harry, "The Nature of Love," *American Psychologist,* Vol. 13 (December, 1958), pp. 673–685.

Hobart, Charles, "The Incidence of Romanticism During Courtship," *Social Forces,* Vol. 36 (May, 1958), pp. 362–367.

Kirkpatrick, Clifford, *The Family* (New York, Ronald, 1955), Chapter 12.

Knight, Thomas, "In Defense of Romance," *Marriage and Family Living,* Vol. 21 (May, 1959).

Martinson, Floyd, *Marriage and the American Ideal* (New York, Dodd, Mead, 1960), Chapters 7 and 8.

Maslow, A. H., *Motivation and Personality* (New York, Harper & Row, 1954), Chapter 13.

Montagu, M. F. Ashley, *The Meaning of Love* (New York, The Julian Press, 1953).

Reik, Theodore, *A Psychologist Looks at Love* (New York, Holt, Rinehart and Winston, 1944).

de Rougemont, Denis, *Love in the Western World* (New York, Pantheon, 1956).

Wallace, Karl, *Love Is More Than Luck* (New York, Funk, 1957).

Winch, Robert, *The Modern Family* (New York, Holt, Rinehart and Winston, 1963), Chapter 14.

Winch, Robert, *Mate Selection* (New York, Harper & Row, 1958), Chapter 3.

Waller, Willard, and Hill Reuben, *The Family* (New York, Holt, Rinehart and Winston, 1951), Chapter 7.

QUESTIONS AND EXERCISES

1. Do you believe that "love at first sight" is possible? Why or why not?
2. Some authorities distinguish between "real" and "spurious" love. Do you agree that it is legitimate to make this attempt? If not, why not? If so, on what basis do you make the delineation?
3. A number of Hollywood couples, once reported to be deeply in love, have found themselves engaged in divorce litigation. Does this mean they were not once in love? Discuss.
4. A number of writers, for example Martinson, and Reik, imply that the immature or poorly adjusted person is more inclined to "fall" in love than the average person. Indicate your stand on this matter.
5. Do you believe that love and sex can be delineated as motives? For both men and women? Discuss.
6. Compose a definition of love which you would find satisfactory.
7. Analyze the love relationship portrayed in a novel of your own choosing.
8. Do a case study focusing on an acquaintance who has recently fallen in love. Analyze the person's change in behavior, emotions, etc.
9. Beigel, de Rougemont, and others disagree strongly on the function of romantic love in our society. Write a paper in which you trace the origin of romantic love and indicate its relationship to premarriage and marriage from your point of view.
10. How can a person be sure that the love relationship between himself and a partner is strong enough for a sound marriage?
11. Write a critique of Maslow's concept of a healthy type of love between the sexes based on a reading of chapters 12 and 13 in the reference cited.
12. Do you believe that it is healthy for a young person to have a number of light love affairs or infatuations before settling down to a more mature type of love? If so, what would be an undue number? Discuss.

8

Serious Mate Selection

WHO MARRIES WHOM?

What social processes appear to determine "who marries whom"? Just how does John happen to choose Mary? These questions involve both general and specific factors upon which research has cast some light.

First of all it is basic to distinguish between processes or factors over which individuals have little if any conscious control, and those over which they can exercise some control. Studies seem to show clearly that some sorts of social processes operate to limit the range of selection to a fairly small and predictable category of eligible prospects. In Figure 4 we have an attempt to illustrate diagrammatically the screening process that seems typical of the U.S. in regard to mate selection.

The factor exercising the greatest influence seems to be race.[1] Some 19 states have laws prohibiting racial intermarriage. Even though northern states are without such prohibitions, few people cross racial lines in choosing spouses. The next selective factor exercising considerable influence in limiting mate selection is religion. Traditionally religious groups have put great pressure on their members to "marry within the faith." In the United States this has operated especially in regard to Protestants, Catholics, and Jews. One study found that 94.1 percent of the Jews, 93.8 percent of the Catholics and 74.0 percent of the Protestants married within their own religious group.[2] While this rate of ingroup marriage is probably above the average for the United States as a whole the process involved is probably typical.

---

[1] August Hollingshead, "Cultural Factors in the Selection of Marriage Mates," *American Sociological Review,* Vol. 15 (October, 1950), p. 627.
[2] *Ibid.*

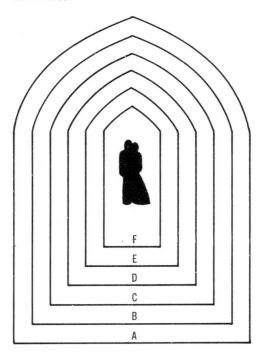

FIGURE 4. *Screening Factors in Mate Selection.* NOTE: *A*. Race, *B*. Class, *C*. Religion, *D*. Ethnic origin, *E*. Ecological area, *F*. Personality. SOURCE: Adapted from August Hollingshed, "Cultural Factors in the Selection of Marriage Mates," *American Sociological Review,* Vol. 15 (October, 1950), p. 627.

Ethnic background is another important factor in restricting mate selection. America has been known as a land of multiple ethnic or nationality groups. Especially where these groups have lived in subcommunities there has been a tendency toward marriage within the group (endogamy). Quite often the two factors of religion and ethnic group have been associated, e.g., Irish Catholic. The combination of the two factors has been a powerful influence affecting marriage patterns. The steady tendency toward assimilation of ethnic minorities has resulted in a lessening of pressures toward ethnic endogamy.

Social class position is another factor associated with mate selection. There is a pronounced tendency for people to marry within their own social class. Men, however, are more inclined than women to choose mates from social ranks beneath themselves. Practically the same statements can be made regarding educational level, which is not surprising since these two factors seem to be associated.

Another factor found to be associated with restrictions on "free" choice of marital partner is residence. In spite of the geographic and social mobility prevalent in modern society an amazing proportion of people select mates from their own neighborhood or residential area.[3]

The exact way in which the above and other factors operate in the mate selection process is not completely clear. It is perhaps best to think of social processes which involve a "sifting" of people into subcategories of "eligibles" as far as mate selection is concerned. These sociocultural factors seem to operate together to create for a particular individual a category of eligible prospective spouses. The individual tends to choose, normally within his own age group, from the available, eligible persons. As Hollingshead puts it, . . . "one's subculture, and one's race, age, and class position in the society effectively determine the kind of person one will marry, but not the individual." [4]

HOMOGAMY VS. HETEROGAMY

It seems clear then that in mate selection the choices are not fully random and uncontrolled. The old questions are raised anew: "do opposites attract," or "do like marry like?"

One study of engaged couples shows quite clearly the tendency for couples to be very similar in social characteristics, at least at the middle-class level.[5] In Table 9 is shown the degree to which, in a sample of 1000 couples, resemblances predominate over differences.

TABLE 9

Similarity of Members of Engaged Couples on Social Characteristics

	Ratio to Actual Expected Similarity
Religious Affiliation and Behavior [a]	
Religious affiliation (Catholic, Protestant, Jewish, none)	2.14
Church attendance	1.69
Church membership	1.43
Sunday-school attendance (stopped before age of 11, at 11–18, at 19 or over)	1.42

[3] See Alvin Katz and Reuben Hill, "Residential Propinquity and Marital Selection: A Review of Method Theory and Fact," *Marriage and Family Living,* Vol. 20 (February, 1958), pp. 34–35.

[4] Hollingshead, *op. cit.,* p. 627.

[5] Ernest Burgess and Paul Wallin, *Engagement and Marriage* (Philadelphia, Lippincott, 1953), pp. 205–207.

TABLE 9 (*cont.*)

Similarity of Members of Engaged Couples on Social Characteristics

	Ratio to Actual Expected Similarity
Family Backgrounds	
Place lived in childhood (large city, small city, suburb, town)	1.49
Nativity of parents (native-born, one foreign born, both foreign born)	1.48
Education (graduate and professional, college, high school or less)	1.37
Present income of parents (under $2000, $2000–$4999, $5000 plus)	1.34
Courtship Behavior	
Age began keeping company	1.55
Persons gone steady with besides fiance(e)	1.27
Discussed engagement (with no one, one, two, three or more persons)	1.25
Previously engaged	1.10
Conceptions of Marriage	
Should fiancee work after marriage (no: yes, if necessary: yes desirable)	1.64
Number of children desired (three or more, one or two, none)	1.42
Attitude toward having children (very much desire, mildly desire, object)	1.31
When spouse ceases to be in love (divorce, separate, continue together)	1.28
Social Participation	
Drinking habits (never, rarely, occasionally, or often)	1.81
Smoking habits (does not smoke, will stop if other objects, will not stop)	1.38
Prefer play or dance (play, dance, don't know)	1.31
Leisure time preferences (stay at home, on go most of time, on go all the time)	1.29
Family Relationships	
Attitude toward father at present (hostile, mildly attached, considerable and strong attachment)	1.11
Attitude toward sibling (none, no attachment, attachment to one or more)	1.15
Rating of parents' marriage (very happy, happy, average, unhappy)	1.14
Attitude toward father as a child (hostile, mildly attached, considerable and strong attachment)	1.14

[a] In all cases the four items in each category with the highest ratios are included.

SOURCE: Adapted from Burgess and Wallin, *Engagement and Marriage,* published by J. B. Lippincott Company, Philadelphia, Penna., copyright 1953.

It is important to note the method of calculating resemblances and differences. A ratio of actual to expected similarity is developed. The authors give a concrete illustration which will be helpful in explaining their procedures.

Usually Catholics marry Catholics, Jews with Jews and Protestants with Protestants. But there are also many unions of those with mixed faiths. It is therefore, interesting to figure the ratio of the actual marrying of "like with like" faith to that which would occur by pure chance. If the 1000 men and the 1000 women in the Burgess-Wallin study had been mated by chance 37.1 percent would be of the same religious affiliation. Instead of this theoretical expectation, actually those with the same religious affiliation (both Catholic, Jewish, Protestant, and none) are 79.4 percent of the couples. The ratio then, of the actual to the similarity expected by chance is then 79.4 percent divided by 37.1 percent, or 2.14. By obtaining this ratio it can be definitely stated that engaged couples of this particular study resemble each other in religious affiliation more than twice as often as the theoretical outcome calculated on the basis of mating by pure chance.[6]

Attention to Table 9 brings out the strong tendency toward homogamy (like marry like) in social characteristics. The greatest similarity was found in religious patterns and the next in family background. The least amount of similarity was found in family relationships and social participation. However, on these latter items there was similarity between the members at well above the level of pure chance. Certainly on the basis of this and other published studies the principle of homogamy or assortative mating operates to narrow the range from which a mate will be chosen.

The Personality Level

What about homogamy in personality characteristics? Burgess and Wallin studied some 42 personality traits of engaged couples. Of these 14 showed a greater than chance tendency toward homogamy. Compared to social characteristics there is only a slight tendency toward similarity.[7] There was a tendency for neurotics to be engaged to neurotics and non-neurotics to non-neurotics. The area of personality characteristics is subtle, however, and before broad assertions can be made there is need for further sophisticated research.

Winch has recently made a strong case for the theory of heterogamy in regard to personality factors or, more specifically, to personality needs.[8] According to Winch, sociocultural factors operate to narrow the range of eligible spouses down to a small "field." Within this narrow field the typical American middle-class individual dates, courts, and eventually narrows the choice to one person whom he marries. But how?

[6] *Ibid.*
[7] *Ibid.*
[8] Robert Winch, *Mate Selection* (New York, Harper & Row), 1958.

The actual choice of a specific mate is motivated by personality needs. These needs may be either conscious or subconscious, although they are primarily of the latter variety. On the basis of his research Winch believes that there is a tendency for an individual to choose a partner whose need patterns are opposite to his own. This theory has become known as the "complementary needs" theory of mate selection.

Again it is to be noted that the sociocultural and personality factors discussed above involve processes which operate to a large degree outside the individual's conscious control. One ordinarily does not choose his ethnic origin, parental residence, social class position of parents, and so forth. Yet from within the pool of social eligibles, individuals have great freedom of mate selection in American society. What then does the individual do to choose a spouse who will be compatible with his own needs?

Winch hypothesizes that "in mate selection each individual seeks within his or her field of eligibles for that person who gives the greatest promise of providing him or her with maximum need gratification." [9] He postulates a series of specific needs based on Murray's approach. These needs and general traits are listed and defined in Table 10.

Winch hypothesizes that the specific need pattern of each partner "will be complementary rather than similar to the need pattern of the other spouse."

Let us assume that there is a chap by the name of Jonathan, and that Jonathan's most distinguishing characteristic is a need to be dominant in interpersonal relationships. We shall assume further that among his acquaintances are two girls, Jean and Jennifer. Jennifer is like Jonathan in being dominant and in being intolerant of differences in viewpoint, whereas Jean does not have strong convictions and is used to being governed by the judgments and wishes of others. If we are informed that Jonathan is about to marry one of these women and if on the basis of the information cited above we are asked to guess which one, probably we should agree that Jean would be the more likely choice for Jonathan to make. This is the sort of thing I have in mind in hypothesizing that if A and B decide to marry each other, their need patterns will be complementary rather than similar. I mean that there will be a tendency for each to see the complementary features of the other as characteristics of more or less endearment. Thus Jonathan should see Jean as a "truly feminine, tractable, agreeable young lady who knows when and how to help a man," whereas to Jean Jonathan might well appear as a "vigorous and decisive tower of strength." I should expect further that Jonathan would be repelled by Jennifer and would see her as bossy, unfeminine, and probably shrewish.

It should not be assumed that all features of the complementariness necessarily register in the consciousness of each spouse. The degree to which these features are conscious is still an open question. It seems reasonable to assume

[9] *Ibid.*, p. 89.

TABLE 10

The Twelve Needs and Three General Traits

Need	Definition
Abasement	To accept or invite blame, criticism, or punishment. To blame or harm the self.
Achievement	To work diligently to create something and/or to emulate others.
Approach	To draw near and enjoy interaction with another person or persons.
Autonomy	To get rid of the constraint of other persons. To avoid or escape from domination. To be unattached and independent.
Deference	To admire and praise a person.
Dominance	To influence and control the behavior of others.
Hostility	To fight, injure, or kill others.
Nurturance	To give sympathy and aid to a weak helpless, ill, or dejected person or animal.
Recognition	To excite the admiration and approval of others.
Status Aspiration	To desire a socioeconomic status considerably higher than one has (A special case of achievement).
Status Striving	To work diligently to alter one's socioeconomic status. (A special case of achievement).
Succorance	To be helped by a sympathetic person. To be nursed, loved, protected, indulged.
General Trait	
Anxiety	Fear, conscious or unconscious, of harm or misfortune arising from the hostility of others and/or social reaction to one's own behavior.
Emotionality	The show of affection in behavior.
Vicariousness	The gratification of a need derived from the perception that another person is deriving gratification.

SOURCE: Adapted from Robert Winch, *Mate Selection* (New York, Harper & Row, 1958), p. 90. By permission of the author.

that where complementary features are not consciously seen by the persons involved there is some good reason, and that the principles are more comfortable if they do not have to face the recognition of such an arrangement. For example, let us assume that Jennifer, the bossy woman we conjured up above, marries a passive, compliant chap—say Herbert (previously presented). Because the pattern of dominance, although complementary, would run counter to the conventional conceptions of sex roles (she being a "masculine" woman and he a "feminine" man), it seems likely that neither party would wish to admit to himself or to anyone else that this pattern of dominance was a bond between them.[10]

[10] *Ibid.*, pp. 97–98.

The complementary needs theory of mate selection has been investigated by a number of researchers. Those who have used formal statistical approaches, such as Bowerman and Day, as against the case and clinical data of the Winch group, have in general not sustained the theory. Recently Kerckhoff and Davis have reviewed the literature bearing on the problem and also reported on their research.[11] They provide a mild confirmation of the theory. These authors suggest that "a series of 'filtering factors' operate in mate selection at different stages of the mate selection process." They agree that social status factors are involved early in the process and that the complementary need factor comes late. In between is the factor of value consensus. Kerckhoff and Davis believe that having common social background is not enough to produce a high degree of consensus on values. This comes, if at all, through interaction over a period of time.

It is suggested that during the initial stages of mate selection there is so much idealization involved that the "true" personality makeup of the partner cannot be assessed. When couples remain together over a period of time, they come to know each other more realistically. At this point complementariness begins to operate. In effect Kerckhoff is suggesting, then, that at the level of social factors and values people are drawn together by similarity.[12] Within this closed circle personality factors begin to operate, there being some evidence that opposites complement each other at this point.

There is also the question of the salience of needs to the personality. Surely not all needs are of equal importance. Presumably the most important needs of the person should be satisfied or complemented by the partner in order to have a satisfactory relationship.

MAKING A RATIONAL CHOICE

Rationality is a complex of many assessments and judgments. First of all, one might attempt to analyze his own conception of an ideal mate. As has often been stressed, the individual seems to develop subconsciously an ideal-mate conception rather early in life. Strongly affected by parental images and standards, the conception probably changes only slightly when the person leaves his parental environment. These images are difficult to objectify because they are subtle and largely unconscious; and even where they are conscious, the person may be unwilling or unable to describe them. Questionnaire studies are, therefore, not necessarily to be regarded as re-

[11] Alan Kerckhoff and Keith Davis, "Value Consensus and Need Complementarity in Mate Selection," *American Sociological Review*, Vol. 27 (June, 1962), pp. 295–303. See also Jerold Heiss and Michael Gordon, "Need Patterns and Mutual Satisfaction of Dating and Engaged Couples," *Journal of Marriage and the Family*, Vol. 26 (August, 1964), pp. 337–341.

[12] Kerckhoff and Davis, *op. cit.*

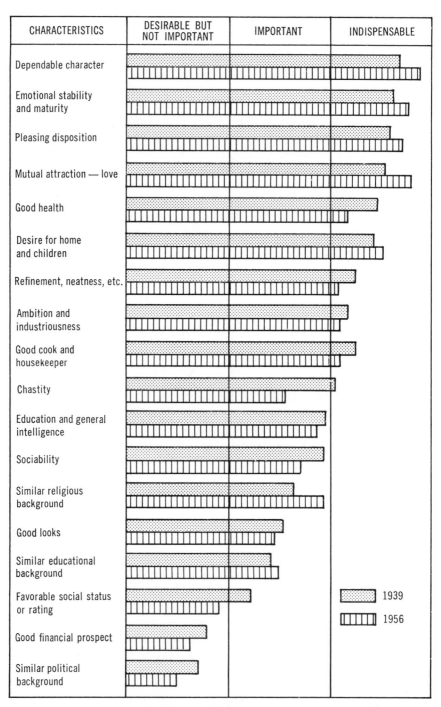

FIGURE 5. *Average Evaluation by Male College Students of Eighteen Factors in Mate Selection: Two Studies.* SOURCE: 1939 Data adapted from Reuben Hill, "Campus Values in Mate Selection," *Journal of Home Economics,* Vol. 37 (November, 1945), pp. 554–557; 1956 Data adapted from Robert McGinnis, "Campus Values in Mate Selection: A Repeat Study," *Social Forces,* Vol. 36 (May, 1958), pp. 368–373.

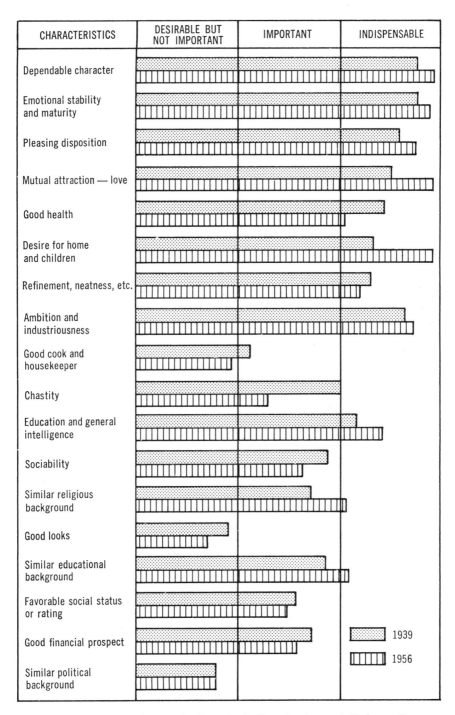

FIGURE 6. *Average Evaluation by Female College Students of Eighteen Factors in Mate Selection: Two Studies.* NOTE: The original study involved 600 students at the University of Wisconsin. The second study, using the same questionnaire, was done seventeen years later; it involved 120 students at the same university. SOURCE: Reuben Hill, *op. cit.* and Robert McGinnis, *op. cit.*

liable. One such study done by Christensen and Hill at Wisconsin revealed an interesting evaluation of the importance of eighteen factors in choosing a mate. The following were rated by both men and women as the six most important factors: (1) dependable character, (2) emotional stability and maturity, (3) pleasing disposition, (4) mutual attraction, (5) good health, and (6) desire for home life and children.

McGinnis has recently completed a replication study in the same campus setting.[13] The results found were very similar to those of the original study. The differences found were interpreted as indicating a companionship as against an institutional orientation toward the family.

The reader may wish to compare his own attitudes with these indicated here. He may decide for himself which items he would stress. Since we are talking about serious interests which will presumably lead to permanent marriage, certain surface items may not be as important as they would be in dating considerations.

THE QUESTION OF "MIXED MARRIAGES"

What should be done if major class, religious, or racial differences appear in the background of a marriage oriented couple? It must be conceded that by American ideals decisions should be made by the individuals themselves as their democratic right and privilege. Some of the possible effects on a relationship, however, may be worth consideration.

Social class differences often pose a problem. A social class position involves a "way of life." General habit patterns, values, attitudes, language, and especially subconscious personal characteristics are the consequence of class affiliation. Differences in class background may, then, result in vexing, often unidentifiable tensions and conflicts. Roth and Peck have analyzed the relationship between social class and marital adjustment for the original Burgess and Cottrell sample. They have found that intraclass marriage had a significantly higher average adjustment than interclass marriages.[14] Many students of marriage think that class or cultural differences tend, other things being equal, to set the stage for marital conflict and tension.

It should be noted that we are not advising people necessarily to follow the conventional social norms, whether the reference is to marriage or to some other area of life. The democratic ethic, supposedly basic in our culture, suggests that individuals be respected as persons in their own right. This can be taken to mean that in mate selection individuals should search

[13] Robert McGinnis, "Campus Values in Mate Selection: "A Repeat Study," *Social Forces,* Vol. 36 (May, 1958) pp. 368–373.

[14] Julius Roth and Robert Peck, "Social Class and Mobility Factors Related to Marital Adjustment," *American Sociological Review,* Vol. 16 (August, 1951), pp. 474–487.

for compatible partners regardless of class and other background factors. Certain religious norms would seem to demand the same type of approach, namely that more attention be paid to the character and personality of the individual involved than to his class level as such.

Further, as we pointed out previously, the type of marital adjustment referred to here is *conventional*. Individuals who wish to cross major class or cultural lines will have to be especially adaptable and creative to develop successful marriage. Perhaps these marriages will of necessity be unconventional,[15] and conventional criteria for their evaluation may not be relevant.

Interracial Marriage

Marriage across racial lines in America is a very uncommon phenomenon.[16] In separate studies both Hollingshead,[17] and Wirth and Goldhamer [18] report the proportion of Negro-white marriages among all marriages involving whites to be less than one percent. Jacobson estimates that the number of Negro-white marriages in a given year in the whole United States is in the neighborhood of 2,000.[19]

These figures reflect practices that are deep-seated in the American mores. As previously stated some states forbid interracial marriage. It is not encouraged in the states which do not specifically outlaw such marriages. In most American communities dating and social relationships are such that most individuals do not meet members of racial groups other than their own under circumstances which would lead to serious mate selection. If the latter takes place, group pressure to discourage involvement is usually forthcoming. The couple which persists is usually forced to associate with interracial groups, and in many cases the courtship is kept secret from friends and relatives. Golden in his study of Negro-white intermarriage in Philadelphia reports that such marriages are usually "irregular." [20] Few have the ceremony typical of their class level, such as formal church ritual and receptions to which friends and relatives are invited. Elopements are fairly common.

Once married, the couple is inclined to identify with the Negro com-

[15] In the novel *Kitty Foyle* Christopher Morley has described some of the difficulties of adjustment which developed when a girl from a modest family married into an old "main line" Philadelphia family.

[16] Robert Bell, *Marriage and Family Interaction* (Homewood, Ill., The Dorsey Press, 1963), pp. 140–141.

[17] Hollingshead, *op. cit.*

[18] Louis Wirth and Herbert Goldhamer, "The Hybrid and the Problem of Miscegenation," in Otto Klineberg (Ed.), *Characteristics of the American Negro* (New York, Harper & Row, 1944), p. 277.

[19] Paul Jacobson, *American Marriage and Divorce* (New York, J. B. Rinehart and Company, 1959), p. 62.

[20] Joseph Golden, "Patterns of Negro-white Intermarriage," *American Sociological Review,* Vol. 19 (April, 1954), p. 144.

munity, although not on a basis that can be considered intimate in most cases. Rather typical is the tendency to associate with other couples whose marriages are of the same type.[21]

Let it be clear that our reference is to present-day America. In a milieu such as that of Hawaii interracial marriage has been accepted for a number of generations. As Adams indicates, all levels of marital adjustment can be found among couples who have crossed racial lines.[22] It must be pointed out that a number of important factors have laid the general groundwork for a tolerant and permissive attitude on the part of many island people toward interracial marriages.[23] Those who wish to promote successful marriages across racial lines on a large scale in a country such as America should not underestimate the magnitude of their task.[24] Marriage involves factors involving both the couple and the society in which the couple will live. Couples willing to risk social disapproval will need to have the resources available to develop a successful relationship without some of the social support which is ordinarily provided from the outside community.

The chance of dating or marrying across religious lines is becoming much greater than it would have been in previous generations. In the early days of our country endogamy was encouraged if not required by the major religious groups and by the sectarians. A general policy of religious toleration, combined with great freedom of mate choice, and along with other factors, has broken down many of the taboos against "mixed marriage." Student attitudes are noticeably liberal, especially in regard to dating. Prince, in a study of the attitudes of 1252 students at the University of Idaho, found very little opposition on the part of students to dating across religious lines and little to going steady with persons outside their faith. The Catholic students were more willing than Protestants to go steady with persons not of

[21] Strauss reports that in American soldier-Japanese marriages in Chicago most couples associated socially with couples similar to themselves. Anselm Strauss, "Strain and Harmony in American-Japanese War Bride Marriages," *Marriage and Family Living* (May, 1954), pp. 99–106. Roberts in his study found this to be true. See Robert Roberts, "Negro-white Intermarriage: A Study in Social Control," unpublished M.A. thesis, University of Chicago Library, 1940. On the other hand, Pavela, in a study of ninety-five Negro-white couples, did not find them associating more closely with other interracial couples than with other community members. See Todd Pavela, "An Exploratory Study of Negro-white Intermarriage in Indiana," *Journal of Marriage and the Family*, Vol. 26 (May, 1964), pp. 209–211.

[22] Romanzo Adams, *Interracial Marriage in Hawaii* (New York, Macmillan, 1937), pp. 224–225.

[23] See Brewton Berry, *Race and Ethnic Relations* (Boston, Houghton Mifflin, 1965), pp. 138–142. For a survey of the factors apparently responsible for the tolerant atmosphere prevailing in Hawaii regarding interracial marriage.

[24] On the other hand Dyer and Luckey found that interfaith marriages for University of Minnesota students whom they questioned in a follow-up study were as successful as were those where the partners belonged to the same religious group. Dorothy Dyer, and Eleanor Luckey, "Religious Affiliation and Selected Personality Scores as They Relate to Marital Happiness of a Minnesota College Sample," unpublished paper, kindly supplied by authors. Further research is definitely called for in this area.

their faith at a ratio of 90 percent to 75 percent. However, many of them were assuming that in the event of marriage the partners would change to the Catholic faith or that at least any children born to them would be brought up as Catholics. See Table 11 for a summary of the student attitudes.

TABLE 11

Attitudes of College Students Toward Dating, Going Steady, and Marrying Outside Their Religious Faith, by Percentage

	Male N-777		Female N-475		Total N-1252	
	Yes	No	Yes	No	Yes	No
Would date outside religious faith	97	3	97	3	97	3
Would "go steady" outside religious faith	80	20	72	28	77	23
Would marry outside religious faith	62	37	52	48	59	41

Forty-one students in the sample indicated no religious affiliation. These were not included in the above N's. Forty of this group would date, go steady or marry from any of the religious groups or non affiliated group. One student indicated he would date and go steady with a person of any religious group but would marry only a person with no religious affiliation.

SOURCE: Alfred Prince, "Attitudes of College Students Toward Inter-Faith Marriage," *The Coordinator* (September, 1956), p. 12. By permission E. C. Brown Trust Foundation, Portland, Oregon.

It seems clear that many students who report that they would marry across major religious lines would not expect to change their faith. In fact Landis found that of students who reported they would marry outside their faith, 37 percent of the Protestants and only 11 percent of the Catholics would willingly change faith.[25]

The relaxing of opposition to interfaith marriages does not mean that in consequence such marriages present no difficulties of marital interaction. Many researchers have reported findings to the contrary indicating that interfaith couples, other things being equal, differ significantly in adjustment from couples where such is not the case. A recently reported study by Peterson involved some 440 persons chosen at random in Los Angeles. Adjustment scores for married couples who were interfaith were compared with those couples where both were Catholic, Protestant, or nonchurch affiliated respectively. The results are summarized in Table 12. It will be noted that couples whose marriages were interfaith had the lowest average adjustment score of any category of couples studied.

[25] Judson Landis, *Building a Successful Marriage* (Englewood Cliffs, N.J., Prentice-Hall, 1953), p. 157.

TABLE 12

Interfaith Marriages Compared as to Adjustment Score with Catholic, Protestant and Non-Religious Marriages by Percentage

Adjustment Score	Catholic-Protestant	Catholic	Protestant	Non-Church
Low adjustment	50	39	20	29
High adjustment	50	61	80	71

SOURCE: James A. Peterson, "The Impact of Objective and Subjective Religious Factors on Adjustment in Marriage," unpublished Ph.D. dissertation, as quoted in James Peterson, *Education for Marriage* (New York, Scribner, 1964), p. 223.

Some of the major areas of difficulty have appeared consistently in the studies. Education and training (including religious training of children) were found to be the greatest problem by Landis. The Roman Catholic Church insists that children be brought up in the Catholic faith when one partner is a member of that faith. In spite of this there is a general expectation that the mother will take responsibility for the religious training of children. One would almost predict on the basis of theory that marriages of Protestant women to Catholic men would be especially vulnerable to divorce. This was found to be true by Landis. The reasoning is essentially that the Protestant or nonaffiliated man will tend to abide by the agreement and allow the wife to proceed with religious instruction of the children without too much complaint. The Protestant mother, on the other hand, must supervise training of children in an alien faith. She will usually default and attempt to bring up her children in terms of her own belief. This is too much for the Catholic father who struggles to gain control.

TABLE 13

Percentage of Marriages Broken by Divorce or Separation, by Religion, Found in Three Given Studies

Religion	Percentage of Broken Marriages		
	Weeks (Washington)	Bell (Maryland)	Landis (Michigan)
Both Catholic	3.8	6.4	4.4
Both Jewish ⎫		4.6	5.2
Both Protestant ⎭	10.1	6.8	6.0
Mixed Catholic-Protestant*	17.4	15.2	14.1
Both no religion	23.9	16.7	17.9

* Mixed marriages of any type

SOURCE: Adapted from Thomas P. Monahan and William Kephart, "Divorce and Desertion by Religious and Mixed Religious Groups," *American Journal of Sociology*, Vol. 59 (March, 1954), p. 457.

As we attempted to demonstrate previously, class position involves a "way of life." So it is with religion. In addition to creeds and rituals, religion encompasses values, attitudes, and other factors. It is not just a matter of where one shows up on the Sabbath morning. One church encourages games of chance, another opposes gambling in any form. One church allows dancing in the church recreation rooms which to another would be unthinkable. In ways too numerous to mention here religion affects the attitudes and behavior of individuals in matters not strictly religious.

Those who take their religion seriously need to explore the situation carefully when they consider interfaith marriage. They should, if possible, project themselves into the future, including the time when they will have children.

We do not wish to imply that people from similar social and cultural backgrounds will have exactly the same standards, ideals, and habits. Kerckhoff and Davis have demonstrated that social similarity does not always produce value consensus.[26] Since individual variation is possible and even probable, it becomes imperative that couples explore their mutual sets of values, standards, and practices to check on compatability and consensus.

TESTING PERSONALITY COMPATIBILITY

So far our discussion has centered on factors that are essentially social. While compatibility in these areas is not simple to test, it is more easily tested than compatibility in more narrowly personal form.

If Winch's theory of complementary needs has any foundation at all, consideration as to how the personalities of the individuals mesh should be taken into account. There are many problems involved here. Kubie suggests that the major problem is the depth of needs or of personality drives.[27] As a psychiatrist he takes the view that, because of faulty rearing and early traumatic experience, most adults have strong neurotic drives which are below the level of consciousness. These drives are so powerful that they override all rational considerations and they operate to keep people from assessing what they want in the way of marriage or of a marriage partner. They further operate in marriage to prevent partners from attaining successful adjustment. Kubie believes that the emphasis on romanticism in America furthers the distortion by rationalizing and beautifying "a neurotic state of obsessional infatuation."

Kubie's suggestions as to how the situation might be remedied are summarized as follows:

[26] Kerckhoff and Davis, *op. cit.*
[27] Lawrence Kubie, "Psychoanalysis and Marriage: Practical and Theoretical Issues," in Victor Eisenstein (Ed.), *Neurotic Interaction in Marriage* (New York, Basic Books, 1956), Chapter II.

We may best approach this problem through:

1. A modification of the romantic tradition, so that we cease to look upon this obsessional state as the highest artistic, aesthetic and spiritual experience in life.
2. A fundamental change in the process of education, so that individuals grow up without the cleavage that occurs at present between the conscious and unconscious aspects of personality.
3. The development of techniques by which such cleavages can be rapidly knit together as they occur in childhood, so as to re-establish the integrity and unity of the personality, as a whole, especially as the young person approaches marriage.[28]

This position is extreme. Many will question the suggestion that so-called normal individuals have marked neurotic drives or deep splits between the conscious and the unconscious. However, Kubie's warning can well be heeded. Those who expect to make use of rational processes in mate selection may be forced to consider romantic illusions and/or strong, deep-seated neurotic drives. As a help in this direction the services of a counselor or therapist may well be necessary. Especially important is the determination of the most basic needs which might be satisfied in marriage by a particular partner. At this point of course, the major question involves the pair. Do we complement each other? It is possible that the need pattern on which the pair relationship is grounded may be basically unsound. For those who can follow him, the writings of Ackerman may be helpful in this regard.[29] Any substantial change in personality patterns will probably require psychiatric help, however. While matrimony may bring out the best (as well as the worst) in people, the marriage bed is not the equivalent of the psychiatric couch.

The possibility that testing and counseling psychologists would be of some help may be considered. Work being done by Harrower and others with such tests as the Verbal Wechsler-Bellevue Intelligence gives some indications that certain types of patterns will blend together better than others.[30] However, until more basic research is done with couples previous to marriage who are then followed into marriage, predictions made on tests of this sort will be rather hazardous, and most psychologists will probably prefer to use clinical judgments.

Presently for those couples who are within the normal ranges of personality, an empirical type of test still offers the greatest possibility of success. Couples must interact together to see how their personalities function. It is especially important that the pair work and play together in all types of legitimate situations. John may be quite the lad on the dance floor or

[28] *Ibid.*

[29] Nathan Ackerman, *The Psychodynamics of Family Life* (New York, Basic Books, 1958).

[30] Molly Harrower, "The Measurement of Psychological Factors in Marital Maladjustment," in Eisenstein, *op. cit.*

football field. What is he like in the classroom, on a hike, or at work? Married life is not going to be one endless round of parties, football games, and coke sessions. Young people with ingenuity will try to approximate as nearly as possible marriage and family situations as they know them to exist for friends and relatives. This takes time and patience. It also demands a degree of rational planning and a toning down of romantic drives and feelings.

Some good sense must be used here. A certain type of antidevelopmental bias can easily creep into our thinking, whereby we hope to make an adjustment which will last for all time. John and Mary at thirty-six are not the John and Mary of twenty-one. Mary may be the person who changes from a vivacious, happy, energetic young lady of twenty-one to the sour, frumpy woman of thirty-six. John will inevitably change—for better and/or worse. Life is not static. It is a process of development. Presumably, however, those couples who have a general agreement on values and objectives in life and a good personality relationship at the time they enter marriage have the best chance to develop together over the years.

THE DEVELOPING PAIR RELATIONSHIP

While each couple has its own pattern of development, there are certain patterns which seem typical among American courting couples. The following pages describe these patterns which may serve as probative models for couples interested in serious appraisal of the mating process.[31]

Involvement usually begins with some form of dating. The original intent may be casual or serious. Be that as it may, the couple continue to see each other and a relationship develops. At first coquetry may be quite prominent. This display invites further involvement, as it suggests adventure and interesting possibilities. If the participants are very young much teasing may take place. This teasing covers up tensions and doubts and stimulates the partner toward further interest.

As the relationship is maintained some doubts and anxieties enter the picture on both sides. The boy, wishing to further the relationship but to allow himself a path of departure, begins to feed the girl a "line." The line involves a pattern of soft words of a complimentary nature. They indicate that the partner is unique and interesting. The girl may respond by a slightly modified type of line of her own to keep the situation interesting.

The "line" has the function of covering up anxieties, tensions, and embarrassments. It enables the couple to inject an implication of seriousness into the relationship to distinguish it from casual dating. Unfortunately it

[31] This discussion bears heavily on Willard Waller and Reuben Hill, *op. cit.,* Chapter 10 and on lectures by Reuben Hill to his classes in the spring of 1957. It applies primarily in the college or university environment.

encourages further doubts, for each partner is suspicious of the other's line and wonders how much of it, if any, is sincere. Eventually the suspense and suspicion become so strong that something has to give. The typical outcome is a quarrel which tends to clear the air. In some cases the affair is broken off at this point. Where such is not the case the situation is clarified and the relationship becomes a more clearly defined and solid one.

After this clarification the partners become more serious with each other, if they have well-developed consciences. Often they engage in mutual confession and in attempts to belittle themselves in each other's presence. The boy suggests to the girl that he is really not worthy of her, that he really isn't very good, and that he has many shortcomings of personality and character. The girl responds by reassuring him, suggesting that comparatively speaking, he is good indeed. She also indicates some of her own faults. It can hardly be said that this is done in too serious a vein, or that the participants really are fully attempting to "tell all." This process serves to further unite the couple and to lead to deeper involvement.

As the process of involvement develops the pair becomes increasingly identified as a unit. This involves both the couple itself and outsiders. The couple develops an *esprit de corps* which includes others to a certain degree. The couple retreats psychologically into a rather socially unreal environment of their own making. Often they attach themselves to objects to which they give undue importance. These may be objects of apparel, rings, or even places which are spoken of as "ours" and have a meaning which others would not understand. In addition to specific objects which have a unique meaning to the couple, a special form of discourse develops between them. They have their own pet jokes and sayings. Particular phrases, gestures, and emphases come to have a special significance which would not be understood by outsiders.

Idealization is involved in the process for many couples. Through the intermittent process of moving toward and away from the partner it is easy to build up a rather unreal conception of the partner. Given a romantic setting and biological drives, the suitor wishes to possess his partner fully and completely. During periods of absence his thoughts dwell upon her. Illusions enter the picture, and in effect many times the suitor falls in love with (to him) the most favorable characteristics of the partner rather than the "real" person.

Emotions are not always positive toward the partner. Periods of moving toward the partner are broken intermittently by times when the person wearies of involvement and wishes for his freedom.[32] The lover wonders at times whether he really wishes to carry through with this process, and whether she is really the one for him. Doubts about the partner, about the desirability of marriage in the immediate future, and about the requirements of marriage flair up occasionally to plague the partners as they move along

[32] Francis Merrill, *Courtship and Marriage* (New York, Holt, Rinehart and Winston, 1949), p. 82.

toward deeper involvement. These doubts lead to quarrels and to a dropping out on the part of some.

Friends and outsiders aid and abet the process. Gossip has it that Joe and Mary are getting serious. Invitations are issued to them as a couple. Rival suitors look for more favorable prospects instead of "cutting in." The meaning of this action is not ignored by the couple. The young people come to feel a general community approval. No longer is the relationship a novel one with those attendant attractions. It is now moving inevitably toward the point where engagement will have to be considered.

EVALUATING THE INVOLVEMENT

Again it must be stressed that each couple has a unique relationship at least in certain areas. Couples who are rationally inclined will not have some of the problems which the extremes of idealization and undue sentimentality bring about. If insincere lines have not been extensively fed, the partners will have had fewer illusions and will be better prepared to assess the relationship on its merits.

Individuals should seriously evaluate their social compatibility, their emotional compatibility, and the positive and negative elements of the relationship in which they are involved. Are we developing a unity which is strong enough that we want to move into formal engagement leading ultimately to marriage? We have been through a testing period. Engagement, or the equivalent, should be the final testing period and also a planning period. Are we ready to move this far, this fast?

A note must be made regarding commitment. Choosing a marital partner involves an act of faith: faith in one's ability and that of his partner to make new adaptations as they move along together through life. The whole developmental task concept implies taking challenges in stride. Accomplishing one means that a better basis is laid to accomplish later tasks than would otherwise be the case. New tasks to be met are always "just over the horizon." The challenge of mate selection seems very clear: make the best choice of a mate that you possibly can, and make what you can of the potentials in the relationship after marriage.

SELECTED READINGS

Barron, Milton L., *People Who Intermarry* (Syracuse, N.Y., Syracuse University Press, 1946).

Becker, Howard, and Hill Reuben, *Family Marriage and Parenthood* (Boston, Heath, 1955), Chapter 8.

Bernard, Jessie, *Remarriage, A Study of Marriage* (New York, Holt, Rinehart and Winston, 1956).

Blood, Robert, *Marriage* (New York, Free Press, 1962), Chapter 3.

Bossard, James, and Boll, Eleanor, *One Marriage, Two Faiths* (New York, Ronald Press, 1957).

Bowerman, Charles, "Assortive Mating by Previous Marital Status: Seattle, 1939–1946," *American Sociological Review,* Vol. 18 (April, 1953), pp. 170–177.

Burchinal, Lee, and Chancellor, L. E., "Social Status, Religious Affiliation and Age at Marriage," *Marriage and Family Living,* Vol. 25 (May, 1963), pp. 219–221.

Burgess, Ernest and Wallin, Paul, *Engagement and Marriage* (Philadelphia, Lippincott, 1953), Chapter 6.

Burgess, Ernest, and Locke, Harvey, *The Family: From Institution to Companionship* (New York, American Book, 1945), Chapters 11 and 12.

Cavan, Ruth, *American Marriage* (New York, Crowell, 1959), Chapters 7 and 8.

Chancellor, Loren, and Monahan, Thomas, "Religious Preference and Inter-religious Mixtures in Marriages and Divorces in Iowa," *American Journal of Sociology,* Vol. 61 (November, 1955), pp. 233–239.

Clarke, Alfred, "An Examination of the Operation of Residential Propinquity as a Factor in Mate Selection," *American Sociological Review,* Vol. 17 (February, 1952), pp. 17–22.

Hewitt, Lester, "Student Perception of Traits Desired in Themselves as Dating and Marriage Partners," *Marriage and Family Living,* Vol. 20 (November, 1958), pp. 344–349.

Himes, Joel, "A Value Profile in Mate Selection Among Negroes," *Marriage and Family Living,* Vol. 16 (August, 1954), pp. 244–247.

Katz, Alvin, and Hill, Reuben, "Residential Propinquity and Marital Selection: A Review of Theory, Method, and Fact," *Marriage and Family Living,* Vol. 20 (February, 1958), pp. 27–35.

Kerckhoff, Alan, "Notes and Comments on the Meaning of Residential Propinquity as a Factor in Mate Selection," *Social Forces,* Vol. 34 (March, 1956), pp. 207–213.

Kirkpatrick, Clifford, *The Family* (New York, Ronald, 1955), pp. 382–389.

Kirkpatrick, Clifford, and Hobart, Charles, "Disagreement, Disagreement Estimate, and Non-empathic Imputations for Intimacy Groups Varying from Favorite Date to Married," *American Sociological Review,* Vol. 19 (February, 1954), pp. 10–19.

Koller, Marvin, "Residential and Occupational Propinquity," *American Sociological Review,* Vol. 13 (October, 1948), pp. 613–616.

Landis, Judson, and Landis, Mary, *Building a Successful Marriage* (Englewood Cliffs, N.J., Prentice-Hall, 1958), Chapter 12.

Pike, James, *If You Marry Outside Your Faith* (New York, Harper & Row, 1954).

Sirjamaki, John, *The American Family in the Twentieth Century* (Cambridge, Harvard, 1953), Chapter 4.

Strauss, Anselm, "Strain and Harmony in American-Japanese War Bride Marriages," *Marriage and Family Living,* Vol. 16 (May, 1954), pp. 99–106.

Sussman, Marvin, "Parental Participation in Mate Selection and Its Effect Upon Family Continuity," *Social Forces,* Vol. 32 (October, 1953), pp. 76–81.

Thomas, John, "The Factor of Religion in the Selection of Marriage Mates," *American Sociological Review,* Vol. 16 (August, 1951), pp. 487–491.

Vedder, Clyde, "Lonely Hearts Clubs Viewed Sociologically," *Social Forces,* Vol. 30 (December, 1951), pp. 219–222.

Wallace, Karl M., "An Experiment in Scientific Matchmaking," *Marriage and Family Living,* Vol. 21 (November, 1959), pp. 342–348.

Winch, Robert, *Mate Selection: A Study of Complementary Needs* (New York, Harper & Row, 1957).

QUESTIONS AND EXERCISES

1. Read the various studies on residential propinquity cited in Burgess and Locke. Write an essay on the adequacy of a theory of mate selection based on this factor.

2. Would you enter an interfaith marriage yourself? If not, why not? If so, on what basis?

3. Invite a group of international students to address your group on mate selection customs in their respective countries. Have them compare the strengths and weaknesses of their system to that of the United States as they see the situation.

4. Collect as many novels as you can which deal with marriage across class lines. Analyze them from some particular frame of reference and write a paper in summary.

5. Invite a Catholic priest, a Rabbi, or a Protestant minister to speak to your group on the position of his particular church on interfaith marriage.

6. How do you explain the statistical prediction that a "mixed" marriage has a greater chance of failure than a "nonmixed" one?

7. What is your position on the adequacy of the theory of complementary needs as a theory of mate selection? Discuss.

8. It is suggested that all persons have an ideal-mate image that develops and changes over the years. Write a paper in which you trace as best you can the development of the ideal-mate image you have.

9. Clyde Vedder (cited reference) joined a lonely hearts club in order to study the types of persons who made use of such an organization. Read this article and write a paper in which you discuss the function of such clubs in present-day America.

10. How much authority do you think parents should try to exercise in mate selection today? Discuss.

11. In this day of modern transportation, the possibilities young people have to meet eligible spouses is sometimes exaggerated. Make a small study in which you have a number of your friends indicate exactly how many persons whom they would consider eligible they have learned to know well enough for purposes of mate selection.

9

Premarital Sex

The question of premarital sex conduct is one that must be raised in any realistic treatment of American dating and mate selection today. Considerable confusion, doubt, and apprehension surround this area of life. It will be our purpose in this chapter to give brief reference to cross-cultural and historical materials for background purposes, and then to analyze some of the problems presently facing young people.

BACKGROUND

All known societies have apparently been forced to concern themselves with the question of sex behavior. None lacks standards relative to what is permissible and what is not acceptable in this phase of human interaction. Contrary to the American stereotyped impression of them, primitive societies were never sexual oases in which sex was completely free and unrestrained. Some have been more restrictive than western societies.

An analysis or enumeration of premarital sex customs around the world would be too detailed for our purposes here. Furthermore, a mere cataloging of sexual practices does not in and of itself lead to much insight. One particular custom must be related to the total configuration or milieu if it is to have much meaning. For example, a society which allows premarital sexual intercourse will ordinarily make full provision for all children which issue rather than consider them illegitimate. Further there may be a great interest in fertility on the part of the wife. What appears on the surface to an outsider to be premarital license may instead be essentially a matter of fertility testing and trial marriage. An isolated custom, in and of itself, has little meaning from a scholarly point of view or otherwise.

150

A perusal of anthropological literature would show that a majority of the preliterate societies do permit premarital intercourse under specified conditions. Murdock writes that of 250 societies which he studied 70 percent allow premarital experimentation.[1] On the other hand in only five societies of the group (2 percent) is adultery condoned. From a strictly comparative point of view, the utility or nonutility of premarital intercourse is much more controversial than is that of adultery. What factors, then, in the background of American society account for the traditional emphasis on premarital chastity? To answer this question it will be necessary to take a brief excursion again into history.

Previous Periods

Basic to the early Hebrew system was differential power between the sexes. The husband had the right to multiple spouses and concubines. He had superior rights regarding divorce. While premarital sex and adultery were forbidden, the man caught in an indiscretion was less severely censored than was the woman. In other words a double standard, favoring the male, existed. Sex was more of a male prerogative than it was a matter of a love relationship between husband and wife.

The New Testament does not have as much to say as the Old Testament regarding sexual conduct as such. This means that in general the Old Testament norms were accepted. Christ, however, seemed to favor a single standard of morality.[2] Paul on the other hand was more traditional, although on the positive side he strongly proposed that both men and women strive to live within the law. Christianity, eventually merging with Roman and Greek civilization, reflects this in its history. Since both the Greeks and the Romans had a double standard of sex morality it was probably inevitable that this approach would become deep-seated in western culture. It did and has been part of our heritage to this present day.

The civilization of Western Europe emerged as a synthesis of Roman-Germanic cultures. Old folk ideas of marriage and premarital behavior slowly but surely came under the domination of the church, state, and general community. Sex expression within marriage came to be held as the only legitimate outlet for the sex drive. However, males might sow a few wild oats—especially with peasant women, foreign women, or prostitutes. In the case of upper-class males a steady relationship with a mistress was generally tolerated as long as it was handled with discretion.

American legal and nonlegal sexual norms reflect their Old World

[1] G. P. Murdock, "Sexual Behavior: What is Acceptable?," *Journal of Social Hygiene,* Vol. 36 (1950), pp. 1–31.

[2] William Cole, *Sex and Love in the Bible* (New York, Association Press, 1959).

background with the ingredient of Puritanism added to the mixture. The Puritans, living under harsh physical and social conditions became greatly agitated about matters of sex. It was presented from the pulpit and public platform as something unworthy of the good, moral person. As is so often true, extreme attention to a subject apparently increases its attractiveness to some. Church sessions, at which wrongdoers confessed their indiscretions in great and elaborate detail, were well attended. Historians are convinced that many people in the pews had mixed motives, some of which were not above reproach. At any rate, moral leaders were not fully successful in stamping out all nonlegitimate sex activities. Calhoun reports, for example, that records of the church at Groton indicated that "of two hundred persons owning the baptismal covenant there from 1761 to 1775, no less than sixty-six confessed to fornication before marriage." [3] Adultery was considered a worse offense than premarital intercourse and while moral living was stressed for both sexes, men were, in practice, granted slightly more leeway than women. There seems to have been no equivalent of the scarlet letter for the male transgressor.

Other groups besides the Puritans have contributed to the American sexual heritage. Eventually the idea developed that sex is both very, very bad and yet very, very enticing. When a culture has this type of background, especially if it moves from a religious to a more secular orientation, it is predictable that it is in for considerable conflict.

After the unsettled frontier period the American family system as our grandparents knew it began to emerge. Courtship customs evolved which depended upon both inner and outer controls. Young men and women were expected to be respectable in their approach to each other. Women especially were taught to be modest and virtuous. Chaperonage and community control "helped" those who lacked personal control. If during courtship "something happened" the young man was expected to do his duty and marry the girl. As educational and general standards rose, middle- and upper-class men were expected to delay marriage until they could properly support wives and children. Since it was understood that this put strain on sexual urges, it was more or less accepted that the man could find satisfaction if necessary by consorting with prostitutes or women of easy virtue in the community. The old refrain "don't go around with college boys" reflects this recognition from the point of view of those girls at the more modest level of society.

Urbanization, the coming of the automobile, two world wars, coeducational practices, and other social factors were to induce great changes. Chaperonage declined and community control of the relations between the unmarried became most difficult. The great American invention of "dating"

[3] Arthur Calhoun, *Social History of the American Family,* Vol. 1 (New York, Barnes and Noble, 1945), p. 133.

developed whereby young people might go around together without necessarily implying that they were serious about marriage. Control of erotic impulses was left to the individuals involved, although it was not to be inferred that the community was suggesting any change in sexual standards as such. What are the results of these changes on erotic behavior? Are all standards being ignored under the liberal system of dating which has been developing? While these questions are most difficult to answer, they are worthy of serious consideration.

In spite of the fact that our culture puts great emphasis on sex, comparatively speaking, clear-cut information on typical sex attitudes or sex behavior is not easy to come by. Serious scientific studies have not been encouraged. However, in the last two decades a number of studies have been published which are of considerable help. They by no means enable us to answer all questions that many would wish to have answered, however.

One recurrent question involves the amount of premarital intercourse in our society today. Some cynics by traditional standards are now suggesting that most of our young people are sexually promiscuous. Such seems not to be the case. Promiscuity is not equal to sex expression. Perhaps a summary of the extent of premarital intercourse as reported by various researchers would be in order. Ehrmann has compiled materials on this phenomenon which are presented below in Tables 14 and 15.[4] Focusing first of all on males, it is quite clear that male premarital intercourse is more frequent than that of female. From the various studies we infer that presently some 60 percent of the male college students engage sometime in premarital intercourse. Indications are strong that for the noncollege population the figure would run in the 70 to 90 percent range depending upon educational and class level.

Whereas perhaps 75 percent of our young males have sexual intercourse sometime before marriage, the figure for women must be set at a lower level. As can be seen in Table 15 the reports range from a low of 2 percent to a high of 47 percent. Here again most of the larger studies had a preponderance of college girls in their sample. It is held by most authorities that girls at the lower socioeconomic levels are more inclined to report that they engage in premarital coitus than are women at the higher levels. It would be reasonable to assume that by the time of their marriage conservatively 20 to 25 percent of the college girls have experienced intercourse and that the figure for noncollege girls would run about twice that, or 40 to 50 percent.[5]

It must be noted that well-known differences in socialization patterns

[4] Winston Ehrmann, *Premarital Dating Behavior* (New York, Holt, Rinehart and Winston, 1959), pp. 33–34.
[5] This is essentially a conservative estimate; See Eugene Kanin and David Howard, "Postmarital Consequences of Premarital Sex Adjustment," *American Sociological Review,* Vol. 23 (October, 1958), pp. 557, 558.

TABLE 14

Incidence of Premarital Sexual Intercourse of Males as Reported by Various Investigators

Investigator	Date	Sample	Incidence %
Exner	1915	518 college students (Western sample), S [a]	36
Peck & Wells	1923	180 college level, 23 S & M [b]	35
Peck & Wells	1925	230 college level, 23, S & M	37
Hamilton	1929	100 college level, M	54
Bromley & Britten	1938	470 college students (questionnaire), 16–23 [c], S	51
Bromley & Britten	1938	122 college students (interview), 16–23, S	52
Peterson	1938	419 college students, S	55
Terman	1938	760 college and high school level, 28, M	61
Porterfield & Salley	1946	285 college students, 18–30, S	32
Finger	1947	111 college students, 17–23, S	45
Hohman & Schaffner	1947	1000 college level, 21–28, S	68
Kinsey et al.	1948	2308 college level, 20, S & M	44
Kinsey et al.	1948	761 college level, 25, S & M	64
Kinsey et al.	1948	202 college level, 30, S & M	68
Ross	1950	95 college students, 21, S	51
Gilbert Youth Research	1951	college students, 17–22, S	56
Burgess & Wallin	1953	580 college and high school level, 26, M	68
Landis & Landis	1953	600 college students, S & M	41
Ehrmann		274 college students (non-veterans), 18–21, S	57
Ehrmann		302 college students (veterans), 20–26, S	73
Ehrmann		50 college students (interview), 19–24, S	68

[a] S indicates single
[b] M indicates married
[c] age range distribution

SOURCE: From *Premarital Dating Behavior* by Winston Ehrmann. Copyright © 1959 by Holt, Rinehart and Winston, Inc. Reproduced by permission of Holt, Rinehart and Winston, Inc.

and in social expectations regarding female behavior could lead to under reporting of premarital sexual activity on the part of women. Furthermore, differences in research methods used in the studies could account for some of the divergent results obtained.

It should quickly be suggested that, especially regarding the females, the figures cited, taken at face value, do not necessarily imply promiscuity.

TABLE 15

Incidence of Premarital Sexual Intercourse of Females
as Reported by Various Investigators

Investigator	Date	Sample	Inci-dence %
Davis	1929	1200 college level, 37, S [a]	11
Davis	1929	1000 college and high school level, 26, M [b]	7
Hamilton	1929	100 college level, M	35
Dickinson & Beam	1934	500 college and high school level, 27, S	12
Bromley & Britten	1938	618 college students (question-naire), 16–23 [c], S	25
Bromley & Britten	1938	154 college students (inter-view), 16–23, S	26
Terman	1938	777 college and high school level, 25, M	37
Landis *et al.*	1940	109 high school and college level, 18–30, S	23
Landis *et al.*	1940	44 high school and college level, 22, M	27
Porterfield & Salley	1946	328 college students, 18–30, S	9
Gilbert Youth Research	1951	college students, 17–22, S	25
Kinsey *et al.*	1953	3303 college level, 15, S, M	2
Kinsey *et al.*	1953	2070 college level, 20, S & M	20
Kinsey *et al.*	1953	487 college level, 25, S & M	39
Burgess & Wallin	1953	604 college and high school level, 24, M	47
Landis & Landis	1953	1000 college students, S & M	9
Reevy	1954	139 college students, 18–23, S	7
Ehrmann		265 college students, 18–22, S	13
Ehrmann		50 college students (inter-view), 18–22, S	14

[a] S is single
[b] M is married
[c] is age range 17–24

SOURCE: From *Premarital Dating Behavior* by Winston Ehrmann. Copyright © 1959 by Holt, Rinehart and Winston, Inc. Reproduced by permission of Holt, Rinehart and Winston, Inc.

For the Kinsey active female sample the following figures are of interest for clarification.[6]

Numbers of partners in premarital coitus	percent
one only	53
fiance only	46
six or more	13

[6] Alfred Kinsey, *et al., Sexual Behavior in the Human Female* (Philadelphia, Saunders, 1953), p. 336.

We have not agreed upon standards as to where the line of promiscuity vs. nonpromiscuity should be drawn. Some using the above figures will argue that the women in the "six or more" category should be considered promiscuous. But can one do so regardless of the time interval? And regardless of whether they were monogamous within each relationship as long as it endured and may have been "marriage oriented"? Since the Kinsey sample had an undersupply of girls of the lower educational levels, the true figure is probably a bit higher. Nevertheless indications are clear that the majority of females who engage in premarital intercourse do so with a small and carefully selected number of partners. And, thus, the "promiscuity" issue is really not relevant anyway.

Have the rates of premarital intercourse been increasing over the years? Terman in 1938 had already become interested in this question.[7] Classifying wives in his sample he found that of those born before 1890 only about 13 percent reported premarital intercourse; for the next two decades the figures jumped to 26 percent and 49 percent respectively. Terman reasoned that virginity at marriage among females was on the decrease and that by the middle of this century it would be essentially extinct as an expectation. Further research has not borne out his prediction. It seems apparent that premarital intercourse rates rose sharply in the periods following both World Wars and then stabilized at higher levels than they had previously been. Especially is this true of females. The rates for males eased up at a less rapid pace but they were and remain higher.

It appears, then, that some stability has evolved in the trends of premarital intercourse in the United States. Whether an upward trend as predicted by Terman will again be in evidence will depend on our general social climate. Predictions are hazardous at this time.

Social Factors

Our discussion at this point would be incomplete without reference to social factors which influence sex activity. A focus upon mere rates as such is too narrow. What factors account for *differences* in premarital sexual activity?

It might be expected that religiosity and sex behavior would be correlated.[8] Expectations on the part of most, if not all, religious groups in this country regarding sex standards would seem to be quite clear. Does religious orientation have an effect in practice? Apparently it does. The Kinsey group found that categorizing their sample into "devout" vs. "inactive" brought more meaning into their data than did focus on differences

[7] Lewis Terman, *Psychological Factors in Marital Happiness* (New York, McGraw-Hill, 1938), pp. 134–137.

[8] Jean Dedman, "The Relation Between Religious Attitude and Attitude Toward Premarital Sex Relations," *Marriage and Family Living,* Vol. 21 (May, 1959), pp. 171–176.

in affiliation.[9] They found that devout Protestants, Catholics, or Jews, within each educational level, had "sex frequency" rates of premarital intercourse which were about two-thirds of those inactive members of these categories, educational level by educational level. Differences among the religious groups were small.

It should be noted that it was necessary to focus on particular educational levels even when making comparisons regarding religion. Kinsey and others found that education and occupation, factors we often associate with social class level, were *more crucial than religion* in distinguishing level of sexual activity.[10] In fact there is a high degree of agreement among scholars that profound differences exist among the classes regarding premarital sexual behavior. In general there seems to be an inverse association between the variables, that is, the higher the class level the lower the percent of people who engage in premarital coitus. The upper levels put a greater stress on "technical virginity" and elaborate techniques of petting have been developed as substitutes for intercourse. So strong is this class difference regarding who will or will not have intercourse that it is a better predictor than is religiosity or religious affiliation.

TWO STUDIES

So much, then, for premarital coitus rates as such. The reader who wishes to press further into questions of the reliability, validity, and other characteristics of the data is advised to study the various research reports in some detail. Two recent studies have opened the way to broader questions than incidence, and they deserve our attention. The first, by Ehrmann, involves an intensive investigation of over one thousand university men and women in regard to their premarital "heterosexual behavior and its control." Instead of a focus on sex as "outlet" from the point of view of the individual, Ehrmann as a sociologist was more interested in the types of *interrelationships* of the two people involved. He was especially concerned with control of erotic aspects of dating behavior with respect to stages of involvement, who initiates it, and who restrains it at particular points if restraint is involved. Elaborate questionnaires were filled out by respondents and intensive interviews were held with a proportion of the sample as a check on the reliability of the answers. Some of Ehrmann's major conclusions are as follows:

1. Premarital heterosexual behavior falls into highly compartmentalized stages of increasing degrees of intensity, as judged by males and females, both with respect to physical contact, at one extreme, on through holding

[9] Alfred Kinsey, *et. al.*, *Sexual Behavior in the Human Male* (Philadelphia, Saunders, 1948), pp. 304 and 472–487.
[10] *Ibid.*, p. 19.

hands, kissing, general body embrace, and the fondling of various portions of the body, to sexual intercourse at the other.

2. Although the males engage more often in extreme sexual activities than the females, a larger proportion of these experiences among males represent sporadic ventures with both peer and deviant companions.

3. The typical and usual heterosexual experience for both males and females is kissing and hugging, and all but a rare few have had this experience.

4. Although the male usually initiates the lovemaking, the females frequently make the first overtures. Female initiation of behavior increases appreciably in the going-steady and the love relationship.

5. The limitation of premarital sexual behavior is primarily female determined.

6. Veteran, non-veteran differences among the males is associated with amount of sexual experiences, but the difference is related to age rather than military service.

7. High frequency of dating many different companions (among the males) appears associated primarily with eroticism and (among females) with popularity, but high frequency of dating one partner among both sexes is related to going steady and being in love.

8. Most members of both sexes limit dating to companions of the same social class.

9. Female sexual expression is primarily and profoundly related to being in love and to going steady. (This is probably the single most important empirical finding of this research.) Male sexuality is more indirectly and less exclusively associated with romanticism and intimacy relationships.

10. The above differences between males and females in regard to sex expression tend to disappear when both partners are in love.

11. The peer code of both males and females is more liberal than the personal code; that is, both sexes are more lenient in their attitudes about what is permissible heterosexual behavior for companions than for themselves.

12. The degree of physical intimacy actually experienced or considered permissible is among males inversely related and among females directly related to the intensity of affection in the male-female relation.

13. Females rarely go beyond the limits set by their codes, whereas males are often not able to go as far sexually as their codes permit.

14. There is a marked difference in the standards of sexual behavior between males and females and within the male group. Most of the females have a conservative single standard, but a minority of the girls have a liberal standard with reference to premarital sexual intercourse. A majority of the males have a single standard; most of these males are liberal in considering premarital coitus permissible and the remainder are conservative in adhering to premarital abstinence. A substantial minority of the males have a double standard by which coitus is considered permissible with a nonlover, but not with a lover.

15. Females find pleasure in dating without petting but in sexual activities more with lovers; and males find pleasure in dating lovers and in sexual activities with all females.[11]

[11] Adapted from Ehrmann, *op. cit.,* Chapter VII.

The second major study to which reference should be made at this point is that of Kirkendall.[12] Long interested in the implications of premarital sex on human relationships this author studied, by an intensive interview-case method, the interpersonal relationships based on 668 premarital sex experiences of 200 college males. His concern was especially with the feelings, attitudes, and motivations of the subjects, their sense of responsibility, and the type of communication involved. After preliminary study a continuum was developed to take into account the various levels of interpersonal relationships. These ranged through the following: (1) prostitute, (2) pick-up, (3) casual acquaintance perceived merely as a potential sexual associate, (4) dating partner who became a sex partner before affectional attachment, (5) partner with whom a relationship of some strength existed, and (6) fiancé.[13] As is true of the Ehrmann study, only intensive reading of the various chapters will give one a full understanding of the ramifications of the various levels of relationships in which young people become involved. Kirkendall for years has been concerned with the implications of premarital sex attitudes and behavior for *constructive human relations*. By such a criterion, elusive as it may be, much of the material reported dealing with levels one through four especially, does not indicate that the criterion is generally being met in premarital relationships if these reported are at all typical. In fact the author lists eight major forces which impede the possible integration of sex into satisfactory interpersonal relationships. These are:

1. *Sexual Exploitation*
   Sex is sometimes used as a commodity. At times it is used to satisfy individual desires. In various ways sex is used to exploit other persons who are used as objects. Suspicion, doubt, and mistrust tend to result.
2. *Difficulties in Communication*
   Internalized taboos prevent frank, objective, legitimate discussion of sex. With adults, conversation among their own sex group tends to be risque or judgmental. Adults cannot therefore communicate adequately with children or young people.
3. *Negative Attitudes and Values*
   For males especially sex experience is associated with symbols of success. Females are under pressure, therefore, to develop a steady relationship regardless of cost and the male is motivated to prove his prowess. Either can exploit the other by unduly pushing toward a particular goal regardless of the effect on the other. The source of these confusions and pressures is in our present cultural climate.
4. *Sex Antagonisms and Hostilities*
   The boy may be driven toward aggressive behavior by reactions

[12] *Premarital Intercourse and Interpersonal Relationships* by Lester A. Kirkendall, The Julian Press, New York 10003.
[13] *Ibid.,* p. 19.

against a felt mother domination (woman) at home and school, or by the privileges and expectations of the double standard. The girl may find it difficult to stem this aggressiveness. Driven to wish to "capture" a male she may let herself be finally "pushed into submission." Frequently each is trying to exploit the partner or take advantage.

5. *Biological and Social Sex Differences*

The masculine role in the reproductive process is relatively simple, involving the depositing of the sperm. The female's whole pattern of living is changed, however, as she becomes pregnant. How she reacts to the experience depends in great part on the attitudes and behavior of the man who impregnated her. Women, therefore, must for practical, biological reasons be more careful than men regarding sex behavior.

6. *Deficiencies in Personal Adjustments*

The purposelessness and disorganization which characterize the loves of many people prevent their handling of sex in a mature, nonexploitive fashion. Neurotic immaturities are related to promiscuity and casual, irresponsible sexual exploration; emotionally healthy persons can enjoy sex, but still put it in a perspective where it will effectively support satisfactory interpersonal relationships.

7. *An Irrational Moral Code*

Strides should be made, says Kirkendall, toward a criterion of interpersonal relationships as the basis for moral judgments. Presently power, material wealth, or position are often used as criteria of success. Focus on motivation, meaning, and consequences of behavior for interpersonal relationships would be more constructive.

8. *Inadequate Social Arrangements*

Successful integration of sex into the social fabric requires the development of supporting features within the society in order to afford a needed measure of protection to its members. If a society were to make premarital intercourse acceptable and at the same time include concern with the improvement of interpersonal relationships, some important features would be necessary. These would include responsibility automatically assumed with participation in sexual relationships, including possible pregnancy, and possible emotional outcomes and developments in other relationships, plus social arrangements to care for unmarried mothers and their offspring.[14]

Both the Ehrmann and Kirkendall studies seem to be in high agreement with the point of view of Le Masters: separate male and female subcultures exist with respect to attitudes and behavior in sex matters. Men are much more open and free about sex than women. They are interested in sex as sex. If they consider a girl as potential timber for marriage they are more inclined to protect her and concern themselves with her feelings, desires, and welfare. Even so, she is expected to set up controls on the relationship and indicate resistance. Girls are more love or romance

[14] *Ibid.,* adapted from Chapter 10, by permission of the Julian Press, New York, 10003, 1961.

oriented than sex oriented as such. When they use a boy it is to obtain status or possible marriage rather than sensuous pleasure.[15]

Boys cross class lines and date beneath themselves in order to seek erotic favors. When lower-class girls cross class lines they are interested in potential marriage partners or in the prestige they may obtain. Middle-class girls do not cross class lines for sex as such.

Further this difference between men and women seems to be characteristic of not only middle-class levels (the primary focus of the Ehrmann and Kirkendall studies) but of the lower classes as well. Lower-class men are more inclined to move toward full coitus and to move more quickly than middle- and upper-class men. Petting short of orgasm seems to be a middle-class or college invention. At all levels double-standard men distinguish between marriageable and nonmarriageable girls. Since lower-class boys do not have a supply of datable girls beneath them the question can be raised: How are marriageable and nonmarriageable girls distinguished? An interesting situation typically develops whereby local girls, or girls the boys think of as members of their own group, are considered "out of bounds" regarding casual erotic demands. Boys aggressively seek out girls of other lower-class groups. In this way a category of acceptable girls is kept available for eventual marriage purposes. It is a case of the "left hand not knowing what the right is doing" and is an interesting social fiction because somebody's girls are going to be vulnerable if most lower-class males vigorously seek out partners.[16] Many girls apparently make themselves available to boys other than those in their own group for sex purposes, from motivations of boredom, escape, a search for romance, and the possibility of marriage if the partner is from a higher status.

It must again be emphasized that both the Ehrmann and the Kirkendall studies dealt with college students. Furthermore, the latter included only boys who had engaged in sexual intercourse. If the Kirkendall findings stand out a bit more sharply it is partly because they focus on the proportion of boys engaging in premarital coitus. The evidence is strong that this includes about two-thirds of the college male population, at least of the larger institutions which draw heavily from the general population.

Along with the two studies discussed in the previous paragraphs, the work of Reiss must be included. A family sociologist, Reiss has been engaged in research on premarital sex standards in America and their integration in the social system. Much of his work is as yet unreported, but in his book *Premarital Sex Standards in America* and in a series of articles, Reiss suggests some emerging standards, formal and informal. These standards, in summary form, are as follows:

---

[15] Kanin and Howard, *op. cit.*

[16] See Arnold Green, "The Cult of Personality and Sexual Relations," *Psychiatry*, Vol. IV (1941), pp. 343–348; also reprinted in Norman Bell and Ezra Vogel, *The Family* (New York, Free Press, 1960), Article Number 48.

1. Abstinence—Premarital intercourse is wrong for both men and women, regardless of circumstances.
2. Permissiveness with Affection—Premarital intercourse is right for both men and women under certain conditions when a stable relationship with engagement, love, or strong affection is present.
3. Permissiveness without Affection—Premarital intercourse is right for both men and women regardless of the amount of affection or stability present, providing there is physical attraction.
4. Double Standard—Premarital intercourse is acceptable for men, but it is wrong and unacceptable for women.[17]

It is suggested that two basic types of orientation to sex may be delineated, namely *body* centered and *person* centered. Reiss believes that permissiveness with affection as a standard is growing more acceptable among young people, although this clashes with our formal standard of abstinence demanded by law and generally supported by religious groups.

In the early part of the chapter we gave brief attention to some of the background and changes that form the basis for our sex behavior and sex attitudes of today. We should briefly refer to the present day regarding the place sex has in our culture before discussing some implications of the previously given data.

SEX IN AMERICAN SOCIETY

Some years ago it was suggested that we are a schizoid culture.[18] This implies that as a society we have so many splits and contradictions that we border on the pathological. Ignoring the controversies as to whether or not it is legitimate to call a whole society sick, we certainly see evidences of contradictions and clashes when our sex values and sex practices are carefully studied. The Puritan heritage is still with us, and there are those who at times would like to brand sexual offenders or to make public examples of them. Few are this extreme, but many persons at times reflect an inner attitude of severity on sex matters in general. Sex is something that is not a subject of polite conversation. We have our laws and our social mores. They should be adhered to—straight down the line.

The laws on the books reflect this basic orientation. The majority of our states declare that rape, seduction, premarital coitus, extramarital coitus, and prostitution are illegal. There are also of course laws spelling out other types of illegal sexual activity. The penalties in some cases are relatively severe and, if the laws were enforced fully, would be of considerable impact on the parties involved. Given our particular tradition, and being

---

[17] Ira Reiss, *Premarital Sexual Standards in America* (New York, Free Press, 1960), pp. 83–84.
[18] Read Bain, "Our Schizoid Culture," *Sociology and Social Research* (January–February, 1935), pp. 266–276.

a religious people, we have codes of sex morality which are also written in the laws. Could a visiting anthropologist stop at this point, if he were trying to gain an understanding of our culture? We know he could not. For while one part of us suggests that sex is to be kept under tight control, another suggests that it is something to which we should turn our attention. Sex is fun and too much restraint is unhealthy.

Disguised only slightly, sex in various forms is purveyed through our mass media in ways that shock people from many other parts of the world. The Hollywood writer who has a straight theme must somehow "jazz it up" with sex interest. The young man who wishes to have an historical novel published must see to it that a seduction takes place, lest the book be rejected for lack of "realism." An author can scarcely get better insurance that his book will be read in satisfactory numbers than to have it "banned in Boston."

At the level of sentiments, then, we have both the elements of stern, restrictive morality and the extremes of permissiveness operating at one and the same time. A father who is rather firm with his own teen-age daughters may also be a committee member of a business group that arranges for a bevy of show girls or even call girls to entertain the visiting firemen. This illustrates the way cultural contradictions can be expressed by or through a particular individual. To an extent, of course, differences in sex standards and practices reflect the multiplicity of backgrounds of our people, but by no means can this confusion we have be attributed to this factor alone.

At the level of legal control it must be noted that our laws on adultery and fornication are seldom taken seriously. The Indiana group suggests that if the laws were vigorously and strictly enforced 85 percent of our young male population would be hauled before the courts on sex charges.[19] While this generalization is possibly exaggerated for effect it cannot be dismissed lightly. In a recent case three marines were charged with *statutory rape* for consorting with a sixteen-year-old girl who encouraged them. However, under the law a girl under age could not give consent because she was *unable to give consent*. That the evidence indicated that the girl had previously engaged in promiscuous behavior had nothing to do with the requirements of the law in that particular state. As Ploscowe points out, girls engaging in sex play out of which they receive money (prostitution, in other words) have been able to secure statutory rape charges against the men involved.[20] Even if charges are thrown out of court the resultant publicity can be very damaging to a boy's reputation.

Attention has been given so far in this chapter to the incidence of premarital intercourse in our society and to attitudes and practices correlated

[19] Kinsey, *et al., op. cit.,* 1948.
[20] Morris Ploscowe, *Sex and the Law* (Englewood Cliffs, N.J., Prentice-Hall, 1951), p. 182.

with it, especially regarding male and female differences. We could not in good faith, if we wished, stop at this point. Interpretations and the assessment of implications are called for. What do these data and generalizations mean? What are their implications?

Social Implications

Implication to whom and from what frame of reference? The parent, the educator, the social scientist, the church, young people, and society all have an interest in questions of premarital sex. Each segment will tend to have a particularized interest. It is clear that many parents do not perceive fully the intensity of the pressures under which young people date today. Many would be shocked were they to understand more fully the knowledge, attitudes, and practices of their children and the dilemmas they face. Perhaps they in some cases do not want to know. At any rate young people consistently report that they find it very difficult to communicate with their parents regarding dating and courtship dilemmas that involve erotic elements.

On the positive side most parents are interested in the long-run happiness of their offspring. In general they feel that their children, especially their daughters, will have the greatest possibilities of long-term success if they reserve sexual intercourse for marriage. Typically they believe that the welfare of children is best served by restrictive codes. On the negative side they fear loss of family status if the daughter becomes promiscuous, and they are naturally concerned about the necessity of supporting an illegitimate grandchild in the event of unwed motherhood. Individual parents have their own ideas and values, especially regarding methods of teaching and control. How effective they are is another question.

School administrators and counselors face many problems when it comes to the question of boy-girl relations under their jurisdiction. Some attempt to evade problems by ignoring them. The more thoughtful ones are not willing to engage in this course of action. Just what they are to do is a difficult question. At the high school level educators are criticized by some parents if they allow any sex information to be presented. At the college level this is no longer true but there are problems in sufficient quantity. How much control should be exercised over the young people? How, and by whom? Should they be supervised regarding activities that potentially involve sex? A policy that seems very restrictive to the students may be viewed as quite liberal indeed by their parents. Public college officials are "on the spot" because their students come from such divergent backgrounds. Private schools have less of a problem on this score, but they on the other hand are usually expected to exercise greater control in the realm of morals. Many a young person is sent to a private college in the hope that the college officials will be able to effect control where the parents have failed. A dean is sometimes challenged by the question: "Why did you let my daughter get pregnant?" One can feel sure that a dean normally hopes to be faced with other types of challenges.

That campus dating may lead to erotic and adjustment problems can hardly be denied. Kirkpatrick and associates asked 291 undergraduate co-eds to indicate the amount and types of "erotic offenses" to which they had been subjected while at college.[21] (See Table 16). A total of 56 percent reported that they were offended in the course of their dating-courtship behavior during one academic year. Most of the offenses grew out of necking or petting behavior. However 21 percent of the girls reported offenses involving attempted intercourse, and 6 percent attempted intercourse with violence.

TABLE 16

Relationship Involvement and Erotic Intimacy Level at Which Offensiveness Occurs, by Episodes

	Necking and Petting Above the Waist		Petting Below the Waist		Attempted Intercourse and Attempted Intercourse with Violence		Total	
	N	Per-centage	N	Per-centage	N	Per-centage	N	Per-centage
Ride home First date Occasional date	411	55.0	60	31.4	25	30.1	496	48.5
Regular or Steady date	295	39.4	104	54.5	43	51.8	442	43.3
Pinned Engaged	42	5.6	27	14.1	15	18.1	84	8.2
Totals	748	100.0	191	100.0	83	100.0	1022	100.0

SOURCE: Clifford Kirkpatrick and Eugene Kanin, "Male Aggression on a University Campus," *American Sociological Review*, Vol. 22 (February, 1957), p. 55.

The data seem to indicate that certain types of problems from the girl's point of view are associated with particular stages in dating. Attempts at heavy petting or attempted intercourse of one type or another are more likely to occur with steady dating than with either random dating or a relationship advanced to the pinning or engagement level. Necking and light petting problems are associated more with casual dating than with greater involvement. In other words, problems become greater with progressive involvement.

What seems to be indicated is a double standard that operates on the

---

[21] Clifford Kirkpatrick and Eugene Kanin, "Male Sex Aggression on a University Campus," *American Sociological Review*, Vol. 22 (February, 1957), pp. 52–58.

various levels of dating involvement. At the casual level the boy may initiate what to him is mildly erotic activity. With a more involved relationship he is more inclined to propose going farther. The authors suggest that the relationships reported indicate male exploitation because the female is relatively unprotected. Girls typically try to set up controls. These are often ignored and under pressure the girls yield. On doing so they are often too embarrassed to turn to friends or adults for help in their dilemma. Discussion with the offender and avoiding him are the major methods of control used, although emotional involvement may lead the girl to continue dating the boy. This continuation of the relationship may be under a redefined situation. Notable is the absence of reported appeal to parents or academic authority. The authors believe that feelings of guilt and stigma lead the girls to fear appealing to college authorities such as advisors, housemothers, deans, and counselors.[22]

The authors suggest that girls should be given education as to what they may be expected to face in the way of problems of this nature. Informed self-reliance seems to them to be the goal toward which all should proceed. However even the self-reliant girl may find herself in need of help and guidance. The authors believe that such a girl might turn to a counselor only if this person is not in a position to exercise punitive sanctions as well as counsel.

The sexual implications of our dating system at the college level are becoming a matter of concern to many. Suggestions for action vary considerably. This is probably inevitable, given our present conflict in values. On the one hand we have some leaders advocating a tightening up of moral standards and behavior along traditional lines. On the other side some are advocating that college authorities recognize the prevailing situation and make liberal adaptations to it. Such a proposal was made by Levine and Pines recently in a widely circulated article.[23]

These authors propose that colleges make sure that contraceptive knowledge is available to students along with information on fertilization, pregnancy, and birth. They believe that colleges should "take into account the sexual activity that exists on campuses today and try to match their policies to deal with it as realistically as possible." It is estimated that over 1000 unmarried college girls become pregnant each year, and it is thought that the majority of these girls make use of abortion rings existing around most colleges. The essence of the position of Levine and Pines is this: "Since they know that a certain number of students will have premarital sex relations despite official disapproval, the colleges should try to make sure that all students know how to avoid the consequences." To do this, required courses in physiology which include material on birth control

---

[22] *Ibid.,* p. 58.

[23] Milton I. Levine and Maya Pines, "The Problem Colleges Evade," *Harper's Magazine,* Vol. 223 (October, 1961), p. 132.

should be offered. Each freshman would be provided with a recommended reading list of reliable, forthright books on birth control and sex.

The challenge presented by this team of writers, the senior author of which is a physician in a well-known medical school, is not to be taken lightly. The present author would strongly agree that no one should reach adulthood without having knowledge of human physiology including methods of birth control. An implication is given, however, that college sexual problems are almost strictly matters involving knowledge of physiology. They are much more than this. This is not to suggest backing for a punitive type of sex education lectures as part of an orientation program. We would feel along with many family life educators that facts and values cannot be separated in an area such as this. If a particular value orientation is to be pushed by a college administration this of course should be made clear to everyone concerned.

While not all will agree with the recommendations given by the above authors, the problem posed can scarcely be denied. Some attention to official or unofficial school policy regarding birth control usage by students will soon be required with the approaching general availability of oral contraceptives. One college physician reported to the author that he was surprised to learn that some girls on his campus were presently taking oral birth control pills under prescription by their local physicians. Presumably these local doctors were convinced that they were needed. One can only conjecture as to whether they felt their patients were promiscuous, "in love," or whether they were simply concerned with general safety.

Space limitations forbid discussion of the orientation of the church and other interested groups and institutions toward premarital sex behavior and of the implications of such behavior as seen by these groups. Instead the author wishes to discuss briefly some implications for our general society and then conclude with reference to the individuals or couples involved.

Social scientists, and particularly sociologists, have traditionally been concerned with the balance between individual and social well-being. This interest is reiterated clearly in Kephart's recent family text. Social science cannot decide moral questions as such, but it can aid in the assessment of particular customs or practices in light of their function within a given value context. Operating upon this assumption, family sociologists as teachers and textbook writers have tended to take a conservative position regarding the general efficacy of premarital sexual intercourse.[24] This is not to suggest that complete agreement prevails. Furthermore, along with professionals among the clergy and elsewhere it is generally agreed that particular extenuating circumstance may alter cases. It has been held, however, that relaxing of our premarital sex conventions would in general put the marriage and family system as we know it under further strain.

[24] See Ira Reiss, "The Treatment of Premarital Coitus in Marriage and the Family Texts," *Social Problems,* Vol. 4 (April, 1957), pp. 334–338.

The author is inclined to agree with this position. It is quite true that premarital intercourse in some societies is integrated into a system of stable marriage and family life. But as numerous social scientists have pointed out, premarital sex behavior in a patriarchal, large family, traditional society is quite a different matter than it is in a modern society. At least it can be asserted that many value and structural changes would be called for in our society were a new integration, including full acceptance of premarital sex behavior, to take place. Further it must be reiterated that some control of sex behavior is inevitable and necessary for group and individual well-being. No organized society, to our knowledge, has ever allowed unrestricted sexual intercourse. Instead it has been held necessary that moral codes governing sex be both internalized by individuals and supported by social sanctions if necessary. We believe this approach is a functional prerequisite of social and individual well-being and not just a matter of tradition. To protect the welfare and rights of young men and women it is necessary that standards have general acceptance and be understood by all concerned. The issue is how much control, what kind, and why?

Kirkendall proposes that a new yardstick be used to evaluate premarital sex relationships. It would involve essentially evaluation of the *quality of the interpersonal relationships* involved. Young people would make decisions by reference to this type of code. Considerations would be given to respect, full communication, rights of others, integrity, etc. With this ideal in mind the author writes regarding his own studies with college students:

> The data indicate that most sexually-experienced young people have had, interpersonal relationship-wise, disappointing experiences. In cases where more positive results are reported the writer questions whether premarital intercourse has added anything of permanent significance to the relationship. Therefore, at this time and in this culture he sees too little being accomplished by premarital intercourse toward the improvement of relationships to justify supporting it as an adjustive solution to the sex problem. The depth of current convictions and the slowness with which change comes leads to the supposition that we will continue to face about the same condition for some time to come. We must, nevertheless, be able to face the possibility that ways may be found to use sex in premarital relationships in a positive, meaningful way. This we will be able to do if we can focus on the really important issue, the creation of sound interpersonal relations.[25]

On the basis of personal observation of conditions and counseling and teaching experience the author is inclined to agree with Kirkendall's assessment of premarital sex relations under present circumstances. Premarital sex relations under the conditions surrounding our whole dating-courtship complex would not measure up to any reasonable ideal we know of,

[25] Lester Kirkendall, "Values and Premarital Intercourse—Implications for Parent Education," *Marriage and Family Living,* Vol. 22 (November, 1960), p. 321.

whether that ideal came from a framework of ethics and morals, mental health, social utility, or some other source.

Our society has relatively more severe norms regarding husband and wife loyalty within marriage. Both our traditional religious ideals and our romantic ideals are clear on this point. While much more basic research is needed before we can be sure of this generalization, it appears from at least the Kinsey and Burgess-Wallin studies that those who are involved in premarital intercourse are more inclined toward adultery than those who do not.[26] This may be a strong argument, to some, for a restrictive premarital code.

A few years ago, at a symposium on the question of acceptable sexual behavior, Murdock, well-known anthropologist, issued a challenge to adult leaders of our institutions and communities.[27] Taking the position that our traditional premarital sex mores are and will be unenforceable he suggested that adult, responsible leaders consider a modification in our ethical codes regarding sex. One need not agree with Murdock's general position in order to appreciate his challenge. The writer also believes that an evaluation of the present situation by responsible people of various persuasions is greatly needed. We believe this would be appreciated by many young people. A warning must be given that the task is a complicated one. An important beginning has been made by a group organized under the auspices of the National Council of Churches. Representatives from churches, colleges, and agencies of various kinds met at a retreat in the spring of 1961 and studied problems and issues relating to sexual behavior in the United States.[28] This report deserves wide circulation and study. Similar work on the local community level may be very helpful as a start. To make a real dent some values and practices will have to be altered, however. Ehrmann, who has given considerable thought to the area about which we are writing, reminds us that social action often induces unanticipated consequences.

Actually any constructive efforts to relieve young people of some of the pressures under which they operate must take into account some major forces which seem to be working at cross-purposes. On the one hand certain encouragement is given to early dating and to going steady even down into the grade school. Coupled with this, probably inevitably, is a trend toward early marriage. Some have felt that early marriage is the solution to the problem of premarital sex behavior. However, the development of both a statistical average and an expected norm of early marriage may serve to

[26] Ernest Burgess and Paul Wallin, *Engagement and Marriage* (Philadelphia, Lippincott, 1953), pp. 362–364. Also Robert Hamblin and Robert Blood, "Premarital Experience and the Wife's Sexual Adjustment," *Social Problems,* Vol. 3 (October, 1956), pp. 122–130; and Lewis Terman, *et. al., Psychological Factors in Marital Happiness* (Englewood Cliffs, N.J., Prentice-Hall, 1938), pp. 383–385.

[27] Murdock, *op. cit.*

[28] Evelyn Duvall, and Sylvanus Duvall, *Sex Ways* (New York, Association Press, 1961).

increase the incidence of premarital intercourse, as Kirkendall points out.[29] With the period in which a girl has a good chance of selecting a mate being shortened and pushed into the teen years girls may be encouraged to use sex as a possible avenue to marriage. The trend toward early going steady as against casual dating would seem to encourage premarital coitus, although the evidence is not too clear on this point. On the other hand, there are counterpressures leading toward demands for more education and training and greater delay before entry into the economic and the professional world. Very few societies encourage or allow intensive courtship behavior before the young people are prepared to assume economic and social responsibilities. Something clearly will be forced to collapse in the long run.

THE YOUNG COUPLE

We have deliberately approached the problem of premarital relationships in a broad context because the issues involved can only be fully understood when approached in this fashion. By no means have we exhausted the subject. Many considerations from the point of view of religion, biology, psychology, and so on could be introduced. We are well aware of the fact that it is difficult to be completely rational regarding a force as powerful as sex.

Regardless of all the general discussion, however, young people are faced with serious pressures in specific cases. "What are we to do?" is a recurrent question. The author believes that at a general level such questions, whether they involve sex or something else, can be answered reasonably by this position: Assess carefully the issues and implications involved, and then make a decision with which *you* can live. Responsible decision-making means taking all pertinent facts into account. Needless to say, the place for personal policy-making is not the back seat of a parked car or a blanket on the beach when emotions are aroused and the situation anything but conducive to objective decision-making.

If the problem of full sex behavior is involved, the question can legitimately be raised to one and all, regardless of background: "What are you working toward as a goal?" Erikson has been attempting to combine the insights of psychiatry and comparative anthropology in his work for a number of years. The basic goal of young adulthood, he says, is intimacy as against isolation. This involves a mature sexuality, genitally based. In our culture at the present time mature genitality if it is to be sound must consist of the following as seen by Erikson: "(1) mutuality of orgasm, (2) with a loved partner, (3) of the other sex, (4) with whom one is able and willing to share a mutual trust, (5) with whom one is able and willing to regulate the

[29] Kirkendall, *Premarital Intercourse and Interpersonal Relationships, op. cit.,* p. 246.

cycles of work, procreation, and recreation, (6) so as to secure to the off-spring, too, all the stages of a satisfactory development." [30]

The position taken by Erikson is highly defensible on both scientific and ethical grounds, the two by no means being identical. Initiation into coitus is in cultures such as ours often traumatic, especially for girls. While folk attitudes toward the role of the deflorator and the process of defloration may be generally erroneous, to ignore the emotional significance these may have for the parties involved may be in error also. Simpson, who in general favors a liberal position on sex matters, quotes with approval an emphasis given by Bonaparte, de Beauvoir, and others to the important role the male plays in the initiation of sexual activity for the female, which activity must take place in a supportive environment if trauma is not to be a probable outcome.[31] He goes on to note that

. . . even if initiation into coitus is not traumatic, some individuals are not quickly capable of coping with the refurbished world of infantile emotions that reappear. The underlying emotional patterns which break forth require for their stabilization conditions which are not generally present in premarital coitus: spatial security, regularity, warmth, assurance, continuity. The absence of such conditions may lead to one of two extremes: a view of coitus as dark and surreptitious, or a revulsion against it as loathsome.[32]

Those who challenge restrictive premarital mores must, if they are realistic, indicate fully how society is to move to the place where the conditions of warmth, regularity, spatial security, and the like are provided for sex relations. Until this is done they cannot be operating on firm ground.

Some may find in examining their own thinking and feeling and in discussion with their partners that Erikson's ideal cannot be achieved for themselves. That does not make it invalid in general or as an ideal. For those who insist on some other ideal, there is backing for alternative positions in the literature cited in our footnotes or in references at the end of the chapter. Jesus, Ghandi, Socrates, and others defied certain conventions of their day. They acted on the basis of principle rather than for personal gain, however, and were willing to take the consequences. As Magoun states,

. . . the acid test becomes whether the individual is concerned with [premarital] intercourse for his own pleasure, or whether, without any personal gain whatever, the individual is willing to fight openly for the right of some other man to have intercourse with his sister or the girl he may later marry. Sincerely held, this second position is one which commands respect no matter how vigorously one may disagree with it.[33]

[30] Erik H. Erikson, *Childhood and Society* 2nd ed., revised and enlarged (New York, W. W. Norton and Company, Inc., 1950), p. 266.
[31] George Simpson, *People in Families* (New York, Crowell, 1960), p. 118.
[32] *Ibid.*
[33] F. Alexander Magoun, *Love and Marriage* (New York, Harper & Row, 1956), p. 160.

SELECTED READINGS

Baber, Ray, *Marriage and the Family* (New York, McGraw-Hill, 1953), Chapters 16 and 17.

Bell, Robert, and Blumberg, Leonard, "Courtship Intimacy and Religious Background," *Marriage and Family Living,* Vol. 21 (November, 1959), pp. 356–360.

Blood, Robert, "Romance and Premarital Intercourse—Incompatibles?" *Marriage and Family Living,* Vol. 14 (May, 1952), pp. 105–108.

Breed, Warren, "Sex, Class, and Socialization in Dating," *Marriage and Family Living,* Vol. 18 (May, 1956), pp. 137–144.

Cavan, Ruth, *American Marriage* (New York, Crowell, 1959), Chapter 10.

Christensen, Harold, "Studies in Child Spacing: I-Premarital Pregnancy as Measured by the Spacing of the First Birth from Marriage," *American Sociological Review,* Vol. 18 (February, 1953), pp. 53–59.

Christensen, Harold, and Carpenter, George, "Timing Patterns in the Development of Sexual Intimacy," *Marriage and Family Living,* Vol. 24 (February, 1962), pp. 30–35.

Dedman, Jean, "The Relationship Between Religious Attitude and Attitude Toward Premarital Sex Relations," *Marriage and Family Living,* Vol. 21 (May, 1959), pp. 171–176.

Duvall, Evelyn, and Hill, Reuben, *Being Married* (Boston, Heath, 1960), Chapter 8.

Duvall, Evelyn, and Duvall, Sylvanus, *Sex Ways* (New York, Association Press, 1961).

Ehrmann, Winston, "Some Knowns and Unknowns in Research into Human Sex Behavior," *Marriage and Family Living,* Vol. 19 (February, 1957), pp. 16–22.

Ehrmann, Winston, *Premarital Dating Behavior* (New York, Holt, Rinehart and Winston, 1959).

Gebhard, Paul, *et al., Pregnancy, Birth and Abortion* (New York, Hoeber-Harper, 1958), pp. 150–160.

Hamblin, Robert, and Blood, Robert, "Premarital Experience and the Wife's Sexual Adjustment," *Social Problems,* Vol. 3 (October, 1956–1957), pp. 122–130.

Hiltner, Seward, *Sex Ethics and the Kinsey Reports* (New York, Association Press, 1953).

Kephart, William, *Family, Society and the Individual* (Boston, Houghton Mifflin, 1961), Chapters 12 and 13.

Kinsey, Alfred, *et al., Sexual Behavior in the Human Male* (Philadelphia, Saunders, 1948).

Kinsey, Alfred, *et al., Sexual Behavior in the Human Female* (Philadelphia, Saunders, 1953).

Kirkendall, Lester, *Premarital Intercourse and Interpersonal Relationships* (New York, The Julian Press, 1961).

Kirkpatrick, Clifford, and Kanin, Eugene, "Male Sex Aggression on a University Campus," *American Sociological Review,* Vol. 22 (February, 1957), pp. 52–58.

Landis, Judson, and Landis, Mary, *Building a Successful Marriage* (Englewood Cliffs, N.J., Prentice-Hall, 1958), Chapter 11.

Le Masters, Ersel, *Modern Courtship and Marriage* (New York, Macmillan, 1957), Chapter 9.

Lindsey, Benjamin, and Evans, Wainwright, *The Companionate Marriage* (New York, Boni and Liveright, 1927).

Ploscowe, Morris, *Sex and the Law* (Englewood Cliffs, N.J., Prentice-Hall, 1951).

Reiss, Ira, *Premarital Sexual Standards in America* (New York, Free Press, 1960).

Stokes, Walter, and Mace, David, "Premarital Sex Behavior," *Marriage and Family Living,* Vol. 15 (August, 1953), pp. 234–249.

Vincent, Clark, *Unmarried Mothers* (New York, Free Press, 1961).

QUESTIONS AND EXERCISES

1. Do you believe there has been a significant increase in premarital sex relations in the United States? If so, to what would you attribute this increase?

2. Oral contraceptives will soon be available to young people in a number of localities. What effect, if any, do you think this will have on premarital relations between the sexes? Indicate the basis for your answer.

3. There has been considerable controversy over the question of the responsibility of the home, church, and school regarding sex education. Write a paper indicating what to you represents a proper balance between the three institutions in this area. Justify your position logically.

4. Cavan (see cited reference) suggests five "yardsticks" to be used to measure desirable degrees of intimacy between young people. Read these and write a short paper indicating which one in your opinion is most desirable and why.

5. What is the rationale for having young men associate with prostitutes and women of easy virtue previous to marriage? What effect does this have on marital adjustment of the persons involved, if any?

6. Baber (Chapter 17) favors early marriage as a "solution" to premarital sex problems. How adequate is this suggestion in your estimation?

7. Make a survey of the attitudes of persons in your group regarding premarital sex matters. On the basis of the knowledge you have of the individuals involved indicate the relationship between attitudes and overt behavior.

8. Read and review Vincent's book on unwed motherhood. What generalizations in the book contradict common sense reasoning?

9. Read and critically analyze the positions taken by Walter Stokes and David Mace regarding premarital sex behavior. (See reference cited). Which man writes the soundest argument? Why?

10. In what types of situations do you believe in "forced" marriages and under what circumstances do you oppose them? Discuss.
11. Read the article by Levine and Pines in Harper's Magazine (cited). Do you agree with the proposals made by the authors as to the policies colleges should pursue in handling sex? Why or why not?
12. Is premarital sex a social problem in America or are there only particular personal problems facing specific individuals and couples? Discuss.
13. Do you agree that major changes would be required in the American social structure were premarital sex relations to become accepted as normal? If so, what would be the nature of these changes?

10

Engagement

Formal engagement has changed considerably through the centuries. Among the ancient Hebrews, betrothal meant virtually the first stage of marriage.[1] This was true also among the Germans of the pre-Christian period. There was some confusion as to whether betrothal meant intent to marry or the equivalent of marriage until well into the Christian epoch in Europe.[2] Eventually the conception of engagement as a binding pledge to marry, a contract, developed. This notion persisted in Western society and in America until recently. The implication was that engagement involved a special, public status and that the individuals concerned had thereby bowed out of the mate selection market. A legal buttressing was provided in the form of breach of promise suits. Since engagement involved a special condition recognized by the community, breaking of the contract involved loss of status, and damages were due to the harmed person.

Engagement is now considered as a final testing and planning period rather than a contract. At least sixteen states have abolished breach of promise suits and even where still legal the popularity of such suits is on the wane.[3] This trend would seem to be in line with the changing status of women and emphasis on compatibility of spouses.

GETTING ENGAGED

In spite of the fact that the engagement is no longer considered a contract, individuals who wish to protect themselves and their partners do not

[1] Willystine Goodsell, *A History of Marriage and The Family* (New York, Macmillan, 1934), p. 64.

[2] Manford Kuhn, "Thinking About Marriage," in Howard Becker and Reuben Hill (Eds.), *Family, Marriage, and Parenthood* (Boston, Heath, 1948), p. 280.

[3] Ray Baber, *Marriage and the Family* (New York, McGraw-Hill, 1953), p. 56.

175

enter it lightly. The stereotype of the suitor on his knees in the parlor "popping the question" to a very surprised maiden does not apply today, if it ever did in the past. If dating and courtship have been experienced the expectation of possible engagement has no doubt been entertained by both parties for a considerable length of time.

Some individuals drift into an engagement, as shown by the following case:

John and I started going steady during the latter part of our freshman year. I know now that this was a mistake. We had no real understanding and just kept going together for a year and a half. During the summer we would both date other people occasionally since we could not be together because of distance involved. During the latter part of our Junior year two of John's buddies gave pins to their sweethearts. Just before we left school in June John gave me his pin. I accepted it without any promise.

During our senior year I know we both considered breaking the relationship but couldn't bring ourselves to do it. We never talked much about the future together but confined our conversation to college affairs and gossip. Well you might know what happened. The first thing we knew spring had rolled around and engagements and forthcoming marriages were being announced throughout the senior dorms. One Saturday night John unexpectedly on my part took out a little box from his pocket containing a ring. He asked me if I'd like to be engaged. I didn't know what to say but finally I said I would like to be, and I took the ring. Everybody else was doing it and it was a lot of fun at the time. I don't know though, whether we'll ever get married or not.

This type of beginning for an engagement, though not unusual, has little to recommend it, although few would suggest going back to the formal proposal of former periods.

WHAT ARE THE FUNCTIONS OF ENGAGEMENT?

The functions of engagement depend quite clearly on the style of life of the particular group involved. Kuhn has suggested the following functions for engagement in our society:

1. It may serve to take one or both of the mates-to-be out of sexual "circulation" and to provide a period of exclusiveness—with or without sexual intimacy—prior to marriage. The equating of the exclusive right to the mate with property rights, which grows out of this period of exclusiveness, may and usually does have the effect of making the consequent marriage more solid and permanent.
2. The engagement period may constitute a trial marriage in which the two live together, testing mutually pleasing characteristics in an attempt to determine whether or not the match should be permanent.

3. The engagement period may be one of culturally enforced sexual abstinence, on the assumption that/this denial will build anticipation and intensify the loyalty between the pair.

4. The engagement may serve no purpose with respect to personality testing or sexual experimentation, existing merely as a concomitant of economic processes and readjustments respecting property arrangements, in which case the ensuing marital relation itself is usually more or less an epiphenomenon of property rights and property exchanges rather than a focal point of gratification, affectional response, and close-knit companionship.

5. Betrothal is often a way of celebrating or symbolizing the placing of a new pair relation in terms of an elaborate network of reciprocal family, clan, or gens, moiety, tribal, locality, or other group relations. As a required ceremony it provides the group with a means of scrutinizing new matches before they have become final and permanent.

6. By defining a new match in terms of status or rank, the engagement may operate to control mobility from one social class to another and to make apparent under what conditions "marrying upwards" in rank is permissible.[4]

Of major importance is final compatibility testing. For some couples the courtship period will involve elements of competition and bargaining, with each partner feeling the urge both to move forward and pull out of the relationship. In the more relaxed atmosphere of the engagement period which ideally prevails, the individuals can subject their relationship to the final test prior to marriage. Now is the last chance to check on compatibility of personality, temperament, standards, values, and habits. Specific items such as attitudes on birth control and family planning, relations with in-laws, education of children, religion, role of the wife outside the home, finances, and other matters of potential conflict may be thoroughly discussed and at least tentative adaptations to possible differences considered.

The engagement period is a time when pair unity may be developed to a higher degree than is ordinarily possible in courtship. The pair relationship begins to become more important than other relationships in case of a conflict of loyalties. Cruel as it may sometimes seem, the roommate, the coke partner, the pal (and perhaps even the sibling or parent) is often put on the periphery of the new little circle, for "three is a crowd." The individuals involved begin to think and act as a unit; they ideally develop a "we" feeling, a feeling of "oneness." This does not mean that each person completely submerges himself in the relationship. A crucial test of engagement (and of course of marriage) involves the ability of two people to develop a unified group within which each can feel free to function.

The engagement is a period of sharing and planning. Very private feelings and attitudes can now be shared. Even in very conservative groups the couple is allowed and expected to interact quite closely. Any bargaining or competitive attitudes which might have prevailed in previous periods now

---

[4] Manford Kuhn, "The Engagement: Thinking About Marriage," in Howard Becker and Reuben Hill (Eds.), *Family, Marriage, and Parenthood* (New York, Heath, 1955), pp. 280–281.

give way ideally to attitudes of mutual helpfulness and sharing. Increasingly the two persons will share joys and sorrows, recreation and work.

Specific plans in regard to the timing of marriage, the wedding service, and the honeymoon will be made during the engagement period. For the status-conscious, middle-class couple much planning is necessary to get a home started. Deciding on or locating a job, buying or renting a house, acquiring of furniture and other household necessities may involve much planning, work, and expense by someone. Custom does not prescribe which partner shall make which decision in regard to these plans, as would be true in some cultures. This sets the stage for possible confusion, bickering, and tension. There is vague agreement that the bride-to-be should exercise her preference in regard to basic household items and that the future husband's preference should be deferred to in connection with the location of the job and the house. In these days of the "democratic" family it would probably be well to lay down no hard and fast rules of premarital decision-making and planning. The couple will by a give-and-take, trial-and-error process develop satisfactory procedures.

In the testing, sharing, and planning process which goes on during engagement the two people will tend to develop habitual roles which eventually form a pattern of adjustment.[5] Since it is probable that many of the roles played during engagement will be played in similar fashion in marriage, role accommodation before marriage is particularly important. Especially in planning phases of engagement will important patterns of mutual adjustment be apparent. Dubious methods may be used to achieve dominance. One party may be unable to face up to real life problems. Or a person may find it difficult to work as a member of a team. Developing a set of interpersonal roles which form an acceptable level of accommodation would seem to be a prerequisite for marriage. Failure to do so should probably mean extension of the engagement or breaking up.

Smooth communication is of the essence if the above mentioned functions of engagement are to be achieved. The Swedish social scientist Karlsson stresses this factor.[6] He delineates three different problems of communication between partners: communication of feelings of admiration and respect; communication of love and tender emotions; and communication of role expectations.

LENGTH AND TYPES OF ENGAGEMENT

Just how long should formal engagement last? Both common sense and professional logic tell us that engagements may be too long or too short to achieve their ideal function. What is a happy medium?

[5] Baber, *op. cit.,* pp. 149–155.

[6] Georg Karlsson, *Adaptibility and Communication in Marriage* (Uppsala, Sweden, Almqvist and Wiksells, 1951), p. 133.

Most of the marital prediction studies have found that a relatively long engagement is associated with marital success. Terman and Landis found engagements "under six months" to be associated with poor marital adjustment. Burgess and Cottrell found that engagements of "under nine months" fell in the same category. Burgess and Cottrell and Terman "found two years and over" to be associated with excellent adjustment and Terman found "five years and over" to have the highest association with marital success.

TABLE 17

Length of Engagement in Relation to Marital Success, in Three Studies

Marital Success Level	Burgess-Cottrell [a] 526 Couples	Terman [b] 792 Couples	Landis [c] 544 Couples
Poor	No engagement, or under 9 months	Under 6 months	No engagement, or under 6 months
Good	9 months to 23 months	6 months to 4 years	6 months to 23 months
Excellent	2 years and up	5 years and up	2 years and up

[a] Ernest Burgess and Leonard Cottrell, *Predicting Success or Failure in Marriage* (Englewood Cliffs, N.J., Prentice-Hall, 1939), p. 168.
[b] Louis Terman, *Psychological Factors in Marital Happiness* (New York, McGraw-Hill, 1938), p. 199.
[c] Judson Landis, unpublished research.
SOURCE: Adapted from Judson T. and Mary G. Landis, *Building A Successful Marriage*, 2nd © 1953. Prentice-Hall, Inc.

Stroup found length of total courtship to be significantly associated with marital adjustment, although he did not focus on engagement as such. This is in line with the other marital prediction studies.[7]

Goode's study of divorced wives in Detroit bears on the question of engagement length and marital success. As can be seen in Table 18, the shorter the engagement the greater the chances for divorce. Over one-third of his sample was engaged less than two months.

Locke compared the length of engagement for his happily-married group with his divorced group sample. Significant differences appeared for both men and women, although the differences were higher for women than for men. Again the differences were in the expected direction. The happily married had the longer engagements.

These findings must be used with care. Very probably the short engagement category includes a number of couples whose prognosis for marital success would be poor on a number of other grounds too. Forced marriages, marriages of the immature, marriages of those who seek immedi-

[7] See Atlee L. Stroup, "Predicting Marital Success or Failure in an Urban Population," unpublished Ph.D. Thesis, The Ohio State University, Columbus, Ohio, 1950.

TABLE 18

*Length of Engagement for 425 Detroit
Divorced Couples*

Period of Engagement	Percentage of Couples
Never engaged	19.0
0 to 2 months	17.0
3 to 6 months	35.0
7 to 11 months	6.0
12 to 23 months	14.0
24 months and over	8.0
Not known	0.2
Total	99.2

SOURCE: Reprinted with permission of The Free Press of Glencoe from *Women in Divorce* by William Goode. Copyright © 1956 by The Free Press, A Corporation.

ate rather than long-run satisfactions, and other poor risks tend to swell the statistics of engagements under six months. A class factor is involved also. Among many lower economic groups formal engagement is not customary. Badly needed are studies which will be able to hold other factors constant in order to measure the effects of engagement as such. It is hardly necessary to suggest that such studies would be difficult to design and carry out.

It is logical that an engagement period can act as both a training period and as a screening device. Either outcome can be helpful to the parties concerned. Those whose engagements are too short miss out on both functions. On the other hand engagement can be too long. As Duvall and Hill put it an engagement ought to be

". . . long enough to act as a screening device to alienate and separate incompatible couples who would otherwise marry, only to separate painfully after some years of marriage. The answer to the question of length of engagement is given best, not as a number of months or years, but in terms of the indefinite "long enough." The engagement, then, should be *long enough* to perform the many functions of testing, discussing, learning, fighting and loving which underlie successful marriage." [8]

Waller and Hill delineate an interesting series of types of middle-class engagement based on two items, time-span and provision for becoming a unified pair. The types are as follows:

1. Short but sweet.
2. Short but brittle.
3. Long but separated.

[8] Evelyn Duvall and Reuben Hill, *When You Marry* (Boston, Heath, 1953), p. 89.

4. Long but inconclusive.

5. Long enough to verify readiness.[9]

These types deserve some comment. The *short but sweet* type, lasting typically from two to six months, does not allow time for the testing, sharing, planning, and other functions usually thought of as necessary for this period. Much time is spent in activity involving showers, teas, parties, and the like. Such activities often separate the two young people, both figuratively and literally, since they usually involve members of one sex only. One counselee recently complained bitterly to the author that the engagement period was serving to separate and alienate him from his bride-to-be. In this case, following a fairly long and successful courtship, the pair became engaged and an early wedding date was immediately set. Conditions necessitated geographic separation of the two until six weeks before the marriage date at which time both young people were to be in the girl's home town. During those last six weeks no less than 18 separate parties were held for the girl, all duly publicized in the local papers. A number of stag affairs were held for the boy by his fraternity brothers and other colleagues, at which many remarks relative to the forthcoming marriage were made. In general the young man seemed to gather from the remarks that he was to be pitied rather than congratulated for his interest in changing his status. The two young people managed with the help of relatives to get wedding announcements sent, an apartment rented, and wedding plans made. There was no time for activities and learning experiences which ideally engagement performs for many couples, a fact bitterly resented by the young man in the case. He seemed to feel that his fiancee's mother exercised undue control during the engagement period, but he was unable to do anything about it.

The second variety, *short but brittle,* lasts about the same length of time but ends with a break up rather than marriage. In this type of engagement one or both parties find that a future life as a member of a married pair does not look as attractive as it previously did. In the Burgess and Wallin study of one thousand engaged couples, almost half of the young women and one-third of the young men had previously had one or more engagements. One hundred and fifty of those couples subsequently broke the engagements current at the time of the study.[10] These engagements should not necessarily be considered nonfunctional. A balanced point of view would envision a "weeding out" process at work at the various stages leading to marriage. Perhaps it is better to have a brittle engagement than a brittle marriage.

The *long but separated* is a third type. Contingencies of service in the armed forces or other governmental branches, advanced academic or pro-

---

[9] Willard Waller and Reuben Hill, *The Family* (New York, Holt, Rinehart and Winston, 1951), pp. 221–224.

[10] Ernest Burgess and Paul Wallin, *Engagement and Marriage* (Philadelphia, Lippincott, 1953), Chapter 9.

fessional training, and other reasons may necessitate, or seem to necessitate, long postponement of marriage. While separation may or may not "make the heart grow fonder" it is doubtful that it performs any beneficial functions. Waller and Hill say, "couples so engaged have achieved adjustments mainly at the letter-writing level, which would be functional in marriage only to a couple in which the husband plans to become a salesman, lecturer, actor, or musician who expects to be away from home a large part of the year." [11] Judging from our few counseling cases of this type we are inclined to believe that it is difficult for close pair unity to develop in this type of relationship, except in a very superficial sense.

In the *long but inconclusive* type the couples somehow get hopelessly stalled. Economic considerations, deference to parental wishes, family responsibilities, and the like seem to be recurring causal factors in the drifting prolongation of engagement. In one such case both parties have widowed parents who stand in the way of the marriage. The "young people" are now passing through their middle thirties and both are committed not to marry until no longer responsible for the aged parents. Local skeptics are inclined to feel that the parties concerned will be ready for retirement and marriage at about the same time. It seems obvious that sexual and other strains would emerge in these types of relationships, and little can be said for them on any ground. It may well be that family loyalty is more important to a particular person than a projected marriage, or at least seems to be. The effect on the person and especially the engaged partner is often deleterious.

The long-enough-to-verify-readiness category appears to be by definition the most useful engagement. Typically lasting between six months and two years it involves a leisurely period during which many functions leading toward pair unity can be adequately performed. Quite often this is the type of engagement chosen by college couples who make commitments during the middle years of college and who expect to marry within a short period after graduation. This type has a number of advantages. Not suffering from the difficulties of too short engagements, it does not result in the premarital purgatory of the long but separated or inconclusive types. Instead the engagement is terminated when readiness has been verified and the couple psychologically is prepared to move into a marital relationship.

The quality of the relationship, however, rather than the time spent in the engagement period seems to be the crucial item.[12] If the engagement is too long for a particular couple the relationship may become stale, since, as the old saying has it, the couple are "dressed up with no place to go." Problems involving sex tension, morale, and boredom often appear if engagements are prolonged unduly. For socially intelligent people who have used the previous dating period for compatibility testing and who use the

---

[11] Waller and Hill, *op. cit.,* p. 223.
[12] Robert Harper, *Marriage,* (New York, Appleton-Century-Crofts, 1949), Chapter 6.

engagement for final testing, sharing, and planning, six months to a year and one-half should probably be the span within which their engagement will ideally fall.

AREAS OF DISAGREEMENT IN ENGAGEMENT

If the engagement period is to be a truly functional one, all will not be sweetness and light. For many couples disagreements will appear and tensions will mount. These will have to be worked out through accommodation, if the prognosis is to be good.

TABLE 19

Agreement of 1000 Engaged Men and Women in Selected Areas of Their Relationships

Extent of Agreement or Disagreement by Percent

Area	Reported by	Always Agree	Almost Always Agree	Disagree [a]	Other Reply [b]
Dates with	Men	70.0	21.9	5.7	2.4
one another	Women	70.6	22.4	4.6	2.4
Demonstration	Men	53.6	33.9	9.7	2.8
of affection	Women	53.3	32.2	11.7	2.8
Arrangements for	Men	50.9	31.1	11.9	6.1
your marriage	Women	53.2	29.0	11.7	6.1
Religious matters	Men	49.8	22.0	16.0	12.2
	Women	50.0	21.4	16.4	12.2
Table manners	Men	48.4	26.2	13.2	12.2
	Women	51.0	22.3	14.5	12.2
Matters of	Men	38.9	33.1	21.8	6.2
conventionality	Women	39.8	32.3	21.7	6.2
Matters of	Men	38.2	46.0	14.3	1.5
recreation	Women	44.9	41.2	12.4	1.5
Philosophy	Men	35.9	34.8	20.5	8.8
of life	Women	38.9	35.5	16.8	8.8
Money	Men	33.8	41.7	17.1	7.4
matters	Women	33.3	43.4	15.9	7.4
Ways of dealing	Men	32.8	33.5	24.6	9.1
with your families	Women	36.0	30.2	24.7	9.1
Friends	Men	29.6	46.2	22.0	2.2
	Women	32.0	45.9	19.9	2.2

[a] Occasionally or more frequently.
[b] Never discussed and a few cases where a given item was not checked.
SOURCE: Adapted from Burgess and Wallin, *Engagement and Marriage,* published by J. B. Lippincott, Philadelphia, Penna., copyright 1953.

Burgess and Wallin furnish us some interesting data on this point. They asked their sample members to check the extent of their agreement in eleven areas. Table 19 summarizes the results. There was some disagreement on every item listed, although complete disagreement percentages ran 25 percent or under.

It may be of interest to note that having dates with one another stands out as the area of most agreement. This seems logical in that this is almost a prerequisite of engagement, except perhaps when the couple is separated. Next come demonstration of affection, arrangements for marriage, religious matters, and table manners, with roughly one-half of the couples indicating complete agreement in these areas. From there the percentages drop to a low of about thirty percent for the item, friends. This latter probably reflects certain difficulties that are almost inevitable during the engagement period. It is impossible for all old friendships to be maintained at the same level that they once were. Yet group ties are difficult to cut. Disagreements at this stage of a pair relationship can be important. Discussion, even sharp disagreement, can clear the air and lead to a more satisfactory mode of accommodation. On the other hand, persistent disagreement will lead many to a reconsideration of the practicality of marriage.

BREAKING THE ENGAGEMENT

Sometimes it seems necessary that an engagement be broken. An increasing number of people are taking the position that it is much better to break an engagement than to move into an unfortunate marriage. If the engagement serves the purpose of a final testing period, it is inevitable that some relationships will not measure up to expectations. Some loss of face is involved, especially for the girl. Parents may feel a stigma if an engagement is broken, once it has been publicly announced. Yet they would suffer greater social embarrassment were their child to experience an unhappy marriage and divorce. It would seem gallant on the young man's part if he were to let the girl announce the separation, since she usually stands to lose a bit more in terms of future marital possibilities. Among student couples both parties often let it be known that he (or she) "dropped" the other partner. Presumably this serves to protect the egos of those involved.

In an unpublished study Landis found the following factors to rank high as specific reasons for broken engagements: (1) loss of interest, (2) separation, (3) incompatibility, (4) family background contrasts, (5) pressure from parents and friends.[13] Burgess and Wallin found relatively the same factors operating to disrupt engagements, with personality problems being an additional factor.

---

[13] Judson Landis, *Building a Successful Marriage* (Englewood Cliffs, N.J., Prentice-Hall, 1953), p. 185.

Those who are engaged may wish to make use of the engagement adjustment scale which follows. Based on the work of Burgess and Wallin with one thousand engaged couples, the test is devised to tap the level of accommodation of roles which has been reached for a particular couple. Readers should be cautioned that the scale was standardized for a middle-class urban group, and that it has no known validity for those from other backgrounds. Test scores should be considered suggestive rather than conclusive. The test should be especially valuable in uncovering areas of disagreement, potential or present, which might be further explored.

ENGAGEMENT ADJUSTMENT SCALE [14]

This is a method of appraising adjustment in engagement which has been devised and applied successfully by Burgess and Wallin of the University of Chicago in a study of one thousand engaged couples. Its merit is that you can compare yourselves as an engaged couple with these typical young people on whom the test was first standardized.

To maximize objectivity you should read the scale and score yourselves separately. When you have added up your score you have a score of adjustment from the man's perspective and one from the woman's perspective. Add your individual scores together and divide by two and you have your score as an engaged couple. You are now ready to compare your score with the couples studied by Burgess and Wallin. The upper quarter of these couples scored 163 or more. They are the best adjusted in engagement. The lower quarter scored 142 or below and are the least well adjusted in engagement. That means that half of the group ranged between scores of 142 and 163. If your score is in the lower grouping you should proceed cautiously because adjustment in engagement has been shown to be related to later adjustment in marriage.

	SCORE FOR EACH ITEM	
	Man	Woman
1. In leisure time do you prefer to be:		
"On the Go" all or most of the time	3	3
Stay at home all or most of the time	10	10
fifty-fifty reply or equivalent	5	5
Emphasis on stay at home	7	7
Man and woman differ	4	4

[14] Adapted for self-administration by Reuben Hill from the research scale presented in the report by Ernest W. Burgess and Paul Wallin, "Predicting Adjustment in Marriage from Adjustment in Engagement," *The American Journal of Sociology*, Vol. 49 (January, 1944), pp. 324–330. Used by permission of The University of Chicago Press, publishers of *The American Journal of Sociology*, and Reuben Hill.

	SCORE FOR EACH ITEM	
	Man	*Woman*
2. Do you and your fiance(e) engage in interests and activities together?		
All of them	10	10
Most of them	6	6
Some of them	2	3
Few or none	0	0
3. Do you confide in your fiance(e)?		
About everything	5	5
About most things	2	4
About some things	0	2
4. Does your fiance(e) confide in you?		
About everything	5	5
About most things	3	3
About some things	0	2
5. Frequency with which fiance(e) shows affection.		
Practically all the time	10	10
Very frequent	8	8
Occasionally	2	3
6. Are you satisfied with the amount of demonstration of affection?		
Both satisfied	7	7
Man satisfied, woman desires more	3	3
Woman satisfied, man desires more	3	3
Man satisfied, woman desires less	2	2
Woman satisfied, man desires less	2	2
One desires less, other desires more	1	1
Both desire more	4	4

7. Indicate your approximate agreement or disagreement with your fiance(e) on the following things. Do this for each item by putting a check in the column which shows your agreement or disagreement. To get the man's score add the scale points for each check he made, e.g. every "always agree" checked is worth eight (8) points, every "frequently disagree" three (3) points, etc. To get the woman's score add the scale points for the items she has checked.

(Score value) CHECK ONE COLUMN FOR EACH ITEM BELOW:	(8) Always agree	(6) Almost always agree	(5) Occasion- ally dis- agree	(3) Fre- quently disagree	(2) Almost always disagree	(0) Always disagree
Money matters	—	—	—	—	—	—
Matters of recreation	—	—	—	—	—	—
Religious matters	—	—	—	—	—	—
Demonstration of affection	—	—	—	—	—	—
Friends	—	—	—	—	—	—
Arrangements for your marriage	—	—	—	—	—	—
Dates with each other	—	—	—	—	—	—
Table Manners	—	—	—	—	—	—
Matters of conventionality	—	—	—	—	—	—
Philosophy of life	—	—	—	—	—	—
Ways of dealing with your family	—	—	—	—	—	—

	SCORE FOR EACH ITEM	
	Man	*Woman*
8. Do you ever wish you had not become en- gaged?		
Never	10	10
Once	5	5
Occasionally	1	1
Frequently	0	0
9. Have you ever contemplated breaking your engagement?		
Never	10	10
Once	5	5
Occasionally	1	1
Frequently	0	0
10. What things annoy you about your engage- ment? List them on a scratch pad and count them.		
Nothing listed	10	10
One thing mentioned	7	7
Two things	1	1
Three things	0	0
If "its length" only is mentioned	9	9
If "being separated" is cited	8	8

	SCORE FOR EACH ITEM	
	Man	*Woman*

11. What things does your fiance(e) do that you do not like? List them on a scratch pad and count them.

	Man	Woman
None	7	7
One thing mentioned	5	5
Two things mentioned	1	1
Three or more	0	0

12. Has your steady relationship with your fiance(e) ever been broken off temporarily?

	Man	Woman
Never	10	10
Once	5	5
Twice	2	2
Three or more times	0	0

13. If you could, what things would you change in your fiance(e)? List them on a scratch pad checking the following points and then count them: (a) in physical condition or appearance; (b) in mental or temperamental or personality characteristics; (c) in ideas; (d) in personal habits; (e) in any other way.

	Man	Woman
No change desires	10	10
One change mentioned	8	8
Two changes mentioned	6	6
Three changes mentioned	4	4
Four changes mentioned	2	2
Five changes mentioned	0	0

14. If you could, what things would you change in yourself following the same outline? List them on a scratch pad and count them:

	Man	Woman
No change desires	10	10
One change	8	8
Two changes	6	6
Three changes	4	4
Four changes	2	2
Five changes	0	0

PREMARITAL COUNSELING

At various points it has been suggested that individual partners or the couple may wish to turn to a counselor for aid in solving problems. The same suggestion holds for those who have problems at the engagement stage. Even couples who have no pressing problems of which they are conscious may find it profitable to consult a marriage counselor for some general preparation for marriage. At The Marriage Council of Philadelphia, for example, a program of premarital counseling has been developed. Usually lasting for one or two interviews, the counseling period is devoted to specific items in regard to the particular couple and also to general preparation for marriage.

A thorough physical examination preceding marriage is to be highly recommended. In the majority of cases people appear for these examinations just before the marriage is to take place. It would be better to allow a period of three or four months before the wedding in order to handle contingencies that might arise. A physician skilled in matters of heredity, sexual adjustment, contraception, organic development, and other such things is indispensable. A blood test to check for transmittable venereal disease is now a standard legal requirement in many states. The needs of some couples go well beyond this and may involve checks made for future difficulty pertaining to the Rh factor, hereditary hemophelia, and other troublesome matters.

Duvall and Hill propose the following as ideally being included in a comprehensive premarital physical examination:

Pre-Marital Physical Examination

1. Medical history including the previous sex history of both the man and the woman, possible hereditary problems in either line, and the menstrual history of the woman.
2. Clarification of any item or questions one or both members of the couple bring in, along with any that arise during the consultation. Selected books may be recommended as helpful.
3. Brief review of the anatomy and physiology of both male and female genital systems in the human (with charts or films if desired).
4. General physical examination, including blood and urine studies, heart, lung, and pelvic conditions, and search for any possible pathologies in both the man and the woman.
5. Pelvic examination of the woman with special attention to the condition of the vaginal orifice and the adequacy of the vagina for sexual intercourse.
6. Possible instruction in hymen dilation, where indicated and compatible with the attitudes of the couple.
7. Examination of the clitoris, and plan for freeing the clitoris as indicated.
8. Laboratory study of cultures from vagina and cervix with especial concern for the presence of gonorrheal infection, with immediate program of treatment if tests are positive.
9. Examination of the male genitalia with laboratory tests and a program of treatment for possible infection. (Sperm count and motility may be included if desired.)

10. Blood tests for the detection of syphilis in both individuals. Positive findings are followed at once by adequate treatment. No evidence of the disease is the clean bill of health required in most states before the license is issued.
11. Discussion of plans for contraception, as requested, with particular reference to the initial period of the marriage and the religious factors that may be pertinent: (a) plan for plotting the "safe period" if rhythm method is to be used, or (b) fitting a diaphragm if religious and personal factors allow it.
12. Specific advice on vagina lubricants and coital procedures as requested and indicated.[15]

It would be desirable if all couples were able to obtain this type of examination, but it is probably only idealistic to expect it at present.

Along with the physical examination and some general marriage counseling, the couple expecting to be married by a clergyman should make this known well in advance of the expected date. Many ministers now wish to have at least one or two sessions with the couple previous to the marriage ceremony. They often wish to explore the couple's religious orientation and their readiness to marry as well as to make specific wedding arrangements. Some religious leaders are now prepared to offer more intensive counseling also, if such is desired.

SELECTED READINGS

Becker, Howard and Hill, Reuben (Eds.), *Family, Marriage, and Parenthood* (Boston, Heath, 1955), Chapter 9.

Bernard, Jessie, Buchanan, Helen and Smith, William, *Dating, Mating, and Marriage* (Cleveland, Howard Allen, 1958), Chapters 4 and 5.

Blood, Robert O., *Marriage* (New York, Free Press, 1962), Chapter 7.

Bossard, James, "The Engagement Ring—A Changing Symbol," *The New York Times Magazine Section* (September 14, 1958), p. 32.

Burgess, Ernest and Wallin, Paul, *Engagement and Marriage* (Philadelphia, Lippincott, 1955), Chapters 5–11.

Cavan, Ruth, *Marriage and Family in the Modern World* (New York, Crowell, 1960), Chapter 7.

Duvall, Evelyn and Hill, Reuben, *Being Married* (Boston, Heath, 1960), Chapter 6.

Koller, Marvin, "Some Changes in Courtship Behavior in Three Generations of Ohio Women," *American Sociological Review*, Vol. 16 (June, 1951), pp. 366–370.

Locke, Harvey, *Predicting Adjustment in Marriage: A Comparison of a Divorced and Happily Married Group* (New York, Holt, Rinehart and Winston, 1951), Chapter 12.

[15] Duvall and Hill, *op. cit.,* p. 123.

Landis, Paul, *Making the Most of Marriage* (New York, Appleton-Century-Crofts, 1964), Chapters 18 and 19.

Le Masters, Ersel, *Modern Courtship and Marriage* (New York, Macmillan, 1957), Chapter 8.

Mace, David, *Marriage* (Garden City, N.Y., Doubleday, 1952), Chapter 2.

Martinson, Floyd, *Marriage and the American Ideal* (New York, Dodd, Mead, 1960), Chapters 12 and 13.

Mudd, Emily H., *The Practice of Marriage Counseling* (New York, Association Press, 1951), Chapters 8–10.

Peterson, James, *Education for Marriage* (New York, Scribner, 1964), Chapter 11.

Popenoe, Paul, "A Study of 738 Elopements," *American Sociological Review* (February, 1938), pp. 47–53.

Simpson, George, *People in Families* (New York, Crowell, 1960), Chapter 5.

Skidmore, Rex, and Cannon, Anton, *Building Your Marriage* (New York, Harper & Row, 1958), Chapter 13.

Sussman, Marvin, and Vincent, Clark (Co-Eds.), Special Issue, "American Adolescents in the Mid-Sixties," *Journal of Marriage and the Family,* Vol. 27 (May, 1965).

Waller, Willard, and Hill, Reuben, *The Family* (New York, Holt, Rinehart and Winston, 1951), Chapters 12 and 13.

QUESTIONS AND EXERCISES

1. Engagement is considered by some to be a period of reality testing in which pretense is dropped and the individuals concerned get to know each other "as they really are." How well is this function performed for the average couple?

2. Why do people tend to resist premarital counseling? Is this deleterious in all cases?

3. Just what of one's past, including experience with the opposite sex, should be discussed with the partner during the engagement period?

4. Where it is possible to do so without hurting feelings or violating confidence, interview some friends or acquaintances who have experienced broken engagements.

   Include the following areas:

   (a) How to break off an engagement with a minimum of trauma and frustration.

   (b) How to adapt socially and emotionally to a broken engagement.

   (c) Circumstances under which an engagement could or should be broken.

5. How long do you think engagements should normally last? Discuss.

6. Read Popenoe's article on elopements. Then write a short paper on motivations leading to elopement. (Keep in mind the period in which the study took place.)

7. Write a case history of a person who has been involved in a number of broken engagements. How do you explain this person's behavior?

8. John and Mary are engaged. Both sets of parents oppose their marriage. They feel that they are well matched but have occasional doubts. What should they do under the circumstances?

9. Do a study of the patterns and functions of engagement in your hometown for the college and noncollege group. Do any major differences appear?

10. Making use of anthropological materials, write a paper on patterns and functions of engagement or its equivalent in 12 cultures.

11. In earlier periods engagements were much more binding on the parties concerned than they are today. Is our present system better or worse? Why?

12. George and Jane attend the same college and become engaged. George is to attend graduate school at the state university while Jane remains behind to finish her senior year, after which the couple plans to marry. What are the pros and cons of either or both being allowed to date while they are separated?

11

Legal and Social Preliminaries to Marriage

Before the couple makes specific plans for marriage they would be well advised to study some of the legal and religious requirements and customs which will affect them. These involve state laws, church policies, and such general customs as the wedding and the honeymoon.

THE STATE AND MARRIAGE

The state as the legal representative of society has assumed that the family is a basic social unit and that its stability and permanence are to be protected at least to a minimum degree.[1] By legislation and through the judicial system the state undertakes to determine conditions for the entrance into marriage and for appropriate behavior within the marriage and family system. It does not as a rule attempt to set ultimate levels of moral behavior to which individuals are to conform. These are left to other institutions. The state sets minimum standards in the interest of basic order and stability. It is assumed that through the influence of the mores and the operation of general social ideals, many or perhaps most people would live up to or above the minimum legally required patterns.

In America each state or territory operates with separate jurisdiction in regard to marriage and family law. There exist both common general elements of law and substantial diversity. The laws reflect both the cultural heritage of the people in a given area and the contingencies existing (at least in the minds of legislators) at the particular time when the legislative action was taken. In general it appears that the state is interested in maintaining

[1] Sarah Knox, *The Family and the Law* (Chapel Hill, University of North Carolina Press, 1941), p. 26.

and supporting monogamous marriage, assuring "legitimacy of issue," and protecting property and inheritance rights of the individuals involved.

With the above as general background we will proceed to a discussion of some typical regulations of marriage appearing in the various jurisdictions. Attention is called to Table 20 for a digest of marriage laws in tabular form as they obtain as of 1963.

IS MARRIAGE A CONTRACT?

The question is often raised as to whether or not marriage is a contract. In the eyes of the law it is a status relationship rather than a civil contract.[2] Marriage resembles other contracts to the extent that there must be mutual consent, the parties must be competent and eligible to enter the arrrangement, and a prescribed form must be met. On the other hand, and importantly, marriage commits the parties involved to a new status. General privileges and duties are prescribed by law as against the ordinary contract in which the privileges and duties of the parties involved must be spelled out in the agreement. Once the marriage is consummated, a marital relationship is legally recognized and cannot be dissolved by mutual consent of the parties as in ordinary contracts. Only the state, through the courts and under conditions set up by legislatures, can nullify a marriage. No one can give a spouse a divorce unless and until a court so rules. Further, in the ordinary contract the persons involved must have reached their majority. This is not true regarding marriage.

Age Requirements

Under common law boys could marry at fourteen and girls at twelve. This corresponds with the onset of puberty as defined by early Hebrew tradition and by Roman law. Presently it would presumably apply only in Washington, all other states having moved to a higher age requirement. The states vary considerably in their age requirements as can be seen in Table 20. In general, however, the age of consent for the boy is eighteen and for the girl is sixteen. Very typically parental consent is required unless the boy is twenty-one and the girl is eighteen. However in many states age limitations may be waived at the discretion of the court. The cause most often used for waiver is pregnancy of the girl. It is rather generally held that such a policy is superior to that of allowing an illegitimate child to be born, although there is by no means full agreement on this point.[3] If the girl is under the age of consent for sex relations a crime has ordinarily been com-

[2] *Ibid.*
[3] *Ibid.*

TABLE 20
American Marriage Laws
As of July 1, 1963

State or other jurisdiction	Age at which marriage can be contracted with parental consent		Age below which parental consent is required		Common-law marriage recognized	Physical examination and blood test for male and female		Waiting period	
	Male	Female	Male	Female		Maximum period between examination and issuance of marriage license	Scope of medical examination	Before issuance of license	After issuance of license
Alabama	17	14	21	18	★	30 da.	(a)	……	……
Alaska	18(b)	16(b)	21	18	……	30 da.	(a)	3 da.	……
Arizona	18(b)	16(b)	21	18	……	30 da.	(a)	……	……
Arkansas	18(b)	16(b)	21	18	……	30 da.	(a)	3 da.	……
California	18(c, d)	16(c, d)	21	18	……	30 da.	(a)	……	……
Colorado	16(c)	16(c)	21	18	★	30 da.	(a)	……	……
Connecticut	16(c)	16(c)	21	21	……	40 da.	(a)	4 da.	……
Delaware	18(b)	16(b)	21	18	★★	30 da.	(a)	……	(e)
Florida	18(b, d)	16(b, d)	21	21	★★	30 da.	(a)	3 da.	……
Georgia	18(b, f)	16(b, f)	21(f)	21(f)	★★	30 da.	(a)	3 da.(g)	……
Hawaii	18	16(c)	20	20	……	30 da.	(a)	3 da.	……
Idaho	15	15(c)	18	18	★	30 da.	(a)	……	……
Illinois	18	16	21	18	……	15 da.	(a)	……	……
Indiana	18(b)	16(b)	21	18	……	30 da.	(a)	3 da.	……
Iowa	18(b)	16(b)	21	18	★★	20 da.	(a)	……	……
Kansas	18(c)	16(c)	21	18	★★	30 da.	(a, h)	3 da.	……
Kentucky	18(b)	16(b)	21	21	……	15 da.	(a)	3 da.	……
Louisiana	18(c)	16(c)	21	21	……	10 da.	(a)	……	72 hrs.
Maine	16(c)	16(c)	21	18	……	30 da.	(a)	5 da.	……
Maryland	18(b)	16(b)	21	18	……	……	……	48 hrs.	……

TABLE 20 (cont.)

American Marriage Laws
As of July 1, 1963

| State or other jurisdiction | Age at which marriage can be contracted with parental consent | | Age below which parental consent is required | | Common-law marriage recognized | Physical examination and blood test for male and female | | Waiting period | |
	Male	Female	Male	Female		Maximum period between examination and issuance of marriage license	Scope of medical examination	Before issuance of license	After issuance of license
Massachusetts	18(c)	16(c)	21	18	.....	30 da.	(a)	3 da.	.....
Michigan	(i)	16(b)	18	18	.....	30 da.	(a)	3 da.	.....
Minnesota	18(d)	16(j)	21	18	.....	.....	.....	5 da.	.....
Mississippi	17(c)	15(c)	21	21	.....	30 da.	(a)	3 da.	.....
Missouri	15(c)	15(c)	21	18	.....	15 da.	(a)	3 da.	.....
Montana	18(c)	16(c)	21	18	★	20 da.	(a)	5 da.	.....
Nebraska	18(b)	16(b)	21	21	.....	30 da.	(a)	.....	.....
Nevada	18(c)	16(c)	21	18	.....	.....	.....	.....	.....
New Hampshire	(k)	(k)	20	18	.....	30 da.	(a)	5 da.	.....
New Jersey	18(c)	16(c)	21	18	.....	30 da.	(a)	72 hrs.	.....
New Mexico	18(b)	16(b)	21	18	.....	30 da.	(a)	.....	.....
New York	16	16(c)	21	18	.....	30 da.	(a)	(n)	24 hrs. (l)
North Carolina	16	16(b)	18	18	.....	30 da.	(m)	.....	.....
North Dakota	18	15	21	18	★	30 da.	(o)	.....	.....
Ohio	18(b)	16(b)	21	21	★	30 da.	(a)	5 da.	.....
Oklahoma	18(b)	15(b)	21	18	★	30 da.	(a)	(p)	.....
Oregon	18	15	21	18	★	30 da.(q)	(r)	7 da.	.....
Pennsylvania	16(c)	16(c)	21	21	★	30 da.	(a)	3 da.	.....
Rhode Island	18(c)	16(c)	21	21	★	40 da.	(s)	24 hrs.	(t)
South Carolina	16(b)	14(b)	18	18	★	.....	.....	.....	.....

South Dakota ..	18(b)	21	16(b)	18	......	(a)	20 da.	......
Tennessee	16(c)	21	16(c)	21	......	(a)	30 da.	3 da.(u)
Texas	16	21	14	18	★	(a)	15 da.	(p)
Utah	16(d)	21	14(d)	18	......	(a)	30 da.	......
Vermont	18(c)	21	16(c)	18	......	(a)	30 da.	5 da.
Virginia	18(b, d)	21	16(b, d)	21	......	(a)	30 da.	......
Washington	17(c)	21	17(c)	18	......	(o)		3 da.
West Virginia	18(d)	21	16(d)	21	......	(a)	30 da.	3 da.
Wisconsin	18	21	16	18	......	(a)	20 da.	5 da.
Wyoming	18	21	16	21	......	(a)	30 da.	......
Dist. of Columbia	18(d)	21	16(d)	18	★		......	3 da.

* Prepared by the Women's Bureau, United States Department of Labor for the *Book of the States*, Council of State Governments (Chicago, 1965), p. 439.

★ Indicates common-law marriage recognized.

(a) Venereal diseases.

(b) Statute establishes procedure whereby younger parties may obtain license in case of pregnancy or birth of a child.

(c) In special circumstances statute establishes procedure whereby younger parties may obtain license.

(d) Parental consent is not required if minor was previously married.

(e) Residents, 24 hours; non-residents, 96 hours.

(f) If parties are under 21, notice must be posted unless parent of female consents in person, but if female is under 18, consent of parent is required.

(g) Unless parties are 21 years or more, or female is pregnant.

(h) Feeblemindedness.

(i) No provision in law for parental consent for males.

(j) Parental consent and permission of judge required.

(k) Below age of consent parties need parental consent and permission of judge.

(l) Marriage may not be solemnized within 3 days from date on which specimen for serological test was taken.

(m) Subject to uncontrolled epileptic attacks, idiocy, imbecility, mental defectiveness, unsound mind, infectious tuberculosis and venereal diseases.

(n) 48 hours if both are non-residents.

(o) Feeblemindedness, imbecility, insanity, chronic alcoholism and venereal diseases. (Also in Washington, advanced tuberculosis, and, if male, contagious venereal disease.)

(p) 3 days if one or both parties are below the age for marriage without parental consent.

(q) Time limit between date of examination and expiration of marriage license.

(r) Venereal diseases, feeblemindedness, mental illness, drug addiction and chronic alcoholism.

(s) Infectious tuberculosis and venereal diseases.

(t) If female is non-resident, must complete and sign license 5 days prior to marriage.

(u) Does not apply when parties are over 21 years of age.

mitted and the man could be prosecuted. Marriage typically relieves the man of liability to prosecution.

Common Law Marriages

As we have previously shown, many common people in Europe resisted attempts to have marriage controlled by church or state. Informal marriages by common law have a long tradition. Finally banned by church and state in the "old country" they were revived on the American frontier. Eventually a number of states declared such marriages null and void. Some others have not seen fit to do so, and the courts have been quite consistent in their interpretation of this point. If a state does not specifically declare common law marriages to be invalid they are held to be valid if they can be proven to meet certain requirements even though the laws of the state regarding statutory marriage are violated.[4] The state of Ohio may be used as an example. The Ohio Code specifies that before a marriage license can be issued a blood test is required, and before a marriage license is granted a period of five days must elapse.[5] However, the courts of Ohio have consistently recognized common law marriages even though there has been no blood test, no minister or justice officiating, no license, and no waiting period.[6] It seems ludicrous that a state should set up certain machinery leading to marriage and then permit people to bypass it at will and without penalty. [To indicate how complicated conditions can sometimes become, the case of Kentucky may be cited.] Until 1866 Kentucky recognized marriages by common law.[7] Informal marriages, if entered after that date, were not to be recognized. However, both by court decision and by statute such marriages are valid for certain specified purposes of the Workmen's Compensation Act. Both for the welfare of the individuals involved and of the general society it would appear that the status "now you're married, now you're not" is so ambiguous that further clarification would be in order. Yet at the present time the exact status of a common law marriage is open to some question.[8] Further there is always the possibility that a court will not

---

[4] See *Common Law Marriages,* Los Angeles Law Library Publication (December, 1959) for an analysis of the statutes regarding common law in the various states.

[5] See Ohio Revised Code Annotated (1958) Chapter 3101 which deals with marriage. Section 3101.05 refers to medical requirements, Sections 3101.06 to licensing, and Section 3101.08 to solemnization requirements.

[6] See Johnson v. Wohlford, 11705.136, 157 N.E. 385 (1927); or Lynch v. Romas, 740.1 Al, 139 N.E. 2nd 352 (1956).

[7] See Kentucky Revised Statutes annotated (1959) Section 402.020 where common law marriage is prohibited. However, section 342.080 gives limited recognition for purposes of Workmen's Compensation cases..

[8] To illustrate the confusion Common Law Marriages, *op. cit.,* p. 7 contains the following notations regarding New Hampshire:

(1) New Hampshire Revised Statutes (1955) Sec. 457:39 declaring that persons cohabiting and acknowledging each other as husband and wife and generally reputed to be such for the period of three years shall be deemed legally married.

(2) Common law marriages are not recognized, Dunbarton v. Franklin, 19 N.H. 257

recognize a particular relationship as being valid. If it does not the possibility of illegitimacy of children and/or prosecution for fornication are always in the offing. Couples who are concerned with order and stability will wish to comply with legal regulations under ordinary circumstances.[9]

Marrying Too Close

Under the common law certain types of marriages were forbidden on the basis of consanguinity or affinity. The first refers to relationship by blood, the second by marriage. The origin of these prohibitions goes back to the Old Testament days. In England the ecclesiastical courts at the time of Henry VIII forbade the marriage of persons closer than first cousins. This line is generally adhered to in all jurisdictions of the United States. Complications arise regarding half siblings, half nieces and nephews. It is at the line of first cousins that the law begins to vary. Thirty-two of our states prohibit marriages between first cousins, and nine prohibit marriages of first cousins once removed or of second cousins.[10] Certain states make clear their opposition to any relationship suggestive of incest. This is illustrated by the law of Indiana. Prohibition extends to grandaunt, grandniece, first cousin once removed, granduncle and grandnephew.

Prohibitions of marriage between certain affinal kin also exist in the various jurisdictions. Ecclesiastical law spelled out prohibitions against a man marrying the following: (1) grandfather's wife, (2) wife's grandmother, (3) father's brother's wife, (4) mother's brother's wife, (5) wife's father's sister, (6) wife's mother's sister, (7) stepmother, (8) mother-in-law, and (9) wife's daughter by previous marriage. A woman could not marry persons of the opposite sex of the corresponding categories. The effect of the ecclesiastical tradition can be clearly seen in a perusal of the various state laws, although some strange inconsistencies do appear.

(1848), but the cohabitation statute, Supra, substantially in force since 1842, gives limited recognition to such marriages under certain and strict conditions stated therein, Delisle v. Smalley, 95 N.H. 314, 63 A. 2nd 240 (1949). We take this to mean that certain common law marriages were, or better could have been, if brought to the attention of officials, granted recognition, but that others were not. In 1955 the law was apparently liberalized to allow a larger proportion of common law relationships to be recognized. Yet most allegedly authoritative sources insist that New Hampshire *does not* recognize common law marriage. Since the question of legal recognition of a marriage is no small matter when it comes to legitimacy of children, inheritance rights, rights of widows under social security, etc., individuals personally concerned are advised to obtain legal counsel in order to clarify the laws of the particular state involved.

[9] Professor Donald Irish has suggested that in certain cultures individuals who cannot afford to be married in minimum style (with the equivalent of at least an upper lower or lower middle-class wedding and start in marriage) will tend to live in *consensual* or nonrecognized unions. He doubts that such motivation is as common in America as it is elsewhere but believes it is not altogether lacking, especially among southern Negroes.

[10] Francis Kuchler, *The Laws of Marriage and Divorce Simplified* (Dobbs Ferry, N.Y., Oceana Publications, 1961), pp. 23–26.

Considerable debate surrounds the whole question of prohibition of marriage between certain affinal kin. It has been assumed by many that the prohibitions were based on genetic considerations and therefore that such laws were ridiculous. The evidence is against this position; the concern has been with family stability. Rightly or wrongly it has been held that the incest taboos that are widely held in the mores and implemented by law are socially beneficial. Murdock writes:

A sexual prohibition that demonstrably serves to bulwark the family must be regarded as scientifically acceptable, even though it is biologically quite restrictive. As a matter of fact, such prohibitions are nearly as universal as the family itself.

Foremost among them are the incest taboos. It may surprise some of you to learn that there is not a single society among the thousands of which we have record—not even the most backward in culture—that does not impose upon its members a strong prohibition of both sexual intercourse and marriage between mother and son, father and daughter, and brother and sister. Individual instances of the violation of these taboos do occur in many if not most societies, but they merely reflect the strength of the sex drive. . . . These prohibitions are commonly supported by quite irrational beliefs, such as our own that the offspring of near relatives are prone to hereditary defects, but the taboos themselves have a high social utility. They inhibit sexual rivalry and jealousy within the family, which might seriously interfere with the adequate performance of the latter's important social functions, and by compelling out-marriage they bind the families of the larger society to one another by ramifying kinship ties. Comparative anthropology warns us not to relax our incest taboos, and even suggests that we not object too strongly to the irrational beliefs that support them.[11]

Murdock's reference is specifically to incest but the general principle to which he refers would seem to apply to any close relationship of either blood or marriage.

Present laws pertaining to consanguinity and affinity can be sharply attacked on two counts. First, they were originally devised when the large family existed in close-knit fashion. Relationships that would cause jealousy and disunity in that type of system are not as probable in the conjugal type family of today. Second, the wide variation in the laws does not seem reasonable. If we wish to draw lines it would seem that a general movement to wipe out the gross inconsistencies would be in order.

The Annulment of Marriage

It stands to reason that if states set up regulations regarding the entrance into marriage some people are going to marry without satisfying all

---

[11] George Murdock, "Sexual Behavior: What Is Acceptable," *Journal of Social Hygiene,* Vol. 36 (1950), pp. 1–31; reprinted in Landis, Judson and Landis, Mary, *Readings in Marriage and the Family* (Englewood Cliffs, N.J., Prentice-Hall, 1952), p. 405.

the legal provisions. What is the legal status of such marriages? While generalizations can be misleading at this point, it is clear that two categories, void and voidable marriages appear in every jurisdiction.[12] A *void* marriage is one which was never valid because it, by definition, could not from its inception be valid. In general, marriages which violate laws regarding incest, miscegenation, bigamy, and the like fall into this class. In the case of *voidable* marriage, action must be taken by the courts in regard to the legal provisions which were not fully met. Until the court annuls such a marriage by declaring it null and void it is a legal marriage, even though it is, or at least was, voidable. The most common categories found in the various states are: (1) fraud or duress used to obtain consent, (2) underage, or lack of parental consent, and (3) mental incapacity or the inability to perceive the meaning or requirements of marriage, or physical inability to perform sexually.

Again from the legal point of view a marriage may be voidable but valid. Suppose an Ohio couple, both eighteen, go to Illinois and indicate to the registrar that the boy is twenty-one, while the girl correctly indicates her age as eighteen; a license is issued after a clear blood test report and the couple is married by a qualified justice of the peace. Could the boy after a few days have a change of heart and back out of the marriage? Could he inform his spouse that he has had an interesting weekend but that he would now admit to lying about his age and obtain an annulment? He could try. It can be said that most judges become concerned with public policy at this point. Under ordinary circumstances they would hesitate to annul this marriage, even though the qualifications were not fully met. Even an irate parent charging that his consent was not obtained might find the court out of sympathy with his plea.

It must be made clear that where conditions are not fully met either party or an outside party can initiate suit for annulment. In general in cases of underage, marriages are theoretically voidable until the parties both are of the required age, at which time they are no longer voidable. However, in some fourteen or fifteen states a marriage may not be annulled after the couple have lived together, even if fraud has been perpetrated or if all requirements were not met.

Miscegenetic Prohibitions

At the present time nineteen states prohibit marriages between Negroes and whites. Thirteen states have laws against whites marrying Orientals. Marriages between those to whom it is forbidden is ordinarily punishable by fine and the marriages are usually void on their face. As might be expected most of the states which prohibit miscegenation are in the South, Southwest, or far West. However, Nebraska, Colorado, Indiana, the

---

[12] Kuchler, *op. cit.,* Introduction.

Dakotas, Utah, and Wyoming also have or have had miscegenation statutes. The constitutionality of these laws may be open to question in the future. The California state supreme court ruled in 1948 that the law in that state was unconstitutional. What the U.S. Supreme Court would do with such a case has not yet been ascertained, but the probabilities are strong that it would take the same position that the California court took.[13]

Still to be fully decided is the question of the unqualified right of the individual to marry, regardless of character, background, or genetic makeup. About half of the fifty-one American jurisdictions forbid marriage to those who are mentally incapacitated. The terms used are not psychiatrically precise. Terms such as lunatic, unstable mind, feebleminded, and insane appear in the various state laws. Part of the confusion reflects the inadequacy of definitions of psychosis and mental deficiency. However, the intent is to discourage marriage among those who could not perceive responsibilities. In other cases the intent was eugenic.

Besides the above prohibitions, laws against the marriage of epileptics, those with venereal disease, and persons with certain other malfunctions appear in some states. In many cases the persons involved are required to indicate any deficiency at the time of application for license. Some prohibited marriages are void if consummated, others are only voidable. Since action is not always brought in the latter case, such marriages often exist even though forbidden by strict interpretation of the law.

THE RED TAPE OF MARRIAGE

All fifty-one American jurisdictions require as typical procedure that those who marry obtain a license and observe other stipulated conditions. The license is issued by the office of the county clerk of courts or the judge. This license is a permit to marry and in most states becomes invalid after a specified period. Further, there is no valid marriage until the various provisions are met including a recording of the marriage. Some three-fifths of the states require a waiting period before the marriage can be solemnized. In some cases this waiting period refers to the time between the date of the blood test and the wedding ceremony. In others the period is between the date of application for the license and its issuance. (See Table 20.)

The logic behind the required waiting period is clear. Hasty marriages are made less possible by this device. In a number of states the waiting period is longer for out-of-state residents. On the other hand, some states have no waiting period whatsoever. Those that do often give the judge the power to waive the requirement at his discretion. When pregnancy is alleged

[13] As of this writing, February, 1966, the U.S. Supreme Court has not directly dealt with the question of the constitutionality of miscegenation laws.

waiver is often granted, and this is common practice during wartime periods. If waiver is granted too readily the law is essentially ineffective.

Most states now require serological tests for venereal disease close to the time of the marriage date. (See Table 20.) These so-called "blood test" laws have become popular within the last few decades. Again they may be waived for "good cause." Further in some states applicants for marriage are only advised that they are carriers of disease, and are not prohibited from marrying. These laws would appear to serve a general purpose, however minimal their effect may be.

Ceremony

Marriages may be performed by either religious functionaries or by civil authorities in all but a few of our jurisdictions. The latter require a religious officiant to perform the marriage. In either type of marriage people must be present who will witness to the marriage. The actual form of the ceremony itself is of little interest to the state. The traditional promise to obey on the part of the girl may be waived without fear of any judicial eyebrows being lifted. The important part of the ceremony is the assent or commitment which each party gives before witnesses, as far as the state is concerned. The young man's mumbled "I do" may be well nigh inaudible, but if the witnesses and the bride are sure that he has so spoken, he is married.

About one-fourth of all couples are married by a civil officer, who is typically a judge or justice of the peace. It is of interest that the early Puritan zeal for civil ceremony has waned to the point where many nonreligious persons prefer a religious ceremony. The businesslike, cold efficiency of the civil ceremony no doubt alienates many couples. Further, the religious ceremony seems to indicate greater status even for those not known for their personal piety or devotion.

SECRET MARRIAGES AND ELOPEMENTS

Since marriage involves a new, publicly recognized status it follows that secret weddings and elopements while quite legal are often considered unorthodox. Very few studies have been published bearing on either type of marriage. Ricards, however, has reported on a study of 8,122 marriage licenses issued between 1920 and 1956 in Isabella City, Michigan.[14] He found that 4.75 percent of these licenses were issued in secret. Michigan is unique in that a license can be obtained from a probate judge without publicity. The license is legally recorded but no publicity is given to its issuance.

Ricards found that a number of secret marriages involved Catholics

[14] Sherman Ricards, Jr., "The Secret Marriage," *Marriage and Family Living,* Vol. 22 (August, 1960), pp. 243–247.

who had secured dispensation from the banns. Otherwise, those seeking a secret marriage tended to be older than average, especially in the case of the female. A number of the cases involved remarriage. Contrary to what might be expected, the clergyman officiated in these marriages more often than did the justice of the peace.

This study focused only on licenses issued, with no follow-up being made to ascertain the success or failure of the marriages which had their origin in this unique fashion. Consequently there is no indication given as to the eventual outcome of the marriages.

Not many studies have been made of elopements, but it seems clear that in a large percentage of cases couples are attempting to bypass or conceal something. This may be parental objection, legal requirements in the home jurisdiction, local publicity, or premarital pregnancy. Popenoe with his students made a study of 738 elopements in southern California. The following motivations were reported:

Parental objection	46 percent
Avoid publicity	20 percent
Economy	12 percent
Pregnancy	8 percent
Miscellaneous	14 percent [15]

Popenoe reports on the success of these marriages as measured by self-report. Three hundred and fifty-six (48 percent) were ranked as happy; 66 (9 percent) were doubtful; and 316 (43 percent) received the ranking of unhappy. If couples who elope are similar to the couples in the Popenoe sample, their chances for successful marriage are not particularly good. It must be pointed out, of course, that we do not know the chances of success for noneloped marriages.

As Christensen points out, we may distinguish two types of elopements or secret marriages.[16] The first involves an act of impulsiveness. There is the desire to flout the law or the general community, or to marry in spite of parental opposition. In many cases there has not been a period of dating and engagement sufficient to serve as a period of testing and preparation for marriage. In some few cases marriages are made to satisfy wagers or when the parties concerned are under the influence of alcohol. In the second type of elopement or secret marriage careful consideration has been given to the unique and unorthodox procedure. If there has been parental opposition it has been taken into account. As a whole this category includes couples whose matches have general approval by friends and relatives. The lack of regular ceremony and publicity is what brings some disapproval.

---

[15] Paul Popenoe, "A Study of 738 Elopements," *American Sociological Review,* Vol. 3 (February, 1938), pp. 47–53.

[16] Harold Christensen, *Marriage Analysis* (New York, Ronald, 1950), pp. 295–296.

Gretna Green Marriages

For many years a small town in Scotland just across the border from England was known as a haven for impetuous lovers, who wished to marry in haste.[17] From the time of the passage of the Hardwicke bill of 1753 until the 1870s when a waiting period law was passed, Gretna Green was well-known. With no waiting period required, all that was necessary was spoken vows with witnesses present who would vouch for the couple. Thousands of marriages were performed for willing English couples at Gretna Green, Scotland until the restrictive laws of the 1870s were passed.

In America many towns such as Las Vegas, Nevada and Elkton, Maryland have been known for their Gretna Green variety of marriages at one time or another. What is required is a particular combination of circumstances, the most important being differentials in state marriage laws. Factors involved include lower age of consent, absence of blood test, and absence of waiting period. Cooperative justices or parsons are also necessary.

Two studies have been made of the rate of divorce among Gretna Green marriages. Kephart and Strohm compared the divorce rate of Philadelphia couples who were married in Elkton, Maryland with those who were married in Philadelphia.[18] Hopson did an analagous study using Tennessee couples who married in nearby states comparing them with couples who married in Tennessee.[19] In both cases the migratory marriages had a higher divorce rate than did the marriages which were performed at home. In spite of the evidence of these studies which is in line with expectations based on theory, marriage mills still exist and will probably continue to do so in the immediate future.

THE CHURCH AND MARRIAGE

The church has a number of the same interests in marriage that the state has at least so far as its own constituents are concerned.[20] The control of relations between the sexes contributes to public morals, in which the church has always shown interest. The stability of the home, the protection of women and children, and the clarification of inheritance are not without religious significance.

At the Council of Trent in 1563 it was decreed that marriage is a

[17] E. S. Turner, *A History of Courting* (New York, Dutton, 1955), pp. 164–166.

[18] William Kephart and R. B. Strohm, "The Stability of Gretna Green Marriages," *Sociology and Social Research,* Vol. 36 (May, 1952), pp. 291–296.

[19] Arthur Hopson, "The Relationship of Migratory Marriages to Divorce in Tennessee," *Social Forces,* Vol. 30 (May, 1952), pp. 449–455.

[20] Henry Bowman, *Marriage for Moderns* (New York, McGraw-Hill, 1960), p. 254.

sacrament if solemnized properly. This position has been retained by the various Episcopalian groups as well as by the Roman church. Most Protestant groups do not consider marriage a sacrament as such. This should not be interpreted to mean that marriage is considered to be a strictly secular formality similar to the negotiation of a business contract. In the eyes of all churches of the Judeo-Christian heritage the man and woman take their vows and are made one in the presence of God. This is the essence of the marriage ceremony. The theology of the particular denomination in question determines whether this event is to be considered sacramental or to be given some other meaning.

Actually for most groups of people the marriage ceremony has a deep religious significance, if a religious orientation prevails to any degree. At such a ceremony people sense, if they ever do, the connection between past, present, and future. Memories and thoughts of those gone before are blended with visions of those to come in the future. Questions regarding the mysteries of life, birth, and death are mixed in the thoughts of participants with thoughts more directly pertinent to the occasion. Durkheim took the position that the essence of religion involves the collective thought patterns of people about the meaning of life. Whether one accepts this position or not it can hardly be denied that a marriage ceremony represents an important rite of passage which has religious significance.

For the particular couple involved, having the backing of the church can be extremely satisfying, if, again, they are religiously oriented. A dignity prevails to a greater degree in a religious ceremony than in a civil ceremony. Many couples have been offended by the casualness with which a justice of the peace has "done his duty" in a few short minutes. Small wonder that many couples who have experienced the civil ceremony complain that they "hardly feel married."

A religious service may also be reassuring to those who still have sexual anxieties. The couple is assured that sexual fulfillment is not only allowed but required. This touch of legitimacy can be reassuring to some, especially brides, who have been taught to curb their sexual feelings. The marriage ceremony suggests that the actions which before would have been improper are now legitimate and proper. It is true that not all people are emotionally prepared to make a quick transition to the new status. Nevertheless an appreciation of the fact that the general society now expects the couple to act as husband and wife can be a powerful incentive to some individuals. In a word the marriage ritual may have an important function.

The Marriage Ceremony

Specific procedural aspects of a religious marriage will vary considerably. In the less formal churches the individual couple and the officiating minister are permitted leeway in devising the exact nature of the ceremony. A general form is ordinarily suggested by the minister's manual for the average ceremony in the denomination. The following is from the Methodist manual: [21]

Dearly beloved, we are gathered together here in the sight of God, and in the presence of these witnesses, to join together *this man and this woman* in holy matrimony; which is an honorable estate, instituted of God, and signifying unto us the mystical union which exists between Christ and his Church; which holy estate Christ adorned and beautified with his presence in Cana of Galilee. It is therefore not to be entered into unadvisedly, but reverently, discreetly, and in the fear of God. Into this holy estate these two persons come now to be joined. If any man can show just cause why they may not lawfully be joined together, let him now speak, or else hereafter forever hold his peace.

† *Addressing the persons to be married, the minister shall say,*
I require and charge you both, as you stand in the presence of God, before whom the secrets of all hearts are disclosed, that, having duly considered the holy covenant you are about to make, you do now declare before this company your pledge of faith, each to the other. Be well assured that if these solemn vows are kept inviolate, as God's Word demands, and if steadfastly you endeavor to do the will of your heavenly Father, God will bless your marriage, will grant you fulfillment in it, and will establish your home in peace.

† *Then shall the minister say to the man, using his Christian name,*
N., wilt thou have this woman to be thy wedded wife, to live together in the holy estate of matrimony? Wilt thou love her, comfort her, honor and keep her, in sickness and in health; and forsaking all other keep thee only unto her so long as ye both shall live?

† *The man shall answer,*
 I will.
† *Then shall the minister say to the woman, using her Christian name,*
N., wilt thou have this man to be thy wedded husband, to live together in the holy estate of matrimony? Wilt thou love him, comfort him, honor and keep him, in sickness and in health; and forsaking all other keep thee only unto him so long as ye both shall live?

† *The woman shall answer,*
 I will.

† *Then shall the minister say,*
Who giveth this woman to be married to this man?

† *The father of the woman, or whoever gives her in marriage, shall answer,*
 I do.

[21] From *The Book of Worship for Church and Home,* copyright © 1964–65 by Board of Publication of the Methodist Church, Inc., by permission of The Methodist Publishing House, pp. 28–31.

† *Then, the minister, receiving the hand of the woman from her father or other sponsor, shall cause the man with his right hand to take the woman by her right hand, and say after him,*

I, *N.*, take thee, *N.*, to be my wedded wife, to have and to hold, from this day forward, for better, for worse, for richer, for poorer, in sickness and in health, to love and to cherish, till death us do part, according to God's holy ordinance; and thereto I pledge thee my faith.

† *Then shall they loose their hands; and the woman, with her right hand taking the man by his right hand, shall say after the minister,*

I, *N.*, take thee, *N.*, to be my wedded husband, to have and to hold, from this day forward, for better, for worse, for richer, for poorer, in sickness and in health, to love and to cherish, till death us do part, according to God's holy ordinance; and thereto I pledge thee my faith.

† *Then they may give to each other rings, or the man may give to the woman a ring, in this wise: the minister, taking the ring or rings, shall say,*

The wedding ring is the outward and visible sign of an inward and spiritual grace, signifying to all the uniting of this man and woman in holy matrimony, through the Church of Jesus Christ our Lord.

† *Then the minister may say,*

Let us pray.
Bless, O Lord, the giving of these rings, that they who wear them may abide in thy peace, and continue in thy favor; through Jesus Christ our Lord. *Amen.*

† *Or, if there be but one ring, the minister may say,*

Bless, O Lord, the giving of this ring, that he who gives it and she who wears it may abide forever in thy peace, and continue in thy favor; through Jesus Christ our Lord. *Amen.*

† *The minister shall then deliver the proper ring to the man to put upon the third finger of the woman's left hand. The man, holding the ring there, shall say after the minister,*

In token and pledge of our constant faith and abiding love, with this ring I thee wed, in the name of the Father, and of the Son, and of the Holy Spirit. *Amen.*

† *Then, if there is a second ring, the minister shall deliver it to the woman to put upon the third finger of the man's left hand; and the woman, holding the ring there, shall say after the minister,*

In token and pledge of our constant faith and abiding love, with this ring I thee wed, in the name of the Father, and of the Son, and of the Holy Spirit. *Amen.*

† *Then shall the minister join their right hands together and, with his hand on their united hands, shall say,*

Forasmuch as *N.* and *N.* have consented together in holy wedlock, and have witnessed the same before God and this company, and thereto have pledged their faith each to the other, and have declared the same by joining hands and by giving and receiving *rings;* I pronounce that they are husband and wife together, in the name of the Father, and of the Son, and of the Holy Spirit. Those whom God hath joined together, let not man put asunder. *Amen.*

† *Then shall the minister say,*
Let us pray.

† *Then shall the husband and wife kneel; the minister shall say,*
O eternal God, creator and preserver of all mankind, giver of all spiritual grace, the author of everlasting life: Send thy blessing upon this man and this woman, whom we bless in thy name; that they may surely perform and keep the vow and covenant between them made, and may ever remain in perfect love and peace together, and live according to thy laws.

Look graciously upon them, that they may love, honor, and cherish each other, and so live together in faithfulness and patience, in wisdom and true godliness, that their home may be a haven of blessing and a place of peace; through Jesus Christ our Lord. *Amen.*

† *Then the husband and wife, still kneeling, shall join with the minister and congregation in the Lord's Prayer, saying,*
Our Father, who art in heaven, hallowed be thy name. Thy kingdom come, thy will be done on earth as it is in heaven. Give us this day our daily bread. And forgive us our trespasses, as we forgive those who trespass against us. And lead us not into temptation, but deliver us from evil. For thine is the kingdom, and the power, and the glory, forever. *Amen.*

† *Then the minister shall give this blessing,*
God the Father, the Son, and the Holy Spirit bless, preserve, and keep you; the Lord graciously with his favor look upon you, and so fill you with all spiritual benediction and love that you may so live together in this life that in the world to come you may have life everlasting. *Amen.*

The essential element is the taking of the vows before the witnesses. It is sometimes said that only in a Quaker marriage do the young people "marry themselves." Strictly speaking they do in any type of ceremony, by the vows of taking each other. The officiant presides and formally introduces the couple as Mr. and Mrs. to the community after the vows are spoken.

Type of Ceremony and Wedding

Actually the mere carrying through of the marriage ceremony is the only necessity as far as either state or church is concerned. The wedding, originally referred to as social ceremonial, is "extra" to the marriage ceremony itself. The two have become confused and fused in popular thinking to the point that they are used as being synonymous. In some circles the nonreligious, social, and commercial elements have entered the church service to the point where terms like "Hollywood show" are not inappropriate. F. H. Ferris has attacked such trends in a forceful manner. Writing on the basis of considerable experience in ministering to upper-middle and upper-class families, Ferris bemoans the pomp and circumstance which detract from the essential dignity of the service.[22] So complicated have things become that a wedding director is needed to keep proper order and decorum. The responsibilities of this director as reported by Ferris are staggering. (The latter term also describes both the father when he first sees the bills and in all too many cases the general state of the ushers at the rehearsal.) The wedding becomes a vehicle of social mobility, ". . . a symbol of worldly success, an assertion of the fact that the family has arrived or an attempt to climb a rung higher."

The service itself is not immune to secularization and commercialization. Romantic music is interspersed with religious, and organ buildups bring to mind Hollywood pageantry. Ferris goes so far as to use the term "racket" and argues that "it is possible to have a church wedding without pomp and circumstance, even in the presence of a considerable gathering." [23] It is easy to sympathize with Ferris' point of view. The pressures become very great to use the wedding as a status device. While both state and church recognize and allow for custom and tradition including merry-making and social festivity, neither requires extravaganza. The latter has developed in status-conscious families and must be judged not only in terms of its status functions, but its religious, moral, and psychological dysfunctions as well.

The Wedding Cost

No adequate modern studies are available which indicate the actual amounts spent for the wedding. Studies if made would most certainly show a wide variation in costs. The range from the simple home or church wedding to the large, formal affairs is very great. Arlitt suggests that the simple home wedding should cost between $585 and $685 depending upon the season, for the bride's family, with the groom being required to spend about $255. For the expenses of the simple church wedding her estimate is from $1405 to $1580 for the bride and $640 to $660 for the groom, depending upon the season.[24] She considers the expenses for the large home or church and club wedding so far out of line for the average family that no rough estimate is suggested.

Customs vary somewhat by region and economic level but Arlitt's figures are probably representative for the so-called middle classes, if all ex-

[22] Frank Ferris, "Of Weddings and Funerals by the Officiating Clergyman," *Harper's Magazine,* Vol. 191 (December, 1945), pp. 496–499.

[23] *Ibid.*

[24] Ada Arlitt, "The Wedding and Honeymoon," in Morris Fishbein and Ruby Jo Kennedy (Eds.), *Modern Marriage and Family Living* (Fairlawn, N.J., Oxford, 1957), Chapter 13.

penses are taken into account. Some may be able to trim a few dollars here and there but the fact that weddings are expensive at best must be faced. Thousands of dollars are involved for those who wish to have the large, formal affair with all the trimmings.

MAKING DECISIONS

The individuals involved must make basic decisions as to their relationship to state, church, and local community regarding the preliminaries and the marriage ceremony itself. In certain states they may marry informally by common law if they so desire. They, under normal circumstances, may travel to another state with more lenient laws, if the laws at home seem too restrictive. They may choose between a civil and religious ceremony. Most assuredly they or their families will choose the degree of ostentation to be displayed in the wedding and reception to follow.

Studies seem to indicate that those who are married in conventional fashion with parental approval have the greatest chances of achieving conventional marital adjustment.[25] This may, of course, simply mean that conventional people have conventional marriage ceremonies and conventional marriages. Nevertheless those who fly in the face of form and control of marriage may find themselves on somewhat shaky ground. If this is done out of strong and firm conviction it is one thing; if attempts are made to bypass law and custom just to escape onerous requirements it is something else again. For example, when serological tests for venereal disease were first proposed many objected to them on the ground of invasion of private rights. A concern with the freedom of the individual as against state control is one to which many will lend an ear. On the other hand, few would defend the right of a prospective groom to infect his bride with syphilis. Actually comparatively little red tape is necessary for entrance into marriage whereas much more is required to exit from wedlock. This differential emphasis may be misplaced.

The couple will need to choose from among alternative patterns just what type of entrance into marriage is to be used. Values and customs of the particular groups to which the couple belong should not be overlooked. On the other hand, questions of degree of "show," and the sacredness vs. secularity of the ceremony are matters in which the two partners have a right to express their individual tastes. It is customary to defer to the bride and her parents on specific matters of the wedding reception. The bridegroom may do well to allow this right to the bride and her family except in cases where on principle he must object. In such an event he will probably wish, as tactfully as possible, to inform the bride of his feelings.

[25] Henry Bowman, *op. cit.,* p. 206.

THE HONEYMOON

The honeymoon has a long history, being known in some form in many parts of the world. Tradition has it that among some groups newly-weds were expected to eat a form of mead or honey for a month, and from this tradition the word was derived. The young people are encouraged to absent themselves from their regular mundane roles and day-to-day tasks in order to make initial adaptations to each other and to marriage. They are also away from friends, relatives, and neighbors who might embarrass them by their presence or by their attempts to make fun of them. Interestingly enough, in modern society many couples seem to want the honeymoon to perform multiple functions. Expecting too much of the honeymoon may result in disillusionment.

The question of location is important. Marriage educators generally agree that the couple should go to a type of location that is familiar to both parties. City-bred individuals who have never climbed or ridden horseback over mountains should probably not attempt to learn these demanding skills at the same time they are attempting to develop skills of marital interaction. Small town and rural couples would hardly be expected to feel relaxed at Miami Beach or in a Broadway hotel. The point.is that the couple should be at a location which provides them anonymity but which does not force them to make adjustments other than to each other. The important item is an atmosphere conducive to uninhibited mutual responsiveness. Unwanted distractions of whatever cause should be kept to a minimum. If the couple wishes to visit the zoo or watch the water go over Niagara Falls, fine. They should not feel compelled to do so by a previously planned schedule. Impulses of the moment should be given free reign in a way they would not be, or could not be in normal day-by-day living.

It is possible that some couples may find the honeymoon sexual experience disillusioning. Various factors may operate to keep the level of sexual fulfillment from reaching a maximum. Among them are postwedding fatigue, inhibitions and timidity, unrealistic expectations, and the like. Satisfactory sexual adjustment may receive an impetus during the honeymoon, but it may take weeks or months of married living to achieve complete mutual satisfaction. Undue concentration on sex to the neglect of other elements of total living during the honeymoon should therefore not be encouraged.

Some criticize the honeymoon on the basis that it is artificial and dysfunctional: [26] the regular requirements of everyday living are suspended to give a vacation-like atmosphere conducive to initial adjustments. If more money is spent than the couple can reasonably afford, or if expectations are unrealistic, then the honeymoon does not serve a useful purpose.

[26] Philip Wylie, "Honeymoons Are Hell," *Redbook* (November, 1952).

Kept within reasonable bounds economically and with realistic attitudes prevailing, the honeymoon can serve as a positive impetus to start a couple out on the marital road.

SELECTED READINGS

Baber, Ray, *Marriage and the Family* (New York, McGraw-Hill, 1953), Chapter 3.

Bell, Robert, *Marriage and Family Interaction* (Homewood, Ill., The Dorsey Press, 1963), Chapter 9.

Bernard, Jessie, Buchanan, Helen, and Smith, William, *Dating, Mating, and Marriage* (Cleveland, Howard Allen, 1958), Chapter 6.

Bowman, Henry, *Marriage for Moderns* (New York, McGraw-Hill, 1960), Chapter 9.

Bradway, John, "What Family Members Should Know About Law," in Howard Becker and Reuben Hill (Eds.), *Family, Marriage, and Parenthood* (Boston, Heath, 1955), Chapter 19.

Brav, Stanley, "Note on Honeymoons," *Marriage and Family Living* (Summer, 1947), p. 60.

Cavan, Ruth, *American Marriage* (New York, Crowell, 1959), Chapter 11.

Clarke, Helen, *Social Legislation* (New York, Appleton-Century-Crofts, 1957), pp. 27–110.

Common Law Marriages, Los Angeles Law Library, December, 1959.

Daggett, Harriet, "Reflections on the Law of the Family," *Annals American Academy Political and Social Science,* Vol. 251 (May, 1947), pp. 120–127.

Duvall, Evelyn and Hill, Reuben, *Being Married* (Boston, Heath, 1960), Chapter 9.

Ernst, Morris and Loth, David, *For Better or Worse* (New York, Harper & Row, 1952).

Ferris, Frank, "Of Weddings and Funerals by the Officiating Clergyman," *Harper's Magazine,* Vol. 191 (December, 1945), pp. 496–499. Also reprinted in Landis, Judson, and Landis, Mary, *Readings in Marriage and the Family* (Englewood Cliffs, N.J., Prentice-Hall, 1952), pp. 133–138.

Hogan, John, and Ianni, Francis, *American Social Legislation* (New York, Harper & Row, 1956), pp. 143–300.

Hopson, Arthur, "The Relationship of Migratory Marriages to Divorce in Tennessee," *Social Forces,* Vol. 30 (May, 1952), pp. 449–455.

Jacobson, Paul, *American Marriage and Divorce* (New York, Holt, Rinehart and Winston, 1959), Chapters 1–6.

Kephart, William, and Strohm, R. B., "The Stability of Gretna Green Marriages," *Sociology and Social Research,* Vol. 26 (June, 1952), pp. 291–296.

Kephart, William, *Family, Society and the Individual* (Boston, Houghton Mifflin, 1966), Chapter 14.

Knox, Sarah, *The Family and the Law* (Chapel Hill, University of North Carolina Press, 1941).

Kuchler, Frances, *The Law of Marriage and Divorce Simplified,* Vol. 24 (Dobbs Ferry, N.Y., Oceana Publications, 4th ed., 1961).

Litwak, Eugene, "Three Ways in Which Law Acts as a Means of Social Control: Punishment, Therapy, and Education," *Social Forces,* Vol. 34 (March, 1956), pp. 217–223.

Martinson, Floyd, *Marriage and the American Ideal* (New York, Dodd, Mead, 1960), Chapter 16.

Moore, Marvin, "The Case for Marriage by Proxy," *Cleveland-Marshall Law Review* (May, 1962), pp. 313–322.

Moss, J. J., and Gingles, Ruby, "The Relationship of Personality to the Incidence of Early Marriage," *Marriage and Family Living,* Vol. 21 (November, 1959), pp. 373–377.

Peterson, James, *Education for Marriage* (New York, Scribner, 1964), Chapter 12.

Pilpel, Harriet, and Zavin, Theodora, *Your Marriage and the Law* (New York, Holt, Rinehart and Winston, 1952).

Radin, Paul, *The Law and You* (New York, The New American Library, 1948), Chapter 3.

Rheinstein, Max, "Trends in Marriage and Divorce Law of Western Countries," *Law and Contemporary Problems,* Duke University School of Law (Winter, 1953), pp. 3–19.

Simpson, George, *People in Families* (New York, Crowell, 1960), Chapter 9.

Vernier, Chester, *American Family Laws* (Stanford, Stanford University Press, 1931–1938), five volumes.

QUESTIONS AND EXERCISES

1. Under what circumstances do you think elopements are justified? Defend your answer.
2. How do you explain the existence of restrictive interracial marriage laws in such states as Indiana, the Dakotas, Nebraska, Colorado, and Wyoming, which are neither southern or western, as such?
3. What are the arguments pro and con for the recognition of common law marriage by the state?
4. Read the appropriate sections in Bradway and Knox cited, then write a paper on the respective legal rights and duties of the husband and the wife in the United States.
5. What to you is the main function of the honeymoon? Under what circumstances may couples dispense with the honeymoon trip?
6. Read Simpson's Chapter 9 entitled "Some Critical Notes on Weddings and Honeymoons." Do you essentially agree or disagree with his analysis? Why or why not?
7. Ask a group of international students to speak to your class on wedding and honeymoon customs in their respective countries. Note the similarities and contrasts between their patterns and our own.

8. Write a report on marriage laws in your home jurisdiction; in what respect are they typical and in what, if any, are they unique?
9. Have a local physician speak to your class on the desirability of having premarital counseling and a premarital physical examination.
10. Make a case study of an annulment which has been granted in your jurisdiction.
11. The Reverend Jones is a minister in a large Protestant denomination. He has been insisting that his own parishioners have at least one premarital counseling session with him before he will marry them. At about 10:30 P.M. Joe and Mary, a young couple from another part of the state, arrive at his door. They present the required legal papers, in proper order, and ask to be married. Should this minister marry the couple? Justify your answer.
12. Read Baber, pp. 75–77 or Kephart, pp. 418–421 in the references cited. Write a paper dealing with the possibilities of a Uniform Marriage Law in the United States. Include the features you would insist be included in the law.

three

Marriage:
The New Family in Formation

12

Achieving Order
in the Family

The honeymoon may extend psychologically into the early months of marriage; in fact, one author speaks of a "psychic honeymoon." [1] During this period, which varies in length depending upon the individuals involved, the partners are living in a world that is only partially real. Eventually they must descend from the erotically tinged clouds to the hard ground of mundane everyday living as a married pair. That this is not necessarily easy can be inferred both from common-sense observations and more scientific evidence.

Landis made a study of 409 couples in which he attempted to determine the length of time it took to achieve adjustment in six aspects of marriage: in-law relationships, mutual friends, religious activities, sex relationships, social activities, and expenditures of family income. The individuals responded independently so it was possible to check on the extent of agreement between the spouses.

The greatest agreement at the beginning of marriage involved mutual friends and religious activities. About three-fourths of the couples fell into this category. The least agreement involved sex relations and spending the family income, with slightly over half the couples reporting agreement from the beginning of marriage on these two categories. The items social activities and in-law relationships fell in between, with about two-thirds of the couples reporting initial agreement in these areas.

Landis found a strong association between the length of time which was required to achieve adjustment and happiness in marriage. Landis interprets this to mean that "the earlier the adjustments are made the more

[1] Willard Waller and Reuben Hill, *The Family* (New York, Holt, Rinehart and Winston, 1951), p. 253.

likely is the marriage to be happy." [2] If this interpretation is correct it is imperative that early adjustments be made in the most vital areas of marriage to secure a foundation on which to build future success. Building a real working relationship sometimes takes effort on the part of a couple. We must not paint too dark a picture, however. As Baber points out, the expectation of success is a powerful motive in itself to propel the couple along.[3] If it is strong and deep-seated, difficult problems are taken in stride and in the more fortunate cases, may not arise.

In this chapter we wish to discuss three major family developmental tasks which face the couple if *order* in the home is to be established (See pages 106 and 107 in Chapter 4). They are the establishment of patterns of emotional attachment, establishment of patterns of sex relations, and establishment of patterns of communication.

ESTABLISHING PATTERNS OF EMOTIONAL ATTACHMENT

Burgess and Wallin, in reporting the results of their study of some 666 marriages, include a section on the intimacy of association in marriage.[4] They theorize that four major factors are subsumed under intimacy of association and are indispensable to marital unity: love, demonstration of affection, emotional interdependence, and satisfactory sex relations. We will rely heavily on their report and consider the first three categories mentioned above as subcategories of emotional attachment. Sex relations will be treated as a separate category. In Chapter 6 we distinguished among infatuation, romantic love, and conjugal love. On the basis of our distinctions conjugal love would have the highest association with marital success. Burgess and Wallin provide a rough test of this hypothesis. Using both a case study and statistical approach they attempt to determine the association between love and companionship in marriage. Statistically they found an association of about $+.40$ which is not high but is above the level of chance. These authors found that many of the more successfully married couples reported their love grew more true, real, stronger, and sensible after marriage as compared with the premarriage period. One couple describes the change in the love relationship as follows:

Husband. I am more in love now. At that time it was a romantic love. Now it is something deeper. It is a mutual understanding of each other, a faith in each other; a companionship. When we are apart we yearn to be together. She has said she is more in love now than ever.

---

[2] Judson Landis, "Length of Time Required to Achieve Adjustment in Marriage," *American Sociological Review,* Vol. 11 (December, 1946), p. 668.

[3] Ray Baber, *Marriage and the Family* (New York, McGraw-Hill, 1953), p. 161.

[4] Ernest Burgess and Paul Wallin, *Engagement and Marriage* (Philadelphia, Lippincott, 1953), pp. 419–421.

Wife. I think I am more in love with him than he with me. He says his love is deeper than before marriage.[5]

The Burgess and Wallin findings and interpretations provide some comfort for those who fear the loss of romance in marriage. In marriage, as Fromme says, the "illusory elements in love are bound to fade." [6] At least some of them are. If the marriage has been built on too many illusions it may be most difficult for the couple to develop a satisfactory and continuing love relationship in marriage. One is reminded of the biblical injunction to build a house on a rock, not on sand. Furthermore, the process of growth must be taken into consideration. Lack of growth is pathological. Ideally a somewhat new and different type of love emerges in marriage, with much or little romance depending on the pair and on the circumstances being retained and with new kinds of companionship being added.

Contrary to some popular opinion love will not solve all problems. A strong case can be made for the reverse assertion. It is practically impossible to maintain cooperation and tolerance in the face of deep-seated clashes in personality or basic family policy, or in the face of lack of respect.

Serious disagreement can take place regarding demonstration of affection. A good case can be made for the hypothesis that individuals carry patterns they have learned from childhood into their new homes. If a person comes from a home in which affection and love were freely demonstrated he will probably tend to expect this in his new home.

Clinical observations incline one to the generalization that in America a desire for more outward demonstration of affection is more typical of women than of men. Burgess and Wallin's findings are in line with this generalization. A counselee once said to the author: "Things certainly have changed. Before I married Joe he couldn't seem to be satisfied no matter how much kissing, embracing, and lovemaking took place. Now you'd think I was a cold potato the way he greets me. Except for sex relations he seldom shows me any affection." There were some unique personality factors involved in this case. Nevertheless the author's counseling experience leads him to believe that the wife's complaint is a fairly typical one.

Some married couples put a great emphasis on family events such as birthdays, anniversaries, and holidays. The absent-minded husband who forgets these events has become a stereotype in middle-class America. While the stereotype may be exaggerated, no doubt many husbands would do well to remember the occasions deemed important by their wives. Women may in turn be expected to reciprocate.

Burgess and Wallin's conclusions may be of interest here. They state that "in general, then, demonstration of affection maintains the marriage

[5] *Ibid.*
[6] Alan Fromme, *The Psychologist Looks at Sex and Marriage* (Englewood Cliffs, N.J., Prentice-Hall, 1950), p. 111.

in its status quo and does not serve as a dynamic factor in the development of the marital relation. Diminution of affection, however, may be an indication of the decline of love in the relationship." [7]

Emotional interdependence is the third facet to be considered. Three patterns are distinguishable: each emotionally dependent on the other, one emotionally dependent on the other, and both emotionally independent. One would expect that the first pattern would provide the greatest marital unity. This seems to be borne out by case studies. Excerpts from a case will illustrate a growing interdependence of a particular couple:

Husband. I do want to get approval and sympathy. She is very good. In fact too good. When I write a paper I ask her to criticize where I could improve it. It is very seldom that she has a negative criticism. She usually says it's very good. Really, I covet the other too. I would appreciate it if she would be more critical. . . . She needs sympathy and encouragement. . . . She needs reassurance that she is doing all right. I feel I am pretty good at it and am improving. In our early married life I didn't realize she needed it . . .

Wife. I need sympathy and encouragement. I think he gives it very well. Better now than when we were first married because we understand each other better. That goes for him too. He needs encouragement. When we were first married I didn't realize I should encourage him about little things such as his writing a paper and speaking in public. He . . . needed sympathy and encouragement.[8]

In other instances one spouse may be self-sufficient while the other is emotionally dependent on the partner.

Focusing on the individual alone, both laymen and social scientists are prone to think that a mature person is a self-sufficient person. Most definitions of maturity make this assumption. It is possible that a point of diminishing returns appears in marriage. Burgess and Wallin believe that an important integration factor is lacking if both spouses are self-sufficient.[9]

We have considered three factors (love, demonstration of affection, and emotional interdependence) that seem to be crucial in the development of emotional attachments in marriage. It should be stressed that adjustments in these areas are begun in the premarriage period and continued through marriage. The early months and years of marriage seem to be especially crucial to later marital success, however. According to our theory, complementary personalities and the absence of extreme cultural differences would be prerequisites to successful emotional interaction. Given this base, it is imperative that the young people strive to develop satisfactory emotional attachments early in marriage if they wish a firm foundation for later success. There is also a body of theory which takes the position that

[7] Burgess and Wallin, *op. cit.,* p. 425.
[8] *Ibid.,* pp. 425–426.
[9] *Ibid.,* p. 429.

one can't "work out" such emotional states, that they are the product of the personality and the basic relationship and that self-conscious "working at it" does more harm than good.[10]

ESTABLISHING PATTERNS OF SEX RELATIONS

The reader will remember that the couples in the Landis study reported that sex presented the greatest difficulty. Almost one-half (47.3 percent) of the couples had at least initial difficulty or disagreed as to whether they had worked out satisfactory adjustment at the beginning of their marriage. Only 12.5 percent of the couples failed to work out a satisfactory sexual adjustment eventually. It should be pointed out that for a certain proportion of the couples the adjustment is a noncreative resignation or acquiescence to frustration.

Clinical findings support the assertion that initial sexual relations are often difficult for couples, even those who eventually will achieve a high degree of success. It may be helpful to discuss some of the major causes of the difficulty and to describe some of the patterns of sex behavior which bring satisfaction to most couples.

Sex Attitudes

Physical aspects of coitus are important. While some of the young people today are ignorant of the physical aspects of sex, most of them in the educated classes of the population are not. Information on the biological aspects of sex is being disseminated in many homes, schools, and other institutions. Social and psychological aspects of sex are less often taught and understood.

Sex values have a varied history in American society. Influences from Catholic tradition, Puritanism, and other sources have been added to a basic Judeo-Christian heritage on which the American family system is based. Small wonder then that within the same country may be found attitudes and values regarding sex behavior which are contradictory. Sex may be considered to be for procreation only. To a few it may be for pleasure only. To some it may be a sinful activity. It may be considered the highest expression of love and tenderness possible between spouses. It may be considered an animalistic impulse. Other conceptions are possible. Differences in conceptions of sex may exist even within the same family, so it is easy to understand why two young people coming together in marriage may have different basic conceptions of the meaning of sex. To the extent that sexual permissiveness before marriage is allowed, these differences will not appear

[10] Controversies exist at present as to (1) the proportion of the basic personality structure which is formed in early childhood, and (2) the degree to which individuals can by self-effort effect any real change in their own personality dynamics.

later, either because no marriage will result or differences will be ironed out.

Families differ also as to the openness with which sex and related factors are discussed and recognized. Other things being equal, children brought up in homes where responsiveness was encouraged and sex matters handled openly and sympathetically will enter marriage with fewer troublesome sex attitudes. But contradictions existing in our culture may still be internalized and reflected in sex problems in marriage.

The breakdown of the double standard combined with greater freedom of women and the accent on lovemaking may have created some general problems unknown in previous generations. Both husbands and wives may have rather high expectations in regard to sexual responsiveness on the wife's part. At the same time some "well-bred" girls will enter marriage relatively unawakened sexually. It is sometimes difficult for young wives to respond with abandon, even though they wish and expect to have very much more active roles in sex play than had their Victorian great grandmothers. Wives more often than husbands have conflicts over their sex behavior. In previous generations the wife was to be relatively passive; sex was primarily for the husband's pleasure. Now the wife may wish to be a very active sex partner but may find it difficult, especially in early marriage, to live up to her own and her partner's expectations.

It should be stressed that both the husband and the wife have the individual developmental tasks of becoming good sex partners. We have been stressing some of the typical difficulties wives have in task achievement. This should be balanced with reference to husbands. Typical male sex experience with promiscuous women often ill prepares them for sex experience with unawakened wives. They lack the patience, understanding, tact, and foresight necessary to lead their wives along toward mutually satisfactory sexual interaction.

Differences between Men and Women

Various studies have dealt with the question of differences between men and women in sex attitudes, desire, and activity. There seems to be rather general agreement that men and women as categories but not always as individuals differ on the following items:

1. Sexual activity before marriage
2. General premarital attitude toward sex
3. Preferred frequency of intercourse
4. Satisfaction from intercourse
5. Frequency of orgasm
6. Frequency of refusal to have intercourse

In one study, on all the items listed above the husbands ranked higher than the wives, with the exception of the last item.[11] Husbands were more

[11] Burgess and Wallin, *op. cit.*, Chapter 20.

active before marriage, had a more favorable premarital attitude toward sex, preferred a greater frequency of intercourse, received greater satisfaction from intercourse, and had more sexual unions resulting in orgasm, compared with their wives. Wives were more inclined to refuse intercourse. Whether culturally or biologically determined, significant differences between men and women appear to exist.

Many implications will be obvious to the reader. In the average marriage, at least in the early years, certain differences are to be predicted. The husband should not be considered abnormal or oversexed because he has frequent interest in erotic pleasures. And the wife should not be considered prudish or Victorian if she differs from the husband and seems less erotically oriented than he.

"Normal" Sex Behavior

Many people become greatly concerned over the question of the acceptability of various sexual practices. Unfortunately the delicacy of the subject makes it rather difficult for people to discuss such matters openly. Newspapers freely use terms such as lewd, pathological, or abnormal in referring to sex acts, so that apprehension arises in the minds of many people as to what is proper and legitimate in marriage and what is not.

It must be stated that there are no consistent conceptions of abnormal or perverted sex behavior. This is found to be true when one examines the literature in social science, biological and medical science, law, and religion. From the point of view of the individual couple, acceptable normal sex behavior might well involve practices which culminate in mutual satisfaction, in most cases orgasm for both parties. A wide variety of techniques are possible for this goal to be achieved. Practices which result in emotional or physical harm should obviously be avoided.

An example of an area where variations in sex practices are typical involves position in intercourse. In Western society the typical pattern features the husband above with the wife reclining. In a number of preliterate societies the reverse is the expected. Fromme's point is well taken when he states that "So long as husband and wife find that whatever they do is mutually agreeable, it makes little difference whether they have their relations standing, sitting, lying down, man above, woman above, face to face or any other way they may desire." [12] Most couples will probably wish to develop a fairly consistent pattern with acceptable variations practiced occasionally for novelty purposes.

Frequency of Sex Relations

Sometimes the question of the frequency of sex relations in marriage arises. Cuber relates a counseling case in which a married woman asked the

[12] Fromme, *op. cit.*, p. 103.

counselor during the initial interview for the name of a reputable lawyer.[13] Interrogation revealed that the client thought that her husband was over-sexed and too demanding of her. It was eventually disclosed that she inter-preted frequency of sex relations of twice a week as indicating pathological desires on the husband's part! Actually this frequency of sex relations was clearly within the range of average sex behavior for the group from which this woman came. Kinsey reports a figure of 3.7 times per week for couples under age twenty, then a progressive decline until the weekly frequency averaged 1.0 at age sixty. At the various age levels there were wide varia-tions, however, with extremes on both sides of this norm being reported.[14]

Most couples will find that after the initial honeymoon and immediate post-honeymoon period they will naturally develop an habitual pattern which is mutually acceptable. If the pattern falls within the range of ten to fifteen times a month it will apparently be statistically normal or average. Deviations from this on either side should not be taken too seriously, unless emotional or physical disturbance is apparent.

Orgasm and Sex Relations

There seems to be general agreement that the inability of the wife to achieve orgasm is a problem in many marriages. Dickinson and Beam report that this was the most frequent complaint of the women in their classical study.[15] In about 25 percent of their cases women were unable to have orgasm. Other studies have found fairly similar results. Some of them have found fairly similar results. Some of them have failed to take the dura-tion of the marriage into account. Clinical findings indicate that wives often find difficulty in achieving orgasm early in marriage but that eventually they are able to do so. The Kinsey study took account of this time factor and the results bear out clinical findings. Kinsey reports that one-half of the wives achieve orgasm once or more during the first months of marriage.[16] This proportion increases fairly consistently until the fifteenth year of marriage by which time about nine-tenths of the wives have had orgasm once or more. As a matter of fact by then the great majority of sexual experiences result in orgasm for the wife as well as the husband.

It is possible that too much stress is put on orgasm. Stone writes:

. . . I should like to stress the fact that if a woman responds actively to the sexual embrace and takes pleasure in the sexual union, her inability to reach an orgasm may not be of serious import. Please understand that even if a

[13] John F. Cuber, *Marriage Counseling Practice* (New York, Appleton-Century-Crofts, 1948), p. 78.

[14] Alfred Kinsey, *et al., Sexual Behavior in the Human Female* (Philadelphia, Saunders, 1953), p. 394.

[15] Robert Dickinson and Laura Beam, *A Thousand Marriages* (Baltimore, Wil-liams and Wilkins, 1931), p. 62.

[16] Alfred Kinsey, *op. cit.,* p. 349.

woman does not attain an intense culmination, it does not mean that she does not derive a great deal of gratification out of the sex act. Some women, indeed, are not at all aware of any orgasm problem until they learn about it from a conversation or book, and then they become greatly worried because they believe that they are not obtaining complete satisfaction from their sex experiences.[17]

Sex is complex and its understanding and analyses should be considered in its emotional, social, and spiritual aspects, as well as in its physical aspect. The physical is an important and legitimate, and for some people an exceedingly crucial aspect of sex. This is not so for others. Nevertheless, orgasm is the ultimate in physical response for most people and there is reason to conclude that it is both a natural and a desired goal of sexual union.

SEXUAL HARMONY AND MARITAL SUCCESS

What relation does success in sex relations have to marital success? Popular thinking sometimes leads one to the conclusion that sexual maladjustment is a major if not *the* major cause of marital difficulty and divorce. Most marriage counselors would tend to dispute this and the results of statistical studies would also. Complications arise however when one attempts to isolate the sex factor. As Terman says:

The problem is complicated by the fact that the testimony of husband and wife regarding their sexual compatibility is influenced by their psychological compatibility. Couples who are psychologically well mated are likely to show a surprising tolerance for the things that are not satisfactory in their sexual relationships. The psychologically ill-mated show no such tolerance but instead are prone to exaggerate in their report on sexual maladjustments. The two sexual factors of genuine importance are the wife's orgasm adequacy and relative strength of sex drive in the two spouses.[18]

It does appear that sexual compatibility is an important expectation in modern marriage, and that where incompatibility exists, marital satisfaction will tend to be lowered. But as Burgess and Wallin say, while "there is evidence indicating that successful marriage and sexual adjustment tend to go together, the evidence does not reveal which is cause and which is effect." [19] The implications for the specific couple are rather clear. Success

[17] Abraham and Hannah Stone, *A Marriage Manual* (New York, Simon and Schuster, 1935), p. 201.

[18] From *Psychological Factors in Marital Happiness* by Louis Terman. Copyright, 1938. McGraw-Hill Book Company, Inc. Used by permission.

[19] Burgess and Wallin, *op. cit.,* p. 676. Our generalization on the relationship between sexual and marital adjustment should be applied primarily to the middle classes. Komarovsky suggests that the relationship between these two variables will

should be sought in the various areas of marriage, not solely in sex. Difficulties should be examined carefully, with outside help if necessary. The possibility that sexual tensions, if they arise, are reflecting other difficulties should be given consideration. Sex problems *and* fulfillment, to the realistic, are unavoidably individual and subjective. The final test of satisfaction is idiosyncratic to the specific pair.

Impotence and Frigidity

Sometimes the husband will be found who is or becomes unable to have sex relations with his wife. This condition is known as impotence. It usually occurs in varying degree. Complete impotence is the organic inability to have sex relations. Occasional impotence is a more common occurrence, while absolute impotence is very rare.

Impotence may be either physical or psychological in etiology, with the latter probably predominating.[20] Since in cases like these the line between the physical and psychic is very thin, medical attention is called for if difficulties persist. Seldom if ever are men constitutionally impotent, but certain diseases can result in physical impotence. More often inhibitions, deep-seated anxieties, or possibly latent homosexual tendencies are involved. Under competent psychiatric treatment the prognosis is usually good.

Sexual coldness is more common among women than is impotence among men. Frigidity, a term used only in reference to females, suggests the inability to respond sexually or to enjoy the coital experience.[21] Absolute frigidity is rare. However, in a study made in the thirties of one thousand married women, some 26 percent of them were sexually nonresponsive, as was previously indicated. Frigidity might well be considered as the level of difficulty a woman has in being aroused sexually.[22] It is a matter of degree. Pearson and English distinguish five categories ranging from painful contraction in the vagina with any coital activity through occasional failure to reach a climax.[23]

The causes of sexual unresponsiveness are biological, psychological, or social. As was previously pointed out, an unknown but important proportion of American women are sexually "unawakened" during the early years of marriage. Probably many reflect a conservative conditioning received in childhood. Correction of this difficulty can come with time,

---

not be as high as might be predicted in the working classes. See Mirra Komarovsky, *Blue-Collar Marriage* (New York, Random House, 1964), Chapter 4.

[20] Abraham and Hannah Stone, *op. cit.,* p. 189.

[21] Albert Ellis and Albert Abarbane, *The Encyclopedia of Sex Behavior,* Vol. 1 (New York, Hawthorn, 1961), p. 450.

[22] *Ibid.*

[23] O. Spurgeon English and Gerald Pearson, *Emotional Problems of Living* (New York, Norton, 1945), pp. 363–365.

patience, and skill on the part of the husband, perhaps aided in certain cases by counselling. Inept treatment may easily worsen the condition. More intensive medical or psychiatric therapy is, of course, indicated if progress on the wife's part is not soon forthcoming.

Birth Control

Most couples in early marriage, if not before, need to consider the question of contraception and conception. Negative control means that unwanted conception will not occur. Positive control suggests that the couple will be able to have children when it wishes to do so. Often instruction in the arts and techniques of contraception will accompany the premarital physical examination.

Birth control is not synonymous with contraception. It refers to all methods of preventing potential pregnancies or births. This can and may include such alternatives as delayed marriage with sexual abstinence, sterilization, and abortion, as well as the use of contraceptives or abstinence during marriage. Contraception, which will form the primary basis for our discussion, involves the use of chemical or mechanical means to prevent the fertilization of the ova by a live sperm.

There are a number of criteria by which a contraceptive method may be judged. Included are that it should be safe, it should result in only temporary prevention of conception, it should be reliable, and it should be acceptable to both parties involved.[24] Factors such as cost, availability, ease and timing required, use by husband or wife, esthetic effect, and others may also be considered. It must be made clear that a method in and of itself is not inherently "good." Account must be taken of the culture, social level of the couple involved, and other variable factors. For our purposes it may be wise to refer to some of the recent information on pregnancy from the Study of Family Growth in Metropolitan America (FGMA) conducted by Princeton University researchers. This will give some indication of the reliability and acceptability of methods among urban Americans during the period from 1950 to 1956.

In Table 21 we note that the two most popular methods, namely the condom and the diaphragm, were also the most reliable. The diaphragm, usually to be used with an additional jelly, has been recommended extensively by American physicians for a number of decades. It must be inserted by the woman before sex relations take place, if it is to be effective. Certain advantages and disadvantages are clear.[25] Especially for middle-

[24] Bernard Greenblatt, *A Doctor's Marital Guide for Patients* (Chicago, Budlong Press, 1964), pp. 75–84.

[25] The diaphragm has been especially popular with Americans of the higher educational levels. It is here that an emphasis on "deferred gratification," on "planning ahead," if you will, is most pronounced. The idea that the method should be under the control of the female has gained its strongest acceptance here. Rainwater notes

TABLE 21

Effectiveness of Contraceptive Method, by Interval,
Per 100 Years of Exposure

Method	Before First Pregnancy		Before Second and Third Pregnancy	
	Months of Exposure	Failure Rate	Months of Exposure	Failure Rate
Condom	3,227	17.1	6,835	12.3
Diaphragm and jelly	1,941	13.6	3,738	14.8
Withdrawal	213	22.5	1,074	15.6
Alternation-other	768	18.8	1,161	19.6
Alternation-douche	245	24.5	618	27.2
Combination-safe period	563	34.1	1,221	43.2
Combination-douche	346	34.7	683	24.6
Safe period	894	57.7	3,285	33.2
Douche	336	60.7	929	33.6
Other	179	60.3	351	41.0

SOURCE: Adapted from C. F. Westoff, *et al.*, *Family Growth in Metropolitan America* (Princeton, Princeton University Press, 1961), Table B-2, p. 362.

class American couples and physicians with high motivation to achieve control over pregnancy the diaphragm has been considered more natural and superior to the condom.

The condom (male sheath) although long criticized because of its alleged unreliability, is a relatively simple method to use.[26] Presumably its effectiveness has been greatly increased in recent years by a general upgrading in quality.[27] Withdrawal (coitus interruptus) has been considered an old folk method of dubious effectiveness, but the Princeton study indicates that it is almost as reliable as either the condom or diaphragm, although not as popular.[28] However, another criterion for judging a contra-

that lower status women raise a number of objections to the use of the diaphragm, however. They fear it will be lost, feel that it is "unnatural" to have an object inside themselves, and prefer that the male have control of the contraceptive. See Lee Rainwater, *And the Poor Get Children* (Chicago, Quadrangle Books, 1960), Chapters 7 and 8.

[26] The condom has a number of advantages, given a certain frame of reference. Rainwater's female respondents mentioned use by the male, its visibility as an external device, and the fact that it prevents the semen from reaching the woman's internal genitalia. Disadvantages are that it interferes with sex pleasure of the man, is subject to breakage, and puts the woman at the mercy of the man in sex relations. See *ibid.*

[27] Christopher Tietze, *The Condom as a Contraceptive* (New York, National Committee on Maternal Health, Inc., 1960).

[28] Stycos sharply attacks planned parenthood personnel and kindred groups for their depreciation of what he considers to be lower-class methods of birth control, including withdrawal. He suggests that the arguments against the latter are pseudomedical, without proven foundation, and overlook the probability that its use was largely responsible for the decline in Western fertility. See his "Critique of the Traditional

ceptive is that it be psychologically as natural as possible. Here is where withdrawal can be severely criticized.

Those who are prohibited the use of chemical or mechanical means of contraception by religious or other reasons may have an interest in the so-called "safe period" of birth control. This method is based on the assumption that a regular rhythm in the menstrual cycle of the woman can be ascertained. In the regular twenty-eight day cycle, ovulation supposedly occurs on the fourteenth day, give or take a few days either way. Since fertilization can take place only when the egg is vital, sex relations on days other than those immediately preceding or following ovulation should theoretically be "safe."

A major difficulty involves the fact that it is not yet possible to predict the exact time ovulation will occur in specific women. By carefully recording the menstrual cycle for six months to a year the relative stability of a particular woman's cycle can be ascertained. Women with regular cycles, with careful use of calendar and temperature charts, are able with a fairly high degree of accuracy to predict the time of ovulation. For those with irregular cycles it is much more difficult. Tietze and associates conclude that "the rhythm method offers a satisfactory degree of protection against unwanted pregnancy to rigorously selected and carefully instructed wives who, with their husbands, are intelligent and strongly motivated. For others and for those to whom pregnancy would be dangerous the effectiveness of the method in preventing conception is not considered adequate." [29]

Why does a couple use a particular method? It is known that motivations vary depending upon the personal preferences of the individuals involved and the circumstances. The Westoff sample of women gave various reasons for preferring a particular method. As can be seen reliability ranked high for over half of those who preferred diaphragm and jelly, condom, jelly, or other techniques. This contrasts sharply with the users of male withdrawal, douche, and safe period who gave other responses as predominating in their choice.

As the authors of the study point out, the reasons other than reliability vary with the method. Diaphragm and jelly users report that they accepted medical advice. When a condom is used it is often suggested that this is the only method known. Interestingly enough and contrary to what has been thought, when withdrawal is used wives are inclined to report that their

Planned Parenthood Approach in Underdeveloped Areas," in Clyde Kiser (Ed.), *Research in Family Planning* (Princeton, Princeton University Press, 1962), pp. 477–496. This criticism is probably most legitimate regarding populations in so-called underdeveloped countries, for which it was intended, although it has some validity in reference to lower-class groups in America. It points to the fact that the orientation toward sexuality, the roles of men and women in its regard, and personal and situational factors are all involved in consideration of the use of contraceptives.

[29] Tietze, *et al.*, "The Clinical Effectiveness of the Rhythm Method of Contraception," *Fertility and Sterility* (September–October, 1951), as cited in Greenblatt, *ibid.*, p. 83.

TABLE 22

*Reasons Given by Wives for Preferring the Single
Method They Are Currently Using*

Reasons for Preferring Current Method	Times Mentioned	Percentage of Wives
Reliable, safest, most effective	388	49
My husband prefers it; doesn't interfere with enjoyment of either spouse; most natural	156	20
Church approves it	152	19
Only method I know; never used any other	127	16
My doctor recommended it	127	16
Convenient, no trouble, easy to use; simple	77	10
Not reported	27	3
Clean, not messy	23	3
Physically safe, not harmful to the body	23	3
Other reasons	13	2
Don't know	4	1
Total	1,117	142

SOURCE: Charles Westoff, *Family Growth in Metropolitan America* (Princeton, Princeton University Press, 1961), p. 364.

husbands prefer this method. Unfortunately we do not have data available indicating the husband's preferences by their own report. That the religious factor is involved when the safe period is used should not be too surprising.

Attention may now be given to some newer methods which were not included in the Metropolitan study. One of these is the contraceptive foam. This method involves the insertion by the female of a chemical similar to the familiar jelly or cream which develops into a foamy substance in the vagina.[30] A modern method receiving considerable attention involves the use of an oral contraceptive or "pill." Synthetic steroid hormones have been found to inhibit ovulation in the female if taken regularly. Starting in 1956 with field trials in Puerto Rico, experimentation has taken place using the oral progestin, as it is known technically, in Britain, Mexico, and some other countries as well as the United States.[31] In 1960 approval for prescription preparations was granted by the Food and Drug Administration. Ten thousand women had participated in trials using some type of oral progestin, and by June, 1965 it was estimated that over six million women in various parts of the world (almost four million in the United States) were using the steroid pill.

[30] Aquiles Sobrero, "Birth Control Report," *Sexology* (July, 1963), p. 797.
[31] Frank Notestein, *et al.*, "The Problem of Population Control," in Philip Hauser (Ed.), *The Population Dilemma* (Englewood Cliffs, N.J., Prentice-Hall, 1963), Chapter 7.

Reports on the reliability of oral contraceptives suggest that if used carefully, effectiveness will be extremely high. The greatest problems apparent at present involve alleged side effects and cost, overlooking religious objections to the method. At the time of this writing (late June, 1965) the National Institute of Health has announced that a large-scale study of the steroid pill's effect on female users will be launched.[32] Steroids to be used by males will soon be developed.

Of major importance at this point is the revival of experimentation with intrauterine contraceptive devices. In the late twenties Gräfenberg and other German obstetricians experimented with rings made from silkworm gut and silver or gold wire. The rings were highly effective, but cases of inflammation of the pelvis were reported as side effects. Western physicians were not receptive and the method quickly came into disrepute. Israeli and Japanese gynecologists kept experimenting during the period from 1930 to 1960, however. By the early sixties some American experimentation was taking place. The Population Council was sufficiently impressed with these developments to consider supporting extensive research projects regarding the use of the intrauterine devices. This is now being done in a number of areas in America and abroad.[33]

American physicians have generally taken a conservative stand regarding the use of the so-called Gräfenberg ring. They will probably continue to do so in the immediate future. It is reported that 15 to 20 percent of the users suffer from irritation from the device, or experience difficulty keeping it in place. For the successful users there are obvious advantages. The device is effective, inexpensive, and after insertion can offer months or years of protection. Only initial motivation for use is required. Acceptability by users at various class and cultural levels is reportedly high. At any time the method can be discontinued, with no impairment of fertility. Reports are optimistic and suggest that the method will meet most of the standard criteria of acceptability, safety, and efficacy. Extensive use of this device for population control in underdeveloped countries can be predicted.

COMMUNICATION

A third major requirement for satisfactory marital life involves the establishment of satisfying patterns of communication. Unfortunately this

[32] See *Proceedings of a Conference: Thromboembolic Phenomena in Women* (G. D. Searl and Co., Box 5110, Chicago, Ill.). This bulletin discusses the alleged relationship between thromboembolic occurrence and the use of Enovid, a popular oral contraceptive. See also Associated Press release by Frank Carey, "Government Probes The Pill for Bad Effects" (*Cleveland Plain Dealer,* Sunday, June 27, 1965), p. A A 1.

[33] See *The Population Council Report,* 1962 and 1963 (New York, The Rockefeller Institute), pp. 11–13.

is one of the most seriously neglected aspects of marriage and family study. This is not to say that communication has been overlooked by social science. Much work has been done in linguistics by psychologists and anthropologists. Mass communication is receiving increasing attention by various kinds of social scientists and others. The same can be said for speech problems. But the *subtle aspects* of communication in marriage are only now emerging as an important subject of social science research.

Communication has been defined by Newcomb as the "process by which a person refers to something, either by pointing to it or using a symbol for it, in such a way as to lead another person to have a more or less similar experience of it." [34] He goes on to say that this presupposes shared frames of reference or norms. This is a crucial point and bears detailed discussion.

Norms develop and exist in a cultural system. All people in modern societies are now somewhat aware of the fact that cultures around the world differ in content. They may not be aware of all the implications of these differences. They may be very ethnocentric about their own way of doing things and not tolerant of others. The story is told of the Englishman who was commenting to friends on his experiences in traveling to various parts of the world. Part of his comments were as follows: "Yes sir, you sure see and hear some peculiar things. Take such a simple item as H_2O. In Germany they call it 'wasser,' in Spain 'aqua,' in China 'shwai,' and so on. Strange blokes some of those people are. After all the stuff is 'water.' "

International and intercultural marriages are obviously faced initially with definite barriers regarding communication between the spouses. The same holds true for marriages which cross subcultural groups in the United States. The latter are becoming much more common. The following case of cross-cultural marriage illustrates the differences which may arise when norms are not shared in marriage.

Mary and Marvin were married after a courtship of several years, during which she taught school in the rural community in which he owned and operated a small business. She was a member of the Presbyterian Church and he a Mennonite. Between their two faiths there was no great theological difference, and Mary was particularly impressed by and eager to participate in the pacifist position of the Mennonites. Their marriage had every expectation of success by reason of their maturity, their long acquaintance, their sharing of common values. When Mary married Marvin she became a member of the Mennonite congregation to which he belonged, taking pride not simply in becoming a member of her husband's church but in becoming a member of a movement which had maintained a vigorous and idealistic peace testimony in the face of persecution for hundreds of years.

But soon her feeling toward the church and toward her husband suffered a change. Although she had been accepted with every sign of friendliness by

[34] Theodore Newcomb, *Social Psychology* (New York, Holt, Rinehart and Winston, 1950), p. 268.

the members of the church and although all the activities of the church were open to her, she felt herself alternately left out of or oppressed by church activities. Mennonite congregations are family affairs; persecution has given them an intense ingroup solidarity which is the strength of the individual Mennonite in a hostile social environment. Mary could feel this intense group loyalty; she could hear the older people talking of events and persons which meant nothing to her.

It was natural for Marvin and herself to take dinner with his family on Sunday when he was courting her. To him it was equally natural to maintain that custom when they had a home of their own. It seemed to her, however, that they did not have a home of their own, but rather that the clan into which she had married simply had another stopping place in town. Their private lives and all their intimate aspirations were going down in a sea of family and kin.

Yet at the same time, she hated to complain to Marvin about the matter since it seemed foolish. Why shouldn't they go out to the farm for dinner after church on Sunday? She had enjoyed doing it in their courtship days. The attention given them by the clan seemed so friendly that she began to wonder whether she was becoming "queer."

Marvin could not but notice the emotional tension under which Mary was laboring. Coming from the stern background of the Mennonites, he did not think of talking the matter over with her. Rather he concluded that she was angry with him, that he had unintentionally failed her in some subtle way. Thus within a year and a half a young couple beginning with many advantages had arrived at mutual distrust and guilty self-condemnation.

The student will note that Mary's difficulty lay not in entering the new fellowship, a step she had been eager to take, but in what that involved with respect to other fellowships in which she had formerly participated. As a Presbyterian she had been free to enter into whatever recreation groups she might choose. As a Mennonite she was expected to refrain from activities in certain recreational groups. Thus entering a different religious fellowship involved a readjustment of her entire system of group allegiances, a matter which she had not bargained for when she entered the Mennonite church. Since her marriage to Marvin was the cause of her entry into that church, and since his long membership there had made him so familiar with its restrictions as to be unaware of them, he had offended her twice: once, by bringing her into a restricting fellowship; and again by failure to perceive the fact that it was restricting for her.[35]

Besides the larger cultural and subcultural differences which may exist as barriers to communication are those reflecting differences in previous family culture. The family develops it own unique and peculiar culture, with shared meanings attached to particular things and events. The members come to share common experiences and to understand one another's views

[35] From Rockwell Smith, "Religion in Family Life," in Howard Becker and Reuben Hill (Eds.), *Family, Marriage, and Parenthood* (Boston, Heath, copyright 1955), pp. 600–601.

and behavior. Bossard, long-time student of the family, has this to say in regard to modes of expression as part of the unique family culture: "modes of expression constitute a distinctive aspect of family situations. Each family has its own words, signs, gestures, pet phrases, humorous references, special words of condemnation, favorite topics, and characteristic forms of expression." [36]

Since the husband and wife are likely to have been socialized in different family cultures, even if they are reared within the same general culture, the possibilities of certain background barriers to communication are always present.

Another barrier to husband-wife communication is laid in the differential conditioning of the sexes in childhood and youth, and in the fact of membership in the sex grouping of "men" and "women" respectively. Hill and associates provide an interesting illustration of this from their well-known studies of fertility planning in Puerto Rico. Under the topic "Barriers to Communication" they say:

From the exploratory study of seventy-two families, the cleavages which make communication difficult have been identified. The differential statuses of male and female are expressed in ideologies which invidiously define the women as weak, naive, and pure, and the man as strong, shrewd, and inherently evil. These ideologies are expressed in differential child rearing practices and in different role expectations for the sexes before marriage. Girls internalize patterns of modesty, low sexual drives, and subservience to males. Boys internalize the patterns of high sex curiosity, strong sexual drives, and assertiveness with respect to women. To maintain this character structure the sexes are segregated in work and play, although exceptions are everywhere seen in the island with the inauguration of coeducation in the schools. There are, however, few opportunities for boys and girls to develop companionship patterns before marriage. Boys run with boys, and girls share their thoughts primarily with their own sex. Courtships are carried out under supervision of chaperons, which minimizes the opportunity for developing patterns of give-and-take discussion before marriage.

Once married, two important barriers to communication are manifested—respect for the husband and modesty of the wife. The first is an important norm of husband-wife and father-child relations. A certain degree of formality is supposed to characterize the relations between wife and husband which would be threatened by discussion of intimate topics of interpersonal relations. One lower-class woman expressed the position poignantly: ". . . I never discuss such things with my husband. I feel too much respect for him." Men, in turn, are hesitant to open up discussion on matters which they have not heard discussed by their own parents. They want to believe that their wives are innocent and too modest to talk about matters of sex and childbirth. Said one husband in this connection: ". . . to my wife, me talk about these

[36] James Bossard, *The Sociology of Child Development* (New York, Harper & Row, 1954), p. 199.

things? Look, man, I couldn't even try. I am not accustomed to talking about these things with women." Modesty operates as a barrier to communication between husband and wife on topics which to an outsider would appear far removed from the tabooed areas of sex and childbirth. In a tabulation of the answers of 150 mothers from the sample of 888 families, the amount of communication between husband and wife on crucial marital issues appears small even for such seemingly neutral matters as child discipline and the husband's work. About a fourth of the 150 women questioned never talked about these areas of family life (Table 23). In general, the more intimate the area, the more attenuated the discussion between husband and wife, with almost half never talking about birth control or sexual relations.[37]

TABLE 23

Extent of Discussion between Husband and Wife of Key Marital Issues, as Reported by 150 Wives* in Puerto Rico by Percentage

	Frequency of Discussion During Marriage			
Topic	Never	Occasionally	Frequently	All Respondents
Husband's work	23.0	42.0	35.0	100.0
Discipline of children	25.0	47.0	28.0	100.0
Religion	35.0	48.0	17.0	100.0
Future plans	35.0	46.0	19.0	100.0
Birth control	47.0	35.0	18.0	100.0
Sexual relations	53.0	34.0	13.0	100.0

* A subsample of 888 wives interviewed.
SOURCE: Reuben Hill, Kurt Back and J. Mayone Stycos, "Intra-family Communication and Fertility Planning in Puerto Rico," *Rural Sociology,* Vol. 20 (September–December, 1955), by permission of the authors and publisher.

While this reference is to a culture rather distinct from that of middle-class United States proper, it should not be assumed that communication difficulties across sex lines exist only in the more traditional cultures. Mead and others have shown that communication between the sexes is often hampered by the differential conditioning of males and females in American society.[38] Harper comments on this point in these words:

Since members of the other sex represent behavior patterns opposed to those each sex is encouraged to develop, boys and girls during the preadolescent years grow up under conditions that lead them to avoid and distrust one an-

[37] Reprinted from *Rural Sociology,* Reuben Hill, Kurt Back, and J. Mayone Stycos, "Intra-family Communication and Fertility Planning in Puerto Rico," Vol. 20 (September and December, 1955), pp. 264–265, by permission of the authors and publisher.
[38] Margaret Mead, *Male and Female* (New York, Morrow, 1949), Chapter 14.

other. The girls come to resent boys, because boys are permitted freedom not granted girls and because boys develop personality traits girls have been taught to think of as not nice. Boys, feeling tensions from frustrations met in their broader and more demanding experiences, come likewise to resent girls because girls manifest interests and attitudes that the boys have been taught are undesirable, and because girls have a socially enforced impunity from male attack. Both sexes, then, move into the period where romantic interest develops with a conditioning that has not equipped them either to understand or to admire the personality traits of the other sex.[39]

It is probably inevitable that there will be some carry-over of hostilities developed in childhood and adolescence into marriage. And the membership of the spouses in the two different social categories of men and women may make for at least minimum difficulties of communication.[40]

Besides the communication barriers which are cultural and social in origin are those of a more individual nature. A number of researchers have commented on the relationship between emotional maladjustment and difficulties in communication. Rogers says, in relation to this question, that

The whole task of psychotherapy is the task of dealing with a failure in communication. The emotionally maladjusted person, the neurotic, is in difficulty first because communication within himself has broken down, and second because as a result of this his communication with others has been damaged. If this sounds somewhat strange, let me put it in other terms. In the neurotic individual, parts of himself which have been termed unconscious, or repressed, or denied to awareness, become blocked off so that they no longer communicate themselves to the conscious or managing part of himself. As long as this is true, there are distortions in the way he communicates himself to others, and so he suffers both within himself, and in his interpersonal relations.[41]

The individual who has a maladjusted personality, then, will ordinarily be difficult to communicate with. Most of us are aware of this. Many have had contacts with mentally ill people whose verbal communications were disconnected and incoherent. Many more of us have had unpleasant contacts with individuals suffering more minor personality maladjustments and have not realized some of the sources of the difficulty. In most communities individuals exist who are recognized by the neighbors and family members as being difficult to communicate with and "touchy." A man occasionally may even publicly exclaim in reference to his wife, "I just can't talk to her," or a wife may complain to a friend, "He gets all up-

[39] Robert Harper, *Marriage* (New York, Appleton-Century-Crofts, © 1949), p. 67.
[40] LeMasters in a recent book sees fit to include a chapter on the female subculture and a chapter on the male subculture in America. See Ersel LeMasters, *Modern Courtship and Marriage* (New York, Macmillan, 1957).
[41] Carl Rogers, "Communication; Its Blocking and Facilitation," in S. I. Hayakawa, *Language Meanings, and Maturity* (New York, Harper & Row, 1954), p. 53.

set whenever we talk about any of our problems in the home. I just have to keep quiet about things."

Bordering on minor maladjustment of personality is a category which might be referred to as the idiosyncratic or unique frame of reference or simply bias. Personality maladjustment is not necessarily involved, but difficulties of communication exist anyway. Take the case of George D. George D. is a Ph.D. businessman from a lower middle-class background. Mrs. Mary D., his wife, has a college degree and was a school teacher previous to her marriage. The couple have three young children. In terms of general social and cultural background and basic value orientation George and Mary are well matched. Both seem well within the range of normality in terms of both personal and social adjustment. Although we do not have the couple's personal rankings of themselves on a marital success scale, close friends rank them average to good on a five-point scale. A factor which stands out in this case is the lack of smooth communication between the spouses. Mary communicates very well with outsiders, while George communicates adequately with them. With his wife George is sometimes difficult because he values his own opinions highly and seems to place little value on hers. Some might say that George is eccentric. Mary has been known to use even stronger adjectives occasionally in describing her husband's behavior. At times Mary simply cannot communicate with George; she says he is like a stone wall. At other times she can get through to him. As a whole we would have to say that communication between the spouses in this family is rather poor, and the barrier seems to involve George D., both as communicator and communicant.

Communication in Marriage Studies

The importance of communication as a factor in marital success has been the concern in two marriage prediction studies by Karlsson and Locke respectively. Karlsson hypothesized the following:

1. Communication of role expectations is associated with marital satisfaction.
   A necessary prerequisite for the adjustment of the spouses to each other is that their expectations are communicated. Otherwise they will not know what to adjust to. On the other hand, communication will be affected by the emotional relations between the spouses and their mutual satisfaction. This follows from the fact that the inhibition from communicating is strongly affected by the feelings.
2. Communication of intentions is associated with marital satisfaction. This is necessary for a reasonable amount of security for the spouses in knowing what the other mate will do.
3. Communication of love and respect is associated with marital satisfaction.
   The important love and respect in the marital process is the love and respect that is communicated to the mate. If not communicated it is of

comparatively little importance, restricted to the feeling person as it is. The main expectation in marriage is that the other spouse is loving and respectful and shows it.[42]

Karlsson found these hypotheses to be generally borne out in his study.

An index of communication was constructed by Karlsson for the purpose of finding out how much the spouses knew about each other's wishes.[43] The items making up the index included finances, work, playing with children, talking about children, etc. The respondent was asked to indicate his satisfaction with the knowledge of his wishes possessed by his mate. He was also asked to indicate his spouse's wishes on each item. The communication index was based on the degree spouses were correct in predicting the wishes of their mates. A rather high correlation between scores on this index and marital satisfaction was found by Karlsson.

Locke also made use of the communication factor in his study in prediction of marital success. He used a broad concept of communication, including face-to-face association, reduction of intimate communication, sympathetic understanding, frequency of kissing, engaging in outside interests together, and talking things over together. Basing his analysis on both statistical associations and case study Locke is led to conclude that marital adjustment is positively associated with the following items of communication: "Intimacy of association, as indicated by frequent kissing, by always, or almost always, talking things over, and by joint participation in all, or almost all, outside activities and interests." [44]

Our common sense generalizations on the importance of communication in marriage seem to be borne out in research studies.

So far we have been lumping all forms of communication together regardless of type. It should be made clear that there are two major types of communication, verbal and nonverbal. (Under verbal we include both spoken and written language symbols). It is difficult to determine which type is the more important in marital interaction. Certainly nonverbal symbols such as gestures, facial expression, and the like are crucial in marriage. Each spouse has to learn to interpret these nonverbal cues which convey meaning in and of themselves and when they accompany verbal communiques. A "no" may mean anything from a strong negative feeling to a mildly affirmative one, given the particular situational context. When husband meets wife at the door as he comes home from work the question may be posed by one spouse, "How did things go today?" The answer "okay" is not very meaningful to anyone but the perceptive spouse who is familiar with the mate's typical modes of communication.

[42] Georg Karlsson, *Adaptibility and Communication in Marriage* (Uppsala, Sweden, Almqvist and Wiksells, 1951), pp. 52, 53.

[43] *Ibid.*, pp. 132–133.

[44] Harvey Locke, *Predicting Adjustment in Marriage* (New York, Holt, Rinehart and Winston, 1951), p. 266.

It seems wise then that each spouse attempt to build channels of communication with the other spouse that can be kept *free* and *open*. It is probable that ability in this realm is more an art than a science. Barriers to communication, social, psychological, or of whatever category, need often to be broken down if marital success is to be achieved. This involves patience, ingenuity, and hard work. It involves the ability to perceive the meaning behind the words spoken rather than the very literal significance of statements. A folk saying in rural Pennsylvania and Ohio goes something like this: "You should take a Dutchman for what he means, not what he says." The same idea is true for the spouse in regard to his mate.

Interpersonal competency, especially empathy, is involved in intra-family communication. The person with this ability in high degree is so able to perceive his spouse's feelings and intentions that he can to a high degree predict his spouse's behavior.

As husband and wife live together over the years they will normally, in a good marriage, be able to communicate with each other increasingly well. This becomes a source of great joy and satisfaction. The approving smile, the loving touch, and the knowing glance all may have a rich meaning. Fortunate are the couples who can communicate for they shall achieve understanding—and more.

SELECTED READINGS

Baber, Ray, *Marriage and the Family* (New York, McGraw-Hill, 1953), Chapter 6.

Becker, Howard, and Hill, Reuben (Eds.), *Family, Marriage, and Parenthood* (Boston, Heath, 1955), Part III.

Bell, Robert, *Marriage and Family Interaction* (Homewood, Ill., Dorsey Press, Inc., 1963), Chapters 10, 11.

Benson, Purnell, "The Interests of Happily Married Couples," *Marriage and Family Living,* Vol. 14 (November, 1952), pp. 276–280.

Benson, Purnell, "Familism and Marital Success," *Social Forces,* Vol. 33 (March, 1955), pp. 277–280.

Bernard, Jessie, Buchanan, Helen and Smith, William, *Dating, Mating, and Marriage* (Cleveland, Howard Allen, Inc., 1958), Chapter 8.

Blood, Robert, *Marriage* (New York, Free Press, 1962), Chapters 9 and 12.

Burgess, Ernest and Wallin, Paul, *Engagement and Marriage* (Philadelphia, Lippincott, 1953), Chapters 14 and 18.

Cavan, Ruth, *American Marriage* (New York, Crowell, 1959), Chapter 12.

Cavan, Ruth, *Marriage and Family in the Modern World* (New York, Crowell, 1960), Chapter 12.

Christensen, Harold, *Marriage Analysis* (New York, Ronald, 1950), Chapter 19.

Corsini, Raymond, "Understanding and Similarity in Marriage," *Journal of Abnormal and Social Psychology,* Vol. 52 (May, 1956), pp. 327–332.

Duvall, Evelyn, *Family Development* (Philadelphia, Lippincott, 1957), Chapter 6.

Duvall, Evelyn, and Hill, Reuben, *Being Married* (Boston, Heath, 1960), Chapter 10.

Foote, Nelson, "Matching of Husband and Wife in Phases of Development," Family Study Center, University of Chicago, paper number 7, 1956.

Himes, Norman and Taylor, Donald, *Your Marriage* (New York, Holt, Rinehart and Winston, 1955), Chapter 11.

Hobart, Charles, "Disillusionment in Marriage and Romanticism," *Marriage and Family Living,* Vol. 20 (May, 1958), pp. 156–162.

Keeley, Benjamin, "Value Convergence and Marital Relations," *Marriage and Family Living,* Vol. 17 (November, 1955), pp. 342–345.

Kephart, William, *Family Society and the Individual* (Boston, Houghton Mifflin, 1961), Chapter 17.

Kirkpatrick, Clifford, *The Family* (New York, Ronald, 1955), Chapter 18.

Komarovsky, Mirra, *Blue-Collar Marriage* (New York, Knopf, 1964), Chapter 2.

Landis, Paul, *Making the Most of Marriage* (New York, Appleton-Century-Crofts, 1960), Chapters 21 and 23.

LeMasters, Ersel, *Modern Courtship and Marriage* (New York, Macmillan, 1957), Chapters 12 and 15.

Levy, John and Munroe, Ruth, *The Happy Family* (New York, Random House, 1938), Chapter 2.

Locke, Harvey, *Predicting Adjustment in Marriage* (New York, Holt, Rinehart and Winston, 1951).

Mace, David, "Personality Expression and Subordination in Marriage," *Marriage and Family Living,* Vol. 15 (August, 1953), pp. 205–207.

Martinson, Floyd, *Marriage and the American Ideal* (New York, Dodd, Mead, 1960), Chapter 17.

Olsen, Arthur, Mudd, Emily H., and Bourdeau, Hugo, *Readings on Marriage and Family Relations* (Harrisburg, Pa., The Stackpole Company, 1953), Part IV.

Simpson, George, *People in Families* (New York, Crowell, 1960), Chapters 11 and 12.

Winch, Robert, *The Modern Family* (New York, Holt, Rinehart and Winston, 1963), Chapters 12 and 16.

QUESTIONS AND EXERCISES

1. Is it inevitable that there will be a "psychic honeymoon" followed by a period of disillusionment during the early part of marriage? Discuss.

2. What are some of the processes involved in early marital adaption? Indicate how they function by referring to specific cases of which you have knowledge, if possible.

3. What patterns of behavior can be carried over from engagement into marriage and what patterns should ideally be dropped? Discuss.

4. Riesman, Whyte, and others have been calling for more "individualism" and less "togetherness." To what degree can this be applied to marriage in your estimation? Is there a danger that individualism will go too far?

5. Invite a few couples who have been married two or three years to speak to your group on adjustments made during the first months of marriage.

6. LeMasters (Chapters 22, 23) suggests that there are important differences in orientation between men and women which must be understood in order to have mutual understanding in marriage. Read the chapters and then write a critique of them.

7. Both Komarovsky (Chapters 3–7) and Burgess and Wallin (p. 618) report that wives are inclined to make more adjustments in marriage than husbands. Is this inevitable? Why?

8. Indicate by example how social mobility may be a source of tension between marital partners. Discuss.

9. Invite a panel of religious leaders (including a minister, a priest, and a rabbi) to explain their churches' positions on the use of birth control.

10. Read the cited Duvall and Hill section (pp. 200–201), then write a paper on the question of whether or not an "Etiquette of Intimacy" is necessary in the early part of marriage.

11. Some clinicians stress the importance of the sexual factor in marriage while some researchers consider it to be secondary regarding overall adjustment. Just how important, comparatively speaking, do you consider sex to be in relation to marital success? Defend your position.

12. Have two or three of your young married friends indicate to you the changes in attitudes, values, and general personality, if any, which they experienced during their first year of marriage.

13. Marriage has been spoken of as "antagonistic cooperation." From your point of view to what degree is this true and to what degree false?

14. Analyze the Mace (1953) article critically regarding personal freedom and mutual support within the marital relationship.

13

Relating to Outside Groups

Man does not live alone, nor does a couple. The concept of an oasis in which the couple will live alone ever after is romantic but not very realistic. The point need not be labored. Besides relations with the extended family network, the couple will need to relate to organizations outside the home, to the business organization or some other source of employment, to the church, and many other organizations and institutions in the community. Our discussion in this chapter will focus first of all upon relations with in-laws and then proceed to friends and associates, the church, and other groups.

One does not marry merely an individual of the opposite sex; one also marries a family, or rather, *into* a family. This family from which the spouse comes and into which he marries has a set of values, mores, and folkways that may or may not be similar to those with which he is familiar. Even though the new couple may live some distance from either family, the folkways of the respective in-laws are still to a certain extent embodied in each spouse.

RELATING TO IN-LAWS

Relations between young couples and their respective parents are seriously affected by the cultural arrangements which have been instituted to regularize the interaction. This can be illustrated by reference to cultures other than our own. In the East, especially in old China, it was understood that the daughter-in-law would be brought in by her husband to live with his relatives. The concept of family line was stressed, as embodied especially in the male. In reality, women were "brought in" to perform a function by continuing the line. The new daughter-in-law had to serve a type of apprenticeship by "waiting on" her new mother, in essence assuming the role of a servant. As time went on, especially if she bore sons, the daughter-in-law was able to assume more authority. Eventually she would become lady of her own household and be able to supervise a daughter-in-law of her own.[1]

In modern times this system has incurred increasing attack throughout the East, under the influence of western ideologies.[2] In the old days, however, the system reportedly worked well within the framework of traditional eastern values. Within such a system the authority of the two generations was defined and relationships were clear-cut.

The western system, particularly in urban America, is obviously based on different principles. Ideally, as everyone knows, the young couple is to leave both sets of parents and strike out on its own. This presupposes economic and emotional maturity on the part of the young people and a willingness on the part of the parents to give up authority over them. Problems can arise on either side. Some parents find that a son or daughter cannot move into marriage freely without emotional or other support from his or her mother and father. On the other hand, young people may find impulsive parents too eager to help them "avoid mistakes."

How Difficult Are In-Law Relationships in Early Marriage?

If relations with in-laws are to be difficult for a particular couple, the chances are that problems will arise during the early years of marriage. Landis studied two different samples of married couples and in both cases inquired into their relationships with in-laws. Those who had been married twenty years on the average mentioned in-law relationships second or third (women and men respectively) among six problem areas in achieving marital success. The other group contained couples who had been married only a few years. These couples placed in-law relationships at the top of their list of problem areas in marriage.[3]

A study by Thomas of some 7,000 Roman Catholic marriages which had failed bears out the principle that in-law problems are more prevalent in the early years of marriage. He reported in-law relations to be the largest cause of trouble during the first year of marriage, but during the later years other factors moved into prominence.[4] Blood and Wolfe confirm these

[1] Francis Hsu, *Americans and Chinese* (New York, Abelard-Schuman, 1953), pp. 125–130.

[2] William Goode, *World Revolution and Family* (New York, Free Press), Chapters V–VII.

[3] Judson Landis, *Building a Successful Marriage* (Englewood Cliffs, N.J., Prentice-Hall, Inc., 1953), p. 303.

[4] John Thomas, "Marital Failure and Duration," *Social Order,* Vol. 3 (January, 1953), pp. 24–29.

findings by Thomas. In a sample of married women from the Detroit area, in-law problems were about twice as prevalent during the early period of marriage as they were at any other time.[5]

It seems plausible that findings such as the above should emerge. Time is necessary to break old habits and establish new ones. In school, factory, army, and other groups, the newcomer is often viewed with some suspicion and even hostility. He must measure up to certain expectations before he is accepted. Families on both sides may adopt such an approach to the new in-law. Especially will this be true if the marriage was opposed in the first place. As time elapses, however, close relationships may be developed. But it often takes a few rough years for a couple to attain a satisfactory equilibrium in their association with the in-laws.

General Bases for In-Law Difficulties

There seem to be various causes of in-law problems. They can be analyzed under two main categories, the sociocultural and the psychological. We shall consider first the sociocultural category.

Sociocultural

Various stereotypes having to do with in-law relationships exist in American society. Most of them seem to have an underlying note of hostility or avoidance. Duvall, who has made the most thorough study of in-law relationships to date, finds that the mother-in-law is the butt of jokes and stereotypes to a greater extent than any other in-law. She delineates eight themes which predominate in all parts of the country:

1. Mothers-in-law talk too much.
2. Mothers-in-law know all the answers—the wrong ones.
3. Mothers-in-law are meddlesome troublemakers.
4. Mothers-in-law are ego-deflating.
5. Mothers-in-law are mean.
6. Mothers-in-law are loathsome objects of aggression.
7. Mothers-in-law come too often and stay too long.
8. Mothers-in-law are to be avoided.[6]

While there is evidence that some individuals are rejecting the mother-in-law jokes and stereotypes, they still negatively condition many of us and provide a rather poor groundwork for smooth interaction between the in-laws involved.

A source of in-law problems is that of cultural conflict between the generations. In a society changing as rapidly as ours culture conflict be-

[5] Robert Blood and Donald Wolfe, *Husbands and Wives* (New York, Free Press, 1960), p. 247.

[6] Evelyn Duvall, *In-Laws: Pro and Con* (New York, Association Press, 1954), pp. 23–24.

tween the generations may be inevitable. Parents tend to have well-established habits and ideas regarding recreation and entertainment, religious practices, and social conventions. Young people exposed to new ideas and new ways of acting outside the home often reject some of their parents' expectations and deviate from them. Dinkle concludes, on the basis of a study of fifty families in Minnesota, that "broadly viewed, conflict of *aged* parents with their children was in large part a clash of different cultures." [7]

Psychological Factors in In-Law Problems

The major psychological factors involved in in-law difficulties of the early marriage period relate to "overattachment" or what is commonly referred to as the problem of weaning or cutting the apron strings. These can be of two types: overattachment of the young married person to one of the parents, or the overattachment of a parent to the newly-married child. It is at this time impossible to say which causes the greatest amount of difficulty.

The first category involves lack of maturity and independence. It is quite natural for a child to be closely attached to one or both parents in the childhood home, and we consider him to be deviant if such is not the case. But an emotional weaning is a necessary process in the movement toward full adulthood and independence. Difficulties in this realm are fairly common and can be inferred from the stories of the young wife who "runs home to mother" when any problems arise, or of the young husband who can't cut his "mother's apron strings." The latter condition has been considered so common by some that it has brought forth a flood of articles and books, of which those by Wylie and by Strecker may be considered typical.[8]

As is well known, Freudian theory suggests that the child will be most closely attached to the parent of the opposite sex. Winch's findings, based on a study of college students, are instructive at this point and indicate that the students tended not to prefer one parent over the other. However, when they did, the mother was more often preferred than the father. Further, sons were inclined to prefer their mothers in greater proportion than were the daughters. As a whole, according to Winch, the mother-son relationship is the "key one." The following are hypotheses resulting from Winch's studies:

I. Offspring of both sexes tend to profess no preference for either parent.
II. Irrespective of sex, those offspring who prefer one parent over the other tend to prefer the mother.

[7] Robert Dinkel, "Parent-Child Conflict in Minnesota Families," *American Sociological Review,* Vol. 8 (August, 1943), pp. 412–419.
[8] See Philip Wylie, *Generation of Vipers* (New York, Holt, Rinehart and Winston, rev. ed., 1955) and Edward Strecker, *Their Mother's Sons* (Philadelphia, Lippincott, rev. ed., 1951).

III. Of those offspring who prefer one parent over the other, sons tend to prefer their mothers in greater proportion than do daughters; daughters tend to prefer their fathers in greater proportion than do sons.
IV. Irrespective of the sex of parent, those parents who prefer children of one sex over children of the other tend to prefer sons.
V. Of those parents who prefer children of one sex over children of the other, fathers tend to prefer daughters in greater proportion than do mothers; mothers tend to prefer sons in greater proportion than do fathers.[9]

Parental overattachment to children or the reverse can set the stage for grave in-law difficulties. Some parents fail to grow and mature along with the growth and development of their children, and are not emotionally prepared to see them embark into new family careers. Especially vulnerable, according to a present theory, is the middle-class mother, who feels she faces a bleak, uninteresting, and unneeded existence after the children have departed from the home. This theory may be overstressed but the mother who does not receive all the affection she desires from her husband is probably most likely to overprotect her children and be less ready to accept the married status of her child.

Which In-Law Relationships Are the Most Troublesome?

Tradition has it that relations with the mother-in-law are the most troublesome of all in-law relationships and that young wives have the greatest amount of difficulty. Research seems to bear out the traditional idea. Duvall's findings are summarized below.

TABLE 24

The In-Law Named Most Difficult by 1337 Persons

	Number	Percentage
Mother-in-law	491	36.8
Sister-in-law	272	20.3
Brother-in-law	72	5.4
Father-in-law	67	5.0
Daughter-in-law	37	2.8
Other female-in-law	22	1.6
"All-in-laws"	20	1.5
Son-in-law	10	.7
Other male-in-laws	1	.1
No difficult in-laws	345	25.8
total	1337	100.0

SOURCE: *In-laws: Pro and Con*, Evelyn Duvall (New York, Association Press, © 1954), p. 188.

[9] Robert Winch, *The Modern Family* (New York, Holt, Rinehart and Winston, 1952), p. 300.

What might be considered ingroup solidarity sets the stage also for potential in-law frictions. The person is reared in his family and under typical conditions develops strong loyalties to this family group. If the family is well integrated, the members have learned to be mutually supportive, and to rally to each other's aid in time of trouble. With marriage comes a break in the ranks, albeit an expected and socially sanctioned one. A struggle may ensue in which (focusing on the family of one of the spouses) an attempt is made either to reject the newcomer or to remake him so that he is acceptable. The rejection process is probably more typical. Neither rejection nor remaking is considered desirable by the set of in-laws concerned. Unless the spouse seems—as the mate interprets it—willing to give first loyalty to the new pair relationship, the partner may become very hostile toward the in-laws.

Hill points out that another source of difficulty is the difference in role expectations between the spouse and in-laws in regard to their child. George is still "their boy" not quite grown up. Jane fully expects George to "act like a man" and carry out the duties of a husband.[10]

The family ingroup also has its own culture, its own set of values, standards, preferences, habits, and rituals. The newcomer cannot possibly know or appreciate all the finer points of the pattern. As a novice he will at best fail to respond to certain subtle cues, to find humor in certain situations, or to know when something calls for a serious demeanor. The cultural clash tends to be more serious in cases of marriage across national, religious, ethnic, or class boundaries but it is by no means confined to marriages of this sort.

Landis found the following relatives most responsible for friction in in-law relationships: [11] (1) mother-in-law, (2) sister-in-law, (3) brother-in-law, and (4) father-in-law. We note that again mother-in-law and sister-in-law are in one and two positions but that brother-in-law and father-in-law are reversed compared to the order in Table 24.

What Major Complaints Are Made against Mother-in-Law and Sisters-in-Law?

While definite differences appear, both the mother-in-law and sister-in-law seem to have a tendency to meddle, interfere, nag and criticize, and be inconsiderate and thoughtless. Especially criticized is the sister of the young husband, who apparently finds it difficult to share her favorite brother with a newcomer, or extends sibling rivalry into the new marital situation. Brothers-in-law and fathers-in-law seem easier to live with. Those who do complain about their brother-in-law refer to incompetence and ir-

---

[10] Willard Waller and Reuben Hill, *The Family* (New York, Holt, Rinehart and Winston, 1951), p. 290.

[11] Judson Landis, *op. cit.,* p. 304.

TABLE 25

*Complaints Made against Mother-in-Law and
Sister-in-Law*

Category	Mother-in-law Order	Sister-in-law Order
Interference	1	1
Possessiveness	2	11
Criticalness	3	4
Indifference	4	2
Immaturity	5	5
Uncongeniality	6	10
Thoughtlessness	7	3
Partiality	8	13
Intruding	9	14
Self-righteousness	10	8
Talkativeness	11	12
Misrepresentation	12	7
Rivalrousness	13	6
Incompetency	14	9
Unconventionality	15	15

SOURCE: Adapted from *In-laws: Pro and Con*, Evelyn Duvall (New York, Association Press, © 1954), p. 246.

responsibility, while the father-in-law is criticized for being ineffectual, uncongenial, talkative, unconventional, and old-fashioned.

It appears that females are more vulnerable to in-law friction than males. Perhaps interpersonal relations within the family are more important to them than to men, whose major interests often lie outside the home. Men may conveniently withdraw from home or conflict by preoccupation with their work or recreational life to an extent which is impossible for women.

The Komarovsky study calls the above generalization into question in regard to working-class families, however. The pattern was confirmed in Komarovsky's sample in which the wives were graduates of high school. One-third of the wives reported serious dissatisfaction with in-law relationships, while the husbands reported relative satisfaction. On the other hand, in the non high school category of their sample, 33 percent of the men as well as 32 percent of the women indicated that the relationship with in-laws was strained.[12]

It is of interest to note that the author was so struck by the unpredicted in-law problems that she saw fit to devote a whole chapter to them, entitled "A Marriage Triangle: The Husband, His Wife, and His Mother-

[12] See Mirra Komarovsky, *Blue-Collar Marriage* (New York, Random House, 1964), pp. 259–260.

in-Law." Stressed as disturbing influences that often appear to be causally involved in the unhappy triangle are:

1. Marriage to a better-educated wife.
2. The antagonisms of the wife to her mother.
3. The wife's emotional dependence upon her mother.
4. Economic and social interdependence, including joint households.

The author believes that the excessive (comparatively speaking) prevalence of in-law problems among those of lesser education is caused by special situational factors. Economic and other conditions often require men to be dependent on in-laws and to become involved in situations which they cannot readily escape.

Living with In-Laws

A folksaying such as "no house is big enough for two women" illustrates the American expectation that married couples should live in separate households. Yet certain conditions make this virtually impossible in many cases. The increasing tendency toward early marriage, housing shortages, military requirements, and other factors induce thousands of young couples to "double up" with in-laws in housing arrangements. Glick, using census data on American families in midcentury, has this to say regarding the establishment of a home by young couples: "Not all married couples are financially able to establish a home of their own immediately after marriage. Perhaps largely for this reason, about one married couple out of every five in the early 1950's postponed setting up a separate home during the first year of marriage, and one out of every eight put off moving into separate quarters for three years." [13]

Class level and race are important in the doubling-up process as is also age at marriage. These factors are of course intercorrelated. When lower-class individuals marry at an early age, living with relatives is not an unusual procedure. In Glick's words

Since younger couples are the ones most likely to be in difficult financial circumstances, the relatives with whom they live no doubt reason that one of the best ways to help them is to share living quarters with them. Data from the 1950 census on family status by income show that among couples living with the husband's or wife's parents, 32 percent of the husbands under 25 had incomes in 1949 of less than $1,000, as compared with 25 percent of those of the same age living with nonrelatives. Among couples living with the husband's parents, 93 percent of the husbands under 18 years of age had less than $1,000 income, as compared with 61 percent of those 18 and 19 years old, and 32 percent of those 20 to 24 years old.[14]

[13] Paul Glick, *American Families* (New York, Wiley, 1957), pp. 60–62.
[14] *Ibid.*

Perhaps fortunately, the majority of young couples who move in with parents during early marriage live with the parents of the young wife. Theoretically this should avoid the most difficult of in-law relationships, that of the young wife with her mother-in-law. It does leave the young man in a very vulnerable position, since it violates the norm that the husband shall be able to provide for and "run" his family.

What effect does living with in-laws have on marital success? One study found that those who had separate quarters of their own were the happiest, by self-report.

TABLE 26

*Living Arrangements of 544 Couples in the Early
Years of Marriage by Self Rating*

| Living Arrangement | Marital Success * | | | Total |
	Very Happy	Happy	Average	
Not together	64%	36%	0%	100%
With parents	66%	30%	4%	100%
Private room, trailer or apartment	75%	20%	5%	100%

* The study involved primarily skilled worker and middle-class, midwestern couples. The validity of the happiness self ratings are open to question since no couples are listed as unhappy. This should not seriously affect the differences in satisfaction with or impact of living arrangements, however.

SOURCE: Adapted from Judson T. and Mary G. Landis, *Building a Successful Marriage*, 2nd © 1953. Prentice-Hall, Inc., p. 316.

One notes in this study that a spouse who had to live alone, due to military service, or some other contingency was practically as happy as one who lived with in-laws. Evidently it is difficult to keep intergeneration relationships running smoothly under such doubled-up conditions. Very probably it is hard for the young people to develop a sense of independence and self-reliance under these circumstances, and in-laws are convenient recipients of projected hostilities.[15]

ACHIEVING SUCCESS IN IN-LAW RELATIONSHIPS

So far we have been focusing on negative and problematic aspects of in-law relationships. We need to analyze the positive aspects of in-law relationships and discuss specific approaches to in-law problems with the idea of minimizing them.

[15] In-law problems are more likely to occur if the daughter-in-law must share the quarters of her mother-in-law, according to Burgess and Wallin. See Ernest Burgess and Paul Wallin, *Engagement and Marriage* (Philadelphia, Lippincott, 1953), pp. 603–606.

First, let it be stressed that most married couples eventually make good adjustments with in-laws. Those who are not able to do so seem to have a general tendency toward nonadjustment in other areas of life. Patience is called for on all sides when a new marriage takes place, because both the young man and the young woman are taking on a new status and a new role. The process of adapting to a new role sequence is not without its tensions. But it can usually be smoothed by good intentions, understanding, and tolerance.

It is unfortunate that in-law stereotypes are perpetuated through jokes and stories. Some young people are ill prepared emotionally to interact smoothly with their in-laws, and vice versa. Persons who wish to get along well with their in-laws will wish to look beyond the traditional stereotypes to the people behind them. That this can be done with helpful consequences is illustrated in the following case excerpt:

In our family, there exists a great deal of love and harmony. A good bit of this happiness can be attributed to my mother-in-law. In my estimation, there is none as grand as she.

Since I have been married to her son, "Mom" has made me feel like her very own daughter. Having lost my own mother at the age of ten, Mom has taken away much of the emptiness I ofttimes felt through the past years.

Mom is a great confidante of mine and is just like one of the girls when it comes to being fun. What else can any girl ask for? Love, humor, confidence, wisdom—all these are part of my Mom.

She's our Queen and 'Long may She Reign!' [16]

It must be expected by parents that a newcomer who marries a child of theirs will not always see eye to eye with them. If they insist on keeping a closed circle with the newcomer on the outside they are asking for trouble. The same can be said if they attempt to "make him over" so he will "fit." To gain his interest they must show that they want to include him in the circle but that he will not be forced. They can manifest their sincerity by recognizing overtly the new status and role their child has assumed as a married partner starting a new family.

In spite of certain expectations in America that the young people should be strictly independent, thousands of them receive great aid and comfort from one or both sets of parents. Sussman, studying the help pattern in the middle-class family, concludes that "apparently the middle-class family, as represented in our sample, is not as independent or isolated a unit as it is generally thought to be. Affectional and economic ties still link the generational families and give stability to their relationships." [17]

Faris also has made the point that many young people suffer materially, culturally, socially, and psychologically by being cut off from their

[16] Duvall, *op. cit.,* p. 126.
[17] Marvin Sussman, "The Help Pattern in the Middle Class Family," *American Sociological Review,* Vol. 18 (February, 1953), p. 28.

families of orientation. Parental families often have invaluable resources at the disposal of their young married children if all the possibilities are realized on both sides.[18]

We really have no research findings on the relation between marital success and the geographic proximity of young married people and their in-laws. However, Sussman found that relations between the two generations were optimum if they were within fifty miles of each other. Logical inference tells us that where there are cultural or other conflicts, physical avoidance through geographic distance may be the only solution. In the absence of the above, it seems ideal for many young people to live in the same area as their in-laws but far enough apart to allow for privacy and independence. This will vary with particular couples and local conditions. For some young couples residence in the same town with in-laws is "too close." Geographic distance, per se, of course is not as crucial as ease of travel between the homes.

Where there is overattachment of parent to child, the opposite spouse must use extreme diplomacy. Overattachment of a young married partner to a parent is, of course, an indication of immaturity. Fortunately time and the requirement of the new role and status often help to induce growth in the person who is otherwise basically secure and emotionally sound. In severe cases some type of counseling or psychotherapy is helpful. It may take all the ingenuity available to the opposite spouse to help bring the mate and the particular parent-in-law involved to a realization of the necessary corrective steps.

Duvall found that one out of four people had no trouble with in-law relationships. The factors stressed most strongly by the respondents were acceptance and mutual respect. While these attitudes cannot be automatically turned on as one snaps on the livingroom light, they are capable of development on the part of individuals concerned. Without them in-law friction is probably inevitable. With them the possibilities for working out very meaningful, supportive, and abiding relationships are great.

MUTUAL FRIENDSHIPS AND ASSOCIATIONS

An old song had words to the effect that "wedding bells are breaking up that old gang of mine." A truism is expressed in the song. Marriage means, at least to a certain extent, involvement in a new social world, and the giving up of many previous relationships. Charles Lamb tells of his difficulties (as a bachelor) in trying to keep up relationships with his former bachelor friends who were no longer single in an essay on "A Bachelor's Complaints of the Behavior of Married People."

[18] Robert Faris, "Interaction of Generations and Family Stability," *American Sociological Review,* Vol. 12 (April, 1947), pp. 159–164.

But this is not the worst; one must be admitted into their familiarity at least, before they can complain of inattention. It implies visits, and some kind of intercourse. But if the husband be a man with whom you have lived on a friendly footing before marriage—if you did not come in on the wife's side—if you did not sneak into the house in her train, but were an old friend in fast habits of intimacy before their courtship was so much as thought on—look about you—your tenure is precarious—before a twelve-month shall roll over your head, you shall find your old friend gradually grow cool and altered toward you, and at last seek opportunities of breaking with you. I have scarce a married friend of my acquaintance upon whose firm faith I can rely, whose friendship did not commence *after the period of his marriage*. With some limitations they can endure that; but that the good man should have dared to enter into a solemn league of friendship in which they were not consulted, though it happened before they knew him—before they that are now man and wife ever met—this is intolerable to them. Every long friendship, every old authentic intimacy, must be brought into their office to be new stamped with their currency, as a sovereign Prince calls in the good old money that was coined in some reign before he was born or thought of, to be marked and minted with the stamp of his authority, before he will let it pass current in the world. You may guess what luck generally befalls such a rusty piece of metal as I am in these *new mintings*.

Innumerable are the ways which they take to insult and worm you out of their husband's confidence. Laughing at all you say with a kind of wonder, as if you were a queer kind of fellow that said good things, *but an oddity,* is one of their ways;—they have a particular kind of stare for the purpose;—till at last the husband, who used to defer to your judgment, and would pass over some excrescences of understanding and manner for the sake of a general vein of observation (not quite vulgar) which he perceived in you, begins to suspect whether you are not altogether a humorist,—a fellow well enough to have consorted with in his bachelor days, but not quite so proper to be introduced to ladies. They may be called the staring way; and is that which has oftenest been put in practice against me.

Then there is the exaggerating way, or the way of irony; that is, where they find you an object of especial regard with their husband, who is not so easily to be shaken from the lasting attachment founded on esteem which he has conceived towards you; by never-qualified exaggerations to cry up all that you say or do, till the good man, who understands well enough that it is all done in compliment to him, grows weary of the debt of gratitude which is due to so much candor, and by relaxing a little on his part, and taking down a peg or two in his enthusiasm, sinks at length to that kindly level of moderate esteem, —that "decent affection and complacent kindness" towards you, where she herself can join in sympathy with him without too much stretch and violence to her sincerity.[19]

Mr. Lamb's experiences can probably be verified by innumerable bachelors from various parts of the world. Marriage takes single men and

[19] Charles Lamb, *Essays of Elia,* "A Bachelor's Complaints of the Behavior of Married People" (Philadelphia, Altemus, © 1893), pp. 230–232.

women out of their old circles into the social world of married couples. If the married man is to be "one of the boys" it will now mean he is a member of a set composed primarily of other married men.

For some reason or other the young woman is not expected to give up her female friends and associates to the same degree when she marries that the man does. Whether or not this popular conception has a basis in fact has not been tested. The theory may well rest on the idea that the man makes a greater sacrifice of freedom in entering marriage than does the woman. This is an old and widely held theory.

The task of making mutual friendships may not be an easy one. It is probably not as much of a problem if both young people are from the same local area. When this is the case they may move more or less naturally into a set of young married couples, many members of which they have known previous to marriage. But for many if not most today, a new circle of mutual friends must be found.

As we saw in the previous chapter, three-fourths of the couples in Landis' study had no trouble agreeing on mutual friends from the beginning of marriage. However, a hardcore group of about 10 percent never made satisfactory adjustment. It is possible that some of these couples included men who could never adapt to marriage or girls whose friendships outside the home were allowed to intrude to the extent that they became divisive.

LeMasters suggests the wives must come to terms with the social world of the male and its importance to husbands. He states that

. . . tavern society is still basically a man's world. The world of the Elks Club, the American Legion, the Moose, are basically male worlds. Luncheon clubs, athletic clubs, veterans' organizations, hunting clubs—all these, within limits, illustrate a way of life that is essentially masculine in our society. We grant, of course, that women share more of this man's world today in the United States than they did fifty years ago, but we think it unwise for women approaching marriage to conclude that male society is now completely open to them, or to condemn their husbands for wanting to participate in the man's world, as he has been accustomed to doing since he can remember.[20]

And further: "It is unwise to approach marriage, even in modern America, with the assumption that modern marriages succeed to the extent that husbands and wives share more and more activities as a pair."

LeMasters is on solid ground anthropologically speaking. In most, if not all societies, certain aspects of the culture are not open to women and vice versa. However, in modern America especially during early marriage, the husband and wife are busy building the solid foundations of a relationship which is to last. If either the wife or husband is made to feel that an

---

[20] From Ersel LeMasters, *Modern Courtship and Marriage* (New York, Macmillan, 1957), pp. 489–492. By permission of the publisher.

outside recreational group takes precedence over the marriage there may be trouble. When the "we" group relationship becomes well knit it can stand some strain, if necessary, from outside friendship groups. Until that time it would seem wise for spouses to curtail relationships that present problems.

Locke has done considerable research on the relation between non-familial friendships and marital adjustment. He makes much of the sociability factor in marital success, and this is one form of sociability which he discusses.[21] Locke found that happily married couples are much more inclined to have many friends in common than couples who had previously been married. The implication is that each couple needs a circle of mutual friends; they cannot live only to themselves.

Locke's research indicates that mutual enjoyment of certain activities is conducive to marital adjustment while participation in others is divisive. As can be seen in Table 27, five activities were enjoyed by a significantly larger proportion of happily-married men and women. These were church, reading, radio, sports, and music. Further, mutual enjoyment of politics and parties was more typical of happily-married men and happily-married women respectively. On the other hand, dancing and drinking were considered mutually enjoyable activities by a significantly higher proportion

TABLE 27

Percentage of Happily-Married and Divorced Men and Women Reporting the Mutual Enjoyment of Given Activities

Activities	Men		Women	
	Married	Divorced	Married	Divorced
Church	77.2	37.8	76.6	31.4
Reading	71.3	48.1	73.1	44.9
Radio	89.2	72.4	90.4	77.6
Sports	50.3	33.3	57.5	37.8
Music	85.0	75.0	92.2	74.4
Politics	19.8	13.5	15.6	15.4
Parties	54.5	50.6	59.9	41.0
Drinking	6.0	23.1	7.2	15.4
Dancing	26.9	37.8	24.0	39.1
Cards	39.5	39.1	38.3	51.3
Gambling	1.2	3.2	2.4	1.9
Movies	65.9	69.2	69.5	74.4

SOURCE: Adapted from Harvey Locke, *Predicting Adjustment in Marriage,* Copyright 1951, Holt, Rinehart and Winston, Inc. Used by permission of the publishers.

[21] Harvey Locke, *Predicting Adjustment in Marriage: A Comparison of a Divorced and a Happy Married Group* (New York, Holt, Rinehart and Winston, 1951), Chapter 12.

of divorced than happily-married men and women, and mutual enjoyment of card playing was also more often reported by women.

Locke gathered data on individualistic orientation, focusing on activities which the spouse *enjoyed alone*. The following categories were enjoyed individually by a significantly larger number of divorced than married men: reading, church, radio, sports, music, parties, drinking, dancing, and card playing. Divorced women were more inclined to enjoy individually the following activities to a significant degree: church, reading, radio, sports, music, politics, dancing, and movie going.[22]

A picture begins to emerge from the Locke findings which may tentatively be applied to other groups. Enduring marriages will tend to be characterized by mutual enjoyment of a number of social activities. The type of activities may be of some importance. In general, however, "the common or shared enjoyment of activities is highly associated with marital adjustment, and individualistic behavior is highly associated with marital maladjustment." [23]

Of course the question of cause and effect cannot be fully answered here. Undoubtedly selective factors operate to bring together spouses who will tend to enjoy the same activities. Strong marriages are built by people who have essentially the same general orientation to the world. Most couples will never agree on everything, including friends and associations. One might suspect the complete domination of one spouse over the other where there was complete agreement. Individualistic behavior, if carried to the other extreme, is often a sign of incompatibility. During the early marriage period the couple will do well to explore mutual interests, even though this has been partially done previous to marriage.

Besides the factor of selectivity, certain types of social activities in and of themselves seem to provoke marital difficulty. For *some,* drinking, dancing, and gambling, whether mutual or individualistic, seem in the long run to lead to marital strain. Gambling in many cases strains the pocketbook, and budgetary tensions often spill over into other areas. In the heat of anger words to the effect that the spouse is acting "like a common gambler" or the like will seldom be taken lightly.[24]

Marriage is a process of sharing. Mutual friendships provide an area in which the young people can become involved as a couple in activities which are binding and supportive. Individual friendships may be continued after marriage and under normal circumstances some will be. They need not strain successful marriages, but they can be divisive, especially in cases where other factors have sown the seeds of discord.

[22] *Ibid.,* pp. 257–259.

[23] *Ibid.,* p. 258.

[24] The cultural and subcultural context must be taken into account at this point. Practices that would probably cause marital dissension in rural Indiana might be considered customary and nonthreatening in other environs. The particular time period should also be noted.

RELATIONS WITH THE CHURCH

The religious background of the couple has implications for their marital adjustment. Burgess and Cottrell found that Sunday School attendance through the teens was highly favorable to marital adjustment. These same authors report church attendance during childhood favorable to marital success as do a number of others.[25]

Locke has studied the effects of religious activity during early marriage on marital adjustment, and he found that regularity of church attendance was pertinent. Locke's findings are summarized in Table 28. For his sample, having a religious rather than a secular ceremony and being active in church affairs both before and after marriage was more characteristic of the happily-married than the divorced group. From Locke's point of view church membership and attendance is an index of sociability and conventionality. The sociable, conventional person has, on the average, less tendency to be involved in difficulties that lead to divorce.

TABLE 28

Regularity of Church Attendance of Happily-Married
and Divorced Men and Women during the
First Half of Marriage, by Percentage

Monthly Attendance	Men		Women	
	Married N 165	Divorced N 162	Married N 167	Divorced N 186
4 or more times	30.9	18.6	43.7	28.6
2 or 3 times	23.0	12.3	13.8	13.4
once or less	28.5	35.1	30.5	27.9
none	17.6	34.0	12.0	30.1

SOURCE: Adapted from Harvey Locke, *Predicting Adjustment in Marriage,* Copyright 1951, Holt, Rinehart and Winston, Inc. Used by permission of the publishers.

Focusing on divorce prevention is still a somewhat negative approach, however. The question is one of the potentialities the church has for the given couple in regard to the good life, however it is to be defined. This leads ultimately to the question of values and philosophy of life which will be dealt within the next chapter. In the church, or at least in some churches, a positive approach to fundamental values of life can be found. Included will be material of particular relevance to marriage and family living.

As has been pointed out many times, a reciprocal relationship exists in that "the family needs the church and the church needs the family." The

[25] See Ernest Burgess and Harvey Locke, *The Family* (New York, American Book, 1953), p. 421.

church as an institution is dependent on the support of individual family members. Without their backing it could not exist. With their backing it can serve not only its constituents but can also reach out to those who may have greater needs.

As is well known, in many communities women are much more regular in church attendance than are men. We have no evidence that wives have been happy about the state of affairs and by inference they have not been. As a matter of fact, many church patterns assume a family or pair activity. Consequently the spouse who appears singly may normally feel a bit out of place. At best such a person will in time tend to be somewhat resentful of the spouse's continued absence. As Burgess and Cottrell point out, the wife more often than the husband has had to make adjustments in marriage. This principle holds true in religious life as well as in many other areas.

Ideally if the marriage is mixed by religious faith, agreements regarding church attendance, birth control, rearing of children, etc., have been made previous to marriage. Unfortunately, often this is not the case, and these problem areas are fully faced only when they arise in marriage. Furthermore, many agreements made before marriage are not honored and the issues are reopened. This happens more often in the case of birth control or rearing of children than in church attendance as such. Whatever the implications about the sincerity of young people in their promises and commitments, the knowledge that many premarital agreements are readjusted in marriage may enable young couples to make the best of the situation.

RELATIONS WITH THE GENERAL COMMUNITY

Relations with in-laws, peer couples, and the church are not sufficient to meet all the needs of the couple for outside relationships. A successful family even in urban areas will ordinarily have reciprocal ties with other community organizations and institutions. Usually the younger couple will not be as heavily involved in community affairs as the one with growing children, but it still needs the community and this need is reciprocated.

The average couple in the establishment stage may not wish to formally evaluate any particular community. Quite often they will have a period of a few years in which the location of the home is determined by the contingencies of military service, graduate school, or new and unstable initial occupational pursuits. Eventually they may wish to exercise some rationality in the choice of community in which to reside and participate. If so, what are some characteristics of communities which may be studied and investigated? Warren, in his useful book, *Studying Your Community*, lists the following as being important:

1. Background and Setting
2. Economic Life
3. Government, Politics, and Law Enforcement
4. Community Planning
5. Housing
6. Education
7. Recreation
8. Religious Activities
9. Social Insurance and Public Assistance
10. Aids to Family Living and Child Welfare
11. Health
12. Provisions for Special Groups
13. Communication
14. Intergroup Relations
15. Associations
16. Community Organization

It is not suggested that each young couple is to organize a social survey of the local area; rather that some relationship between the individual family and many of the areas indicated above is inevitable and functional. The couple that wishes to make long-term plans for a reasonably successful and stable life will be forced to take community factors into account. By this same token, a community is roughly a group of families. It is not by some definitions a full, real, or active community until the families act cooperatively together.

Communities differ, as Sanders points out, in (1) kinds of social organization, (2) types of leadership, (3) types of social ranking, (4) methods used to make individuals conform, and (5) systems of social value.[26]

Many couples have found to their despair that a particular neighborhood or community was not what they expected it to be. It is not unusual for a young pair to move into a community composed mainly of middle-aged people and then to complain that there are no children with whom their children can play.

As the young couple begins to interact in a given community the question of conforming with community norms and standards will almost inevitably arise. We shall discuss this point further in Chapter 14. The couples must decide, however, to what degree and in what ways they will attempt to "keep up with the Joneses." As Blood states, "by example, by gossip, and by direct-suggestion, neighbors apply pressure to conform." [27] Few indeed are the families which will not be sensitive to this kind of pressure. Deci-

[26] Irwin Sanders, *Making Communities Better* (Lexington, University of Kentucky Press, 1952).

[27] Robert Blood, *Anticipating Your Marriage* (New York, Free Press, 1955), p. 447.

sions eventually have to be made as to ways these pressures and standards will be handled. They cannot be completely ignored.

A positive approach will involve seeking out and making use of the desirable features of the community of their choice. Students of American life tell us that much of the old neighborliness has gone and that most of us are now destined to live our lives in an impersonal atmosphere. While this may be true in general, couples with sociability drives will attempt to make use of the human and material potentials of their local communities for the good life as they define it.

SELECTED READINGS

Albrecht, Ruth, "Relationships of Older Parents with Their Children," *Marriage and Family Living,* Vol. 16 (February, 1954), pp. 32–35.

Bell, Robert, *Marriage and Family Interaction* (Homewood, Ill., The Dorsey Press, Inc., 1963), Chapter 11.

Bernard, Jessie, *American Community Behavior* (New York, Holt, Rinehart and Winston, Inc., 1950).

Biddle, William, *The Cultivation of Community Leaders* (New York, Harper & Row, 1953).

Blood, Robert, *Marriage* (New York, Free Press, 1962), Chapters 15 and 16.

Bossard, James, and Boll, Eleanor, *Ritual in Family Living* (Philadelphia, University of Pennsylvania Press, 1950).

Buell, Bradley, *Community Planning for Human Services* (New York, Columbia, 1952).

Burchinall, Lee, "Marital Satisfaction and Religious Behavior," *American Sociological Review,* Vol. 22 (June, 1957), pp. 306–310.

Cavan, Ruth, *American Marriage* (New York, Crowell, 1959), Chapter 18.

Christensen, Harold, *Marriage Analysis* (New York, Ronald, 1950), Chapter 10.

Dinkel, Robert, "Parent-Child Conflict in Minnesota Families," *American Sociological Review,* Vol. 9 (August, 1943), pp. 412–419.

Duvall, Evelyn, *In-Laws: Pro and Con* (New York, Association Press, 1954).

Duvall, Evelyn, and Hill, Reuben, *Being Married* (Boston, Heath, 1960), Chapter 21.

Dyer, Dorothy, *The Family Today: A Guide for Leaders* (Minneapolis, University of Minnesota Press, 1950).

Himes, Norman, and Taylor, Donald, *Your Marriage* (New York, Holt, Rinehart and Winston, 1955), Chapter 24.

Komarovsky, Mirra, *Blue-Collar Marriage* (New York, Random House, 1964), Chapters 9, 11, and 12.

Martinson, Floyd, *Marriage and the American Ideal* (New York, Dodd, Mead, 1960), Chapter 28.

Merriam, R. E., *Going into Politics, A Guide for Citizens* (New York, Harper & Row, 1957).

Moore, Bernice, and Sutherland, Robert, *Family, Community and Mental Health* (Austin, Hogg Foundation, 1950).

Neisser, Edith, *How To Be a Good Mother-in-Law and Grandmother,* Public Affairs Booklet 74 (1951).

Nimkoff, Meyer, *Marriage and the Family* (Boston, Houghton Mifflin, 1947), Chapter 9.

Peterson, James, *Education for Marriage* (New York, Scribner, 1964), Chapter 17.

Reuss, Carl, "Research Findings on the Effects of Modern Day Religion on Family Living," *Marriage and Family Living,* Vol. 16 (August, 1954), pp. 221–225.

Skidmore, Rex and Cannon, Anton, *Building Your Marriage* (New York, Harper & Row, 1958), Chapter 9.

Sussman, Marvin, "The Help Pattern of the Middle Class Family," *American Sociological Review,* Vol. 18 (February, 1953), pp. 22–28.

Woods, Sister Frances Jerome, *The American Family System* (New York, Harper & Row, 1959), Chapter 15.

Zimmerman, Carle and Cervantes, Lucius, *Marriage and the Family* (Chicago, Regnery, 1956), pp. 100–125.

QUESTIONS AND EXERCISES

1. What type of relationship with your former, nonmutual friends do you wish to maintain in marriage? What would you consider ideal for your spouse?

2. Why is it, in your estimation, that the relationship between the wife and her mother-in-law is reported to be the most difficult of in-law relationships? Discuss.

3. Under what circumstances would you move in with your relatives or your spouse's relatives?

4. Analyze a case involving a young married couple and their parents and parents-in-law which involves a minimum of tension. Do the same for another case involving considerable tension. Postulate some possible sources of the variation in tension level.

5. Analyze critically the thesis that in-law problems are partially an outcome of our type of family system.

6. Why does it seem to be true that religion is in some cases integrative and in some cases divisive? Discuss.

7. Do you expect to render assistance to any voluntary agencies after your marriage? Why or why not?

8. Do a case history of an adult person who has not been able to emancipate himself or herself from the parents. Isolate and discuss any basic causal factors involved that come to your attention.

9. Indicate and discuss the type of relationship with the community you wish your family to have after you marry.

10. Organize a group of young people who are interested in community

service projects. By dividing the work load, interview administrators of social agencies in order to ascertain the possible uses of volunteer help as seen by these leaders.

11. Interview some members of the local clergy in order to ascertain what special provisions, if any, are made particularly for young married couples.

12. Community and political activity may seem very unrelated to marriage. Justify or criticize the inclusion of such topics in a marriage and family text.

14

Establishing a Philosophy
of Life

One of the most important developmental tasks of the early period of marriage is that of establishing a mutually satisfying philosophy of life. To achieve something more than a minimum level of marital integration and adjustment it will be helpful for the couple to set up criteria by which marital activities can be evaluated. In a word, some agreement on basic values becomes imperative.

THE PROBLEM OF VALUES

What do we mean by values? Values are criteria for judgment. In the abstract, they are measuring sticks or standards by which actions and behavior may be judged.[1] Values, as we are using the term here, are not goals or objectives as such, but rather they are the basic criteria by which goals or objectives may be selected. Values are central, both as symbols of solidarity and as coordinating forces, to increase group cohesion. Values result in approval or disapproval of certain practices because the practices are considered central to the welfare of the group, as, for example, integrity, responsibility, or loyalty. Values exemplify the core ideals toward which basic institutions point, ends or goals to which people aspire, and things to which they are driven to give attention because of social pressures. Values, then, are criteria which express basic meanings.

In our discussion we have been referring to values shared by the individuals in the group. Obviously, all values attributed to a particular society are not shared equally by all individuals. For example, in Russia religious

[1] Harry Johnson, *Sociology* (New York, Harcourt, Brace & World, 1960), p. 49.

265

ideas and practices in the traditional sense are allegedly out of step and forbidden in that country; yet numbers of people in Russia worship publicly and follow certain religious practices. In spite of this apparent inconsistency present-day Russia is clearly a communist country. The point is simply that values may be dominant and yet not be shared equally or even by a majority of the members of the society. Sociologists often use the term *subculture* to refer to societal islands in a larger society, such as the Amish, "beatniks," Mormons, bohemians, and so on. Within each of these, however, the values tend to be group-enforced and this is what gives each subculture its distinctiveness and contributes to the group's solidarity.

VALUES AND THE INDIVIDUAL

How does the individual obtain his value orientations? Each person is born into a particular social setting. His family exposes him to certain beliefs and practices and isolates him from others. Whether or not the parents are completely aware of the process in rearing their child they will be impressing upon him selective value orientations. The parents will tend to reflect the same orientations which are found in other families in their society. For example, the belief in monogamy or the belief in personal freedom or initiative would be espoused in almost any Western household. Likewise an interest in economic competition and in individual fulfillment will tend to be emphasized. A child brought up in the Orient, on the other hand, would be subjected to stress on ancestry, protocol, good form, and decorum.

The family acts as a mediator between the individual child and the surrounding culture. The basic values of the society will ordinarily be disseminated to the child through the parental family. To these influences are added those of the peer group, the church, and other influences with which the developing child comes into contact. It must, of course, again be noted that subcultures exist in the United States. The Amish child will be subjected to certain values that are distinct from those found in the more general American society. He will be taught that warfare under any condition is immoral. He will learn that the good life is to be lived in the rural areas only and that the city is a center of corruption and worldliness. Other unique religious, ethnic, occupational, and regional groups in America will come to the mind of the reader as examples.

There are also unique family subcultures.[2] A particular upper middle-class family in a suburban area characterized by a "conspicuous consumption" may itself stress frugality and simplicity, thus being an exception to the general rule of the community. Individuals also have unique experi-

---

[2] See Ruth Cavan, *The American Family* (New York, Crowell, 1963), Part II for a description of ethnic and class differences in family systems in America.

ences. The individual cannot be expected to be an exact carbon copy of others in the group in which he holds his membership. Unique experiences for the individual can accrue as day-by-day increments or they can be crucial and traumatic experiences. In either case their significance depends much on the way the experiences are perceived and reacted to by the individual.

Attempts have been made in recent years to delineate and analyze basic values in American society.[3] A perusal of these writings reveals a general consensus of opinion on the following: materialism, success, progress, rationalism, equality, and freedom. Note that the analysis of values at this point is at a very abstract level, and the ties between these values and average families may not be obvious. As we have repeatedly stated, however, family life takes place in a total context. If the culture places great stress on success and competition, and if the criteria of judgment are materialistic in nature, individual families will be affected by this. A young man may, for example, graduate from medical school expecting to serve in some rural or mountain area where medical services are nonexistent. He is idealistic, almost missionary, or service oriented to his associates. Assume that this young doctor then marries a woman who aspires to high status in society, with the material comforts and conveniences that a successful doctor could afford. The potentials for conflict are obvious. Yet the values of materialism and humanitarianism are both basic to American culture. One might assume that such differences in value orientation should have appeared in the courtship period. Yet they often do not. This leaves the couple with a major rift in their value orientation.

CRITIQUES

In recent years a number of social science writers have taken occasion to severely criticize some of the major value orientations in America. One of the most penetrating analyses has been made by the psychiatrist Horney. Horney sees the seeds of neurosis in the conflicting configuration of American values.[4] We have, on the one hand, the stress on humanitarianism, brotherhood, love, and unselfishness. On the other hand, we have the values of success, status, material gain, and aggressiveness. These contradictions may become internalized. The typical neurotic individual in our society manifests these contradictions, according to Horney. He is torn between the desire to make good for himself, and the desire to be good to others. The fear of failure becomes intense, since a limited number of

[3] See the works of Williams, Gillin, Kluckhohn, and Graham, cited in the Selected Readings.
[4] Karen Horney, *The Neurotic Personality of Our Time* (New York, Norton, 1937), Chapter 15.

people can be successful. On the other hand, success may mean some degree of isolation from others and resultant pain and guilt. The individual is literally damned if he does and damned if he doesn't!

Riesman thinks that a change is taking place in the American character.[5] Formerly, many individuals were "inner-directed" persons who relied finally on moral and ethical principles when making choices and decisions. Now the "other-directed" type is coming to the forefront. This type of person makes much use of a sort of built-in radar screen which is primarily attuned to the opinions of others around him. Unable to function solely under his own power, the individual needs always to be sure of the attitudes of his associates before he makes a move. He lacks the fortitude to take an unpopular position or to move against the crowd. He may even be unable to see alternative modes of thought and action.

Proceeding in somewhat the same vein, Whyte is also very much concerned with the tendency toward external conformity which he sees developing in this country.[6] Whyte sees the source in the developing and enveloping bureaucratic social order as it affects the individual. Writing with a sharp pen, he develops the thesis that most of our organizations are no longer looking for the independent and self-reliant American. The big question instead is, "Will he get along in our group?" So concerned are many large business organizations with this problem that they have invaded the domestic scene. Even "the Mrs." must be screened lest she fail to be a good "company wife." If she cannot pass acceptably the husband may not get the position to which he aspires. If there are some rough edges which can be smoothed out, the wife is processed to the point where she is more acceptable.[7]

A different type of analysis which has been made by Myrdal also illustrates confusion in our value system. Writing with a focus on race relations, Myrdal suggests that a hiatus exists between our basic values expressed as ideals and our actual behavior. Myrdal describes what he calls the "American creed" which is a composite of our ideals of freedom, democracy, and justice. He believes that these values do exist in America and that we do not just give lip service to them. On the other hand, our treatment of minorities, especially Negroes, contradicts the ideals set up as models.[8]

Some caution is in order at this point. Those who write critiques may throw out the babies with the bathwater. The exact degree of individualism

[5] Riesman, David, *The Lonely Crowd* (New Haven, Yale, 1950).

[6] William H. Whyte, *The Organization Man* (New York, Simon and Schuster, 1956).

[7] William H. Whyte, "The Wife Problem," in Robert Winch and Robert McGinnis (Eds.), *Marriage and the Family* (New York, Holt, Rinehart and Winston, 1953), p. 278.

[8] Gunnar Myrdal, *An American Dilemma* (New York, Harper & Row, 1944). Actually, Ralph Linton, *The Study of Man* (New York, Appleton-Century-Crofts, 1936), Chapter XVII preceded Myrdal in popularizing the distinction between culture as ideals and actual behavior. He may not have been the first to do so.

or conformity existing in a particular country at a given time is difficult to ascertain. One must especially be suspicious of comparisons with the "good old days" when allegedly people had more of this or that. Nostalgia and selective memory may cause one to focus upon certain items or proportions to the neglect of others more objectively true.

The matter of conformity to the group involves complex problems of analysis. American history impresses one with the spirit of individualism which has prevailed, in contrast to other societies. This presumably reflects the impact of certain philosophical ideas resulting from the various religious, political, and social revolutions of Western Europe. The frontier was not without its effect. As Waller and Hill point out, however, "the *rugged individualism* of which our political orators speak was actually a *rugged familism.*" [9] Early American life was family centered, not individually centered. A significant revolution in the United States has involved the shift from family goals to individual goals. If Riesman is correct, it means that no longer are individuals internalizing family standards as they once were. No longer receiving clear-cut standards which they can accept as their own, people are now reaching anxiously to those around them for the security no longer provided by their own convictions.

The small village in the "old days," however, demanded a type of conformity that was stifling to many individuals. For many, the basic motive behind the trek to the city has been the lure of anonymity offered by city life. It is true, however, that a bureaucratic society makes its special demands upon the individual. A society worried about external and internal threats will probably not tend to sanction much deviation. It can hardly be denied that strong pressures to conform exist in America. Making precise comparisons of their degree and effects in relation to former periods of history and to other societies is a task that demands very careful scholarly attention.

The Myrdal type of critique brings to the fore the problem of the relation between the ideal and the real. Do verbalized values merely provide convenient window-dressings? Are they merely aids in rationalization? The analysis is provocative and cannot be dismissed lightly. It is difficult to find societies, groups, or individuals where a gap between their ideal pattern and their actual behavior is nonexistent. Realistically some discrepancy is to be expected. Yet gross discrepancies present logical and practical problems and often lie at the base of both mental illness and serious domestic discord.

The foregoing brief discussion has focussed upon overall value problems in American culture. Attention should now be given to the types of *marriage* value systems in our society, realizing that ours is a mixed value

[9] Willard Waller and Reuben Hill, *The Family* (New York, Holt, Rinehart and Winston, 1951), p. 15.

heritage rather than one with a consistent ideal of marriage or anything else agreed upon by everyone.

The American marriage and family system has ancient roots upon which have been added various branches. It is perhaps possible to summarize some of the main features of our heritage by delineating a small number of typologies. This has been done in a very interesting fashion by Martinson, who suggests that there are three marriage models in American culture from which couples formulate their own personal conceptions: The Judaic-Christian, the romantic, and the rationalistic. The following table presents his summary:

TABLE 29

Marriage Models in American Culture

Aspect of Marriage	Judaic-Christian	Romantic	Rationalistic
Origin of marriage	God	Man	Man
Structure of marriage	Monogamous	Monogamous	Monogamous
Essential basis of marriage	Mates freely chosen through personal confrontation	Impelled by love	Mates freely chosen with aid of rational mate selection processes and techniques
Reality of marriage	Two become "one flesh," act of God: oneness	Two become one through union of love spirits or souls: oneness	Two remain two: togetherness
Functions of marriage	Unitive, companionship, procreation, outlet for sex desire	Ecstasy	Mutual happiness, mutual adjustment, companionship
Permanence of marriage	Indissoluble	Dissoluble if love dies	Goal is stability but marriage dissoluble

SOURCE: Reprinted by permission of Dodd, Mead & Company from *Marriage and the American Ideal* by Floyd Martinson © by Dodd, Mead & Company, Inc., 1960, p. 62.

According to the traditional Judaic-Christian model, marriage is instituted for the glory of God, as is implied in the traditional words of the standard marriage ceremony: "We are gathered in the sight of God . . . to join together this man and this woman in holy matrimony which is ordained of God and is to be honored by all men." It is blessed for man and is for his own good. The two partners become one in mystical union and the partnership is not to be dissolved by man. The basic functions of marriage involve companionship for the partners, provision for sex release, and procreation of children.

The romantic model for marriage does not imply a relationship instituted for the glory of God. The impelling force which brings the partners together is an intense feeling of affection for each other. There is the underlying assumption that somehow the partners were "made" or "born" for each other, or at least uniquely suited to one another emotionally.[10] The two become one, again in a mystical union, but without the theological overtones which obtain in the previous model. In the stereotyped sense in this marriage concept the couple lives "happily ever after" in a "dream cottage." Children are born from the ecstasy of the love between the two partners. The couple remain together as long as their love for each other lasts. If it dies they are allowed to separate and to go their own ways or to remarry. It is at times even suggested that it would be immoral for the partners to remain together, if their love subsides. Stress is placed on individual rights and prerogatives, not on traditional loyalties to church or to kin.

The rationalistic model for marriage is a product of Western pragmatic trends and the emphasis is on reason as against mere romantic feelings or trust in God. Mates are chosen on the basis of the potentialities that seem to forecast a successful marital relationship. The object is a particular type of partnership or "togetherness" which is mutually satisfying to both parties.

In this model the goal is a stable, adjusted marriage. If such does not develop, the marriage can be dissolved after sufficient rational attempts at reconciliation. Children are expected as a regular outcome of sexual relationships on a planned basis.

Martinson's approach is provocative and worthy of attention. A few comments may, however, be in order. The models are to be considered as typologies which are clear-cut only in the abstract. As we move from abstraction to real people in their actual living, we note the ambivalence and lack of clarity with respect to implementation of the models. The Roman Catholic church, for example, grants annulments if one member of a couple refuses to have children. Many Protestant ministers, in lecturing and advising their young people in preparation for marriage, present

---

[10] There is a degree of predestination that appears in the romantic ideology. To trace its source it would be necessary to go back to the Greek Gods and Goddesses who presumably were concerned with making appropriate matches. If one pursues this point it appears that only in the rational model is man as such fully in charge of mate selection processes.

materials from all three models in a combination which is not by any means well synthesized.

Actually these ideologies all represent verbal systems that are part of our total heritage. Again, while the Amish are not exposed to great degree to influences of the romantic or rationalistic ideologies, most of us are socialized to some extent in all three systems in this pluralistic culture. By giving some conscious attention to the value choices available, however, the American couple may be helped to develop a more definitive value blueprint of its own.

CLARIFYING VALUES

What can be done by the couple to move toward a personally fulfilling yet ethical and moral philosophy of life? A first step may be to consider values in a hierarchy: high-level ultimate values, the more day-by-day, mundane value choices, and those that fall between these two extremes.

Three Levels of Values

First there are the higher-level, fundamental values which some people consider most significant. Such considerations are discussed in a wide range of books dealing with ethics, religion, and philosophy. One book which may be of help is by Morris. He suggests that there are thirteen major value orientations to the world:

1. Preserve the best that man has attained
2. Cultivate independence of persons and things
3. Show sympathetic concern for others
4. Experience festivity and solitude in alternation
5. Act and enjoy life through group participation
6. Constantly master changing conditions
7. Integrate action, enjoyment, and contemplation
8. Live with wholesome, carefree enjoyment
9. Wait in quiet receptivity
10. Control the self stoically
11. Meditate on the inner life
12. Chance adventuresome deeds
13. Obey the cosmic purposes [11]

These brief statements do not do justice to the conceptions, but lack of space prevents us from including them in detail. However, the following illustration describes alternate Way 1: preserve the best that man has attained:

[11] Reprinted from *Varieties of Human Values* by Charles Morris by permission of The University of Chicago Press. Copyright, 1956, p. 15.

Way 1: In this 'design for living' the individual actively participates in the social life of his community, not to change it primarily, but to understand, appreciate, and preserve the best that man has attained. Excessive desires should be avoided and moderation sought. One wants the good things of life but in an orderly way. Life is to have clarity, balance, refinement, control. Vulgarity, great enthusiasm, irrational behavior, impatience, indulgence are to be avoided. Friendship is to be esteemed, but not easy intimacy with many people. Life is to have discipline, intelligibility, good manners, predictability. Social changes are to be made slowly and carefully, so that what has been achieved in human culture is not lost. The individual should be active physically and socially, but not in a hectic or radical way. Restraint and intelligence should give order to an active life.[12]

Couples might find it illuminating to work through Morris' questionnaire without collaboration, and then compare results.

Another approach which may be found beneficial by couples is a study of the Allport-Vernon-Lindzey theory of values.[13] Based originally on Spranger's theory of personality types, this approach isolates six major subcategories of value which are of importance. They are (1) theoretical, (2) economic, (3) aesthetic, (4) social, (5) political, and (6) religious. By taking the tests indicated in the book each spouse can obtain a "Profile of Values" showing his ranking in the various areas discussed. Probably most couples would do well to discuss the results with a professional person competent to deal with this particular test. Given proper attention the results may suggest areas of value difference which can bear considerable exploration.

Figure 7 indicates in graphic form the scale values of Mr. X and Mrs. X, a couple who sought marriage counseling help because of difficulties which gave rise to considerable tension between them. The following brief notes will demonstrate some of the potential kinds of conflict between the spouses.

Mr. X, age twenty-seven, is the son of a family which has been in business for years, with moderate to good success. The father had been a self-made man of little education. John (Mr. X) was the youngest of three children who always had the best of everything at home. In college, Mr. X went through a phase of rebellion against his parents. He joined a liberal political club as a sophomore and experimented with what for him were new and challenging ideas. By the time he was a senior he had "settled down" from his father's point of view. After graduation he went into his father's firm, where he has been reasonably successful.

Mrs. X (Mary) was brought up on the mission field. She was sent away to school for months at a time and never learned to know her parents well. Sent home to college in the States, Mary met John during her junior

[12] Morris, *op. cit.,* p. 15.
[13] Gordon Allport and Phillip Vernon, *Study of Values* (Boston, Houghton Mifflin, 1931).

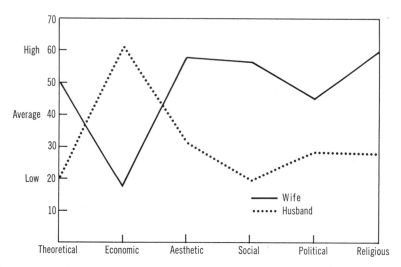

FIGURE 7. *Value Scale Scores for Mr. and Mrs. X.* [a] The solid line stands for the wife's score and the dotted line for the husband's score.

year, and they became engaged as seniors. In college Mary showed great interest in social science, religion, and philosophy. Soon after graduation she and John were married.

At the time they sought marriage counseling help Mr. and Mrs. X had been out of college for four years. They had one child of whom both were very fond. However, they seemed to be growing apart. Mr. X was very status-conscious and was attempting to move to the top in the business. He felt that he and his wife should join the country club in order to make and keep contacts. Mrs. X had no interest in social success and did not wish to join the country club. Instead she often expressed interest in "service" projects at home and abroad. At the time of the first interview Mrs. X was suggesting that the family consider going abroad on a special project (what would be similar to a Peace Corps program). As can be seen in Figure 7, the couple is rather far apart in basic values as measured by the Allport-Vernon-Lindzey scale, which was administered by the counselor.

Books that discuss value orientations from various frameworks can be found in most of the larger and better libraries. The list in the selected readings at the end of the chapter is suggestive. Persons who belong to organized religious groups may wish to investigate the background and history of their particular denomination rather carefully and critically and then compare the general orientation of the group with others available. On this basis they may obtain a better understanding of the value systems to which they have been exposed and in which they may have been indoctrinated. As adults they should choose for themselves whether or not they will finally and fully espouse these values which have been inherited from previous generations.

A number of suggestions may be made. A thorough study of American values and ideals is a possibility. The works of Williams, Whyte, and Graham should be helpful. Attention should be given to Wood's *Cultural Values of American Ethnic Groups.* For both minority and nonminority Americans this book can be illuminating in that it discusses subgroup values that are often imperfectly understood by the average person.

For those who wish to pursue an analysis of American marriage and family values, the works of Sirjamaki,[14] Cavan, Martinson, and Wood should be considered. In order to gain full perspective on them it is probably advisable to adopt the cross-cultural approach and study carefully the values of a number of other cultures as well. The second edition of *The Family in Various Cultures* by Queen, Adams, and Habenstein can be highly recommended in this regard.

Having provided this type of base and background the two spouses may then analyze the value orientations of their respective families. It is suggested that each analyze as carefully as possible his own family background and then cross-comparisons can be made.

At the lowest level of abstraction and generality are found the day-by-day things to which preference is given. Whether one prefers a bread, meat, and potatoes diet or one emphasizing vegetables and fruits will illustrate this level. Some readers may well wonder if this level deserves to be treated within the same framework that the other two levels were. Are not the other levels so much "higher" that an inclusion of values of this sort borders on the vulgar? On the contrary, there is a fundamental association between the various levels of values. The higher, more ultimate ones have little meaning in and of themselves. Man does not live by bread alone, but first of all by bread.

Couples can to some degree, and if possible rationally, consider the values they wish to espouse at all levels of abstraction. The question can often be raised as to the motivation behind the purchase of a particular style of garment or of a specific brand and design of automobile. In a very provocative book, Packard illustrates the lengths to which modern advertisers will go to appeal to and develop the tastes of the American public.[15] He makes it clear that fundamental utility is not by far the only criterion many persons have in mind in making a purchase.

It would be a grave error to suggest that what has been proposed in this chapter will involve simple tasks. The perceptive reader will already

---

[14] John Sirjamaki, *The American Family in the Twentieth Century* (Cambridge, Harvard, 1953).

[15] Vance Packard, *The Hidden Persuaders* (New York, McKay, 1957).

have realized that a number of intellectual and other problems will beset those who self-consciously attempt to establish a working philosophy of life which will be based on an intelligent appraisal of value orientations. Kirkpatrick's concept of dilemma is deserving of attention. He demonstrates that goals (values) exist as dichotomies. In choosing values or value positions dilemmas arise because each position or choice demands its price. Whether one is focusing upon groups or upon the single individual, value choices exact their pound of flesh.

Dilemmas of Making Choices

Below are listed some goals and dichotomous categories which are taken from Kirkpatrick:

Dilemmas (Goals)

1. Order	1. Freedom
2. Specific and stable goal expectations	2. Free expression of age, sex, and individual potentialities
3. Child rearing	3. Personal self-expression
4. Family loyalty	4. Community loyalty
5. Casual association	5. Restrictive, intensive association
6. Sex linked to family stability	6. Free sex expression

Descriptive Dichotomies

1. Authoritarian	1. Democratic
2. Familism	2. Individualism
3. Sacred	3. Secular
4. Patriarchal	4. Equalitarian
5. Duty	5. Happiness
6. Respect	6. Love [16]

The first value dilemma listed is a very old one and has been reflected in the writings of various social, religious, economic, and political philosophers. As Kirkpatrick implies, choices between these alternates must be made at both the larger societal levels and the more narrow individual family levels. The latter will form the base for our discussion.

As has been pointed out previously, freedom is a blueprint which has been highly emphasized in America. Without question the concept of individual freedom, first applied in the economic and political realms, has in America increasingly been applied to the family realm as well. In this day and age young people are insisting on freedom of choice of mates, and in choice of place of residence. Furthermore, wives are insisting on individual

[16] Clifford Kirkpatrick, *The Family, As Process and Institution* (New York, Ronald, 1955), Chapter 4.

prerogatives which would have been unthinkable in the more orderly, husband-dominated families of previous generations.

The more traditional concept of order also demands its pound of flesh. An orderly and efficient household provides for many individuals a sense of security and stability most difficult to match. With each member of the household having a clear-cut role to play, a higher degree of efficiency can be expected. But as Waller and Hill indicate, a person may carry a certain role, while his whole personality cries out against it.[17] Many a spouse lives a life of "quiet desperation" even though his outward appearances would give no indication of this.

An approach of this type can be used by the reader to analyze the other value approaches listed above. Perhaps each of these could be considered the ends of a continuum. Spouses may wish to consider the type of balance which will be most satisfactory to them. It should be noted that as those are listed by Kirkpatrick, there is a general tendency for American families to move toward the concepts listed on the right. We are not suggesting that couples will wish to take positions always synonymous with those typical of surrounding groups. As a matter of fact, we are suggesting an approach which, if followed, will make each couple somewhat unique.

Most people, as groups and as individuals, have not carefully evaluated and thought through the values they follow. Justification for this view is to be found in a community study entitled *Crestwood Heights*.[18] This suburban North American community was carefully analyzed by a team of social scientists, with exceptional cooperation being given by the families, school officials, and various other institutional representatives involved. The authors first of all show that men and women vary considerably regarding values which are to be emphasized. Basically the men are more conservative, competitive, and means-oriented. They stress production, achievement, and order. Women on the other hand stress tolerance, democracy, and happiness, and they are more interested in persons than in things. They are more concerned with ends rather than means, and with freedom rather than order. Such sex differences, *if* they exist generally in the society, cannot be completely overlooked. Seeley discusses "antagonistic cooperation" at one point.[19] This seldom becomes a short-cut struggle, however. Instead ". . . a kind of gentle, guerilla-like action is carried on, intermittently, and for limited gains—indeed without total victory even as an objective."[20] It would appear that efforts to reconcile some of the differences to the point where the marriage would involve a minimum of guerrilla warfare tactics would well be in order.

At another level, however, families in Crestwood Heights reflect "con-

---

[17] Waller and Hill, *op. cit.*, Chapter 15.
[18] John Seeley, *et al., Crestwood Heights* (New York, Basic Books, 1956).
[19] *Ibid.*, Chapter 12.
[20] *Ibid.*, p. 398.

fusion, internal contradiction, and incompatibility in belief within persons and between them," in the realm of general beliefs and values.[21] The old order is gone. Adults have broken with their parents. Often they have broken ideologically with their ethnic and religious groups. Feeling that the leaders of the latter have little to offer that is realistic in terms of modern conditions, they turn to school leaders and functionaries for guidance.

As Riesman points out in his introduction to *Crestwood Heights,* the picture one gets is in some ways disturbing. Here are people who theoretically "have it made." The schools and community services have officially been ranked high. The level of education is far above average. In terms of room and space per family, conditions are exceptional (20 percent of the houses have ten rooms or more, with only 7.1 percent having less than six rooms). A high percentage of the families are intact; divorce and separation rates are low. However, the incidence of mental health problems found was higher than would have been predicted by a mental hygienist. As has already been suggested, beneath the surface of outward calm rage conflicts that are deep-seated. In the words of the authors the conflict between the pursuit of *maturity* (democracy, tolerance, emotional security) and *success* (status) is especially profound. The authors suggest that the supports of inertia, habit, and a stable social structure are functional necessities. Without them the tendencies toward personal disorganization would be extreme.

Since many in the United States seem to aspire to a style of living embodied in Crestwood Heights, some careful thinking, at its very best, is in order. The authors do not claim that this study is typical of upper middle-class suburbia, but Riesman suggests that it is in many ways. At any rate couples who wish to live the good life with an absence of deep-seated value conflicts within themselves or between themselves and others and who wish to live in a Crestwood Heights will have their work cut out for them.

Middle-class couples especially must be warned of the extreme difficulties inherent in a program of deviation from community norms, as well as the penalties of abject conformity. Through subtle and sometimes not so subtle pressures many deviant couples find that what they considered to be matters of personal choice are not so considered by their associates.

The middle class, whose values dominate our society in large part, may address their attention less to 'public' and more to 'private' behavior, with particular emphasis to conformity to the norm. . . . Its members may not be so much concerned with the plight of the under privileged as with their own adjustment to a society that demands conformity as the price of success. Many of the social conditions that originally gave rise to 'public' problems have changed, although these problems are by no means completely eliminated. In their place has risen an emphasis upon conformity, adjustment to the group,

[21] *Ibid.,* p. 394.

and the minimization of individuality. The new (and unforgivable) problem behavior may be nonconformity.[22]

PSYCHOTHERAPY AND IDEOLOGY

Our discussion would be incomplete if ended with the implication that couples, working actively together, can always build a mutually satisfactory philosophy of life without help. This assumes a naive and unjustified faith in the rational approach to problems.

The Freudians and others have demonstrated beyond a doubt that much human behavior has nonrational bases. The wellsprings of human motivation run deep, and many an individual finds it impossible to probe these depths, at least without skilled professional help. In many cases a value to which an individual thought he was fully attached can be shown to be a part of an irrational defense system. Pull out two or three fingers from the dike and the whole system collapses. Many individuals find it necessary to avail themselves of professional counseling help, if they are to embark on a program as suggested in this chapter. Only in this way can they bring their irrational impulses under control and reduce their sense of anxiety and insecurity.

Having done this, however, they are only ready to develop a satisfactory working philosophy of life. Psychotherapy or marriage counseling cannot and should not be expected to provide a person or a couple with a value orientation by which to live. Psychotherapy may help an individual to understand the sources of much of his behavior. Marriage counseling at its best may help with the next step. The skilled marriage counselor, working with both partners (not necessarily in joint session), may be able to help them identify their value differences and aid in movement toward a mutually satisfactory new configuration. One is on shaky ground if he thinks that by turning to psychiatry, social science, or some other type of science he will find his ultimate values. This is to confuse means with ends. Science is instrumental. It may help us achieve ultimate goals, if we know how to use it, but it can never create them.

A number of leaders in various fields have issued warnings along this line. Mowrer, the learning psychologist, believes that Freudian psychiatry has been demonstrated to be inadequate in both its clinical program and the ideology of life which it implies.[23] Redlich, the psychiatrist, would not accept Mowrer's first point, but does not believe it proper that psychiatry attempt to provide values. He states, "If the quest for therapy becomes a quest for ideology, it is bound to be disappointed . . . because psycho-

[22] Francis Merrill, *Society and Culture* (Englewood Cliffs, N.J., Prentice-Hall, 1957), p. 565.
[23] O. H. Mowrer, *The Crisis in Psychiatry and Religion* (Princeton, Van Nostrand, 1961).

analysis cannot provide an ideology." [24] It is the latter point that we especially wish to stress. The scientist or the clinician can assess the general and particular possibilities of man. Inconsistencies, logical fallacies, new knowledge, and new techniques can be provided. But in the long run individual couples must finally and often painfully make their own choices of values to live by and must accept the consequences of those choices. Much of the thrill of the human experience would be lost were this not so.

SELECTED READINGS

Ashen, Ruth (Ed.), *The Family: Its Function and Destiny* (New York, Harper & Row, 1960).

Becker, Howard, and Hill, Reuben (Eds.), *Family, Marriage, and Parenthood* (Boston, Heath, 1955), Chapters 11, 20.

Blood, Robert, *Marriage* (New York, Free Press, 1962), Chapters 12, 16.

Bowman, Henry, *A Christian Interpretation of Marriage* (Philadelphia, The Westminster Press, 1959), Chapter 2.

Cavan, Ruth, *The American Family* (New York, Crowell, 1963), Chapter 1.

Duvall, Evelyn and Hill, Reuben, *Being Married* (Boston, Heath, 1960), Chapter 21.

Fairchild, Roy and Wynn, J. C., *Families in the Church: A Protestant Survey* (New York, Association Press, 1961).

Farber, Seymour, *et al., Man and Civilization: The Family's Search for Survival* (New York, McGraw-Hill, 1965).

Foote, Nelson, and Cottrell, Leonard, *Identity and Interpersonal Competence* (Chicago, University of Chicago Press, 1955).

Gillin, John, "National and Regional Values in the United States," *Social Forces,* Vol. 34 (December, 1956), pp. 108–110.

Graham, Saxon, *American Culture* (New York, Harper & Row, 1957), Chapter VII.

Horney, Karen, *The Neurotic Personality of Our Time* (New York, Norton, 1937).

Jacob, P. E., *Changing Values in College* (New York, Harper & Row, 1957).

Kephart, William, *Family, Society, and the Individual* (Boston, Houghton Mifflin, 1961), Chapter 8.

Kirkpatrick, Clifford, *The Family* (New York, Ronald, 1955), Chapters 4, 8.

Kluckhohn, Florence, "Dominant and Substitute Profiles of Cultural Orientation," *Social Forces,* Vol. 28 (May, 1950), pp. 376–393.

Komarovsky, Mirra, *Blue-Collar Marriage* (New York, Random House, 1964), Chapters 1 and 14.

Levy, John, and Munroe, Ruth, *The Happy Family* (New York, Knopf, 1948), Chapter V.

Mace, David, and Mace, Vera, *Marriage East and West* (Garden City, N.Y., Doubleday, 1960).

[24] In J. Masserman (Ed.), *Psychoanalysis and Human Values* (New York, Grune & Stratton, 1960), p. 88.

Martinson, Floyd, *Marriage and the American Ideal* (New York, Dodd, Mead, 1960), Part I.

Morris, Charles, *Varieties of Human Value* (Chicago, The University of Chicago Press, 1956), Chapters 1–4.

Pepper, Stephen, *The Source of Value* (Berkeley, University of California Press, 1958).

Peterson, James, *Education for Marriage* (New York, Scribner, 1964), Chapters 1 and 18.

Riesman, David, *The Lonely Crowd* (New Haven, Yale, 1950).

Seeley, John, *et al., Crestwood Heights* (New York, Basic Books, 1956), Part III.

Sutton, Francis, *The American Business Creed* (Cambridge, Harvard, 1956).

Thomas, John, *The American Catholic Family* (Englewood Cliffs, N.J., Prentice-Hall, 1956), Part II.

Tillich, Paul, *The Courage to Be* (New Haven, Yale, 1952).

Waller, Willard, and Hill, Reuben, *The Family* (New York, Holt, Rinehart and Winston, 1951), Parts I and III.

Whyte, William H., *The Organization Man* (New York, Simon and Schuster, 1956).

Williams, Robin, *American Society* (New York, Random House, 1960), Chapter 11.

QUESTIONS AND EXERCISES

1. Read carefully Martinson's Chapter 3 including the discussion of the three marriage models, namely the Judeo-Christian, romantic, and rationalistic. Which model would you essentially prefer for your own life and why?

2. Justify or criticize the inclusion of a chapter on "Building a Philosophy of Life" in a marriage and family text.

3. Arrange a forum on "An Adequate Philosophy of Life" which includes both a secular philosopher and a member of the clergy.

4. Why is it that the churches are not as critical of romanticism as they were in the Middle Ages? Discuss.

5. Justify the idea of building a set of values after marriage. Are not our values internalized when we are children? Shouldn't couples agree on values previous to marriage?

6. In attempting to build a family value system how much attention should young couples pay to the values and traditions of their parental families and the groups from which they came?

7. Study a group of young couples who as yet do not have children. Find out how far they have attempted to go in deliberately building a system of values and practices to which they wish to expose their future children.

8. To what values are you most strongly committed? Why?

9. Should members of religious minorities or other subgroups attempt to perpetuate themselves? Why or why not?

10. To what extent can spouses disagree on basic values and still maintain a successful marriage?

11. Happiness, stability, integration, adjustment, companionship, and personality development have all been used as criteria to measure success in marriage. How would you rank these in importance? Justify your answer.

12. Just how rational do you think couples can be in their attempt to build a system of values? Discuss.

15

Physical Maintenance of the Pair

Finding a method of obtaining the wherewithal to provide the couple with the basic necessities and some of the luxuries of life becomes an important developmental task of early marriage. Since it is the normal expectation that the husband will be the major breadwinner, some attention should be given to his occupational pursuits. However, since a growing proportion of young wives are also employed outside the home, some attention will be given to this phenomenon also.

RELATING TO THE OCCUPATIONAL WORLD

Many husbands at first will be young and have limited occupational experience and/or training. As has already been indicated, the median age of marriage has moved steadily down since 1890, although it is presently in the process of stabilizing. This trend has taken place in the face of an opposing trend, namely the stepping up of educational and occupational training requirements. It is now suggested in many quarters that technical skills and training will be standard prerequisites for most general industrial jobs! [1] Those who wish more advanced positions will be required to have a background of advanced education. We are thus suggesting that many young couples are marrying with the possibility of a number of years of advanced technical training or education still ahead of them. In the immediate future at least this pattern will persist. Most assuredly educational requirements are going to remain high.

Advanced education is desirable from a purely monetary point of

[1] Editors of Fortune, *America in the Sixties* (New York, Harper Torchbooks, Harper & Row, 1960), Chapter 2.

283

view. In Figure 8 we get an indication of the occupational opportunities which will be available to men in relation to education and technical training. While those with little formal education may be able to step into a job with good pay initially, they usually soon reach a leveling off point above which they will find it most difficult to rise. On the other hand, the person with advanced education can, on the average, look forward to a rising level of income until the later years. As even the liberal arts colleges are now pointing out, "education pays."

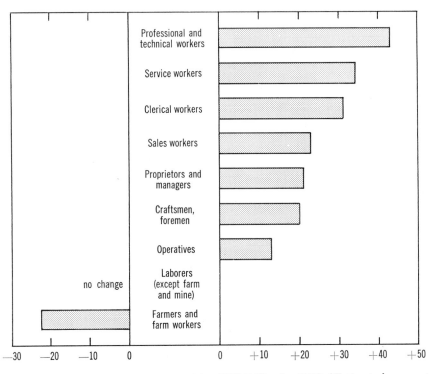

FIGURE 8. *Occupational Opportunities Will Differ in 1970 (Estimated percent change 1960–1970)*. SOURCE: American Women: Report of President's Commission, Women's Bureau, Department of Labor, Washington, D.C., 1963. Based on Employment Projections, by Industry and Occupation, 1960–1975 (U.S. Department of Labor, Bureau of Labor Statistics), Special Labor Force Report No. 28, p. 244, Table 2.

This is not to suggest that financial considerations as such should determine career choice. Interest, aptitude, and appeal are also important and basic. Moreover, if young men and women are to prepare for positions of leadership in public life, including even those of a service or missionary nature, advanced training is also a necessity.

It may be helpful to consider the typical course of income earned by men in their career cycles in the various occupations. Those in the unskilled categories reach their earning peak early and then face a period of decline. Men in the skilled and professional groups begin their substantial earning period at a relatively late time because of required education and training. However, they can look forward to a higher earning power, and a lower income decline at a later age compared to other income groups.

Many young couples thus may experience a financial "squeeze" that will require them to consider methods of supplementing the husband's income. The old concept of parental subsidy has not been adapted to modern urban living in America to the point where it is standard or accepted. Nevertheless many young couples find it necessary to accept some aid from their parents in order to get established. There are inherent difficulties in such plans under modern conditions, but with good judgment used by all parties concerned, tension can be kept at a minimum.

Very commonly these days in all but the upper class the young wife works outside the home to supplement income. Census reports show that during the first year of marriage in over 40 percent of the families this will be the case.[2] In the Blood and Wolfe Detroit study the rate of working outside the home was even higher, as shown in Figure 9. If trends continue in the present direction, most wives below the upper class will be working outside the home for a year or so after marriage.[3]

Some typical problems can be identified. Even though the young wife is full of enthusiasm and energy, she can scarcely be expected to handle two jobs at the same time. If married to a tradition-oriented husband who feels that all work around the house is women's work, she may find herself overwhelmed by all the requirements of her double role. Blood and Hamblin found that while 85 percent of the housework is done by wives who remain at home, working wives still carry about 75 percent of the housework.[4] Fortunately there is evidence that young men are beginning to adapt themselves to modern conditions, for many are willing to carry their share of household obligations without grumbling. A number of older married couples state that they developed a strong sense of camaraderie and fellowship through a cooperative approach to household tasks during the early years. This might not have happened, had the wife carried these tasks alone.

Attitudes are especially important here. If the husband's pride is injured because he cannot support his wife the way he wishes, she may need

[2] Paul Glick, "The Life Cycle of the Family," *Marriage and Family Living,* Vol. 17 (February, 1955), p. 8.

[3] Attitude studies reveal some subdivisions on this matter. See however, O. E. Thompson, "What is the High School Student of Today Like?" *Journal of Secondary Education,* Vol. 36 (April, 1961), pp. 210–219. See also, Reece McGee, *Social Disorganization in America* (San Francisco, Chandler Publishing Company, 1962), p. 148.

[4] Robert Blood, and Robert Hamblin, "The Effect of the Wife's Employment on the Family Power Structure," *Social Forces,* Vol. 36 (May, 1958), p. 351.

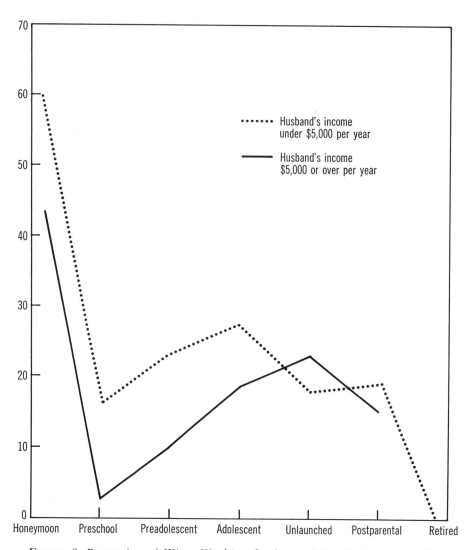

FIGURE 9. *Proportion of Wives Working, by Stage of Family Cycle and Husband's Income.* NOTE: Percentage of wives working in each subcategory of the sample according to income differential. SOURCE: Reprinted with permission of The Free Press of Glencoe from *Husbands and Wives* by Robert Blood and Donald Wolfe. Copyright © 1960 by The Free Press, a Corporation.

to be very tactful about her reference to her job, her contributions to the larder, etc. Each partner's conception of the proper role of the husband and the wife will tend to be reflected in the way situations such as these are approached. Regardless of their values, it would seem incongruous for the wife to contribute handily to the joint income only to have the husband exercise sole authority over its disposal. Inevitably when the wife works, there will be pressures toward a more democratic type of family organization, not only in economic but in other matters as well.

Practical impediments arise also. Federal and sometimes state income tax rates will be very high on the wife's earnings. Also allowance must be made for the cost of extra clothes, for lunch expenses, and for transportation to and from work. Often the wife's working results in extra meals being taken outside the home, additional laundry and cleaning bills, and other expenses. One report attempted to estimate how much could be saved by the wife working.[5] Assume the wife earns $3900. A couple without children, with the husband having an income of $5000, will be able to save about $2200 out of an income of $3900 which the wife brings in, by present tax rates. On the other hand, if the husband earns $15,000 the couple will only be able to realize $1785 out of the $3900 the wife earned. Some will doubt that the extra money the wife can earn is worth the effort, although at the lower income levels, it may mean that a certain number of luxuries or necessities, depending on the point of view and circumstances can be obtained, which otherwise would have to be foregone. The wife may, of course, prefer to work for other than monetary reasons.

The type of occupation for which the wife has training is a matter of some importance. With no particular skill the net return for her efforts outside the home may be small indeed. Furthermore, she may not be able to receive any concessions in regard to special hours or the like where occasionally necessary. The wife with an occupational skill which is in demand has a number of advantages. The possibility of part-time work or work at favorable hours is strong. Furthermore, she may be able to find employment no matter where her husband is located.

The biggest problem for the trained woman seems to be the question of a career line. The untrained woman has little psychological or economic stake in a job outside the home. Usually she views her employment merely as necessary to raise the level of living for the couple. For the trained or professional woman it is another matter. Such a woman may develop a professional interest in her job and be reluctant to give it up to have a child or to move with her husband to a new location. If she wishes to be a career wife, careful planning will be necessary on the part of both spouses so that this will not interfere with the marriage.

Since there are a fixed number of hours in a week, it is impossible for both spouses to work outside the home, do all their own housework, and compete with their neighbors in social activities. Something will have to give way. While young and full of vitality, a couple may require a minimum

[5] "Does it Really Pay for the Wife to Work?" *U.S. News and World Report,* Vol. 42 (March 15, 1957), pp. 154–158.

amount of rest and relaxation. Over a long period hard choices may be necessary.

HOW MUCH INCOME

How much money may the young couple realistically expect to earn? This obviously depends upon the characteristics of the couple, the general state of the nation's economy, and other factors. It may be worthwhile to give brief attention to reports of family income for the nation as a whole to give perspective. The Conference on Economic Progress, a nonprofit economic research organization, has developed five categories of living, based on considerable study. They are as follows: (1) poverty, (2) deprivation, (3) deprivation-comfort, (4) comfort-affluence, and (5) affluence.[6]

These divisions at best are somewhat subjective, but they are by no means arbitrary either. The categories are correlated to a degree with the "modest to adequate" budget series developed by the Department of Labor in its ongoing studies of family expenditures in American towns and cities. Poverty is defined as total *family* income under $4000. In 1960 about 23 percent of the nation's families lived at the poverty level. The status of the rest of the families in the country is shown in Figure 10. In this chart comparisons are made with the late twenties, the depression period, and two other postwar periods, based on 1960 dollars.

Many college couples will be starting out in the "deprivation" level or the lower part of the deprivation-comfort category, by 1960 dollars. Naturally, where the husband is trained in a scientific or technical field the beginning salary will be somewhat higher. In many cases, however, he will be working a number of years at a fairly low level if he is furthering his education or getting started in such a field as teaching, the ministry, or the law.

It must be noted that the majority of families in the categories listed are composed of more than three persons. A couple can live better at the corresponding income level than might be implied by Figure 10. However, unless some of the earnings are saved the advent of children can bring financial pressure, if not crisis, particularly if the pregnancy is not anticipated.

Disbursing the Income

Regardless of the amount of income, some method of managing it must be agreed upon. There are three major methods of arranging for the handling of money. They are:

[6] See *Poverty and Deprivation in the United States* (Washington, D.C., Conference on Economic Progress, 1962).

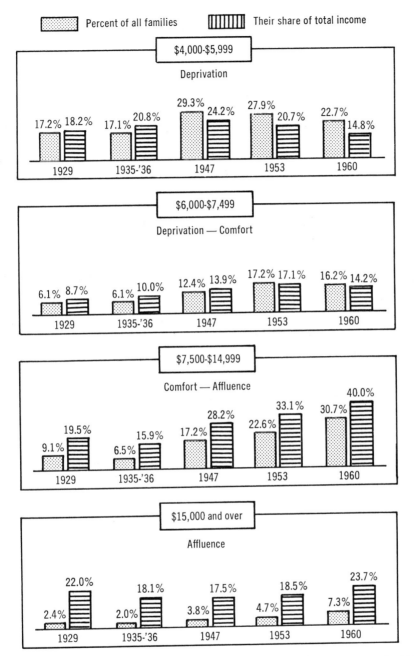

FIGURE 10. *Percent of Multiple Person Families with Annual Incomes of $4,000 and Over, Before Taxes, and Their Share of Total Family Income, in 1960 Dollars.* NOTE: Includes in addition to cash income the monetary value of food and fuel produced and consumed on the farm, and other nonmoney income. SOURCE: Leon H. Keyserling, Poverty and Deprivation in the United States (Washington, D.C.) Conference on Economic Progress, April, 1962), p. 37.

1. Control by one spouse.
2. Control by one spouse and an allowance to the other.
3. Joint control.

Where one spouse is in charge of dispensing the income it traditionally has been the husband, but today this is not necessarily true. As in any system of monopoly control there are some advantages. If the person assuming leadership is the most efficient manager this may be the most economical method of operation. If both spouses agree, no other value may be lost in the process. Otherwise this method comes under attack on a number of grounds.

Under plan two, one spouse controls the income (ordinarily the husband) but the wife is granted a fixed amount each month for the household and her own personal expenses. Some wives consider this an improvement over a patriarchal version of plan one, but many would still feel that the dignity which rightfully belongs to the wife is not granted her under this system.

If the husband fails to give his wife a large enough allowance for necessities she may find that she has nothing available for her personal use. On the other hand, the wife may, at least from the husband's point of view, skimp on necessities in order to increase the amount used for her own benefit. The possibilities of tension and conflict inhere in this method as in all others.

A variation of the plan is an allowance for the husband. Usually this means that he will pay some of the major bills and have a personal allowance which he uses as he sees fit.

Joint control in some form appears to be increasing, and this would seem logical in that it embodies the principles of equality and democracy to a greater degree than the other methods. For some this will mean a joint bank account from which each can freely draw. Its possibilities and problems are apparent. Under joint control each marital partner can exercise major authority in expressing his or her opinion on the eventual use of the *family income*. When children come and reach a reasonable level of maturity they can also be involved. Each person feels that he is making a contribution to the family enterprise and that he has a right to a share in decisions affecting distribution of goods and services.

Some maturity is demanded if couples are to avoid problems in the handling of their money. Attitudes and motivations are heavily involved. As Kirkpatrick indicates, a young wife who is "free and easy" with the joint bank account may be reacting to an overrestrictive childhood. If Winch's theory of complementary needs were carried to an extreme, the spendthrift would tend to select the miser as a marital partner. Whether in actual practice the two would nicely complement each other remains to be empirically demonstrated.

It seems reasonable that the "tail should not wag the dog," that money should be only a tool that the couple uses to meet its collective needs. If disputes over finances mount to the place where there are monthly or more frequent battles, it would seem that the dog is no longer master of the tail.

Income Management

Many couples will wish to develop some systematic plan to determine how their financial resources may best be used. Such a form of financial or income management would obtain the maximum benefits or return for the couple.

What are the advantages of planning? Bigelow, an economist who for years has specialized in family economics, thinks that the majority of people do not have the money sense to operate efficiently without some rather detailed planning of their finances.[7] Without this, the average person tends to be very vague as to how much money has passed through his hands, and for what it was spent. It is true that some couples are able to operate very efficiently with informal planning, as Bigelow admits. But most are overwhelmed by the financial labyrinth in which they are forced to operate today. It would appear that many couples will need to make rather detailed and careful plans by which their income is dispensed, if they are to achieve efficient use of their resources.

Objections are often based on misleading conceptions of what planning means. To some it implies an inflexible system, devised by "experts," a limiting or restricting plan. To others it arouses feelings and resentments reminiscent of the dictates of childhood. Actually in some ways it would be emotionally advantageous for some couples if they could "pass the buck" to some management authority who could plan for them and make them happy with the results. However, since such an expert does not exist, each couple must do its own planning in terms of its unique needs and goals.

This is not to discourage the use of model plans or the study of the spending patterns of other families, some of which are reported in governmental and other reports. These can be helpful in furnishing ideas and checks against bizarre patterns in particular instances. They must be handled with some statistical sophistication if they are to be of any positive value. They represent the summation of what a number of families in previous years have actually done with their money. If the figures reported refer to changes in proportions of income spent for items such as food or rent the discerning student can get some idea of the effects of recessions, full employment, or inflation. One must be careful to note the size of families in the sample, and the income level from which these were derived.

Again there is no substitute for creative planning for the future. Past

---

[7] In Howard Becker and Reuben Hill (Eds.), *Family, Marriage, and Parenthood* (Boston, Heath, 1955), Chapter 13.

experiences of others can be helpful but they do not make decisions in and of themselves.

Steps in Management of Income

The following steps are necessary in any systematic planning of disbursement of income:

1. Determine marital goals.
2. Determine a planning period.
3. Determine the types and amounts of income available for the period.
4. List the fixed and variable expenses for the period.
5. Put the plan to work.

Determination of Goals. The developmental task of determining and delineating general goals in marriage is discussed in detail in Chapter 14, and the reader's attention is called again to this. Certainly a couple can ignore the building of a philosophy of life and the attempt to give some rational control to its life and destiny. If so, financial planning can become compulsive, and an end in itself, rather than a means to an end.[8] Furthermore, in such cases it has been found that it is rather difficult to plan finances. Couples unwilling to give careful thought and attention to ultimate, long-term goals often find it most difficult to be systematic in the financial realm. At any rate, it is impossible to plan without setting up some goals and making some decisions among possible alternatives.

Here class factors and style of life of parents will enter the picture. Night club activity for one young couple will be so important that it will be willing even to skimp on food or housing. To a neighboring couple such a choice might seem questionable, to say the least.

It is sometimes said that people are judged by the way they spend their money. If so, it is implied that a couple will wish to be rather clear as to what it wishes to emphasize through its spending program.

The Planning Period. Some couples will wish to plan for a year, some for six months, or shorter or longer periods. Since certain categories of employed and salaried people are now being paid on a monthly basis, many couples will want to use some combination of months for their overall planning unit.

There will always be those for whom irregularity of income will be typical. This will vary from the couples who have seasonal employment through the ranks of farm, business, and certain types of salaried people for whom there are possibilities of bonuses or commissions. Various plans have been suggested which usually involve estimates of minimum predic-

[8] Paulena Nickell and Jean Dorsey, *Management in Family Living* (New York, Wiley, 1950), Chapter 10.

tions for half-year or year periods. It appears that it is easiest to estimate minimum income, and it is probably wisest to plan for this level and then make adjustments if estimates were too low. In reality this means that the couple is attempting to approximate the consistent receipt of wages or salaries which are typical in other groups.

By planning on an annual basis the couple can take account of some of the major fixed expenses more handily. Taxes, dues, insurance, and other such items do not come each month. Many will be annual or semi-annual in form. Since many of these bills must be paid promptly couples must find some method of having extra money available when needed. A "leveling off" during these periods of high expenses seems to work best for most couples. Whether this be done by saving so much per month, or by some other method is a decision for the couple. If no planning is done it may be necessary to borrow or allow bills to lag because no forethought was given to the problem of payments due in certain critical months.

Types and Amounts of Income. There are three major types of income which may be cited. They are *money* income, *real* income, and *psychic* income.[9] Money income used in this connection represents actual purchasing power over a given period of time and is in the form of dollars and cents or the equivalent by some other standard. For the average young couple the main source of this income will be the job, although of course they may receive additional amounts through inheritance, gifts, and dividends. The latter are ordinarily not as predictable as wages or salary, and it would be wise to focus planning essentially on the steady salary. Dependence on the windfalls of inheritance or gifts may turn out to be hazardous. Of course, income from an endowment or a share of stock may be highly predictable in a specific instance. The couple may wish to treat it in the budget as the equivalent of salary and apportion it out accordingly.

Real income is composed of the actual goods and services available. Its source is money income or services and wealth produced by the individuals in the household for use by family members. For example, the wife may add to the real income by furnishing food from a garden, or by being efficient in ironing and washing, doing her own washing, and the like. Real income then refers to services controlled by members of the family. The more efficient the use of the skills and services available, the greater the real income. Abilities of family members in management and planning are crucial in this regard.

It takes imagination and effort to make efficient use of all the sources of real income readily available. Services made available by the community should not be overlooked at this point. While each family member theoretically is paying for any public or private agency service through taxes or

<hr>

[9] *Ibid.,* p. 211.

welfare contributions, often the services and commodities available for use will far exceed the subsidy which a young couple is giving them.

Many will wish to increase their educational background through the use of public libraries, evening college classes, and the like. These opportunities are often of considerable value when viewed in terms of their full potential.

Psychic income is the personal satisfaction which comes from the use of the real income. Wealth and services of various kinds are obtained by the couple and used for various purposes. While no precise measuring stick is available to measure such a subjective phenomenon, psychic income here seems to be the most important, ultimate, and intrinsical of the three types of income described.

In this category much depends on the emotions and attitudes of individuals concerned. For example, some individuals do not avail themselves of services that are available to the general public. Apparently these are too "common" for them, and their pride would be so hurt that any potential satisfaction (psychic income) would thereby vanish. Any reader will be able to give examples of couples who derive great satisfaction out of a simple life on modest means, and also of those who, in spite of above average wealth or income, are apparently not able to satisfy their psychic needs. Clearly, individual differences are such that it would be most difficult to predict what psychic income a given object or action would bring to an individual picked at random. *The Gift of the Magi* by O. Henry comes to mind at this point. The wife put great value on her long, golden hair while the husband treasured his gold watch. To other individuals these items might be very mundane and of trivial significance and value.

The Fixed and Variable Expenses. To develop a financial plan the couple may list the items for which the costs are essentially the same yearly or monthly. Such a category will include insurance, taxes, installment payments, and the like. Following these, there is a list of items which are relatively fixed, and which will vary only slightly on a monthly or yearly basis. Included would be such items as utilities, laundry, dry cleaning, and food. Finally, the variable expenses such as recreation, education, and clothing may be listed, since it can be shown that expenses will vary on these items to a greater degree than on the other items.

The total plan might look something like this:

Fixed Expenses

Taxes—Federal, state, local
Social Security
Insurance—Accident, fire, health, liability, life
Housing—Mortgage, upkeep, and repair or rent
Dues—Professional or union fees and assessments

Pledges—Commitments to religious and charitable institutions
Contingency Fund—Fund for emergencies and savings

other————————————————

Semifixed Expenses

Food
Utilities—Fuel supplies, electricity, water, telephone etc.
Household services—Laundry, cleaning
Personal services—Care of hair, shaving, beauty, toilet and personal supplies.

other————————————————

Variable Expenses

Clothing—Garments, accessories, repair
Health—Hospital, doctor, dentist, drugs
Transportation—Automobile, other travel expenses
Household upkeep—Repairs, addition of small equipment, etc.
Education—Books, magazines, fees, supplies
Recreation—Admission fees, vacation, travel, newspapers, magazines, music,
    records, etc.

other————————————————

The young couple starting out housekeeping will not have previous yearly records to aid them in their planning. This means that they will have to estimate expenses in the various categories. Some will wish to seek assistance from older married couples within their circle of friends, while others will turn to published resources for help in their planning. One excellent source is the Heller Committee of the University of California, which publishes three budgets for families of four persons—man, wife, boy of thirteen, and girl of eight years, where the father and wage earner is an executive and a white-collar worker, respectively.[10] See Appendix (Figure 22).

For newly-married couples budgets will be somewhat distinct from those of couples married longer. Therefore this type of chart is not as suitable for the young couple as another might be. It does have the advantage of being up-to-date, as reports are issued annually and are based on studies of the previous year. This gives the couple some basis for planning which can be adapted to their own use.

Once income and expenses have been estimated, a balance must be made between the two. If the income exceeds expenses the problem will be

[10] See *Quantity and Cost Budgets for Two Income Levels* (Berkely, Heller Committee for Research in Social Economics, 1962).

small. If the income is smaller than estimated expenditures either the wants will have to be pared down or the income increased. If income cannot reasonably be supplemented in the immediate future a reassessment of values and a new ranking of priorities are necessary. First things must be put first. Items thought of as necessities will be listed first while others will be arranged in order of preference. After the necessities will come the important wants, to be followed by the luxury items. In most cases every want cannot be met, and some items may have to be deferred for a year or so.

To increase the income it may be necessary for the wife to take employment outside the home, or for the husband to find additional part-time employment. Here again personal, social, and economic factors influence the feasibility of these alternatives.

Putting the Plan to Work. A plan on paper remains just that if nothing else is done. In order to have the maximum results it is necessary to put the plan into operation. It is possible that through the process of plan-making some things will be learned which will have a carry-over effect. But best results are obtained when actual spending is regularly checked against the plan.

It is clear that more attention needs to be given to the semivariable and variable items than to those that are essentially fixed. There are different methods of doing this, even including separate pocketbooks for each category. Probably most couples will prefer to use an account book of some sort for such a purpose. There are many such forms available. State and county extension services usually have booklets available at minimum cost and couples are well advised to contact such sources for lists of publications. Interestingly enough, farm families seem more inclined to use accounting methods than city families, probably because they must engage in record keeping for tax and other purposes.[11]

The spending plan is to be a guide, not a policeman. For most couples only a flexible plan is workable. Changing price and wage scales, unexpected contingencies, and other occurrences may make the best-laid plans difficult to follow. If the changes which occur are drastic the overall plan may need revision. Such a couple is in a better position to make needed adjustments than if it had no plan to adjust.

MAJOR EXPENDITURES

Acquiring Housing

One major task for the young couple is the location of suitable housing facilities. The type of housing initially selected will depend on a num-

---

[11] *Guiding Family Spending* (U.S. Department of Agriculture, Miscellaneous Publications, No. 661), p. 13.

ber of factors. When the husband is not settled in his occupational pursuit —a rather typical circumstance of today's marriage—the couple will probably not wish to purchase a house. If both spouses are employed outside the home, a small apartment will probably be more suitable than more spacious quarters. If the wife does not work and if the couple expects to remain a number of years in the same location, a larger apartment or a house may be preferable.

Young people usually find it necessary to start housekeeping in furnished quarters. After a period of time they are able to accumulate enough money to furnish their own apartment or house. Since in many cases mobility is advisable during the early years of marriage, the absence of quantities of housekeeping equipment has definite advantages.

Should the couple buy a home during the early years of marriage? The general merits of buying versus renting will be discussed in a later section. The question for concern here deals with couples who will buy eventually, and the factor of importance is timing. One recent marriage text suggests that they should buy very quickly if at all possible.[12] The arguments are rather clear-cut. Building costs have been rising and the predictions are that they will continue to do so. It is probably true that inflated housing prices will be with us for some time to come. Other things being equal, a delay in buying of a home probably costs additional money. Things are not equal, however, when the new husband and wife are compared with couples in other later stages of the family cycle. Home ownership involves considerable responsibility and risk. If the husband is occupationally mobile he may find it necessary or advantageous to move quickly, perhaps a considerable distance. When one is forced to place his home on the market and to sell quickly he is at considerable disadvantage.[13] Often he must suffer a loss of one to three thousand dollars under a forced sale. When this contingency is coupled with the real estate broker's fee, the presumed savings involved in buying during the very early period of marriage may be spurious.

Furthermore, the very young couple has not had time to develop an appreciation for all the elements involved in home ownership and neighborhood living. Some features which are stressed by an overzealous salesman may not be the items the couple will be interested in after two or three years of married living and experience. Once obtained, a house has to be given attention if depreciation is not to be excessive. To find himself negotiating with plumbers, carpenters, painters, tax assessors, and a host of other functionaries may be a rather disorganizing experience for the young spouse. It is possible that such responsibilities could best be left to a landlord for a year or two until the couple has had the chance to make a

[12] Ersel LeMasters, *Modern Courtship and Marriage* (New York, Macmillan, 1957), p. 433.
[13] Editors of Fortune, *op. cit.,* Chapter 8.

number of necessary adjustments in other areas of life. Home ownership is really not a simple matter.

How much can a couple safely spend for housing? A study of various budgets will show that from 15 to 25 percent of the income should be allowed for the housing item. In order to get quarters that they consider comfortable or desirable many families may be forced to go above that level. However, it can be said that the young couple who expects to operate an automobile, and to dress and eat well, may find it necessary to keep rental costs under control if they are to remain solvent.

Household operating costs must not be forgotten. While they tend to run around 5 to 10 percent in the lower and middle income group they can, if exaggerated, help swell the housing allotment to rather large and unexpected proportions.

Food

A check of suggested budgets and of family expenditure studies will show that food usually ranks at the top of the itemized categories. The percentages allotted for food will vary from 30 to 40 percent at the lower income levels and be scaled down a bit with rising income. Naturally this item is dependent on the number of children in the family and the class level of the family. As children are added, the *average* spent *per person* naturally drops off.

The young couple will be forced to experiment with its food budget until some agreeable pattern can be developed. Food habits and preferences differ considerably from one group to another. Actually it is possible to serve nutritious food which is still fairly reasonable in price by present economic standards. Many, perhaps most people, are more concerned with taste and preference than with nutrition, as such. Nutritionists actually claim that many Americans are not adequately nourished in spite of the fact that our per capita food consumption cost is among the world's highest.

To be specific, the couple must come to a decision on such matters as to whether choice cuts of meat are to be bought, how much expensive fruit is to be eaten out of season, or how much prepared food is to be purchased. Achieving agreements may not be a simple matter. If college students are representative of sex preferences for food, it is to be expected that the adult man and woman will not see eye to eye. Food service departments of colleges report that men wish ample servings of meat and potatoes while the girls prefer lighter foods such as salads. What to a young bride may seem perfectly adequate and nutritionally correct may imply to the husband a diet sufficient only for a yearling goldfish or songbird. By compromise on food preferences, by careful shopping, and by preparation (canning, freezing) of some food at home the couple can achieve material savings in food bills.

Bigelow suggests that it is better to estimate food costs by focusing on the expenditure necessary per day per person in the family.[14] By doing this the couple can quickly arrive at weekly and monthly averages. If the home manager then notices that food expenditures have been particularly heavy during a given period it may be necessary to suggest that the next week be a "hamburger and beans" rather than a "steak and caviar" week to keep the food budget in line.

Clothing

A third major item of expenditure is clothing. Naturally this item will be especially affected by class, income level, and occupational pursuit. It may be of interest to note that for years a rather consistent proportion (irrespective of income level) of family income was allocated to clothing in a wide variety of budget proposals and income studies. The percentage usually was between 13 and 15 percent.

At the present time many standard budgets suggest holding the clothing item to 10 percent or under if possible. Transportation and income taxes have moved ahead of clothing costs to the point where clothing is in fourth place in the budgets of many families. It must be remembered that these figures reflect averages, and that item purchases in given time periods will vary considerably. This is true both when a particular couple compares its purchases in one period with another, and when two couples compare expenditures for clothing during a stated period. The reason behind this is clear. Articles of clothing are expected to last several years on the average, but if it becomes necessary to buy several major items of clothing during a particular period the expenditures will be unusually high.

Some advisors suggest that clothing purchases be so planned that no more than one major item will be bought in a given month or period. This method has advantages, but does not allow for purchases at special sales or for acute need. It appears logical that clothing needs should be projected over an extended period of time, so that it is possible to take advantage of special or seasonal sales. By purchasing a good quality garment it may be possible to obtain an extra year or so of wear.

If the couple expects to have a large number of children, the wife may wish to learn to sew so that she can make and redesign clothing. With care she may be able to make an attractive garment for herself for a modest cost. And when children come along, the advantages of home production will be noteworthy.

Not every wife will find that home sewing results in a substantial saving. As is true of many do-it-yourself projects, considerable skill and equipment are necessary if the finished projects are to look other than amateurish

[14] In Morris Fishbein, and Ruby Jo Kennedy (Eds.), *Modern Marriage and Family Living* (New York, Oxford University Press, 1957), p. 295.

and low-grade. Given the ability to read directions carefully, the proper equipment, and strong motivation, however, home sewing has its advantages.

Home economists have shown that the housewife should have considerable knowledge and good judgment if the couple is to be efficient in clothing purchase and management. Among the responsibilities listed are:

1. Analyzing the family's clothing needs.
2. Determining the proportions of the budget which may be spent for clothing.
3. Following market conditions as they pertain to clothing.
4. Developing a rationale for clothing choice.
5. Learning how to build up a wardrobe within a reasonable budget.
6. Learning to recognize various levels of quality in commercial clothing.
7. Developing good habits of care, upkeep, and storage of clothing.
8. Developing skill in construction of new clothing and mending of old if this is to be handled in the home.
9. Teaching children acceptable methods of clothing purchase, storage, etc.[15]

Not all of this knowledge is necessary for the first years of marriage, since each spouse will usually already possess a fairly complete wardrobe. However, clothing will wear out or be out of style in time, and when children begin to arrive, a reevaluation of family needs will quickly become necessary. Development of skills in clothing management cannot come too early in marriage.

Miscellaneous Items

Besides the basic factors of food, clothing, and shelter, many miscellaneous items will enter the picture. Among them, transportation, health, recreation, and education will stand out. Today many couples find transportation and health will actually involve respectively a larger portion of the budget than clothing. Recreation and education will cost about half as much as these two items.

A major question involves the ownership of an automobile. It seems clear that the automobile, while often essential, is a very expensive commodity and that the average couple would do well to consider use of public transportation.[16] That such an assertion will seem heretical, even outside of Detroit, can be taken for granted. The couple nevertheless should recognize four important factors in appraising the actual cost of an automobile: (1) initial cost, (2) general upkeep, (3) depreciation, and (4) insurance and license. In addition there is the question of a new versus used car, and a large versus small car.

Health has become a major budget item in the last few decades. Our standards have risen and the general level of physical health has improved.

---

[15] Partially based on Nickell and Dorsey, *op. cit.,* Chapter 20.

[16] See Editors of Fortune, *op. cit.,* Chapter 11, for a discussion of possible developments in public transportation.

Advances have come especially in the field of drugs and in new medical techniques, both of which are, however, very expensive. Either through insurance or through budgetary procedures the couple can spread potential expenses over extended periods. If this is not done, health contingencies may be very difficult to meet.

Other items, such as recreation and leisure pursuits, are of such nature that the couple can spend as much money on them as is available. The possible alternative choices are so great that it is most difficult to generalize about them. By their nature they are highly subjective, since so much depends on the wants and tastes of the individuals concerned. To one couple a simple picnic in a public park, involving a minimum expenditure for food, is a great delight, while to another couple only a theater engagement coupled with dinner in an expensive restaurant could bring the same satisfaction.

Couples obviously will be forced to choose between alternatives. Available money can be stretched only so far. With ingenuity many do an amazing job within the limits of their resources. Apparently there will always be some who, as the old saying goes, have "beer pocketbooks but champagne appetites."

NEEDS, WANTS, AND AMERICAN SOCIETY

It may be in order to consider the relationship among needs, wants, and social imperatives. For generations scholars and social practitioners have been concerned with the question of the necessity versus the luxury. It is now apparent that no objective measuring stick can be developed. Standards of living are highly relative to historical period, place, class level, and other factors.

This is not to say that the needs and wants of individuals are solely products of social conditioning; a bio-psycho-social theory best explains the complex of need and want patterns found in any individual. In America at least, consumptive habits no longer bear any close relationship to minimum needs to sustain life. Knight was able to state as early as 1925: "Even our food and clothing, in all their concrete content, and by far the larger part of their money cost, represent social and esthetic and not biological values." [17]

Americans are now living in what Bernard calls a "context of abundance" and what Galbraith refers to as an "affluent society." Our society has a level of living that is, for the average family, the highest in the world. We are especially blessed in terms of food, clothing, shelter, health facilities, mechanical conveniences, and labor-saving devices. Compared to other

[17] F. H. Knight, "Economic Psychology and the Value Problem," *Quarterly Journal of Economics,* Vol. 39 (May, 1925), p. 401 as cited in Kyrk, *op. cit.,* p. 386.

parts of the world and to past periods of history, we have a small amount of real poverty and want.

It should follow then that American young couples, at least those who are above the poverty and deprivation level, should feel free from pressure and frustration as far as material factors are concerned. All available evidence is to the contrary. We should perhaps give brief attention to the reasons for this.

One theoretical approach to the dilemma has been suggested by Galbraith when he states that "the urgency of wants does not diminish appreciably as more of them are satisfied. When man has satisfied his physical needs, then psychologically grounded desires take over. These can never be satisfied or, in any case, no progress can be proved." [18] And further, "Without going as far as Duesenberry in reducing goods to the role of symbols of prestige in the affluent society, it is plain that his argument fully implies that the production of goods creates the wants that the goods are presumed to satisfy." [19] Here we have the suggestion that at least in our kind of social context many individuals are dissatisfied with their level of consumptive behavior, and furthermore will continue to be so even if our level of production keeps increasing indefinitely in the future.

In his analysis Galbraith suggests that two basic factors are causally behind the increase of consumer demands: (1) increased production, and (2) advertising. Also involved somewhere in the causal chain is the "reference group" to which an individual or family relates. Gross National Product (GNP) is a relatively meaningless symbol to many of our solid citizens even though it appears in charts of their daily newspaper with regularity. Changes in the level cause little popular concern. But raw production becomes meaningful when one's associates begin to exhibit new products in their homes and in the neighborhood. To get down to cases this means that while the average young couple is going to have a higher level of consumptive behavior than was true a generation ago, it will still feel as if it is in the proverbial squirrel cage.

The factors of social acceptance and social mobility also affect psychic income. For many people, the "Joneses" set the standards which must be emulated and some future, if mythical, life style defines their aspirations.

Basically young people will be forced to make some important value choices and policy decisions in regard to consumptive patterns. The style of life they wish to maintain will be involved, with all that this implies. Taxes will be increasingly high, and prices will probably continue to rise also. It is inevitable that many young American couples, even in an age of abundance, will feel financially pinched. This paradox will presumably be with us for an extended period of time, if not always.

---

[18] John Galbraith, *The Affluent Society* (Boston, Houghton Mifflin, 1958), p. 143.
[19] *Ibid.*, p. 155.

SELECTED READINGS

Baber, Ray, *Marriage and the Family* (McGraw-Hill, 1953), Chapter 12.

Baker, Elizabeth, *Technology and Womens' Work* (New York, Columbia, 1964).

Becker, Howard, and Hill, Reuben (Eds.), *Family, Marriage, and Parenthood* (Boston, Heath, 1955), Chapter 13.

Beyer, Glenn, *Housing: A Factual Analysis* (New York, Macmillan, 1958).

Bigelow, Howard, *Family Finance* (New York, Lippincott, 1953).

Blood, Robert, *Marriage* (New York, Free Press, 1962), Chapter 14.

Bowman, Henry, *Marriage for Moderns* (New York, McGraw-Hill, 1950), Chapter 12.

Bradley, Joseph, and Wherry, Ralph, *Personal and Family Finance* (New York, Holt, Rinehart and Winston, 1957).

Cole, Robert, *et al., Consumer and Commercial Credit Management* (Homewood, Ill., Irwin, 1960).

Crandall, Elizabeth, "Newer Aspects of Home Management," *Journal of Home Economics,* Vol. 48 (October, 1956), pp. 631–634.

Consumer Bulletin (Consumer's Research, Inc., Washington, D.C.), monthly bulletins.

Consumer Reports (Consumer's Union of the U.S., 256 Washington Street, Mt. Vernon, N.Y.), monthly reports.

Duvall, Evelyn, and Hill, Reuben, *Being Married* (Boston, Heath, 1960), Chapters 5, 12, 13.

Feldman, Frances, *The Family in a Money World* (New York, Family Service Association of America, 1957).

Fishbein, Morris, and Kennedy, Ruby Jo, *Modern Marriage and Family Living* (New York, Oxford University Press, 1957), Chapter 21.

Fortune, *America in the Sixties* (New York, Harper Torchbooks, Harper & Row, 1960).

Graham, Benjamin, *et al., Security Analysis* (New York, McGraw-Hill, 1962).

Gross, Irma, and Zwemer, Evelyn, *Management for Modern Families* (New York, Appleton-Century-Crofts, 1965).

Hanson, Arthur, and Cohen, Jerome, *Personal Finance* (Homewood, Ill., Irwin, 1955).

Jacobson, Allvar, "Conflicting of Attitudes toward the Role of the Husband and Wife in Marriage," *American Sociological Review* (April, 1952), pp. 146–150.

Kyrk, Hazel, *The Family in the American Economy* (Chicago, The University of Chicago Press, 1953).

Landis, Paul, *Making the Most of Marriage* (New York, Appleton-Century-Crofts, 1964), Chapters 26 and 27.

LeMaster, Ersel, *Modern Courtship and Marriage* (New York, Macmillan, 1957), Chapters 19 and 20.

Lippitt, Vernon, *Determinants of Consumer Demand for House Furnishing and Equipment* (Cambridge, Harvard, 1959).

Mack, Ruth, *Consumption and Business Fluctuations* (New York, National Bureau of Economic Research, 1956).

Mazur, Paul, *The Standards We Raise: The Dynamics of Consumption* (New York, Harper & Row, 1953).

Morgan, James, *Consumer Economics* (New York, Prentice-Hall, 1955).

Peterson, James, *Education for Marriage* (New York, Scribner, 1964), Chapter 18.

Smith, Paul, *Consumer Credit Costs* (Princeton, Princeton University Press, 1964).

Troelstrup, Arch, *Consumer Problems* (New York, McGraw-Hill, 1957).

Wolff, Janet, *What Makes Women Buy?* (New York, McGraw-Hill, 1958).

Worthy, Beatrice, "Part-Time Working Mothers, a Case Study," *Management Record* (National Industrial Conference Board, 1960), pp. 15–20.

QUESTIONS AND EXERCISES

1. Do a questionnaire study of the expected income level your classmates have in mind for their early years of marriage. Compare your results with the latest census data available relating income to occupational level. Do your colleagues seem to be realistic or not?
2. Write a short paper dealing with the pros and cons of installment buying.
3. As practice for your married life of the future, make a budget which you will follow for an academic year. Break it down into yearly, semester, and monthly units. Follow the budget for the year, keeping a record of your expenditures, and report your experience at the end of the year.
4. Have a real estate representative speak to your class regarding the advantages and disadvantages of renting as against purchasing a home during the early period of marriage.
5. By what method should young couples come to an agreement on the system of money control which they will eventually use?
6. Under what circumstances should the young wife work outside the home in your estimation? Remain in the home? Discuss.
7. Organize your class and make a survey of the prices of homes and rentals in the various areas of the town or city in which you are located. Prepare a summary report. Indicate whether or not your results are surprising to yourself and other members of the class.
8. Invite an economist to your class to discuss the possibilities if inflation and deflation occur in the American economy during the next decade. Have him spell out some of the implications of either type of trend for families at various stages of the life cycle.
9. Many people fail to realize that the ownership and use of an automobile often costs $1000 or more per year. Is the automobile a necessity or luxury for the average young couple? Discuss.
10. According to the Federal Reserve Board, about 70 percent of our young couples in the twenty-five to thirty age range live above their incomes. Is this figure "normal" or are present-day young people living "too high?" Discuss.

11. In ever-increasing numbers workers are being replaced by machines, which generally perform more efficiently and less expensively than human beings. In a few years it is probable that automation will actually displace many categories of white-collar workers. Discuss thoroughly the implications of automation for the maintenance of the family at various class levels in our society; or do the same for the various stages of a typical family life cycle.

16

Allocation of Resources, Division of Tasks and Responsibilities

A marriage is a small social unit of a society—a social system in its own right too. Any group that is going to last will find that certain things must be accomplished. In the case of a family, besides obtaining the basic necessities of food, clothing, and shelter, which were discussed in Chapter 15, some division of labor is necessary so that tasks may be accomplished.

Were this book being written for the Old Order Amish, it would hardly be necessary to include such a chapter. A young Amish girl of eighteen knows exactly what a wife should and should not do. She also knows what her husband-to-be will expect her to do. Both will acknowledge the husband as head of the house and the final authority on all general "policy decisions." The wife will not consider challenging the husband's authority nor will the husband allow it to be challenged. In a word, the roles of the spouses among the Amish or similar groups are sharply defined. Even some ethnic and religious minorities no longer have such clearly established roles for husband and wife.[1] A precise division of responsibilities will emerge only after a trial-and-error period, if at all.

A reasonably well-integrated home life, in any society, however, requires agreement as to "who does what, when, and how." We will discuss this under three major topics:

1. Establishing procedures to determine "who does what" (compatible roles).
2. Establishing patterns of accountability and authority.
3. Establishing a routine and schedule for completing tasks and services.

[1] Robert Blood and Donald Wolfe, *Husbands and Wives* (New York, Free Press, 1960), Chapter 2.

ESTABLISHING COMPATIBLE ROLES

The new bride comes to marriage with a general conception of what she wants to do and be as a wife; the same principle holds for the bridegroom as a husband. It is generally conceded that both will have a more clear-cut picture of the husband's future role than of the wife's. As was pointed out in Chapter 3, roles for women have been changing more rapidly than for men in American society, both outside and within the family. The chances are that some initial conflict will develop between the spouses until thoroughly compatible roles are developed.

What is a role? A role is in simple terms a part one plays in the real drama of life. Now a part presumably has a script. In this case the roles for a husband and wife exist as expectations in the reference group and hence in the spouse as to what is proper behavior for a husband or wife. The expectations of friends, relatives of the couple, and members of the general community are usually the important reference groups.

The drama of American married life, however, allows a number of possible roles to be played by married partners, especially the wife. There is not one single script which she must accept. In a brilliant essay, Clifford Kirkpatrick describes the three major role types available as alternatives for American wives today, each

. . . carrying certain privileges and certain responsibilities and obligations: [2] (1) The wife-and-mother role is the traditional role of the married woman. It implies as privileges security, the right to support, alimony in the case of divorce, respect as a wife and mother, a certain amount of domestic authority, loyalty of the husband to one who has borne him children, and a more or less sentimental gratitude from husband and children. Corresponding obligations include bearing and rearing children, making a home, rendering domestic service, loyal subordination of self to economic interests of the husband, an acceptance of a dependent social and economic status, and the acceptance of a limited range of interests and activity. (2) The companion role is essentially a leisure-class phenomenon. The privileges pertaining to this role include sharing pleasures with the husband, receiving funds adequate for dress and recreation, having leisure for social and educational activity, and the receiving of a certain amount of chivalrous attention. On the other hand, it implies as obligations the preservation of beauty under the penalty of marital insecurity, the rendering of ego and libido satisfaction to the husband, and the cultivation of social contacts advantageous to him, the maintenance of intellectual alertness, and the responsibility for exorcising the demon of boredom. (3) Finally, there is the partner role, corresponding to a new definition of the cultural situation which is gradually emerging. This entails the privileges of economic independence, equal authority in regard to family finances, acceptance as an

[2] Clifford Kirkpatrick, "The Measurement of Ethical Inconsistency in Marriage," *International Journal of Ethics*, Vol. 46 (July, 1936), pp. 440–460. Reprinted with permission of author and Journal.

equal, exemption from one-sided personal or domestic service to the husband, equal voice in determining locale of residence, and equality in regard to social and moral liberty. The obligation side of the balance sheet would include renouncing alimony save in the case of dependent children, complete sharing of the legal responsibilities of the family, willingness to dispense with any appeal to chivalry, and equal responsibility to maintain the family status by success in a career.

As described, these roles involve very general scripts existing in the larger society. But each family will have its own version of the more general social expectations, and a child within the family will acquire his or her own unique version of what an ideal or proper marital role should be. In fact, it is in the parental family that many of the individual's earliest role-expectations are formed.

In a very interesting article, Bossard and Boll show that in large parental families many role-types may develop.[3] They are: (1) the responsible one (dutiful, helpful), (2) the popular one (sociable, well-liked), (3) the socially ambitious one ("social butterfly," usually a girl), (4) the studious one (quiet, hard-working), (5) the family isolate (self-centered, withdrawn), (6) the irresponsible one (the nonparticipant in the family), (7) the sickly one (physically defective or hypochondriacal), and (8) the spoiled one (sometimes the lastborn).

It is to be understood that these roles are not always found and that they are not the only ones possible. They are roles that may be chosen in childhood and they no doubt have an effect on later adult behavior. It would seem logical that there would be a carry-over from childhood roles into roles enacted at later adult periods. Can the "social butterfly" settle down to a somewhat traditional wife-mother role when she marries a relatively conservative man? Will the "sickly one" develop to the extent that she can become an active companion, wife, and mother of four children who takes everything in stride inside and outside the home? While people can and do change, certain habits and attitudes tend to develop around early roles to the extent that they are not easy to change. Regardless of childhood roles played, marriage involves certain demands. Reciprocal roles which are mutually satisfactory must be developed by the young couple if the marriage is to be successful by any standard. What role especially, is to be chosen for the wife?

It may be helpful to evaluate some implications of the respective choices of roles delineated by Kirkpatrick (above). The traditional wife-mother is the one most often referred to in Mother's Day sermons, and she most often receives medals. It is this type of whom Solomon wrote the famous passage.[4]

[3] James Bossard and Eleanor Boll, "Personality Roles in the Large Family," *Child Development*, Vol. 26 (March, 1955), pp. 71–78.
[4] Proverbs 31 : 10–31.

Who can find a virtuous woman? for her price is far above rubies. The heart of her husband doth safely trust in her, so that he shall have no need of spoil. She will do him good and not evil all the days of her life. She seeketh wool, and flax, and worketh willingly with her hands. She is like the merchants' ships; she bringeth her food from afar. She riseth also while it is yet night, and giveth meat to her household, and a portion to her maidens. She considereth a field, and buyeth it: with the fruit of her hands she planteth a vineyard. She girdeth her loins with strength, and strengtheneth her arms. She perceiveth that her merchandise is good: her candle goeth not out by night. She layeth her hands to the spindle, and her hands hold the distaff. She stretcheth out her hand to the poor; yea, she reacheth forth her hands to the needy. She is not afraid of the snow for her household are clothed with scarlet. She maketh herself coverings of tapestry; her clothing is silk and purple. Her husband is known in the gates, when he sitteth among the elders of the land. She maketh fine linen and selleth it; and delivereth girdles unto the merchant. Strength and honour are her clothing; and she shall rejoice in time to come. She openeth her mouth with wisdom: and in her tongue is the law of kindness. She looketh well to the ways of her household, and eateth not the bread of idleness. Her children arise up, and call her blessed; her husband also, and he praiseth her. Many daughters have done virtuously, but thou excellest them all. Favour is deceitful, and beauty is vain: but a woman that feareth the Lord, she shall be praised. Give her of the fruit of her hands; and let her own works praise her in the gates.

Poets, painters, and statesmen do her honor, and musicians write songs of praise. Would it not be logical for young married women to choose this role?

It is no secret that many of our urban middle- and upper-class wives do not aspire to the traditional wife-mother role. While the causes for this are complex we suggest three major reasons for this role rejection. First, while the role may be extolled by many leaders, it is no longer purveyed as ideal by our modern mass media of communication. Few Hollywood actresses or Who's Who subjects receive their fame because of their traditional virtues. Secondly, advanced educational institutions do not prepare women for or idealize this type of pattern for women. Vocational training, liberal arts, and general education courses all tend to assume a nonhomemaking career. Finally, carry-overs from the feminist movement of former eras make this type of role *en toto* unacceptable to a democratically oriented, romantic, sophisticated, active woman. She is apt to find it too circumspect and limited.

The most popular role among middle-class women seems to be that of companion. It is considered preferable by the majority of students, both male and female, questioned by the author. Some adaptation of this will probably be considered by the co-ed readers of this book. The companion role as described above is a general framework into which may be fitted women who differ to a considerable degree.

What are some of the problems that appear when, in actual practice, a given couple attempt to develop a mutually acceptable system of role relationships?

WORKING OUTSIDE THE HOME

As has been suggested, in the middle and lower classes a surprising number of younger housewives are now working outside the home. Their motives vary but outstanding is the desire to raise the level of living higher than it would otherwise be.[5] Younger men tend to be in lower-paying jobs, or are still preparing through formal education for more specialized positions. In one way or another many are "apprentices," which means there are great pressures on the wife to work outside the home.

Some women are bored with housework and feel the necessity to be creative outside the home. This is particularly true of educated women. If they are career-trained or career-minded the motivation to keep one foot in the professional door may be strong.

A very typical pattern as well as the relatively uninterrupted career role, is that of working "before and after children." To some the "after" will mean when the children are in school, to others when the children are grown. In any case the wife modifies the straight companion role with some type of partial career. Many of the strains of such an arrangement will be obvious. Partial careers are not as easily carved from the occupational tree as full ones. Jobs take not only time, but energy. If the wife devotes sufficient time and interest to her position, the husband may feel that she is neglecting her wifely duties.[6] She may become so involved in her career that she wishes to put off childbearing, and in effect, assume a partner role. If this is satisfactory to both spouses well and good; but if the husband is expecting his wife to work just a few years, he may express a negative attitude.

Difficulties may arise if the husband has traditional expectations concerning his wife's activities around the household, but under pressure agrees to having her work outside. He may still expect the wife to assume the same obligations his mother did when she remained in the home. Clearly some semblance of agreement between the spouses is called for, not only as to whether or not the wife works outside the home during the early marital period, but also what the individual and shared tasks will be inside the home.

The partner role for the wife probably seems the most extreme to the average person, even the sophisticated one, for it stresses her productivity outside the home, and career recognition in her own right. For those who

[5] Mirra Komarovsky, *Blue-Collar Marriage* (New York, Random House, 1964), Chapter 3.
[6] *Ibid.*

cannot or do not wish to have children, it is a logical alternative. To combine it with motherhood is to take on a series of tasks of considerable magnitude. In spite of the fact that many noted women have chosen this path, at present it is a rocky one, untraveled except by a hardy few in the educated classes. Since it does not have general social recognition, the possibilities of conflict between the spouses, and of frustration because of unachieved goals seem rather strong.

ROLE INCONGRUITY

Kirkpatrick makes the point that many husbands and wives wish to both "have their cake and eat it," in regard to privileges and obligations of marital roles.[7] The wife may wish all the old-fashioned love and respect that great grandmother had but be unwilling to have a large number of children or care adequately for children, husband, and household. She may wish to receive romantic attention and admiration but not render herself attractive or interesting, but instead allows herself to "go to seed" in terms of personal beauty and social and intellectual alertness.

The husband may want and expect an unfair distribution of obligations and privileges. He may wish his wife to be as circumspect and domestic as great grandmother was when around the kitchen, as attractive and alluring as a mistress when in the bedroom, and adept and competent in arranging social contacts for him in the proper social circles. If he by chance finds such a gem of versatility such a man may still find it difficult to grant her all the rights and privileges she deserves.

Kirkpatrick concludes that "there is reason to think that there is a disposition for women to desire the privileges of more than one role, and for men to be ethically inconsistent in expecting the fulfillment of obligations in more than one role." [8] Note that he speaks of this type of incongruous behavior as "ethical inconsistency." While they may not use such formal terms to describe their frustration, spouses who sense injustice of the type here described can be expected to react in negative fashion.

We have been describing general roles and focusing on the wife. As Cottrell shows, individuals play a number of roles in marriage rather than one.[9] Susan may at one time play the nagging sister and at another time the loving protective mother, as far as George is concerned. George may at times be the domineering father and at other times the spoiled, protected younger brother. Unfortunate as it may seem, especially in early marriage, inappropriate role responses learned in the parental family may be forth-

---

[7] Kirkpatrick, op. cit., pp. 447–448.

[8] Ibid.

[9] Leonard Cottrell, "Roles and Marital Adjustment," Publications of American Sociological Society (1933), pp. 107–115.

coming when the spouse provides familiar cues. We might add that this occurs unknowingly. Eventually, by trial and error, spouses may learn what responses to expect from the playing of certain types of roles on their own part. The point to be made is this: Spouses must somehow, consciously or otherwise, work out reciprocal general and specific roles which are basically satisfactory if their marriage is to succeed. This is a difficult game at which to play, and the stakes are high.

Individual personality factors should not be overlooked. A wife may, because of expectations of others, play a somewhat traditional role but find that she feels like the proverbial bird in a cage. A neurotic drive may so condition a person's responses that he cannot fulfill general expectations which even he himself may intellectually accept. Barring serious neurotic drives in either or both partners, and assuming a reasonable degree of complementariness of personalities, the couple through mutual effort should be able to achieve a "meshing" of roles which will be functional and satisfactory.

AUTHORITY AND ACCOUNTABILITY IN MARRIAGE

Given any social group, including, of course, a family, some method of control over the direction the group will go develops. The possibilities range from authoritarian (dominance by one party) through equalitarian (shared control) to laissez-faire (oscillating control, no consensus).

The husband-controlled authoritarian type has been the most typical in traditional Western society. Something approximating it may be found in those families in the United States which are highly conservative. This arrangement has been more typically rural than urban and more characteristic of certain religious groups than others. It is no surprise that in a study of American family life by the department of agriculture the Amish family and the Hispano family (old Spanish in New Mexico) were found to be most patriarchal. In both cases rural residence is combined with a traditional religious conception of proper family government.

The latter two types (equalitarian and laissez-faire) are to be found anywhere in the United States, with something approaching the equalitarian type being common in many quarters, especially among the more educated classes.

Some comments on these types are in order. An authoritarian relationship with the husband having the control is the Pauline standard, if such verses as the following in the *New Testament* are to be taken literally as role prescriptions.[10] "For the man is not of the woman; but the woman of

[10] I Corinthians 11:8–9 and 14:34–35.

the man." "Neither was the man created for the woman; but the woman for the man."

Many traditionally oriented students of the family take the position that the patriarchal family of old was more orderly and stable and much better integrated when the husband dominated the spouse and children. It is difficult to challenge the basic thesis that in a traditional society where the norms are clear-cut and where imperatives strongly support husband-father dominance marital relations are more orderly. By inference we can draw false analogies from other social spheres. When Mussolini took over in Italy the trains were more often on schedule than they had previously been, labor disputes became less numerous, and general social conditions became more orderly. That hardly proves that Mussolini's dictatorship was totally good for the Italians.

Any system has its price; Peter is often robbed to pay Paul. The price paid in individual freedom and initiative in Italy hardly requires comment, as the facts are generally known. It follows that the structural advantages of authoritarianism in marriage must be balanced by an account of the psychological toll which may take place. A required deference of one party to the other, when not wanted, is taken as an insult by a modern, sophisticated person. Over a long period of time it often results in frustration, hostility, disillusionment, or in similar negative reactions of the ego, if the relationship is not severed.

This is not to imply that our ancestral great grandmothers became neurotic because their husbands dominated family life. Living in a stable society where the roles were well defined, they apparently accepted their husband's leadership in basic family policy-making without particular question. As a matter of fact, a woman in a traditional society who married an acquiescent man was considered by all, herself included, to have obtained a "lemon." Women who became so frustrated with their husbands resorted to greater activity in kitchen, church, and neighborhood.

Today American society generally does not give the traditional support to husband dominance. A norm seems to be emerging which implies a rough equality rather than dominance by one spouse over the other. However, since we are still in a period of transition, husbands and wives may and do choose from various models and form varying role combinations without fear of social reprisal unless they be extreme.

One modern type of role pattern is that of wife dominance. When the old-fashioned system of male dominance became broken to the extent that other patterns were possible, it was inevitable that some marriages would involve a reversal of the traditional pattern. Psychologically this would seem probable in certain cases. A man may be so dominated in his childhood by his mother that he "needs" a mother substitute for a wife in order to function at an adult level. Mace notes that "there are people who *want* to be dominated and not all of them are women." He says further that:

. . . so long as extremes are avoided, there is evidence that departures from the 'normal' pattern of personal interaction in marriage do not matter, if the partners contrive to satisfy each other's needs. The marriage of a strongly dominant person and an exceptionally submissive person may be successful where unions between two dominants or two submissives fail. We must be careful to leave room for these wide individual variations, and not to apply rigid criteria. Successful marriages display a remarkable variety of patterns.[11]

It must be pointed out, however, that a reversal of traditional roles in a marriage may bring social pressure, especially on the husband. A man who allegedly is "bossed" at home by his womenfolk is teased unmercifully by his male colleagues at work. Remarks such as "she is wearing the pants," or "he is henpecked," may be continually dropped in his presence. As a matter of fact, the theme of a popular syndicated comic strip involves a character, "Dagwood," who is inept in carrying a role of leadership in his family. In many circles it would appear that while old-fashioned male authoritarianism is frowned upon, female authoritarianism is also considered very unacceptable. A dilemma is posed here for matches of a certain type. Psychologically, even if a relationship with wife-dominance may be most satisfactory, it may bring frustration because of outside reaction. If the relationship is subtle enough to be hardly noticeable outside the family it may be successful.

According to most students of the family, there has been a general if also irregular trend toward democracy in the American family system. Supposedly this trend has been most pronounced in the middle classes, but is affecting other class levels as well.[12] Just what is meant by an equalitarian or democratic system of authority and accountability in the marital sphere? Democracy implies a cooperative venture, first of all.[13] This means that the members assent to share together and work together toward common goals. It is not anarchy, the condition which may occur in a laissez-faire approach. It implies a system containing both rights and privileges for a member, with at least a rough equality of status. Every system demands some authority if anarchy is not to prevail; the democratic family is no exception. As Fromm points out, it rests on "rational authority."

Rational authority has its source in competence. The person whose authority is respected functions competently in the task with which he is entrusted by those who conferred it upon him. He need not intimidate them nor arouse their admiration by magic qualities; as long as and to the extent to which he is competently helping, instead of exploiting, his authority is based on rational grounds and does not call for irrational awe. Rational authority not only permits but requires constant scrutiny and criticism of those subjected

---

[11] David Mace, "Personality Expression and Subordination in Marriage," *Marriage and Family Living,* Vol. 15 (August, 1953), pp. 205–207.

[12] Komarovsky, *op. cit.,* Chapters 3 and 5.

[13] Christine Beasley, *Democracy in the Home* (New York, Association Press, 1954), Chapters 2 and 3.

to it; it is always temporary, its acceptance depending on its performance. The source of irrational authority, on the other hand, is always power over people. This power can be physical or mental, it can be realistic or only relative in terms of the anxiety and helplessness of the person submitting to this authority. Power on the one side, fear on the other, are always the buttresses on which irrational authority is built.[14]

The implications of this for the relations of spouses are many. If other than a pseudodemocracy is to be achieved the partners must function on the basis of their competence. This means that if the wife is competent in a certain sphere she will lead out in that direction. The husband will exercise leadership in another. The major developmental task under this system would involve developing agreed upon spheres of influence in which the spouses operate with authority.

Miller and Swanson suggest that while a general equalitarianism is developing in modern marriage, this does not mean that the roles of husband and wife are identical. They have coined the term *colleague* family in which there is a general democratic ethic in operation but with a recognition of separate spheres of interests and obligations.[15]

Laissez-faire is a third type of authority in marriage. It implies in its extreme, lack of cooperative effort. The relationship between the spouses is not structured under this system and the roles are not defined or agreed upon. Each person seeks his goals by his own sights and may not be concerned with group ends and values, immediate or ultimate.

As Baber points out, laissez-faire in modern marriage has become more common during a period when it has been in a decline in another of our major institutions, the economic system.[16] It also becomes more prevalent at a time when allegedly conformity and group-mindedness have been increasing in other areas outside the home. If the interpretations of men like Riesman, Whyte, and others are sound then we have here a contradiction of importance.

From one family development point of view, full-fledged laissez-faire is dysfunctional. Assessment of authority and responsibility implies a systematic allocation of tasks and responsibilities to the extent that orderly relationships prevail and marital goals are achieved. Laissez-faire by definition implies a lack of mutual sharing and cooperation.

What relationship do these types of authority patterns have to success in marriage? Unfortunately few researchers have explored this specific area. In an early study Popenoe found that a democratic relationship was rated happier than one in which either the husband or the wife dominated. The results of this work are shown in Table 30.

[14] Erich Fromm, *Man For Himself* (New York, Holt, Rinehart and Winston, 1947), pp. 9–10.

[15] Daniel Miller and Guy Swanson, *The Changing American Parent* (New York, Wiley, 1958), pp. 200–201.

[16] Ray Baber, *Marriage and the Family* (New York, McGraw-Hill, 1953), p. 215.

TABLE 30

Authority Patterns in a Sample of American Marriages

Authority Pattern	Happy Percentage	Unhappy Percentage
Husband-dominated marriage	61	24
Wife-dominated marriage	47	31
Fifty-fifty (democratic)	87	7

SOURCE: Paul Popenoe, "Can the Family Have Two Heads?" *Sociology and Social Research* (September, 1933), p. 13.

Later studies have tended to confirm the results of this early one, that the equalitarian or democratic marriage is the most successful one in our culture. This would include findings, at least by inference, from studies by Jacobson,[17] Terman,[18] Luckey,[19] Yi-Chuang Lu,[20] and Locke[21] among others. Locke found that leadership varied within the happily-married couples more often than it did among the divorced. Happily-married husbands would lead out sometimes and wives at other times, in such areas as disciplining of children, religious activities, affectionate behavior, and recreation. There was less sharing of leadership among the divorced couples. Husbands and wives who reported a feeling of equality rather than superiority toward the spouse were more inclined to be happily-married, as had been found in an earlier study by Kelly.

While further research is very much needed it would appear that, other things being equal, the chances of marital success are greater if a given couple attempts to set up a democratic system of authority within the household, with the principle of mutual cooperation toward common goals dominating the relationship. This is especially true for educated couples in the United States.

The Making of Decisions

The making of innumerable decisions becomes the task of the young couple as it undertakes the practice of married living. Dozens of issues

[17] Allvar Jacobson, "Conflict of Attitudes Toward the Roles of Husband and Wife," *American Sociological Review,* Vol. 17 (April, 1952), pp. 146–150.

[18] Louis Terman, *Psychological Factors in Marital Happiness* (New York, McGraw-Hill, 1938).

[19] Eleanore Braun Luckey, "Marital Satisfaction and Its Association with Congruence of Perception," *Marriage and Family Living,* Vol. 22 (February, 1960), pp. 49–54.

[20] Yi-chuang Lu, "Marital Roles and Marriage Adjustment," *Sociology and Social Research,* Vol. 36 (August, 1952), p. 365.

[21] Harvey Locke, *Predicting Adjustment in Marriage: A Comparison of a Divorced and a Happily Married Group* (New York, Holt, Rinehart and Winston, 1951), pp. 263–265.

which require attention may arise in a given week. How in general are these decisions made in American homes?

Research on decision-making by couples is sparse indeed, and the area seems to be a fertile one for future social scientists. Our discussion will draw on the studies available and on analogies to decision-making in other groups and situations.

It seems clear that the old-fashioned method of decision-making whereby the man could allegedly decide all important issues is on the wane. No longer is the husband the old patriarch that his grandfather was or at least could have been. Does this mean that conditions have changed so much that the wife now dominates the picture and makes the major decisions? The following well known joke would seem to imply so. It concerns Mr. Averageman who asserts: "I make the major decisions in our household. My wife makes the little ones such as which house to buy, when to buy a new car or refrigerator, and how much life insurance to carry. I make the big decisions, such as whether to admit Red China to the U.N., how much foreign aid Congress should vote, and what income tax rates should be."

The actual situation is not this extreme. The old patriarchal power is gone. In its place has not always come either anarchy or female dominance. Instead, a wide variety of possibilities has emerged ranging from dominance by either spouse to more equalitarian forms of decision-making processes. Before these possibilities are spelled out and illustrated, a suggestion of the meaning of the transition away from patriarchal rule is in order. Bierstedt and others distinguish between power and dominance, and this distinction should be helpful here. Power involves authority sanctioned in a given position by the community. In a fully patriarchal society the father has authority because he is father. The role requires his leadership in decision-making. Dominance, on the other hand, allows individual characteristics of personality to predominate in a given situation. This means that in the more intimate interpersonal relationships of marriage and the like, dominance, if there is any, comes because one person is able to control the situation and the other party allows it.

In present American marriages it is expected, then, that particular personal characteristics will be expressed in decision-making within the home. On an experimental or pragmatic basis the couple will work out a satisfactory system which suits them even if it differs from that of the neighbors across the street. In actual practice certain decisions are made more often by the husband and others by the wife. In the Detroit study, out of eight decision-making areas, the husband tends to predominate in two, the wife in two others, and the remaining are divided or joint decisions. Results of this study are summarized in Table 31.

The type and location of job, and the purchase of the car are the two decision areas in which the husband has greater influence. Apparently the

TABLE 31

Allocation of Power in Decision-making Areas
(731 Detroit Families)

	Decision							
Who Decides	Hus-band's Job	Car	Insur-ance	Vaca-tion	House	Wife's Work	Doc-tor	Food
(5) Husband always	90%	56%	31%	12%	12%	26%	7%	10%
(4) Husband more than wife	4	12	11	6	6	5	3	2
(3) Husband and wife exactly the same	3	25	41	68	58	18	45	32
(2) Wife more than husband	0	2	4	4	10	9	11	11
(1) Wife always	1	3	10	7	13	39	31	41
N. A.	2	1	2	3	1	3	3	3
Total	100	99	99	100	100	100	100	99
Husband's Mean power *	4.86	4.18	3.50	3.12	2.94	2.69	2.53	2.26

* The mean for each column is computed on the basis of the weights shown e.g. "Husbands always" = 5.

SOURCE: Reprinted with permission of The Free Press of Glencoe from *Husbands and Wives* by Robert Blood and Donald M. Wolfe. Copyright © 1960 by The Free Press, a Corporation.

husband's work role is considered so basic that practically all wives leave the final decision to the men. Somehow control of the car is still considered the male prerogative. Perhaps a carry-over from the old days when the male was in charge of heavy nonhousehold implements exists. On the other hand, work around the home involving decisions about meals, planning and buying food, household purchases, or even the calling of a physician, are interpreted most often as being primarily the wife's concern. As a whole this division of spheres of influence seems logically tied to the division of labor discussed under the previous section.

The other decision areas tend to be less sex-role specific; joint decision-making is more often involved. In some sort of give-and-take manner decisions are hammered out, depending upon the strength of personality and capabilities of the individual partners involved.

If custom no longer dictates that the husband is the maker of family decisions, does it mean that young couples will experience some confusion before they are able to settle into comfortable patterns of behavior? Research evidence seems to point in this direction. Kenkel has experimented with undergraduate married students on an American campus. On simulated problems (involving finances) husbands tended to have the greatest influence in the decisions made.[22] Wives played subordinate and associate roles by encouraging and humoring their husbands and by facilitating the discussion. Those who were best at playing this kind of supportive role achieved the greatest influence.

It is reported, however, that conceived or predicted approaches which the couples thought they would use did not correspond too closely with what they did when given the problems.[23] If this was true in regard to money problems it would appear that more confusion might obtain in other, more ambiguous areas. Furthermore, in a recent survey of families in various parts of the U.S. it was shown that the older established families made less use of joint decision-making and had more definite ideas of which partner was to make what decision.[24]

This means then that young couples will have the task of deciding what form of decision-making is most suitable to their tastes. For those who ideologically lean toward democracy at all levels there seem to be two possible approaches available as suggested in Oeser and Hammond.[25] In the one case decisions are made jointly by the spouses. This is called "syncratic." In the other approach, spoken of as "autonomic," separate decisions are made by partners in equal numbers. The only American study which relates these two types of roles to marital satisfaction is the Detroit study. The syncratic arrangement received a rank of higher satisfaction than did the autonomic. (Of the four types, husband-dominant was third and wife-dominant fourth). This suggests that wives are most satisfied when they are fully involved in the decision-making process. They want to count for something. Sharing to the point of having separate spheres of decision-making is not as meaningful as being copartner in joint effort.[26]

For the particular couple it is a question of what is most suitable for them and gets decisions made rather than what is average or typical in outside groups. Decisions must be made and life must go on. Allowing issues to remain unsettled unduly long is frustrating to most couples.

Allotting the Tasks

In the old days on the farm the work of the men and women was rather clearly differentiated. Men felled the trees and worked in the fields. In general this involved the heavier labor. Women did the work around the

[22] William Kenkel, "Influence Differentiation in Family Decision Making," *Sociology and Social Research,* Vol. 42 (September, 1957), pp. 18–25.

[23] William Kenkel and Dean Hoffman, "Real and Conceived Roles in Family Decision Making," *Marriage and Family Living,* Vol. 18 (November, 1956), pp. 311–316.

[24] Elizabeth H. Wolgast, "Do Husbands or Wives Make the Purchasing Decisions?" *Journal of Marketing,* Vol. 23 (October, 1958), pp. 151–158.

[25] O. E. Oeser and S. B. Hammond, *Social Structure and Personality in a City* (New York, Macmillan, 1954).

[26] Bloode and Wolfe, *op. cit.,* p. 258.

house and barn, and supervised the younger children. At harvest and other pressing times women (and children) aided the men in the fields.

Of what help is this backlog of tradition for a division of labor in the present home? Have conditions changed so much that none of the old patterns should apply? Apparently not. In general the wife stays by the fireside and carries the regular home duties, and the husband goes away to work. In the Blood and Wolfe study it can be seen that the men still carry, in the urban environment, many of the tasks considered somewhat masculine in nature. These researchers asked housewives to indicate the division of labor regarding eight tasks ordinarily performed in most families and which could be performed by either husband or wife. Below are their results in summary form:

TABLE 32

Division of Labor, by Household Tasks
(731 Detroit Families)

Who Does It?	Task							
	Re-pairs	Lawn	Walk	Bills	Gro-ceries	Break-fast	Living Room	Dishes
(1) Husband always	73%	66%	61%	19%	7%	16%	1%	1%
(2) Husband more than wife	11	9	13	6	7	5	1	2
(3) Husband and wife exactly the same	6	6	8	34	29	4	17	13
(4) Wife more than husband	3	6	7	11	20	7	15	12
(5) Wife always	3	7	7	30	36	66	65	70
N.A.	4	6	4	—	1	2	1	2
Total	100	100	100	100	100	100	100	100
Wife's mean task performance *	1.46	1.71	1.81	3.27	3.72	4.04	4.44	4.52

* The mean for each column is computed on the basis of the weights shown e.g. "Husbands always" = 1.

SOURCE: Reprinted with permission of The Free Press of Glencoe from *Husbands and Wives* by Robert Blood and Donald M. Wolfe. Copyright © 1960 by The Free Press, a Corporation.

As can be seen, husbands tend to do the repairing and to work with lawn and garden. Wives most often do the cooking, dishes, and cleaning and straightening of the living room. Keeping track of the money and paying the bills may be the responsibility of either spouse, but more often belongs to the wife. Following the author's line of reasoning what is behind the division of labor in the typical family?

While women can mow lawns and shovel snow, the extra size and strength of the male is a decided advantage on these jobs. Also, his alleged knack with machinery should make him a better prospect for do-it-yourself repairing than his wife. In fact, the reverse is often true. While cooking and cleaning are not necessarily correlated with any obvious aspects of female physical structure, they have usually been associated with the role of wife and mother. It has been suggested that the great enthusiasm for patio and outdoor cooking is the clever wife's way of working her husband into some of the cooking chores!

The paying of bills and purchasing of groceries seem more neutral, and practices on these items varied. Handling of bills is tied up with household operations and the latter is associated logically with shopping for groceries. It should not be surprising that wives who do more of the housework are inclined to handle money and pay the bills.

Does this mean that husbands and wives are so conservative that they follow traditional customs of division of labor just because of tradition? Blood and Wolfe think not. The answer is primarily specialization and contributions by each partner on the basis of time and skill. The husband still retains those tasks that involve brawn or some technical skill or training. The wife focuses on tasks associated with childbearing, child rearing, homemaking and related functions. If there are special contingencies the one partner is expected to help out the other, even if this is not the way it was done in grandfather's day.

There is food for thought in the Blood and Wolfe study and young married couples could well read the whole book. For a particular couple facing the problem of allotting tasks early in their marriage, what are some implications and aids which may appear? The principle of justice appears as the standard by which each partner should be allotted his "package" of tasks and responsibilities. Ethics demand that the wife who works outside the home receive some help with household tasks. In the Detroit sample she typically gets it. However, the question of the time (and energy) available from the husband cannot be dismissed. If the husband is a "moonlighter" he has less time to come to the wife's aid and typically is not expected to do so. Each couple must raise the question, "What would be an equitable arrangement of tasks based on our given personal preferences, time, and energy, within the general framework of the community?" Justice would seem to demand that each partner put his best into the arrangement. This means that each will attempt to put his best foot forward in offering his time, skill, and interest in the tasks which have to be accomplished. Some initial give and take will be called for. It may be found that after a period of fumbling efforts by the husband, the wife has more expertness in the repairing of small household fixtures than the husband. Perhaps the husband has had considerable bookkeeping experience and enjoys keeping household accounts. Experimentation and discussion, with mutual interest, initiative, and good humor, should allow the couple to work out a *modus operandi* of task arrangement which will get the necessary work done with the least amount of frustration.[27]

The importance of role clarification and agreement on methods of decision-making during this early period of marriage can hardly be over-emphasized. The couple is young and more adaptable than it will be in later years. It has no backlog of habits which must be changed or modified. Further, there are implications for future child-rearing years. It is more difficult to experiment when children are in the family circle. This is not to say that roles and decision-making processes must remain fixed throughout the life cycle. Rather it is to suggest again that initial adaptations which are successful lay the groundwork for later successful task performance and adjustment.

ROUTINES AND SCHEDULES FOR COMPLETING TASKS AND SERVICES

To a degree man is a creature of habit. Were it not so social living would be well nigh impossible. Thus most people require the development of at least a minimum plan for the use of their time and energy. The setting up of a routine has a number of advantages. Among them are the following:

1. Through the use of a schedule tasks can be shared equitably by both marital partners. Otherwise one partner actually may be forced to carry more than a fair proportion of the load and responsibility.
2. A priority rank can be given to the various tasks and duties. In this way things that are most important can receive the attention they deserve and not be crowded out because of time given to more nonessential activities.
3. Energy can be budgeted through use of a schedule. Some tasks obviously require greater amounts of physical or nervous energy than others. By planning, a satisfactory combination of tasks requiring heavy, moderately heavy, and light expenditures of energy can be obtained.
4. Through scheduling, time can be allotted to recreational, social, and general family and personal activities. In some homes there is the continual complaint of the lack of time for other than "work." In others the family members complain about having long periods of time on their hands with "nothing to do." Scheduling of activities with due allowance for those of an intellectual, social, or recreational nature may help people handle either the demon of boredom or the lack of time for other than work.

We are not advocating slavery to a schedule or routine. Any plan for the use of time must be flexible to allow for many contingencies and excep-

---

[27] Homans seems to feel that a general norm of reciprocity or "distributive justice" develops in dyadic relationships where there is continual social exchange. See George Homans, "Social Behavior as Exchange," *American Journal of Sociology,* Vol. 63 (May, 1958), pp. 597–606. Such norms seem to have operated in the sample of semiskilled couples studied by Komarovsky. See Komarovsky, *op. cit.,* Chapter 3.

tions or it will be useless and impractical. Except for the couple who wishes to live a Bohemian type of life under unique circumstances, a minimum of routine is prerequisite to marital integration and probably also to marital happiness. Tasks and services must be performed by someone. Breakfasts must be cooked and served, beds made, clothes washed and ironed, and the cat fed *ad infinitum*.

How can a couple go about this process of setting up a routine and schedule of activities which will be reasonably satisfactory to them? A listing of daily, weekly, and seasonal or special activities would resemble the following:

A list of daily needs:
    preparation and serving of meals
    making of beds
    disposing of garbage and wastepaper
    some cleaning and tidying of house
    regulation and care of heating mechanisms
    dishwashing
    personal care and grooming
    reading, rest, relaxation
    recreation and social activities
A weekly list for the couple would include the following items, along with others:
    general cleaning of rooms and floors
    social and recreational activities
    market trip for food purchases
    shopping trip for general purchases
    religious activities
    record-keeping and banking
    baking and special cooking
    other weekly and special activities
The third list would include seasonal or special activities and tasks such as:
    thorough cleaning of all rooms
    thorough cleaning and waxing of all floors
    installation and repair of storm windows and screens
    canning and freezing of foodstuffs
    cleaning and rearranging of cupboards, drawers, closets, etc.
    special holiday and anniversary activities
    cleaning and inspecting of heating and other basic equipment [28]

Once a division of activities into daily, weekly, and seasonal or special categories has been accomplished, some synchronization is possible. It is suggested that a typical day and a typical week plan be set up which can be used as a guide.

There should be flexibility in the making of any set of plans. They

[28] See Paulena Nickell and Jean Dorsey, *Management in Family Living* (New York, Wiley, 1959), Chapter 6, for an alternate listing of activities.

need not be too binding. It is to be remembered, however, that basic tasks must be accomplished sometime. They do not vanish into thin air just because they are put off on a certain day. An orderly schedule has an advantage in that one can almost see at a glance some free time to which an unexpected contingency can be assigned.

The couple cannot expect to reach a satisfactory equilibrium in a few short weeks or months. It takes time to develop mutually satisfactory routines which integrate all of the activities of the couple into a reasonably balanced pattern. With time, effort, work, and good faith on the part of both husband and wife it can be successfully done.

SELECTED READINGS

Barnes, Ralph, *Motion and Time Study* (New York, Wiley, 1958), Chapters 1–5.

Beasley, Christine, *Democracy in the Home* (New York, Association Press, 1954).

Bee, Lawrence, *Marriage and Family Relations* (New York, Harper & Row, 1959), Chapters 15 and 16.

Bernard, Jessie, Buchanan, Helen, and Smith, William, *Dating, Mating, and Marriage* (Cleveland, Howard Allen, 1958), Chapters 9 and 10.

Buerkle, Jack, Anderson, Theodore, and Badgley, Robin, "Altruism, Role Conflict, and Marital Adjustment: A Factor Analysis of Marital Interaction," *Marriage and Family Living,* Vol. 23 (February, 1961), pp. 20–26.

Carey, Henry, "This Two-headed Monster—The Family," *Harper's Magazine* (January, 1958), pp. 162–171.

Dalton, Robert, "Developing Control for Democratic Living," *Journal of Home Economics,* Vol. 39 (January, 1947), pp. 1–4.

Dornbusch, Sanford, and Heer, David, "The Evaluation of Work by Females, 1940–1950," *The American Journal of Sociology,* Vol. 63 (July, 1957), pp. 27–29.

Foote, Nelson, "Matching of Husband and Wife on Phases of Development," *Transactions of World Congress of Sociology* (1956), pp. 24–34.

Fitzsimmons, Cleo, *The Management of Family Resources* (San Francisco, Freeman, 1950).

Gilbreth, Lillian, Thomas, Orpha and Clymer, Eleanor, *Management in the Home* (New York, Macmillan, 1955).

Gross, Irma and Crandall, Elizabeth, *Management for Modern Families* (New York, Appleton-Century-Crofts, 1954).

Hacker, Helen, "The New Burdens of Masculinity," *Marriage and Family Living,* Vol. 19 (August, 1957), pp. 227–233.

Kenkel, William, and Hoffman, Dean, "Real and Conceived Roles in Family Decision Making," *Marriage and Family Living,* Vol. 18 (November, 1956), pp. 311–316.

Komarovsky, Mirra, *Women in the Modern World, Their Education, and Their Dilemmas* (Boston, Little, Brown, 1953).

Martzloff, Thomas, "The Challenge of Work Simplification to Management," *Journal of Home Economics,* Vol. 46 (December, 1954), pp. 720–721.

Massey, Leila, "Selecting Kitchen Utensils for the Job to Be Done," *The Kitchen Reporter,* Kelvinator publication, 1952.

Moore, Bernice, "Time, Tension, and Mental Health," *Journal of Home Economics,* Vol. 49 (December, 1957).

Nadler, Gerald, *Work Simplification* (New York, McGraw-Hill, 1957).

National Manpower Council, *Woman Power* (New York, Columbia, 1957).

Nickell, Paulena, and Dorsey, Jean, *Management in Family Living* (New York, Wiley, 1950).

Peet, Louise, and Thye, Lenore, *Household Equipment* (New York, Wiley, 1955).

Slater, Eliot, and Woodside, Moya, *Patterns of Marriage: A Study of Marriage Relationships in the Urban Working Classes* (London, Cassell, 1951).

Strodbeck, Fred, "Husband-Wife Interaction over Revealed Differences," *American Sociological Review,* Vol. 16 (August, 1951), pp. 468–473.

Wolgast, Elizabeth, "Do Husbands or Wives Make the Purchasing Decisions?" *The Journal of Marketing,* Vol. 23 (October, 1958), pp. 151–158.

National Manpower Council, *Work in the Lives of Married Women* (New York, Columbia, 1958).

QUESTIONS AND EXERCISES

1. Many European observers of the American scene suggest that men are being feminized by being forced to do housework, help with children, etc. Do you agree with their criticism? Why or why not?

2. What is the most ideal arrangement of authority within the household? Defend your position.

3. Select from fiction or history a marriage partnership that is to you ideal. Indicate the basis of your choice.

4. Read Part 2 on "time and energy" management in Nickell and Dorsey cited in the readings. Do you believe that time and activity plans should be made for the home? Why or why not?

5. Read Komarovsky's book dealing with the education of and the roles of modern women (cited in the readings). Do you agree with her essential position? Discuss.

6. Should the newly married couple have regular family council sessions for purposes of decision-making? Why or why not?

7. Make a case study, if possible, of a couple which seems exceptionally successful in marriage. Analyze the role and authority patterns and the decision-making process used by the couple.

8. Read and critically analyze the article by Whyte on wives of management.

Do you think modern corporations expect too much of the wives of their management personnel? Why or why not? *

9. Many people seem by their actions and attitudes to depreciate the home-maker role. In your opinion is this an inevitable corollary of modern democratic trends or is it a temporary phenomenon? Discuss.

10. Make a time study of your own activities for one week. Are you satisfied with the allotments being given to study, recreation, sleep, etc.? Are "first things" being put first in your program? If not, how can the situation be remedied?

* William H. Whyte, Jr., "The Wife Problem," in Robert Winch, *et al., Selected Studies in Marriage and the Family* (New York, Holt, Rinehart and Winston, 1962), p. 111.

17

Maintenance of Morale

Young couples tend to enter marriage with a burst of enthusiasm. If the marriage has an inadequate base the psychic honeymoon is soon over and the bedrock of reality is found to be hard indeed. Many in this category flounder for a time, and some of them separate or file for divorce. The majority remain together, but many of them still have their difficulties. A major task facing the young couple, or the couple of any age, is that of maintaining morale. Therefore, in this chapter we shall explore some of the typical reasons for the lowering of morale and suggest some possible adaptations which may be beneficial.

GENERAL PREREQUISITES TO A SOUND MARITAL STRUCTURE

Understanding the Basic Relationship

Marriage involves a "unity of interacting personalities." This is another way of saying that marriage involves a group structure even though the pair relationship involves the smallest group possible. As is true of any group, marriage involves the balancing of forces that sometimes seem to be in direct conflict with each other. Sumner spoke of marriage as being characterized by "antagonistic cooperation." The opposing forces can be isolated in at least two ways. First, there is the fact that the two partners concerned are individuals with egos. Under the most ideal of circumstances there will be a bit of jostling for position and influence between the two partners. Although we frown on viewing marriage in this manner we must recognize that any group relationship sets the stage for some competition.

327

From another orientation we have the factors of individual or private goals. If the latter are the stronger and more powerful sources of motivation it may be rather difficult for the couple to work toward the goals of the marriage as distinct from their own personal goals.

Keyserling spoke of marriage as being a "tragic state of tension." [1] He had in mind the opposing forces at work in a relationship. Those on the one side make for integration and unity, and on the other side disintegration and destruction. It is suggested, then, that any relationship has inherent within it the seeds of tension and strain. On the other hand, isolation also eventually brings its own problems, and the drive to affiliate with others in intimate interaction seems so basic and powerful a human motive that for most people, marriage, with all its problems, offers the greatest potential for growth and development.

The problem in this chapter is that of getting an effective group organization but at the same time maintaining a high degree of morale in the relationship. Effectiveness as used here refers to task performance. What can be done to build an effective, functioning pair relationship involving generally high morale?

Building an Identification

The first item of importance which is basic to a successful marriage is identification of the partners with each other and with the marriage. Identification has been receiving increased attention in recent years to the point where one social psychologist wishes to use it as a base for a whole theory of motivation.[2] Certainly marriage involves putting most if not all of one's eggs in one basket. The identification called for is such that the person must have a genuine feeling of oneness with the spouse. Empathic abilities come into play at this point. Some persons are better able than others to reach out toward their partners with real feeling and understanding.

The identification must be twofold. It involves identifying both with the marriage as a marriage and with the partner as a person. In this process, called *reification,* the marriage relationship is endowed with reality. Starting in the courtship period, the identification of the partner as a person develops during engagement and reaches its culmination in marriage. Identity is built by a series of experiences, both positive and negative. A sense of accomplishment comes when the pair is able to achieve some of the goals toward which it has moved. A strong identity may also develop from the common experience of meeting crises and misfortunes.

[1] Hermann Keyserling, *The Book of Marriage* (New York, Harcourt, Brace & World, 1926), pp. 47–48.

[2] Nelson Foote, "Identification as the Basis for a Theory of Motivation," *American Sociological Review,* Vol. 16 (February, 1951), pp. 14–21. See also Robert Winch *Identification and Its Familial Determinants* (Indianapolis, Bobbs-Merrill, 1962).

Besides being something which is created by the individuals themselves identity of the couple is furthered by the support of the community.
Bernard has analyzed this process in the following manner:

When the family was the producing unit of society, the identity of interests of all members of the family was perhaps itself sufficient to create and
maintain the feeling of unity essential to primary-group relationships. But the
unity between husband and wife in our society does not necessarily appear,
like Minerva, fully developed, at marriage. It must grow and mature, and when
it appears it is often as much a product of the outer world's reaction as of
their own.

The relationship between two people may exist as much in the minds
of the outside world which associates them together and treats them as a unit,
as in their own minds. . . . A feeling of unity may . . . be created between
two persons simply by treating them as a unit and thus giving them this common interest.

In marriage the association of two people in the minds of the outside
world imputes a unity and solidarity to them which the married persons may
not themselves feel. Sometimes it is the fact of being treated as a unit that
finally develops the feeling of unity in them. The woman is treated no longer
as Mary Brown but as Mrs. John Smith, and according to Cooley's principle
of the looking-glass self, she comes in time to think of herself as Mrs. John
Smith.

The success of a marriage often depends not only upon the young persons involved but also in large measure upon the attitude and behavior of
their friends and relatives, since the feeling of unity essential to successful marriage is largely dependent upon the way the two people are treated. We have
no experimental evidence on this point; but popular fiction, the example of
Hollywood, urban-rural and regional differences in divorce rates are all suggestive in this connection. It may happen in certain instances that two persons
marry against social odds, sacrifice friends and relatives, and consider the
world well lost. The feeling of unity is engendered by their very behavior.
This is truly in the romantic tradition. But in by far the largest proportion of
cases marriages need the support of friends and relatives if they are to function effectively and develop the necessary feeling of unity. . . . Many Hollywood marriages are reported to have gone on the rocks because of gossip. If
outsiders treat married persons not as married persons but as individuals still
free to respond to them, the feeling of unity necessary for primary-group relationships may not develop and the marriage may fail.[3]

The Will to Succeed

Common sense tells us that some individuals are more concerned that
their marriages be successful and functional than are others. Presumably

[3] Jesse Bernard, *American Family Behavior* (New York, Harper & Row, 1942),
pp. 3–4.

the variation is related to many factors including the will to succeed in marriage. Will is a concept which is not particularly popular in social science. Yet Rank, the psychoanalyst, made it the central concept of his theory of personality. Certainly it cannot be doubted that determination to succeed is *a* factor, whether one is referring to success in one's occupation, in academic work, or to marriage. Presumably it varies greatly in intensity and may not always be present.

It is asserted that many, if not the majority, of young people today are marrying on a trial basis, with the reservation that they will try again if the marriage does not meet with their expectations. The proposition is probably overstated. Expectations of success are strong for most couples. There is reason to suspect that this expectation is a naive one for some, of course. The road to marital hell is often paved with good intentions. A determination to succeed when the going gets rough is required, or at least very useful, for many marriages. Measured by such a standard, some people do seem to lack the drive necessary to sustain them in marriage as well as in other situations characteristic of the average human life.

Developing Reciprocal Roles

There is overwhelming evidence that groups are not successful in performing their tasks unless an interdependence of roles can be established. This applies to industry and education as well as to the family. The relation between the type of group structure, productivity, and morale is a very complicated one, and we have only the bare outlines of a theory at this point.[4]

It does seem rather clear that a cooperative arrangement is superior for most couples to one of dominance-submission or one of laissez-faire individualism. Studies by Maller [5] and Deutsch [6] show that greater productivity results when group members work cooperatively for group goals rather than competitively for their own individual goals. Many studies of industrial and educational groups report opposite findings, of course. But it must be remembered that incentive systems in education and especially in industry are oriented to private goals. It should follow that competitive, individualistic behavior toward strictly private goals would effect strains that most marriages could not endure.

Although based on Deutch's experiments with classroom groups rather

---

[4] See Ralph Stogdill, *Individual Behavior and Group Achievement* (New York, The Oxford Press, 1959), for the best work to date on this matter. We are indebted to him for a number of ideas expressed in this chapter.

[5] J. B. Maller, "Cooperation and Competition," *New York Teachers College Contributions to Education,* No. 384, 1925.

[6] M. Deutsch, "An Experimental Study of the Effects of Cooperation and Competition Upon Group Process," *Human Relations,* Vol. 2 (July, 1949), pp. 199–232.

than married pairs, Riecken and Homans' comments on group structure and the individual seem relevant to marriage.

It is through a particular structure of rewards that integration is achieved between individual motives and group goals. In a cooperatively organized group, Deutch's theory points out, no individual can move toward his own goal without also forwarding the progress of other members toward their goals, while the converse is true of competitive organized groups. In cooperation, when one swims, all swim—when one sinks he draws the rest with him. This is by way of saying, in a different form, that group goals and individual goals are identical—or at least, that maximum harmony has been achieved. Individual needs are not "subordinated" to the welfare of the group but, rather, the group is an instrument for the satisfaction of individual needs. In competitively organized groups, the group may or may not be such a means, or may be so in varying degree.[7]

Importance of Technical Skill

Performance of a group on particular tasks cannot be considered unrelated to technical skill, and the marriage situation is no exception. A group of men in a welding shop might be so organized that it seems efficient. The men are all congenial. If, however, the majority of the group members are lacking in welding knowledge and skill it is predictable that the group will not be an efficient group. It could not achieve the goal for which it existed. It could not meet the private goals of the members (pay, prestige as good welder) and consequent lowering of morale and motivation would follow.[8]

It is hazardous to generalize from industrial or other groups to the marital pair, but it seems logical and justifiable at this point. Clinical impressions of the author incline him to believe that both efficiency and morale of many marriages could be raised by a change in the technical skills of the members and better organization of the couple.

Reference to technical competency has been made previously in reference to reciprocal roles (Chapter 16). If the wife seems to be the most capable purchaser of food and clothing perhaps she should be the one to handle such tasks even though this was not done in her childhood family or that of her spouse. The important thing is to develop a concept of interdependence which will result in task efficiency.

There is no substitute for knowledge. In our present complicated social system it is not a simple matter to keep the wheels of the family machinery turning. It would appear that husbands and/or wives should

[7] Henry Riecken and George Homans, "Psychological Aspects of Social Structure," in Gardner Lindzey (Ed.), *Handbook of Social Psychology* (Reading, Mass., Addison-Wesley, 1954), p. 810.

[8] *Ibid.*, p. 814.

have a minimum knowledge of law, consumer economics, bookkeeping, business administration, first aid and home medicine, restaurant and hotel management, mechanical and electrical engineering, as well as of the general social and psychological sciences, to function adequately. And the surface is only being scratched with the above list. This is not to suggest that the homemaker should be an expert in any of the above. Rather it would be ideal to have minimum knowledge at least so as to know when a particular task falls within the range of his knowledge and when indications call for consultation with an expert. Good judgment proceeds from a base of sound knowledge out of which alternatives can be posed for final selection and action.

Finally, the proof of the pudding is still in the eating. A wife may have read a dozen sex manuals and still be inept as a sex partner. Knowledge and understanding of mother's methods of cooking and household administration are no guarantee of skill on the part of the young wife, although they may provide a good basis for her. Only practice under actual circumstances makes perfect. The applied sciences of social work, teaching, and psychiatry have programs of internship by which the fledgling works under supervision. The practice is sound, and in a sense we have the equivalent in the supervision of the child in the parental home. There is an important difference. Interne programs involve adults working in life-like settings, such as clinics, hospitals, and schools. In the parental home the recruit receives training and experience before he is in full adulthood, and he is on the wrong side of the desk, so to speak. He is more like a client receiving aid and help from a professional than a person experimenting with administration and leadership himself.

Of course in ideal homes the child is helped to project himself into marital roles, and training under such conditions has been the best type obtainable for future marriage. It still may be. One sometimes wishes that young couples could become apprentices to some of our more successful families, but no one has proposed any workable program of this type as yet.

Skill can be developed, although obviously there will always be differences in proficiency. From trial-and-error and from the example and advice of others, spouses can increase their technical capabilities and thereby become more proficient in performing the tasks that accrue to them as couples and individuals.

INDIVIDUAL PROBLEMS

It is inevitable that marriage will at times become frustrating and that morale will become low. No relationship can be completely devoid of problems. It is our purpose to examine some of the typical emotional maladjustments which may arise in marriage and to offer constructive possibilities for handling them.

Tremendous Trifles

First, attention must be given to the small irritations that crop up. These are items which appear of little consequence to the casual observer, but as a steady diet in a particular marriage they become unbearable. The following have been reported to the writer in various cases:

1. Burns toast every morning
2. Has dirty fingernails
3. Clothes are never picked up
4. Repeats old jokes *ad nauseum*
5. Can't get out of bed in the morning
6. Leaves dirty dishes in the sink
7. Slip is always showing
8. Never puts used razor blades away

Some of these irritations will seem more important than others. The point is that we are dealing with items that must be taken *in context*. In one household burnt toast is served every morning without a murmur. Why all the fuss in the other? What makes a trifling matter no longer a minor irritation?

A minor irritation can become a large one, if aggravated. The wife who expects animated conversation at the breakfast table may at times reach the point of exasperation when her husband consistently reads the stock market reports and the sports page. Once or twice is one thing; daily another. Actually in many cases the process of conditioning is involved. The particular act of behavior objected to sets off at first a mild negative reaction. It probably is related to criticism or punishment received in childhood for acts of behavior of a similar nature. Eventually it happens that the stimulus, whatever habit of behavior it might be in the spouse, sets off a response of anger, hostility, and frustration.

It seems important that spouses try to eliminate as many of the smaller annoyances as possible. On the other hand, some tolerance of personal idiosyncracies is required if one is to live intimately with another.

Grievances

Terman made a thorough study of grievances which the husbands and wives had in his sample of 792 couples. In the following table these complaints are listed in order of seriousness as they appeared to couples at the time of the study.

It may be helpful for couples to give some thought and study to the grievance list of the Terman couples. If some difficulties are appearing in their own marriages the couples may find it beneficial to open up discussions by using this list as a base. Naturally the important thing is not whether they fall into Terman's typical group or not but rather the significance their own grievances have to their relationships.

TABLE 33

Rank Order of Grievances of Husbands and Wives
According to Seriousness

Grievance of the Husbands	Rank Order	Grievance of the Wives
w. nags me	1	h. selfish and inconsiderate
w. not affectionate	2	h. unsuccessful in business
w. selfish and inconsiderate	3	h. untruthful
w. complains too much	4	h. complains too much
w. interferes with hobbies	5	h. does not show his affection
w. slovenly in appearance	6	h. does not talk things over
w. quick-tempered	7	h. harsh with children
w. interferes with my discipline	8	h. touchy
w. conceited	9	h. has no interest in children
w. insincere	10	h. not interested in home
w.'s feelings too easily hurt	11	h. not affectionate
w. criticizes me	12	h. rude
w. narrow-minded	13	h. lacks ambition
w. neglects the children	14	h. nervous or impatient
w. a poor housekeeper	15	h. criticizes me
w. argumentative	16	Poor management of income
w. has annoying habits	17	h. narrow-minded
w. untruthful	18	h. not faithful to me
w. interferes in my business	19	h. lazy
w. spoils children	20	h. bored with my small talk
Poor management of income	21	In-laws
In-laws	22	h. easily influenced by others
Insufficient income	23	h. tight with money
w. nervous or emotional	24	h. argumentative
w. easily influenced by others	25	Insufficient income
w. jealous	26	h. has no backbone
w. lazy	27	h. dislikes to go out with me
w. gossips indiscreetly	28	h. pays attention to other women
w. has much poor health	29	h. has poor table manners
w. has too many social affairs	30	Preference for amusements
Preference for amusements	31	h. quick-tempered
w. too talkative	32	h. attitude toward drinking
w. no interest in my business	33	h. untidy
w. extravagant	34	h. too wrapped up in business
w. too interested in clothes	35	h. intellectual interests

SOURCE: Adapted from *Psychological Factors in Marital Happiness* by Louis Terman, *et al.,* Copyright, 1938. McGraw-Hill Book Company, Inc. Used by permission.

Individual Reactions to Frustration

If grievance and frustration are bound to develop in most marriages, the question becomes, what can be done to adapt with the least amount of emotional pain?

It is very important to understand that frustration is inevitable and natural. As a matter of fact, in one sense, it is desirable. If we were all to go through life as contented as Borden cows or emasculated Tom Cats it would be a dull life indeed. Norman Vincent Peal notwithstanding, peace of mind without any problems of frustration is pap rather than the real bread of life.

Frustration *can* be destructive, however, and methods of dealing with it are necessary to maintain mental health. Frustration tolerance is one important adjustment. It suggests the development of what psychologists call appropriate and adaptive, as against inappropriate and nonadaptive, behavior. What are some typical methods of reacting to frustration, and are they appropriate or inappropriate?

Compensation. This is a form of substitution. The drive toward a particular goal is blocked, and the individual moves toward another goal which presumably will offer the equivalent satisfaction. As used by some authorities it refers to aggressive action to cover up for a shortcoming.

Sublimation. This again is a form of substitutive behavior. Blocked in the achievement of a particular goal, pressures toward a socially nonacceptable one build up. The individual, however, is able to redirect these pressures into more acceptable channels. For example, a young woman can turn toward promiscuity if she finds herself unable to attract men in regular social relationships. Through the process of sublimation, however, the drive can be channeled into nursing, teaching, or some other occupation which will at least be partially satisfying as a substitute goal.

Identification. This mechanism of adjustment is very familiar to students of adolescent behavior. By playing the role of the other vicariously the individual can achieve goals and sense satisfactions which have been denied to him. It has been suggested the daily soap operas of radio and television allow this outlet to thousands of frustrated and bored housewives. Be that as it may, identification is engaged in at times by most if not all of us who find it necessary to obtain some borrowed satisfaction.

Daydreaming. Closely allied to identification is daydreaming. It involves a realization of satisfaction in a make-believe world which exists only in fancy. By this mechanism the shop girl can imagine herself being elected May Queen or being married to the boss' son.

Rationalization.   Unable to reach a certain goal, the rationalizer tries to convince himself that he did not wish it in the first place. When inadequacies exist, the person may attempt to cover up by "making excuses." Thus the husband, who had strong hopes of being promoted to a higher position but was passed over may be able to lessen the blow by reference to the extra headaches and inconveniences which would have been involved in the wanted position.

Repression.   The Freudians have made much of this concept. It involves the pushing out of the conscious level thoughts and impulses which are of questionable validity in terms of the person's particular standards. The person tries to hold down any thoughts or desires which might be embarrassing to him if they were known to others. Sometimes the individual may try to deny to himself that the unworthy desires exist.

Regression.   This method of adaptation involves the adult who, frustrated in his ability to reach his goals, reverts to childlike behavior. It is as if the person withdraws from the rough competition of the adult world to an environment where the competition is on a less difficult level. Unfortunately a delusion is involved, for the child's world is difficult enough *for the child.* Remembering the pleasant aspects and forgetting the problems the person may find behavior at the more simple level attractive.

The above mechanisms of adjustment are both fairly common and understood. The more severe and disruptive adjustments categorized as neurotic and psychotic are not within the realm of this discussion. The standard mental health literature will serve the interested reader who wishes to delve further into the subject.

Our position is that the effects of the adjustment mechanism should be judged by two criteria: (1) What is the emotional outcome for the individual involved, and (2) What effect does the mechanism have on the interpersonal relations of the actors? In our particular context the question becomes one of the effect on the marriage partner and the marriage. Take for example the matter of aggressive behavior. Overaggressiveness will in most cases cause damaged interpersonal relations. As Mowrer and others have shown, the average man will realize this and not act aggressively in the office even though he would at times like to literally "wring some necks." He may upon occasion redirect these aggressive impulses toward his wife since she can't get him fired. He does, however, face a dilemma. On the one hand, it is imperative that the husband work out his aggressive feelings somehow, lest he develop too full a head of steam. If the home is not a safe place in which to vent feelings, where does such a place exist? On the other hand, how many wives will be able to receive positively some verbal brickbats which were really meant for the boss or the office clerk? Some will be able to accept the barbs without disturbance and to play a very therapeutic role thereby. Others will be inclined to fire them right back to the thrower.

The point is, adaptive mechanisms must be judged in context with emphasis on their effects. It is in error to attempt to set up rigid categories such as normal or abnormal, healthy or unhealthy. Here especially the interpersonal competency component, judgment, can come into play. In his calmer moments the marital partner can attempt to evaluate his typical reactions to frustration and their ultimate effects. If he finds himself unable to do this adequately, he may wish to seek some professional assistance.

In this discussion we have been focusing on the individual partner and the personal irritations with which he may have to deal. Our focus should now turn to the pair and to their interaction as a pair.

PROBLEMS IN THE PAIR RELATIONSHIP

Conflict and Tension

Only a very naive or overly idealistic person would take the position that the presence of any conflict in a marriage is abnormal. The more realistic view is that some conflict, at least at certain periods in marriage, is inevitable. The reasons for this will be readily apparent to even the casual student of marriage. Temperamental differences in the spouses, the clash of deep-seated wishes and motives, the building up of minor irritations all may be involved. Burgess and Locke suggest that in our modern day, conflicts may be increasingly cultural in origin rather than personal.[9] Whatever the source, differences seem bound to crop up in the best of homes.

Conflict should be distinguished from tension.[10] Conflicts develop and eventually the problem is solved. The basic structure of the relationship remains intact. Tensions are unresolved conflicts. They refer to conflicts which exist and persist over time to a point where the emotional force is affecting the marital relationship or will do so.

Further it is suggested that conflict may be either overt or covert. Here class differences enter the picture, as well as ethnic and other variations. Overt conflict to the point of fist cuffs may be typical in certain neighborhoods among couples who are having marital difficulty. This does not always mean that these couples are near divorce. A housewife may be heard to say something like the following: "Sure, I bashed his d____ head in with a skillet. He doesn't need to think he can treat me that way. I'll do it again if he comes home half drunk and gives me that line of malarkey."

[9] Ernest Burgess, Harvey Locke, and Mary Thomes, *The Family* (New York, American Book, 1963), Chapter 18.
[10] *Ibid.*, p. 388.

One would wish to know something about the class patterns as well as the individuals concerned before judging the seriousness of the situation.

Covert conflict, more prevalent in educated circles, can be as deadly as overt, if not more so. Take the case of Mrs. Jones. The writer interviewed her as a prospective sample member for a research study a few years ago. We talked about her background and some things about her marriage were briefly discussed. The picture which at first emerged was that of a conventional, stable, successful professional family. It would appear that associates of the couple type them as ideal. They present a solid front publicly.

When the initial interview was closed, Mrs. Jones agreed to fill out a questionnaire and to return it by mail. As we left her company she hinted that a few items might come as a bit of a surprise. This was the only indication we had that the marriage was not what it appeared to be on the surface.

The process of responding to marital success items in the questionnaire apparently opened the floodgates for Mrs. Jones. She complained bitterly of her mate and of the emotional aspects of her marriage. The following series of questions with her answers, including added remarks, will indicate the degree of feeling the woman has regarding her marriage. Her added comments have been set in parentheses.

Question: In leisure time husband prefers?

    __X__a. To be "on the go"   (alone)
    _____b. To stay at home

Question: In leisure time wife prefers?

    __X__a. To be "on the go"   (with husband—but since he re-
    _____b. To stay at home   fuses to take me—if I go, I go
                                        alone)

Question: Do you confide in your husband-wife?

    __X__a. almost never   (no—He would embarrass me by
    _____b. rarely   airing them before mutual friends.)
    _____c. in most things
    _____d. in everything

Question: Do you wish you had not married?

    __X__a. frequently
    _____b. occasionally
    _____c. rarely
    _____d. never

Question: What things annoy and dissatisfy you most about your marriage? Lack of partnership, the sulking of husband—he will never provide conveniences for wife in house, yet he spends large amounts on himself in pleasures, clothes, cars, trips etc.

Question: What things does your husband (or wife) do that you do not like? He expects me to be his "Mother" as it were—always giving and doing for him yet never expects to return them even in support, affection, courtesy, or consideration. He even takes the money I earn if he can get hold of it.

Question: Describe your husband's (or wife's) disposition as well as you can.

He is egocentric and domineering and sullen (and) nontalkative. If I try to talk he tells me to keep still, he'll do the talking in this house.

Question: If your marriage is an unsuccessful one, what do you believe to be the chief cause of its failure?

Selfishness, also his reversion to his type of life and association of his childhood. He now isn't "at home" among educated and refined people. He went to college on an *athletic* scholarship, was a star in college in football, basketball, baseball. He has no education background. I was brought up in a different setting of friends as well as a home life. I want our home to be the center pivot of our life together. To him it's only a place to eat, sleep and start from. He had no home ties as a boy and never went there unless he had to. I think it's a mistake to marry unless of like background—my marriage has proved it.

Question: What is the principle source of trouble between you and your partner?

Finances.

Question: Have you any habits to which your partner seriously objects?

_____a. Yes

_____b. No (Not that I know of—I suppose I do.)

Unfortunately we've had no follow-up to this case. It is our judgment that this couple will remain together in this "tragic state of tension." At least many of this sort do.

Some spouses are very clever at devising subtle ways of striking at their mates in such manner that they can hardly be questioned or called to task. One woman in mixed company has been heard to say on a number of occasions: "I keep telling Joe that he is not as young as he used to be and that he'll just have to curtail his golf and tennis." It seems pretty clear that continual repetition of this type of treatment is rather devastating.

The Effects of Quarreling

If it is agreed that some conflicts will arise between marital partners for one reason or another, the question of the function of overt quarreling presents itself. Among the experts two divergent schools of thought have developed. The one holds essentially that the ultimate effects of quarreling in marriage will be negative. The other rejects this point of view. Briefly the argument of the first group goes something like this:

In a quarrel there will be more heat than light. A person will begin by being somewhat guarded in his remarks but as the process proceeds he will begin to release the pent-up hostilities which may have their source outside the marriage itself. The spouse responds in kind. Soon references are no longer being confined to specific issues but they are touching on the shortcomings of the spouse, his family, or friends. Each partner, not to be outdone by the other, adds fuel to the fire. Barbed comments are thrown which are not really meant literally, but which will have an effect.

Perhaps the wife will be forced to tears and the couple will then "kiss and make up." While some things may have been learned in the process and some compromises made, certain scars remain which can never be erased. Some temporary relief has been obtained, but nothing is really settled. The next quarrel will probably be more vigorous and damaging and eventually the couple will find itself driven apart.

The second theory has essentially a psychiatric base, and takes the position that the individual must be able to release his feelings. It is assumed that repression in the long run is conducive to mental ill health, and that bottled up feelings will eventually explode with great destructiveness. Writing on this Duvall and Hill say:

> There needs to be some place, however, where the individual can give vent to his annoyances and be himself, and that place seems to be in marriage. If there is that kind of cantankerousness in a marriage, the couple should chalk it down as proof that their marriage is performing one of its main functions— providing a place to let off steam and reestablish emotional balance. If a marriage is so fragile that it must be maintained by the same kind of artificial manners that keeps an office force functioning, it is pretty precariously based. One insightful authority has stated in positive terms, "one of the functions of marriage is to weave a rope of relationships strong enough to hold each person at his worst." [11]

It is suggested that only through quarreling can spouses perceive each other's true feelings, however irrational they might seem at first.

Relying on the same concepts originally suggested by Binckley, Waller and Hill suggest the distinction between productive and destructive quarreling.[12] In productive quarreling the process is delimited to issues at hand. The spouse does not attack the integrity of his partner by dragging in extraneous items. Furthermore he does not undercut by threatening to dissolve the relationship. Besides being delimited to specific issues at hand, by definition some minimum decision in the way of compromise must emerge. In other words new ground has been gained; the quarrel has not resulted in a stalemate.

[11] Evelyn Duvall and Reuben Hill, *When You Marry* (Boston, Heath, 1945), pp. 187–188.
[12] Willard Waller and Reuben Hill, *The Family* (New York, Holt, Rinehart and Winston, 1951), pp. 309–312.

Destructive quarreling becomes increasingly ego-involving and personal. Instead of focusing upon the issues at hand the partners shift toward the soft and exposed parts of the opponent's ego and move toward these vulnerable areas. The analogy of the boxer sparring with his opponent seems appropriate and the picture of loving spouses engaged in building a sound relationship seems to fade in the background.

A real dilemma is posed here. Frustration must be alleviated, differences settled, and pressures drained off. Few will deny this. Can spouses develop codes and patterns whereby they will be able to confine themselves to productive quarreling? In our judgment some will be able to and some will not. Probably at this point the emotionally healthy and the neurotic must be distinguished. Some kinds of neurotic individuals, or couples, will tend to use a destructive approach.[13] When the chips are down this temptation to fight with no holds barred will be too strong to resist. Some emotionally healthy couples will be able to make use of sometimes heated discussions which will enable them to reach a higher level of identification and consensus. This will require resolution and a basic sense of fair play.

The functional test may legitimately be used in this connection. Couples can realistically attempt to assess the outcomes of quarrels. If they find that the results for both parties concerned are consistently negative they may wish to attempt to change their approach. The analysis by Magoun might be helpful in producing an orientation toward the handling of conflicts constructively.

I. Both husband and wife must have a self-respecting status.
   In order to be self-respecting one needs:
   A. To be self-governing.
   B. Opportunities for self-fulfillment.
   C. Recognition as belonging and being wanted.

II. Both husband and wife must have a continuing and healthy understanding of how the desires and the performance of each are affecting and are affected by the performance and desires of the other in every situation as it occurs. This can be accomplished by:
   A. Open channels of communication by which to recognize each other's legitimate need and no refusal to negotiate.
   B. Proper adjustment between one's selfish impulses and the community of needs arising from the partnership.
   C. The sure feeling that each person's legitimate wants will be satisfied without the necessity of fighting for them.

III. Both husband and wife must have confidence in the availability of and the effectiveness of adequate good method in working out acceptable solutions for the inevitable disagreements which arise. Adequate good method requires:

---

13 Some types of neurotics are too passive to be capable of conflict.

   A. A constructive rather than a destructive approach to conflict.

   B. Not only an attempt at "solution with" but an intelligent, realistic approach.

   C. Effective solutions, honestly arrived at.

   D. A minimum of self-assertion.

IV. Both husband and wife must accept mutual responsibility for results, and yet recognize clear-cut lines of authority so that their activities do not conflict. This requires:

   A. A satisfactory division of labor.

   B. Efforts that fit together.[14]

MAINTAINING SATISFACTIONS

In the previous sections we have attempted to indicate some of the major prerequisites for a productive, efficient marital structure which will at the same time allow a high degree of morale and member satisfaction. The latter now deserves some attention. Many of the points we wish to make have already been made or implied in other contexts.

The famous Lewin, Lippitt, and White studies indicate that member satisfaction in a group is highest when the group structure is intermediate rather than at either an authoritarian or anarchical extreme.[15] This does imply that a definite assumption of leadership is taken by *someone*. By trial and error and eventual mutual agreement leadership-followership patterns and spheres of influence can be developed by the couple to insure the highest degree of satisfaction possible. Satisfaction with the marriage is to a degree a function of the expectations which each partner brings to the marriage. A woman marrying mainly for social status can hardly be satisfied with a relatively good marital relationship if the couple cannot crack the social circle to which the wife aspired. In a case known to the author a young woman married a man who presumably was on his way to a departmental chairmanship. When subsequently he was not granted the position the wife entered suit for divorce. A person very strongly committed to a "champagne" style of life may find it most difficult to be satisfied with a marital "beer" pocketbook.

One of the alleged difficulties of the typical early marriage is the tendency to have unrealistic standards based on an idealistic, naive, romantic ideology. Expectations can be unrealistic at any age but they probably have a greater tendency to be so during the younger years.

---

[14] Adapted from F. Alexander Magoun, *Love and Marriage* (New York, Harper & Row, 1956), pp. 322–326.

[15] Kurt Lewin, Ronald Lippitt, and R. White, "Patterns of Aggressive Behavior in Experimentally Created Social Climates," *Journal of Social Psychology,* Vol. 10 (August, 1939), pp. 271–299.

Burgess and Locke correctly point out that satisfaction in marriage may be relatively high, even though there are tensions and conflicts.[16] In the following case the wife expressed satisfaction with her marriage even though there was considerable conflict in the relationship.

George is a good man. He works hard and always sees to it that we have enough money for food and clothing. He never beats the children but is always kind to them. Yes, George is alright.

How do we get along? Well I'll tell you. George really doesn't know a woman's feelings for things. When we were first married he would bring me things from Woolworths. He even brought me some flowers once. Now he never remembers my birthdays and he hasn't bought me a present in years.

And he's so jealous. If I look at another man he about goes crazy. I guess he thinks he can't trust me. All I want is a good time now and then. I'm not interested in other men. The thing is, you can't expect too much. I know what my mother had to put up with. Marriage isn't a bed of roses. You have to take the bitter with the sweet. I'm as happy as any wife on the block even if George and I don't see eye to eye on many things. Women just have to put up with a lot, that's all.

Providing Mutual Support

Marriage is supposed to mean that each partner has the other to whom he can turn when in trouble. In the typical ceremony the mate is chosen "for better or for worse." Some days or periods in marriage will be worse or more difficult than others. Can one turn to the spouse for support, or as Blood and Wolfe use the phrase, for "therapeutic utilization," or for a "mental-hygiene function"? [17] This will depend upon a number of factors, including the personalities of the individuals involved and the type of relationship developed. In their Detroit study the above authors found that working-class women in general turn more freely to their husbands with their troubles than do wives of the middle and upper classes.[18]

The meaning of this is not fully clear. However, it appears that the educated wives are more "selective" in deciding when to turn to the husband for support. In some cases realism no doubt tells the wife to refrain from "bothering" her husband with her seemingly small problems when he himself has big ones with which he is contending. She may also be subtle enough to know when to pick a time when she will stand the best chance of obtaining maximum results.

[16] Burgess, Locke, and Thomes, *op. cit.*, p. 292.

[17] Robert Blood and Donald Wolfe, *Husbands and Wives* (New York, Free Press, 1960), p. 194.

[18] The relationship appears to be a complicated one. The authors point out that wives in the poorer classes tend to split into two groups, those who turn to their husbands and those who do not. It is reasoned that they are not selective in turning to their husbands as are the upper-class wives. When consistently repulsed, they retreat from interaction with their husbands.

TABLE 34

Therapeutic Utilization of Husband After a Bad Day, by Occupation of Husband

| Frequency Wife Tells Husband Her Troubles | Husband's Occupation | | | |
| | Blue Collar | | White Collar | |
	Low	High	Low	High
Always	25%	23%	19%	17%
Usually	23	20	34	24
Half the time	23	26	30	32
Seldom	16	21	10	21
Never	13	10	7	6
Total	100	100	100	100
Mean *	2.32	2.24	2.49	2.26
Number of families	173	173	88	157

* Mean represents the average number of shared troubles. A four-point scale is used.

TABLE 35

Husband's Therapeutic Response, Relief Felt by the Wife and Her Resulting Satisfaction

Husband's Therapeutic Response	Percentage of Total Sample	Effect on Wife of Husband's Response *	Wife's General Satisfaction with Understanding
1. Help toward solution of problem	6%	3.31%	3.83%
2. Help in withdrawing from the situation	3	3.80	3.70
3. Sympathy, affection	28	3.63	3.59
4. Advice, discussion of how wife can solve problem	20	3.63	3.54
5. Passive listening	18	2.92	3.27
6. Dismissal as unimportant	7	2.79	3.27
7. Criticism and rejection Wife never tells her troubles	9	—	3.22
N. A.	3	—	—
Total	100		
Number of families	731		

* Code "Wife feels much better"–4 points; "a little better"–3 points; "sometimes better-sometimes worse"–2 points; "about the same"–1 point; "worse"– 0 points.

What can the husband do to facilitate some relief of the wife's problem in order to help rebuild her morale? Table 35 indicates the responses typically used by the husbands in the Detroit study and the immediate effects of these responses. Also indicated is the wife's satisfaction with the husband's understanding of her feelings and problems as she sees them.

We are reminded of the factors of interpersonal competence discussed in Chapter 6. Among them empathy, judgment, and adaptability would be most appropriate here. The spouse who is high in empathic ability will be able to *verstehen*. This means to *fully* understand and perceive. If this is combined with good judgment and adaptability the husband will be able to help his wife to move toward an adequate solution of her difficulties. This may involve either a head-on attack or withdrawal from the situation. Good judgment helps to determine the best approach, taking into account personal feelings, and the possibilities of change in the situation.

Quite a high proportion of the husbands offer sympathy and affection or advice regarding solutions to the problem. While these are not appreciated to the degree that the methods cited above are, they result in a generally high level of satisfaction on the part of the wife. They do indicate an interest on the part of the husband and a willingness to take the situation seriously.

Listening passively, dismissing the problem, or criticizing and rejecting the wife are the most difficult for her to take. Often this means casting blame explicitly or implicitly. While a wife may already feel that she herself is partly to blame for her troubles, she usually does not appreciate someone's pointing it out to her.

Data are not available on the tendency of husbands to turn toward the wife after a bad day at work. It is known, however, that hundreds of men turn to other women with the pleas that their wives do not understand them.[19] No doubt rationalization is involved in many cases. Nevertheless the outside competitor not only offers new romantic possibilities but often is willing to listen, which many a wife is unwilling or unable to do.

Young married couples will be forced to experiment with various types of approaches or rebuild waning morale and relieve tensions. They lack the wisdom regarding each other which comes with the experience of living together over a long period. They do, on the other hand, have the enthusiasm, ingenuity, and vibrancy of youth. Furthermore, they are not locked in mutual habit patterns which those who have been married longer may be. By creatively searching and by exploring alternatives, morale builders and tension relievers may be found. In particular cases techniques will work which would seem completely out of place in others. In one instance the purchase of a new hat will work wonders for the morale of the lady of the house. A relative of the author finds it necessary to spend a month in the Canadian bush country each summer in order to keep his equilibrium. During this month he is displeased if he meets people other

[19] Clark Vincent, *Unmarried Mothers* (New York, Free Press, 1961), Chapter 11.

than the Indians. After the month away he can come back to his job and family. Without this month away from civilization he would, he feels, be impossible as a husband or colleague. Four hours on the golf course with a good friend may be the answer for a tense father and husband. For others it is the peace and quiet of a boat on a lake with a fishing rod for company.

Maturity cannot be ruled out of the picture. Spouses will come to find that some things cannot be changed. Clinicians are in rather thorough agreement that attempts to reform the marriage partner usually have deleterious results. The ability to perceive what must be accepted and what can be changed by persistent effort is a very precious commodity and in rather short supply. Nevertheless wise couples will make use of that which they have available to achieve the highest level of morale obtainable for them.

SELECTED READINGS

Angell, Robert, *The Family Encounters the Depression* (New York, Scribner, 1936).

Baber, Ray, *Marriage and the Family* (New York, McGraw-Hill, 1953), Chapters 6, 7.

Bell, Norman, and Vogel, Ezra, *The Family* (New York, Free Press, 1960), Part VI.

Blood, Robert, and Wolfe, Donald, *Husbands and Wives* (New York, Free Press, 1960), Chapter 7.

Blood, Robert, *Marriage* (New York, Free Press, 1962), Chapter 10.

Bossard, James, and Boll, Eleanor, "Marital Unhappiness in the Life Cycle," *Marriage and Family Living,* Vol. 17 (February, 1955), pp. 10–14.

Burgess, Ernest, and Cottrell, Leonard, *Predicting Success or Failure in Marriage* (Englewood Cliffs, N.J., Prentice-Hall, 1939), Chapter 3.

Burgess, Ernest, and Locke, Harvey, and Thomes, Mary, *The Family* (New York, American Book, 1963), Chapter 18.

Cavan, Ruth, and Ranck, K., *The Family and the Depression* (Chicago, The University of Chicago Press, 1938).

Cavan, Ruth, *American Marriage* (New York, Crowell, 1959), Chapter 17.

Christensen, *Marriage Analysis* (New York, Ronald, 1950), Chapter 10.

Duvall, Evelyn, and Hill, Reuben, *Being Married* (Boston, Heath, 1960), Chapter 14.

Goode, William, *After Divorce* (New York, Free Press, 1956).

Hill, Reuben, *Families Under Stress* (New York, Harper & Row, 1949), Chapters 1–3.

Hollis, Florence, *Women in Marital Conflict* (New York, Family Service Association of America, 1949).

Horney, Karen, *The Neurotic Personality of Our Time* (New York, Norton, 1937).

Katz, Irvin, *et al.,* "Need Satisfaction Perception and Cooperative Interaction in Married Couples," *Marriage and Family Living*, Vol. 25 (May, 1963), pp. 209–214.

Karlsson, Georg, *Adaptability and Communication in Marriage* (Uppsala, Sweden, Alqvist and Wiksells, 1951), Chapter 7.

Komarovsky, Mirra, *Blue-Collar Marriage* (New York, Random House, 1964), Chapters 6, 7, 8.

Koos, Earl, *Families in Trouble* (New York, King's Crown, 1946).

Landis, Judson, and Landis, Mary, *Building a Successful Marriage* (Englewood Cliffs, N.J., Prentice-Hall, 1953), Chapter XII.

Lantz, Herman, and Snyder, Eloise, *Marriage* (New York, Wiley, 1962), Chapter 16.

Le Masters, Ersel, *Modern Courtship and Marriage* (New York, Macmillan, 1957), Chapters 12 and 13.

Levy, John, and Munroe, Ruth, *The Happy Family* (New York, Knopf, 1938).

Locke, Harvey, *Predicting Adjustment in Marriage: A Comparison of a Divorced and Happily Married Group* (New York, Holt, Rinehart and Winston, 1951), Chapter 4.

Martinson, Floyd, *Marriage and the American Ideal* (New York, Dodd, Mead, 1960), Chapter 21.

Mowrer, Harriet, *Personality Adjustment and Domestic Discord* (New York, American Book, 1935).

Peterson, James, *Education for Marriage* (New York, Scribner, 1964), Chapter 20.

Pineo, Peter, "Disenchantment in the Later Years of Marriage," *Marriage and Family Living*, Vol. 23 (February, 1961), pp. 3–11.

Waller, Willard, and Hill, Reuben, *The Family* (New York, Holt, Rinehart and Winston, 1951), Part VI.

Winch, Robert, and McGinnis, Robert, *Selected Studies in Marriage and Family* (New York, Holt, Rinehart and Winston, 1953), Chapter 18.

QUESTIONS AND EXERCISES

1. Discuss the implications of the following statement: "Quarreling has functional as well as nonbeneficial effects in the pair relationship."
2. Individual reactions to frustration in the pair relationship can be played up or largely repressed for the good of the marriage. What general position would you adopt in this dilemma? Discuss, making specific references to situations in the marriage relationship.
3. There is an old if somewhat trite saying, "Where there's a will, there's a way." Discuss the application of this statement to marriage, using outside information as well as that supplied in the text.
4. Have several members of the class present case studies of marriages that have "gone on the rocks." In the discussion that follows, the class should attempt to determine as specifically as possible the chief causes of the difficulty.

5. On a more positive note, discuss the particular strengths demonstrated in certain case studies presented by members of the class.

6. Morale considerations in marriage have changed a great deal in the last fifty years. Discuss this statement making specific references to significant factors in America's social change.

7. Another comparative approach involves an analysis of morale in American marriage along side of morale in other cultures. Individual reports might be given to determine whether this concept plays as important a part in marriage and whether the emphasis is similar in other lands.

8. Some couples enter marriage imbued with idealism; Keyserling, at the other extreme, considers marriage a "tragic state of tension." Relate your own position to the two stated above.

9. In one household a husband is irritated by his wife's failure to have a suit cleaned, but no incident results. On the other hand, a similar situation in another family produces open conflict. Discuss the reasons for such divergent situations.

10. As a project the class might attempt to devise schemes for building (and rebuilding) morale. Small groups should be assigned to work on specific situations; their conclusions should be reported to the class for general discussion.

11. How far should a spouse go in subordinating himself or herself to the marriage if this subordination is burdensome? Discuss.

18

Facing the Realities of Pregnancy

The great majority of young couples will expect to have and will have children. On the average, pregnancy will occur during the first few years of married life.

ATTITUDES TOWARD CHILDBEARING

It is interesting that on the matter of the desirability of having children, traditionalists, middle-of-the-roaders, and radicals are in essential agreement. The traditionalists are inclined to think of the bearing of children as a duty to God, church, and country. Liberals, affected by the child-centered orientation of our culture, think of children as the natural outcome of a happy marriage. Those in the middle range of orientation may have mixed reasons for desiring children, but in America they tend to favor them. Although the meaning of childbearing may differ, people of various persuasions consider children essential to a successful marriage.

Do children facilitate success in marriage? This is an interesting question to which there is as yet no clear-cut answer. Studies by Davis, Bernard, Locke, Terman, and Williamson find no significant relationship between the presence of children, or the number of children, and marital success.[1] Monahan has assessed some of the pertinent literature dealing with this question, and he thinks that an attitude of caution must be exercised by those who feel strongly that children prevent divorce or insure marital success. He says: "A more complete answer to the question of the relationship between marital instability and children must await the compilation of more refined data on divorce, desertion, and domestic discord,

[1] These and other studies are reviewed in Ernest Burgess and Paul Wallin, *Engagement and Marriage* (Philadelphia, Lippincott, 1953), Chapter 21.

349

and the characteristics of stable families in the population as a whole." [2]

Jacobson has also been concerned with this problem. He found, in examining divorce records, that the difference in divorce rate between childless couples and couples with children was not consistent throughout the marital cycle. He found that ". . . divorce is much more frequent among those without children in the early years of marriage, and the differential diminishes rapidly thereafter." [3] Since control of pregnancy has become more and more a reality, it is probable that the ability to control fertility is more significant than presence or lack of children or numbers per se. Reed, in a Milbank Memorial Study, found that couples who were able to control fertility as they desired were the best adjusted. Those couples who were unable to achieve fertility control and who therefore had unwanted children tended to be more poorly adjusted.[4] Studies by both Burgess and Cottrell and Burgess and Wallin support the above finding. In both cases it is concluded that couples who desire children and have them tend to have a higher level of marital adjustment than those who have children they did not desire.[5] It appears, then, that attitude toward having children and ability to control their coming to a degree are more crucial than the number of children as such, or absence, or presence of them.

In writing primarily for couples in the educated classes one assumes ability and willingness to exercise control over conception except where religious objections intercede. Such an assumption may not be fully warranted, but as a whole it seems reasonable.

Rainwater's recent study indicates that among working-class families four categories of couples appear: (1) early planners, (2) late, desperate users, (3) nonusers, and (4) sporadic or careless users. The first two are effective in family planning and the latter two are not.[6] It is suggested that especially for the very poor, family planning represents a problem difficult to comprehend and master. They operate in a confused world in which they feel somewhat helpless and lost. Attempting vigorously to determine the number of and spacing of children calls for more concerted effort than they are capable of mustering.[7]

Many modern couples who are realistic will wish to be in the category of early planners. They will attempt to use the latest available scientific

[2] Thomas Monahan, "Is Childlessness Related to Family Stability?" *American Sociological Review,* Vol. 20 (August, 1955), pp. 446–456.

[3] Paul H. Jacobson, "Differentials in Divorce by Duration of Marriage and Size of Family," *American Sociological Review,* Vol. 15 (April, 1950), pp. 235–244.

[4] Robert Reed, "The Interrelationship of Marital Adjustment, Fertility Control, and Size of Family," Part VIII, *Social and Psychological Factors Affecting Fertility* (Indianapolis, Millbank Memorial Fund, 1948), pp. 422–424.

[5] Burgess and Wallin, *op. cit.,* pp. 716–718.

[6] Lee Rainwater and Karol Weinstein, *And the Poor Get Children* (Chicago, Quadrangle Book Company, 1960), Chapter 3.

[7] *Ibid.,* see also Roy Greep (Ed.), *Human Fertility and Population Problems* (Cambridge, Schenkman, 1963), Chapter 6.

information on control of conception and will try to master not only negative control (prevention of conception) but positive control (ability to induce conception when desired) as well. If they are successful, present indications are that they will have greater chances of marital success and happiness with their children.

Our concern in this chapter will be with the "pregnant pair." [8] Whether the pregnancy was planned or not, the average couple during the latter part of the second year of marriage finds a baby is on the way. If so, certain developmental tasks accrue to the couple during this important period.

FEELINGS ABOUT AND ATTITUDES TOWARD PREGNANCY

Pregnancy is a state of the mind as well as a matter of physiology. There is a growing feeling on the part of many authorities that the attitudes of the wife and the husband toward the impending event are of crucial importance for all concerned.

If Winch is correct, the basic needs of the two spouses are being gratified before the pregnancy if the marriage is reasonably successful. Ordinarily, however, there will also be a desire for children to fulfill other goals of the marriage. If this is true, and for both spouses, it is probable that pregnancy will not as a rule present serious problems. If the husband and wife are still in the process of adapting to each other emotionally and otherwise, if one or the other is not yet ready for a pregnancy, or if they are unrealistic about the change which pregnancy brings, or if unusual medical problems arise, then pregnancy may result in emotional difficulties of some intensity.

The above implies that if the couple is emotionally, socially, physically, and economically ready to have a child before pregnancy occurs, problems which arise can ordinarily be handled without undue difficulty. If a mature type of love has been attained by the couple, they are much better prepared to anticipate the arrival of a child. Those wishing to have children only from a romantic impulse may find it difficult to cope with some of the contingencies of pregnancy. Mature love is less exclusive and concentrated. In somewhat technical language, it must embrace a new constellation. The new baby means three persons in the home, not two. No longer will the husband receive full and exclusive affection and attention from his wife, nor she the same from him.

Clinicians tell us that the couples they see often have weak motives for

[8] Family life educators are now beginning to use the term "pregnant pair" and the concept "we are pregnant" in order to emphasize the husband's social and psychological role in the process. See William Genné, *Husbands and Pregnancy* (New York, Association Press, 1956).

having children. Many, faced with marital difficulties and possible separation or divorce, turn to pregnancy as a possible solution to their emotional and adjustment problems. Evidence indicates that typically problems are compounded rather than solved by such action. It is not difficult to see that a crying, colicky baby, night feedings, formula-making, dirty diapers, and a disorderly house might aggravate the already strained relationship.

Few careful research studies of pregnancy have concerned themselves with the emotional and social side of the experience. One of the few is by Newton, who interviewed some 190 mothers in the rooming-in wards of the Jefferson Hospital in Philadelphia.[9] Mothers were asked to indicate their feelings regarding pregnancy, childbirth, menstruation, breast feeding, satisfaction with woman's role in life, and the wish to be a man. Their answers to these questions were related to various social and personal measures. Some of the findings may be of interest.

The mothers were divided into two categories, namely those who had negative feelings toward pregnancy and those who reacted positively. The following differences appeared between the two groups.[10] Women somewhat negative toward pregnancy were more likely to have fewer motherly desires and to wish they were men. On the other hand, women who indicated a positive approach to pregnancy were less inclined to wish they were men and more inclined toward the expression of maternal drives. Women who regarded pregnancy negatively sometimes showed dissatisfaction with the sex of their child and complained about the procedure of rooming-in. This negative group not only produced no more children than the positive group even though the women were older, but it was also more inclined to prefer the small family as an ideal.

Among social factors studied, economic standing most influenced the couples' feelings and attitudes toward pregnancy. The higher income group was more receptive to pregnancy than the lower income group.

In their research studies, Robertson,[11] Kroger and De Lee,[12] and McCammon [13] refer to nausea and vomiting. Newton's informal observations are upheld in line with the findings of these studies. Nausea and vomiting seem to be associated with emotional attitudes, disturbed sexual functioning, or excessive dependence of the wife on her mother.[14]

More thorough research is needed regarding the emotional, social, and

---

[9] Niles Newton, *Maternal Emotions,* Psychosomatic Medicine Monograph (New York, Hoeber-Harper, 1955).

[10] *Ibid.,* Chapter 4.

[11] G. Robertson, "Nausea and Vomiting in Pregnancy," *Lancet* (September, 1946), p. 336.

[12] W. S. Kroger and S. T. De Lee, "The Psychosomatic Treatment of Hyperemesis Gravidarum by Hypnosis," *American Journal of Obstetrics and Gynecology,* Vol. 51 (April, 1946), pp. 543–545.

[13] C. S. McCammon, "A Study of Four Hundred Seventy-Five Pregnancies in American Indian Women," *American Journal of Obstetrics and Gynecology,* Vol. 61 (May, 1951), pp. 1159–1166.

[14] Newton, *op. cit.,* p. 29.

physical impact of pregnancy. On the basis of present knowledge and findings from her study, Newton offers the following practical suggestions to the husband, friend, or professional who is concerned with the pregnant wife's feelings about pregnancy.

At present a pregnant woman may be helped by applying a few suggestive thoughts we do have. They can be encouraged to talk about how they actually feel about pregnancy and the idea of having a baby. 'How do you like the idea of being pregnant?' or 'Are you kind of glad or kind of sorry you are going to have a baby?' may be all that is necessary to start a normal woman expressing her mixed feelings about pregnancy. The second prenatal visit to the physician may be an opportune time for such discussions since it may take some time after the diagnosis of pregnancy before the full emotional impact develops.

Once doubtful feelings are voiced, reassurance can be given by pointing out (1) that unhappiness during the first months of pregnancy is a usual occurrence and, (2) that most women find themselves eager for the baby before it actually arrives despite their earlier feelings. Financial anxieties tend to disappear after the birth of the baby even if there is no more money.

Problems of nausea and vomiting may be helped by calling attention to the possible causes. Is the woman particularly nauseated the day after having intercourse with her husband? Is she more prone to vomit when she has been in close touch with her mother?

If pregnancy continues to seem hard, thinking together with a pregnant woman along the following lines might be helpful: 'How does she feel about becoming a mother?' 'Does being a mother mean something nice or something rather disagreeable to her?' 'How does she feel about her own mother?' 'Has she ever wished to be a man?' 'If so, might not this feeling in some ways be related to the feeling that pregnancy is awful?' 'Does she feel a little helpless and dependent and does she resent this feeling?'

Such a series of direct questions sprung at a woman one after another would of course, not be helpful. The pregnant woman first needs to feel that the person she is talking to is deeply interested in how she feels and will continue to think well of her regardless of what she says. Under the circumstances an appropriate question or two may help to lead her thinking along surprisingly fruitful lines. To spend a few minutes in such discussion is to recognize the obvious fact that the average normal woman experiences pregnancy, emotionally as well as physically, and needs watching and perhaps a little help in both areas.[15]

Pregnancy is not wholly an abnormal condition for the married woman. Strange as it may seem this is a relatively modern notion. Old wives tales in times past emphasized the wife's "delicate condition" and implied that she was ill or mildly neurotic. A much healthier attitude exists today. Physicians encourage the young wife to take pregnancy in stride emotionally and socially, and in general, the associates of the couple will encourage the same type of attitude and approach. It should be understood,

15 *Ibid.*, p. 28.

however, that while pregnancy is a natural and not an abnormal phenomenon, it is a unique event for the couple. Both husband and wife will need to be especially sensitive to the emotional needs and frustrations of this particular period.

Sexual Adjustment

It is obvious that sex relations during the period of pregnancy will have to be somewhat modified. The specific type and amount of modification necessary will depend essentially on various factors involved in the particular case. Naturally the physician should be the final authority on the subject. If there is reason to believe the wife might have trouble holding the fetus in the uterus, vigorous sex activity may be discouraged. Especially is this true during the early months of pregnancy in those periods when the wife would ordinarily menstruate. The physician often discourages full sex relations during the last month of pregnancy, because of possibility of infection in the birth canal and the danger accruing from vigorous muscular activity on the part of the wife.

Even with these constraints the average couple will be able to have fairly normal sex relations during the greater part of the pregnancy period. Naturally the wife may be more sensitive at times than she ordinarily would be. On the other hand, clinicians report that some wives are inclined to refuse their husbands during pregnancy, but in such cases refusal is quite often an index of shortcomings in either the marriage or the emotional adjustment of the wife, or both. Some women find greater enjoyment in sex relations during pregnancy, probably because the fear of becoming pregnant has been removed.

Few research studies have been made of sexual adjustment during pregnancy. Landis and the Poffenbergers report on the effects of first pregnancy on a sample of 212 newly married college couples.[16] For both sexes about one half (58 percent) reported the pregnancy had no effect on sexual adjustment, while about one fourth of the couples experienced an unfavorable effect. Of the husbands, 19 percent reported favorable effects and 17 percent of the wives gave the same response.

In this study, sex desire seemed to be related to the phase of pregnancy. All but a minority of the women reported a decrease in sex interest as the pregnancy progressed. About one fourth experienced a decrease during the first three months. By the last three months over three-fourths noticed a decrease in desire. The authors interpret this as an indication that psychological as well as physiological factors influence sex desire.[17]

---

[16] Judson Landis, Thomas Poffenberger, and Shirley Poffenberger, "The Effects of First Pregnancy upon the Sexual Adjustment of 212 Couples," *American Sociological Review,* Vol. 15 (December, 1950), pp. 766–772.
[17] *Ibid.*

Communication

Society, with gentle and sometimes not so gentle pressure, has helped prepare the young woman for the role of motherhood. Pregnancy for her involves physiological change and significant emotional experiences. For the husband the latter factor only is involved. These emotions may be positive or they may be negative. If the wife has wanted a child, pregnancy represents a hoped for accomplishment. For some, motherhood may connote the greatest contribution they can make to the universe. Some women will feel that this is what they have been waiting for to give meaning to their lives. Others, perhaps the most healthy, want children simply because they like children, because childbearing is natural, and because they and their husbands have an interest in this kind of mutual fulfillment.

Prospective fathers may also have positive feelings regarding approaching fatherhood. In many if not most societies, sexual prowess is considered a manly attribute. The presence of a child is presumed to be prima facie evidence of this prowess. When such is the case the knowledge of the first pregnancy may make the husband "feel that he is now a man."

On the negative side of the ledger either husband or wife may be subject to many doubts and fears. The wife may fear the loss of her figure, difficulties in carrying the child, the possibility of pain, or even death at childbirth. Some women will be bothered by nausea, especially when arising in the morning. Others may find they have all-consuming appetites for foods that did not particularly interest them before or that the beloved cauliflower is the most foul smelling mess in the world.

It is important that the young couple keep open the channels of communication at this important period in their lives. They will vary as to whether they can express their positive or negative emotions more easily. Some wives can share their great expectations at "Kaffee Klatsches" but are unable to relate in similar fashion to their husbands. Some husbands may be better able to discuss their prospective fatherhood with the office secretaries than with their wives. When this is the case communication between the spouses becomes exceedingly important and should have special attention.

ADAPTING TO OUTSIDERS DURING PREGNANCY

Pregnancy calls for many adaptations and adjustments within the home. It also demands adaptations in relating to relatives, friends, and others outside the marital circle.

In-laws may evidence a smothering and unduly inquisitive interest in the married couple when they find that a grandchild is expected. In general, however, they may have either a positive or negative effect on the couple. On the positive side, in-laws usually look forward to the advent of a grandchild, and it often brings a sense of self-fulfillment and joy. In many cases any reservations they may have had about the acceptability of the new son-in-law or daughter-in-law diminish and the outsider is now fully accepted. Without the responsibility to care for and provide economic support of them, grandchildren have all the attractive points and few of the liabilities associated with one's own children.

Many grandparents, their own responsibilities permitting, are willing to give considerable help to a couple after the birth when mother and child are first home from the hospital. Their experience with such matters may be a stabilizing influence on the young couple who is passing this way for the first time.

On the negative side there can be in-law problems which come to a head at the time of the approaching birth of the first child. In one case known to the author, the young wife was of a different religious background than the husband. A strained but relatively satisfactory accommodation developed between the couple and the two sets of in-laws during the early period of marriage. Pregnancy precipitated discussions regarding the religious affiliation of the child still to be born. After the birth of the child, when the mother was still recuperating, the paternal grandparents took action. They had the infant baptized by the priest of their choice. This act produced a strained relationship which has, as yet, not been basically changed.

Another type of problem involves the advice grandparents give to the prospective parents. Ordinarily it is based on the folk wisdom and experiences of the past. If the prospective parents are attempting to obtain the latest medical knowledge to guide them the chances are strong that it will not coincide with that given by members of the older generation. The ramifications of this situation are many and while not too difficult to understand may be vexing indeed. The grandparents can easily interpret the young couple's disregard of their advice as criticism of their own competency as parents, and hurt feelings may result.

A word may be said about the pregnant couple's relating to the general community. Rarely is it any longer customary for the pregnant wife to withdraw from public life. In earlier times the wife "in her condition" was advised to keep herself from public gaze. Fortunately a much more wholesome attitude prevails in most communities today. The extent of the wife's social interaction will depend both upon her previous habits and upon her health and feelings in the matter. If, especially in the latter stages of pregnancy, she feels conspicuous, it' may be sensible to absent herself from public events. Otherwise, if her health and interests are normal it is probably most desirable that she maintain at least a minimum of social and community contacts. Usually both the couple and the general community understand that pregnancy along with other life experiences is no cause for isolation.

One type of community activity in which couples are engaging increasingly is attendance at expectant parents' classes. These classes, formerly for expectant mothers only, are now attracting increasing numbers of prospective fathers as well. The success of these ventures appears to rest on certain sound principles of group dynamics. Couples who have felt somewhat alone and isolated with their problems find relief in noting that other couples have similar problems.[18]

Quite typically, classes for prospective mothers were developed by hard-pressed physicians who felt that instruction to groups of their female patients would be time-saving as against individual instruction. From this modest beginning have developed the classes for expectant mothers, and sometimes for expectant fathers as well. Their popularity seems to attest to their value.

The expectant couple's relationship with a competent physician is extremely important. Whether or not a specialist is chosen as against a general practitioner is a matter of preference, availability of personnel, budget considerations, and other factors. The specialist has the typical advantage he offers in other areas. In cases of special difficulty his greater knowledge and experience suggest greater ability to cope with any contingency. Most important is to have a physician in whom the couple and especially the prospective mother can have full and complete confidence.

PREPARING TO REALLOCATE ROLES, TASKS, AND RESPONSIBILITIES

Quite possibly the young wife has been working outside the home previous to pregnancy. If so she and her husband have no doubt developed a system whereby the tasks of the household are accomplished. Now with the birth of a child in the offing a reworking of roles and reevaluation of habit patterns in the home become practical. Some wives will hope, of course, to take "time out" only for maternity leave and then return to outside work. What are the possibilities for this type of approach?

First of all, it should be noted that some American employers still do not encourage the employment of married women with very young children.[19] Childbirth is viewed by many as a handicap. If a woman is working in a job which requires little training she may find that some competitor will move into the job during her maternity leave. Women with training or

---

[18] Under the able leadership of David Treat, the Clara Elizabeth Fund for Maternal Health of Flint, Michigan has been especially successful in sponsoring this type of program.

[19] Ray Baber, *Marriage and the Family* (New York, McGraw-Hill, 1953), pp. 393–395. On the other hand, in Sweden the employer is required by law to grant a maternity leave and to hold the position for the mother.

needed skills fall into a special category. Employers are more inclined to make exceptions and to accept them after the birth of a child on a full or even part-time basis. It should be clear, however, that a middle-class woman with a small child at home faces many obstacles in returning to work. Community and family sentiment seldom support her.

At this point it may be necessary for the husband and wife to make some changes and for the husband to take on some new tasks. The more equalitarian husbands are quite willing to make the adaptations without resenting them. The more traditional husbands find it rather difficult to involve themselves in what they consider to be "women's work." If the household budget permits they may prefer to have some household help rather than to scrub floors themselves. Actually with her first pregnancy the wife will ordinarily be able to handle most of the housework which she has been regularly doing even though tasks that require stooping, bending, and lifting may need to be reassigned. Most important is an attitude of cooperation on the part of the husband. His willingness to do some special things will help the wife feel a sense of identification which is most important for her at this period.

MAINTAINING MORALE AND MOTIVATION

Physical difficulties which sometimes occur during pregnancy are well-known and understood, and they can be rather serious. Frequently they are of an emotional rather than a physical nature. The new medical emphasis on psychosomatic medicine reveals that physical and emotional factors are closely associated. If such is the case, then at times physical upsets during pregnancy may cause emotional disturbance. Conversely it becomes important that the wife's emotional adjustment be as good as possible in order to allow her physiological processes to proceed undisturbed.

As shown in Chapter 17, it is contended that morale and motivation cannot be considered solely individual characteristics. There are group connotations as well. This means that the maintaining of morale and a high level of motivation of the pair is of considerable importance at this point.

Does the couple want the new baby? Are they prepared to make some sacrifices in order to have a more complete home life? Much depends initially on the basic values of the couple and their ability to adapt to new conditions and new situations.

Many a woman will have depressed and anxious periods because she fears the rigors of the pregnancy and childbirth experience. Individual sessions with her own physician and attendance at motherhood classes can be of great help in boosting morale. During the first pregnancy, going as a couple to the doctor's office or to the group sessions stresses the team approach which is sometimes helpful in maintaining morale.

Reevaluation of work responsibility is also important for morale. If there is agreement as to who is to do what, and when, morale tends to be maintained. If there is lack of agreement and indecisiveness, morale tends to suffer.

It is fairly typical for a pregnant woman to spend more time than she ordinarily would in sitting and daydreaming. If she is not careful this will eventually mean that dirty dishes, clothes, and dust will begin to accumulate. While standards differ it is not conducive to the wife's morale to have such overt evidences of needed work continually "staring her in the face." By careful evaluation of work roles, the husband and wife can integrate their efforts and accomplish the minimum tasks necessary for the maintenance of an orderly household. Sometimes scheduling is important, for by careful timing and allowing intermittent rest periods, the wife may be able to accomplish much more than she would have thought possible when pregnant.

Human beings seem to hope for rewards for their accomplishments of whatever nature. Expectant mothers are no exception. During this period the husband will find that it is especially crucial to reward his wife in any legitimate and acceptable fashion. He will expect to defer a bit more to his wife's wishes and desires, especially where her comfort is concerned. If he is the type who typically spends many hours at the lodge or with male friends at the gym or golf course, he may find it wise to modify this activity and spend more time with his wife. Greater attention and respect seem to be expected.[20] Fortunately our social life is organized to aid and abet this process. Parties, baby showers, and the like give the wife (and indirectly the husband) some needed recognition and reward.

Spouses reciprocally will attempt to fulfill each other's needs throughout their married life. It is well recognized that wives may have special needs during the pregnancy period. In the middle of the night she may suddenly develop a strong hunger for a coke or sandwich. Overlooking dietary hazards, the thoughtful husband may be willing to go to the refrigerator to retrieve said objects without grumbling. After all, pregnancy doesn't occur every year in most families.

It is to be expected that the wife will occasionally regress during pregnancy and have a strong need to be protected and cherished. This should not be considered pathological. The wife is being forced to come to grips with new reality and at times the potential responsibility seems overwhelming. The strong protecting arms of the husband can be reassuring to her and will calm her feelings of isolation and fear.

Patterns of handling tensions and conflict need to be strengthened during this period. Grievances can easily be magnified out of proportion by

[20] Shirley Poffenberger, Thomas Poffenberger, and Judson Landis, "Intent Toward Conception and the Pregnancy Experience," *American Sociological Review,* Vol. 17 (October, 1952), pp. 616–620.

either spouse, but especially by the wife. If either is only grudgingly ready to accept the new baby or if either or both reject the idea of parenthood, they are in for trouble. It is easy for the wife to blame the husband. After all he "got her that way." The husband in turn may believe the pregnancy would not have occurred had the wife "been more careful." While such reactions seem to the outsider rather unrealistic they are by no means atypical.

A corollary point may be made with regard to quarreling. If the couple can concentrate on the issues at hand and always arrive at a constructive solution, such will not be harmful. If they resort to ego attacks and excursions into all areas of the marital relationship trouble is predictable. This is not to suggest that partners put on an act during the expectant period. Such an act would be naive, dangerous, and unrealistic. Rather they may be well advised to follow the biblical injunction to live as peacefully as possible.

Again the will to succeed must be stressed. It may take drive and work for some to prepare to be good parents. Attention and thought must be given to many areas to prepare for the new baby and the triadic relationship which will develop. A wife may "sit and mope" about her present troubles and the potential work she will eventually be forced to do. The husband may be overwhelmed with the potential expenses and be disturbed about the new household arrangements which a baby will require. If instead of this negative approach, the spouses can vigorously and positively prepare themselves for the event which is to take place in their household, a great part of the struggle is won.

FEARS OF THE CHILDBIRTH PROCESS

One problem in the maintenance of morale on the part of the wife is her projection forward to the time of birth. Fears may involve the possibility of her or her child's death. Fortunately statistics show that in the United States these fears are relatively groundless (See Figures 11 and 12). As can be seen, rates for either maternal or infant deaths have dropped sharply since 1915. United States rates are now low in comparison with the rates in other nations.

Fear of the birth process itself is another matter. Childbirth will never be a simple procedure for the average woman, especially in the case of the primapara. It is now held by some authorities that emotional and social factors are involved in making the process more difficult than it should be. Dershimer is one who leans toward this point of view. He states,

. . . other physiological functions such as eating, coitus, defecation, and so on are naturally pleasant and easy. . . . The usual ease with which they naturally occur may be completely destroyed by the development in the indi-

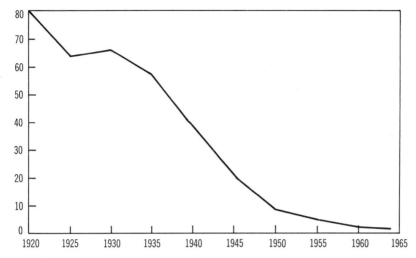

FIGURE 11. *Maternal Death Rates, 1920–1964 (Rates per 10,000 live births).*
SOURCE: *Statistical Abstracts of the United States, 1961,* No. 57, "Maternal
Deaths, Infant Deaths (Under 1 Year of Age), Fetal Deaths, and Neonatal
Deaths by Color; 1915 to 1960" (Washington, D.C., United States Government
Printing Co., 1961), p. 57; and "Monthly Vital Statistics Report," Vol. 13, No.
13 (Washington, D.C., U.S. Department of Health, Education and Welfare,
July, 1965), p. 10.

vidual of certain emotional attitudes in connection with them. Analogy suggests
that labor should be naturally pleasant and easy and when it is not, the common cause of a similar state affecting other functions should be taken as the
most likely cause until proved otherwise.[21]

Later in the same article Dershimer states the following: "Society in
general makes every possible effort to prevent the pregnant woman from
accepting pregnancy and labor as a natural physiological function. The
same amount of attention to eating would make most of us have nervous
indigestion." [22]

The English physician, Read, on the basis of clinical work and a review of social science literature on pregnancy and childbirth developed the
so-called "natural childbirth" technique to minimize negative feelings
toward childbirth and to cut down the actual amount of pain experienced.[23]

Read stressed the negative effects of fear. An increase of tension ac-
companies fear, and with this tension come muscular spasm and increased
pain. Fear and apprehension are reduced when the mother understands the
childbirth process. This leads to reduced tension and to lower incidence of

[21] F. W. Dershimer, "The Influence of Mental Attitudes in Childbearing,"
American Journal of Obstetrics and Gynecology, Vol. 31 (March, 1936), p. 444.
[22] *Ibid.*
[23] Grantly Dick Read, *Childbirth Without Fear* (New York, Harper & Row,
1953).

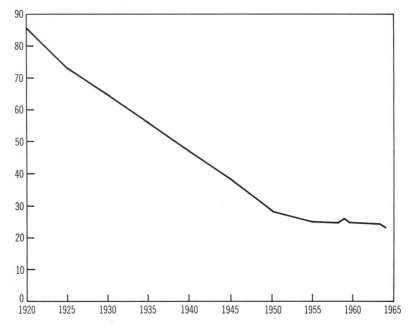

FIGURE 12. *Infant Mortality Rates, 1920–1964 (Rates per 1,000 live births)*. SOURCE: *Statistical Abstracts of the United States, 1961,* No. 57, "Maternal Deaths, Infant Deaths (Under 1 Year of Age), Fetal Deaths, and Neonatal Deaths by Color; 1915 to 1960" (Washington, D.C., United States Government Printing Co., 1961), p. 57; and "Monthly Vital Statistics Report," Vol. 13, No. 13 (Washington, D.C., U.S. Department of Health, Education and Welfare, July, 1965), p. 11.

pain. The mother is taught how to relax her body and also the techniques of rapid chest breathing and slow abdominal breathing. These are used when appropriate during labor.

The approach stresses the following points. The prospective mother is to develop a close relationship with a physician in whom she has confidence. Through a series of office sessions she will be given information regarding physical and psychological factors correlated with childbirth. This includes specific and detailed information on matters of diet, exercise, control of muscles, breathing, position during the process of labor, and the like.[24]

Research by Thoms [25] and by Miller [26] report reduction in fears, easier and shorter average labor, and less need for use of drugs when the

[24] Freely adapted from Niles Newton, *Maternal Emotion* (New York, Hoeber-Harper, 1955), pp. 31–32.

[25] H. Thoms, *Training for Childbirth—A Program of Natural Childbirth with Rooming-in* (New York, McGraw-Hill, 1950).

[26] H. L. Miller, *et al.*, "Education for Childbirth in Private Practice," *American Journal of Obstetrics and Gynecology,* Vol. 63 (April, 1952), pp. 792–799.

method is followed. On the other hand Callahan,[27] Davidson,[28] and Mandy [29] in separate reports all indicate poor or at best moderate success. More research will be necessary before the efficacy of the method can be fully assessed.[30]

ADAPTING TO GETTING AND SPENDING OF INCOME

Very often the young wife has worked outside the home until pregnancy occurs. Now the possibility of giving up this outside work must be faced, although maternity leaves of absence are beginning to come in some areas. For quite a number of couples this experience is more traumatic than had been expected. If the young wife is interested in her job, and if both she and her husband have learned to appreciate and depend on the extra income, adjustments may be difficult.

In financial planning, the more successful couples use the young wife's earnings to help assemble the basic furniture and other objects in anticipation of family expansion or for extras and nonessentials. When this is done, in place of living temporarily at a spuriously high level, the couple will find it easier to adapt to the expenses of the new baby.

How much do babies cost? Obviously this question cannot be answered simply. We should consider not only initial cost but projections ahead. Both will vary on the basis of the class level, the region in which the couple live, and other factors. In general, the physician's initial fee will run from one to two hundred dollars, including prenatal care. Hospital fees of course will vary with the area, the length of hospitalization, and whether or not special facilities or medicines are needed. A minimum of thirty-five dollars per day can be anticipated in most instances.[31]

Blue Cross and Blue Shield insurance plans will now cover regular delivery and hospitalization charges. It must be noted that these will not always be covered in full, and that the costs are still there, albeit they are being met over an extended period rather than by direct payments.

Besides a few hundred dollars for these initial expenses there are the costs for clothing and equipment needed for baby. For the first child

[27] J. T. Callahan, "A Physician's Viewpoint on Preparation for Childbirth," *Transactions of the Fifth American Congress on Obstetrics and Gynecology* (1952).

[28] H. B. Davidson, "The Psychosomatic Aspects of Educated Childbirth," *New York State Journal of Medicine* (November, 1953), p. 2499.

[29] A. T. Mandy, *et al.,* "Is Natural Childbirth Natural?" *Psychosomatic Medicine,* Vol. 14 (1952), p. 431.

[30] It should be noted that the use by the physician of a particular technique tells us more about the physician than about the technique at this point.

[31] According to a report by the American Hospital Association, the average daily cost per patient rose from $15.62 in 1950 to $41.58 in 1964, for the United States as a whole. See *Boston Globe,* Sunday Edition (August 1, 1965), p. 17.

there is no equipment to be handed down from a previous baby. Some couples will be fortunate to have in-laws and friends who will help out with needed items.

It can be expected that family expenses will increase gradually as the child matures and as new children enter the family. The peak years of expenses will come when the children are in high school and college. It is now being suggested that a fairly precise estimate of the cost of rearing a child to college age is that of three times the father's average annual income for the total childbearing period. For illustrative purposes we may take a hypothetical case. Suppose a couple has four children, the first three born two years apart and the third and fourth, four years apart. The first child is born in 1960 and the last in 1970. Assuming that all the children are launched into their own occupations at age twenty, by 1990 the last child will be launched. Let us assume that the father's income averages $9,000 for the total twenty-year period. That means that his total income for the thirty-year period of child rearing is $270,000. Using our formula, $108,-000 or 40 percent of this would be spent in raising the four children. It must be noted that these manipulations do not include tuition payments of any kind. Were all four children to be sent through four years of college, a minimum of $32,000 would have to be added to the $108,000.[32] Naturally projections such as these are subject to change if great fluctuations occur in our economic order and style of living. Nevertheless a figure tied to the father's salary seems entirely reasonable.

A consideration of the finances of pregnancy and future child rearing leads naturally to the next category. Projections involving thousands of dollars lead the sensitive, thoughtful persons to reassess their values and goals in life. Some will wonder if parenthood is worth the cost in material outlay and in other ways.

THE PHILOSOPHY OF LIFE

It has been suggested that rather early in marriage the young couple needs to come to grips with the basic values by which it is to live. If this has been done previous to pregnancy there should be few problems. However, if this task has not been fully accomplished, some additional evaluating becomes necessary.

Some young men who have been rather noncommittal about church attendance begin to attend when a child is on the way. The wife whose greatest intellectual endeavor has been bridge-club chatter or the reading of the society page, may now exhibit an interest in "the better books."

---

[32] Perhaps it is unwise to introduce such items of high finance at this time. After a classroom discussion in which similar figures were used, a student was heard to comment, "If that's how much they cost, I know I'm not having any."

Superficial though some of these actions may be, they indicate at least half-hearted attempts by the individuals involved to come to grips with forth-coming responsibilities.

Sensitive couples realize that a child may force changes in some basic patterns in their homes. Pregnancy may produce real soul-searching, even demoralization, when both young people are fully career oriented, for example. Projecting plans for future education of the children, obtaining life insurance, and many other activities are more general forms of value-changing in which many couples engage at this period.

For those who wonder whether children are worth their cost Bossard has some interesting comments.[33] He suggests that at this time parents become sensitive to matters they had previously tended to overlook. These will include problems of family finance, insurance, home ownership, community conditions, and conditions of the school system which should have been attended to earlier.

Besides these there are other important contributions. The child gives emotional satisfactions and interests of long duration. The emotional satisfactions multiply as the children and their parents grow older. With the passing of years the changing of circumstances and the greater need for emotional satisfactions from without, parents normally identify with the developing lives and careers of their children. Children then offer insight into basic life processes and insight into' the essential meaning of life. Bossard, who devoted more than three decades to intensive study of parent-child relations, speaks as follows on the latter point:

What parenthood brings to one, in the ultimate analysis, is some comprehension of the meaning of life and of the individual's role in the cosmic scheme of things. Stated in its simplest form, it is this: Each person is but a temporary trustee of the life stream.

One comes to sense this first, perhaps, with one's possessions. Yesterday, you owned them absolutely. You gave them the care that such absolute possession deserved, for their preservation was as signally important as your own life; they became as vital as the maintenance and development of your own personality. Today, your child uses them carelessly, and destructively perhaps. You squirm a bit at first, but, after all, it is *your* child violating *your* possessions; and you resolve the conflict finally so that the violation of what was yours dissolves into the development of your child that is. These possessions may be your old toy, your book, your chair, your watch, or your house. Somewhat later, you experience the same changing evaluation of your energy. Originally your energy was yours, to expend for your pleasure and your development. It was so insensibly a part of you that your use of it could not be conceived of except in terms of yourself and your interest. With continuing parenthood, this, too, shades gradually into the feeling that every parent knows, where your energy and even your life blood become the small change

[33] James Bossard, and Eleanor Boll, *The Sociology of Child Development* (New York, Harper & Row, 1960), Chapter 7.

you pay to satisfy the passing needs of your children. It is at such moments, when a parent has given his all to the insatiable demands of his child, that there comes the true meaning of one's relation to life: that each generation is but a trustee of life for all its values and all its possessions. Thus, in the larger sense, we never own anything; for everything that can be owned belongs to time, and time is endless. This, then, is the real end of life, that we receive, as it were, the torch from one generation, to carry it and perchance to brighten it, but ultimately always to turn it over to the next generation. This it is that the child brings, in some varying form of expression, to each parent who has the capacity to perceive it.[34]

SELECTED READINGS

Blattner, Russell, "Rubella During Pregnancy," *Journal of Pediatrics,* Vol. 54 (February, 1959), p. 257.

Bowers, P. A., "Husbands in the Delivery Room," *Child-Family Digest* (April, 1952).

Corbin, Hazel, and Van Blarcom, C., *Getting Ready to Be a Mother* (New York, Macmillan, 1940).

Davidson, H., "The Psychosomatic Aspects of Educated Childbirth," *New York State Journal of Medicine* (November, 1953), p. 2499.

Dershimer, F., "The Influence of Mental Attitudes in Childbearing," *American Journal of Obstetrics and Gynecology* (March, 1936), p. 444.

Donnelly, James, "Toxemia of Pregnancy," *American Journal of Nursing,* Vol. 61 (April, 1961), pp. 98–101.

Eastman, Nicholson, *Expectant Motherhood,* 3rd. ed. (Boston, Little, Brown, 1957).

Eastman, Nicholson, and Hellman, Louis, *Williams Obstetrics,* 12th ed. (New York, Appleton-Century-Crofts, 1961).

Genné, William, *Husbands and Pregnancy: The Handbook for Expectant Fathers* (New York, Association Press, 1956).

Giblin, Elizabeth, and Osmond, T., "Nursing Care in Toxemias of Pregnancy," *American Journal of Nursing,* Vol. 54 (December, 1954), pp. 1488–1489.

Goodrich, F., *Natural Childbirth* (Englewood Cliffs, N.J., Prentice-Hall, 1950).

Guttmacher, Alan, and Rovinsky, J. (Eds.), *Medical, Surgical, and Gynecological Complications of Pregnancy* (Baltimore, Williams and Wilkins, 1960).

Heardman, Helen, *A Way to Natural Childbirth* (Edinburgh, Livingston, 1951).

Hirning, J., and Hirning, Alma, *Marriage Adjustment* (New York, American Book, 1956), Chapter 17.

Koos, Earl, *Marriage* (New York, Holt, Rinehart and Winston, 1957), Chapter 16.

Krugman, Saul, and Ward, Robert, "The Rubella Problem," *Journal of Pediatrics,* Vol. 44 (May, 1954), pp. 489–498.

[34] *Ibid.,* p. 143–144.

Landis, Paul, *Making the Most of Marriage* (New York, Appleton-Century-Crofts, 1960), Chapter 28.

LeMasters, E. E., *Modern Courtship and Marriage* (New York, Macmillan, 1957), Chapter 24.

Lewis, Abigail, *An Interesting Condition: The Diary of a Pregnant Woman*, Garden City, N.Y., Doubleday, 1950).

Newton, Niles, *Maternal Emotions* (New York, Hoeber-Harper, 1955).

Read, G. D., *Childbirth Without Fear* (New York, Harper & Row, 1954).

Rock, John, and Roth, David, *Voluntary Parenthood* (New York, Random House, 1949).

Stone, Abraham, and Himes, Norman, *Planned Parenthood* (New York, Viking, 1951).

Taylor, Katherine Whiteside, "The Opportunities of Parenthood," in Becker, Howard, and Hill, Reuben, *Family, Marriage, and Parenthood* (Boston, Heath, 1955), Chapter 16.

Thompson, L., "Attitudes of Primiparae As Observed in a Prenatal Clinic," *Mental Hygiene,* Vol. 26 (April, 1942), p. 243.

QUESTIONS AND EXERCISES

1. Do you consider children an essential part of marriage? Defend your answer.
2. Would you consider adopting a child? Why or why not? Under what circumstances?
3. Would you consider having a child in the first year of marriage? What would be your arguments for or against?
4. Do you agree with the use of the concept "Pregnant Pair"? Why or why not?
5. List the ways you think a husband can bolster and support his wife during pregnancy.
6. What curtailment of social life do you deem necessary and proper for the "expectant pair"?
7. What are some ways a wife can reassure her husband during the prenatal period, or should this be a one-way street?
8. What is your attitude toward the advice and help offered by parents of the couple? Would you accept help? What kind and on what terms?
9. How would you go about the task of choosing a physician to handle prenatal care and delivery?
10. Make an itemized list of basic expenditures that will be necessary to see a couple through pregnancy and birth including the essential clothing and furniture needed for the first months of the baby's life. Use local hospital and doctors' fees in your list.
11. What would you want to have included in a class held for expectant parents? Do you think such a class should be held for both parents? Separately or together?

12. If you were an employer would you want a pregnant woman to continue working as long as she was able? Give arguments to support your answer.
13. From a husband's viewpoint would you want your wife to work during pregnancy? How long and under what conditions?
14. What are some of the sacrifices you forsee necessary after the addition of a child to the family circle, especially a first child?
15. What are some of the compensations and contributions made to the family circle by the child?
16. Considering the degree of maturity necessary for meeting the challenges of marriage and parenthood what do you think of the idea of having children when you are young and growing up with them?

19

The Physiology of Reproduction*

This chapter will deal with the basic mechanisms that lead to pregnancy and childbirth. To some readers of this book the material will be repetitious, having been covered in biology or other subjects. It still may be useful as review material. There will probably be some new information for everyone, since medical and biological researchers are constantly adding to our knowledge, refining information, and challenging misinformation.

THE FEMALE GENITAL SYSTEM

The *female genitalia* are a system of numerous structures and organs both internal and external. Due to its double purpose of producing the ripe ovum and the nurturing of that ovum through pregnancy and birth, the female genital system is vastly more complex than that of the male. Although there are internal and external parts to the female system, the major organs are internal.[1]

The external organs consist of the outer lips or labia majora, the inner lips or labia minora, the clitoris, and the breasts. The *labia majora* are firm folds of flesh which form a funnel-like entrance to the vagina. At puberty these outer lips become covered with hair. Lying beneath are the *labia minora* which consist of long flabby folds of mucous membrane and serve as a protective covering to the vaginal opening. They contain a network of blood vessels and nerves and are very sensitive. Just above the

[1] In this chapter extensive use has been made of Nicholson Eastman and Louis Hellman, *Williams Obstetrics,* 12th ed. (New York, Appleton-Century-Crofts, 1961).
* Written in collaboration with Paul K. Jentes, M.D., obstetrics and gynecology.

point where the labia minora come together is the clitoris, usually covered by the labia majora.

The *clitoris* is a spongy tissue of elongated cylindrical form. It is extremely sensitive to gentle touch and like the male penis becomes engorged with blood during sexual excitement. It is often described as a vestigial penis and is of the size of a small bean.[2] It is covered by foreskin called the *prepuce*. The labia majora, minora, and the clitoris are collectively termed the *vulva*. Two sets of glands, the *paraurethral* near the urethra and the *Bartholin* near the vagina, secrete a lubricating substance which provides for the easy and painless intromission of the penis during intercourse.

The breasts, although not always included in the listing of female genitalia, perform three functions: the first is the suckling of the newborn, the second is the sexual stimulation of the wife when caressed, and the third is the erotic effect of the caressing activity on the husband in cultures where this practice is common.

The *hymen,* long considered the true index of virginity and surrounded by mystery, myth, and folklore, is a membrane which partially covers the vaginal opening. It is difficult to class this particular structure as either external or internal. The structure, size, and thickness of the hymen vary greatly from individual to individual. It varies from the one extreme where the membrane is so loose and easily stretched that it survives childbirth to a thick, tough membrane which must be surgically snipped to permit initial intercourse. Somewhere between these two extremes lie the majority of cases. Doubt and worry about this structure can easily be dispelled by a physician during the premarital examination in the average case. Very few cases require any treatment and those that do may be cared for in the doctor's office, or they may involve a more intensive procedure including hospitalization and general anesthesia. The absence, presence, size, or strength of the hymen is not a good index to be used by the groom to determine the bride's virginity.

The internal organs are the vagina, uterus, the two fallopian tubes and the two ovaries. It is this internal group of organs which produces the egg and houses and nourishes the developing fetus.

The *vagina* is a musculomembranous passageway connecting the external and internal organs. Through this passageway travels the unfertilized egg and the menstrual flow and the newborn child. Into this passageway the penis enters during intercourse to deposit the sperm. The vagina is an elastic muscular tube from three to three and one-half inches in length. Because of its elasticity it can painlessly stretch during intercourse to about six inches. The vagina is moist although it has no glands

[2] F. Alexander Magoun, *Love and Marriage* (New York, Harper & Row, 1956), p. 261.

for the secretion of lubricating mucous. This is supplied by the glands in the cervix.[3]

The *cervix,* about an inch in length, is located at the tip end of the uterus and is the opening into the vagina. The cervix is especially vulnerable to cancer and may also be the seat of bacterial infections and erosions. We will pay more attention to the cervix in our description of the birth process.

The muscular, hollow, inverted pear-shaped organ which lies at a right angle to the vagina is the *uterus* (commonly called the womb), which is lined with mucous membrane. The uterus furnishes a safe, nourishing environment for the fertilized egg during the gestation period. The muscles of the uterus are controlled by the autonomic system of nerves and are therefore not influenced or voluntarily controlled.[4]

At the upper, larger end of the uterus on either side are two small openings into the fallopian tubes, also known as *oviducts.* These slender

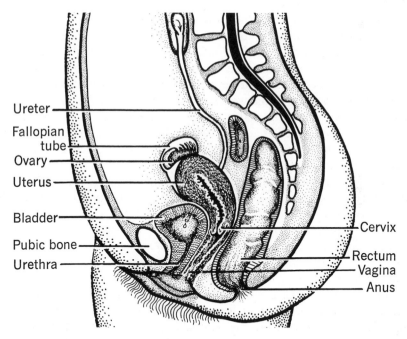

FIGURE 13. *The Female Sex Organs.* SOURCE: Adapted from *Biology,* 2nd ed., by Alfred M. Elliott, and Charles Ray, Jr., assisted by Edward L. Davis (New York, Appleton-Century-Crofts, 1965), p. 656.

[3] Erna Ziegel and Carolyn Blarcom, *Obstetric Nursing* (New York, Macmillan, 1964), p. 18.
[4] Barry King and Mary Showers, *Human Anatomy and Physiology* (Philadelphia, Saunders, 1963), p. 412.

tubes are about three and one-half inches long on the average and about 1/100 of an inch across at the opening into the uterus. They widen and end in a number of finger-like projections near the ovaries.

The *ovaries* are the female sex glands or gonads. These almond-shaped glands which are about four to five cm. in length and one cm. in thickness perform two major functions. At birth each ovary contains 25,000 or more immature ova. At puberty the ovaries begin ripening and release an ovum or egg about every twenty-eight days for a period of about thirty years. The ovaries usually alternate in this function. When a pregnancy occurs the ovaries cease ripening and expelling ova for the duration of the term and they will again revive this function after the pregnancy is terminated.

The ovaries are also responsible for the production of the important female hormone, *estrone,* which controls the development of female characteristics and a second hormone, *progesterone,* which causes the uterus to make ready to receive and nourish the fertilized ovum should fertilization take place.

One body function peculiar to women is menstruation. Menstruation, when understood and accepted as an orderly rhythmic bodily process, should lose all the connotations of sickness or curse, etc. with which it has been viewed. It is true that some women experience discomfort and certainly some inconvenience. However, the menstrual period should be a cause for little distress in the woman who is in good health. When painful it is termed *dysmennorrhia* and is usually cause for consulting a physician. We will not attempt to discuss the causes for this disorder. Barring such abnormalities the trend of modern young women is to go about a normal, active routine during the period.

We have already mentioned that the ovaries mature and discharge (ovulate) an egg every twenty-eight days on the average. This egg travels into the fallopian tubes, then on into the uterus. If it has not been fertilized it will die. During the time the egg is ripening the uterus is being prepared for a pregnancy. The walls are built up with a spongy material. If fertilization or implantation does not occur then the spongy material is not needed; it and mucous are sloughed off in a flow or discharge. Very little blood is actually lost. The average is about two ounces during the three to five day period. Menstrual blood differs from regular blood in that it lacks the clotting substance, and therefore can be discharged easily. The length of average period will sometimes be prolonged in case of illness. Again we stress these figures are average and variations are not to be construed as abnormal. Extreme emotional disturbances can cause upset and temporary cessation of menstruation. Before the period of menstrual flow is over another egg is maturing and the uterus will again make ready for a possible pregnancy. This period from the maturing of an egg, its ovulation, menstrual flow to maturing egg is called the *menstrual cycle.*

Somewhere between the age of thirty-eight and fifty women will cease to menstruate. This event is termed *menopause* and indicates the end of the childbearing period. The ovaries no longer mature and discharge ova or produce female hormones; therefore the uterus ceases to prepare for a pregnancy. The menopause is only one phase of the bodily changes which take place at this time. The aggregate of changes is termed the *climacteric*.[5]

THE MALE GENITAL SYSTEM

The *male genitalia* are a somewhat simpler system than that of the female and to a greater extent external. The visible male organs which lie outside the body are the penis and testes (testicles). The *penis* is a muscular structure with a network of blood vessels. On the underside is a tube, the *urethra,* through which the urine passes from the bladder. This same tube is also the outlet for the seminal discharge during intercourse.

On either side of the penis suspended in the *scrotum* (a skin pouch) lie two ovoid bodies, the *testes*. These are the male gonads or sex glands. They perform two important functions similar to those performed by the ovaries for the female. The first is the production of the sperm. Parallel to the female, the male is born with a complete set of immature sperms (primordial stem cells). The male produces sperm from puberty into old age. Several billion sperm are produced in a month by a healthy man. Nature has provided well for the production of the sperm. The testes are located outside the body cavity where the temperature is several degrees cooler. Internal body temperature is too high for sperm production. The second major function of the testes is to manufacture *testosterone,* the hormone which influences the development of male secondary sexual characteristics, and also has an effect on metabolism.

Outside and above the testes but still within the scrotum lies a storage area known as the *epididymis*. The epididymis finishes the sperm and adds a fluid. From here the sperm are moved into the *vas deferens*. These muscular tubes with minute channels extend from the testes to the opening of the urethra. The upper end of the vas deferens widens into a storage recepticle known as the *ampulla*. Here the sperm reside until mixed with the fluids and mucus provided by the prostate and seminal vescicle glands. They are thence expelled during ejaculation through the urethra.

The prostate gland secretion is a milky alkaline substance which counteracts the uric acid which has passed through the urethra previously and would be destructive to the sperm. The teaspoon of semen which is expelled contains from 200 to 500 million sperm but the bulk of the semen is the fluids provided by the glands.

The purpose of these fluids is to provide a conveyance for the sperm

[5] See Ziegel and Blarcom, *op. cit.,* pp. 40–41.

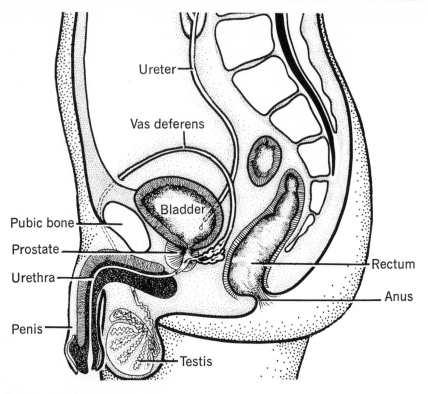

FIGURE 14. *The Male Sex Organs.* SOURCE: Adapted from *Biology,* 2nd ed., by Alfred M. Elliott, and Charles Ray, Jr., assisted by Edward L. Davis (New York, Appleton-Century-Crofts, 1965), p. 656.

and to activate the sperm into whipping-lashing movement. Up to this point the sperm are moved along their way by muscular action but in order to reach an egg in the fallopian tube they must be self-mobile. Mention should be made of *Cowper's glands* located where the vas deferens empty into the urethra. They too secrete a lubricant which facilitates the sperm's progress.

THE PROCESS OF CONCEPTION

For a new being to be conceived it is necessary for one live sperm to meet and penetrate one live ovum.[6] This appears simple but there are places

---

[6] There may be an exception here on rare occasions. See R. R. Race, *Medical News* (British), Vol. 128 (1965), p. 18. Dr. Race, head of the Medical Research Council Blood Research Unit in London, claims that dispermy can exist as a condition whereby two sperms apparently arrive at the egg at exactly the same moment, and both enter the egg. The two sperms need not come from the same man.

Race suggests that individuals born in such fashion would tend to possess two

where the sperm in its circuitous journey can encounter mortal danger. The ovum too is subject to blockades in its path or conditions which are lethal.

Follow the route of the sperm on the diagram in Figure 14 from the sperm factory, the testes and epididymis, into the pin-sized channels of the vas deferens, stored for a time in the ampulla and then through the urethra.

During ejaculation in intercourse the sperm are deposited in the vagina and cervix. All this transportation has been provided by muscular activity. Now the sperm through its own efforts must move into the uterus, through its cavity, and enter the fallopian tubes. The meeting with the ovum will ordinarily take place in the fallopian tube. We have already mentioned the minute size of the tube openings into the uterus.

The ovum which has been ripened bursts from the blister (grafian follicle) on the ovary and is set free. It should be picked up by the finger-like projections of the fallopian tube and there meet the sperm. The ovum is sometimes lost in the body cavity and there disintegrates. Only one sperm will penetrate the ovum. The instant a sperm head penetrates the covering of the ovum the tail drops off. The covering of the ovum becomes impenetrable to all other sperms.

Period of Fertility

The timetable for this meeting is a close one. It will vary from individual to individual as to exact time but the time span is similar. The ovum is released about the ninth to the thirteenth day as counted from the first day of the last menstrual period. Unless it is penetrated by a sperm it dies and disintegrates. The time of its viability is still subject to conjecture but may be as short as twelve hours or as long as two days. Sperm are thought to retain some motility for as long as twenty-four hours after they are ejaculated and to maintain their fertilizing power for as long as forty-eight hours after entering the genital tract. We see that survival for a sperm and an ovum depends on their meeting and fusing.

Infertility

A disappointment which plagues about one out of ten married couples is their inability to conceive children. Great inroads have been made on the problem by medical science and numerous couples have found help. Some couples may be temporarily unable to conceive. Other couples are found to be permanently sterile. Probably 10 to 15 percent of married couples fall

---

different kinds of blood as revealed by genetic characteristics. He reports that the council has established the existence of dispermy in four human beings. While Dr. Race does not suggest that any of the four may have had two fathers, he does report his own belief that many individuals must have had two fathers over the span of man's long tenure on earth.

into this category.[7] The husbands are found to be the cause in about one third of the cases. If the couple is seriously interested in remedying the situation both husband and wife will be cooperative in submitting to the fact-finding tests.

Sound and advisable behavior for a couple which has been unable to effect a pregnancy in a long period of time is to seek out an infertility clinic or a specialist in gynecology. Of those couples who come to such clinics about one fourth to one third of them have conditions which are remediable. The couples' efforts ultimately result in pregnancies. If couples are found to be permanently sterile they can begin to orient their way of life to a childless home or initiate adoption procedures.

Signs of Pregnancy

When an ovum and sperm have transcended all difficulties and successfully united, changes take place in the mother's body. The signs and symptoms of pregnancy are classified into three groups:

1. *Presumptive*. These are subjective in character and may be experienced at various periods. Included are cessation of menses, changes in the breasts, disturbances in urination, and morning sickness, among others.
2. *Probable*. Among these are enlargement of the abdomen, changes in the cervix or in the size and shape of the uterus, and positive hormonal tests.
3. *Positive*. These are usually detected only after the fourth month. Included in this group are x-ray of the fetal skeleton, movements of the fetus which can be felt, and hearing and counting of the fetal heartbeat.[8]

Tests of Pregnancy

Various hormonal tests have commonly been used since the late twenties to verify suspicions of pregnancy. First female mice or rabbits were used; later toads, frogs, and rats. With use of these animals inaccuracy rates of 3 to 5 percent are common. A recent test, the U.C.G., which is based on the principle of hemagglutination inhibition, has appeared.[9] This test is simple in that routine laboratory procedures only are involved. Inaccuracy rates are reported to be slightly lower than those which require laboratory animals.

Usually there is no great urgency to establish pregnancy on the part of the married couple, and most wait out the several months to diagnose with the usual signs.

[7] Abraham Stone, "World Conference on Human Infertility," *Marriage and Family Living,* Vol. 15 (August, 1953), pp. 231–233.

[8] Eastman and Hellman, *op. cit.,* Chapter 9.

[9] A. L. Southam, *et al.,* "Evaluation of a Rapid Immonologic Test for Pregnancy," *American Journal of Obstetrics and Gynecology,* Vol. 85 (February, 1963), pp. 495–499.

Gestation Period

The period of growth from fertilized ovum to full-term, delivered child is frequently termed the *gestation period*. The length of time required from fertilization to birth is 270 to 280 days, ten lunar months or nine calendar months. Expectant mothers are usually supplied with a tentative date by their doctors. However, to expect prompt action on that particular date is only to leave oneself open to disappointment. The length of pregnancies will vary and termination may come a few days earlier or later than anticipated. Neither of these variations is unusual and is certainly not to be considered abnormal. The period of pregnancy is frequently divided into three parts or stages, namely germinal, embryonic, and fetal.[10]

Germinal Stage.   This is the shortest of the periods lasting about two weeks. Following fertilization the ovum continues down the fallopian tube toward the uterus. Fertilization usually takes place high in the tube near the ovary. The journey through the tube takes from three to seven days. When the *zygote* (as the fertilized ovum may be called) reaches the uterus it remains unattached for a few days. The single fertilized cell has already begun to divide but changes little in size. After several days the zygote literally ingests some of the uterine wall and becomes imbedded and in a fixed position. Cell division continues at a rapid rate and the zygote becomes encased in an amniotic sack filled with *amniotic fluid* (commonly termed bag of waters). This protective system will insure the growing child against bumps, shocks, changes of temperature, and so forth. Some of the cells which have developed become the placenta, some the umbilical cord, and some the fetus. These three form a unit and are not a part of the mother. We will consider what happens to the placenta and umbilical cord when we discuss the birth process.

The *placenta,* when fully developed, is a plate-shaped organ weighing about a pound, is seven to nine inches across and about an inch thick in the center. On the side attached to the uterus are many *villi* which penetrate the uterine tissues. Through these villi will pass the food and oxygen supply necessary for the growth of the fetus. There is no interchange of blood between fetus and mother. Each maintains its own blood system independently. The food and oxygen are transferred from the maternal blood through the membrane of the villi to the fetal blood by the osmotic process. Waste from the fetus is handled in reverse order from fetal blood to maternal blood and then excreted by the mother with her own waste. The fetus is attached to the placenta by the *umbilical cord*. The blood vessels in the villi converge to form two large arteries and a vein which run through the umbilical cord to the fetus.

[10] King and Showers, *op. cit.,* p. 433.

At the end of the germinal period the developing organism is about one fouth of an inch in length. Except to the expert it would not be distinguishable as a human embryo. Organs have started to form but this will be accomplished to a greater degree in the next stage of development.

Embryonic Stage.   The embryonic stage lasts from the end of the two-week germinal period until the beginning of the third month. This is roughly a six-week period. Gesell refers to this period as a period of "structural organization." [11] In a brief span of six weeks the embryo attains a length of one inch. It has rudimentary arms, legs, and fingers. The muscles begin to form. The heart, lungs, and kidneys are distinguishable. The heart begins to beat about the fourth week. Facial features such as eyes, ears, and mouth are apparent. The external genital organs appear but are difficult to identify. The basic systems are present but incomplete. By the end of the eighth week the head has increased in size to the point where it is almost as large as the rest of the body.

Fetal Stage.   From the third month to the end of the ninth month or birth the term *fetus* is used in referring to the unborn child. This is the finishing period. It is a time for greater differentiation of structure and function. By the end of the fourth month the heartbeat can usually be heard through a stethoscope and the mother may be able to feel the quickening as the child moves about. This is more apparent to the mother carrying her second child. This is probably due to the early fluttering movements which can easily be mistaken for gas rumblings by the woman who has never experienced them before. The fetus is about six to eight inches long and weighs about six ounces. Eye lashes and eyebrows appear. At the end of five months weight has increased to a pound, fingernails are apparent, and hair has appeared on the head. Should the fetus be expelled at this time it could not survive.

The next three months are marked by a good increase in weight. If the fetus were born at the end of the seventh month it could survive with special care. Chances for survival are greatly increased with each passing week. The baby gains 50 percent of its birth weight in the last two months.[12]

BIRTH PROCESS

At the end of the gestation period when the fetus is developed and capable of independent functioning the uterus will expel the fetus. What sets the birth process in motion is not yet understood. It is thought to

[11] Arnold Gesell, *et al., The Embryology of Behavior* (New York, Harper & Row, 1945).

[12] Ziegel and Blarcom, *op. cit.,* Chapter 5.

be some sort of hormonal enzymatic interaction. Several weeks prior to the birth the fetus will usually have assumed a head down position and settle into the birth canal. This dropping or "lightening" as it is sometimes called indicates the birth is approaching. This will also give the mother some relief in breathing and she frequently has a more comfortable feeling. It is not unusual for uterine contractions to occur at this time. They are sometimes mistaken for the onset of labor.

The birth process is usually divided into three stages and is termed *labor*. The first stage (dilation) begins with the first regular uterine contractions. This is the tedious period and lasts about thirteen to sixteen hours for first babies but is somewhat shorter for subsequent deliveries. The labor pains or contractions are rhythmic contractions of the uterus which feel like abdominal cramps. The early contractions are usually light and twenty to thirty minutes apart. As time goes on they become more regular, more frequent, and more intense. The contractions serve to push the head of the fetus against the cervix causing it to thin and dilate. Toward the end of the pregnancy the cervix will have dilated some but complete dilation to about

FIGURE 15. *Before the Onset of Labor—Full Term.* SOURCE: Reproduced with permission from the *Birth Atlas* published by Maternity Center Association, New York City.

FIGURE 16. *In Labor, Cervix Dilating.* SOURCE: Reproduced with permission from the *Birth Atlas* published by Maternity Center Association, New York City.

a four-inch opening is necessary. The pressure exerted by the contractions will force the amniotic sac (bag of waters) to protrude through the cervix. It may rupture, releasing the amniotic fluid through the vagina. A bloody show is discharged from the vagina. This is composed of mucus and some blood from the capillary ruptures in the cervix. The timetable for these events will vary with the individual.

When the cervix is completely dilated the second stage of labor (expulsion) begins. This is the moving of the fetus down the birth canal and the expelling of same. This period lasts about an hour although this may vary again and is usually shorter with a second delivery. This stage is truly labor. During this time the mother can assist the progress by "bearing down" with the contractions. In about 95 percent of births the baby will emerge head first. In the other 5 percent the feet or buttocks will emerge first. It is sometimes possible for the attending physician to turn the baby in the uterus by manipulation externally or internally through the vagina. When the head appears the rest of the body is expelled quickly. This is the end of the second phase. When the umbilical cord which is still attached to the baby and the mother stops pulsating it is tied in two places and severed

FIGURE 17. *Head Deep in Birth Canal, Cervix Dilated.* SOURCE: Reproduced with permission from the *Birth Atlas* published by Maternity Center Association, New York City.

between the ties. The baby is now an independent organism and must breathe, eat, digest, and excrete for itself.

The third (placental) stage of labor is short, lasting ordinarily up to thirty minutes. This is the expulsion of the placenta and umbilical cord both of which have served their purpose and are now excess baggage. The placenta pulls away from the wall of the uterus and is expelled through the birth canal. It is called the "afterbirth." The large blood vessels of the uterus which supplied the placenta are now exposed, open ends. The uterus contracts strongly, squeezing the ends of the blood vessels together to stop bleeding. It is now routine procedure to administer hormones which aid in loosening the placenta and produce prolonged contraction of the uterus.

Mention should be made of the use of forceps. At one time this type of delivery was clearly the exception. Now it is almost routine with some obstetricians, even though it is still classed as an operative delivery. Indications for the use of forceps are those relating to the condition of the baby and those relating to the condition of the mother. Involved causally are poor contractions of the uterine muscles, toxemic circulatory disease, and

FIGURE 18. *Head Emerges—Body Will Follow Quickly.* SOURCE: Reproduced with permission from the *Birth Atlas* published by Maternity Center Association, New York City.

exhaustion. Signs of fetal distress, such as changes in the rhythm or rate of fetal heartbeat, are used to determine forceps use as far as the baby is concerned.

A Caesarean section is called for in certain cases. The most common primary indications are cephalopelvic disproportion and antepartum bleeding.[13] The latter often involves the placenta's loosening too soon and/or coming previous to the baby. An incision is made through the abdomen and uterus and the child and afterbirth are lifted from the uterus. Caesarean sections are more hazardous than normal vaginal deliveries. They are however, increasingly accepted by the medical profession. A recent study indicates that some 5 percent of the deliveries in a sample of metropolitan hospitals were of this type.[14]

Puerperium Period

The *puerperium period* (period of recuperation) lasts about six weeks. In this time the genital organs return to nearly their original size and shape.

[13] Eastman and Hellman, *op. cit.,* pp. 1182, 1183.
[14] *Ibid.*

If the attending physician's instructions for exercise, diet, and rest are followed the new mother need not suffer from overweight or protruding abdomen. The first menstrual period following delivery signals a return to a pre-pregnancy state. It is again possible to conceive and start the whole cycle over again. The return of the monthly periods varies but is accomplished in three or four months in the nonnursing mother. Usually menstruation does not resume during the lactation period but it can occur. The obstetrician will conduct a thorough examination about six to eight weeks after delivery to determine the condition of the genital organs and check for any infections. A good bill of health at this time indicates complete physical recovery and the couple can feel free to engage in sexual intercourse.

Lactation Period

The first substance produced by the breasts is called *colostrum*. This is a thin watery liquid with slight laxative properties. Colostrum seems to have a beneficial effect on the baby's digestive tract. From two to five days after the birth the breasts begin producing milk. If the mother chooses to breast feed her baby the sucking will stimulate the production of milk and the supply will continue for many months. If the mother does not nurse her baby the breasts will soon cease to produce milk. It is possible also for the physician to prescribe drugs for the discouraging of the milk-producing function. The decision to nurse her baby should be made by the woman in consultation with her doctor and her husband. We will not pretend to give advice or persuasion on this moderately controversial point.

PREGNANCY FAILURE

Not all pregnancies result in full-term babies. *Abortion* is the term used by the medical profession to indicate the termination of a pregnancy before the fetus is capable of sustaining life. This is generally accepted as the beginning of the seventh month.

The term abortion has various—sometimes unpalatable—connotations. There are three recognized types or classes of abortion. The *criminal abortion* is an illegal termination of an undesired pregnancy.[15] The operation is often performed by an unscrupulous doctor, or an unskilled person with attendant risk from infection or a poorly executed operation. The *therapeutic abortion* is the termination of a pregnancy in order to preserve the life or health of the mother. This operation is performed only after professional considerations indicate the operation is warranted. It is performed

[15] See Robert Hall, "Therapeutic Abortion, Sterilization, and Contraception," *American Journal of Obstetrics and Gynecology,* Vol. 91 (February, 1965), pp. 518–532 for a thorough, recent study of therapeutic abortions in some sixty leading hospitals. He makes the point that many indications are being used which are not within the specific intent of the law.

in the aseptic conditions of a hospital with skilled surgeons in attendance and good postoperative care. The *spontaneous abortion* occurs without operative interference. The termination of a pregnancy in this manner is termed by the layman as a "miscarriage."

About one out of ten pregnancies ends in spontaneous abortion. Approximately one third of these are due to abnormal fetuses according to Greenhill.[16] What is a disappointment at the time may be considered a blessing in disguise. Abnormalities in the reproductive system are responsible for some abortions and in some cases no apparent cause can be determined. Threatened abortions can sometimes be averted. Vaginal bleeding and cramping during pregnancy are danger signals and not to be considered inconsequential. Physicians may prescribe rest and administer vitamin E and hormones such as thyroid, estrone, and progesterone.

MULTIPLE BIRTHS

Couples who find themselves the parents of twins might well wonder what happened. In these days of modern obstetrics most couples have been made aware of the possibility of multiple births before the expected date of delivery. The physician through various signs obvious to him such as being able to detect two heart beats, is able to give warning of the plural "blessed event." After the first surprised shock, parents are usually excited and proud at the prospect of twins.

What are the statistical probabilities of having twins? Lentz quotes the following figures for multiple births in the United States as of 1954. "Twins are born once in 85 births; triplets, one in 7,000; quadruplets, one in 50 million; and quintuplets, one in 57 million." [17] Aside from the strictly statistical probability of having twins, young couples who can point to twins in the wife's family have a greater probability of producing twins themselves.

Twins come in two varieties. About one third of all twins born are of the identical type. The other two thirds are fraternal twins. The explanation of the two types of twins lies in their origin. The identical twins are the product of a single fertilized ovum which early in its development splits and forms two individuals rather than one. Identical twins are always of the same sex and because of their single egg and single sperm origin have exactly the same genotype or inheritance. This is the fact which makes them

---

[16] J. P. Greenhill, *Obstetrics in General Practice* (Chicago, The Year Book Medical Publishers, 1948), p. 77. David Carr, *Obstetrics and Gynecology,* Vol. 26 (1965), p. 308 reports that gross chromosome abnormalities are more than fifty times more common in a series of spontaneous abortions studied than they are reported to be in regular live-born babies.

[17] John Lentz, "Two for One," *Today's Health,* Vol. 26 (September, 1958), pp. 26–27, 69.

so desirable as subjects for genetic and environmental studies. Despite their genotypic likeness their phenotypes may differ somewhat and this makes it possible for those closely associated with them to easily distinguish them from each other. Fraternal twins are the results of two ova being released at the same time from the ovary and being fertilized by two sperms. Both fertilized eggs implant themselves in the lining of the uterus and develop as a single pregnancy would. Fraternal twins are no more alike than any other two siblings in the family except for their sharing of the same small apartment for nine months and birthdate. Fraternal twins can be of the same or different sex. Their coloring can be as different as day and night and it is not unusual to see quite a difference in body type. All of these differences point to the individuality of their respective beginnings, separate eggs and sperms. According to Lentz older women are more likely to produce twins or multiple births than younger women.[18]

PRENATAL INFLUENCES

Some cursory attention should be given to a number of factors which can adversely affect or influence the prenatal environment. In explaining the protective system which develops to enfold the fetus during its development we noted the carefully controlled temperature, the chemical balance, and the protective amniotic bag and fluid. The most vulnerable point of attack on the fetus appears to be via the placenta and umbilical cord. Although as noted there is no crossing of blood supplies between the mother and the child it is possible for certain chemical substances to cross the barrier in the same manner that oxygen and food supply do. We shall mention briefly four divisions of maternal conditions which may affect the unborn child.

Maternal Malnutrition

Severe malnutrition of the mother is a general condition which can affect the food supply of the fetus and therefore affect its development. In such case the lack of proper food supply may result in retarded development, deformity, or abortion. In the reports of a study made in Italy in 1945 on 680 women it was found that there was a definite increase in stillbirths, abortions, toxemias, and other complications.[19] A study was made in Toronto, Canada using a sample of clinic maternity patients whose diets

[18] *Ibid.*
[19] Emma Kyhos, *et al.,* "Effects of Malnutrition Upon Mothers and Infants in Naples, 1945," *American Journal of Digestive Diseases* (December, 1949), pp. 436–441. This was of course a time of poor diet and starvation rations for the general population in Italy due to the ravages of World War II.

were known to be inadequate.[20] Some of the women were given supplemented diets. This control group continued for the whole period of pregnancy on their usual inadequate diets. The two groups were compared on a number of points. The babies born to the mothers of more adequate diet had better health records during the first two weeks after birth and also fewer incidences of major illnesses such as pneumonia, rickets, anemia, and ills such as colds, bronchitis, etc. during the first six months of life. It must be stressed that if the carefully prescribed diet, any principles which the physician will give his patient, are followed, there is little danger from this situation.

Emotional State

We have stressed the complete separation of the blood systems of the fetus and mother. The same separateness is true of the nervous systems. There is, however, a direct way that the mother's emotional state can affect the fetus. It is held that such emotions as rage, fear, and anxiety result in the release of excess amounts of chemicals into the blood stream by certain glands, especially the adrenals. These chemicals can pass through the placenta and enter the fetal blood stream.[21]

Sontag of Fels Research Institute has done considerable research in this area of fetal environment.[22] He has reported his findings in numerous articles. Sontag has established that an excess of hormones released during an emotional disturbance in the mother is upsetting to the fetus. The fetus responds to this chemical imbalance by greatly increased muscular activity. Sontag noted that such increase ran as high as several hundred percent and such increased activity lasted as long as the emotional disturbance in the mother continued. He further believes that long periods of emotional strain can have a prolonged effect on the child. To bear out this premise it is noted that children born to emotionally disturbed women weigh less and are inclined to have high activity levels. He states:

Such an infant is from the beginning a hyperactive, irritable, squirming crying child, who cries for his feeding every two or three hours, instead of sleeping through his four-hour feeding period. Because his irritability affects control of his gastrointestinal tract, he empties his bowels at unusually frequent intervals, spits up half his feedings and generally makes a nuisance of himself. He is to all intents and purposes a neurotic infant when he is born—the result of an unsatisfactory fetal environment.[23]

[20] J. H. Ebbs, et al., "The Influence of Improved Prenatal Nutrition Upon the Infant," Canadian Medical Association Journal (January, 1942), pp. 6–8.

[21] Gladys Schultz, "The Uninsulated Child," Ladies Home Journal (June, 1956), p. 61.

[22] L. Sontag, "The Significance of Fetal Environmental Differences," American Journal of Obstetrics and Gynecology, Vol. 41 (December, 1941), pp. 996–1003.

[23] L. Sontag, "War and the Fetal-Maternal Relationship," Marriage and Family Living, Vol. 6 (Winter, 1944), pp. 3, 4.

Maternal Disease

There are several maternal diseases now known to have adverse effects on the unborn fetus. German measles (rubella) although not a serious disease for the mother has been found to be a villain in its attack on the embryo.[24] During the second world war some alert physicians in Australia noticed the coinciding epidemic of rubella and the unusual number of birth anomalies in newborn infants some months later. Rubella is particularly devastating in the embryonic period or the first two months of pregnancy. This period was previously referred to as that of "structural organization." So much development of the various organs takes place in this brief span of time that it is a particularly vulnerable period. If rubella is contracted by the mother at this time the organ or organs which are at their peak of development will be arrested and there is no time to catch up. For example if the viruses from the mother enter the embryo at the peak of development of the visual system the child may be born blind or with impaired vision. Babies who have encountered this disturbing element in their prenatal environment during the embryonic period may be born with blindness, deafness, heart lesions, or mental deficiency. The effects of German measles have been well publicized. Pregnant women are happy to be able to relate a case of rubella in childhood to their obstetricians and the doctors are just as relieved to include it in the case histories. Mothers are becoming aware of the desirability of their daughters' having a fully diagnosed case of German measles before they are married and ready to have families. It is one of those diseases for which a strong case of deliberate exposure can be made.

In times past syphilis was one of the most important infections of the fetus. In fact it was at one time responsible for as many as one third of the fetal deaths in major hospitals. Today, however, syphilis plays a minor role as an etiologic factor in fetal deaths.[25] The effect of fetal syphilis is concentrated largely on the lungs, liver, spleen, and long bones.

On rare occasions the placental barrier does not screen other maternal diseases. There have been cases where infants were born suffering from such infectious diseases as smallpox, chickenpox, mumps, or measles which were contracted from the infected mother prior to birth. It must be stressed that this is a rare occurrence.

Drugs and Narcotics

It has been established that along with the nutrient substances and metabolic waste of the fetus which permeate the placenta membrane it is

---

[24] Eastman and Hellman, *op. cit.,* p. 1107.
[25] Eastman and Hellman, *op. cit.,* p. 1094.

possible for other substances to get through. Such is the case with some drugs, including alcohol and nicotine.

In an article published in the *Journal of the American Medical Association* reference is made to studies which have been conducted on animals.[26] In these studies the stillbirth rate of animals who were exposed to the nicotine equal to that in twenty cigarettes per day was ten times higher than in animals receiving no nicotine. The amount of nicotine which the fetus receives from a chain-smoking mother has not been determined. It has been determined that the heartbeat rate of the fetus increases when the mother smokes. This does seem to indicate that the toxic products of smoking can and do pass through the placenta.

A recent study of 4,440 postpartum women representing 16,158 pregnancies focused on the relationship between smoking habits and pregnancy outcome. It was found that the incidence of prematurity is greater in smokers than nonsmokers, and that infants born to mothers who smoke were significantly lighter in weight at birth. The rate of abortion was slightly higher among smokers also. There was, on the other hand, no significant increase in stillbirths, major fetus anomalies, or maternal complications.[27]

Narcotics when used by the mother can be carried by the maternal blood and enter the fetal blood system. This has the effect of temporary dysfunctions in the fetus but with no apparent permanent damage. Among newborn infants whose mothers have been given drugs during labor, signs of sedation and respiratory difficulties are sometimes noted. Realization of this factor has caused doctors to be more conservative in their use of drugs during labor and for some mothers to be less demanding of heavy sedation during labor and delivery.

Rh Factor

Brief attention must also be given to the problem of Rh incompatibility between mother and child.[28] Named for its discovery in the Rhesus monkey, hemolytic disease of the fetus and newborn is commonly termed

[26] Staff, "Smoking and Drinking During Pregnancy," *Journal of American Medical Association,* Vol. 154 (January, 1954), pp. 154–186.

[27] Paul Underwood, *et al.,* "The Relationship of Smoking to the Outcome of Pregnancy," *American Journal of Obstetrics and Gynecology,* Vol. 91 (January, 1965), pp. 270–276.

[28] Eastman and Hellman, *op. cit.,* pp. 1073–1094. However, the original Rh concept suggested by Wiener and Landsteiner and also Levine and co-workers has been found to be oversimplified. There is now some confusion in both nomenclature and genetic theory. Most marriage and family textbook explanations are far from adequate, technically speaking. This is understandable. Allen and Diamond, *Erythroblastosis Fetalis* (1957), note that there are forty-nine human blood group factors known. Any attempt then to explain the possible combinations of these which may cause damange to the fetus in one or two simple diagrams is foredoomed from the start. Fortunately Wiener's suggestion that eight combinations of genotypes would account for most of the Rh types has proved to be correct.

erythroblastosis. The disease is typically caused by incompatibility between an Rh negative mother and an Rh positive fetus. Antigens from the fetus enter the blood of the mother. She builds up antibodies which then circulate in the fetal system, having passed through the placenta. Harmless to an Rh negative fetus, the antibodies cause hemolytic disease in the infant who is Rh positive. Isoimmunization of the mother is gradual. It is largely a phenomenon of multiple pregnancies. Roughly 75 percent of those who become sensitized to the point of trouble do so by the fourth pregnancy.

Where the fetus is in apparent danger *in utero,* early delivery may be used, the exact timing of which is controversial. For the infant with hemolytic disease, exchange blood transfusion is used. The decision involves a difficult clinical judgment, and is based primarily on the concentration of antibodies in the mother's blood, and the degree of anemia and jaundice shown in the infant. Fortunately, using modern clinical methods the probabilities of successful outcome preventing serious complications from Rh incompatibility are high.

A number of mysteries still remain in regard to the whole area of human reproduction. A minimum understanding of the process of fertilization, the pregnancy period, and the birth process should be standard for the modern, educated person. Such understanding should enable a person to meet the developmental tasks that obtain at significant periods in his marital career.

SELECTED READINGS

Bowman, Henry, *Marriage for Moderns* (New York, McGraw-Hill, 1960), Chapter 18.

Crow, Lester A., and Crow, Alice, *Child Development and Adjustment* (New York, Macmillan, 1962), Chapter 3.

Dickinson, R. L., and Belskie, Abram, *Birth Atlas* (New York, Maternity Center Association, 1940).

Gebhard, Paul, *et al., Pregnancy, Birth, and Abortions* (New York, Hoeber-Harper, 1958).

Gentry, Elizabeth, "Caring for Mother and Child Before and After," in Becker, Howard, and Hill, Reuben, *Family, Marriage, and Parenthood* (Boston, Heath, 1955), Chapter 15.

Gesell, Arnold, *Infant Development: The Embryology of Early Human Behavior* (New York, Harper & Row, 1952).

Goodrich, Frederick, *Natural Childbirth* (New York, Prentice-Hall, 1950).

Greenhill, J. P., "The Birth of the Baby," in *Modern Marriage and Family Living,* Fishbein, Morris, and Kennedy, Ruby Jo (Eds.) (Fairlawn, N.J., Oxford University Press, 1957), Chapter 28.

Guttmacher, Alan, "Abortions," *Modern Marriage and Family Living,* Fishbein, Morris, and Kennedy, Ruby Jo (Eds.) (Fairlawn, N.J., Oxford University Press, 1957), Chapter 29.

Himes, Norman, and Taylor, Donald, *Your Marriage* (New York, Holt, Rinehart and Winston, 1955).

Hooker, D., *The Prenatal Origin of Behavior* (Lawrence, University of Kansas Press, 1952).

Hutt, Max, and Gibby, Robert, *The Child, Development, and Adjustment* (Boston, Allyn and Bacon, 1959), Chapter 2.

Klein, Robert, and Schuman, B. J., *How to Have a Baby* (Baltimore, Williams & Wilkins, 1951).

Merrill, Francis, *Courtship and Marriage* (New York, Holt, Rinehart and Winston, 1959), Chapter 17.

Miller, Daniel, and Swanson, Guy, *The Changing American Parent* (New York, Wiley, 1958).

Miracle of Growth, The (Chicago, Museum of Science and Industry, and University of Illinois Professional Colleges, University of Illinois Press, 1950).

Mussen, Paul, *et al., Child Development and Personality* (New York, Harper & Row, 1963), Chapter 3.

Peterson, James, *Education for Marriage* (New York, Scribner, 1964), Chapter 15.

Potter, Edith, *Fundamentals of Human Reproduction* (New York, McGraw-Hill, 1948).

Read, Grantly Dick, *Childbirth Without Fear* (New York, Harper & Row, 1953).

Stone, Joseph, and Church, Joseph, *Childhood and Adolescence* (New York, Random House, 1957), Chapters 1 and 2.

QUESTIONS AND EXERCISES

1. Arrange for an obstetrician to discuss childbirth processes with special attention to such things as natural childbirth, hypnosis, and use of anesthetics.

2. Obtain from the local bureau of vital statistics the infant and mother mortality rates. Chart or graph the statistics for a period of years to see if there is a trend.

3. Arrange for the showing of the film, *Labor and Childbirth,* Medical Films Inc. of San Francisco, or some similar film.

4. Read several of the supplemental readings on maternal influences on prenatal environment. Should a woman modify her usual habits such as smoking and drinking during her pregnancy?

5. List, if any, the misconceptions and misinformation you were able to discard following the reading and discussion of this chapter.

6. What is your position on the validity of the so-called "natural childbirth" theories? (See the footnotes and readings.) Defend it.

7. Write a paper on "the problem of therapeutic abortion in the United States."

8. Write a paper on "the role of the midwife in the United States."

9. Analyze the work of the Maternal and Child Health Section of the World Health Organization since its establishment in 1948.
10. To what degree should a courting couple ascertain possible childbirth or genetic problems such as Rh incompatibility, the possibility that both family lines carry hereditary hemophelia, diabetes, and the like? Discuss.
11. Write a paper on the possible relationship between the use of the newer drugs by infertile couples and multiple births.

four

Parents and Children

20

Preschool Family Tasks

With the actual coming of a child the couple no longer is merely a "married pair." A family has emerged. The parents are entering a developmental sequence of childbearing and child rearing which normally is to last over a period of twenty-five years.[1] Even after this twenty-five years has passed there will still be visiting with children and grandchildren and continuing correspondence. Family life is beginning for the couple and it will not end until their deaths.

The infancy and preschool stage is a very busy one. The husband and wife are required to learn the roles of father and mother, and very quickly. If they are typical they will have a second child before the first has entered school. This means that a series of developmental tasks for themselves and for the children will present themselves for urgent consideration. Truly the husband and wife will never again be as carefree as before.

EARLY ADAPTATIONS TO THE NEW SITUATION

A certain degree of disorganization often prevails when the new baby first comes home from the hospital. No longer can the focus be just on the routine going to work and coming home of the husband, with evenings and weekends given over to work around the home and to recreation. The schedule now must revolve around the baby's needs and wants. The home becomes baby-centered rather than husband- or wife-centered as it previously had been.

That many parents find this adaptation to parenthood a crisis should

[1] Paul Glick, "The Life Cycle of the Family," *Marriage and Family Living,* Vol. 17 (February, 1955), pp. 3–9.

perhaps not come as a surprise. While, as has been suggested, this is a child-centered culture, people are not necessarily fully or well prepared for all the demands of parenthood. Young people in previous generations probably had more responsibility in caring for younger siblings than do teen-agers today, especially in the middle and upper classes. One study of a middle-class sample of forty-six couples revealed that 83 percent of them experienced extensive or severe crisis in adjusting to the first child. Some comments from the report of the study are as follows:

The mothers reported the following feelings or experiences in adjusting to the first child: loss of sleep (especially during the early months); chronic "tiredness" or exhaustion; extensive confinement to the home and the resulting curtailment of their social contacts; giving up the satisfactions and the income of outside employment; additional washing and ironing; guilt at not being a 'better' mother; the long hours and seven day and night weeks necessary in caring for an infant; decline in their housekeeping standards; worry over their appearance (increased weight after pregnancy, et. cetera).

The fathers echoed most of the above adjustments but also added a few of their own: decline in sexual response of wife; economic pressure resulting from wife's retirement plus additional expenditures necessary for child; interference with social life; worry about a second pregnancy in near future; and a general disenchantment with the parental role.

The mothers with professional training and extensive professional work experience (eight cases) suffered 'extensive' or 'severe' crisis in every case. In analyzing these cases, it was apparent that these women were really involved in two major adjustments simultaneously: (1) they were giving up an occupation which had deep significance for them; and (2) they were assuming the role of mother for the first time.[2]

This study was replicated by Dyer and the findings confirmed.[3] LeMasters suggests that over-romanticizing parenthood is probably a most important factor in bringing about this state of affairs. If these findings are typical of urban middle-class couples, they point to a need for more thorough preparation for the early adjustments of parenthood than most young people are presently getting. Fortunately LeMasters was able to report that the great majority of the parents apparently made a successful adjustment to parenthood, even though they found the transition a difficult one.

Adapting Emotional Attachments

Whatever the nature of the love relationship between the spouses it will be subjected to test with the advent of the first baby. As virtually every-

---

[2] Ersel LeMasters, "Parenthood as Crisis," *Marriage and Family Living,* Vol. 19 (November, 1957), pp. 352–355. Used by permission.

[3] Everett Dyer, "Parenthood as Crisis: A Restudy," *Marriage and Family Living,* Vol. 25 (May, 1963), pp. 196–201. See also Daniel F. Hobbs, "Parenthood as Crisis: A Third Study," *Journal of Marriage and Family,* Vol. 27 (Aug., 1965), p. 367. In this study findings were in opposition to those of LeMasters and Dyer.

one now realizes, babies need loving. Ribble,[4] Spitz,[5] and others have stressed the tremendous need of the young infant for love and affection. Spitz found that a disease called *marasmus* occurred among young children who received no mothering in hospital wards but were cared for by nurses who engaged in no emotional interchange with the children. These children became apathetic and did not develop normally in the physical, emotional, and social realms. On the other hand, children in similar institutions whose mothers cared for them developed in much superior fashion.

It is now common practice in hospitals for nurses to respond with affection to tiny babies, and parents are encouraged to do the same. Children's home supervisors are also encouraged to place children in foster homes where, hopefully, individual love and attention can be given to them. Compared to the twenties and thirties, great stress is put these days on creating a loving and accepting climate for the well-being of the child.

The reader may ask: "Is this a difficult problem? Do not parents naturally love their children and accept them wholeheartedly?" The answer must be a qualified "no." Hundreds of cases of neglect and nonacceptance of children come to the attention of social workers and child guidance centers every year. In many cases the parents simply are unable to set up an accepting and loving environment sufficient for the demands of the child.

Is it possible to give the child too much love and attention? Here the question must be asked as to the *type* of love and the *conditions* of the love. Levy [6] found that an inadequate love life and/or social life on the part of the mother tended to intensify the mother-child relationship to the point where it was unhealthy. This becomes maternal overprotection or absorption, and it is considered unhealthy for the child. Essentially it can be said that the love between the parents in such cases is neurotic, and the consequent relationship of the child to the parent also tends to develop in some neurotic fashion. Freud comments on the relationship between the love-starved mother and her child in this fashion: "She is over-tender and over-anxious in regard to the child, to whom she transfers her need for love, thus awakening in it sexual precocity." [7]

What is needed is a type of relationship between the parents which can be enlarged to include the new child, without at the same time stifling him or absorbing him. Fortunately many parents are able to do this to at least an acceptable degree. Noteworthy are reports of case after case in which parents risk life, limb, and fortune for the benefit of the child. The little tot arouses positive emotions in a healthy adult by his very nature. The sentiments can soon become stronger and more deep-seated.

[4] Margaret Ribble, *The Rights of Infants* (New York, Columbia, 1943).

[5] Rene Spitz, "The Role of Ecological Factors in Emotional Development in Infancy," *Child Development,* Vol. 20 (September, 1949), pp. 145–155.

[6] David Levy, *Maternal Overprotection* (New York, Columbia, 1943).

[7] Sigmund Freud, "Civilized Sexual Morality and Modern Nervousness," *Collected Papers,* Vol. 2, p. 97.

Sexual Adjustment

After the birth of the child an interval of from four to six weeks will be necessary before the wife may engage in sexual intercourse. By this time the effects of the childbirth experience have been diminished and the wife is ready to enjoy intercourse again.

The Freudians and others make much of the principle that after the birth of a child the wife may be able to participate more freely in sexual intercourse than she had before. By this it is suggested that childbirth hastens biological and psychological maturity. Certainly there is considerable clinical evidence that this is true. Women who have secretly resented men, or who have been emotionally tied to their parents and who have had slight feelings of guilt about sexual activities may find that such feelings are worked out during the pregnancy and birth experience. On the other hand, women with deep-seated sexual anxieties may have their guilt feelings exaggerated by pregnancy and childbirth. In some cases therapy seems to be the only remedy available. Some wives suffering from fatigue and concern about the welfare of the new baby find it difficult to wax enthusiastic about sex.[8] Occasionally the wife is found who discourages her husband well after the birth of the child. Ordinarily a few weeks' time is sufficient to solve the problems which have developed. Wives should be cautioned against playing martyr roles or diverting all their attention to the baby. The baby's needs and wants must be satisfied, and ungrudgingly, if he is to get off to a sound start, but the husband-wife relationship must also be maintained and reactivated if a solid basis for the future family is to be maintained.

Couples with a new child in the home do find that they cannot be quite as free in following their impulses as they previously had been. As a number of writers have pointed out, the baby can break up the most tender embrace. Mature husbands and wives learn to take these interruptions without undue grumbling. The sex drive is strong enough in most cases not to be thwarted by a half hour of baby tending. After a time the parents develop new schedules which parallel those of the youngster and which allow them some precious moments to themselves, even if they must by necessity be around the midnight hour.

With the birth of one child the couple is faced more starkly with the question of future family planning. In terms of possible pregnancy the wife is very vulnerable. An old wives' tale suggests that the wife is "safe" as long as she is nursing a baby. While there seems to be some scientific basis for this supposition, many a wife has found it to be invalid in her case. Both the husband and wife, but especially the wife, will feel more free to have sex relations if conception can be more specifically controlled. It is very important in such cases that the wife receive competent medical advice as

---

[8] Mirra Komarovsky, *Blue-Collar Marriage* (New York, Random House, 1964), Chapter 4.

to the best contraceptive method for the couple at this time. After having one child the couple will usually wish to give attention to the spacing and numbers of future children. Study after study has shown that young people today want two to four children.[9] Statistically, the average interval between births is about two years. Studies of college graduate families indicate that the interval between children increases with subsequent children.[10] No doubt parents attempt to "catch their breath" before embarking on new endeavors. It would seem logical that a year or so should elapse before the new mother is involved in another pregnancy. Just as newly-married couples often want and need a period of time to adapt to each other, so the new parents need a bit of time to experiment with their new parental roles. Full mastery of negative conception control at this point may be extremely helpful.

Physicians are interested in the medical implications of repeated pregnancies in rapid succession. Although experimental evidence is hard to come by, many physicians suggest that a reasonable period of time should elapse after the birth of a baby before a new pregnancy in order to give the mother ample time to recover. In a survey of the attitudes of practicing physicians on this matter, the doctors on the average favored a lapse of twenty-three months between pregnancies.[11] Considering all the factors involved, their attitudes seem realistic.

EXPANDING THE COMMUNICATION SYSTEM

The young husband and wife spend much time, whether they are conscious of it or not, in developing a system of communication. By the time the new baby arrives they have worked out some elementary type of system, satisfactory or not as the case may be. With the advent of a child the system of communication must be changed and expanded. This presents itself as a developmental task of the first order which should not be ignored. Empathic spouses learn to make use of various cues to serve as indices of the needs, wants, and feelings of their partners. Through daily living together they learn to infer meaning from the symbols which are being used by the partner. These symbols may be in the form of words but they also may be in the form of gestures or other types of cues. The old joke about the husband tossing his hat in the door before he enters to test his wife's humor is using one of these unspoken cues in jest. The young couple de-

[9] Charles Bowerman, "Attitude Norms About Optimum Size of Family," *Coordinator,* Vol. 4 (March, 1956), pp. 8–12.

[10] Gerald Leslie, Harold Christensen, and Glenn Pearman, "Studies in Child Spacing," *Social Forces,* Vol. 34 (October, 1955), pp. 77–82.

[11] Alan Guttmacher, "The Attitudes of 3,381 Physicians Toward Contraception and the Contraceptives They Prescribe," *Human Biology,* Vol. 12 (March, 1947), pp. 1–12.

velop a system of symbolic interaction which is meaningful and understandable to them.

Including the Child

An important facet of communication is developing an anticipation or expectancy, that is a preparation to react to stimuli. The psychologists use the term "set" to describe this emotional readiness. Spouses learn to anticipate certain things and to predict what the behavior of the partner will be. The new baby must also learn to develop a "set" or readiness to react which will be proper for his stage of development. He first learns to expect response when he cries. He learns to open his mouth for food. He learns to respond when picked up or approached. He learns very quickly, in effect, some of the elementary forms of communication.

As the child progresses he begins to use more complex cues and gestures and eventually sounds and words to indicate his feeling and thinking. By fifteen months he will often be able to indicate what he wants by pointing and some vocalizing.[12] By twenty-four months he understands much of what is said to him and can use some simple words "with remarkable effectiveness." By three years "his increased ability with, and interest in language help him to be a delightful companion, an interesting group member. His own vocabulary and ability to use language have increased tremendously in most cases. Now he can not only be controlled by language, but he can be entertained and himself can entertain." [13] By age four the toddler can judge to a certain degree the appropriateness of the use of words. It has been found by the Gesell researchers that the four-year-old typically uses bathroom and elimination words accompanied by much silly laughter, an indication that he appreciates the inappropriateness of such usage. Wise parents give attention to the ability of the child to communicate at his particular level and behave accordingly. They realize that the words and gestures they use and the way they use them are going to make deep impressions on the young child. In cases where the family is of subcultural membership the question of the use of the traditional language or dialect enters the picture. Groups such as the Amish use little English around their very young children, hoping in this way that the children will retain some basic features of their way of life. On the other hand, socially mobile parents often try to teach their children to use better language than they, the parents, use. The latter seldom have satisfactory results. Parents have to decide what position they will maintain in regard to the use of dialects, Old World languages, and profanity in the home. They set patterns which the

[12] Frances Ilg, and Louise Ames, *Child Behavior* (New York, Harper & Row, 1955), Chapter 2.

[13] James Bossard and Eleanor Boll, *The Sociology of Child Development* (New York, Harper & Row, 1954), Chapter 9.

child will tend to reflect as he goes out into the world to interact with those outside his home. By the time the child goes to school his basic method of communicating has already been formed. Contrary to an old saying, talk is not cheap. Both individually and as a couple, parents will find it advisable to spend time talking with the child. No longer do we believe it wise that he "be seen but not heard." The child needs both the chance to talk out his anxieties and disgusts and to share the elation of his triumphs and new interests. Besides the opportunity of expressing emotions and feelings the child needs the chance to have his sights raised by communicating with adults. Children can learn much by listening to their parents and other adults around the table and in the living room. They can learn more if they at times can participate rather freely.

Naturally the parents must learn to adapt their conversation to a degree in order to incorporate the child into the picture. New parents sometimes find this a bit difficult to accomplish. The tendency is often to set the level too "high," or to make the opposite error of engaging only in "baby talk" when Johnny is around. A middle course seems most appropriate for all concerned. By the use of the common but less abstract words the parents are able to carry on a meaningful conversation without giving Johnny the feeling of "being left out." This is not to say that the child is always to be included in adult conversation. Some parents seem to think this is necessary. A few get to the position where they give the child the center of the stage anytime he demands it. In our opinion either extreme position is in error, the latter representing the logical extreme of a reaction against the old-fashioned approach. A reasonable approach would seem to suggest that the parents should make it clear to the child that at times the conversation will be adult-centered. While no longer is papa "all," it is good training for adult life to learn to defer at times when it is proper and appropriate.

ADAPTING TO OUTSIDERS

With the coming of a child the couple is also forced to reevaluate its relationship with in-laws and with others outside the immediate family circle. Sometimes in-law problems can develop or be accentuated during this period. Frequently relatives aid the young couple with household duties until the mother is on her feet and able to stand the new routine. Fortunate is the couple which has a grandmother or aunt with the time and interest which enables her to keep the household equilibrium reasonably intact. Relatives often take more interest in the "little things that count" than do servants. When relationships with in-laws have been smooth this help from relatives can be a tremendous boon to the young family. Duvall, in her well-known study of in-law relationships, includes such case excerpts as the following in which the young parents seemed to appreciate very much the aid of their in-laws.[14] "When my child was born my mother could not be with me and although my mother-in-law, who is in business for herself and finds it hard to get away, was at the time needed at home, she came to me and saw me through it all."

"My husband and I have been married five and a half years. At first I resented my mother-in-law. Our first baby was born a year after we were married. She came five hundred miles to help care for me and the baby."

Members of the older generation have experienced the developmental stage the young parents are going through, and they can give valuable aid and counsel. Sussman found evidence of this in his study of help patterns in the middle-class family.[15] Parents are often able to help the young folks "to get started" financially. They frequently provide assistance in purchases of such major items as house, household furnishings, and automobiles. It was brought out that many parents find that indirect giving is more successful than direct giving of subsidies in that it is less likely to induce conflict with the head of the new family.

Conditions change, and each couple has to meet its own problems in its own way and in its own day. Ideas of child rearing which the young people have picked up from college classes and their reading may be quite foreign to what the parents knew. Sussman found that the relationship between the two generations depends to a degree on whether the older parents had been traditional or developmental in their own child rearing practices. As Sussman put it:

Parents who raised their children developmentally, i.e., growing with them as they passed through successive age periods, and who encouraged them to become independent and self-reliant, but to continue affectionate ties with family members, had an easier time in adjusting to their child's marriage status than those who reared their progeny traditionally. Elders in using the latter method tended to keep a strict control over their children, and to retard their emancipation by creating a dependent relationship between them and parents. Upon the children's marriage they had difficulty in severing the emotional ties with them, and as a result were prone to interfere unduly in their married life.

Parents have illustrated these generalizations by the degree of ease or difficulty they have in assuming new roles upon their child's marriage. They who raise their children in a traditional way tend to constantly advise their child, and discourage his independence. Hence, these elders are less apt to recognize that the changed marital status of the child calls for a cessation of control. Their relationships after marriage of the child, as a result, are often marked by discord, frequently caused by their excessive interference into the activities of their child's family. Conversely, parents using a developmental pattern appear to be less insistent during the rearing period that their child invariably accept their advice, and are more likely to encourage him to make

[14] Evelyn Duvall, *In-Laws: Pro and Con* (New York, Association Press, 1954), pp. 94–95.
[15] Marvin Sussman, "The Help Pattern in the Middle Class Family," *American Sociological Review,* Vol. 18 (February, 1953), pp. 22–28.

his own decisions. Thus, they are better prepared to accept his marriage and recognize his independence of them. Furthermore, they refrain from interfering unduly with their married child's activities, hence making for friendlier relationships.[16]

The implications from this study are fairly clear. Parents who are more developmentally oriented are somewhat better able to move along with their children and to allow them further measures of independence. When the children are launched into families of their own the older parents find it easier to grant full independence and not to interfere unduly. If one set of parents is very tradition oriented, or if the marriage partners come from families who differ considerably in cultural background (and are very traditional in orientation) the stage is set for trouble when the grandchild arrives on the scene. This makes it imperative that the young parents work out an agreed-upon formula by which they can develop an acceptable pattern of interaction with the grandparents. Besides conflict which reflects the cultural orientation of the grandparents is that which reflects personality and role conflicts on the part of one or both grandparents. If the grandparents are the type whose focus was on their children, it may be very difficult for them not to reassert this focus on new grandchildren. Most authors stress the overprotective mother as against the father, but either sex can find it possible to go overboard in a relationship with a grandchild in attempting to fill an emotional void. Where such is the case ingenuity on the part of the young parents will be called for.

Besides relating to in-laws the new parents must now readapt some of their familiar patterns of interaction with the general community. Even with one child, social, religious, and recreational pursuits take on a different tone. The problem of adequate baby-sitting will be immediately faced. Some couples are fortunate to have built-in baby sitters available in the form of willing relatives or friends. While the Sussman study shows that there are a greater percentage of such arrangements still in existence than most of us would have believed, many couples will not be so situated that relatives are available.

The possibilities in baby-sitting will vary with the neighborhood. At best the expense is a severe handicap for young parents. Competent sitters are often scarce. Fortunately young couples are able to find perhaps one or two acceptable high school girls or widows who do not overcharge. Some couples are experimenting with cooperative arrangements which seem to hold considerable promise. In most societies and in most times the paid "baby-sitter" as we know her did not exist. Children usually were cared for by relatives at times when the parents were away from them. It would appear that, if they were willing to do.so, young couples could act as substi-

[16] Marvin Sussman, "Family Continuity: Selective Factors Which Affect Relationships Between Families at Generational Levels," *Marriage and Family Living,* Vol. 16 (May, 1954), p. 116.

tute relatives in sharing mutual burdens of child care in order to allow each other some badly needed time off. Some of the problems involved in this type of plan are obvious. Essentially, such plans involve a concept of local community and neighborhood life which seems to have vanished in urban middle- and upper-class circles. Whether the individual couple can find neighboring couples willing to cooperate is something it will be forced to find out by trial and sometimes, unfortunately, by error.

Couples with young children will sometimes feel that a conspiracy exists against them in community institutions, including even the church. It is difficult to understand the naivete which is exhibited by some religious leaders who wonder why all the young families have disappeared.[17] An examination of local church practices will show that many of them really discourage participation by families as families. For those who wish to participate in church and community activities, persistence in insisting on arrangements for families in all stages will often help not only the particular couple but many others as well. Few couples can isolate themselves fully and completely from the community without harm to themselves, to say nothing of the concomitant loss to the community.

REWORKING THE PHILOSOPHY OF LIFE AND DEVELOPING

Adequate Training and Socializing Procedures

With the coming of the child the value system or philosophy of life of the couple becomes increasingly significant. As the couple will soon realize, inconsistencies, dilemmas, and differences between the parents on basic goals will become increasingly apparent when the task of training the youngster is actually faced. In the formal language of social science the training process in all its aspects is termed *socialization*. All agree that the socialization of the child is one of the most crucial tasks faced by the family. Recent research has shown that many young parents are confused as to how they will approach the manifold tasks involved in socializing their children. Living in a day when many traditional value systems are under attack, they are uneasy as to how they wish to do it. That such is the case should perhaps come as no surprise to students of contemporary society or to those who have studied the development of parent education. Sensitive policy-makers in charge of the various institutions in most modern communities will usually be found to exhibit doubts and anxieties about their policies. Why should sensitive parents be expected to be much different?

Unfortunately the experts have not been in agreement on goals and

[17] Regina Wieman, *The Modern Family and the Church* (New York, Harper & Row, 1937), Chapter VIII. See also Roy Fairchild and John Wynn, *Families in the Church* (New York, Association Press, 1961).

techniques of child rearing during the past few decades. Traditional methods of handling children came under severe attack by Watson and his fellow behaviorists during the twenties.[18] The Watsonians stressed an objective approach by which children were to be treated as young adults. Stress was put on order and scheduling, with the goals to be defined by the parents. A developmental approach appeared in the thirties and forties which stressed a child-centered permissiveness. This newer approach has held sway among many child psychologists, public educators, and parent educators down to the time that this is being written. There is some evidence that some modifications are appearing here and there among parent advisors, but as a whole the developmental position is still accepted.

Duvall has done pioneering research regarding conceptions of child rearing.[19] She used the following questions with a sample of mothers: What is a good mother? What is a good child? On the basis of these questions she found that their answers fell into two rather clear-cut categories, *traditional* and *developmental*. Traditional conceptions of motherhood include making the child "good," training the child physically and to regularity, keeping house, and disciplining. From such a program the child is supposed to learn to work well, be religious, neat and clean, obey and respect adults, and fit into the program of the family. Developmental approaches, on the contrary, emphasize the mother's role in guiding the child with understanding and love, training him for citizenship and self-reliance, helping him develop emotionally and socially, while at the same time remaining a calm and growing person in her own right. From such an approach the child is expected to be happy and contented, to share and cooperate, to love and confide in his parents, develop health and well-being, and grow as a person.

As yet the relationship between the conceptions parents hold of child rearing and what they actually do in practice is not clear.[20] The inference is that the more traditionally oriented will make more use of the so-called old-fashioned methods of child rearing than will the developmental. Not only will their techniques differ somewhat, but their basic end goals will differ. Essentially they are concerned with the adaptation by the child to the norms and standards of the adult world, and this as quickly as possible. The developmental approach has adult standards in the background. Stress is on the needs of the child and his orderly development.

Connor, Johannis, and Walters made a study in which fathers, mothers, and adolescents were asked to indicate their conceptions of the good father and the good mother. Their responses reveal the dichotomy

[18] John Watson, *Psychological Care of Infant and Child* (New York, Norton, 1928).

[19] Evelyn Duvall, "Conceptions of Parenthood," *American Journal of Sociology,* Vol. 52 (November, 1946), pp. 193–203.

[20] At the time of this writing the author does not know of any studies which compare the rankings of parents on the traditional-developmental continuum with their actual, day-by-day practices in child rearing.

between the traditional and developmental role conceptions rather neatly, as can be seen in Tables 36 and 37.

TABLE 36

Typical Responses of Respondents Revealing Traditional and Developmental Conceptions of a Good Father

Respondent	Conceptions of Traditional Role	Conceptions of Developmental Role
Father	1. Provides adequate financial support	1. Helps provide a harmonious home atmosphere
	2. Teaches the child right from wrong	2. Cultivates the child as a pal
	3. Is active in church and makes children active in church	3. Spends as much time as possible with the children when home
	4. Furnishes good advice	4. Keeps in touch with school and community as they relate to child growth
	5. Sets an example; is the man in the family	5. Helps with the household duties
Mother	1. Is a good provider	1. Builds up wholesome family relationships
	2. Corrects the children when they are at fault	2. Tries to follow interests displayed by the child
	3. Provides a religious background	3. Includes the child in social activities in which the parents participate
	4. Provides for the child's education	4. Is loving and kind and interested in the children's personal problems
	5. Sets a good moral example	5. Strives to understand the child's point of view
Adolescent	1. Provides enough money for the family to live comfortably	1. Shares in the development of the child
	2. Is responsible for the discipline of the children	2. Gains a close relationship with children and mother
	3. Provides material security	3. Considers the child's problems as serious as he does his own
	4. Gives wise advice	4. Does not teach by threatening, fear, or distrust
	5. Sets a good example	5. Does his share of the household tasks

SOURCE: Adapted from Ruth Connor, Theodore Johannis, Jr. and James Walters, "Parent-Adolescent Relationships," *Journal of Home Economics,* Vol. 16 (March, 1954), p. 189.

TABLE 37

Typical Responses of Respondents Revealing Traditional and Developmental Conceptions of a Good Mother

Respondent	Conceptions of Traditional Role	Conceptions of Developmental Role
Father	1. Keeps the home properly	1. Gives the child of her time in way the child wishes
	2. Teaches daughter home-making	2. Educates the children to think independently
	3. Is a good cook and house-keeper	3. Leads the family into co-operative planning
	4. Teaches the child religion	4. Helps the father understand the daughter
	5. Provides wholesome meals	5. Has outside interests, PTA etc.
Mother	1. Tries to teach children proper manners	1. Attempts to understand the child and his needs
	2. Puts family needs and welfare ahead of her own	2. Builds up wholesome family relationships
	3. Cooks good healthy meals	3. Shares and cooperates with the child
	4. Teaches religious values	4. Strives to understand the child's point of view
	5. Sets a good example	5. Aids in civic ventures for betterment of community
Adolescent	1. Cares for the house and cooks	1. Respects children's feelings and listens to their troubles
	2. Is a good wife and mother	2. Plays and has fun with children
	3. Keeps the house neat and clean	3. Allows children to share family pleasures and responsibilities
	4. Teaches children right from wrong	4. Provides children with plenty of love and affection
	5. Is a good example	5. Tries to keep up with current times and ideas

SOURCE: Adapted from Ruth Connor, Theodore Johannis, Jr. and James Walters, "Parent-Adolescent Relationships," *Journal of Home Economics,* Vol. 16 (March, 1954), p. 189.

What are the effects of holding certain child rearing ideologies or of the use of particular methods of child training on the personalities of the children involved? We have no sure answer to the question. Under the impact of Freudian theories of personality development, pediatricians and other child development specialists began a few decades ago to advocate what are essentially developmental child rearing practices as we have been using the term. Stressed have been breast feeding, late weaning, self-demand rather than scheduling, permissive bladder training, and the like. Research studies have not borne out the assumed relationship between these practices and healthy personality development of the child. Orlansky, after a careful survey of the literature, concludes that "social scientists have failed to produce a definitive answer to the question of the relation between infant disciplines and character development. . . . We are led to reject the thesis that specific nursing disciplines have a specific invariant psychological impact upon the child." [21]

Research studies since Orlansky's survey have as a whole brought no major changes. Sewell, for example, studied a sample of children and parents in Wisconsin. Child rearing practices were related to personality variables. No consistent relationships were found.[22] The author supervised a project in which the thesis that the marital adjustment of the mother would be highly correlated with the personality of the child was tested. No associations between these two variables was found, and the hypothesis had to be rejected.[23] In a follow-up study Burchinal, Hawkes, and Gardner found results in the same direction as our own.[24] What are we to make of this situation? [25] Are we to gather that one type of child training practice is as efficacious as another? This position would be too extreme and of doubtful validity. The suggestion, instead, is that this whole topic is complicated and that further research and careful interpretations are needed.

Sears *et al.*[26] interviewed mothers of kindergarten age children regarding their child rearing practices, the children's behavior reactions, and their feelings about the whole process. After assembling their data on the

[21] Harold Orlansky, "Infant Care and Personality," *Psychological Bulletin,* Vol. 46 (January, 1949), pp. 38–39.

[22] William Sewell, "Infant Training and the Personality of the Child," *American Journal of Sociology,* Vol. 58 (September, 1952), pp. 150–159. See also William Sewell, and Paul Mussen, "The Effects of Feeding, Weaning, and Scheduling Procedures on Childhood Adjustment and the Formation of Oral Symptoms," *Child Development,* Vol. 23 (September, 1952), pp. 185–191.

[23] Atlee L. Stroup, "Marital Adjustment of the Mother and the Personality of the Child," *Marriage and Family Living,* Vol. 14 (May, 1952), pp. 109–113.

[24] Lee Burchinal, *et al.,* "Marriage Adjustment, Personality of Parents and Personality Adjustment of Child," *Marriage and Family Living,* Vol. 19 (November, 1957), pp. 366–372.

[25] It must be noted that Baruch using a clinical approach in her studies, found marital tensions, especially regarding the mother, to be associated with the maladjustment of children. Other clinicians formally and informally report such findings. On the other hand, a recent study reported by Brim, *et al.,* obtained findings in line with our own. (See Orville Brim, *et al.,* "Relations Between Family Problems," *Marriage and Family Living,* Vol. 23 (August, 1961), pp. 219–226). Further careful work needs to be done to check on the discrepancies between the results of these research and clinical studies.

[26] Robert Sears, Eleanor Maccoby and Harry Levin, *Patterns of Child Rearing* (New York, Harper & Row, 1957).

interrelationships between their major variables, they isolated seven major patterns or dimensions through the use of factor analysis:

(a) Permissiveness—strictness
(b) General family adjustment
(c) Warmth of mother-child relationship
(d) Responsible child-training orientation
(e) Aggressiveness and punitiveness
(f) Perception of husband
(g) Orientation toward child's physical well-being [27]

It is suggested by these researchers that the above patterns or dimensions are underlying traits in mothers. Their effects are diffuse. For example, the warmth of the mother-child relationship was found to be more important in arousing disturbance in the child regarding toilet training than the level of severeness of the training. The factor of warmth was also highly (inversely) related to problems of aggression, bedwetting, conscience development, and problems of feeding.

The sex of the child, his ordinal position, and the way he typically perceives phenomena all are important factors. This was brought out in an earlier study by Sears et al.[28] It was found that the effects of punitiveness by the mother were not the same for boys and girls, the girls being more affected than the boys. According to the authors the explanation was to be found in the differences in identification with the mother. Girls identify more closely and therefore are more affected by the mother's punitiveness.

Young parents are forced to choose between competing ideologies of child rearing, whether they are explicitly aware of this fact or not. Once they have taken a general position at this level, specific techniques and practices can be more easily decided upon.

One of the first items demanding attention is that of eating habits. The question of whether to breast or bottle feed, and the question of scheduling of feeding is perplexing to many. While it is impossible to find scientific evidence that breast feeding is superior to bottle feeding, given present-day substitutes for mother's milk, many physicians will encourage it. Most parents cooperate with their physicians on this matter. Either way, stress will be put on the close, warm relationship which is possible when feeding the baby.

The question of permissiveness in feeding is bound to come up. Parents will find that most literature stresses "self-demand" as against rigidity at the present time. Actually some misinterpretation may be involved here. Many pediatricians, by self-demand, do not mean complete lack of sched-

[27] *Ibid.*, Chapter 13.
[28] Robert Sears, *et al.*, "Some Child-Rearing Antecedents of Aggression and Dependency in Young Children," *Genetic Psychology Monographs*, Vol. 47 (1953), pp. 135–234.

ule. Rather, they wish the mother to aid the infant in moving toward his own schedule, which ordinarily he will do fairly rapidly.

The modern attitude on bowel and bladder training is also on the more permissive side. It is held by many child development experts that many middle-class parents cause too much frustration and hostility in the child by early attempts at conditioning. The basis for this thinking has to do with the development of both physical and emotional readiness for training. The child must be able to control the sphincter muscles regulating elimination, and he must wish to attempt to do so. Undue stress on the part of the mother may cause the child to make attempts before he is ready, with corollary development of irritation, guilt, and hostility. Firm but gentle help by the parent, when the child is ready for it, seems to be the best advice available for either bowel or bladder training. Again we are reminded that the attitudes of warmth and acceptance on the part of the mother may be more crucial than the specific timing.

Adjustment of Space Relations and Locations

With the coming of a child the couple is forced to take space and location factors into account. Without children, and especially if the wife is working, the couple may live adequately in a small apartment. With just one child added, "the cute little apartment" may now seem to be the "tight little box" that the family is packed into. Couples are usually amazed at the demands on space which one small child makes. Not only does he require a place to sleep, but he requires much additional equipment, which is also space-consuming.

As the child grows he needs space in which to maneuver. A little child cannot sit still. He needs room in which to explore freely. Often the couple is forced to move to a larger apartment or to adopt makeshift adjustments until it can see the way clear to a larger apartment, rented house, or possibly a future home of its own. Originally the apartment is often chosen on the basis of easy access to the husband's and wife's work or because of its low rent. Such apartments may have undesirable features for child rearing. There may be dangerous steps or windows, open gas heaters, and the like. Unfortunately with the wife unable to work, the young couple may find it financially impossible to move to more adequate quarters until the husband is more solidly established in his occupation. With the trend toward early marriage and early childbearing the housing squeeze on young families is truly significant.

Within the house itself, adjustments taking into account that an active child is around must be made. Here again, the general orientation to child rearing is basic to what the parents will do and how they feel about the situation. In a very provocative study Blood examined the consequences of permissiveness for the parents of young children. Permissive parents had to endure the following to a greater degree than nonpermissive parents:

1. Disturbances of their activities by children's noisiness
2. Lack of parental privacy
3. Damage to living-room furniture
4. Frequent cluttering of living room
5. Difficulty in controlling children's activities [29]

Blood did find that permissive parents make necessary adaptations to the situation through a process dubbed "child proofing." Breakable items are placed out of the child's reach. Expendable, secondhand items are often used. Slipcovers are used for large items of furniture when possible. Emphasis is put on allowing all members of the family to enjoy the living room and other major rooms, not just the adults. If by chance visitors come unexpectedly they are welcomed with little ado or apology. As Blood says ". . . concern about one's own social status is discounted and the emphasis is placed on personality interaction rather than on the symbolic or representational function of the living room. Developmental parents can thus experience with a minimum of embarrassment or guilt a situation which would precipitate a traditionally-oriented parent into a frenzy of apology and attempted remedy." [30]

We see again that the central values and emphases that couples wish to stress in their lives are basic to such mundane items as living-room space. Each couple must make choices as to the type of child-proofing it wishes and the type of limitations on behavior it will require inside specific rooms in the home. This much can be said, however: Small children cannot be expected to exhibit the same type of restraint possible in the adolescent or the adult. Heirlooms, fancy objects, and the like may well be put away until the children have reached an age when they can treat them with the care the parents expect them to receive.

Spending Income

The new person in the household will soon make himself obvious, economically speaking. Money will be needed for additional food, clothing, medicine, doctor bills, etc. What with the wife's being unable to work outside the home as she formerly did, the strain may be great. What can the parents do to make ends meet? Most couples find that some of their previous luxuries must go. Perhaps in their early married life they were accustomed to expensive steaks and to making the rounds of shows and night clubs, expensive parties, and the like. On an average single salary such a

[29] Robert Blood, "Consequences of Permissiveness for Parents of Young Children," *Marriage and Family Living,* Vol. 15 (August, 1953), pp. 209–212.
[30] *Ibid.*

style of life is almost impossible to maintain if children are to be reared properly. To give up some luxuries and recreational pursuits may seem unjust at times, and occasionally the young mother and father may feel that if it were not for baby they would be well off. Such feelings are natural if they are not too frequent, but wise and mature parents will try to put first values first. If they make the choice of having a baby, he must be cared for, no matter what the sacrifice.

It may indeed be fortunate that child-proofing a home involves the use of secondhand furniture equipment as against modern and expensive furniture. If young parents can accept this orientation and live with it, the budget will stretch much farther and the pressure on the child will also not be as great. Many couples with young children have saved enough from their early years of marriage to buy basic equipment and carry themselves when the wife remains home to care for the baby. If they have not been this far-sighted, they may be forced either to borrow or to accept assistance from relatives.

Deciding how much they can reasonably borrow is a task to which young couples may have to devote considerable time. In effect this means assessing the chances for salary raises, taking into account possible inflation or deflation, and hedging against various types of contingencies. Being forced to do this may be of great help to the couple in finally deciding what comes first in their lives, in solving the problem of eventually buying a home as against renting one, for example.

Many, perhaps a majority of young couples, are now making use of installment buying.[31] Competent consumer economists warn that many families are overextending themselves by making commitments which will be most difficult to honor. With experience young couples may learn how difficult it is to make regular, high payments on material objects which have a high rate of depreciation.

Roles and Responsibilities

By the time the first child arrives the average couple will have had a few years' time in which to develop patterns of responsibility and authority

---

[31] Many couples fail to realize the high rate of interest they are paying when they buy on the installment plan. One type of loan used by banks, sales finance companies, and retail sellers involves subtracting the interest charges from the loan at the time it is granted and the borrower repays the full amount at the end of the stipulated period. A person borrows $500 for one year at discount rate of 7 percent. The amount received will be $465. The full $500 is to be repaid at the end of the year. The actual interest paid is about 7½ percent ($35÷$465). Suppose the same $500 is borrowed at the discount rate of 7 percent to be repaid in twelve equal monthly payments. Since the money is being repaid over a year period the borrower has the use of about half the money for the year. The interest rate in this plan is about 15 percent ($35÷$465).

2

within the home. The wife will often have worked outside the home, but with a child needing twenty-four hours per day supervision, attrition of roles becomes obligatory. The couple is pushed into a traditional mold with the husband as provider and the wife as mother and homemaker. Often there is considerable strain involved for couples in making the necessary adaptations. Many middle- and upper-class girls have developed outside-the-home interests and orientations which have led them to devalue homemaking. According to some authorities our educational system has tended to further this process rather than to prepare women intellectually and emotionally to assume primary homemaking responsibilities. Regardless of this, certain responsibilities press. At least when children are young, it will ordinarily be the wife who will have the greatest responsibility within the household itself. Young children require constant care. In spite of the fact that everyone realizes this, many young mothers have reported that they were overwhelmed at first with all the tasks they were required to perform. The feeding and bathing of the baby and laundering of his clothing may seem like enough to keep mother busy most of the day. Add to this the routine of cleaning, cooking, and shopping and one comes up with a very full day's work. Mead suggests that we expect more of our young mothers, despite all their labor-saving devices than has been the case in most traditional societies.[32] In the large, extended family system the grandmother, aunts, and other relatives often assumed the care of the child during the daytime, or helped out with household tasks. It is a great help to the mother if someone can step in today to do so, but under modern conditions this is not often possible. When it isn't, the husband may find it necessary to modify his own program in order to take on certain home tasks, at least temporarily. In some households the tasks of mopping and cleaning and some of the tasks involving heavy lifting are left for the husband for Friday evenings or Saturday afternoons. This is a needed sacrifice, if it allows the wife to retain her health and emotional well-being.

When the husband defines his role as that of provider only, it will be difficult for him to accept new tasks around the house. Especially is this true if he feels that help with household tasks or baby-tending are beneath him. If such is the case, basic discussion between the spouses is called for in order to arrive at some consensus on a new arrangement of responsibility. Fortunately many people are capable of adapting to new situational requirements when it becomes necessary.

As the small child begins to grow he can soon be made a part of the family system of task performance. Learning to dress himself, to pick up toys, and to do other simple tasks is a very important part of his upbringing. The child can quickly observe that work must be done cooperatively if the family is to live happily together. By assigning small but definite tasks

[32] Margaret Mead, "The Contemporary American Family as an Anthropologist Sees It," *American Journal of Sociology,* Vol. 53 (May, 1948), pp. 453–459.

to the young child the parents can make him feel that he is a needed member of an ongoing team. This process can hardly be started too early. It is highly doubtful that many modern parents of the educated classes will be too demanding and require too much too early. They will probably tend to err on the opposite side.

Parents will find that the interrelationship within the home becomes much more complicated with the addition of children. Bossard has demonstrated that this development is not a simple arithmetic one. In what he terms the Law of Personal Interrelationships the principle is stated as follows: "With the addition of each person to a family or primary group, the number of persons increases in the simplest arithmetical progression in whole numbers, while the number of personal interrelationships within the group increases in the order of the triangular numbers." [33] Mathematically speaking the formula is as follows:

X = the number of personal interrelationships
Y = the number of persons
$$X = \frac{Y^2 - Y}{2}$$

A series to illustrate this principle is as follows:

Number of persons	2	3	4	5	6	7
Number of personal relationships =	1	3	6	10	15	21

While the addition of one child does not complicate the network of relationships greatly the effect is felt. It has been demonstrated that in three-person groups there is a tendency for two to pair off and exclude the third. This research has not been done with parents of young children and therefore it is of dubious value at this point. The possibility of coalitions which will leave one member isolated is definitely there, however, and must be taken into account as the parents attempt to redefine the role structure in their home. The possibility of providing a playmate and confidant for the new child often leads parents to have a second child within a few years after the birth of the first.

Reorganization of Routine

When he is small the baby demands constant oversight and attention. The adage "a woman's work is never done" begins to strike home. Many couples, when systematically examining their programs and schedules, find that they can make certain changes with a resulting increase in efficiency and satisfaction. Some women find that experiment station and home economics extension bulletins can be helpful in enabling them to schedule

[33] James Bossard, and Eleanor Boll, *The Sociology of Child Development* (New York, Harper & Row, 1960), pp. 134–138.

systematically and organize their basic work tasks. Such bulletins are not panaceas, however. Each family must plan in terms of its own needs, abilities, and desires in its own situational context. But by adapting sound principles to specific circumstances it can simplify many tasks. In effect we are suggesting that parents make at least rough job analyses for themselves. As an aid in moving in this direction Fitzsimmons suggests the following principles:

1. Deciding on consuming and producing activities which must be fitted into each division of time so that they can be accomplished without undue effort or use of time, and the life family members lead will result in production which must be carried on; enjoyment of satisfactions desired; and the achievement of goals considered worthwhile.
2. Forming the habit of scrutinizing proposed activities or, from time to time, activities already undertaken to evaluate their worth for the individual or the family.
3. Discarding those which do not appear to offer sufficient returns in product or satisfaction to make them worth doing.
4. Improving the methods of doing the jobs which are retained.
   a. Setting reasonable standards for the product or outcome of all work processes whose attainment is possible in the time and with the amount of energy which can be devoted to that end.
   b. Developing standardized procedures for all jobs which are repeated frequently and performing them each time according to this procedure.
   c. Developing standardized procedures for all jobs which take a great deal of work, many operations, or a long time to perform.
   d. Developing standardized procedures for consuming, as well as producing, activities where these are repetitive in nature. Examples are dressing, bathing, and preparing oneself for bed.
5. Watching for changes in goals which may make necessary some change in the choice of activities to be undertaken by family members.
6. Watching for changes in methods of performing tasks, new equipment or possible changes in working places which might enable family members to do their work with still greater reduction in expenditure of motions and time.
7. Making allowances for leisure and unassigned time, according to individual preferences, so that the process of planning, trying out, and continuing the best use of motions and time will not prove burdensome.
8. Relating activities consciously to goals desired so that feelings of fatigue may be reduced by awareness of progress toward goals.
9. Being aware that fatigue is a natural result of physical and mental effort and even of boredom.
10. Arranging a plan for time use which will provide work periods that are not so long as to cause excessive fatigue and free periods in which suitable rest or relaxation can be obtained.[34]

[34] Cleo Fitzsimmons, *The Management of Family Resources* (San Francisco, Freeman, 1950), p. 423.

MAINTAINING MOTIVATION AND MORALE

We have previously referred to LeMasters' point that parenthood is for many couples a "crisis." If such is the case special measures to increase motivation to succeed and to maintain morale may be helpful. The husband may be having problems because of the combined pressures of home and job. The new baby makes him more conscious of his breadwinner role and the responsibilities attached thereto. He may begin to assess the long-run potentials of his job, and to consider the possibility of transfer to another position. In this evaluation process he will need the encouragement, understanding, and sympathetic backing of his wife. If she has no time to discuss the husband's problems, and if she cannot empathize with him at this point, he may feel lonely and resentful. The adaptable wife can help stabilize her husband by her interest and psychological support. In so doing she will be less likely to feel isolated and anxious about her own situation. The husband who feels that he has his wife's full support will be more likely to use good judgment in making occupational decisions which affect the whole family.

Apparently it is more often the wife, however, who becomes disillusioned. The following description by a young wife is typical:

Let us peek in again without the rosy spectacles supplied by the nationally advertised brands. Mary Jane's frock for mornings at home looks a little frayed and faded. Her apron has definitely seen neither Lux nor a harsh washing soap for several days. She scrapes dispiritedly at the breakfast plates, slightly repulsive with congealed egg yolk and slimy cold bacon grease. For the fourteenth time she exhorts Junior to stop dawdling and eat his cereal. She is not, at the moment, enjoying her marriage very much. Why should she? Washing dishes day in and day out is not the same thing as canoeing in the moonlight with your heart's beloved. . . . Mary Jane is remembering five o'clock with Jim waiting at the corner, of dinner with dancing, of going to the movies, or a concert, or the theater, or just a long ferry-boat ride. Of the difficult goodnight kiss and the ecstatic knowledge that soon she would have Jim all the time for always. She is thinking rather wryly of how entrancing, how full of promise, this battered dishpan looked when it first emerged from pink tissue paper at the shower the girls gave her. She may even think, a little cynically, as she surveys the grey, grease-pocked surface of her dishwater, of the foaming pans of eternally virgin suds she expected from her perusal of the advertisements. Well, she's married now. She has her own house, her own dishpan, her husband, and her baby. All the time and for always. She doesn't even go to the movies any more because there is no one to stay with Junior. She speaks so crossly to the child now that his tears fall into the objectionable cereal. Why on earth won't Jim let her get Mrs. Oldacre in to stay evenings? He'll be earning more soon; Mr. Bayswater practically told him he would be put in charge of the branch office as soon as old Fuzzy retired. Five dollars a week savings—much good that does anyway. Mary Jane's thoughts about her husband become quite uncharitable. 'If he only had the least understanding of the kind of life I have, but all he notices is Junior's shoes are scuffed out, and he would not even try that Bavarian cream I fixed yesterday. It's all very well for him to think Jimmy Junior's cute when he sneaks out of bed—he doesn't have him all day and all night and nothing but Jimmy Junior.' [35]

It is imperative that the husband help the wife overcome such disillusionment as much as possible. It may be in order at this point to refer to a psychological experiment on the effects of boredom. Subjects were paid to lie on beds for 24 hours a day, taking time out only for eating and using the bathroom. They wore visors which allowed them only slight vision. Their auditory perception was severely limited in that they rested their heads in rubber pillows and air-conditioning equipment sounds were fed continuously into the room. The reactions of the subjects to this monotonous environment were extreme. They developed marked irritations, found it difficult to concentrate, and experienced "very unpleasant" periods of restlessness. It is probably extreme to draw a parallel between this type of experimental situation and the situation obtaining for the mother and small child. The reader can point to many differences. The point is that for some women the full responsibility for a small child, day in and day out, becomes overwhelmingly tedious. They have a feeling of being restricted in what has been termed by Lewin "the space of free movement." Commenting on the type of situation involved in the above experiment, but probably applying also to our distraught mother's situation, Thibaut and Kelly are led to say: "Life becomes empty and monotonous. The necessity for making choices among different behaviors becomes largely eliminated, and, as a result, the ability to make decisions may become dulled. Under these conditions, some individuals make creative and clever use of the resources at hand or resort to complicated fantasy life; others slump into an inactive, stuporous state." [36] One might suspect that these comments apply unfortunately to housewives who are given the full charge of small children. For those who make the negative adaptations some method of making some changes in their outlook, their environment, or both is a prime necessity in order to further their mental health and that of their children.

The suggestion has been made that older couples help out young couples in their own neighborhood or church, even though they are not related to each other. Grandparents perhaps can occasionally help by acting as baby-sitters for children in the neighborhood. If handled properly such a program might be organized locally as a means of meeting the needs not only of the young parents who need an occasional evening of relaxation and fun, but of the older adults as well, who often feel unneeded and "on the shelf."

[35] Reprinted from *The Happy Family* by John Levy and Ruth Munroe by permission of Alfred A. Knopf, Inc. Copyright, 1938 by Ruth Munroe Levy, pp. 59–61.

[36] John Thibaut, and Harold Kelly, *The Social Psychology of Groups* (New York, Wiley, 1959), p. 173.

SELECTED READINGS

Ausubel, David, *Ego Development and the Personality Disorders* (New York, Grune & Stratton, 1952).

Baldwin, Alfred, "The Effects of Home Environment on Nursery School Behavior," *Child Development,* Vol. 20 (June, 1949), pp. 49–62.

Barclay, Dorothy, "Safety Without Fears for the Active Child," *The New York Times Magazine* (November 3, 1957), p. 75.

Bernert, Eleanor, *America's Children* (New York, Wiley, 1958).

Bernhardt, Karl, "How Permissive Are You?" *Bulletin of the Institute of Child Study* (1956), pp. 1–6.

Blood, Robert, "Consequences of Permissiveness for Parents of Young Children," *Marriage and Family Living,* Vol. 15 (August, 1953), pp. 209–212.

Bossard, James, and Boll, Eleanor, *The Sociology of Child Development* (New York, Harper & Row, 1960).

Dameron, Laurence, "Mother-Child Interaction in the Development of Self-Restraint," *Journal of Genetic Psychology,* Vol. 86 (June, 1955), pp. 289–308.

Elkin, Frederick, *The Child and Society* (New York, Random House, 1960).

Erikson, Erik, *Childhood and Society* (New York, Norton, 1963 rev.).

Escalona, Sibylle, *Understanding Hostility in Children* (Science Research Associates, 1954).

Hadfield, J., *Childhood and Adolescence* (Baltimore, Penguin, 1962).

Hirschberg, J. Cotter, "Some Comments on Religion and Childhood," *Bulletin of the Menninger Clinic* (May, 1954), pp. 141–186.

Jacobs, Leland, "What Shall We Read to Our Children?" *National Parent-Teacher* (November, 1956), pp. 34–36.

Koch, Helen, "The Relation of Certain Family Constellation Characteristics and Attitudes of Children Toward Adults," *Child Development,* Vol. 26 (March, 1955), pp. 13–40.

Krogman, Wilton, "The Physical Growth of the Child," in Morris Fishbein and Ruby Jo Kennedy (Ed.), *Modern Marriage and Family Living* (New York, Oxford University Press, 1957), pp. 417–425.

Lasko, Joan, "Parent Behavior Toward First and Second Children," *Genetic Psychology Monographs,* Vol. 49 (February, 1954), pp. 97–137.

Marshall, Helen, and McCandless, Boyd, "Relationships Between Dependence on Adults and Social Acceptance by Peers," *Child Development,* Vol. 28 (December, 1957), pp. 413–419.

McCandless, Boyd, *Children and Adolescents* (New York, Holt, Rinehart and Winston, 1961).

Newson, John, and Newson, Elizabeth, *Patterns of Infant Care* (Baltimore, Penguin, 1965).

Putney, Snell, and Middleton, Russell, "Effect of Husband-Wife Interaction on the Strictness of Attitudes Toward Child Rearing," *Marriage and Family Living,* Vol. 22 (May, 1960), pp. 171–173.

Ribble, Margaret, *The Rights of Infants* (New York, Columbia, 1943).

Ritchie, Oscar, and Koller, Marvin, *The Sociology of Childhood* (New York, Appleton-Century-Crofts, 1964).

Sewell, William, Mussen, Paul, and Harris, Chester, "Relationships Among Child-Training Practices," *American Sociological Review,* Vol. 20 (April, 1955), pp. 137–148.

Taylor, Katherine, "The Opportunities of Parenthood," in Howard Becker and Reuben Hill (Eds.), *Family, Marriage, and Parenthood* (Boston, Heath, 1955), Chapter 16.

Witmer, Helen, and Kotinsky, Ruth (Eds.), *Personality in the Making* (New York, Harper & Row, 1952), Chapters 1 and 3.

Wolf, Katherine, *The Controversial Problem of Discipline* (The Child Study Association of America, 1953).

QUESTIONS AND EXERCISES

1. Discipline is undoubtedly necessary in a number of child training situations. However, imaginative parents can devise numerous techniques whereby the necessity for discipline is circumvented. Discuss.

2. Discuss the function of age-graded, situationally oriented punishment.

3. What kind of home climate is necessary in order to keep children secure and happy? Must they always be allowed to do as they wish?

4. What type of sex guidance would you expect to give your children in the preschool period? Discuss.

5. How do you personally feel about the use of the family council? Would you include preschool children in the council? Discuss.

6. Arrange to do a case study of an individual child. Include references to his self concept, his level of skill in group leadership, etc.

7. Arrange a meeting to which you invite a child psychologist. Have him speak on personality assessment during the preschool years.

8. What can the parents do to help the older child get ready for a new baby brother or sister? Is some sibling rivalry inevitable? Discuss.

9. The late James Bossard was a strong proponent of the idea that children should have pets available in the home. What advantages and disadvantages are involved when cats or dogs are made members of the family circle?

10. What types of stories did you enjoy during your early childhood? What kinds of stories do you expect to use with your own children? Do you believe that it is legitimate to invent tales in order to satisfy the children?

11. Mental hygienists warn against the development of excessive fears. However, the child who is not cautious when caution is called for may suffer severe harm. How can proper cautionary fears be developed in the child without at the same time injuring his mental health?

12. Do you think parents should attempt to teach their children to read before they reach public school age? Discuss.

21

Development of the Infant and the Preschool Child

The fortunate child has been born into a home in which his coming was anticipated with joy and satisfaction. He is given food, clothing, shelter, love, and attention to provide for his basic needs and development. Such is the optimum family environment of the child. It does not, however, guarantee that he will develop and mature. The child from his early months on faces tasks that must be met and handled if he is to progress toward independent adulthood. Very quickly he must learn to eat, sleep, eliminate, and respond to his parents. Other tasks follow. Successful completion of them will form the basis for mastery of the later tasks.

Below are listed in detail the various locomotor, sensory, and behavior developments typical for the child at the various ages from one month through the second year. These items are from a scale used by Griffiths to measure and test "mental development." [1] The scale represents norms developed from the study of 600 children of London, England. Careful contemplation of the items on the scale can hardly help but make one conscious of the many and varied tasks which must be performed by the infant as he proceeds during his early months and years.

We now turn to a consideration of the major developmental tasks facing the infant and preschool child. A discussion of them will enable us to sense more fully the complexity of the tasks as they involve maturation of body and mind, attitude, knowledge, and skills.

GIVING AND RECEIVING AFFECTION

It seems quite clear that one of the most important tasks for the young child is to learn to give and receive affection. Whether or not there is an inborn need to love and be loved may be debatable, but life without affec-

[1] Ruth Griffiths, *The Abilities of Babies: A Study in Mental Measurement* (London, London University Press, Ltd., © 1954).

420

TABLE 38

The Griffiths Mental Developmental Scale
Complete Inventory of Test Items

Months of Age	A — Locomotor	B — Personal-Social	C — Hearing and Speech	D — Eye and Hand	E — Performance
1	1 Lifts chin when prone.	1 Regards person—momentarily.	1 Startled by sounds.	1 Follows a moving light with the eyes.	1 Grasps examiner's finger.
	2 Pushes with feet against examiner's hands.	2 Quieted when picked up.	2 Quieted by voice.	2 Looks at ring or toy momentarily.	2 Reacts to paper. I—Generalised physical movements.
	3 Holds head erect for a few seconds.	3 Enjoys bath.	3 Vocalisation other than crying.	3 Looks steadily at bell-ring held still.	3 Hand goes to mouth.
2	4 Lifts head up when prone.	4 Smiling.	4 Listens to bell.	4 Follows moving bell-ring horizontally.	4 Shows energetic arm movements.
	5 Kicks vigorously.	5 Visually recognises mother.	5 Cooing—one syllable.	5 Follows ring vertically.	5 Reacts to paper. II—Vigorous head turning.
3	6 Active in bath—kicks.	6 Vocalises when talked to.	6 Searches for sound with eyes.	6 Glances from ring to bell.	6 Holds doll.
	7 Lifts head when in dorsal position.	7 Follows moving persons with eyes.	7 Listens to music.	7 Follows moving bell-ring in a circle.	7 Plays with own fingers.
	8 Rolls from side to back.	8 Returns examiner's glance with smiling or cooing.	8 Makes z + different sounds.	8 Watches object pulled along by string.	8 Looks at box on table.
4	9 Back firm when held in sitting position.	9 Friendly to strangers.	9 Searches for sound with head movements.	9 Grasps ring when given.	9 Resists doll withdrawal.
	10 Lifts head and chest when prone.	10 Resists adult who tries playfully to take toy.	10 Laughs aloud.	10 Visually explores new environment.	10 Clasps cube put in hand and holds it.
	11 Holds head erect continuously.	11 Frolics when played with.	11 Turns head deliberately to bell.	11 Reaches for ring and grasps.	11 Drops first cube for second.

421

TABLE 38 (cont.)

The Griffiths Mental Developmental Scale
Complete Inventory of Test Items

Months of Age	A Locomotor	B Personal-Social	C Hearing and Speech	D Eye and Hand	E Performance
5	12 Lifts head and shoulders, *dorsal*.	12 Stops crying when talked to.	12 Listens to tuning-fork.	12 Carries ring to mouth.	12 Reacts to paper. III— Pulls it away.
	13 Rolls from side to side.	13 Turns head to person talking or singing.	13 Coos or stops crying on hearing music.	13 Clutches at dangling ring.	13 Shows interest in box.
6	14 Plays with own toes.	14 Anticipatory movements when about to be lifted.	14 Talks (babbles) to persons.	14 Secures dangling ring.	14 Takes toy from table.
	15 *Crawling Reaction (I)* Draws up knees, etc.	15 Holds a spoon.	15 Manipulates bell.	15 Hands explore table surface.	15 Holds two cubes.
	16 Sits with slight support.	16 Stretches to be taken.	16 Makes 4 different sounds.	16 Plays with ring—shaking bells, etc.	16 Grasps box.
7	17 Can roll from back to stomach, etc.	17 Drinks from a cup.	17 Responds when called.	17 Reaches for and picks up string—any method.	17 Manipulates cube or toy.
	18 Stepping reaction (*a*): Dancing movements.	18 Manipulates cup or spoon in play.	18 Two-syllable babble.	18 Looks for dropped toy.	18 Reacts to paper. IV— Reaches for and takes.
8	19 *Crawling (II)* Tries vigorously to crawl.	19 Reacts to mirror image— 1. Looks at.	19 Shouts for attention.	19 Strikes one object with another.	19 Passes toy from hand to hand.
	20 Sits alone for a short time.	20 Knows strangers from familiar friends.	20 Listens to conversations.	20 Watches examiner scribble.	20 Drops one cube for third.
	21 Stepping reaction (*b*): One foot in front of the other.	21 Prompt reaction to situations, e.g. at table.	21 Singing tones.	21 Secures ring by means of string.	21 Manipulates 2 objects at once.

#	A	B	C	D	E
22	9 Crawling (III) Can turn around when left on floor.	Displaced if toy is taken away.	Babbled phrases: 4 syllables.	Forefinger and thumb partly specialised.	Reacts to paper. V— Plays with, crumples, etc.
23	Can be left sitting on floor.	Helps to hold cup for drinking.	Says Mama or Dada, etc. (one word clear).	Fine prehension.	Lifts inverted box in search of toy.
24	Crawling (IV) Makes some progress forwards or backwards.	Pulls off hat.	Listens to stop watch.	Dangles ring by string.	Rattles box.
25	10 Stands when held up.	Reacts to mirror image—11. Smiles at, or plays with.	Shakes head for "No!"	Plays pulling ring or toy by string.	Clicks two bricks together. (Imitation.)
26	Sits well in a chair.	Waves bye-bye.	Says two clear words.	Throws objects.	Lifts lid off box.
27	11 Pulls self up by furniture.	Gives affection.	Short babbled sentences.	Thumb opposition complete.	Finds toy under box.
28	Can stand holding to furniture.	Finger feeds (thumb and forefinger).	Rings bell.	Can point with index finger.	Tries to take cubes out of box.
29	12 Crawling (V) Creeps on hands and knees, etc.	Plays with cup, spoon, and saucer.	Reacts to music vocally.	Interested in motorcar.	Accepts third cube without dropping.
30	Side-steps round inside cot or play-pen holding rails.	Obeys simple requests: "Give me cup," etc.	Babbled monologue when alone.	Can hold pencil as if to mark on paper.	Removes both cubes from box (shown).
31	Can walk when led.	Plays "Pat-a-cake" (claps hands). Puts small objects in and out of cup at play.	Says three clear words.	Uses pencil on paper a little.	Manipulates box, lid and cubes.
	Total Items Passed: A	Total B	Total C	Total D	Total E ....

423

TABLE 38 (cont.)

The Griffiths Mental Developmental Scale
Complete Inventory of Test Items

Second Year	A Locomotor	B Personal-Social	C Hearing and Speech	D Eye and Hand	E Performance
13	32 Climbs on a low ledge or step.	32 *See Ch. XII, Introduction.	32 Tries definitely to sing.	32 Likes holding little toys.	32 Unwraps and finds toy or cube.
	33 Stands alone.	33 Tries to help dressing —arms into coat, etc.	33 Looks at pictures for a few seconds.	33 Preference for one hand.	33 One-circle board—two trials.
14	34 Walks alone.	34 Can hold cup for drinking.	34 Knows own name.	34 Plays rolling ball.	34 Opens two boxes.
	35 Kneels on floor or chair.	35 Uses spoon himself—spills some.	35 Likes rhymes and jingles.	35 Can hold 4 cubes in hands at once.	35 Puts two cubes back into box when encouraged to do so.
15	36 Climbs stairs (up).	36 Shows shoes.	36 Uses 4 or 5 clear words.	36 Plays pushing little cars along.	36 Two-circle board—one in.
	37 Likes pushing pram, toy horse, etc.	37 Tries to turn door-knob.	37 One object in box identified.	37 Places one lid, box or brick upon another.	37 Puts cubes in and out of boxes in play.
16	38 Trots about well.	38 Cleanliness—asks.	38 Uses 6 or 7 clear words.	38 Scribbles more freely.	38 Square board—two trials.
17	39 Stoops.	39 Manages cup well—half-full.	39 Long babbled conversations—some words clear.	39 Pulls paper or cloth to get toy.	39 Two-circle board—two in.
	40 Climbs on a low chair.	40 Can take off shoes and socks.	40 Enjoys picture-book.	40 Constructive play with boxes or other materials (E).	40 Can put lid back on box.

424

No.	A	B	C	D	E
41	Can walk backwards.	Likes adult to show book.	Two objects in box identified.	Tower of three.	Three-hole board—one in, two trials.
42	Walks pulling toy on string.	Parts of body—1.	Uses 9 words.	Can *throw* a ball.	Puts two cubes into box, lid on, all complete.
43	Climbs stairs (up and down).	Bowel control complete.	Four objects in box identified.	Tower of four.	Circle and square board together.
44	Jumps.	Uses spoon well.	Vocabulary 12 words.	Enjoys vigorous straight scribble.	Three-hole board—two in.
45	Runs.	Bladder control by day.	Picture vocabulary (1).	Can pour water from one cup to another.	Three-hole board—three in.
46	*Walks* upstairs.	Tries to tell experiences.	Word combinations.	Circular scribble (imitation).	Two-circle board rotated.
47	Climbs to stand on a chair.	Asks for things at table by name.	Picture vocabulary (2).	Tower of five or more.	Circle and square boards rotated.
48	Can jump off a step.	Parts of body—2.	Listens to stories.	Perpendicular stroke.	(Credit two points.)
49	Can seat himself at table.	Parts of body—3.	Vocabulary 20 words clear.	Train of three.	Assembles three boxes.
50	*Walks up* and *down* stairs.	Parts of body—4+.	Eight objects in box identified.	Throws ball into basket.	(Credit two points.)
51	Can kick a ball.	Can open a door.	*Names* 4 toys.	Making a brick or toy walk.	Can turn a screw.
52	Can be trusted on stairs alone.	Helps actively to dress or undress.	Uses sentences of 4+ syllables.	Horizontal stroke.	Can reassemble screw-toy.

Total Items Passed:
A .... Total B .... Total C .... Total D .... Total E ....

Source: Ruth Griffiths, *The Abilities of Babies: A Study in Mental Measurement* (London, University of London Press, Ltd., copyright © 1954).

425

tion of any sort is not human. The little child receives pleasurable sensations at first from any manipulation of his erogenous zones. At this early
stage he has no concept of himself, as distinct from others, and therefore
he cannot perceive that his mother or others have helped him obtain
pleasure. As early weeks and months go by the child begins vaguely to perceive that others are helping him achieve pleasurable states. Possibly
through an elementary stimulus-responsible cycle he learns to associate
mother with food, warmth, and dry diapers. He soon learns that crying will
bring a response from her.

The average child will typically begin to reach out toward others
fairly early in life if encouraged. From time immemorial mothers have
cuddled and fondled their children and the children have responded with
affection. With encouragement provided, it is only the exceptional child
that will not develop an interest both in giving and receiving affection during the first year or so of his life.

Once this interest in or feeling for affection is developed, the child
must move toward the ability to give to as well as to receive affection from
others, if he is to mature. It would appear that, given the proper stimulation on the part of the mother, he will inevitably respond to her with
affection and wish to receive more in return. The child who cannot do this
at a minimum level has probably developed a sense of mistrust which
makes him withdraw from intimate interaction with those around him.

During the early childhood years the youngster learns also to love his
father and other members of his immediate family or neighborhood. If
the Freudians are at all correct this period can be a rather difficult one for
the average child because he must learn to "share" mother with both his
father and a new baby, and he should also love them both. The transition
is often difficult for obvious reasons. The growing child no longer receives
the attention he did during his early months. Furthermore, he eventually
perceives that his mother belongs also to his father. That he should develop
mixed feelings toward father and siblings should not be surprising.

The parents will be required to use all the ingenuity at their command
when the second child arrives. Since the mother-child relationship is still
intense during the second and third year the mother may find it rather
difficult to make the necessary adjustments required for the new emotional
constellation when the new baby arrives. The chances of the child's adapting
to the new situation are better if the mother can adjust her relationship with
relative ease.

THE DEVELOPMENT OF THE SELF

An important task for the small child is the development of a concept
of self in relation to others. By self we mean that which is the object of
reference when the common terms "I," "me," or "myself" are used. The

development of the self is a twofold process, one outside the person and the other within. The child interacts with his mother and others and usually finds pleasure in this interaction. At first he is not conscious of himself and others as objects—he simply reacts in a conditioned response pattern. Eventually he begins to note that certain behaviors on his part bring a pleasurable reaction (smile, gesture of approval, etc.) while other actions bring disapproval on the part of mother. He begins to distinguish vaguely between the "me" and the "not-me." As time progresses the "not-mes" become more clear-cut objects in and of themselves, and of course this reinforces the distinctiveness of the "me."

Cooley [2] and Mead [3] have stressed the role that associates play in the development of selfhood in the person. Cooley suggests that eventually the child begins to imagine how he appears to others. On the basis of this he imagines the judgments others make of what they see of him. Finally the child develops, as a result of the previous two cognitive processes, feelings of self-worth or shame. This is known as the "looking-glass self" concept.

Mead suggested that the child is moving along toward selfhood when he can vicariously view himself as an object. The child does this by role-taking. When little Mary can play the role of mother and have her doll be "Mary" she is able to take an "outside" position and view her own thoughts, feelings, and behavior somewhat objectively.

According to Mead, the child really develops a self through three stages. The first is the *preparatory stage*. In this stage the child is not able to view his own actions objectively. He can imitate others and is pleased when they indicate a favorable reaction to this behavior. The second stage is known as the *play stage*. Here the child plays various roles as described above. Finally, there is the *game stage* in which the child must learn to react to, and in accordance with the expectations of a number of persons. This stage involves the early school years and will be discussed in a later chapter. During the preschool period the youngster is encouraged to develop a sex identity and to be able to differentiate age-graded sex roles. At the appropriate time the little boy's curls are cut because he is beginning to "look like a girl." Birthday and Christmas presents involve airplanes, railroad trains, and athletic toys. At the same time the girl is encouraged to be feminine, to play house, and to cringe at the sight of snakes and mice.

Learning his sex identity is not necessarily an easy process for the child in spite of the typical encouragement received. As Parsons points out, the symbols for the various possible roles and role relationships are more complicated than would at first be imagined.[4] Typically the boy develops a

---

[2] Charles H. Cooley, *Human Nature and the Social Order* (New York, Scribner, 1922).

[3] George H. Mead, *Mind, Self, and Society* (Chicago, The University of Chicago Press, 1934).

[4] Talcott Parsons and Robert F. Bales, *Family Socialization and Interaction Process* (New York, Free Press, 1955), Chapter 2.

close relationship with his mother. In a sense he identifies with her. As he grows he comes to the point where he is encouraged to distinguish girl and boy, male and female. Presumably the boy discriminates between father and mother and boy and girl at about the same period in his development. As he progresses he is encouraged to identify with his father on the basis of maleness as against femaleness represented by his mother and any sisters he may have.

Identification can be problem-ridden and confusing for the child. The boy can go only so far in identifying with his father. Vicariously playing the husband role to mother is difficult although the boy may try it occasionally, especially if encouraged by his mother. The result is, of course, guilt feelings and, according to some authorities, anxiety lest father use drastic measures to reduce the competition. It is also difficult for the small boy to identify today with his father's occupational role. Father leaves in the morning to go to the big office downtown. What he does there and how he does it is not very clear to Johnny. Nor is it too clear as to how it differs from what a woman might do away from home.

It seems clear that the small child needs help in clarifying his maleness or femaleness. Parents can be of help in a number of ways. Most important is to establish, in as clear-cut and consistent a fashion as possible, role-images which are held before the child. This includes the establishment of a home in which there is reasonable order, cooperation, and fair play. Besides this, attention must be given to the questions children ask in regard to sex roles and sex matters. The normal child will be curious about items of sex differences, childbirth, and similar matters. It is now held by many clinicians that these questions need not produce anxiety and undue frustration if they are handled naturally and routinely by parents. Trouble comes when parents are evasive or when they react with feelings of guilt and embarrassment. In many cases this no doubt suggests an inadequate adjustment to sex roles and sex functions on the part of the parent. The sensitive child will perceive the anxiety of the parent and in turn will become confused and troubled.

This means that parents must learn to handle sex questions in a manner which is natural for themselves, and they must be as consistent as possible. Children, like the proverbial elephants, have long memories. Fourth- or fifth-grade children who recall stories of childbirth that included storks, cabbage heads, the doctor's black bag, or other animate or inanimate phenomena in the process may well suspect either their parents' veracity or their basic intelligence. It should come as no surprise if they are motivated to turn elsewhere later for reliable information on intimate matters.

Learning to Communicate

To learn to communicate effectively is a necessity if the child is to develop a selfhood and to become a functioning member of a human group.

The small child soon starts this process by vocalizations of various kinds. At first the crying and other utterances may be partially random. Within a month or so, however, most parents seem able to discern from these utterances if the child is satisfied, if he is frightened, or if he is in pain or discomfort.

What is often referred to as "babbling" will then develop within a few months in most children.[5] This involves a type of circular conditioned response in which a particular sound serves to stimulate its repetition. During this babbling period, roughly from the third to the ninth month, the child usually exhibits a wide variety of sounds. This sets the stage for the imitative period which is to follow. In the imitative stage the child is able to repeat sounds he hears made by adults. Naturally there are certain limitations on the child involving the maturation of jaws, the mouth, and the vocal chords. The imitation stage is an enjoyable one for parents or siblings in the ideal home environment. Parents vie with each other in trying to get the child to imitate big words, and the child enjoys being the center of attention.

Finally, what is called "true speech" develops. Authorities are pretty well agreed that it develops sometime during the first half of the second year.[6] By true speech it is meant that the child is able to relate a specific sound to a specific referent, even though it may not be quite proper in the adult sense.

From this state on, the child's abilities in speech develop rapidly. Environmental influences must not be overlooked, however. Children in orphanages under six months of age vocalize less than those in family homes.[7] There are indications that these effects are pronounced, at least until the adolescent years.[8] Abundant evidence indicates that the child in the middle-class home will progress more rapidly in language development than the child in the lower-class home. Presumably this difference results mainly from the greater amount of attention the individual child can receive in the home and the type of language stimuli to which he is exposed.

Learning the intricacies of language is no simple matter for the preschool child, and he needs plenty of encouragement. When one considers the difficulties that thousands of college freshmen have each year in demonstrating satisfactory performance in the use of the King's English, one wonders how the small child of three can be expected to perform at all. Yet from the age of about three years until he is ready for grammar school the average child will have progressed in truly startling fashion. Starting at this

[5] Marian Breckenridge and Lee Vincent, *Child Development* (Philadelphia, Saunders, 1944–1960), p. 409.

[6] Elizabeth Hurlock, *Child Development* (New York, McGraw-Hill, 1953), Chapter 6.

[7] A. J. Brodbeck and O. C. Irwin, "The Speech Behavior of Infants Without Families," *Child Development,* Vol. 17 (September, 1946), pp. 145–156.

[8] W. Goldfarb, "The Effects of Early Institutional Care on Adolescent Personality," *Journal of Experimental Education,* Vol. 12 (1943), pp. 106–129.

period with a vocabulary of under 300 words, the child by age six has a vocabulary of over 2500 words.[9]

When one realizes the immensity of the task facing the child in building a language he may feel that this is the most difficult task obtaining for the preschool child. As Davis and Havighurst point out, however, this task may not be as difficult as learning to control the bladder and bowels or to perform other needed tasks. This is because the learning of a language does not do great violence to the natural impulses of the child, but is basically in harmony with them.[10]

The child's language will reflect the particular subcultural accents of the family, if any, and also the peculiar usage of words as used only in a given family. Habitual use of slang, swear words, and the like will also be reflected as many a parent has learned in the presence of the visiting minister, teacher, grandmother, or gossipy Mrs. Grundy, the next door neighbor.

Learning the Family Value System

The young child, from the point of view of the social scientist, is amoral. He has no sense of right or wrong, no sense of value. Although religious groups may differ as to whether the child will reflect original sin or whether he is born free of such taint, all groups and societies over the world agree that the child must be taught something. In actuality the family in a given society becomes the mediating agent between the general society and the child. This means that the child is exposed to the value system of the community at large and the value system of his particular family.

This process of socialization or education in the broad sense is something that is both important and difficult for the child. The normless child would be hopelessly out of place in the nursery school and in later public life. But learning one's own way of doing, thinking, and feeling about things is anything but simple for the child.

Fortunately certain processes develop rather naturally in the majority of homes which aid the children in their learning of "how things are done." Young children are prone to imitate adults. With slight encouragement they attempt to imitate mother's and father's behavior. What actually takes place is that the child identifies with the role of the parent and attempts to act as does the parent. The boy dresses up to go to work, hunting, or golfing; the girl cooks, wears long dresses, and puts the doll baby to bed. According to a number of authorities, full identification with parents of the opposite

---

[9] M. K. Smith, "Measurement of the Size of the General English Vocabulary Through the Elementary Grades and High School," *Genetic Psychology Monographs* Vol. 24 (1941), pp. 311–345.

[10] Allison Davis and Robert Havighurst, *Father of the Man* (Boston, Houghton Mifflin, 1947), p. 109.

sex will not come at the preschool period. Regardless of the merits of their position, the small child will begin or can begin his primary identification with the parents during the period from his second to fourth year.

The Freudians use the term "superego" to refer to the social norms of the community which are internalized in the child. For the young child internalization means that he begins to develop some moral sense and also a conscience which will give him pleasure when he "behaves" and will induce guilt feelings when he "does wrong." Slowly but surely the child begins to perceive the value system of the household and his part in the system.

The child may be encouraged to learn appropriate behavior by reward, punishment, or some combination of the two. The wise parent makes use of the positive reward approach as much as possible. We are told that in the middle-class family the typical negative approach involves the threat of the withdrawal of love. Eventually the child develops inner controls which raise objections whenever the improper drives become strong. When this takes place we say that the child has developed a "conscience," or in Freudian terms a "superego."

At the preschool level most of the standards by which the child is directly confronted will be those of the parental family. He must learn "how things are done in our family." In our house children do not climb on the good furniture, even though they do in the house across the street. We see to it that children learn early to respect adults and property. In this home our children are taught to be little ladies and gentlemen. The child gradually learns, sometimes the hard way, the prevailing value system in his household.

Learning "how to behave" is not a simple matter for the child. Impulses to strike out aggressively, to be defiant, or to regress and act like a baby are at times irresistible to him. From his limited point of view the restrictions imposed upon him are often arbitrary, unfair, and unreasonable. Yet some type of discipline and supervision of the child is essential for his well-being. A child who was not given some training and limits at home would find social living outside the home impossible. Clinicians who work with male delinquents consistently report that the boys suffer from the lack of adequate role-models. Often they have no active fathers in the home whom they trust or on whom they can rely.

What type of punishment is used by parents of preschoolers in order to bring about expected behavior? One of the more thorough studies of the subject is that of Radke.[11] She found that the most commonly used methods were isolation, spanking, rewards and praise, verbal appeals, allowing the behavior to take its course, and depriving the children.

Radke states that ". . . most of the devices are aimed at undermining the power of the child or restricting his freedom, either physical or

[11] Marian Radke, *The Relation of Parental Authority to Children's Behavior and Attitudes* (Minneapolis, University of Minnesota Press, 1946).

psychological." [12] Reasoning, praise and rewards, and positive verbal appeals are among the least restricting and power reducing.

Interviews of the children by Radke indicated the ambivalence that children often feel in regard to the discipline used by their parents. The children do not believe that the punishment used makes them resolve to do better. About half of them report a dislike for parental punishment and interference with their play. On the other hand, they respect the right of their parents to be in authority over them and in general, accept as valid the types of punishment used.

Since children are very adaptable and ingenious, they develop counter-methods of control. Table 39 below indicated the methods used by the children, and their success or failure as they perceived them.

TABLE 39

Percentage of Children Attempting Various Methods of Controlling Parents

Method Used	With Mother		With Father	
	Boys	Girls	Boys	Girls
Pays no attention to parent's request				
Success	26	25	39	29
Failure	74	75	61	71
Cries, has tantrums				
Success	21	26	17	14
Failure	79	74	83	86
Refuses parent's requests				
Success	50	26	41	19
Failure	50	74	59	81
Whines, begs, etc.				
Success	47	39	53	33
Failure	53	61	47	67

SOURCE: From: *The Relation of Parental Authority to Children's Behavior and Attitudes* by Marian Radke. Child Welfare Monograph, No. 22. University of Minnesota Press, Minneapolis. Copyright 1946 by the University of Minnesota.

Appeals to the generosity of the parents are apparently the most successful techniques used by the children, especially the boys. Ignoring or refusing of requests also brings considerable success. It appears that boys, for some reason or other, have greater success in controlling their parents. Is this because they are more persistent and aggressive? Are parents more forceful in demanding that daughters conform?

Erikson's theories of development may be relevant at this point. He postulates a series of stages which reflect the development of the healthy personality. Erikson takes the position that at each stage of development

[12] *Ibid.*

certain potential conflicts must be handled and certain tasks accomplished. These problems are never solved to the extent that they do not reappear. Rather their solutions at a particular time lay the groundwork for progress to the next stage and personality stability for the future.

		1	2	3	4	5	6	7	8
VIII	Maturity								Ego integrity vs. despair
VII	Adulthood							Generativity vs. stagnation	
VI	Young Adulthood						Intimacy vs. isolation		
V	Puberty and adolescence					Identity vs. role confusion			
IV	Latency				Industry vs. inferiority				
III	Locomotor-genital			Initiative vs. guilt					
II	Muscular anal		Autonomy vs. shame, doubt						
I	Oral sensory	Basic trust vs. mistrust							

FIGURE 19. *Erikson's Eight Ages of Man.* SOURCE: Reprinted from *Childhood and Society,* Second Edition, Revised and Enlarged, by Erik H. Erikson. By permission of W. W. Norton & Company, Inc. Copyright 1950, © 1963 by W. W. Norton & Company, Inc.

The midcentury White House Conference on Children and Youth made extensive use of the Erikson approach to personality growth and development. Below is a brief discussion of the first three stages as the Conference interpreted them:

1. The sense of trust.

    During the first year of a baby's life, the sense of trust is developed. This component of a healthy personality emerges from the direct satisfaction of the infant's basic needs, in particular experiences associated with feeding. When these needs are ineptly or neglectfully attended to, mistrust can develop.

2. The sense of autonomy.

At the age of twelve to fifteen months, following the completion of the first stage, begins the sense of autonomy. At the same time as his muscle-system maturation, the infant desires to undertake a multitude of new and difficult tasks. Although restrictions must be placed on numerous activities, it is very important that the child be allowed to make an increasing number of decisions himself to establish his autonomy. An area of study which has received particular attention during this stage is bladder and bowel control.

3. The sense of initiative.

When the child has enjoyed about a year of autonomy, the sense of initiative commences. At age four or five, the child wants to discover what he can do. Enterprise and imagination characterize this phase, as well as the origination of conscience. The parental object at this time is to regulate the child's initiative without producing an excessive, inhibiting guilt. Enterprise should be encouraged, and punishment should be reserved for occasions where it would be particularly beneficial. The skill that is ultimately being developed is an ability to select and pursue social goals.[13]

The conference group considered the first three stages to be the most basic. This of course is open to controversy. If the stages have any degree of validity, however, ability to meet and perform the tasks which accompany them provides an important groundwork for the future.

Later developmental phases in Erikson's scheme, as reproduced in Figure 18 will be cited in the following chapters and appropriately documented at such times. (Note that Erikson now speaks of "ages" rather than "stages" in his revised work.)

Eating, Toilet Training, and Dressing

Major developmental tasks for the small child center around his eating of food, control of bowels and bladder, and learning to dress himself. In regard to the eating of food, obviously the hunger drive will usually spur the child on at any age to seek food. The basic task of learning eating habits that will be satisfactory in his parental home is no simple task, however.

The young child can develop acceptable eating habits more readily if parents provide certain aids for him. Parents above the poverty level can provide foods that will furnish the basis for sound health. While evidence is not completely conclusive, it appears that children, if left to their own initiative, will choose a wide variety of nutritional foods.[14] Good food should be presented to the child as a matter of course. Children will eventually imitate many parental habits of eating. If the atmosphere is free and easy it will tend to encourage the children to eat. The wise mother sub-

---

[13] Helen Witmer and Ruth Kotinsky (Eds.), *Personality in the Making* (New York, Harper & Row, 1952), Chapter 1.

[14] Boyd McCandless, *Children and Adolescents* (New York, Holt, Rinehart and Winston, 1961), Chapter 1.

stitutes a new dish now and then when everyone is in good humor and hungry. In most cases children will sample the food if encouraged to do so and if all the adults do the same.

Individual differences will inevitably appear in food intake, preferences, and the like. Undue variations from the average should be checked with the child's physician.[15] Often severe eating problems are reflections of emotional difficulties in the home. It is said that middle-class children are more inclined toward psychosomatic difficulties connected with digestion than are lower-class children.[16] The latter may at times actually be provided with nutritionally inadequate diets.

Control of Elimination

During the days when behavioristic child psychology was popular, children in the middle classes were conditioned at a very early age. It is reported that some mothers held their children on the "potty" as early as the age of three months. It should go without saying that this must have been a frustrating experience for both parent and child. Some "success" occurred, but in most cases it was the mother who became trained rather than the child. She learned to detect the necessary cues and to respond accordingly.

Present pediatric theory suggests that the child in the long run will be better adjusted if he is given considerable leeway in developing his own habits of elimination. In the first place, it is difficult for him to control himself until his nervous system has developed to a certain level. Control of elimination demands certain developments both in the control nervous system and in the nerve endings. When the child's nervous system has developed to the point where control of elimination is possible, he will be able to control himself. He is not really prepared to do so before this time.

In the second place, undue emphasis on toilet training may bring more tension and frustration than it is worth. This is not to say that the author is a "diaper determinist" or that he believes that Hitler was what he was because he was severely trained. Rather it seems reasonable to make elimination as natural and nonemotional a process as possible. If parents react to "accidents" with great concern it will be almost inevitable that the child will develop feelings of guilt or anxiety. The child needs supervision, help, and reassurance in order to learn to control himself. He does not need undue emotional stress.[17]

One problem which often arises has to do with the coming of younger children. Often parents are putting on the pressure for the child to control

[15] See Francis Ilg and Louise Ames, *Child Behavior* (New York, Harper & Row, 1955), Chapter 4 for a description of typical eating behavior of children at particular age periods.

[16] Robert Blood, *Anticipating Your Marriage* (New York, Free Press, 1955), p. 389.

[17] McCandless, *op. cit.*, Chapter 3.

himself at the same time that a new brother or sister is being introduced
into the family. This doubling of pressures may very well result in a retrogression of behavior.

Learning to Recognize Hazardous Situations

The young child must learn to adapt himself to the physical and geographic limitations which obtain for him. Naturally these limitations will
depend much upon the style of living of the parental family. The class level
of the parents, whether they live on the farm, in the small town, or in the
city, and the parent's attitude toward personal property in relation to the
child will all be factors that will help determine the limits within which the
child must operate.

If there is any drive in the average child that is "natural" it is the
drive to be inquisitive or adventuresome. As parents well know, by about
age two youngsters can manipulate doorknobs and other such instruments.
From that time on until the child has a fully developed sense of inherent
danger, the possibilities of bumps, cuts, bruises, and worse, defy the imagination.

Regardless of the values of the parents, the young child needs the help
of the parents who can manipulate a reasonable physical environment for
him. While not all parents will wish to adopt a formal program of "child
proofing," there are many practical adjustments that they can make which
will enable the child to explore his surroundings and also maximize his
safety.[18]

Eventually the child learns the potential dangers of stairways, electric
fixtures, tools, and various other phenomena. He learns to roam freely
within the household and the yard. By the time he is three years of age he
will be wanting to roam more widely and to investigate more interesting
areas. Sometimes it would appear to a sensitive observer that we in America
no longer care for our boys and girls. No longer can they wander across the
neighbor's lawn and across the road with freedom and relative safety. The
child must be helped in his efforts to learn how to adapt to situations that
inherently are full of danger. This means that at an early age the child must
learn to recognize stop signs, sidewalks, and highly traveled roads. He must
also learn the boundaries of his immediate neighborhood, the distances he
can safely travel from home, the heights he may reasonably climb, and so on.

Developing Appropriate Motor Skills

If the child is to be able to enjoy the many potentialities available to
him he must develop the motor abilities and skills available to him for his
age. To do this he needs an environment which allows him to mature at

[18] See the suggestions in Evelyn Duvall, *Family Development* (Philadelphia,
Lippincott, 1957), p. 205.

his natural pace and also provides learning experiences which will help him advance.

Section A of the Griffith Mental Development Scale indicates the locomotor development and abilities of the average child during the infancy period. Inspection of this will lead one to note that development proceeds following what is called the cephalo-caudal principle. Briefly stated, this involves the muscular development of the child starting with the head and neck, extending to the arms and upper trunk, and then proceeding to the lower back, legs, and feet.

During the preschool period the child increases his abilities in the motor skills already started and develops new ones. Increasingly his muscular activities are differentiated. At first his behaviors or responses are diffuse or mass movements. Eventually they become more specific or individuated. For example, when the two-year-old throws a ball he rather clumsily throws it forward with much use of his whole torso. By the time he is five he can make a short throw of the ball, overhand or underhand, without much movement of the torso.

By the time the child is three much of the uncoordinated and clumsy behavior of infancy has passed.[19] The child can run with greater smoothness, turn sharp corners, and go upstairs alternating his feet. He feels ready to give up his "kiddy car" and other baby toys to ride his more advanced tricycle. By the time he reaches the age of four the child has moved still further. He can run with still greater smoothness. He negotiates the tricycle well and attempts to "stunt" with it, to the dismay of his mother. He is developing a proficiency in skipping and jumping, although he usually is unable to hop. By five years of age the child is developing motor controls which will suffice for many coordinations. His movements have become still more differentiated. His sense of balance and rhythm is good and this is reflected in the confident way he asserts himself. He skips and jumps smoothly.

It seems clear that maturation is a factor in motor performance and that the child proceeds through a succession of stages of development at which periods his performance becomes more and more advanced. A question is raised. What are the effects of training or learning on performance? Answers to this question are not easily arrived at. Separation of the effect of maturation and learning is not a simple matter. Studies made by researchers do allow us to make certain observations.[20] The simple or so-called universal skills of human beings are little affected by coaching or training. The child must reach a certain level of maturation before he can respond in the motor activity. When he reaches this level he will typically initiate the activity.

[19] Catherine Landreth, *The Psychology of Early Childhood* (New York, Random House, 1958), Chapter 4.

[20] George Thompson, *Child Psychology* (Boston, Houghton Mifflin, 1962), Chapter 4.

In regard to the more specific type of skill, it appears that here again the child cannot profit from an experience until he is ready for it. But if he is neuromuscularly ready (the parallel to the "teachable movement" in regard to nonmotor learning) then coaching will enable him to learn more readily than he otherwise would.

Maturation and learning through practice are not fully separate factors. Maturation sets the stage for learning. Without maturation no learning is possible. Some parents bring on frustration in the child by trying to push him too hard too fast. Not only will the desired motor activity not be forthcoming, but fears and anxieties will build up in the child which may prevent him from initiating activity when he is mature enough for it. On the other hand, some parents by their negative approach do not stimulate a child to develop normally and in some cases children are actually deterred by parents. Landreth not only sums up what is known about the possibilities of coaching in this area but also indicates the optimum environment for the child's motor development:

. . . benefits of practice are related to the particular kind of practice given, the particular skill practiced, and the level of maturity, pre-practice level of skill, and characteristics of the particular child involved. Simple skills in which a child already has a fair level of pre-practice skill show little improvement as a result of additional practice. Practice involving only repetition by a child is less effective than practice following demonstration by an adult, or practice directed by specific, encouraging, unhurrying verbal directions, or practice involving successful kinesthetic experience on the part of the child. As for demonstrations, these are more effective when both demonstrator and child have the same physical orientation to the performance and when the demonstration is accompanied by statements which direct attention to the processes involved.

The implications from these generalizations for giving praise and encouragement and specific suggestions to any child attempting a new motor coordination, such as feeding or dressing himself, would seem obvious. Unfortunately, it is in these very performances that many young children are most handicapped by negative, general, reproving, and hurrying directions.

As demonstration, praise, encouragement, and specific direction help children to develop motor skills not universally acquired by the human species, the selection of skills encouraged in any society is an important factor in young children's motor development.[21]

DEVELOPING AUTONOMY AND INDEPENDENCE

During the period of infancy the child is and must be in a state of complete dependence upon the parents. Compared to lower animals the

[21] Landreth, *op. cit.*, pp. 113–114.

human infant is in a very precarious position if left to fend for himself. During the age period of three to five years, however, change takes place. The child faces the task of developing a minimum degree of autonomy and independence to the point where he can in satisfactory fashion manage much of his own behavior comfortably.

Paradoxical as it seems, the child, during the second year, reaches a peak of dependency on his mother.[22] This seems to be the result of emotional maturation and development. The child develops a stronger emotional attachment for the mother and this makes him wish to depend on her for the protection and attention she can give. It is during this period that the child is usually being pushed to learn to control his bowels and bladder. The pressure from his mother induces frustration on the part of the child. His identification with her makes him wish to satisfy her and to control himself. The hostilities stemming from his frustration give rise to mixed feelings or ambivalence. If the mother does not exert undue pressure, however, the child will gain some satisfaction and feeling of independence from his ability to control himself.

In general the ability of the child to exercise more independent control over his own behavior increases during the years three to five. He takes more and more responsibility for dressing himself. He assumes more responsibility for his toys and other objects that belong to him. He learns to play comfortably by himself out of sight of his parents. At the same time he can play comfortably with other children and will invite them to play with him.

What type of parental environment is conducive to independence? One of the first studies which raised such a question was that of Levy.[23] Using an intensive case study approach, Levy found a strong association between maternal overprotection and the lack of independence. Specifically he found three subcategories of overprotection present in cases leading to overly dependent behavior. They were prevention of independent behavior, infantilization, and excessive contact. These terms require some explanation. In the first case through subtle or direct methods the mother kept the child from playing with other children, from taking responsibility, etc. Infantilization means that the mother prolonged her techniques of feeding, dressing, and mothering the child unduly, by average standards. Excessive contact refers to situations in which the mother keeps, cuddles, and fondles the child, holds him on her lap, and in general "treats him like a baby." Often the mother finds it difficult to engage in normal social intercourse because she cannot leave the child. Another important factor was in the picture. This was "excessive dominance." This combined with the three

---

[22] Paul Mussen and John Conger, *Child Development and Personality* (New York, Harper & Row, 1956), p. 184.

[23] David Levy, *Maternal Overprotection* (New York, Columbia, 1943).

subfactors above showed a strong tendency to produce dependency in children.

The recent study by Sears, Maccoby, and Levin of 379 Boston mothers and their five-year-old children focused heavily on childhood dependency.[24] At the time of the study the children were reported to be as a whole relatively independent. Over half of them no longer tried to follow or cling to their mothers or seek to be near them. About 37 percent still manifested considerable dependent behavior, however.

How did mothers handle dependency? Some expressed faith in punishment. Evidence regarding the success of this was negative. When punishment was used, or when mothers reacted negatively, dependency increased. The authors reason in this fashion. The child develops habitual ways of acting. He uses these to reassure himself that his mother loves and accepts him. If the mother rejects this turning toward her, if she threatens to withdraw her love, or if she punishes his aggressive tendencies, the child will increase his effort to secure his mother's approval and affection. He will, in other words, become more dependent. The authors suggest that the relationship between the mother's approach and the child's reactions is a complicated one. They say:

We are skeptical that there is any single direction of cause-and-effect relations in the child-rearing process. True, the mother's personality comes first, chronologically, and she starts the sequence of interactive behavior that culminates in the child's personality. But once a child starts to be over-dependent, or is perceived as being so by his mother, he becomes a stimulus to the mother and influences her behavior toward him. Perhaps, within the present group (sample) of mothers, over-dependency of their children increased the mother's rejective feelings, made them more angry and hence more punitive for aggression. The whole relationship could be circular. An enormous amount of pains-taking research will be required to untangle these phenomena.[25]

The child can be aided in his drive toward independence and autonomy by having understanding parents who know how to bring out the best in him. They will know that at times it is necessary for the child's development that he be what seems to them rather negative. His "no" may be a reflection of his feeling that he should do a particular thing for himself, and the adept parent will sense this. The child is caught betwixt and between. His autonomy can only be a matter of degree during childhood and he will always need some help and supervision. The child needs, above all, understanding as he takes his initial steps on the thin ice of independent activity. Gradually the child comes to feel that he is an individual in his own right. As he progresses he finds that other people have rights also. It is good if he

[24] Robert Sears, Eleanor Maccoby and Harry Levin, *Patterns of Child Rearing* (New York, Harper & Row, 1957), pp. 160–175.
[25] *Ibid.,* p. 175.

can learn to stand on his own feet and view the world around him without anxiety.

DEVELOPING INTELLIGENCE

Unfortunately we do not have full agreement as to what we mean by intelligence. The reader is referred again to Chapter 6 where intelligence as a subcategory of interpersonal competency was discussed. If the child is born with a certain level of potential it becomes necessary at the various stages of development to learn how to make use of this potential.

The world to the infant is, according to William James, "a great, big, blooming, buzzing confusion." His abilities of perception are weak and his verbal and abstract reasoning and memory powers are undeveloped. However, the infant quickly begins the process of adaption. Within a few weeks he is sensitive to mother's touch and words of assurance. Soon he will listen to the sound of an animal or a machine. Eventually he learns to tie the sounds with the objects in a meaningful way. During the early years the development of the child's sense organs and locomotor equipment is extremely important for later intellectual development. While it is possible for a Helen Keller to learn under optimum conditions, her opportunities were as extreme as her handicaps. The child needs, if possible to, have impressions coming to him via the various sense organs. While he cannot interpret them, they form the foundation for later emotional and intellectual development.

Learning to vocalize is extremely important for the child's intellectual development. He learns to give names to objects, which is important in the development of his thinking process. By building a vocabulary the child is preparing himself for later mental exercises in which abstractions are primarily used.

During the first few years, then, the child is establishing the foundation for the various intellectual competences which he may develop in later years. As can be seen by the Griffith scale, there are no measures of memory, logical reasoning, and so on during the first two years. Instead the items involve essentially motor skills or abilities. Since the association between motor abilities and the more abstract abilities found in regular child and adult intelligence tests is not very high, so-called infant IQ's should not be taken too seriously.

From ages two through five the child begins to move in his ability to use his intellect. His vocabulary grows by leaps and bounds. He learns first to put short sentences together and then longer sentences. He learns elementary rules of grammar. Since later school experiences (and intelligence tests) are based so much on vocabulary and use of language, it is imperative that the child form this foundation quickly.

According to Strang, the major ingredients of intelligence are perception, memory, judgment, the ability to see relationships, and the ability to solve problems. Perception is basic.[26] It depends on sensory-motor development but is aided by abilities in memory, and in drawing associations. Perceptions involve first of all the use of the various sense organs in the development of individual sensations. Eventually these are integrated into meaningful wholes.

The child learns to perceive size, shape or form, color, weight, distance, time, number, etc., somewhat in the order of complexity as given here. Through the use of projective tests some understanding of the developmental process can be gained. During the early years the child responds more to the total Gestalt or configuration than to specific details. As a whole there is "a change from the global approach to the ability to differentiate parts, an increase in creativity and imagination, and more control over emotionality without inhibiting a spontaneous reaction to environmental stimuli." [27]

Seeing Relationships

It is more difficult to observe or draw relationships between phenomena than simply to observe them or be able to identify or name them. Nevertheless children develop this ability increasingly during the preschool period. The child learns to attach names to objects and note what they are like and how they are or can be manipulated. After this he is ready to draw relationships between these objects or phenomena.

Perception of relationships is built first upon concepts of size and space, and then later upon texture, weight, distance, and time if these are involved. Elementary understanding of space comes in the prenursery period. The ability to judge distance comes during the third- to sixth-year period.[28] Children first learn to perceive objects in relation to themselves. Later they begin to see the relationships between the particular objects involved.

Concept Development

Concepts of size, form, and space are really abstractions. They develop from the child's experience with actual phenomena. But the short attention span which obtains for the child allows only a few properties of the object or situation to be perceived. Furthermore the child's ability to

[26] Ruth Strang, *An Introduction to Child Study* (New York, Macmillan, 1959), pp. 149–151.
[27] *Ibid.*
[28] *Ibid.*

relate stimuli logically is limited. He therefore may focus upon unimportant aspects of a particular object and lump them with more important properties of another. Thus any four-legged, furry animal may be a "kitty." When eventually the child can name an object he is usually able to distinguish its major properties and to relate them to properties of other objects in the same class. This ability usually comes in the later preschool years at which time the attention span is longer allowing the child to react to more stimuli or properties of the object.

The small child finds it difficult to comprehend abstract ideas. He can understand in elementary fashion at least concepts that are related to things he can hear, smell, and feel around him. Concepts of God, justice, truth, and the like can really not be understood by the preschooler to any great degree.

Problem-Solving Ability

Children are handicapped in their ability to solve problems by their undeveloped powers of perception and by their lack of experience. They learn especially through trial and error. It is doubtful that the child learns as much by adult explanations or solutions to problems as he does by his own trial-and-error deductions. It is suggested that adults who wish to help should offer encouragement to the child to help him stay with the problem, and that they can direct the child to some particular area of the problem without fully revealing the solution.

LEARNING TO HANDLE EMOTIONS AND IMPULSES

There has been considerable disagreement in the child development literature in regard to the concept of emotion. Watson's classical categorization of love, rage, and fear as primary emotions is not well accepted today. It is agreed that under favorable conditions the child will begin to develop patterns of emotional responses which become more and more specific and occur more often in reaction to external stimuli as time goes on.

While certain emotional predispositions may be genetic, it seems clear that the child develops his emotions and learns to express them in response to the environment around him. Tender loving care, or what some psychologists would refer to as a nonstressful situation, will tend to provide the best basis for emotional growth and maturation. Under such conditions the child learns to develop positive emotions of affection and love, and to have a smaller number of negative responses.

In any environment some frustration for the child is inevitable. The very small child kicks, squirms, and cries in somewhat uncoordinated fashion. This type of reaction should probably not be called anger but is preliminary to anger which will come with maturation. Furthermore these responses are essentially random or unlearned. As these responses are rewarded they tend to be repeated, and eventually become habitual. Dollard and Miller point out that these emotions are reinforced or rewarded in the following ways:

> . . . there are two sets of circumstances in which the responses involved in the anger pattern are likely to be rewarded. In one, habits motivated by a drive and leading to a reward are blocked by the intervention of another individual. Under these circumstances, responses of aggression are likely to cause the other individual to get out of the way and thus allow the reward to be secured. Another condition is that in which a motivated response usually leading to reward is prevented by some sort of a physical obstacle, such as a sticking door. Both of these conditions will be recognized as the type of situation usually referred to as a frustration.[29]

The small baby reacts in a generalized way to frustration. As he grows, his emotional reactions become more and more differentiated, following the same type of developmental sequence as in the realm of motor abilities. Thus anger, fear, disgust, and jealousy emerge as differentiated emotions from the general distress of an earlier period.

Anger and aggression appear in general, then, to be reactions to frustration. The small child expresses his anger more or less at random. As he grows older it tends to be directed toward the parent, the playmate, or some object. Some years ago Goodenough made the most thorough study on anger which has yet appeared.[30] She classified anger into three categories: (1) undirected energy, (2) motor or verbal resistance, and (3) retaliation. In general children moved from one through three as they matured. It appears that anger, as well as other emotions, is related both to the individuality of the particular child and to the environment around him. Goodenough found that such conditions as the amount of sleep the child has had, the time of day, the presence or absence of unusual conditions in the home, and the like were related to the outbursts of anger.

In general, however, the child develops some inner controls from his third to his fifth years. Temper tantrums, tendencies to try to "boss" others, and the like may appear, and may be considered as evidence that the child's drives are being turned away from outbursts of anger and aggressiveness. It is consistently reported that boys will, on the average, be slightly more aggressive than girls. Certainly much of the difference must have a cultural base in the different expectations and controls used by parents and in the differential process of identification.

[29] John Dollard and Neal Miller, *Personality and Psychotherapy* (New York, McGraw-Hill, 1950), pp. 83–84.

[30] Florence Goodenough, *Anger in Young Children* (Minneapolis, University of Minnesota Press, 1931).

What help is needed by the child in order to enable him to develop adequate control of his emotions? We will again depend heavily on the Boston study of 379 mothers' patterns of child rearing in making tentative suggestions at this point.[31] Some type of middle ground seems to be most appropriate. To tone down aggression, the parents make it clear that aggression is frowned upon and they stop it when it occurs, but if possible not through the use of punishment. The effects of punishment are complicated. It may stop aggressive outbursts temporarily but it will tend to generate more hostility and lead to further outbreaks. Sears writes that:

the most peaceful home is one in which the mother believes aggression is not desirable and under no circumstances is ever to be expressed toward her, but who relies mainly on nonpunitive forms of control. The homes where the children show angry, aggressive outbursts frequently are likely to be homes in which the mother has a relatively tolerant (or careless!) attitude toward such behavior, or where she administers severe punishment for it, or both.[32]

During the last few decades a recognition by many educated people of the negative side effects of punishment has led to what is almost a cult of permissiveness about aggression.[33] The goal has been to avoid repression, permit free and easy expression of impulses on the part of the child, and thus prevent the development of aggression-anxiety, with accompanying displacement projections and, in some cases, uncontrollable fantasies.

Good as the goal may be, there is a question whether it can be achieved by a high degree of permissiveness for expression of aggression toward parents. There is no indication in the Boston data that a permissive attitude, with a consequent freer expression of aggression, decreases the strength of projective fantasies. Permissiveness does increase the amount of aggression in the home. This results in upset siblings, retaliation on their part, and frustration for the parents. The angry child is not necessarily the happy child nor is he the one who received affection and willing companionship from others.

These comments may seem to encourage a conclusion that parents will find it to their advantage to be somewhat nonpermissive of aggression that is directed toward themselves. This can be a dangerous conclusion if the kind of permissiveness we mean is not clearly understood.

Therefore, let us be as clear as possible about the aspect of permissiveness we have in mind. A child is more likely to be nonaggressive if his parents hold the value that aggression is undesirable and should not occur. He is more likely to be nonaggressive if his parents prevent or stop the occurrence of aggressive outbursts instead of passively letting them go on, but prevent them by other means than punishment or threats of retaliation. If the parent's nonpermissiveness takes the form of punishing the child (and thus leading the

---

[31] Sears *et al., op. cit.,* pp. 266–268.

[32] *Ibid.,* p. 266.

[33] The following is essentially paraphrased freely from *Ibid.,* p. 266–268.

child to expect punishment) for aggressive behavior, then nonpermissiveness will not have the effect of reducing the child's aggression. On the contrary the instant that punishment enters, all the consequences of punishment . . . may be anticipated, including that of increasing the child's level of aggression.

One caution: we are not suggesting that parents should band together in omnipotent suppression of every justifiable angry response the child makes. The right to be angry without fear or guilt is as inalienable as any other, and more important than some. But since anger interferes with constructive action in the face of many, if not most problem situations that the child and his family face, parents are understandably anxious to keep it within reasonable bounds; and our interest has been in showing what parental actions are likely to have desired effects and what actions are likely to have undesired side effects.[34]

CONCLUSION

Now that many of the major tasks facing the preschool child have been delineated and discussed, some general considerations may be in order. What do children need from parents and others to aid them in facing their various tasks? Are there some general statements which can be made which will be helpful yet which will allow sufficient leeway for individual differences?

Frank, a few years ago, wrote a pamphlet on the fundamental needs of the child, as he saw them.

The child needs:
1. to be protected from unnecessary pain, deprivation, and exploitation.
2. to be accepted as a unique individual.
3. to be allowed to grow at his own rate.
4. to receive emotional satisfaction in feeding during infancy.
5. to receive constant reassurance during toilet training.
6. to receive extra affection when the new baby arrives.
7. to receive help in regulating his emotional responses.
8. to receive help in accepting his or her own sex.
9. to receive constant reassurance and simplified enlightenment on questions of sex and procreation.
10. to receive help in learning how to behave toward persons and things.
11. to receive help in accepting authority.
12. to receive the affectionate personal interest of an adult in order to create a constructive ideal of self.
13. to receive education that does not arouse hostility and aggression.
14. to receive wisely administered regulation or direction.

[34] *Ibid.*, p. 268.

15. to receive a clear-cut definition of a situation and of the appropriate conduct.
16. to receive the warmth of mothering at home and in nursery school.
17. to receive help in meeting life tasks.[35]

It must be stressed that no child is going to have all of his needs met as set forth in the above list to optimum degree at any one time. These statements can, nevertheless, serve as guidelines for students of children, parents, and others involved in responsibility for their welfare.

SELECTED READINGS

Allen, Fredrick, "The Dilemma of Growth for Parents and Children," *Child Study* (Spring, 1958), pp. 4–7.

Ausubel, David, *Ego Development and the Personality Disorders* (New York, Grune & Stratton, 1952).

Baldwin, Alfred, "The Effect of Home Environment on Nursery School Behavior," *Child Development,* Vol. 20 (June, 1949), pp. 49–61.

Barclay, Dorothy, "Safety Without Fears for the Active Child," *The New York Times Magazine* (November, 1957), p. 75.

Bernhardt, Karl, "How Permissive Are You?" *Bulletin of the Institute of Child Study* (1956), pp. 1–6.

Blake, Florence, *The Child, His Parents, and the Nurse* (Philadelphia, Lippincott, 1954).

Brim, Orville, "Evaluating the Effects of Parent Education," *Marriage and Family Living,* Vol. 19 (February, 1957), pp. 54–60.

Castaneda, A., Palermo, D., and McCandless, B., "Complex Learning and Performance As a Function of Anxiety in Children and Task Difficulty," *Child Development,* Vol. 27 (September, 1956), pp. 327–332.

Davis, H., Sears, R., Miller, H., and Brodbeck, A., "Effects of Cup, Bottle, and Breast Feeding on Oral Activities of Newborn Babies," *Pediatrics,* Vol. 3 (1948), pp. 549–558.

Freud, Anna, and others, *Psychoanalytic Study of the Child* (New York, International Universities Press, 1954).

Martin, William, "Effects of Early Training on Personality," *Marriage and Family Living,* Vol. 19 (February, 1957), pp. 39–45.

Mussen, P., and Conger, J., *Child Development and Personality* (New York, Harper & Row, 1956), Parts II and III.

Piaget, Jean, *The Moral Judgment of the Child* (New York, Harcourt, Brace & World, 1932).

Ribble, Margaret, *The Personality of the Young Child* (New York, Columbia, 1955).

[35] Lawrence K. Frank, *The Fundamental Needs of the Child,* National Association for Mental Health, Inc., 1952. This copyrighted material was originally produced by the National Association for Mental Health, 10 Columbus Circle, New York, N.Y. 10019.

Sears, R., Maccoby, E., and Levin, H., *et al., Patterns of Child Rearing* (New York, Harper & Row, 1957).

Sewell, William, "Infant Training and the Personality Adjustment of the Child," *American Journal of Sociology,* Vol. 58 (September, 1952), pp. 150–159.

Spock, Benjamin, *The Pocket Book of Baby and Child Care* (New York, Pocket, 1954).

Stendler, Celia, "Possible Causes of Overdependency in Young Children," *Child Development,* Vol. 22 (June, 1954), pp. 125–146.

Stone, Joseph, and Church, Joseph, *Childhood and Adolescence* (New York, Random House, 1957), Chapters 3–7.

Stroup, Atlee, "Marital Adjustment of the Mother and the Personality of the Child," *Marriage and Family Living,* Vol. 18 (May, 1956), pp. 109–113.

Vincent, Clark, "Trends in Infant Care Ideas," *Child Development,* Vol. 22 (September, 1951), pp. 199–209.

QUESTIONS AND EXERCISES

1. Comment on Erikson's series of stages referred to in this chapter. Do you believe that Erikson's schema is more adequate than the Freudian theories on child development? Discuss.

2. Arrange to observe a new baby for a period of time. Describe and record all his movements during this period of time. Attempt to indicate the possible source of each movement.

3. Does the month-old child have a human personality? Why or why not?

4. Arrange to spend a series of sessions observing children in a nursery school situation. Compare the boys with the girls in terms of social behavior and motor activity.

5. "It is generally harmful to the child if the parents bicker and argue in his presence, and disagree openly on methods of discipline." Discuss the validity of this statement.

6. What can be done to bring out a child who is shy, introverted, and lacking in self-reliance?

7. Are temper tantrums in young children normal or pathological? Discuss.

8. How did you express anger and hostility as a child? Do you openly express anger and hostility more or less as an adult? Have you made progress with increasing age in this regard?

9. Organize a group and have two or three sets of young parents in to speak on life with young children as they see it.

10. Children often engage in telling "tall" stories. At what age should parents interfere in order to bring a sense of reality into the picture? Or should they ignore such behavior? Discuss.

11. How can parents best encourage the development of self-reliance and initiative in young children?

12. Since child development specialists do not agree on the practices and techniques which should be used in child rearing, do you believe parents should fall back on folklore and tradition? Why or why not?

22

The Family During the Expansion Period

The preschool period is a very busy one. But almost before it can catch its breath the family becomes a school-age family. At this period new tasks appear while old ones, in a multichild family, still remain.

PROVIDING ADEQUATE SPACE AND TIME

With a growing family of children, at least one of whom is in school, the typical family finds itself under pressure regarding shelter and space.[1] Often the family has initially been in an apartment or small house. Now the quarters are just too cramped. The children are growing by leaps and bounds. Father has no safe place for his tools, guns, golf clubs, and books. Mother's personal belongings are distributed in various corners and closets throughout the house, for she has no one place that she can literally call her own. The family must have more space.

The family with such pressures faces difficult decisions. Is a move to be made to a developed suburb or to a new housing development? Is it now the time to buy? What features are to be emphasized in the new house?

---

[1] As was suggested in Chapter 4, our schema of family development does not do full justice to the complexities involved. When the first child enters school a new period is opening up for the family. At the same time in the great bulk of cases there will be a younger child in the home. In effect the family is forced to cope with both the school and preschool stage in simultaneous fashion. All we can do in a treatment of this type is to analyze the particular periods as systematically as possible. Future research may well suggest that a different system of stages, based upon a refined approach to the family configuration, is in order. See Roy Rodgers, *Improvements in the Construction and Analysis of Family Life Cycle Categories* (Kalamazoo, Western Michigan University Press, 1962).

The family in choosing a house is also choosing an environment, both physical and social. Included will be the type of school the children attend, the availability of playground and playing space, the provision of public services and facilities, and so forth.

Having once decided on the general type of environment wanted, the family must answer more specific questions regarding house and lot. Will the new house provide adequate sleeping facilities? Will the bathroom facilities prove adequate even during the morning period of stress? Are the kitchen and laundry facilities functional in reference to location, amount of space, availability, and possibilities for efficient and step-saving work?

The children will be growing and needing space for play, homework, and rest. Unless the family is well above average in income, some squeeze will be felt and dilemmas will appear. If father is to have a study to himself, the children may have to double up on bedroom space. Is the family to have a large dining room and living room area for socializing activities? If so, it may mean sacrificing an extra bath or bedroom. Dozens of questions such as the above arise as practical questions or dilemmas which must be solved in trying to accommodate a growing family to physical and spacial realities.

Space and scheduling are correlated problems, and the latter will be discussed in a later section. The age and stage differences of the children will mean that a wide range of activities must go on in the household. In late afternoon or evening it may be necessary for Johnny to practice his music lesson while at the same time Susie needs to do her homework. The fact that Joe, aged two, may be relatively unsupervised by Mother at the same time, due to dinner preparations, will add to the pressure for separate facilities to which people can go to pursue their individual tasks.

The general philosophy and value system of the family are also heavily involved in the question of the location of housing. Is the family trying to "crack" a particular social circle? Is it willing to mortgage heavily in order to live in an exclusive section? The particular decisions made regarding housing have broad implications.

FINANCES

As Bigelow shows, the high school and college period will bring the greatest pressures on the family purse.[2] However, during the elementary school period the cost of family upkeep will continually expand. Mother will notice that one can or dish of food will no longer suffice as it once did. Clothing for school and other activities will take an increased proportion of the budget. And it will seem that the "free" public school will demand

[2] Howard Bigelow, "Financing the Marriage," in Howard Becker and Reuben Hill, *Family, Marriage, and Parenthood* (Boston, Heath, 1955), Chapter 13.

a quarter for each child every other day. In short, the couple will begin during this period to realize what it is finally "in for" regarding the rearing of a brood of children, even though the worst is yet to come.

Many dilemmas will occur. By this time the husband-father is becoming established in his occupational role. If he is not in a niche which seems promising, he may wish to explore the possibilities of a transfer. While some new avenue may hold more promise for the long run, for the short run the family may have to face loss of income and security. The implications for the family are rather clear. Expenses continue even though father may be "between jobs" or temporarily on the lower rung of a better ladder.

These days a typical dilemma involves the question of mobility within the larger company structure. So often it appears that a man must go to two or three branches before he lands in Detroit. Once there, he may be offered the "big chance" at another outlying area. While in some cases the company will pay transportation and sometimes certain other costs, such moves may upset even the most careful financial planning. Problems of buying and keeping furniture, or renting versus buying, are correlated to a degree with questions of vertical and horizontal social mobility of the family.

Physical maintenance of the family at this period also involves guarding against accident and disease. Children by this age are bound to roam about. Unfortunately all parents except those of great means will be forced to allow the children to go about in the neighborhood adjacent to home. For many this means walking and playing within yards or feet of moving vehicles, dangerous electric equipment, and sharp objects of various sorts. No ideal solution to the situation seems possible under present conditions of planning. Persistent and consistent training and warning will cut the rate of accidents for whole categories, but this fact is not of much solace to the parents of a child who forgot caution for one crucial moment.

SOCIALIZATION

During the public school period the family's value system is exposed in a way it never was before. The child at that age will be old enough to notice alternative ways of acting and doing. He will want to know the reasons behind some of the family's standards and practices, and is inclined to press the parent to explain his rationale. This puts the parent "on the spot." No longer can he appeal to tradition as his parents and grandparents before him did. In a pragmatic, rapidly changing society children are all "from Missouri." They must be "shown" and references to what used to be done may bring forth accusations of being an "old fogey" or "old-fashioned."

One consultant describes some of the problems that parents have related to him in these words:

Let us turn now to the question of what values to transmit to one's children. One problem is that of personality versus skill. In the past our society rewarded the person who became highly skilled, who was a hard worker, and who developed primarily his working abilities. More and more we have seen that it is not always the hard worker who receives reward, promotion, or financial success, but rather the person with the type of personality that enables him to get along easily with other people. Recently I interviewed a man who pointed out that, in the promotions that had taken place in his office over the last ten years, a number of individuals, who were actually less able accountants than he, had been promoted—they were now his chiefs—primarily because they had out-going personalities. The question arises, what should such a parent emphasize with his child? His child argues that he does not have to put as much work into obtaining good school marks or into earning achievements as the father thinks he should, because as long as he has a passing grade and is a well-liked, 'well-rounded' type of person who gets along easily with everyone, he will go just as far as the bookworm. He argues that playing football, working on the school paper, being active in the dramatic club, and so on, are actually more important than grades and homework. The parent who sees the child's arguments borne out in his own office, and who at the same time still highly values the more traditional concept that one's skills and one's ability to study and to know a subject are more important than anything else, is in a dilemma; he is not quite sure that his child is really gaining more by social promotion than by the attainment of scholastic standards. The feeling of being caught in this dilemma may cause apathy and may diminish the parent's effectiveness as a culture-bearer.

The value of conformity is an American culturalism, and the parent who fears that too much conformity at times may be harmful to individuality is in a quandary as to which is more important to give his son, the outer security of excessive conformity or the inner security of individuality.

The parent who places value on health also finds himself in a dilemma since he has been made conscious of the importance not only of physical health but also of mental health. For example, in the past the parent felt quite comfortable about ordering his child to put on his rubbers in order to avoid colds. Now he questions whether or not he should make an issue of putting on the rubbers, particularly when he is told that having a cold may have something to do with emotions or that nagging the child may affect his emotional health. In the past many parents felt quite comfortable about the idea that a child should have a bowel movement every day in order to maintain his physical health. Now they have been made conscious of the fact that one may encourage anal fixations by overemphasizing the bowels. Parents may change their behavior to fit the times, but still worry about whether or not they are endangering their child's physical health.

Many medical and social problems, such as venereal disease, mental breakdown, alcoholism, gambling, stealing, and even the subject of sex, were handled traditionally by the simple concept of, and simple word, "sin." With the greater appreciation of the complexity of these problems, the parent at times finds himself in a conflict between the religious teachings that have been handed down to him from the past and modern science.

Speaking of religion, we must not forget the problem faced by the parent who belongs to a minority sect or denomination regarding religious principles versus social acceptance. The parent who is aware of the effect on his child of pressure by the child's peer group and the desire of his child to want to be like everybody else may wonder how forcefully he should pass on to his child the tenets of his particular religious group.[3]

Compared to British parents, many American parents apparently are stressing the value of getting along with others. Farber asked samples of both British and American middle-class parents to respond to the statement: "a properly brought up child should be." Respondents were asked to indicate the qualities which were considered to be predominantly American or predominantly British. His results are included in Table 40.

Farber notes that in a sense American parents want to have their cake and eat it. While they stress social skills, there is evidence of a fear that socialization will destroy individuality and originality. Whatever the conflicts parents may have at this more abstract level, the parents must and will stand for something. Besides working along with the children toward clarification of the values to be stressed in their particular family, they will find it necessary to help the child reconcile any divergence which may obtain with norms held by outsiders. Often conflict will involve the expectations of peers. "All the other kids are doing it, why can't I?" can be a powerful appeal. Obviously people are going to differ as to how they handle such situations. Children must be able to get along with others and to have friends in order to develop into healthy adulthood. But both to prevent the characterless conformity about which Riesman speaks and to preserve its own integrity, the family will often be forced to take a stand.

A somewhat more personal problem will arise for many parents. During this period if the school situation is ideal, the child will come to consider the teacher the final authority on things important. Difficult as this may be, it would no doubt be more disconcerting to find that the child had no respect at all for the teacher.

DEVELOPING NEW PATTERNS OF RESPONSIBILITY

As children move into the school period the family division of tasks and responsibilities will ordinarily be changed. It will seem that work requirements will increase by geometric rather than arithmetic progression as the children grow year by year. How is all the work to be done to keep the household running smoothly? Perhaps something can be learned from

[3] Philipp Sottong, "The Dilemma of the Parent as Culture Bearer," *Social Casework,* Vol. XXXVI, No. 5 (July, 1955), p. 305. Permission for reproduction granted by the Family Service Association of America, New York, N.Y.

TABLE 40

*Percentage of British and American Respondents
Listing Various Qualities as Desirable in
a Properly Brought-Up Child*

Qualities Hypothesized as Predominantly American (previous to testing)	British	American
Respect for parents, adults, authority	19	30
Sincere, honest	12	22
Getting along with others, mixing well	0	11
Unselfish	0	9
Well-behaved	3	7
All-aroundness	0	4
Individuality, originality	6	15
Neatness	3	5
Influenced by religion	6	11
Loving	3	6
Feels loved by parents	0	4
Not spoiled	0	4
Genial, good-natured	0	2
Intelligent	0	2
Taught about sex	0	2
Qualities Hypothesized as Predominantly British (previous to testing)		
Good manners, politeness, courtesy	53	43
Obedience	31	20
Thoughtfulness about others	16	12
Self-reliance	19	1
Create no nuisance	16	0
Hold his own without aggression	6	0
Self-control	6	0
Kindness	13	2
Kindness to animals	9	0
Total number of respondents	(32)	(81)

SOURCE: Maurice Farber, "English and Americans: Values in the Socialization Process," *Journal of Psychology,* Vol. 36 (October, 1953), p. 245.

the traditional family of the frontier. There everyone was expected to assume certain responsibilities from the age of five or six. The assigned tasks were graded according to age and ability. The little girl of six would carry a jug of cider or water to the fields to the thirsty men. The boy of ten or twelve was given considerable responsibility and was occasionally sent to a neighboring work crew in place of an adult man. Under modern conditions it is much more difficult to find tasks which can be assigned to the child which will both aid the family and contribute to the child's development. If the first criterion is not met, the latter is nonexistent. While play work is often of interest to the child, real work although at times boring and discouraging, is in the long run more satisfying and meaningful.

Two problems which often arise involve misplaced emphasis. The first is the general American approach to child labor. The fear persists that if children are asked to work the neighbors will be reminded of the early industrialists who exploited children. Naturally we are not contending that children should be overworked. Our criticism is directed toward those parents who deprive their children of wholesome training and feelings of achievement regarding tasks well done.[4] The second problem is essentially one of status. Many men seem to feel that it would be ideal if they could make enough money so that servants could do most of the work and the children would not be required to lift a hand. Such attitudes probably reflect in many cases insecurities born of depression upbringing. Whatever their origin and whatever their value in bolstering feelings of status, these attitudes are not helpful in providing an optimum environment for the growing child.

The parents who wish to have a home in which a cooperative group gets the tasks accomplished will have their work cut out for them. It is not as easy to find suitable work tasks for children today as it was a generation or two ago, especially for boys. Tradition oriented fathers may fear that asking boys to help with housework will make them "sissies." Realism suggests that such fears are not warranted if other areas of the environment are normal for the children. It will, however, take all the creativity the parents can muster for them, working with the children, to arrange a program of mutual sharing of home tasks which are beneficial to all concerned.[5] There will be times when it would be much simpler and easier for the parent to do the task rather than have the child attempt it. Eating daughter's first cake or pie may seem like a sacrifice to father and older brother, for example. But it will be a necessary part of the picture if daughter is to move along toward a future homemaking role, even though mother's pie may taste better.

Economic Responsibility

It is universally recognized that children must be helped to gain a sense of responsibility in the use of money or its equivalent. Even the most idealistic person will grant that the child must gain some sense of the value and use of money. How to arrange optimum conditions for the development of this on the child's part is the question posed.

[4] Maurice Farber, "English and Americans: Values in the Socialization Process," *Journal of Psychology,* Vol. 36 (October, 1953), pp. 243–250.

[5] Note again the emphasis Erikson puts on industry at the school (latency) period; see Chapter 21. See also Ernest Osborne, "How to Teach Your Child About Work," Public Affairs Committee, 1955, pamphlet No. 216 for practical considerations in this area.

Stress on general responsibility in the cooperative work roles, discussed above, sets the stage for more specific training regarding money, in that the concept of general responsibility is stressed. It would be hard to teach economic responsibility without this. Within this framework and within the general value system which forms the basis of their operations, the parents will make plans to allow the child to have money which he can handle and control. Strong arguments are made for and against the allowance. Parents must decide whether an allowance is to be regularly given or whether the children are to be "paid" for their chores. Perhaps the most important element is the practice in decision-making which the child gains by dispensing his own money rather than the method of obtaining it.

If the child is to learn, the parent will be forced to hold his tongue and permit mistakes to be made. The child learns the hard way that money spent for trivia can never be reclaimed. Looking back, the parents and children will often say that the money was well spent in terms of the lessons learned.

When an allowance is given it will be necessary to take into account changing needs and circumstances. It would be unrealistic to give a thirteen-year-old boy five dollars per month and expect him to handle all his school, transportation, lunch, and clothing expenses within this budget by present urban standards. Some discussion will be necessary as to the scope of activities which must be covered by the allowance.

The question of participation by the children in discussion of the family's total financial situation and in financial decision-making is a problem for many. Will Johnny relate the size of the mortgage to the neighbors if he learns of it? Will he be overwhelmed by the immensity of the problems faced by the family from which he could be spared? One is reminded again of sex matters. It seems to be in order here also that children be given knowledge and responsibility which they can reasonably handle, on a developmental basis. If particular types of information prove disturbing, parents may wish to bide their time until a greater degree of maturity will allow for the information to be absorbed. As to decision-making, parents can aid the development of an *esprit de corps* by allowing the children to exercise some authority in financial matters. Whether the family takes a vacation or spends the equivalent cost on some wanted household objects can be a matter for a family council. Such limited problems can be posed with children who are in the preadolescent age category, and their solution can be a valuable learning experience. Ingenious and observant parents are able to judge the level of problem which can be handled by the children involved.

Considerations of economic decision-making raise the broader question of accountability and authority regarding the school age child. Questions of the extent and type of discipline will arise even though the parents thought they had previously been settled. These questions will have to be solved in some way. They essentially involve a reevaluation of the method of enforcement of expectations which the parents have previously instituted. Quite often parents relax a bit as the second child moves along the pathway which the older child opened up.

REORGANIZATION OF SCHEDULES

With children in school the juggling of activities to fit into any orderly schedule becomes a complicated task. Johnny has homework assignments to complete in the evening which must be sandwiched in along with music practice, sports, and TV programs, to say nothing of the chores mother expects him to get done. Gretchen's favorite TV program falls in the period from 6:00 to 6:30 P.M., the most suitable time for the evening meal in view of father's tight schedule. Further, financial pressures are such that the family finally decides it has two alternatives. Either mother works part-time, or father takes on extra work. With either alternative further pressure is put on an already tight schedule.

A cooperative arrangement again seems the only solution to the many schedule dilemmas, with attention given to priorities. If the parents expect the schoolwork to be done, time for it must be allotted somewhere. Perhaps a better use of school time will mean that schoolwork need not be brought home in such great quantities every evening. At least the child may be helped to envision alternatives whereby a reasonable balance can obtain among the various activities.

THE EMOTIONAL CONSTELLATION

With children in school and with a toddler or two in the preschool stage, it is clear that the emotional constellation in the family becomes complicated. How can there be enough love and affection to go around? The stage seems set for some problems. According to the Freudians the school child will often have unresolved oedipal conflicts which push him at times into extreme behavior, although as a whole the period will be a smoother one than the adolescent period to come. It is a period in which the older children will turn often to peers and others for affection, only to return and demand response from parents at unexpected moments. The younger children at home are treated at times as unwanted nuisances and on other occasions with unabashed affection.

The children in a family will differ as to their affectional needs, and the sensitive parent finds it difficult to achieve a balance which is fair to all the children and to the spouse. Children resent favoritism, yet one child at a particular time may have a special need for extra love and attention.

Somehow parents must get it across that each person in the family is loved, wanted, and cherished. This sense of basic acceptance and love probably has to come earlier than the school period in most cases but it must be re-established from time to time and exhibited in new form as the children mature. If a general feeling of warmth and love prevails in the home the stronger siblings cannot allow only the parent or parents to give special attention to the emotional needs of a given child but they may at times be motivated to give aid themselves.

The husband-wife relationship must not be overlooked. According to the Kinsey figures the wife should typically achieve the peak of her sexual desire and activity during this period, and sex should be a factor which helps relieve emotional tensions and hostilities. Initial inhibitions and diffi-culties should have subsided by this time and the relationship should ideally be a satisfactory one. Such is not always the case, of course. Rainwater and Weinstein report the following case involving a couple with three children. The wife reports to the interviewer as follows:

[How did you learn about sex?] I didn't learn nothing. I was told about men-struation when it happened. My foster mother told me that it would happen every month and that I'd have to wear a pad; that's all she ever said. I read a lot about it in my sister-in-law's [nursing] books, and while we were engaged we talked about what I was reading. I was scared to go home with him. He was very understanding and assured me everything would be all right. [Now?] It isn't too often, only about every two or three weeks.

I don't enjoy it because I heard nothing but filth about it when I was young. It's hard for me. I can't relax. I know it isn't sinful, but I remember the bad things I heard. My husband is understanding. [How do you know his desires?] I can tell as soon as he walks in the door when he wants it. They always pat you on the tail, and he wouldn't argue about anything when he wants it.

[What are the changes since you were married?] I'm a little more re-laxed; I still don't want it, but I know it's my duty. He doesn't try too often because he understands. I could always live without it; I just don't need it. If I could just relax it might be better. My husband is very understanding about sex; he holds his urge back for my benefit. He does it because he enjoys it; I do it because it's my duty. If I had to do it for a living, I'd starve.[6]

When the husband-wife relationship becomes monotonous and routine or worse, the stage is set for trouble. While it is perhaps at a later stage that the husband is especially vulnerable to the charms of a young girl in his environment he is by no means immune at this period. Furthermore, a dead-level relationship may be difficult to revive during the middle years when the children are gone and husband and wife are thrown back upon each other. Not to be considered lightly is the role-model parents present

[6] Lee Rainwater and Karol Weinstein, *And the Poor Get Children,* Chicago, *Quadrangle Books,* 1960, pp. 114–115.

to their children. The children's basic attitudes toward sex, sex roles, love, marriage, and parenthood are based partly on what they observe in their parent's behavior.

THE SEX ROLE

According to the Freudians the elementary school period is a "dormant" one. By this is meant that the oedipal strivings of the previous period have either been repressed or worked through. The child is then free to identify with the parent of the same sex and with the sex role appropriate to him. Leaving aside any criticisms of the Freudian hypothesis it appears that this period is a crucial one for the child's development even though the adolescent period may be the most difficult. This period involves "the beginnings of identity" as Erikson phrases it.

Values enter the picture to a degree here. There are those who feel that male and female roles are becoming so blurred in America that soon no clear-cut role-image can be presented to our children. Both foreign and American writers have been having field days regarding the deleterious effect that can be expected when women become more "mannish" and men become more "womanish." Most of these reports are journalistic and exaggerated, as Hartley points out,[7] but not necessarily far wide of the mark. Actually sex role changes have been taking place for at least two generations, and there is no more reason to expect these changes to be disorganizing to children than any other areas of social change. Nevertheless parents must to an extent decide the type of emphasis they wish to give to particular sex roles. As Mead suggests, a child of one sex may be driven away from interest in an occupational pursuit if parents define it as appropriate only for the other sex.[8] The school-age period is one in which early occupational expectations can well be discussed; it is not necessary to wait until the adolescent period, if no pressure is put on by parents toward too early a commitment, and because occupation is only one aspect of sex role.

More specifically comes the question of aiding the developmental process of identification. According to role theory the child will identify with the parent of the same sex. By this time of development, the male child is absorbing many things from his environment and it is clear that he vicariously "plays at" being a "man." Questions are now being raised about the lack of role-models in the environment for the boy to emulate. One emphasis is on the fact that our nursery and elementary schools are dominated by women. A second emphasis stresses the absence of the father

[7] Ruth Hartley, "Some Implications of Current Changes in Sex Role Patterns," *Merrill-Palmer Quarterly* (April, 1960), pp. 153–163.

[8] Margaret Mead in public speeches as quoted in major newspapers in the Spring of 1962.

from the home. Allegedly mothers and teachers will overstress decorum and nonaggressiveness to the point where boys of the future will be "soft" and "sissified."

In our judgment the fears and criticisms again are somewhat exaggerated, for a number of reasons. First of all there is plenty of evidence that adults, regardless of sex, treat children differentially on the basis of their sex.[9] This is true of both parents and is true of teachers and other adults regardless of sex. Postulate a viewing of a Saturday afternoon football game around the TV by father, children, and a few men in the neighborhood who have somehow escaped from their yardwork and related chores. Comments such as "What will you play?" are addressed always to male children in the group. When a little girl is brought into the conversation it will be through references to her potentials as a spectator, band member, or majorette. If women are also participating the process will not vary in any important aspect. Day by day this process of holding appropriate role-models and reacting differentially to the behavior and personality of the child continues.

It is of course true that children of both sexes need adult models of both sexes available in their environment in order for them to acquire their optimal sex roles. For that reason a balanced ratio of teachers by sex, from the primary grades on would seem ideal. Evidence suggests that in cases where the father is absent from the home through divorce, death, or for long periods as in the case of sailors the children will be adversely affected.[10] The picture is not clear in regard to the actual number of hours the parent should be around the child. Presently it appears that it is the type of relationship rather than the time per se which is most crucial. Boys especially seem to need a male authority-figure in the home to emulate in order to establish their essential maleness. Certainly, however, the image the boy has of his father is eventually carried by the boy during the father's absence.

Only males can lead the boy into the male world or subculture, and females are necessary for the initiation of the little girl into the feminine world. This is rather well understood and hardly requires comment. At times the boy will appreciate an intercessor who explains the male point of view on sports or some other area when he seems to be threatened by feminine domination. Similar situations develop for the growing girl although presumably not as frequently since the mother has the more direct contact in child rearing. Certain problems do arise which are not simple to

[9] Hartley, *op. cit.,* See also Boyd McCandless, *Children and Adolescents* (New York, Holt, Rinehart and Winston, 1961), p. 337.

[10] D. B. Lynn and W. L. Sawrey, "The Effects of Father Absence on Norwegian Boys and Girls," *Journal of Abnormal and Social Psychology,* Vol. 59 (Fall, 1959), pp. 258–262. See however, Alan Crain and Caroline Stamm, "Intermittent Absence of Fathers and Children's Perceptions of Parents," *Journal of Marriage and the Family,* Vol. 27 (August, 1965), pp. 344–347.

answer, however. Just what are parents and others holding up to their children as ideal roles? There is evidence that many boys are taught that they are superior to girls in all ways, and that they must not be caught doing anything remotely feminine. Such ideas fly in the face of realities of the schoolroom and the general community at the present, let alone the future. Parents will do well to ponder at length on the type of men and women they wish their sons and daughters to be in terms of the world in which the children will live as adults.[11] If a child seems to deviate too far toward "sissiness" or "tomboyishness" as the case may be, they can take action which seems to them appropriate at the time.

Sex Knowledge and Attitudes

As children struggle with problems of identity, the question of sexuality will arise. Some will be experimenting with masturbation. Boys will often have concerns about it arising from conflicts between what they may have heard from other boys and what they think their parents' attitudes are regarding the practice. But, relatively speaking, the school period is a "quiet" one as sex matters go.

A developmental approach would suggest that parents enter the picture directly when the time is appropriate. Again it is to be understood that much teaching regarding sex is indirect rather than direct. The adroit parent can sense the child's need or problem and arrange to present the information or deal with the attitude in question tactfully. Certainly, for example, the girl should be prepared for menstruation during the prepubertal period. No instance as clear-cut can be cited for the boy, although the incidence of nocturnal emissions at the same period involves a rough corollary.

The concept of the "teachable moment" is basic. It is important that information and interpretation be given at the time when it will be beneficial. Mace suggests that many parents who rank high in other realms fail in the job of teaching sex knowledge and sex attitudes, especially the latter. He reasons that we may be forced to reappraise the notion that this instruction must always be handled by the parents.[12] Perhaps the incest taboo prevents parents from opening up areas which would be found to be impossible to handle once attempted. It may be that outsiders will always have to play a part in the sex education of at least a certain portion of our children. Mace's comments are thought provoking. The question of responsibility immediately comes up. Does the responsibility fall to the school, the church, or some other institution? How are we to determine which children need extra parental instruction and which do not? Other questions will occur to the reader following Mace's logic.

11 McCandless, *op. cit.,* p. 339.
12 David Mace, "Some Reflections on the American Family," *Marriage and Family Living,* Vol. 24 (May, 1962), pp. 109–112.

COMMUNICATION

Communication becomes a more complicated process as the older children go through school and the younger ones fill in their places at home. There are many things to talk about and yet it may be difficult to "get everything out" so to speak. The children all want the parents' attention at times, and yet at other times one child may retreat into his own world and become almost noncommunicative. Bossard has stressed the family meal-time as an important period for discussion.[13] It is here that at least once a day all family members can interact together. The great temptation on the part of the older members is to dominate the discussion completely so that the younger members cannot get a word in edgewise. This is not necessarily harmful in all its aspects. Younger children can learn much by being sensitive listeners. Family attitudes toward sobriety, education, work, and dozens of lesser topics are portrayed directly or indirectly through table conversation. Sometimes the process is deliberate. Father refers to the unfortunate Mr. Jones who lost his business because of his lack of diligence and his appetite for strong spirits. Mother backs him up with a remark to the effect that she cannot understand a man who will run around and neglect his family. Even small children will get some kind of message from such a discussion.

If the adults tend to dominate the table conversation, care must be taken to allow all family members to have their chance at verbal interaction. For the most part, the children will be able to achieve satisfaction in play activities with their siblings and friends. At times they will wish to relate to mother, father, or to both. The principle of equity would seem to demand that somehow these needs be honored. Perhaps most important is a feeling on the part of the youngster that at a critical time he can turn to someone who loves him and receive a sympathetic response.

In reference to the older children, the level of communication will need to change to accommodate their growth and development. The children appreciate the chance to discuss their schoolwork and play activities. In the nonthreatening environment of the home the child can express some of his fears and anxieties without the fear of humiliation that would come were they expressed before classmates or teachers. Where two children of the opposite sex are of school age, family conversation can serve to convey both the masculine and feminine point of view on the matter at hand, if there is a difference. This function can be important to the child who at school and play interacts mainly with members of his own sex. Children of this age also need the advantages of engaging in the more adultlike conversation which they cannot get in peer interaction. By choosing the appro-

---

[13] James Bossard and Eleanor Boll, *The Sociology of Child Development* (New York, Harper & Row, 1960), Chapter 13.

priate symbols, adults can bring school-age children into discussions of politics, religion, finance, and recreation, at levels which are "higher" than they were in previous years. Certain risks obtain of course; a mention of "Social Security" may require a long and detailed explanation of insurance, retirement, general governmental policy, and numerous other details before the conversation can abate. Not all parents have the stamina or knowledge necessary for such excursions. The ability to give explanations that are informative and satisfying, appropriate and to the point but not unduly lengthy, is for parents, an art well worth practicing. It will not only contribute to their own peace of mind but will aid in the children's development as well.

RELATING TO PERSONS OUTSIDE THE FAMILY

During the school period the child and the total family are increasingly exposed to the larger world outside the home. The ubiquitous PTA, the church, and the local and the wide community beckon the family to participate and play its part in the ongoing social process. Certainly, to the socially sensitive person, community needs are such that the calls are difficult to ignore. This is especially so when one's own children are actively participating in the wider community. This is brought home when issues such as a drive for a new school building or community agency is underway. Typically, families with children actually or potentially involved carry the burden of the drive if it is to be successful. Community organization experts tell us that they are forced to appeal to already overworked parents to fill volunteer posts if they are to get them manned successfully.

Riesman, Whyte, and others protest that we are overorganized. By implication they plead that families need more time for privacy and reflection. Others in some communities suggest that the school, for example, makes too many outside demands on the children. (This involves the high school more often than the grade school.) How much is too much? Some families do get so involved in outside-the-home activities that they have no time left for home life. Others might find that involvement in community activities to a greater degree would provide them with new insights and help lift them out of ruts into which they had progressively sunk.

If it is conceded that good schools, efficient and humane government, adequate social agencies, and active churches have their place, it follows that many families will have to participate in community activities. This is not the same as suggesting that we need more so-called do-gooders who neglect their home responsibilities in order to advise others how to live. Instead, it is suggested that for the common good it is necessary that many families extend their activities at times beyond their own boundaries. In so doing they may find that there is truth in the ancient maxim which suggests that life can be found only by losing it.

The family will continue relating to in-laws and relatives during this period if they are available in the community. Visits with aunts, uncles, cousins, and grandparents can be constructive for the children and beneficial to the parents if the relationships are of a positive nature. As Bossard and Boll indicate, the child learns the nature of the parents and parental roles by comparing them with others and observing similarities and contrasts. Reporting on a study based on 400 case records they are led to make the following statements regarding childhood visits, most of which involved relatives:

These visits gave varied insights into life—the nature of adults compared with your parents, dissentions among relatives, "queer" people, new food, different home surroundings, "strange" family customs, new ideas and values in family living. Evaluated in terms of the learning process, these insights were of two different kinds. First there were those that were disillusioning—people, relatives, families, playmates, were not as you thought they were. One-quarter of those who visited as children saw or had experiences of a sexual nature which they apparently had difficulty in assimilating. The other kind were more constructive in nature, teaching something useful later on—ways of dealing with people, of entertaining, of handling difficult situations, and, what was equally important, how not to do certain things.

Visiting away from home invariably led to comparisons between one's home and family and those visited. We human beings early learn to make comparisons, and when young children go visiting they see how "the other half" lives, metaphorically speaking. It is interesting to note that the majority of informants in the study had experiences, still fresh in their minds after a period of years, which led them to appreciate their own homes and parents more than they did before they went visiting. "We had a nicer life at home." "In our family we had better manners." "I discovered there were parents who didn't speak nicely to their children." The most-emphasized feature of home life was food and Mother's cooking. The stress in present-day pediatric care would seem to produce a strong emotional complex about food in the later years. In a minority of cases, the comparisons were not favorable to the home base. These experiences seem to have been particularly well remembered.[14]

It can, of course, be seen that from the point of view of the parents, the experience of visiting will not always be a positive one. Just as is true in relation to house guests or servants in the household, the parent has some control over the learning experience for the child. If the parents are upwardly mobile they may be ashamed of their relatives' old-fashioned or deviant customs, and try to shield their own children from them. It is probable that such a practice will backfire in that guilt feelings will be induced which may eventually have negative effects on the child. As a whole, it appears that the child has a greater chance of establishing a firm identity

[14] *Ibid.,* p. 180.

and feeling of security if he is allowed to visit and interact freely with in-laws, relatives, and friends.

MAINTAINING MORALE AND MOTIVATION TO CARRY OUT FAMILY TASKS

As the children mature the parents have the problem of maintaining a satisfactory system of discipline and order. That this is a complex task is quite clear. The children are not yet at the stage of the so-called adolescent rebellion in which they may at times seem to challenge every act of the parents. Yet that they can be very trying to their parents and other adults at this age is known to all who have sustained contact with normal children of intermediate age. What approach is appropriate for this period?

For a number of years child development writers seemed to be advising parents to be "pals" with their children. In place of the old patriarch who stood above the children as lord and master it was suggested that father now be on the child's level. As is so typical in child study, it was probably inevitable that voices would be raised in protest of this point of view. They have been. It is now being suggested that there are negative aspects involved if parents attempt to play only the pal role with the children. Lynn speaks to the point in the following fashion: ". . . . the father is a better representative of manhood if he does not neglect his role to 'just being a pal' to his son. The father should represent the adult male, not the boy's peer group." [15] It should be noted that Lynn emphasizes not just being a pal. Fathers who are on a firm footing can at times relax and play a pal role with the children. The criticism is against a practice in which this is the only role carried.

The basic problem of discipline and control seems to be that of balance. Children can be controlled to the point where all initiative and drive is pushed out of them. While this may produce docile conformists whose behavior is overtly satisfactory at home and school, the chances are great that initiative and independence will not emerge in adulthood to the degree usually demanded. This approach seems to be used by parents labeled as authoritarian. Although the evidence is still somewhat contradictory, the authoritarian approach seems to produce the following types of personality characteristics in children: hostility, anxiety covered by surface bravado, intolerance of ambiguity, prejudice against minorities, rigidity and conformity.[16] In general, nonauthoritarian parents have children who have

---

[15] D. B. Lynn, "The Husband-Father Role in the Family," *Marriage and Family Living,* Vol. 23 (August, 1961), p. 296.

[16] See T. W. Adorno, *et al., The Authoritarian Personality* (New York, Harper & Row, 1950). An extensive literature exists regarding the so-called authoritarian personality, some of which is rather critical. For a good discussion of child rearing and authoritarianism, see McCandless, *op. cit.,* Chapter 12.

essentially the opposite personality characteristics as far as overall profiles are concerned.[17] There are definite problems which arise when the various studies are assessed, however, and we must be very tentative here. It appears that the nonauthoritarian is inclined to use love oriented techniques of child rearing and that the authoritarian parent is inclined to use other techniques of control. The danger lies in assuming that only the latter can be "manipulative." It now appears that especially in the upper classes, mothers typically use love oriented techniques, especially with boys.[18] However, the threat of love withdrawal is often used as a method of discipline. Both clinicians and research scientists are coming to agree that the use of the threat of love withdrawal technique can have a crippling effect on the growing personality. There is the suggestion that this approach is at least partially responsible for the development of general anxiety and tendencies toward conformity referred to as characteristics of so many American young people of today. It certainly seems clear that the use of love withdrawal is a form of manipulation which can be ruthless if carried to extremes. It may well be that this approach can have as crippling an effect on the psyche of the young child as the use of extreme methods of corporal punishment and rigid discipline.

As the children move away from the family into the wider community, it is inevitable that they will incur certain frustrations and problems. At times they will need special support at home as they try their wings for size away from the parental nest. Fortunate is the child who has the feeling that no matter how difficult the day on the playground or in the classroom, home will provide an atmosphere in which he can recoup in order to face the world another day. Many a child is like the proverbial Indian who "leaves the fight and runs away to return and fight another day." He must, for development of security feelings, know that at home he will always be basically accepted. Perhaps advice, chastisement, or other pressures will be forthcoming. They can be endured because this after all, is home, where, as Robert Frost says, they have to take you in.

The Parents' Morale

The spouses' task of maintaining not only their own morale but that of each other must not be overlooked. What Blood terms a mental hygiene

[17] See especially J. Howard Kauffman, "Interpersonal Relations in Traditional and Emergent Families Among the Midwest Mennonites," *Marriage and Family Living,* Vol. 23 (August, 1961), pp. 247–252. In this careful study of a sample of Mennonite families it was found that the "emergent" (companionship) family structure was associated with positive, nonauthoritarian personality characteristics in children while the "traditional" (authoritarian, patriarchal) family structure produced more rebelliousness and compulsiveness in the children. See also the various studies by Sears and associates.

[18] Robert Sears, *et al., Patterns of Child Rearing* (New York, Harper & Row, 1957).

or therapeutic function is still important in this period of development. He reports that the preadolescent stage shows a drop in therapeutic function of the husband compared to the previous periods, but the use of the husband in such fashion is still high.

As was shown in Chapter 17, wives appreciate help toward the solution of their problems given in positive fashion. Perceptive husbands are able to sense quickly when their wives have bad days. One can bring humor into the situation by a few well-chosen remarks. Another pitches in to help the wife clear the kitchen in order to help calm her nerves, or plays with the children in order to quiet things down. While these approaches offer only temporary relief, their function should not be taken lightly. Although in the Detroit report there is no formal statement spelling out the relationship between the marital adjustment of the couple and the therapeutic use of the husband, Blood and Wolfe comment to this extent:

> Because understanding is related to companionship and to love, marriages which are generally satisfactory to the wife or which are rated by outside observers as very cohesive tend to be characterized by the same patterns of therapeutic response. Not a single husband who actively helps his wife solve her problems or helps her withdraw from the situation has a poor marriage from either point of view. These active husbands go to the most trouble to free their wives from the burdens they are carrying. Either they take part of the load upon themselves, or they go out of their way to give their wives a popularized form of play therapy. The latter may not prevent the occurrence of the problem in the future, but it gives her hope that if things get as bad again, she can count on a recreative break whenever she needs it.[19]

Unfortunately, no comparable data are available which would indicate the importance of therapeutic activities wives engage in to help restore the wounds of their husbands. Clinical impressions lead one to infer that the function may be fully as important to the male as to the female. The ability of the wife to help the husband get some things off his chest after a hard day without having him upset the whole household in the process is a precious commodity if possessed in sufficient degree.

Empathy, the will to help, and command of the appropriate responses would seem to be the vital factors necessary for a person to fulfill the mental-hygiene function in his marriage. Empathy is necessary in order for him to perceive the problem, since the spouse may hesitate to make it known. Once he understands the partner's feelings he can consider appropriate action. Given these two conditions, trial-and-error experimentation will help him know what is helpful to the spouse in a particular situation. Considerations of equity and justice enter the picture at this point, lest one

---

[19] Reprinted with permission of The Free Press of Glencoe from *Husbands and Wives* by Robert Blood and Donald Wolfe. Copyright © 1960 by The Free Press, a Corporation.

partner expect more than his fair share of help which he does not reciprocate.

SOME GENERAL CONSIDERATIONS ON CHILD REARING

It will be our purpose in the remaining section of this chapter to pose some general problems for consideration by prospective parents or for present parents. As a whole these problems do not have implications for any particular developmental stage.

For a generation or two many parents in America have begun to reject the advice and practices of their elders and to turn increasingly toward science for problem-solving information. In so doing, some have come to expect too much too quickly. First of all, some parents are now looking to science for ends or goals rather than means. This is to ask the impossible. As was previously suggested, science essentially contributes to means rather than ends, although it can be used to help clarify ends or goals.[20] In effect this results in some parents coming to depend unduly on experts or books. Many of us are familiar with the cartoon of the exasperated parent holding the child over a knee while feverishly thumbing pages of The Book trying to find the right solution to the problem. Such an exaggeration helps clarify the point we are pursuing.

It must again be stressed that at the present time we do not have a full-fledged science of child rearing. Medical, biological, psychological, and sociological studies dealing with marriage and family life are now becoming quite numerous and impressive. Yet fundamental, basic questions remain unsolved. Unfortunately, this is not fully understood by many persons in American society today. The confusion is compounded by many of our popular writers who tend to extend themselves well beyond the realms of professional competence. Popular writers often use individual case histories but without detailed reference to some of the important circumstances obtaining; thus generalizations are drawn which are far-fetched, if not worse. Especially overlooked are two points: (1) Scientific generalizations can stand only after careful research including replication studies, and (2) One can apply a generalization to his own specific case only when all the important variables or conditions are similar. These qualifications are not stressed or made clear. Our statements apply to writings from the various disciplines. A careful study of the materials in the government bulletin *Infant Care,* for example, indicates quite clearly that changes in medical advice regarding feeding, weaning, and toilet training practices are cyclical and not based on changing research evidence. Yet this bulletin is among the best of its type.

[20] Jules Coleman, "Mental Health Education and Community Psychiatry," *American Journal of Orthopsychiatry,* Vol. 23 (April, 1953), pp. 265–270.

At present a curious phenomenon exists. More and more people are turning to science for answers to problems but they are not willing to support the research needed to give more definitive answers to their problems. The situation is changing but very, very slowly. However, when we get more solid information available in the various areas of parent-child relations we will have at best, a clarification of means to achieve particular ends or values. As Brim points out by way of example, the question can be raised as to whether ". . . It is desirable for a child to be sensitive to group demands, to conform to socially accepted customs, in contrast to being independent of group demands; or in Riesman's terms, the degree to which it is desirable to be other-directed rather than inner-directed. Current research on the origins of conformity motivation suggest that in the near future we may be in the position to describe those child rearing practices which produce relatively greater desire for conformity on the one hand, as opposed to independence on the other. Given such knowledge, the ethical choice is posed." [21]

Thoughtful, sensitive parents, then, can make effective use of what science has to offer in child rearing, if they are discriminating in their approach. It will be required that they periodically evaluate what they are actually doing and accomplishing. For example, at the present time, great stress is being put on excellence and achievement. But recently a number of learned people have raised voices of concern lest we overlook the possibility of some unanticipated consequences. Among them is Bronfenbrenner:

The prospect of a society in which socialization techniques are directed toward maximizing achievement drive is not altogether a pleasant one. As a number of investigators have shown . . . high achievement motivation appears to flourish in a family atmosphere of "cold democracy" if initial high levels of maternal involvement are followed by pressures for independence and accomplishment. Nor does the product of this process give ground for reassurance. True, children from achievement oriented homes excel in planfulness and performance, but they are also more aggressive, tense, domineering and cruel. . . . It would appear that education for excellence if pursued single-mindedly may entail some sobering social costs.[22]

Social science methods can be of help to parents in the clarification of their goals and objectives, but they do not relieve them of dilemmas. Furthermore they cannot make incompatible goals such as initiative and dependence compatible. Often one characteristic of personality or character must be slighted, if another is to be accentuated.

A specific type of warning may be given parents who are trying to use information on child development. Suppose they are making use of the

---

[21] Orrville Brim, *Education for Child Rearing* (New York, Russell Sage Foundation, 1959), p. 92.

[22] Urie Bronfenbrenner, "The Changing American Child: A Speculative Analysis," *The Journal of Social Issues,* Vol. 17 (January–February, 1961), pp. 6–18.

materials supplied by the Griffiths or Gesell people. These involve information on what to expect in the various areas of development for the child at the various stages or levels. First of all, strictly speaking, this information applies only to the child from the same class level as the experimental groups used. This is not always made clear. Secondly, assuming the norms are appropriate for your children, it must again be stressed that they are medians or averages. This suggests that many children in a typical group will vary on each side of the norm, whatever it may be. But alas for little Johnny, from the parent's point of view, if he isn't right on the middle line, especially in a middle-class household! The parents may be permissive in general compared to grandfather's standards, but little Johnny must catch up with the norms or else.

In effect this means that Johnny may be worse off in certain ways because his parents have some knowledge of developmental norms. More specifically, many middle-class parents are attracted to modern psychological or psychoanalytical theories of child rearing. They may subscribe to them in theory. But the underlying competitiveness of middle-class life may drive the parents to nullify in practice, in one way or another, the possible positive effects of a developmental philosophy which is intellectually accepted.

There is no "passing of the buck" as far as parents in the small family system are concerned. The children are their responsibility. All the ingenuity at their command will be taxed at times. They will find it necessary to sift through the chaff of writings on child development in order to find the grains of wheat which can be applied to their specific situation. The ability to search out adequate, well-trained child development experts from the various disciplines when specific advice is needed will be a valuable asset.

It must be stressed that the child is a product of his heredity and his environment *and* his unique experiences. The first is fixed at conception, and the latter are subject to rational control by parents only to a degree. It is possible for parents to become too self-conscious, fearful, and stilted in their approach. Effective parents will sense that the only thing they are able to do is to obtain all the information they can from responsible sources and attempt to apply it appropriately in view of their circumstances.

SELECTED READINGS

Aberle, David, and Naegele, Kaspar, "Middle-Class Father's Occupational Role and Attitudes Toward Children," *American Journal of Orthopsychiatry,* Vol. 22 (April, 1952), pp. 366–378.

Behrens, Marjorie, "Child Rearing and the Character Structure of the Mother," *Child Development,* Vol. 25 (September, 1954), pp. 225–238.

Bossard, James, and Boll, Eleanor, *The Sociology of Child Development* (New York, Harper & Row, 1960).

Brim, Orville, *Education for Child Rearing* (New York, Russell Sage Foundation, 1959).

Brim, Orville, Fairchild, Roy, and Borgatta, Edgar, "Relations Between Family Problems," *Marriage and Family Living,* Vol. 23 (August, 1961), pp. 219–226.

Child, Irving, "Socialization," in Gardner Lindzey (Ed.), *Handbook of Social Psychology,* Vol. II (Cambridge, Addison-Wesley, 1954), pp. 655–692.

Earle, Alice, *Child Life In Colonial Days* (New York, Macmillan, 1937).

Eells, Kenneth, Davis, Allison, and others, *Intelligence and Cultural Differences* (Chicago, The University of Chicago Press, 1951).

Escalona, Sibylle, "A Commentary Upon Some Recent Changes in Child Rearing Practices," *Child Development,* Vol. 20 (September, 1949), pp. 157–162.

Hadfield, J., *Childhood and Adolescence* (Baltimore, Penguin, 1962).

Harris, Albert, *How to Increase Reading Ability,* 4th ed. (New York, McKay, 1961).

Hunter, E., "Changes in Teachers' Attitudes Toward Children's Behavior Over the Last Thirty Years," *Mental Hygiene,* Vol. 41 (January, 1957), pp. 3–11.

Kawin, Ethel, *Parenthood in a Free Nation,* 3 Vols., Vol. 1, *Basic Concepts for Parents,* Vol. 2, *Early and Middle Childhood,* Vol. 3, *Later Childhood and Adolescence* (New York, Macmillan, 1963).

Kerr, Jean, *Please Don't Eat the Daisies* (New York, Doubleday, 1957).

Koch, Helen, "Children's Work Attitudes and Sibling Characteristics," *Child Development,* Vol. 25 (September, 1954), pp. 209–223.

LeMasters, E. E., *Modern Courtship and Marriage* (New York, Macmillan, 1957), Chapter 25.

Martin, William, and Stendler, Celia (Eds.), *Readings in Child Development* (New York, Harcourt, Brace & World, rev. ed., 1959).

McCandless, Boyd, *Children and Adolescents* (New York, Holt, Rinehart and Winston, 1961), Chapter 3.

Miller, Daniel, and Swanson, Guy, *The Changing American Parent* (New York, Wiley, 1958).

Miller, Daniel, and Swanson, Guy, *Inner Conflict and Defense* (New York, Holt, Rinehart and Winston, 1960).

Spector, Samuel, "Climate and Social Acceptability," *Journal of Educational Sociology,* Vol. 27 (November, 1953), pp. 108–114.

Stone, Joseph, and Church, Joseph, *Childhood and Adolescence* (New York, Random House, 1957), Chapters 8–9.

Tasch, Ruth, "The Role of the Father in the Family," *Journal of Experimental Education* (June, 1952), pp. 319–361.

Thom, Douglas, and Newell, Nancy, "Hazards of the High IQ," *Mental Hygiene,* Vol. 29 (January, 1945), pp. 61–77.

Wolf, Katherine, *The Controversial Problem of Discipline* (New York, Child Association of America, 1953).

QUESTIONS AND EXERCISES

1. Form a panel composed of several members of the class to analyze the significance of extraparental influence in child development. One particular subtopic might be the beneficial effects school teachers might have on the development of minority group and lower-class children.

2. How far should parents and teachers go in using extrinsic motives (outside incentives) in order to get children to study, practice on the piano, etc.?

3. How significant are IQ tests in your estimation? Do you believe that intelligence can ever be changed by individual effort? Discuss.

4. What can parents do to increase social sensitivity in their children?

5. Write a brief paper describing the system of discipline to which you were subjected during your childhood, and the subsequent reactions you had.

6. How far may parents go in indoctrinating their children in a particular religious faith?

7. Under what circumstances should children be paid for working around the home?

8. Arrange to visit a local PTA meeting in order to discover ways parents are aiding the school and teachers are contributing to the home. Write a brief account based on your observations.

9. What habits and beliefs do you have which can be attributed to the specific cultural group in which you were reared?

10. How far should parents go in interfering in the school program if they feel that their child is being improperly handled? Discuss.

11. How far can you go in accepting the Freudian hypothesis that early experiences cause later disorders? Discuss.

12. Why does the concept of multiple causation make child rearing seem more difficult to the parent? Must this inevitably be so?

13. Arrange for a sociodrama in your class. Participants are Fred and Sarah, the parents of a boy John, age nine, and a girl Susan, age six. Fred is a somewhat "traditional" father while Sarah is more "modernistic," or developmental in her orientation. Fred feels that Sarah is too lenient with John and that she should punish him consistently for his misdeeds during the day. Sarah thinks that Fred is a good father but that he is overly strict with the boy. The scene opens at 9:00 P.M. in the living room after the children have gone to bed. Fred had come home at 5:30 P.M. on that particular day to find that John had broken a good saw which he was forbidden to use. Fred switched John a few times and ordered him to stay in his room after supper. As Fred enters the room he exclaims: "Sarah, we're going to have to do something about that boy!"

23

The School-Age Child

With school attendance the child embarks on a new adventure. Some previous tasks are continued, some discontinued, and some new ones are added. If the child has been unsuccessful in accomplishing earlier tasks he enters this period sorely handicapped. Regardless of the circumstances, the period must be faced and the challenges somehow met.

PHYSICAL DEVELOPMENT AND HEALTH

The school-age period is one of continual growth and development for children. Both boys and girls delight in games which require greater use of the finer rather than the gross musculature. The early grade-schooler has difficulty with the use of the smaller muscles but as he proceeds through this period his skills increase. Boys will be slightly stronger on the average through this period, and will indicate greater ability in the use of the large muscles. On the other hand, girls are their equals and are sometimes superior on the tests which measure the finer muscle and mechanical skills.[1]

This is a period in which boys and girls with a little encouragement take to group games, to the use of bicycles and roller skates, and to climbing and manipulating play equipment. With practice, movements become more coordinated and rhythmic, and control of muscles becomes more efficient.

Physical development is important for the child. While brute strength is not particularly an asset in industrial societies, physical health and well-

[1] J. Murray Lee, *The Child and His Development* (New York, Appleton-Century-Crofts, 1958), p. 70.

being are. Endurance, energy, coordination, dexterity, etc. are necessary if the potentialities of the individual are to be put to maximum use. If play activities involving motor control are not part of the life of the child they will ordinarily not be taken up later at the adult level. Motor control and activity are related also to other areas of the child's life. There is evidence that brighter children are more active in play and in use of motor skills than dull children, on the average, during the grade-school period. Furthermore, relations with peers and the self concept are involved. Boys and girls are required to have some physical ability and coordination to participate in many of the group games and activities. The children who cannot keep up are often forced to sit on the sidelines or are assigned the roles lowest in prestige. They are the last ones to be chosen for a side. In softball the child who is inept is, if he is lucky, assigned a position far, far out in right field. If possible, his turn at bat is conveniently taken by someone who is more able. Adept parents and teachers can aid the situation by both cutting down on the competition, and also aiding the individual child in acquiring the necessary skills. Children can be taught that they must come to terms with their own bodies and that in most cases practice makes for improvement, if not for perfection. There are very few children who cannot become reasonably proficient in motor control and in typical children's games and sports, if they receive encouragement, are willing to use initiative and in certain cases special aid.

The question of competitive sports at the elementary level is a complicated one. They do provide incentive and training, yet the stress on winning to the neglect of learning and sportsmanship is a constant problem. It tends to further separate those who are mature and already partially skilled from those who lag behind, yet each child needs encouragement regarding maximum use of his body potentials, regardless of whether or not he is to make "the team."

The Proper Use of Physical Development Norms

Height and weight tables for measuring the physical development of children came into extensive use a generation ago. Their use, or rather misuse, has now come under some attack. Especially to be discouraged is the expectation that a particular child will fall right at the *norm* or fiftieth percentile rank. Perhaps the greatest error is committed by comparing weight to height, overlooking body build. In an attempt to provide a more reliable method of checking growth the Wetzel Grid was developed. This grid takes into account physique (body build), height, weight, and basal metabolism. Seven channels are delineated to take into account various types of body build from the stocky to the slender.

This approach seems to be superior to the use of standard height-weight charts. When the child's progress is entered on the chart his development in relation to other children can be ascertained. But more than this, lines indicating his own process of development are indicated. If a child moves out of his "channel" the possibility of special attention is suggested.[2]

Other approaches used involve measures of arm girth, chest depth and width, calf girth, and bones (by x-ray).[3] Again, it must be understood that both group and individual variables contribute to differences in growth and development scores. Japanese children tend to be shorter than American children.[4] Upper-class children tend to be taller and heavier than lower-class children. Environmental factors, including diet, are probably at work here. Within group categories the genes contributed by the particular family lines are heavily involved. Among the poorer elements of the population inadequate diets may contribute to a stunting of growth. Malnutrition because of unbalanced food intake, however, can be a problem at any class level in an affluent society. According to nutrition experts, many middle- and upper-class children apparently suffer from an overemphasis on fats and starches to the neglect of the other food elements.[5]

During the early part of the school period the heights and weights of the boys will be slightly higher than those for the girls. However, by about age eleven the girls will be spurting ahead, to remain ahead for a couple of years. This differential development accentuates certain social and emotional problems which will be referred to later. During the teens the boys catch and surpass the girls again. It must again be noted that there will be considerable variation in patterns within the two sexes. The greatest attention to the question of differential maturation has been given in the California studies of children under Jones and others. The early maturer among boys, according to the California study, would seem to have considerable social and personal advantage over his age mates. He has a greater chance of success in late grade-school competitive sports. He can catch up with girls physically and start to date them more easily if he wishes. He has a greater chance to be chosen for formal leadership or for informal relationships. The late maturing boy has a disadvantage, which he may try to

[2] See Marion Breckenridge and E. Lee Vincent, *Child Development* (Philadelphia, Saunders, 1960), pp. 269–271 for information on the Wetzel Grid and graphic examples of its use. Pediatricians report that the Wetzel approach involves too many variables for use with most parents, however. In its place have come more simplified charts which use height, weight, and a few other items with suggested ranges of "normal" deviation from projected growth channels. See for example, the "Anthropometric" Charts developed by Harold Stuart, M.D., and his associates, Department of Maternal and Child Health, Harvard School of Public Health, Boston, Mass. for the Children's Medical Center of Boston. With proper use, records kept on charts such as the one developed by the Stuart group should be very helpful.

[3] *Ibid.,* Chapter 7.

[4] W. W. Greulich, "A Comparison of the Physical Growth and Development of American-Born and Native Japanese Children," *American Journal of Physical Anthropology,* Vol. 15 (December, 1957), pp. 489–515.

[5] H. V. Meredith, "Relation between Socio-Economic Status and Body Size," *American Journal of Disturbed Children,* Vol. 82 (1951), pp. 702–709.

compensate for either by attention-seeking behavior or, less often, by withdrawal.[6]

California data for the girls as a whole shows the early maturing girls at a disadvantage. They tend to be stockier and heavier than the ideal of their peers. They tend to be larger than boys of their school class. If they associate with them they must take the lead, which violates standard norms. If they date older boys they are often prematurely led into petting and precocious activities.

The total child is, of course, a product of more than his early or late maturing growth pattern. His social and personal adjustment is also based on constitutional factors and growth patterns plus significant interactions with others. Suppose for example a small boy wishes to emulate a favorite uncle who was a football star. Early maturity will be to his advantage in that he will have a greater chance to succeed in this sport if he is well-developed and well-coordinated. Work and drive will tend to bring success, which will bring favorable reactions from peers. This should lead to a stronger self concept and to greater social adjustment, unless the process goes too far and results in undue confidence on his part. As McCandless suggests, in commenting on results of the California studies, "It is probable that the differences in adjustment and social behavior noted between groups of early and late-maturing boys are socially mediated—that is, they are a function of the way society reacts to the mature and the immature fourteen-year-old, rather than of the physiological or biochemical factors making for maturity or immaturity." [7]

RELATING TO VALUE SYSTEMS

During the school period the child has the task of expanding his value system in relation to his ever-expanding environment. The child is "introduced to the world" during this period. He comes in contact with new ways of doing things in his relations with teachers and other adults in the school and community and in his relations with his peers in the school setting and neighborhood groupings. The probability of discrepancies existing between the standards of the home and those of the school are rather high. As many observers have pointed out, the general and official value system prevailing in the public school is that of the middle classes. This is especially true in regard to standards of morality, decorum, achievement, orderliness, aggressiveness, self-discipline, and language. This means that both the high upper class and the lower-class child will suffer a degree of "culture shock"

[6] Mary Jones and Nancy Bayley, "Physical Maturing Among Boys as Related to Behavior," *Journal of Educational Psychology,* Vol. 41 (March, 1950), pp. 129–148.

[7] Boyd McCandless, *Children and Adolescents* (New York, Holt, Rinehart and Winston, 1961), p. 301.

in the school environment. Problems are obviously most acute for the lower-class child, since in many communities upper-class children are sent to private schools. The child senses that his language, dress, and general behavior are somewhat looked down upon by his teachers and peers. If he begins to turn toward the values of the school he runs the risk of being considered "sissified" or "soft" by family members and lower-class play-mates. The attitude of the teacher is crucial. If the teacher is especially warm and accepts him he may start to identify with middle-class values even though they be in conflict with home and friends. If he feels rejected by the teacher he will tend to be apathetic or belligerent in school, thus arousing more criticism from teachers and classmates. Thinking especially of lower-class children and those of ethnic and subcultural backgrounds, Bossard and Boll write as follows:

> Whatever one's personal loyalties to the cause of education, the fact re-mains that, in our contemporary society, the school is often the creator of cultural conflicts for the child. At a very tender age, a child is taken away from his home to enter this specialized institution, which develops its own dual culture: that of the classroom and that of a more purely social world. Development of conflict between the schematized teaching of the school and the pervasive influences of the home is but the more obvious aspect of a much larger conflict situation. Some of this larger culture conflict is due to the cultural diversity of our population, some of it to the rapidity with which our culture undergoes change and the relative place of successive generations in that change. It is much aggravated when the school undertakes, as some educators insist that it shall do, to educate for cultural discontinuities rather than for cultural continuity.[8]

Comparatively speaking, the middle-class child will find the least con-flict between the general values of his home and the school. Given the diversity which exists in American society, he will still find discrepancies existing which will require considerable adjustment on his part. The Quaker, Brethren, or Mennonite child may find that the teacher's views on militarism are in sharp contrast to those prevailing in his home or meeting house. The oversheltered child may be in for considerable adjustment simply because the school must operate on a group basis and cannot give the individual attention which can be given at home. The child learns not only in the official culture of the school, but also in the unofficial peer culture set up by his classmates. On the playground, in the classroom and halls, and after school he is exposed to the values of this world of his peers. The group has, to a degree, language and standards of its own to which the child is exposed. The sheltered child may hear terms that are both new and to an extent shocking to him. Its values at times may be in conflict with

---

[8] James Bossard and Eleanor Boll, *The Sociology of Child Development* (New York, Harper & Row, 1960), p. 569.

both school officialdom and the home. The child then has the dilemma of reconciling these values and still remaining in good standing in all three.

The peer group can have an important role in the development of the child, and it is not necessarily harmful or antisocial. Composed of members of a similar age it has some advantages over the family as a learning environment. In a sense, the members learn by doing, together. They develop group codes, standards, and controls. Based on an ingenious series of observations and experiments with children's play groups, Piaget came forth with a theory of child development.[9] He shows that in the early school period the concepts of morality and justice exhibited by children are based almost entirely upon parental authority. But during the middle school period (roughly eight to eleven years of age) a general equalitarian justice prevails in which the needs and rights of other children as well as themselves are given consideration. By the eleventh or twelfth year the children sense the necessity of norms and rules as prerequisites of group life. They impose them upon themselves willingly.[10]

One can quickly grasp from the above that Piaget is suggesting that children in their play groups relive the human race's history of moving from a more authoritarian, rigid morality to a more flexible one based on justice and equity. More careful research will be necessary before we can be sure of his hypothesis. Assuming tentatively that Piaget is to any degree correct, we are led to the position that play in congenial groups is an experience which is of critical importance to the growing child.

The school child has the task of learning how to interact with others without the direct support of his family while at the same time realizing that he is responsible to his family for his actions. In later years he will have both the chance and the responsibility of moving out on his own.

SELF-DEVELOPMENT

The interactionist concept of self-development was discussed in a previous chapter. It suggests a progressive development of self-attitudes based particularly on reflections of the attitudes of others. If such is the actual process, the role of the child in the peer group and the school as well as in the home is important to his continually developing concept of self. Within the play group divisions are made and roles assigned. Struggles for leadership develop and children are divided into leaders and followers. The group develops its "sissy," its "show-off," and unfortunately, its "goat." [11] Sometimes younger members must go through an apprenticeship

---

[9] Jean Piaget, *The Moral Judgment of the Child* (New York, Harcourt, Brace & World, 1932), pp. 17–30.

[10] *Ibid.*, pp. 160–190.

[11] Bossard and Boll, *op. cit.*, p. 535.

during which time they are assigned the "dirty" and uninviting jobs. Holding a lower status is not particularly deflating to the younger child since he feels that he is lucky to be included in the group at all. On the other hand, being forced to play an inferior role can be rather difficult for the boy who is a full member of the group.

Important lessons in reality testing can be learned by the child in this interaction with his fellows. Just as the child must first learn to be completely dependent and then later move toward independence, so he must learn to interact with the peer group. He must come to terms with the problem of self-reliance and integrity versus conformity. The fortunate child has a home environment in which he feels accepted and loved for what he is. In such a case he may feel strong enough to at times run the risk of ostracism and ridicule in going against the pressures of the group. This will often be necessary for the exceptionally studious boy, for example, in the average public school. The child who feels so helpless and alone that he must conform always and at all cost is developing, if such a phenomenon exists, a neurotic need. As an adult he stands a good chance of becoming the extreme organization man we hear so much about.

Most persons must feel that some group ranks them well and gives them decent status, however, if they are to have an adequate self concept. For this reason some frustrated children will turn from one group to another in an attempt to achieve some measure of satisfaction. Learning to live with his strengths and weaknesses is an important part of self-development for the child. Unfortunately, stereotyping by children and adults may lead a child to believe that he is unworthy and without talent in a given area when the potential is actually there.[12]

ACCEPTING RESPONSIBILITY AND AUTHORITY

The problem of living with adult expectations of responsibilities and authority is difficult for the child at the school level although it will perhaps be greater at the later period of adolescence. Many impulses of the child lead him to be egocentric, and to want immediate rather than delayed gratification of his wishes. As he grows progressively older he is expected to curb his egocentric impulses and to work cooperatively with family members to achieve long-range goals. Ideally the child lives in a paternal

[12] This seems to be precisely what takes place with some of our underprivileged children, according to research reports which are now available. Full attention to this area is outside the scope of this book. Frank Riessman, *The Culturally Deprived Child* (New York, Harper & Row, 1962) analyzes some of the results of action projects with culturally deprived children, with emphasis on the Higher Horizons project of New York City. It seems quite clear that many children have untapped potentials which are not developed for various reasons, some of which are discussed in the Riessman book.

environment where parents are able, by a wise balance of rewards and punishments, to encourage him to wish to accept increasing responsibility. A basic principle is involved which has broad implications: One is able to exercise increasing authority (or obtain increasing decision-making power) by accepting more responsibility. The child must show that he is able and ready to handle increased responsibility. This reciprocal process is a very delicate one and there will of course be many individual variations. If the child shows a tendency to wish for more authority than his carrying of responsibility would deserve, the parents should not be unduly shocked. Lack of firmness in encouraging and expecting increasing competency would seem to be in the long run harmful, however, in view of the reactions the child can be expected to receive in similar situations in the outside world. But some leeway must be allowed and parents and teachers should be careful lest they stifle initiative and natural enthusiasm that most children seem to have for activity and accomplishment.

One task for the school-age child is the development of responsibility in the use of money. According to one group of authorities the child will have the greatest chance of learning how to handle money if parents make use of the following principles:

1. Begin giving a child an allowance as soon as he understands the use of money in getting things he wants.
2. Have an understanding with the child as to what the allowance is to cover. At first it might relate only to such things as toys and special treats, with additions from time to time in the size of the allowance and in its use. Many teen-age boys and girls can handle an allowance that covers their clothing. By this time they should have had some responsibility for looking ahead and saving for special things.
3. Make the child's allowance a fair share in terms of family consumption. The amount should take into account what playmates have, and not be so markedly less that the child by daily contrasts feels constantly deprived. On the other hand, it should not be greatly in excess of what playmates get or the child may be tempted to swagger.
4. As the child gets older give him a part in deciding what his allowance should be. This may be done by having him share in a family round table on the spending plan so he will gain a greater appreciation of fair sharing.
5. Give the child responsibility for spending his allowance, although consultation may be required for some things and is invited at all times. If he makes mistakes he should come to recognize his responsibility for them and to put up with the results of his mistakes. In unusual situations he may be helped out perhaps by an advance of next week's allowance.
6. While the child is learning to plan ahead, give the allowance for short periods, perhaps first by the day, then by the week, and later for somewhat longer periods. Very early, children should learn where money comes from and the effort that earning it entails. Their spending should be made in part dependent on their own efforts. Children can often be taught the

simple lessons of earning and spending by being paid for some household tasks. Parents should be careful not to carry this too far, or the child may acquire the habit of putting all helpfulness on a 'pay me' basis.[13]

In following through such a program, self-control by parents is very important. Careless generosity and mistaken kindness are often stumbling blocks to a sound program. They may interfere with a child's development and lead to later demands on the family purse that must be denied to a child not prepared for such a refusal. In addition, it is sometimes hard to let the children go ahead and make what to their parents are great mistakes, to let them use their allowance for such things as gaudy clothes or numerous comic books that seem a great waste. There seems, however, no other method to us if children are to gain in self-confidence and self-expression. Persuasion should be limited to discussion, including suggestions that other things might well be considered and their merits weighed. At the same time it may be important to try to develop a better understanding of the child's choices if they seem strange or undesirable.

DEVELOPING HEALTHY EMOTIONAL-AFFILIATIVE TIES TO PARENTS

The child during the school period has the task of developing and maintaining healthy emotional ties with both parents. While there is not complete agreement on what a healthy situation for this period really means, some general comments can be put forth to attempt some clarification. As previously indicated, according to the Freudians, the preschool emotional relations will differ for the boy and girl. The girl will first have a close association with the mother. Then during the later preschool period she turns toward her father and tends to react negatively toward the mother. This turning away is caused partly by her lack of a male sex organ (for which she blames her mother) and partly by erotic attraction toward the father. As she gets a bit older and moves into the school period she realizes she cannot possess her father and with some feelings of guilt and shame for wishing to violate the incest taboo, she turns back toward her mother. The boy also first relates lovingly to his mother. As he enters the phallic period his increasing sexuality makes him wish to possess his mother. Since he senses that only father can do this he develops ambivalent feelings toward father. He begins to fear his father because of father's power to remove a threat (via castration). Essentially because of this fear he turns back to his father, repressing incestuous desires he may have toward his mother.

The school period is a period of latency as far as the Freudians are

[13] Adapted from *Guiding Family Spending*, U.S. Department of Agriculture, Miscellaneous Publication No. 661 (March, 1949), pp. 11, 12.

concerned. That is, latent emotional-sexual drives are kept in the background, or more precisely in the unconscious, from whence they will burst forth with new energy at the onset of puberty.

The strict Freudian interpretation of psychosexual development has been challenged by scholars, including Neo-Freudians. Detailed analysis of the criticisms are beyond the scope of this book. Commonly the assumptions in regard to penis envy and castration fears have been challenged. Further, it is doubtful that erotic interests are as submerged as the more traditional Freudians would have them be. The Freudians have, however, provided a start toward a comprehensive theory of psychosocial sexual development which will eventually emerge from scholarly work.[14] Especially provocative is the emphasis on the relationship between the child and the parent. A more refined analysis would take into account the various reciprocal relationships in a household plus the relation of the particular individual under focus to the total emotional and structural configuration.

To a great degree the parents control the environment for the child, and the child must react within this context. That this can at times be extremely difficult for him need only be suggested. By at least the middle school years the child may be able to perceive that a particular parent is seductive or overindulgent. He may be able to sense that, for example, he is caught in a marital crossfire.[15] A particular child may realize that his mother both wants him to show manliness and to remain "mama's little boy." Usually he would be only vaguely aware of these discrepancies, of course. Regardless of the extent of his intellectual awareness, the child must live with his parents as they are and not as he or someone else would have them be.

Not to be overlooked are the experiences outside the family and their effect on the child's ties to his family. Outside contacts provide him with expectations and understandings. He notes the derisive words used in describing the boys who are allegedly "tied to mother's apron strings." In the case of the boy the idea that a real boy is circumspect in his behavior with girls and women is brought home to him. Certain corollary processes are at work for the girl. The expectations of outside groups are applied, in other words, to the roles the child plays everywhere, including at home. They can be disturbing or corrective as the case may be, but they cannot be completely ignored.

The child, during the school period, becomes more aware of counterpressures prevailing upon him to act in certain ways. He is forced to seek some type of equilibrium between his own inner desires and the outside expectations of parents and friends. The unfortunate child suffers from

[14] See J. A. Hadfield, *Childhood and Adolescence* (Baltimore, Penguin, 1962), p. 221.
[15] See Irving Kaufman *et al.*, "The Family Constellation and Overt Incestuous Relations between Father and Daughter," *American Journal of Orthopsychiatry*, Vol. 24 (April, 1954), pp. 266–277.

such overwhelming and inconsistent demands on him that there is no healthy resolution of them. Such a situation develops well above chance in the middle-class American home, according to Green.[16] The child deep down is felt to be a burden, keeping the parents from achieving desirable social goals. The father, with feelings of guilt being present at times, tends to ignore the child and to go about his business. The mother cannot do so and gives much attention to the child. In fact she busies herself with him while at the same time giving him considerable love.

The technique of discipline used is love withdrawal. Love is freely given only if the child complies with mother's wishes. Not to do so means that love will be taken away. For the child especially, this type of situation plants the seeds of neurosis. He suffers from being exposed to contradictory emotional pressures. In the words of Green:

Any striving is painful for it violates the initial submissive adjustment. But he feels equally guilty for not making the effort to achieve. This is a key to much of his contradictory and self-blocking behavior; his desire to be the last man in the last regiment and his desire to conquer the world; his demand that everyone shall love him, and his settled conviction that no one could love a person as base as he; his inability to erect a hierarchy of values; his endless debate over the value of his own goals. He is damned if he does and damned if he doesn't. He is embraced by a psychological Iron Maiden; any lunge forward or backward only impales him more securely on the spikes.[17]

How typical this situation is remains a matter of debate. It can certainly be said that anything approaching it will not be conducive to the successful emotional development of the average child.

IDENTIFICATION AND THE SEX ROLES

The child has the task during the school period of developing a sex role considered appropriate for that period. A discussion of this topic follows naturally after the previous section, and much of what was said will apply here. It seems clear that in the early years both boys and girls tend to identify with their mothers. By the time of the late preschool period the boys are beginning to shift toward their fathers a bit, although they still retain some identity with their mothers. The further development of the process of identification is not well agreed upon, although there is less disagreement about the outcome. As shown by McCandless, as well as others, there are the Freudian, learning, and power (role) theories, all of which have rather logical explanations of the process of identification. These are indicated in the following graphic form:

[16] Arnold Green, "The Middle-Class Male Child and Neurosis," *American Sociological Review,* Vol. 11 (February, 1946), pp. 31–41.
    [17] *Ibid.,* p. 41.

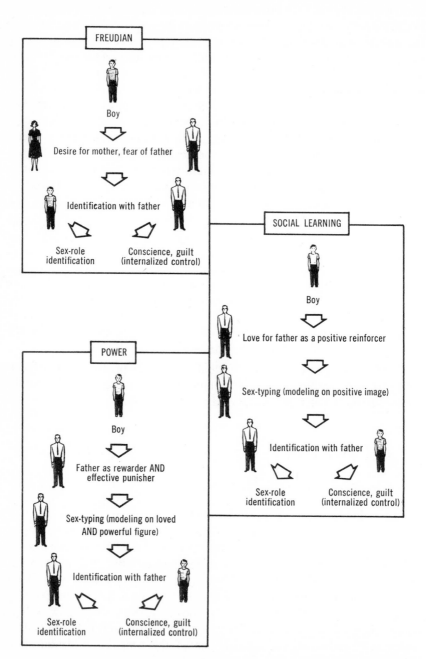

FIGURE 20. *Contrasting Motives for Male Identification.* SOURCE: Boyd McCandless, *Children and Adolescents* (New York, Holt, Rinehart and Winston, 1961), pp. 344–345. The Freudian theory stresses fear; social learning stresses love; power theory stresses love plus respect, with respect possibly tinged with fear.

As is indicated, Freudians hypothesize that guilt and fear motivate the boy to identify with his father. Social learning theorists stress the love the boy has for his father plus the rewards the father gives as reinforcement for appropriate behavior. The power theory suggests that father is both a person to be loved and a person who is an effective manipulator of punishment as well as other things.

In the author's opinion somewhat more stress must be put on the total society in which this process takes place than is indicated by McCandless. For example, in the old German patriarchal family the typical boy must assuredly have developed intense antagonisms against his father. One could logically predict that the boy would identify with his mother and become rather effeminate. Evidence does not sustain this logic.[18] Reason suggests that the stereotype role for the male was held so firmly in German society that all sorts of cultural pressures operated to counter what would seem to obtain logically in the home.[19] Perhaps a society in which the male role is not as clear-cut would have a different impact on the home environment. Evidence to support this is found in at least one study. Mussen and Distler found that highly masculine kindergarten boys had fathers who were more affectionate toward them than those who were low on masculinity.[20] It must be noted here, however, that this involved a middle-class sample and that we really do not know from the study whether the affectionate fathers were also powerful or not. In another study these same authors found that highly masculine boys had fathers whose power (nurthurance plus punishment) was significantly higher than did the less masculine boys. As McCandless says, "Although the number of subjects is small, this study suggests rather clearly that boys identify with strength, that parental strength is a combination of reward and punishment (a sensible enough conclusion); and that, possibly, an excess of reward over punishment is conducive to appropriate identification. . . ." (the last conclusion by McCandless).[21]

Not as much attention has been given to sex role identity of the younger girl as to the identity of the boy. According to the Freudians the girl must shift from an identification with the mother to an identification with the father and then back again to mother and women in general. It is maintained that this process is difficult for the girl psychologically. It is also suggested by some that society attaches greater prestige and privilege to the male role and does not punish girls as readily for adopting aspects of the male role compared to the punishment of boys for the reverse. On the

[18] Bertram Schaffner, *Father Land: A Study of Authoritarianism in the German Family* (New York, Columbia, 1948).

[19] See Robert Winch, *The Modern Family* (New York, Holt, Rinehart and Winston, 1952), pp. 39–44.

[20] Paul Mussen and L. Distler, "Masculinity, Identification, and Father-Son Relationships," *Journal of Abnormal and Social Psychology,* Vol. 59 (Fall, 1959), pp. 350–356.

[21] McCandless, *op. cit.,* p. 340.

other side, the expectation that small girls should be "sugar and spice and everything nice" persists both inside and outside the home. Furthermore, mothers and female teachers offer convenient models for girls. Whatever the comparative causes, however, girls on the average make later sex role identifications than do boys.[22] More of them can be expected to show some aspects of "tomboyishness" during the years six to ten than boys will show "femininity" during the same period. By the end of the school period the great majority of children will show at least outer adaptation to their appropriate sex roles, even if they are emotionally not fully at home with their respective roles. Contradictory pressures will make for plenty of confusion and anxiety on the part of many children of both sexes as they grow through this period, and they will need all the help and counsel they can get from adults who are vitally interested in them.

DEVELOPING APPROPRIATE INTELLECTUAL SKILLS

This topic cannot be adequately discussed without opening up a complicated subject, that of the ubiquitous IQ. Clearly a full understanding of this concept demands thorough study. We will in no way pretend to give this full coverage, but will attempt a general discussion which should be helpful to prospective parents or parents who may go further into the subject if they so desire.[23]

The intelligence test was developed originally by Binet to serve as a predictor of school success. He defined intelligence as invention, comprehension, direction, and censorship. Work in this country to adapt the test to American traditions by Terman, Thorndike, and many others modified the concept in the direction of abstract thinking and ability in language. Actually in terms of the original goal of Binet, the tests have done and still do rather well. They are rather highly correlated with academic school performance. A number of things must be noted, however. Do these tests indicate "native ability?" One wonders if this question can ever be satisfactorily answered. At present it is pretty well agreed that intelligence tests for preschool children are not as reliable as those developed for older children. Certainly it is clear that by the time a child is in school his ability reflects both nature and nurture. At present at least, there is no way of getting inside the organism at birth to test the child's potential before he has been influenced by experience.

[22] M. L. Hutt and R. G. Gibby, *The Child: Development and Adjustment* (Boston, Allyn and Bacon, 1959), p. 232.

[23] A voluminous literature on intelligence testing exists. Most standard child development texts provide an adequate coverage of the subject. See for example, Paul Mussen and John Conger, *Child Development and Personality* (New York, Harper & Row, 1956), pp. 368–380, and McCandless, *op. cit.,* pp. 209–214.

Intelligence tests present problems to be solved. They tend to deal with abstractions and to reflect verbal abilities, although performance tests making use of other facilities are sometimes also used. Thus, a group of test-makers devise a set of problems for children to solve. If the background of the child tested is such that his experiences have been similar to those of the test-developers, he should have a fair chance on the test. If his experience is quite different, he will be handicapped. There is now considerable agreement that intelligence tests are developed by middle-class, intellectually oriented test-makers, whose tests can best be taken by children being subjected to the same type of social situations. Evidence accumulates that children from lower-class homes, or from subcultural ethnic and racial backgrounds will not be able to compete as well on such tests.[24] Not to be overlooked are factors of motivation, morale, fear of the testing situation, and so forth.

It is quite generally agreed that any one test score may be highly inaccurate. More faith can be put in the average of a series of test scores over a period of time. It is also apparent that many children have untapped potential abilities. The problem is to provide the environment where through training and interest these potentials will be actuated as real competencies.

Present tests do have considerable diagnostic value as far as present school conditions are concerned. From these, counselors, teachers, and parents can get information which should be helpful in indicating the general range within which a child should be able to operate, especially regarding intellectual matters. They are particularly helpful in indicating gross deviations from what could reasonably be expected in individual cases.

On a group basis, society (the school board, the school personnel, and parents) has the problem of establishing general policies which will bring out the potential of its young people. But this is a reciprocal process. As he moves along, the child has the task of developing his general intellectual abilities toward the level considered appropriate for his age. It is the job of the schools with parental encouragement to arrange age-graded tasks which can be achieved in a learning situation for the individual child. It is his job to master them progressively.

The subject of intellectual development of children is a complex one which can only be briefly touched upon here. Continual study is being made of the problem-solving ability of typical children at various age levels. Included in this, or contributing to it, are studies in learning and perception. Recently a provocative study was made with Detroit school children. It is an example of the type of research which may be increasingly helpful to

[24] A group has developed which insists that intelligence tests must be "culture-free," that is, not culturally biased. See Kenneth Eells, *et al., Intelligence and Cultural Differences* (Chicago, The University of Chicago Press, 1951). See McCandless, *op. cit.,* Chapter 7, for a critique of this group's approach.

parents and educators. The researcher attempted to check the relationship between the development of perception and thought processes on the one hand and ego-development on the other. Much use was made of game behavior of the children, following Piaget, to whom we previously referred. However, the concern was with mental and social development and not play as such. One interesting aspect of this study is the comparison of a normal group of children and a mentally retarded group (both of middle-class background). The following generalizations are made by Bobroff to describe the typical stages for the two groups studied:

Stage I (age 6—normal subjects; age 8—mentally retarded subjects)
1. The child acts upon his impulses, with apparently little or no predeliberation.
2. Relationships among objects are determined by such elementary classification or organizing principles as proximity.
3. The child does not differentiate between what are rules (which regulate the behavior of interacting individuals) and what are habits (which one practices as an individual).
4. The child's game behavior consists of either repetitive motor actions or expressions of personal fantasy.
5. The child's game behavior is self-oriented, even when he is joined by others in play.
6. The child appraises situations in a personal, subjective way. There are wider variations among children in their descriptions of the same phenomenon.

Stage II (age 8—normal subjects; age 10—mentally retarded subjects)
1. The child tries to use the criteria utilized by adults for evaluation of events, but his successful adaptation of these criteria is hampered both by his limited facility to understand the nature of relationships and by his lack of experience.
2. The child does not perceive cause and effect operating in human relations. Hence, he views outcomes as fortuitous in nature and independent of purposeful action.
3. The child tends to express his feelings with minimal self-restraint. The desire for approbation and fear of reprobation constitute the forces which help the child gain control of some impulses.
4. The child accepts the proscriptions of authority figures as "desirable" while showing little understanding of the roles, functions, or feelings of these persons.
5. The child is eager to learn the necessary group rules, but he is neither completely cognizant of them nor thoroughly persuaded of their purposes and functions.
6. The child wishes to behave acceptably. However, he does not yet understand why certain behaviors are expected of him and hence he often acts as if unaware of external demands.
7. The child prefers games of short duration, although he may play for extended periods of time. With limited anxiety tolerance, he appears to enjoy a succession of short-term goals.

8. The child is attached to many personal possessions and is unwilling to relinquish such objects to other children for the dubious rewards of group fun. For example, children at this age seldom play marbles for keeps.

Stage III (age 10—normal subjects; age 12—mentally retarded subjects)
1. The child often tries to modify some of his feelings in accordance with the demands of his school, family, social group, etc.
2. Curbs upon the child's behavior are still in large part foisted by the existence of external sanctions. Concomitantly, however, the child is developing a set of his own individual, inner controls.
3. The child is beginning to recognize and understand, with considerable objectivity, many of the aspects of adult roles. He tries to incorporate the point of view of his "models" as a basis for forming his judgments.
4. The child respects those whom he considers to be in authority and looks beyond himself for guidance in solving his problems.
5. The child wants to and is able to master the details of the rules to games and to follow them correctly.
6. The child appears willing to work toward more distant goals. He is able to forego immediate satisfactions for the greater pleasures in meeting longer-term objectives.
7. The child begins to seek the many values afforded by group association. He is willing to subvert some of his private inclinations in order to facilitate team activity.

Stage IV (age 12—normal subjects; age 14—mentally retarded subjects)
1. The child can articulate his feelings within the alternate modes society provides for their expression.
2. The child is in the process of developing a more mature inner control system through internal commitment to a hierarchy of values.
3. While the child recognizes the (often primary) importance of his own point of view, he tries to understand adult attitudes and opinions.
4. The child demonstrates a belief that, in general, calculated action produces predictable outcomes.
5. The child is more able to understand reasons for rules in terms of the interrelationships among groups of people.
6. The child can view reality more objectively, and he is better able to grasp causal relationships.
7. The child is able to compromise some of his private desires in the interests of group functioning without submerging his individuality.[25]

Some comments are in order. The stages delineated represent norms, and do not include the many individual variations which were found. The problem still exists; how much of the change would come about naturally regardless of the type of pressure or encouragement used by adults, and how much represents systematic teaching and external aids? Nevertheless such patterns as these, if found to stand by future research, can provide

[25] Alan Bobroff, "The Stages of Maturation in Socialized Thinking and in the Ego Development of Two Groups of Children," *Child Development,* Vol. 31 (The Society for Research in Child Development, Inc., Summer, 1960), pp. 321–338.

useful indications of the type of intellectual or social experience appropriate for the general run of children as they move along through the school period.

Much of the child development literature seems to imply that the school-age period is a quiet one as far as problems of discipline and control are concerned, and that adolescence will bring the real problems. Actually, the child in the middle years of school often goes through phases of rebellion and disobedience which call forth controls but at the same time perplex the parents.[26] It must be remembered that the child has to experiment at this stage to find out many things for himself. Without limits set by parents he would no doubt be anxious and troubled. In the long run the child is probably convinced (in the average home) that a system of rewards and punishment is necessary and that the one against which he is rebelling is basically fair and sound. Both hostility and a drive toward independence encourage him to challenge the system and by implication the parents themselves.

Large-scale studies of the attitudes of school-agers toward parental child rearing techniques are notable for their absence. One study focusing on the adolescent period may be helpful at this point. Bowerman and Elder, in a study of a large sample of students from grades seven through twelve, found that seven different types of approaches to child rearing are possible. They are autocratic, authoritarian, democratic, equalitarian permissive, laissez-faire, and ignoring. Moving from the autocratic to the ignoring approach, there is a progressive decrease in parental direction of the child's behavior and an increase in self-direction. One question in particular which bears on our present discussion is the perception the students had of the fairness of the child rearing policy of their parents. Certainly the type of child rearing structure as the authors describe the seven orientations listed above indicates in a general way the type of control system in vogue in the home even though it does not indicate the specifics. The following table shows the preferences of the students for the alternative approaches.

One can easily see that the adolescents in the sample below reject both parental domination and the lack of parental influence for a moderate approach in between, although if given a choice they apparently would strongly prefer to set their own controls as against being dominated by parents. Interestingly, as a total sample, they expect or allow father to be more authoritarian than mother.

Closely related to the feelings of the students regarding fairness of parental approach is the question of feelings of rejection as related to type of child rearing structure used by parents. Table 42 indicates the findings on this score. The implications for the sample seem fairly clear. The child has the greatest probability of feeling rejected if his parents ignore him or

---

[26] Fritz Redl and David Wineman, *The Aggressive Child* (New York, Free Press, 1957), Chapter 2.

TABLE 41

The Fairness of Parental Child Rearing Policy as Related to Types of Child Rearing Structures, as Perceived by the Children

Type of Child Rearing Structures	Percent of Adolescents Who Consider Parental Child Rearing Policy to be Very Fair	
	Mother	Father
Autocratic	55.1 (367)	50.7 (668)
Authoritarian	58.9 (667)	74.9 (942)
Democratic	85.5 (2237)	85.1 (1966)
Equalitarian	82.8 (1081)	77.1 (817)
Permissive, laissez-faire and ignoring	80.4 (1471)	74.6 (1051)

SOURCE: Glenn Elder, Jr., "Structural Variations in the Child Rearing Relationship," Appendix, revised version of a paper read at the American Sociological Society Meetings in St. Louis, September, 1961. This is a part of the University of North Carolina Adolescent Study directed by Dr. Charles E. Bowerman. Reprinted in adapted form in *Sociometry*, Vol. 25 (September, 1962), p. 258.

TABLE 42

Feelings of Maternal and Paternal Rejection as Related to the Types of Child Rearing Structures

Parent	% of Adolescents by Types of Child Rearing Structures					
	Auto-cratic	Author-itarian	Demo-cratic	Equali-tarian	Per-missive	Laissez-Faire Ignoring
Mother	41.7(277)	25.7(239)	10.9(283)	11.0(143)	11.1(190)	56.8(46)
Father	40.1(525)	17.6(220)	8.4(193)	11.1(117)	11.0(140)	58.0(80)

SOURCE: Glenn Elder Jr., "Structural Variations in the Child Rearing Relationship," revised version of paper read at the American Sociological Association Meetings in St. Louis, September, 1961. Reprinted in adapted form in *Sociometry*, Vol. 25 (September, 1962), p. 258.

are inclined to allow him to do about as he wishes. Somehow on the other side of the wheel, the autocratic parent also encourages a fairly high degree of feelings of rejections in the child. One would assume that the dynamics involved in producing the resultant feelings are different here in relation to the two types of home climate. Again, a moderate to firm parental environment seems to offer the best base from which the child can operate.

Such studies as the above should be replicated with children in the younger-age categories. It is possible that preadolescents tend to view family policy somewhat differently than do adolescents. However, the findings are in line with those found by the Sears group, the Gluecks, Watson, and others for children ranging from preschool through the grade-school age.

Unfortunately again it is difficult to isolate variables involved. It is our impression that children reared in a warm, accepting, stable home with rather firm discipline and occasional punishment would be only mildly critical of the discipline at the grade-school level, especially if liberal use of rewards were typical. Take away the warmth and acceptance on the part of the parents and on the average the punishment would probably seem more severe to the receiver. On the other hand, lack of firm discipline and direction to the point of giving the child full sway produces mixed feelings.[27] As far as the method of discipline is concerned, from the perceptive viewpoint of the child, it may be identified as rejection. The child seems to prefer being treated a bit harshly as against being ignored or shunted if forced to choose from these two possibilities. At any rate, it is difficult to consider discipline in the abstract without tying it into a maze of other factors.

CONCLUSION

Our focus has been on the parent-child relationship in general. We have not been able to encompass fully the total pattern of interaction taking place when a number of children of both sexes in various age categories are in the home. Actually, with minor exceptions, studies with a focus on total family interaction have yet to be made. Much of our child development literature reflects an individualistic focus, which while important, is not sufficient. Research and theory which have a configurational orientation are sorely needed.

A fairly substantial literature exists dealing with sibling position and its impact on child behavior and personality.[28] At present the results of the various studies are inconclusive. Further work along these lines should be encouraged.

We have been assuming in this chapter a typical, so-called normal family of husband, wife, and children, which has never been broken. Actually increasing numbers of children are not being reared in such environments. In a recent study Bowerman and Irish found that in samples of public school children in North Carolina, Ohio, and Washington the proportions of stepchildren were 5.4 percent, 7.5 percent, and 12.2 percent

[27] John Levy and Ruth Munroe, *The Happy Family* (New York, Knopf, 1938), pp. 310–312.

[28] See Atlee L. Stroup and Kathryn Jamison Hunter, "Sibling Position in the Family and the Personality of the Child," *Journal of Marriage and the Family,* Vol. 27 (February, 1965), pp. 65–68 for a short review of the literature; see also Walter Toman, *Family Constellation* (New York, Springer Publishing Co., 1961), p. 6.

respectively.[29] These have been affected by divorce, desertion, or death. Children in "broken" homes could be singled out for attention, as could those who are brought up as bilinguals or those who otherwise are living in relatively unique conditions. A total description of the world of children would be very complicated indeed, and well beyond the scope of this book. It is in order to remind ourselves occasionally, however, that many thousands of children live in environments which are not average or normal.

SELECTED READINGS

Adorno, Theodore, *et al., The Authoritarian Personality* (New York, Harper & Row, 1950).

Banham, Katherine, "Obstinate Children Are Adaptable," *Mental Hygiene,* Vol. 36 (January, 1952), pp. 84–89.

Barker, Roger, and Wright, Herbert, *Midwest and Its Children* (New York, Harper & Row, 1954).

Barry, H., III, Bacon, Margaret, and Child, Irving, "A Cross-Cultural Survey of Some Sex Differences in Socialization," *Journal of Abnormal and Social Psychology,* Vol. 55 (February, 1957), pp. 327–332.

Bayley, Nancy, "On the Growth of Intelligence," *American Psychologist,* Vol. 10 (December, 1955), pp. 805–818.

Bossard, James, and Boll, Eleanor, *The Sociology of Child Development* (New York, Harper & Row, 1960), Part VIII.

Bronfenbrenner, Urie, "Socialization and Social Class Through Time and Space," in Maccoby, Eleanor, Newcomb, Theodore, and Hartley, Eugene (Eds.), *Readings in Social Psychology* (New York, Holt, Rinehart and Winston, 1958), pp. 400–425.

Cattell, Raymond, and Coan, Richard, "Personality Factors in Middle Childhood as Revealed in Parents' Ratings," *Child Development,* Vol. 28 (December, 1957), pp. 439–458.

Davis, Allison, and Havighurst, Robert, "Social Class and Color Differences in Child-Rearing," *American Sociological Review,* Vol. 11 (December, 1946), pp. 698–710.

Davis, Allison, and Havighurst, Robert, *Father of the Man* (Boston, Houghton Mifflin, 1947).

Davis, Allison, and Havighurst, Robert, "The Measurement of Mental Systems (Can Intelligence Be Measured?)," *Scientific Monthly,* Vol. 66 (April, 1948), pp. 301–316.

Erikson, Erik, *Childhood and Society* (New York, Norton, 1950).

Gesell, Arnold, and Ilg, Frances, *The Child from Five to Ten* (New York, Harper & Row, 1946).

Gritzner, Florence, "Why Parents Annoy Us," *National Parent-Teacher,* Vol. 51 (May, 1957), pp. 29–31.

[29] Charles Bowerman and Donald Irish, "Some Relations of Stepchildren to Their Parents," *Marriage and Family Living,* Vol. 24 (May, 1962), pp. 113–121.

Handel, Gerald, and Hess, Robert, "The Family as an Emotional Organization," *Marriage and Family Living,* Vol. 18 (May, 1956), pp. 99–101.

Harris, Dale, and others, "Personality Differences Between Responsible and Irresponsible Children," *Journal of Genetic Psychology,* Vol. 87 (September, 1955), pp. 103–109.

Krogman, Wilton, "Biological Growth as It May Affect Pupils' Success," *Merrill-Palmer Quarterly* (Spring, 1955), pp. 90–98.

Langdon, Grace, and Stout, Irving, *The Discipline of Well-Adjusted Children* (Day & Company, 1952).

Loomis, Mary Jane, *The Preadolescent* (New York, Appleton-Century-Crofts, 1959).

McCandless, Boyd, *Children and Adolescents* (New York, Holt, Rinehart and Winston, 1961), Chapter 10.

Neisser, Edith, *The Eldest Child* (New York, Harper & Row, 1957).

Paulsen, Alma, "Personality Development in the Middle Years of Childhood: A Ten-Year Longitudinal Study of Thirty Public School Children by Means of Rorschach Tests and Social Histories," *American Journal of Orthopsychiatry,* Vol. 24 (April, 1954), pp. 336–350.

Plant, James, *Personality and the Culture Pattern* (New York, Commonwealth Fund, 1937).

Prescott, Daniel, *The Child in the Educative Process* (New York, McGraw-Hill, 1957).

Sewell, William, and Haller, A., "Status and Personality Development," *American Sociological Review,* Vol. 24 (August, 1959), pp. 511-520.

Stouffer, George, "Behavior Problems of Children as Viewed by Teachers and Mental Hygienists, A Study of Present Attitudes as Compared with Those Reported by E. K. Wickman," *Mental Hygiene,* Vol. 36 (April, 1952), pp. 271–285.

QUESTIONS AND EXERCISES

1. Write a paper describing the child rearing techniques used by your parents in rearing you, and some of their general effects.
2. Read and comment on Bossard and Boll's Chapter 31 (cited reference) entitled "The Changing Status of Childhood in the United States."
3. Review the literature dealing with the only child. Write a summary paper presenting your findings.
4. Write a critique of Strecker, *Their Mother's Sons,* in which a well-known psychiatrist develops a causal analysis of male neurosis in American society which puts "mom" in a vulnerable position.
5. After observation and study, write a report on the environment for children in a subcultural neighborhood of your town.
6. How far should outside persons go in attempting to interfere with parents who seem to be rearing their children improperly? When should health or welfare authorities step into the situation?

7. What to you are the responsibilities of outside agencies in sex instruction of children during the grade-school period, if any? Discuss.

8. Why is it that parents tend to become greatly agitated when their children do not develop in line with Gesellian or other such norms? What to you is the best solution to this problem?

9. Outside observers often suggest that the American child is "spoiled." How valid is this position? Discuss.

10. Erikson stresses the development of habits of work and industry during the preadolescent period. How can this be accomplished consistently in our type of society?

11. What effects will the mother working outside the home have on the school-aged child? Discuss.

12. Write a critique of Toman, *Family Constellation*.

five

Completion of the Cycle:
Disorganization and Proposals
for Reorganization

24

Later Stages of the Family Cycle

This chapter discusses the last phase of the developmental cycle. Material on the later stages of the family cycle is often not included in a marriage and family text intended for young people. We believe, however, that the material *is* relevant to young people in today's world. Many of them will have grandparents living, but even if not, projecting ahead to the problems and potentialities of the later stages of their own family cycle should be beneficial to the perceptive and responsible young adult.

THE FAMILY WITH TEEN-AGE MEMBERS

The family eventually finds itself moving into the "teen period." Although some of the previous periods held problems, this forthcoming period often seems difficult indeed. A friend of the author relates that he and his wife could scarcely wait for their oldest boy to get through his grade-school years so that the boy could "act grownup." Now these parents look back on all the previous stages as being relatively calm compared to the "storm and stress" of the teen years.

There is an abundance of material dealing with problems of adolescence and youth in the United States. Very few authors seem to be restrained by the lack of good research. Sweeping statements are often made without regard for differences due to varying class levels, or ethnic associations. It seems that anyone who can get into print or onto the public platform is an authority on adolescence and youth.

THE TEEN-AGE PERIOD

In all societies there will be a transition period between childhood and adulthood, however short. In Western society and especially in the United

States, this transition period, known as adolescence, is relatively long. Furthermore, neither the beginning nor the end of the period is clearly delineated. Biologically, puberty signifies a change in sex function with corollary changes in other physical areas. But does adolescence start with puberty? Socially, we are not quite sure when it starts nor what is mature and proper behavior for the period. There is agreement, however, that adolescence is a period of storm and stress. Must it be so?

For many years it was assumed that the *Sturm* and *Drang* of adolescence had essentially a biological basis.[1] Mead in her original work and other anthropologists following her, challenge this and suggest that the way a culture handles adolescence is more crucial than the biological changes per se.[2] The bulk of social science work on adolescence in the last two decades substantially confirms the more social interpretation. What, then, are some of the characteristics of American culture which make this period a trying one?

Ambiguity characterizes the expectations we have for the adolescent. He is expected to indicate evidences of growth toward maturity but is not allowed the fruits of maturity. The middle-class adult world does not give him authority as a citizen, as a full member of the labor force, as a family member, or as a student in school. It does expect him to conform to certain expectations and to prepare for authority in a future role. For many of our young people this period preceding adulthood seems to be unduly prolonged and is difficult to take.

The Teen-age Way of Life

The teen-age life reflects the affluence which is characteristic of our present culture. The youngster has had an ample supply of good clothing and other paraphenalia and, in the case of the boy, access to a car. Many hours are spent in leisure-time activity, including dating. The focus of much activity is around the school, although such a focus is not necessarily on the strictly academic activities. Extracurricular activities correlated with sporting events receive considerable stress. For the high school group, scholarship comes out a poor second when compared with athletic participation or interest, although it is not ignored by all.[3]

Social class makes itself especially felt by the early teen years. Many lower-class students do not finish high school, but the general expectation for the middle classes is completion of high school and college. Even lower-class youth who drop out of school find it difficult to enter the labor market

[1] Richard Simpson and Ida H. Simpson, "The School, The Peer Group, and Adolescent Development," *The Journal of Educational Sociology,* Vol. 32 (September, 1958), p. 37.

[2] Margaret Mead, *Coming of Age in Samoa* (New York, Morrow, 1928).

[3] James Coleman, *The Adolescent Society* (New York, Free Press, 1961).

actively during their teens. However, many more lower-class youth marry during the teen period than do middle-class youth, in spite of their occupational difficulties.

There develops, then, an adolescent subculture with its own norms and values.[4] If teen-agers cannot be fully accepted (as adults) in the adult world they will develop a world of their own. Does this involve an essential rejection of general societal norms? Bealer and Willits say it does not.[5] In their studies of urban, rural farm, and rural nonfarm young people there were some differences on conservatism and radicalism in reference to American society. However, they had about the same types of attitudes toward their parents. What the young people really want is adult authority and status.

Erikson suggests that the major developmental task of the adolescent period is the establishment of ego identity, as was pointed out in Chapter 21. It is inferred that young people band together in a protective manner because they have trouble establishing clear-cut identities in relation to the adult world. He believes that the inability to establish definitive sexual and occupational identifications, especially the latter, accounts for much adolescent anxiety. The opposite of identification is role diffusion. If a young person cannot identify with particular roles in a satisfactory manner considerable frustration will ensue.[6] The identification will of necessity be vicarious in nature, and projections far into the future will be required for many professional and higher level occupations.

The difficulties of choosing a future occupational role cannot be minimized. The range of occupational choices presenting themselves today, at least theoretically, to all young people is almost shocking to those of a former generation. Furthermore, the choice has much to do with the amount of income, circle of friends, and life style which the person will enjoy. Yet there is considerable evidence that occupational planning is often haphazard and unrealistic for many an adolescent. Obviously class, sex, intelligence, and other factors enter the picture here. The consistency with which many adolescents indicate interest in white-collar occupations leads one to suspect that many of them, especially in the lower-class levels, are rather unrealistic about their potentialities for the jobs to which they

[4] Coleman suggests essentially that there is an adolescent subculture which is controlled largely by the young people themselves. This idea is disputed by some; see Frederick Elkin and William Westley, "The Myth of Adolescent Culture," *American Sociological Review,* Vol. 20 (December, 1955), pp. 680–684. Coleman probably represents the more general position held by social scientists.

[5] Robert Bealer and Fern Willits, "Rural Youth: A Case Study in the Rebelliousness of Adolescents," *Annals of American Academy of Political and Social Science,* Vol. 338 (November, 1961), pp. 63–69. This whole issue is devoted to "Teenage Culture" and edited by Jessie Bernard.

[6] Erik Erikson, *Childhood and Society* (New York, Norton, 1963), Chapter 7. See also Robert Hess and Irene Goldblatt, "The Status of Adolescents in American Society: A Problem in Social Identity," *Child Development,* Vol. 28 (December, 1957), pp. 459–468.

aspire.[7] However, a recent study involving a random sample of California high school students indicated a fairly high degree of realism involved in student occupational choices.[8] In general, students making average grades indicated an interest in occupations conforming to their academic ability as measured by achievement. Many were interested in white-collar occupations who might well be headed for unskilled or semiskilled laboring positions. Students of above average academic ability were taking college preparatory courses and were especially interested in the professions.

Whatever may be the case with the average student, there certainly are many in any large group who are confused and unrealistic. Of interest are the free responses of students to the topic, "How it feels to be growing up," given in a study by Strang. Forty-six percent of the students in grades seven through nine indicated "concern about vocation, or about the future." [9] This was the highest percentage of any response category. For the whole high school group, considerations of independence, morality, and responsibility loomed larger than the vocation category, which was in fourth place out of thirteen possible rankings. It is not difficult to agree with Erikson that sex role and occupational role identifications are two major tasks facing the adolescent today.

THE ADOLESCENT AND HIS FAMILY

It is in the family environment that much of the storm and stress of adolescence is exhibited and dealt with in one manner or another. Some authorities believe that a conflict between the generations is inevitable, given our fast-changing culture. Inevitable or not, conflict is very much in evidence. The difficulties may stem from culture conflict or they may reflect personality factors specific to the situation. At the time the adolescent is beginning his strivings for maturity, the parent may be facing personal problems of his own. As the child begins to mature physically, to date, and to enter the social whirl, unachieved goals of the parent may reassert themselves. A mother who was not too successful at the teen-age level in her own love life may try to relive the period by vicariously identifying with her attractive daughter. A father, somewhat concerned about his own diminishing virility, may resent the son's ability to date a large number of attractive girls. Identification is a process that can act both ways. It can be said that parents who are personally well-adjusted and who have taken their own developmental tasks in stride will be best able to identify with their children in legitimate ways. That which is legitimate identification for a parent

[7] See W. E. Myers, "High School Graduates Choose Occupations Unrealistically," *Occupations,* Vol. 25 (March, 1947), pp. 332–333.

[8] O. E. Thompson, "What is the High School Student of Today Like?" *Journal of Secondary Education,* Vol. 36 (April, 1961), pp. 210–219.

[9] Ruth Strang, "Adolescents' Views on One Aspect of Their Development," *The Journal of Educational Psychology,* Vol. 46 (November, 1955), pp. 423–432.

with the child will vary, and only general suggestions can be made here. The important thing is that the child must move along toward maturity, meeting the challenges and tasks that come. If the parent can aid and guide but at the same time allow and encourage growth, he is probably in the right groove. From the psychiatric point of view it is not legitimate for the parent to seek gratification of a neurotic need through the child. Trying to satisfy a frustrated desire to be a successful love object, athletic hero, scholar, or whatnot, can sometimes involve using the child in an unfair way. If, on the other hand, the parent can be happy because the child is happy and can feel a sense of satisfaction because the young person has achieved what for the time being he wanted to achieve, he would seem to be on more solid ground. Certainly everyone will grant the parents a bit of pardonable pride at the time the child receives public recognition, as in the school, church, or elsewhere. The legitimate pride is in "the job well done" in the rearing of the child.

It is the task of the adults to cushion the impact of the transition period between childhood and adulthood, which is what adolescence is. This means that thoughtful parents take into account individual differences, needs, and circumstances. Susie suddenly exhibits an interest in science and dreams of becoming a medical missionary. To her hardbitten businessman father, this sounds absurd. It might be well that he dampen his realism for the time being at least. He could note that some women have been quite successful in scientific fields of various kinds. Further, should Susie continue in her interest, the chances are greater that she will become a technician in a local laboratory than that she will become the first assistant in Dr. Schweitzer's hospital. Still, who knows Susie's future and would it be too bad if she became a medical missionary and went to a distant country? The fact that Susie's great, great grandmother dreamed of far away places may partially account for the location of Susie in the American Midwest rather than in a small, European peasant community. Dreams and aspirations are the stuff of youth, and parents, assisting their children in reality testing, will do well not to smash all dreams, and to weigh individual aspirations carefully.

Evidence on occupational striving is somewhat disconcerting. It appears that those who become oriented toward the greatest achievement often are unsatisfied at home, whereas those who are less oriented toward achievement upward from that of their parents are often satisfied with their home life.[10] More research is needed to discover the dynamics behind these findings, since many will hope that it is possible to have some high levels of aspiration developed in families where the relationships of the people involved are harmonious. Whatever the association between successful home life and upward mobility striving, however, many parents can play valuable

[10] See the review of the various studies relating home environment and child rearing practices to achievement motivation in David McClelland, *The Achieving Society* (Princeton, Van Nostrand, 1961), Chapter 9.

roles in helping their adolescent children clarify their occupational prospects. In some cases this will mean encouraging the use of guidance and occupational counselors. It may mean suffering with them as they try out various part-time jobs as best they can. If the children wish to enter certain fields it will mean either assuring them of the possibilities of financial support or aiding them in their search for scholarships, loans, and part-time work. It will also mean that the parents, if they have not done so by example, will need to get across to the adolescent what is formally called the concept of "deferred gratification." This is, it must be made clear, that in order to achieve the fruits of a particular job or profession it is necessary to spend many years of study and labor that are sometimes tedious, as against receiving more immediate gratifications.

FAMILY TASKS OF TEEN-AGE PARENTS

The nature of the teen years presents a challenge to all concerned, as we have tried to demonstrate. After a short discussion of some major problem areas, attention can now be turned to a consideration of some major family tasks of the period, outlined below.

1. Expanding the home and achieving maximum usage of all its potentials.
   A. Arranging the space in the home to provide room and equipment for parties and informal entertainment of friends by the teen-age family member.
   B. Utilizing all available extra space for parents and siblings in order to meet their needs for leisure and recreation, work, study, etc.
   C. Making necessary rearrangements or additions required in adapting bedroom facilities to different age and sex combinations of all the children.
2. Refining and maintaining an adequate philosophy of life which will provide a meaningful base for the adolescent and younger children in the family.
   A. Aiding the adolescent in his struggle to develop a set of personal ideals and goals which he can call his own.
   B. Providing adult role-models which are worthy of emulation by the growing adolescent.
   C. Discussing conflicting behavior patterns and standards with the adolescent and mutually noting their potentials and implications.
   D. Encouraging the adolescent in his growth toward an adult heterosexual role.
   E. Helping the child to accept his own body with its particular appearance, strength, and limitations.
3. Adapting the relationship to the adolescent in order to facilitate his progressive cutting of the apron strings.
   A. Providing a more flexible pattern in the independence-dependence relationship.

    B. Aiding the unstable adolescent by providing for his needs; at times supplying security and direction but aiding him and encouraging him in general to move toward independent behavior.

    C. Accepting the indications of adolescent independence rather than being threatened by them.

    D. Recognizing that there will be regressions on the part of the adolescent at times, but that full dependence behavior during adolescence should be a warning signal rather than an evidence of proper character.

4. Reallocating patterns of authority and accountability to take into account the adolescent's increasing capacity for responsibility.

    A. Assisting the adolescent to develop a general sense of responsibility.

    B. Aiding the adolescent's development by allowing and encouraging him to carry certain specific responsibilities by himself.

    C. Providing wider limits on behavior than those set for earlier years, against which the adolescent may feel compelled to strive but which also provide an element of security.

5. Granting the adolescent greater authority in the decision-making process in the family.

6. Reorganizing patterns of income and spending with regard to possible fluctuations of intake and changing demands characteristic of the adolescent family.

    A. Achieving and maintaining an optimum and distinct economic standard of living.

    B. Building the groundwork for the preparation of the eventual achievement of each adolescent as he matures.

    C. Aiding the adolescent in his search for occupational possibilities by indicating sources of information regarding alternative occupations.

    D. Aiding the adolescent along with teachers, occupational counselors, and others in his assessment of his real capabilities and potentialities.

7. Reestablishing and adjusting emotional ties in the home in preparation for the adolescent's departure and the maturing of the younger children.

    A. Rerelating oneself to one's spouse as a person, with particular attention to changing needs and emotions.

    B. Working together as a couple to discover interests and activities which will bring both individuals new emotional satisfactions and zest for living. Accepting and adjusting to the physiological changes in store with approaching middle age.

    C. Adjusting to the personalities of the friends of the adolescent.

    D. Accepting emotional independence in the adolescent.

8. Adjusting to the pressures of changing sex patterns coming from adolescents and parents.

    A. Adapting sexual habits and interests to one's own biological changes.

    B. Adjusting sexual habits in relation to the spouse's changing biological needs.

    C. Maintaining oneself as an attractive sex partner rather than allowing oneself to overlook matters of personal attractiveness.

    D. Aiding the adolescent in his efforts to cope with resurging sexual needs and interests.

9. Establishing and maintaining a pattern of communication suitable to a growing adolescent.
    A. Struggling to understand the adolescent frame of reference in order to communicate intelligently with him.
    B. Providing a "sympathetic ear" to which the adolescent can at times turn to discuss pressing problems.
    C. Encouraging the open discussion of conflicting standards and dilemmas facing all adults in the modern world.
    D. Through communication allowing the growing adolescent to share to a greater degree the family successes and problems, perceived by the parents.

10. Adapting the relationship with outside groups to include patterns of communication with peer groups of the adolescent and other groups and organizations in the community.
    A. Accepting responsibility for the development of the civic and social interests of one's children.
    B. Keeping abreast of changing social currents and thought.
    C. Achieving and accepting adult civic and social responsibility.
    D. Encouraging the adolescent to discover the potentialities available in religious and other human betterment institutions as well as the more narrow social and recreation oriented ones.

11. Maintaining family morale.
    A. Achieving and maintaining a family structure which is conducive to strong morale, individually and collectively.
    B. Providing an environment of mutual encouragement and support which will be beneficial to both adults and adolescent family members.
    C. Maintaining or developing tension-relieving devices which are appropriate to the family constellation of adults, adolescents, and young children.
    D. Maintaining stable general morale in the face of the ups and downs of the adolescents.[11]

DEVELOPMENTAL TASKS OF THE ADOLESCENT IN AMERICAN CULTURE

Mother and father as individuals and as parents have challenges which must be met as the older members of their brood move into the teen years.

[11] For the description of the tasks outlined in this chapter we depend heavily on the work of students of Reuben Hill's seminar groups who have developed material entitled "Basic Tasks of the Family as a Social System Particularized for Specific Developmental Stages of the Family Life Cycle," mimeographed and wall chart, kindly supplied by Dr. Hill. We also give credit to Evelyn Duvall and Reuben Hill (Eds.), *Report of the Committee on Dynamics of Family Interaction* (National Conference on Family Life, Inc., 1948) mimeographed, Parts V, VI, VII. For a parallel approach see Evelyn Duvall, *Family Development* (Philadelphia, Lippincott, 1957), Chapters 11–14.

Rich or poor, strict or permissive, old-fashioned or modern, the home environment has been fashioned by the parents and the children have essentially adapted to it.

Now at the teen level, the child will feel pressure to challenge and reject the home environment at times and to fall back on it for security at other times. Whatever its strengths or weaknesses the home environment still is an important arena for the teen-ager. Within it he will work at certain tasks. From it he will go out in an attempt to master others in the larger community environment. Some of the major tasks the adolescent will face are presented below in outline form.

1. Building a workable, mature value system.
    A. Developing a satisfactory philosophy of life.
    B. Moving away from simple hedonistic motivations for behavior toward behavior related to principles.
    C. Exploring the possibilities available in religious and other institutions.
2. Freeing himself from his parents so that significant steps toward full independence can be taken.
    A. Breaking by degrees the "silver cord" holding him to his parents.
    B. Freeing himself from reliance upon the parents for security and moving toward a position of self-reliance.
    C. Developing a full adult relationship with parents and other adults.
3. Achieving a full acceptance of and identification with his own sex role.
    A. Working through any wishes to be of the opposite sex and coming to grips with the requirements and potentialities of one's own sex role in society.
    B. Establishing emotional relationships across sex lines.
    C. Coming to grips with adult sexuality.
4. Developing a more mature sense of responsibility and its attendant privileges.
    A. Learning to relate responsibility and its attendant privileges.
    B. Developing intellectual skills and concepts necessary for civic competence.
    C. Carrying one's share of family duties and responsibilities.
5. Coming to grips with his physical self, its appearance, potentialities, and limitations.
    A. Appreciating the fact that one's body is the only one he will ever have, and the implications of this.
    B. Taking the changes of puberty in stride.
    C. Learning to control and make maximum use of one's physical potentialities.
6. Learning to relate to various peer groups and circles of friends.
    A. Learning to communicate as an adult with peers and other groups.
    B. Adapting to various types of groups in the community.
    C. Learning to relate to group values without the necessity of compulsive conformity.

7. Moving toward a satisfactory occupational role.
   A. Learning to make a realistic assessment of one's occupational poten-
      tialities.
   B. Exploring a wide range of occupations and narrowing the possibilities
      sharply over time.
   C. Making practical preparations for a future occupational role.
8. Developing more adult relationships with members of the opposite sex.
   A. Learning to understand the basic orientations of members of the op-
      posite sex.
   B. Through experiences with various types of persons, learning the type
      of person to whom one is attracted.
   C. Making specific preparations to leave the parental family and establish
      one's own home.

Evidence that task accomplishment is not always a simple matter for
the adolescent population can be gathered from a number of sources. Juvenile delinquency reports and comments on these reports are available in
abundance.[12] Just what they can really tell us is a complex question. Leaving this extreme group as representative still of only a small (but growing)
minority of adolescents, what problems are typical for the more average
categories? A number of studies have been made using problem inventories
of various types to which young people are asked to react. One recent one,
using 500 adolescent girls as a sample, found three major "clusters" or
problem areas.[13] They were as follows: (1) *General personal anxiety and
insecurity.* Included in the cluster were items such as "people don't understand me," "I'm afraid of making mistakes," and "I'm often restless." (2)
Tension involving relations with others. Specific items often checked were,
"I'm nervous when I talk to people," "I'm not good at talking to people,"
and "I'm nervous in front of the class." (3) *Problems in getting along with
parents.* Some specific items often checked were: "My (father) (mother)
is always criticizing (blaming) (nagging) me," "I can't discuss things with
my (mother) (father)," and "My (father) (mother) is always expecting
too much of me." While these findings are reported only for girls, there is
no reason to believe that results for boys would be extremely different. The
conclusions are in general in line with results reported in the *Annals* study
of teen-age culture.[14] Brown, studying self-portraits of young people as
revealed in their music and literature, found them to be worrying over shy-
ness, alleged personality quirks, and how to get along with members of the

[12] See William Kvaraceus, *et al., Delinquent Behavior: Principles and Practice*
(Washington, National Education Association of the United States, 1959) for a good
survey treatment of the area.
   [13] Richard Schutz, "Patterns of Personal Problems of Adolescent Girls," *The
Journal of Educational Psychology,* Vol. 49 (February, 1958), pp. 1–5. Also reprinted an article number 57 in Lester Crow and Alice Crow, *Readings in Adolescent
Psychology* (New York, McKay, 1961), pp. 339–345.
   [14] Jessie Bernard, Ed., "Teen-age Culture," *Annals of American Academy of
Political and Social Science,* Vol. 338 (November, 1961).

opposite sex. The above report also found that deviates and rejectees exist. Some seem to be or feel out of place, the "wallflowers" in the case of girls or "clods" in the case of boys.[15] Not belonging to some group seems to be about the worst possible fate in the eyes of the teen-ager. Some suggest that lower-class delinquents individually and as groups feel rejected by organized society and therefore band together as a defense mechanism. Membership in a lower-class family or ethnic group and unacceptable individual traits or characteristics make it difficult for some to be accepted in certain groups.

Hill *et al.,* peered beneath the surface of adolescent behavior through the use of projective tests and continuous observation. The following description of the personality maladjustment of adolescents in their sample (from a small southern town) is a rather disturbing one:

I. Parents are differentially perceived as coercive in some situations and succoring when ill, but always as powerful figures with whom only two courses of action are possible, disobedience and taking the consequences in punishment, or running away.

II. Problems are dealt with in one of three ways, by fatalistic acceptance of come what may, by running away to let someone else handle it, or by wishful dreaming.

III. Fantasies show high incidence of morbidity and trouble.

A. Boys particularly see life as a great battle between superior and inferior forces; the world is hostile and frightening.

B. Girls are more likely to view world as beneficent and to see father as helpful and succoring.

IV. Fantasies with respect to trouble show little free-floating creativity freed of tradition.

V. In the adolescent's view of his community people are divided into those who are superordinate to him and subordinate to him; there is no evidence of equality conceptions among his picture stories.

VI. The adolescent is, however, very person-centered, quite conscious of interpersonal relations and pictures his relations with people as determined primarily by sex expectations and age expectations.[16]

It would seem, from the standpoint of mental health, that the typical adolescent's personal adjustment in that particular town leaves much to be desired. Perhaps the general social environment described as being rather rigid and sterile has brought on more inner rebellion and apathy than would be typical. When one notes that such young people will soon be marrying and rearing families of their own it is easy to become discouraged or cynical about the country's future. Pictures such as these, coupled with the data on illegitimacy, delinquency, and other evidences of personal and

[15] Charles Brown, "Self-Portrait: The Teen-Type Magazine," *Annals of American Academy of Political and Social Science,* Vol. 338 (November, 1961), pp. 13–21.

[16] Reuben Hill, *et al., Eddyville's Families* (Chapel Hill, Institute for Research in Social Science, University of North Carolina, 1953), pp. 409–410.

social disorganization can add up to a rather bleak picture. It would be out of order to stop here, however. Keeping all factors in mind, one could easily argue that the incidence of personal maladjustment among young people is low. Caught by age in a period of transition, and by chance in a period of social upheaval, adolescents must prepare to adapt to a troubled world. That some of them reflect the overall social disorganization in their own personalities is predictable and logical. That the great majority of young people are meeting most of their developmental tasks and handling them suggests that their adaptability as a whole is greater than we have sometimes been led to believe.

THE FAMILY IN THE MIDDLE YEARS

This particular stage of family life is one which lacks conceptual clarity and also suffers from a lack of research attention. There are essentially two stages involved. The first is the period during which the children are being launched into the occupational world or marriage (or both). The second is the period which starts when the last child leaves home and ends when the age of occupational retirement of the husband is reached. They can well be classed as separate stages if this is desired, but for our purposes they will be considered as one stage.

THE FAMILY AS A LAUNCHING CENTER

A major developmental task for the family is that of serving as a center from which the young person can be launched into marriage. It is at this point that some parents seemingly long for the old days. How can the parent sit back when the son or daughter is facing loss of status if not ruin as the parent sees it? The parent feels that he has had more experience and that he is more inclined to take the long-term point of view. The young person, on the other hand, wishes to make his own individual choice of dates or prospective marriage partners and resents any implication that he is not mature enough to do so.

There are indications that the status factor is often involved in cases where parents object strongly to the companions of their youth. If the child seriously considers a prospective partner below the class level of the parents or the level to which they aspire, objections may be raised. Bossard and Boll, in *The Sociology of Child Development,* cite the case of an upperclass family in which the son was dating a lower-class girl whom the mother considered quite beneath the family. The mother arranged to have the boy bring the girl in question to what was presumably to be an evening of informal entertainment involving the family. Secretly the mother arranged to have many of the son's upper-class friends in for the evening. The girl could not measure up to the demands of the occasion and the mother had no further "trouble" of this sort.

Mixed marriages sometimes involve potential loss of status, although this is not the only basis for parental objection. When the prospective partner is of the same social status, parental objections usually involve factors of character or general stability. Parents tend to feel that young people focus on more superficial aspects of personality.

It seems clear that the role of the parents during the courtship period of their children needs to be clarified in America. Many parents are caught between the desires to assure their children's success and also freedom of choice. There is no obvious way to solve this problem. Parents must realize, however, that most of their active control of the children comes before this period. For good or ill, by the time of the launching period, children are going to demand the right of decision-making for themselves.

Launching into the Occupational World

In the colonial days preparation for the adult occupational role started in the tender years and was pursued until marriage. At the proper time the parents of the boy would indicate that he could have the "south forty," a few farm animals, and certain farm implements. Combining these with the household equipment and the linens brought by the bride, the young couple were ready to establish themselves. Today it is much more difficult, if not impossible, to pass the needed technological skill and equipment on to the next generation. Certain corollaries of older methods are still with us, however. Skilled workers help their sons and nephews get accepted into apprentice programs. They pass on knowledge gained by long experience regarding roles of foreman, superintendents, and other functionaries. They impart the information they have acquired regarding work conditions, technical skills and attitudes, and trade union practices.

It should not be assumed that middle- and upper-class parents are uninvolved in this process. Ways of training for a business or profession, getting established, and meeting the public can be discussed with youngsters who are assessing alternative occupational pursuits. Questions of the dangers of overextension, of down payments, of loan-making, and hundreds of other things can be discussed by parents and relatives on the basis of their background and experience. At the upper-class level a vast amount of lore involving management of larger business or estates, investments, and supervision of subordinates is made available to younger sons who wish to make use of it for occupational purposes.

The question of "following in father's footsteps" has always been somewhat controversial. The boy who wishes to step in and take over his father's role in business often has economic advantages which his competitors do not have. On the other hand, many if not most men eventually wish to demonstrate to their peers and the world that they can "stand on their own feet." Frequently young people resent being known as "chips off the old block." Motivations of independence and self-reliance often lead young men to turn down, or consider turning down, occupational possibilities which might at first glance seem most promising. Most American young men follow occupations other than those of their fathers. However, they are more inclined to enter their father's occupational *category* than any other.

The important question would seem to be the interests and wants of the child in terms of his perceptions of reality, individual and social. To make a son or daughter over completely in the image of the parent is neither freedom nor intelligence. Parents can function best by providing a generally sound home base from which the child can move in his own direction, in terms of his own potentials. Given this, they can be of great help to the young person in backing him in his search to "find himself." The parents can help to obtain pertinent occupational information and to obtain a reasonably reliable picture of the young person's capabilities. Encouragement can be given to the young person who has an overromanticized conception of certain occupational pursuits. By helping him discuss the particular occupational role with persons who are in the field, the parent can contribute reality testing at a time when it is crucial.

The parent further exercises an important influence by his attitude toward education. Outside of the independent small business, most occupational areas now require education beyond high school as a base for promotion up the ranks. Questions of how much advanced training, how it will be paid for, of parental subsidy after marriage, and the like are often interrelated. Falling back on what was done in grandfather's day or even in father's day a generation ago is no longer very appropriate in view of present conditions. Especially critical will be the question of parental subsidy after marriage while higher education is being pursued.

Financing the Launching Center

The problem of meeting financial pressures of this period is often great. Not only will the parents be struggling to help the older children get educationally or occupationally established, but also they will be responsible for younger children. Small wonder that this period is spoken of by Gutheim and others as the *peak* period.[17] Parents are vulnerable for tuition fees, initiation fees, wedding fees, and professional or union fees until the last child is fully launched. It is the father at this time who ought to be allowed a touch of ambivalence without criticism. While he may wish at

[17] Frederick Gutheim, *Houses for Family Living* (New York, The Woman's Foundation, 1948).

times to slow down the years in order to keep the children at home, there must be other times when he looks forward to the period when the last child is on his own with anticipated feelings of relief.

Ingenuity and persistence are required of parents to meet the financial demands of this period. Part-time or summer work by children may offer possibilities, depending upon both general economic circumstances and on specific local conditions. In many cases these efforts are not sufficient to meet needs, and the mother often reenters the labor market. The 1955 census report showed that 43.5 percent of the wives in the labor force were in the age category twenty-five to forty-four.[18] This was the highest proportion of married women working in any age category. We may be sure that many of the mothers work outside the home in order to help launch the children into the occupational world or into higher education, or both.

College costs have been rising sharply. Presently it costs from $1500 to $2500 or more per year to send a young person to college away from home. These costs can be expected at least to double in the foreseeable future.[19] For many working-class and middle-class families the total cost may be expected to run from one fourth to one third of the father's gross yearly income, depending upon the type of college or university. Report after report suggests that most families are not realistic in their expectations as to what it means to launch children into the professions via college or into the business world at really competitive levels. Farming is even worse. To back a son to the point that he can compete successfully in the dairy farm, beef cattle, or grain area means the investment of thousands of dollars.[20]

It is not suggested that all families can or must launch their children at the levels discussed. Many will be unwilling or unable to do so. Unfortunately many expect to, without adequate sense of what it will mean financially, and otherwise. Somehow children are launched and the family is reduced again to the nuclear couple. We turn now to this postparental period for a discussion of some of its features.

THE POSTPARENTAL PERIOD

According to the 1960 census, in the typical American family the last child will be launched when the husband is fifty years of age or so and the

18 David Kaplan, "The Labor Force in 1975," in Donald Bogue (Ed.), *Applications of Demography: The Population Situation in 1975* (Oxford, Ohio, Scripps Foundation for Research, 1957), Chapter XIII.

19 Based on projections from trends in college tuition raises over the past two decades.

20 Arnold Rose, "Factors Associated with the Life Satisfaction of the Middle-class, Middle-aged Persons," *Marriage and Family Living,* Vol. 17 (February, 1955), pp. 15–19.

wife, forty-seven to fifty years of age. The postparental period is the inter-mediate period between this launching and the beginning of old age. While this period has received a minimum of attention, there are certain gener-alizations that can be made which may be helpful.

A recent study by the Carnegie United Kingdom Trust focused on the problems of 25,000 cases recorded over a three-year period in Marriage Guidance Centers in England and Wales. The concern was with the change in types of problems being presented by those who had been married for some time as against those who had been recently married. There are con-sequently two categories—those married less than three years and those married eighteen years or more. The following table indicates the overall findings.

TABLE 43

Presenting Symptoms in 25,000 Marriage Guidance Council Cases by Percentage

Symptom	Couples Married 3 Years or Less	Couples Married 18 Years or More
Sex	40	15
Living conditions	24	7
Parental influence	22	9
Ill health	14	29
Incompatibility	12	23
Infidelity	6	26
Income	3	6

SOURCE: Address at the 1962 Groves Conference on Marriage and The Family by A. Joseph Brayshaw, General Secretary, The National Marriage Guidance Council, London, England. The table is based on information obtained in a study supported by the Carnegie United Kingdom Trust.

As can be seen, early problems of sex adjustment, adapting to living conditions, and parental influences had been alleviated for the older couples. Looming large as problems are ill-health, incompatibility, and infidelity. What are some of the causal factors underlying these statistics? We can tentatively suggest certain underlying tensions. Health problems are perhaps inevitable for the average couple during these years. Bodily proc-esses change, the joints begin to ache, and endurance is not what it previ-ously was. In the case of the woman, the menopause may be traumatic. How much this is a physiological and how much an emotional problem is a matter of debate. The husband may also deplore his loss of vigor and power.

This period is one in which individuals are forced to come to grips with certain fundamentals. The husband senses that he has reached the peak of his economic career. Boredom, frustration, or insecurity may drive him to seek emotional satisfaction outside the home. He may pursue younger women in order to prove that he is still attractive and manly. Worry about health, infidelity, and incompatibility may well be interwoven causally to the point that it is difficult to isolate cause and effect.

It has been suggested that the wife has a greater risk of problems during this age than does her husband.[21] It is she who must make great adaptations to the absence of the children from the home. The husband's occupational role outside the home continues for a number of years, even though his financial contributions are not as greatly needed. With her in-the-home role severely curtailed, the wife may be driven to engage in outside activities. If this is to involve productive employment, she may find that her previous skills are rusty and unmarketable. Volunteer work in community services and social activity outside the home may or may not fill the void left by the departure of the children. Many women in the later middle-age category either remain employed outside the home if they have been, or enter employment. For those who have been working to aid in the support of the family the departure of children means that the pressure to work outside the home is not as great as it previously was. Many still prefer to work as various studies have demonstrated.[22] Kaplan estimates that by 1975 women in the labor force in the forty-five to sixty-four age bracket will form about 35 percent of the female working force.[23] He notes, however, that many of these will be only part-time workers and that they have a greater tendency to move in and out of the market and from one place of employment to another.

One study of a sample of fifty upper middle-class women from the ages of forty-seven to sixty-five bears on the matter of employment and the basic adjustment of women in this category.[24] All wives were college-trained and living with their husbands in either urban or suburban areas and none had worked full time during the childbearing years. These women would not seek guidance, occupational or otherwise, during the postparental period. Those who worked outside the home often "stumbled into" positions because they were approached by someone in their geographic area. They were not intensively seeking outside-the-home activity.

The authors of the study believe that work outside the home would be helpful to some dissatisfied women in this category. This would necessitate programs to convert the experience of the women into presently marketable skills. A sizeable group of older women are entering teacher train-

[21] See Alfred McClung Lee and Elizabeth Briant Lee, *Marriage and the Family* (New York, Barnes and Noble, 1961), p. 276.

[22] *1960 Handbook on Women Workers,* Women's Bureau Publication No. 275 (Washington, D.C.; Government Printing Office, 1960), p. 36.

[23] Kaplin, *op. cit.*

[24] Ida Fisher Davidoff and May Elish Markewich, "The Postparental Phase in the Life Cycle of Fifty College-Educated Women," *Digest of Doctoral Thesis for Teacher's College* (New York, Columbia, 1961).

ing programs to prepare for public school teaching. At the National Institute of Mental Health, Pines is experimenting with intensive training of wives for posts in psychotherapy.[25] Obvious practical problems will appear to the reader which need not be discussed at this point. There are many community needs which could well be met by able women of this age whose childbearing experience and general maturity make them valuable. In many cases their own marriages and sense of well-being would be aided in the process.

Not all work outside the home need be for pay. As Glasser points out, many organizations would scarcely be able to function without the help of women volunteers.[26] According to the Davidoff and Markewich study, however, many of the wives curtailed their volunteer activities in order to give more attention to their mates and friends. The authors believe that the volunteer activities often had served the latent functions of giving the mothers a chance to be away from their children for brief periods in the company of adults. Now that this escape was no longer needed, the activities were curtailed.

Unfortunately this study was done on a nonrandom sample of women in comfortable environments. However, three fourths of them were adapting in a satisfactory manner to the postparental period. The departure of the children was not traumatic, their health was better than might be expected, and the marital relationship was being rebuilt along new lines. For the minority with poor adjustment, the authors suspect "cultural emphases on achievement, lack of role definition, intra-psychic problems, unsuccessful children, a poor parent-child or marital relationship." [27]

The results of the above study are in line with those of Axelson, who reports on a study of parents in the middle years. In general, the interpersonal relationships and personal satisfactions of the postparental couples were as satisfactory as those of couples who still had children in the home.[28] There was an increase in loneliness of women in the postparental period. Interestingly these same mothers engaged in a decreasing number of community activities compared to former periods in their lives. There was also a greater concern with health. The men in general were better adjusted in the postparental period than they had been in the immediate period preceding it.

Sussman warns that we must not assume that all postparental couples are socially maladjusted and must be "helped" into activities of one kind or

[25] Maya Pines, "Training Housewives as Psychotherapists," *Harper's Magazine,* Vol. 224 (April, 1962), pp. 37–42.

[26] Melvin Glasser, "What Makes A Volunteer?" *Public Affairs Pamphlet,* No. 224 (New York, 1955).

[27] Davidoff and Markewich, *op. cit.*

[28] Leland Axelson, "Personal Adjustment in The Postparental Period," *Marriage and Family Living,* Vol. 22 (February, 1960), pp. 66–68.

another.[29] In his study of 103 middle-class families in this stage, joint activity patterns developed slowly after the children were launched. Those who lived within driving distance of their children experienced little basic change in their activity patterns. Partners were drawn closer to each other with the wives feeling a greater need for increased activity than the husbands. The couples were more free to undertake intended trips or projects than they had been when encumbered with children.

More intensive research with random samples of all class levels is needed at this point. We know that some couples adapt successfully to this period, some moderately so, and some poorly. The predisposing factors involved for these categories are not clear, and they should be studied. It does seem clear, however, that the so-called "empty nest" period need not be so bleak as we have sometimes been led to believe. The postparental period does offer many possibilities to couples if they can make use of them. The children no longer restrict their activities as they once did. In many cases income is sufficient for some travel and other uses of leisure time. In terms of history these couples are now comfortably situated. It behooves couples of this category to work toward models of family living for the postparental period which are meaningful and satisfactory.

THE FAMILY IN THE LATER YEARS

There is no real agreement as to when this category logically starts in the family life cycle. Perhaps as logical as any is the period after the husband retires from his occupation.

Anyone who gives scholarly attention to the aged in our society is struck by a number of factors. First, the aged are increasing both in gross numbers and in their percentage of the total population.[30] Presently the category sixty-five and over includes about 9 percent of the population. Predictions are that it will run between 9 and 10 percent for the next two decades. This means, in round numbers, that there will be twenty million older people by 1975, a sizeable figure, to say the least.[31] The significance of this can perhaps be better appreciated by noting that one hundred years ago slightly less than 3 percent of our population fell in this same category.

A second factor is compulsory retirement from the labor force. In 1850 only 5 percent of the men still living at sixty-five and over were retired from their work. By 1950 the corresponding figure was 55 percent and it will be about 70 percent by 1975. While the proportion of people in

[29] Marvin Sussman, "Activity Patterns of Postparental Couples and Their Relationships to Family Continuity," *Marriage and Family Living,* Vol. 17 (November, 1955), p. 341.

[30] Bruce Waxman, "The Aged Population in 1975," in Bogue, *op . cit.,* Chapter 19.

[31] *Ibid.*

our population sixty-five and over has been steadily increasing, there has been no accompanying tendency to raise the retirement age.

The differential sex ratio for the period sixty-five and over should be noted. In 1955 the ratio of males to females was 86.6 (or about 87 men for every 100 women). By 1975 it is predicted that the sex ratio for the same category will be 72.6.[32]

Ours is a culture which stresses the values of youth. The vigor, aggressiveness, beauty, and vitality of youthfulness are more highly valued than are the wisdom, stability, and experience which older persons are presumed to have. Senior citizens are considered to be "behind the times" and "old-fashioned" rather than wise counselors who can speak with the authority of maturity and experience.

Another factor which adds to the problems of the aged is a high rate of social change. Most senior citizens presently living were socialized in an agrarian or small town type of culture. Emerging urban folkways and mores are at times difficult for them.[33]

Given this brief attention to the cultural and social setting in which aging families live, attention may turn to some of the major problems with which they must cope.

ADJUSTMENT OF THE AGED

In the introduction, attention was briefly given to some of the general features of the social context in which aging takes place. This may now be followed by a few more pertinent considerations before attention is turned to a brief analysis of the role adjustments of the aging.

The impact of rapid social change without a doubt aggravates intergenerational relations in our society. As has been pointed out, many elderly people have been reared in small town or rural cultures, whereas their children have been exposed to urban ways. The possibilities of severe clashes regarding child rearing, recreation, dress, consumptive patterns, and dozens of other things have their source in these differences in cultural orientations. Dinkel, who completed one of the early studies on the relationships between the generations, found this difference to be the basis for much parent-child conflict.[34]

It is now being suggested that with the cessation of immigration and the decline of the rural population, conflicts stemming from this type of source should rapidly diminish. Logic tells us that in a society changing as rapidly as ours, differences of basic orientation to life may continue, but take new forms.

[32] *Ibid.*
[33] Duvall, *op. cit.*, p. 453.
[34] Robert Dinkel, "Parent-child Conflict in Minnesota Families," *American Sociological Review*, Vol. 9 (August, 1943), pp. 412–419.

ROLE, STATUS, AND SELF-ESTEEM

Married men and women who have experienced parenthood have achieved at least minimum recognition and status simply by the fact of completed parenthood. The man has a relatively clear-cut role as husband-father-provider. Typically he has an occupational role and status. The woman through the middle years has the role of wife-mother-homemaker with all that this entails. Among their social peers and in the community in general the parents as individuals and as a couple are ranked from low to high on the basis of occupational and social prestige, adequacy of their child rearing, and so on. The father is known as bank cashier, church deacon, or local ward captain as well as the head of a particular family. He is rated on all of these categories. The wife gains her status to a degree through her husband but also in her own right in terms of her community contributions and her role as mother.

Over the years the conception of self becomes adapted to the various roles played. One has an occupational self, a father self and so on. The middle years are probably more difficult for the woman because she is often forced to reevaluate her "mother self" and her "sex partner self." The husband has his "occupational self" which may be his area of preoccupation and so he is able to get through the middle years fairly well. If the wife handles well the tasks facing her during the middle years she may be better prepared for the later period than he, however. She has a homemaking-nursing function which she may carry until she is completely enfeebled. If the man has centered his interests in his work (has emphasized his occupational self) to the neglect of other roles, the loss of status and self-esteem at retirement may be very great. This process is further accentuated if he moves geographically and breaks former social ties. An older person finds it difficult to carve out new roles in a strange community, although it can be done.

In their search for status and self-esteem older persons often expect too much of the family. Suddenly and abruptly for the man, experiences with the wife, children, and grandchildren are expected to compensate for the loss of occupational and community status. That some frustration might develop is predictable. In the case of the woman, while the children are gone and with them the mother role, the wife-homemaker role with which she started marriage still remains, albeit in more limited form. However, the woman who has only a home and family self may expect too much more from the family. Without outside interests she may make more of the grand-mother role than is legitimate, with resulting frustration and disillusionment.

Sometimes for varied reasons families choose to live together as three-generation households. Koller's more recent study confirms some of Dinkel's earlier findings and offers insights into some of the difficulties involved.[35] Reporting on three studies he finds that families ofen endure value conflicts, being forced to choose between the norm of providing aid to aging parents on the one hand and the desire for independent homes of their own on the other. A power conflict often develops between the two generations, the older parents wishing to retain their authority of the past and the younger generation challenging this in their quest for authority of their own. The grandchildren often sense this conflict and may add fuel to the fire but also may be confused by it. Persistently pressing for freedom and authority of their own, they help put the middle generation in a precarious and difficult position.

The logic of this study's results and those of Dinkel would seem to suggest mutual avoidance patterns as the only successful mechanism of facilitating smooth interactions between the generations. Such suggestions are oversimplified, however. Von Hentig [36] and others suggest positive contributions which can be made by grandparents, especially to grandchildren. Albrecht reports data from her studies in a Midwestern town in which many of the families had developed smooth relationships between the generations.[37] A convergence of findings from her studies and those by Sussman [38] and by Havighurst seems to be developing.[39] It appears that parents who have been somewhat flexible in their rearing of their children are better able to move into the grandparent role than those who have been more traditional and authoritarian. Sussman finds family continuity is optimum if moderate patterns of mutual aid are developed. He finds that being geographically located within a range of fifty miles or so is conducive to family continuity if the two generations have gotten off to a good start. If not, greater geographic distance becomes a necessity in order to keep peace. Albrecht finds that in situations where the two generations are mutually independent but are able to maintain a satisfactory social and affectional relationship the parents can accept and treat their children as adults, and in the case of in-laws, as family members.[40] Havighurst suggests that intensification of activities in some roles and reduction in others is necessary for the aged.[41] This depends to a degree on the ability to modify habits,

[35] Marvin Koller, "Studies in Three-Generation Households," *Marriage and Family Living*, Vol. 16 (August, 1954), p. 206.

[36] Hans Von Hentig, "The Sociological Function of the Grandmother," *Social Forces*, Vol. 24 (May, 1946), pp. 389–392.

[37] Ruth Albrecht, "Relationships of Older Parents with their Children," *Marriage and Family Living*, Vol. 16 (February, 1954), pp. 32–35.

[38] Marvin Sussman, "Family Continuity: Selective Factors Which Affect Relationships between Families at Generational Levels," *Marriage and Family Living*, Vol. 16 (May, 1954), pp. 112–120.

[39] Robert Havighurst, "Flexibility and The Social Roles of the Retired," *The American Journal of Sociology*, Vol. 59 (January, 1954), pp. 310–311.

[40] Albrecht, *op. cit.*, pp. 31–34.

[41] Robert Havighurst, "Middle-Age—The New Prime of Life," in Clark Tibbitts and Wilma Donahue (Eds.), *Aging in the Modern World* (Ann Arbor, University of Michigan, 1957), pp. 31–36.

or on flexibility. He thinks that to have the greatest chance of role flexibility in the later years, reasonably successful experience in a variety of roles during the middle years is necessary. Outstanding success, interestingly enough, may in some cases be associated with rigidity in the later years. He suggests the deliberate cultivation of role flexibility during the middle years through the cultivation of various interests and activities.

It would appear that the ability to adapt to new exigencies and situations is especially important to middle-aged and older persons.[42] This brings us to the personal, rather than the social level. A fairly extensive literature exists dealing with psychiatric and physical problems to which the aged are especially vulnerable. An analysis of this is beyond the scope of our discussion here, which is in no way meant to deny its importance. It has been our purpose to refer to some of the recurrent problems and typical conditions of the aged period. Since general attitudes and practices toward the aged are so important, it may be in order to refer at this point to the report of the 1961 White House Conference on Aging. In adapted, outline form we indicate below a summary of the changes in the environment and general climate of aging in the next two decades, as seen by the conferees:

1. The aged of 1980 may be quite different from the aged of today.
   A. Most of today's oldsters were born and trained in the 19th century.
   B. Those of two decades hence will be 20th century products with different values and possibly different social characteristics.
   C. The pioneering of today's older people is establishing new precedents which will be of inordinate value to new generations.
2. The later years will be longer and more healthy and vigorous.
   A. Concepts of positive health will encourage better habits of nutrition, exercise, activity, and periodic checkups.
   B. Research will yield greater knowledge of the aging and chronic disease processes.
   C. Diagnostic and treatment centers will utilize new restorative techniques focusing on the total person and his circumstances.
   D. Most suffering and early death from heart and circulatory diseases and cancer will have been prevented, and few will experience the agonizing pains of arthritis and rheumatism.
   E. Custodial care will have given way to rehabilitive services attached to community hospitals, active home-care and home-service programs, and health maintenance activities in centers of congregate living.
3. Incomes for our elderly people in the 1980's will be geared to their needs and style of living.
   A. National income will have nearly doubled and the average per capita income will have increased almost as much.
   B. Workers will set aside larger percentages of their incomes for retirement through pension, insurance, and savings programs, public and private.

[42] Evelyn Duvall, "New Family Roles in Middle Life," in Tibbitts and Donahue, op. cit., pp. 87–104.

    C. Escalator provisions may well be built into insurance and retirement programs.

    D. Special attention will have been given to the financial circumstances of the rapidly increasing number of widows.

    E. Burdens of support on many young families today will have been removed so that they may plan for their own retirement years.

    F. Comprehensive insurance against the hazards of long-term illness and mental decline will have been established.

4. Attitudes toward retirement will have changed by the 80's.

    A. Retirement, earned after a specified period in the work force (determined by the total volume of goods and services required) will be an accepted and common expectation of all who desire it.

    B. Systematic preparation for retirement and gradual retirement plans will be common.

    C. Optional continuance in paid employment for those able to work or with needed skills will be available, assuming continual financial growth.

    D. Vocational retraining will be available for all those with obsolete skills and for middle-aged women returning to employment.

    E. Part-time employment will exist for more retirees or mature women who can work only part-time.

5. The concepts of leisure and retirement will have been reevaluated and changed.

    A. Retirement will mean shifting to one or more self-satisfying activities chosen by individual initiative, though often with aid of counseling services, as against the present concept of withdrawal.

    B. More use will be made by the aged adult of education and the arts and crafts.

    C. Ample facilities will exist for social, recreational, and friendship activities of the elderly.

    D. Many thousands of middle-aged and older people will give volunteer service to community services and participate actively in politics.

    E. Many will find outlets in travel, attendance at lectures and concerts, but some will wish to read and some just to sit.

    F. There will be a gradual acceptance of the legitimacy of leisure, which can then be enjoyed with less guilt.

6. The older people in the population will have developed a new subculture of their own, with some of the following emphases:

    A. Increasingly higher values on leisure and freedom of movement.

    B. Greater concern for the purchasing power of retirement incomes.

    C. Pressures for expansion of facilities and services through which their needs can be met.

    D. Demonstration of desire to serve as their own interpreters of their needs and styles of life.

    E. Positive life styles for later age categories will replace stereotypes based on deterioration and withdrawal.

7. Independence in living arrangements will be highly prized.

    A. Appropriate housing, stressing privacy, independence, controlled lighting and climate, safety, and convenience will be available.

    B. Housing for older persons will be located with ready access to shopping centers, medical, religious and other institutions, all of which will have special services for older people as they do for other generations.

C. Many institutions of higher education will encourage the development of retirement communities where the retired can take advantage of their educational and cultural programs.

D. Current cultural conflicts over intergenerational responsibilities will have been resolved, freeing both adult children and their older parents from feelings of guilt.

8. Society will have clear-cut expectations for its older people. It will have become generally recognized that middle-aged and older people have primary responsibility:

A. For maintaining their own health and well-being.

B. For planning their affairs to enable them to move easily through the later stages of the life cycle.

C. For helping their communities through voluntary service and political and civic participation.

D. For granting their adult children freedom of self-determination but for sharing their own experience when it is sought.

E. For retaining their own independence of action and decision-making as long as they are able to do so.[43]

It can be observed that some of the above items are predictions and some represent hopes of the various committees of the White House Conference on Aging. Many of the projections will emerge only if certain policy decisions are made. The ramifications of such policies, and the possible conflict of values are beyond the realm of this discussion. Many persons reading this material will be involved, however directly or indirectly in action affecting the probabilities that the changes forecast above will become realities. On that basis, the whole White House Conference report and similar materials are worthy of considered attention by serious-minded citizens.

SELECTED READINGS

Albrecht, Ruth (Ed.), *Aging in a Changing Society* (Gainsville, University of Florida Press, 1962).

Ausubel, D. P., *Theory and Problems of Adolescent Development* (New York, Grune & Stratton, 1954).

Axelson, Leland J., "Personal Adjustment in the Postparental Period," *Marriage and Family Living,* Vol. 22 (February, 1960), pp. 66–68.

Bernard, Jessie (Ed.), "The Culture of Youth," *Annals of American Academy of Political and Social Science,* Vol. 338 (November, 1961).

Birren, James, *Handbook of Aging and the Individual* (Chicago, The University of Chicago Press, 1960).

Burgess, Ernest (Ed.), *Aging in Western Societies* (Chicago, The University of Chicago Press, 1960).

[43] Robert Kean, *et al., Aging in the United States* (White House Conference on Aging, 1961), U.S. Government Printing Office, Chapter VI.

Christensen, Harold, "Lifetime Family and Occupational Role Projections of High School Students," *Marriage and Family Living,* Vol. 23 (May, 1961), pp. 181–183.

Crow, Lester, and Crow, Alice, *Adolescent Development and Adjustment* (New York, McGraw-Hill, 1956).

Drake, Joseph, *The Aged in American Society* (New York, Ronald, 1958).

Erikson, Erik, *Youth* (New York, Bain Books, 1963).

Glassberg, Bert, *Teen-age Sex Counselor* (Woodbury, Mass., Barron Company, 1965).

Glasser, Paul, and Glasser, Lois, "Role Reversal and Conflict Between Aged Parents and Their Children," *Marriage and Family Living,* Vol. 24 (February, 1962), p. 46.

Gross, Irma (Ed.), *Potentialities of Women in the Middle Years* (East Lansing, Michigan State University Press, 1956).

Havighurst, Robert, Bowman, Paul, *et al., Growing up in River City* (New York, Wiley, 1962).

Kastenbaum, Robert, *New Thoughts on Old Age* (New York, Springer, 1964).

Koller, Marvin, "Studies of Three-Generation Households," *Marriage and Family Living,* Vol. 16 (August, 1954), pp. 205–206.

Lane, Robert E., "Fathers and Sons: Foundations of Political Belief," *American Sociological Review,* Vol. 24 (August, 1959), pp. 502–511.

Levine, Lena, and Doherty, Beka, *The Menopause* (New York, Random House, 1952).

Litwak, Eugene, "Geographic Mobility and Extended Family Cohesion," *American Sociological Review* (June, 1960), pp. 385–394.

Moore, Elon H., *The Nature of Retirement* (New York, Macmillan, 1959).

Mussen, Paul, *et al., Child Development and Personality* (New York, Harper & Row, 1956), Chapters 13 and 14.

Orbach, Harold, and Tibbitts, Clark, *Aging and the Economy* (Ann Arbor, University of Michigan Press, 1963).

Phillips, Bernard, "A Role Theory Approach to Adjustment in Old Age," *American Sociological Review,* Vol. 22 (April, 1957), pp. 212–217.

Rose, Arnold, *Aging in Minnesota* (Minneapolis, University of Minnesota Press, 1963).

Tibbitts, Clark, *A Handbook of Social Gerontology* (Chicago, The University of Chicago Press, 1960).

Tibbitts, Clark and Donahue, Wilma (Eds.), *Aging in Today's Society* (Englewood Cliffs, N.J., Prentice-Hall, 1960).

Wilson, Alan, "Class Segregation and Aspirations of Youth," *American Sociological Review,* Vol. 24 (December, 1959), pp. 836–845.

QUESTIONS AND EXERCISES

1. To what degree should the parents consider themselves responsible for the launching of the child into the occupational world? Discuss, focusing on particular class levels.

2. Davis, Coleman, Dinkel, and others discuss the discrepancies in values held by the members of the different generations. To what extent should older parents be expected to adapt to their married children, and vice versa? Discuss thoroughly.

3. It is clearly necessary that all people in the later age categories make some adaptions to the aging process. To some extent, however, "old age" is societally determined. What general measures can be taken in American society to make the last period of life a vital one?

4. Arrange a panel discussion on teen-age life. Invite a number of youth leaders from the community to serve as panel members.

5. Arrange to do a survey in a local community focusing on community resources available for the teen-age group.

6. In comparison with other periods of married life there has been very little research or writing devoted to the "middle years" of married life. How do you account for this?

7. Do you agree with Erikson that the major problem of adolescence is that of the achievement of a sense of identity? If so, what measures can be taken by parents and institutional leaders to be of greatest aid to young people in regard to the building of clear-cut identity?

8. After the children are launched from the home what types of ties should be maintained between the two generations? Discuss.

9. Read and comment on Havighurst's paper, "Middle-Age—The New Prime of Life" (Footnote 41). Do you agree that middle age is the new prime-of-life period?

10. Read the full text of the summary statement of the 1961 White House Conference on Aging (Chapter 6 of reference in Footnote 43). Which predictions do you consider unrealistic and which do you feel have a strong chance of materializing?

11. The average life span is growing longer in the United States. On the other hand, it is estimated that by 1975 70 percent of our men over sixty-five will be retired. What to you are the pros and cons of a fixed retirement policy set at age sixty-five?

12. We usually, when discussing the later years, focus on adaptations people will be required to make. What special resources can our older people contribute to our community life?

13. What are the advantages and disadvantages of living in a three-generation household? Discuss fully.

14. Make a community study of services and facilities available to all classes of older persons in the area.

25

Crises and Problems

Many families have problems which are disturbing them. Some clinicians working in therapeutic settings have decided that most families are sick or maladjusted. While this point of view probably reflects the contacts of clinical professionals, surely family problems and maladjustments are so common that a treatment of marriage and family living requires some attention to them.

ADEQUATE FAMILY FUNCTIONING

At the outset we must note that there is no complete agreement as to the categorization of family success or failure. The following categories are found abundantly in the literature:

Happy	—Unhappy
Normal	—Abnormal (deviant)
Organized	—Disorganized
Adjusted	—Maladjusted
Integrated	—Disintegrated
Stable	—Unstable
Well	—Sick
Adequate	—Inadequate
Solid	—Broken
Adequate functioning	—Inadequate functioning
Competent	—Incompetent

For none of the above, however, is there complete agreement on the criteria by which success or failure can be measured. It has been asserted that conventional professional concepts often reflect a particularistic definition of morality, and that a practice or condition is labeled abnormal, mal-adjusted, or deviant simply because it doesn't measure up to what the one making the diagnosis considers desirable. It can hardly be doubted that such charges contain a measure of validity. Yet some measuring stick, rough though it may be, should be developed with which we can measure or at least identify family success or failure. It must be admitted though, that no completely satisfactory one has yet been developed.[1]

In spite of conceptual difficulties it can surely be agreed that some families handle their tasks and meet their challenges more adequately than do others. What do we know about adaptation to problems, conflicts, and crises which may be of general benefit?

First, we must note that any adequate method of analysis will encompass the threefold nature of family organization and action. The family as a family interacts with society or the community at large. As a unit, it is a group with particular, reciprocal roles being carried. Finally, each family member is an individual in his own right, with his own personal rights, needs, and idiosyncracies. None of these can be ignored in any complete and balanced discussion of family difficulties.

Perhaps a concept of family equilibrium has merit. Through trial and error the young couple relate to the outside and to each other in fairly systematic ways. As children come along, grow and mature, some adaptations and adjustments are made. A certain balance of forces and pressures is achieved which works. Another family, because of different expectations, abilities, and combinations of the sexes, develops a somewhat different approach to life and yet has roughly the same amount of balance or equilibrium.

An approach along this line is that of Hess and Hendel. Using an intensive case study approach, in their book *Family Worlds,* they describe the psychosocial structure of the various families which they have studied. Essential processes in the establishment of a style or type of family world as they see them are:

1. Establishing a pattern of separateness and connectedness.
2. Establishing a satisfactory congruence of images through the exchange of suitable testimony.
3. Evolving modes of interaction into central family concerns or themes.
4. Establishing the boundaries of the family's world of experience.
5. Dealing with significant biosocial issues of family life, as in the family's

---

[1] For an interesting attempt to measure the adequacy of family functioning see the published reports of the Family Centered Project of St. Paul, Minnesota. One example is Ludwig Geismar and Beverly Ayres, *Measuring Family Functioning,* Greater St. Paul Community Chest and Councils, Inc., 1960. The primary focus, however, is on minimum standards of competency in various areas of family living. Whether this scale could be used to measure families at other levels is another matter.

disposition to evolve definitions of male and female and of older and younger.[2]

These researchers find that unequal attention is given to particular emphases which the families, particularly the adults, have used to achieve their own integration or type of balance. For example, the Lansons stress equanimity, tranquility, and harmony. These are values achieved essentially through cooperation. Selfishness and individual prerogatives are frowned upon. A type of "democracy" prevails but the parents are firmly in control of the system. Emphasis is placed on outward expressions of stability and harmony. The children are maturing, but it is doubted (by the observers) that they will demonstrate creative independence in their adult years. Aggression is to be socialized into acceptable forms.[3]

The brief descriptions of the Hess and Handel case above should give us some idea of the complexities involved in achieving family integration or equilibrium. Thinking of some of the dilemmas such as freedom versus order or independence versus dependence, choices must be and are made. The Lansons have developed their type of world (equilibrium) by stressing certain factors. But something has to give in the process. In the words of Hess and Handell, "The world feels more comfortable—easier to cope with, conducing to equanimity. But a great deal of inner life has to be sacrificed to maintain such a stable psychosocial order, and the Lansons are not oblivious of the cost. Mrs. Lanson feels she is "too meek and dull," criticizing herself for "lacking courage in experiments." Her husband feels that in this type of life perhaps he misses something. "Maybe I'm too meticulous and a stickler for details. I've always been a bit retiring, not agressive. I'd like the girls to be a little bit more aggressive, but not obnoxious." [4]

In the Newbold family discussed by Hess and Handel, the stress is on an active, mastering approach to challenges and situations and it works well for the Newbolds as a whole. At the same time it has produced a "black sheep" in Curt. His very existence is an evidence, in a sense, that the Newbold's equilibrium, while strong, is not as adequate as they might wish it to be.

We also note in these cases something of the relationship between family balance and personal adjustment. The two are so interlocked and interwoven that it is ridiculous to focus on personal adjustment as if the individual lived in a family vacuum. Hess and Handel suggest that "the intrapsychic organization of each member is a part of the psychosocial structure of his family; the structure of a family includes the intrapsychic organization of its individual members." [5]

[2] Reprinted from *Family Worlds* by Robert Hess and Gerald Handel by permission of The University of Chicago Press. Copyright, 1959.

[3] *Ibid.*, Chapter 5.

[4] *Ibid.*, Chapter 3.

[5] *Ibid.*, p. 3.

We are suggesting that the type of organization or equilibrium which the family has developed has much to do with the adaptation the family will be able to make to pressures that develop. Hill has classified some typical and severe pressures which often bring on crises in the family at least for a short period.[6]

A Classification of Family Breakdowns

DISMEMBER- MENT ONLY	ACCESSION ONLY	DEMORALI- ZATION ONLY	DEMORALI- ZATION PLUS DISMEMBER- MENT OR ACCESSION
Loss of child	Unwanted pregnancy	Nonsupport	Illegitimacy
Loss of spouse	Deserter returns	Progressive dissension	Runaway situations
Orphanhood	Stepmother, stepfather additions	Infidelity	Desertion
Hospitalization	Some war reunions	Sense of disgrace, reputation loss	Divorce
War separation	Some adoptions		Imprisonment, suicide, or homicide

Not all authorities agree on systems for classifying family breakdowns.[7] A simple breakdown would involve source of the pressure which caused the difficulty—pressures from outside versus difficulties which stem primarily from within the family circle. We are again reminded that the concept "cause" is very complicated, and at times it is difficult to isolate the causal chain or network with any precision. Nevertheless we cannot overlook either the outside environment or the internal structure of the family in any attempt to understand family troubles. The family achieves a type of relationship with the outside world and also an internal set of interrelationships or organization. Outside changes or pressures may upset the structure or balance which has been achieved internally in the family. However, any family has some ability to cope with certain types of changes in order to maintain a reasonable balance. Families differ in their ability to react to external or internal pressures. What accounts for this? Fulcomer

[6] Reuben Hill, *Families Under Stress* (New York, Harper & Row, 1949), p. 10.
[7] See Reuben Hill and Donald Hansen, "Families Under Stress," in Harold Christensen (Ed.), *Handbook of Marriage and the Family* (Chicago, Rand McNally, 1964), Chapter 19, for thorough discussion of conceptual and practical problems involved in classifying family breakdown.

and Koos make use of the term of *family inadequacy*.[8] They believe that there are a great many causal factors involved but that certain important causes can be delineated as basic. In graphic form their theory is that a crisis is represented by the following equation: A (the event) plus B (additional factor) produces X (the crisis). The B factor is necessary to produce the crisis. Not all families have difficulty in adjusting to certain pressures from the outside. One family takes the particular event in stride while another's organization collapses like a stack of cards. The inadequately organized or the overorganized family is vulnerable to crisis. Perhaps the most important factor, the so-called "B" variable, is the type of family organization or balance which has obtained.

It is stressed that none of the factors isolated represents the cause per se. Instead an initial cause produces ramifications which in turn produce conflicts. In the words of the authors,

For example, cultural disparity may cause a lack of sexual satisfaction because of the differing ideas and standards of sex behavior, which in turn may lead to suspicion of the mate and lack of cooperation as breadwinner or homemaker, which in turn may create conflicting roles in the family and draw individual members into new positions of responsibility in the family at the expense of other members, all of which so weakens the affectional relationships and integration of the family as to render it unable to meet even the simple departure from its ordinary life patterns; the result, when an out-of-the-ordinary event occurs, is a crisis.[9]

Much more research needs to be done both on the types of major events which produce crises in some families and on the reactions of families to these pressures. More research has been done on the impact of the depression on the family than on any other major "event," and discussion of this type of crisis may be helpful to our understanding of family dynamics.

ECONOMIC CRISES

The so-called Great Depression and its effects have been adequately described and interpreted by historians, economists, and others. Coming in 1929, it broke a wave of prosperity and postwar enthusiasm. Industrialization, accentuated by the war, had been pulling families into towns and cities for a number of decades. When economic activity slowed down to a halt, thousands of families suffered crude and unexpected shocks.

While the depression hit families at various socioeconomic levels, its

[8] David Fulcomer and Earl Koos, "Family in Crisis," in Evelyn Duvall and Reuben Hill, Co-chairman, report of committee on *Dynamics of Family Interaction,* National Conference on Family Life (February, 1948), Chapter VIII, p. 11.

[9] *Ibid.,* p. 11.

meaning and impact varied somewhat according to the level at which a particular family operated. To the very poor, family troubles were an old story. A depression meant more of the same and a curtailment of a possible improvement in status. It is the classes above this level that felt the greatest impact, at least in terms of their aspirations and desires. Among the stable working-class families were many who had formerly always had employment in the small town or on the farm. The American dream had assured them that if they could not rise in the world, their children probably could. A depression forced a reassessment of these hopes and dreams and threatened a descent into the chasm of deprivation and hopelessness.

According to many experts on social stratification it is the middle-class family which is especially vulnerable to the impact of an economic depression. At this level the American dream is already partially realized. A step has been made from the farm or regular factory job. Employment has been obtained in the business office, the lower professions, or in the world of small business. There is always the hope, however faint, that the family's ship will come in and that a step upward will be made. There is, hidden not too deeply under the surface, but shunted aside if possible, a lurking fear that a son or daughter might not measure up and that the family or its extension will then not move ahead. A depression shatters dreams of upward mobility and brings threats of permanent lowering of status.[10]

The wealthy have to a degree the availability of various methods of cushioning the effects of an economic depression. However, in some cases whole fortunes are wiped out and in others thousands of dollars are lost. For those used to life on a high plane this may be a severe threat. To a family intent on reaching a particular economic level or on "cracking" a particular social set, a stock market crash can cause disturbance, as is borne out by the incidence of suicides among men whose financial assets were still strong.

Burgess and Locke have summarized the general types of reaction of working-class and middle-class families to the depression as follows:

1. The first reaction was to think of the depression as temporary and to attempt to tide over this period by tapping such available financial resources as savings, by accumulating debts at the grocery store, and by borrowing on life insurance or on assets, such as furniture, or from relatives, or occasionally from friends.
2. Another early reaction was the willingness to curtail the family's expenses, plans, and objectives. This involved securing cheaper rent, giving up movies, and material goods, and postponing sending a child to college.
3. Cheaper rent generally meant small and more crowded living quarters.

[10] W. L. Warner, et al., Social Class in America (New York, Science Research Associates, 1949), Chapter 1.

Less money for recreation led to more staying at home and less contact with people outside the community.

4. Many families doubled up. Previously independent families moved in with the in-laws; a newly formed family lived with the in-laws, generally with the wife's parents. Both situations were potential sources of conflict.

5. Some families, faced with poverty, accepted relief gratefully, with little disorganization.

6. The reaction of a considerable number of families was for the members to rally together under the impact of the Depression crisis. Cavan and Ranck found that in 27 of the 100 families studied there was evidence that new group responsibility was developing, and this in turn increased the unity of the family.

7. Many families expressed worry and discouragement which, in view of the seriousness of the crisis, was not especially excessive.

8. In a few families one or more members were so worried and depressed that they had a nervous breakdown and/or thought of, attempted, or committed suicide.

9. A small number of people became demoralized and violated standards of conduct previously accepted by the person or by his family.

10. A few families became disintegrated; the members drifted apart and the husband and wife separated or secured a divorce.[11]

These categories represent degrees of adaptation to the potential crisis. The first five indicate modes of reaction which were positive in nature. The depression was taken by them with relative equanimity. The sixth indicates the opposite of what common sense would indicate. A depression (or other crisis) may bring about adaptions in the family to the point where a new and stronger unity is developed. The last four categories indicate increasing degrees of disorganization and imbalance. Other pressures besides the depression, of course, may have been involved in the family disturbance.

What factors account for the differing ability to weather the depression? A strong emphasis is placed on the type of organization obtaining in the particular family. Angell, after careful study of fifty families and their adjustments, came to the conclusion that *integration* and *adaptability* are the two key factors on which to focus.[12] Using a slightly different approach, Cavan and Ranck tended to confirm this.[13] Some of the important items contributing to this integration were bonds of affection, common interests, and a feeling of economic interdependence. Others were family ideals, familism as against individualism, involvement in family plans to reach particular goals such as seeing a child through school, and a focus on the

[11] Ernest Burgess, Mary Thomes, and Harvey Locke, *The Family* (New York, American Book, 1963), pp. 435–436.

[12] Robert Angell, *The Family Encounters the Depression* (New York, Scribner, 1936).

[13] Ruth Cavan and Katherine Ranck, *The Family and the Depression* (Chicago, The University of Chicago Press, 1938).

family as a source of recreation and interest. Reciprocal roles in which each member was satisfied with his own role and those played by others also were a feature of the integrated families.

Adaptability was found to be more crucial than integration. It involves the ability of a family to shift its defenses and make necessary adjustments. Standards have to be modified, expenditures curtailed, belts tightened, and so on. Roles must at times be modified in order to meet family needs. It should be noted that adaptability as used here is a collective term, not an individual one. It refers to the ability of the family *as a family* to muster its reserves, rethink its strategy through collective discussion and decision-making, and adapt as best it can. Specific elements of adaptability delineated by Cavan and Ranck were: adaptability of roles, nonmaterialistic philosophy of life, lack of traditionalism, habits of responsibility, and previous experience in meeting a crisis.

A recurring problem centers on the husband-father role. So strong have been the expectations that he shall provide that an interruption of this competency has many and serious ramifications. In some cases his authority was challenged when he no longer "brought home the bacon." [14] Often personal frustration over his inability to carry a satisfactory economic role affected his activities to the point where he could scarcely function at any level. Especially threatening was the situation in which the wife or one of the children became sole breadwinner. This tended to throw the systems of authority, decision-making, and general family interaction into serious imbalance.

Some of our knowledge of family reactions to a severe depression can be helpful in contributing to our understanding of crises in general. Fortunately we have not had need for such knowledge on a mass scale as applied to a great depression since the dark days of the thirties. What we need now is more knowledge of the concomitants of unemployment in a period of general affluence, for this unemployment may be more severe during affluence, albeit to fewer people.[15] At the present time our official unemployment rate is about 4 percent. It is being suggested that it will be difficult to get the rate below 4 percent even with an expanding economy. The causes of this state of affairs are not agreed upon, but automation and resultant technological layoffs most assuredly play a part. At present young people of low education, in minority groups (especially those who also fall in the previous category), without marketable skills, and over forty-five are among those most vulnerable to unemployment. Falling into this category during a period of general expansion may be more disorganizing in some ways than is the impact of a great depression. At the latter time the

[14] Mirra Komarovsky, *The Unemployed Man and His Family* (New York, Holt, Rinehart and Winston, 1938).

[15] See Jessie Bernard, *Social Problems at Mid-century* (New York, Holt, Rinehart and Winston, 1957) for a thorough discussion and treatment of economic problems in an age of relative abundance.

discrepancy between one's own status and that of one's neighbors is not so great. Research both on ways of controlling the event and on methods of adaptation to it is sorely needed.

More attention might also be given to the impact of sudden affluence on family life. While it seems that such events should not bring on crises, apparently at times they can. A sudden external change can force a reorganization of habitual ways of living, acting, and thinking. While an unexpected windfall may seem like a God-send to a family, its results may not be so in all cases.

At one level of theory it may be improper to single out types of events and discuss them. Almost any conceivable event may precipitate a crisis in a particular family. Research and study of predictable and probable troubles are surely worthwhile, however. Kirkpatrick suggests that the term "crisis" be restricted to events which are atypical and/or premature.[16] Death of the aged, the launching of children, and the onset of the menopause would be considered predictable and should be included in the crisis category only if they meet one of the criteria.

MARITAL MALADJUSTMENTS

Spousal difficulties constitute a special subcategory of family maladjustment. The marital pair relationship represents an important core of family life. It is the original *raison d'etre* of the family. It precedes the family and again emerges after launching of the children. The pair has special and lasting significance.

Much of what has been indicated above regarding family organization and imbalance applies here. Any thorough analysis must take into account societal context, the pair relationship, and the individuals as separate personalities. Society provides an undergirding for marriages in its expectations and general support of them. It also stresses (and fails to stress) certain types of marital behavior as ideal. The governmental institution provides the legal groundwork for marriage and its possible dissolution. The economic institution provides the financial basis for marriages. As individual units, marital pairs adjust to society rather than the reverse.

The following factors have been indicated by various writers as being basic general causal factors in the production of marital discord:

1. Loss of former family functions to other institutions.
2. Increasing secularization of society.
3. Urbanization of modern life.
4. Growth of the philosophy of hedonism.
5. Change in the status of women.
6. Rapidity of social change.

[16] Clifford Kirkpatrick, *The Family* (New York, Ronald Press, 1955), Chapter 20.

7. Increase in romanticism.
8. Increasing emphasis on sex.
9. Shrinking of family functions.
10. Decline in general morality.

Other factors have been identified by various theorists. Parsons, for example, suggests that emotional demands on the nuclear family are upgraded as it becomes isolated. The problem of marital maladjustment is so complicated that there will probably never be complete agreement on the subject. Although this is true, it does not provide a justification for ignoring the societal factors when studying marital disorganization. The best we can do at present is resort to the familiar view of multiple causation, with the hope that eventually more precision will emerge.

When we come to a specific couple, even more precision is required. In essence the question is this: What type of resources did the particular couple bring to the marriage and what use was made of the resources? Researchers and clinicians are in general agreement that as a rule common social background tends to provide greater chances of marital success. As has been indicated before, cultural or subcultural background is important because of the configuration of values and attitudes typically associated with a given cultural position which becomes embodied in the personality of the individual. This configuration is not shorn from the person as he enters marriage, but is carried with him. Expectations as to what is a legitimate level of living, what is and is not moral behavior, or what is proper (for men and women), reflect the general background to which the marital partners have been exposed. Marriage as a joint enterprise involves at least minimal agreement on style of life and way of living, if it is to be successful.

Mowrer distinguishes two types of cultural conflicts in marriage. The first is called *general cultural conflict* and results "from the marriages of persons coming from areas in which the cultures are different." [17] The second type is known as *specific cultural conflict*. This is not a resultant of general cultural background of the partners, but of "differing interpretations of culture superimposed on the general background by the specific family and nonfamily groups to which they belong." [18]

It is difficult to prove which of these types of cultural divergence is most often associated with conflict. It is our impression that the latter is becoming more prominent in the United States. Errors are often made in assuming that because people are of the same class level or economic level, their expectations and orientations toward specific situations will be the same.[19]

[17] Harriet Mowrer, "Discords in Marriage," in Reuben Hill and Howard Becker, *Family, Marriage, and Parenthood* (Boston, Heath, 1953), p. 381.

[18] *Ibid.*

[19] See Alan Kerckhoff and Keith Davis, "Value Consensus and Need Complementarity in Mate Selection," *American Sociological Review*, Vol. 27 (June, 1962), pp. 295–303, for a demonstration of this point with a student sample.

ROLE CONFLICT

Whatever the background of the couple, marriage involves two partners coming together to establish a new relationship. As described in Chapters 10 through 15, initial adaptations must be made, work must be allocated, authority patterns must be delineated, and so on. Even though the partners have been well "trained" prior to marriage, they will have some difficulty in organizing their home to the point of full, mutual satisfaction. At least minimum conflict is predictable for most couples and should be considered normal. Folk sayings referring to marriage make use of phrases such as "learning to travel in double harness" and "bearing the double yoke" and not without reason. It must be pointed out also that these sayings developed during periods when roles were clear-cut and not as much leeway was allowed by the community as is allowed today.

Kirkpatrick's reference to rights and privileges deserves reemphasis at this point. Husband and wife must develop role relationships which they carry out in practice. This means responding at the proper times to actions of the partner. The fact that a partner sometimes fails to perform because of indifference, laziness, boredom, or some other motive is understandable. As a consistent pattern it may be understood, and yet be increasingly disconcerting. Take for example a situation in which the husband enjoys well-cooked, relatively heavy food, attractively served. By chance the wife is familiar with the necessary techniques for such cooking, but she lacks an interest in it. She prefers to grab a sandwich and piece of fruit "on-the-run" rather than to cook a substantial meal. She also likes light salads and fruit. If the partners are well-mated in general, chances are the wife will eventually be found cooking in the more traditional fashion, if only to please her husband. But one can venture the assertion that there will be times when the husband's morale will be low, even though he can empathize with her fully.

LOVE AND SEX

Clinical findings encourage at least brief attention to the category of love and affection, including sexual response. It can be accepted that love and sex are closely fused in the average woman, and to a lesser degree in the average man.[20] Even for the man we consider love and sex as one category for analytical purposes as far as marriage partners are concerned. Actually the sex response can be tied closely to the concept of role accommodation. Each person has a part to play, and there are both general prescriptions of proper behavior and individual definitions of what is desirable

[20] Herman Lantz and Eloise Snyder, *Marriage* (New York, Wiley, 1962), p. 74.

and proper. Especially in our romanticized society, the sexual act symbolically represents the couple at its best.[21] This results in high expectations being centered upon the realm of sex and intimate response on the part of many, if not most, couples. Far from the "concept" of outlet in the Kinseyian sense, sexual response patterns become heavily associated with many aspects of the total marital relationship.

If sex does become highly interrelated with other areas of the marital relationship it stands to reason that difficulty in other areas will be reflected in the sexual realm and vice versa. This viewpoint is borne out by both clinical and research findings. Eisenstein writes:

Clinical experience indicates that a good sex life does not assure a happy marriage, nor do sexual difficulties necessarily cause marital breakdown. Sexual symptoms occur in the context of either manifestly harmonious or frankly discordant relationships. There is no question, however, that happy marriages, by and large, are marked by a greater incidence of sexual satisfaction, while unhappy marriages have a much higher incidence of sexual conflicts.[22]

Burgess and Wallin reached generally similar conclusions. They found that a good sex adjustment score was ordinarily associated with a high (general) marital success score, for either men or women. A modifying fact was introduced in that they found a sizeable group of persons having low sex adjustment scores but high marital success. These authors come to the conclusion that "although good sexual adjustment increases the chances of marital success poor sexual adjustment by no means precludes it." [23]

We must use some care in making causal inferences. In an otherwise successful marriage, sexual difficulties may be carried (although presumably the level of marital success might be lowered by the sex factor). The sex factor itself on the other hand will not as a rule carry a marriage alone. Even the well-known analyst Kubie can make the following statement: "I have never seen a marriage made or broken by sex alone, except in the case of frank perversions." [24]

THE PROBLEM OF CAUSATION

It has been suggested above that sexual or affectional problems may be related to other areas of marriage and vice versa. The same can be said for factors other than sex. We are involved in a network of interrelationships which are often very complicated in their workings. Problems that

[21] Willard Waller and Reuben Hill, *The Family* (New York, Holt, Rinehart and Winston, 1951), p. 334.

[22] Victor Eisenstein (Ed.), *Neurotic Interaction in Marriage* (New York, Basic Books, 1956), p. 101.

[23] Ernest Burgess and Paul Wallin, *Engagement and Marriage* (Philadelphia, Lippincott, 1953), p. 692.

[24] Lawrence Kubie, in Victor Eisenstein, *op. cit.,* p. 26.

reflect cultural differences, role incongruities, sex and affectional difficulties, and certain others are noted with such great frequency by clinicians and researchers that it is legitimate to give them time and attention. There is always the danger that these will become fixed in our minds to the point that we will "see" particular difficulties appearing in given cases and neglect to focus on other important phenomena which may be there too. This is especially dangerous if one is attempting diagnosis of a given marriage. It is also possible for popular writers, ministers, judges, and others to make judgments and statements which are misleading, especially regarding alleged "cures" for marital maladjustments. One judge on the basis of his experience sees sex and drinking as being the two basic causes of marital trouble. Another lists money problems, jealousy, and in-law difficulties. We are not suggesting that these men fabricate their experience. Rather it is probable that they have seen recurring patterns appearing in the cases before them and they have grown especially sensitive to certain factors. Were any of us to see the same series of cases we might come to conclusions vastly different from those of the particular judge. We are faced with the problem of a network of causes in a given situation. Let us illustrate the problem by reference to a case.

John Clausen was born and reared in a small Midwestern hamlet. As only son, he was systematically but somewhat permissively reared by his working-class, Protestant parents. John's parents were a hard-working, law-abiding couple who enjoyed the respect of their neighbors and peers in the community. The father smoked occasionally but never drank.

John's grade and high school years were relatively uneventful. He dated very little, preferring to run around with boys. Except for a Halloween escapade or two he was never in trouble. Upon graduation from high school he was drafted and subsequently was sent to Germany. In the army John became more "sophisticated." He drank frequently with the boys and started dating frauleins. One of his dates was a small, shy girl whose parents were rather strict. On the occasion of his second date the girl's parents invited him to Sunday dinner and he accepted. Soon John was taking his Sunday meals regularly at the Schopfers and within a few months he and Hanna Schopfer were married. There were complications in that Hanna was Catholic.

John and Hanna lived together in Germany and their initial adjustment was fair to good in most categories. When John's transfer to the States came through a minor crisis developed. Hanna found it rather difficult to leave her parents in order to accompany her husband. She did so, however, and she and John eventually landed back in Chambersburg, John's hometown.

In Chambersburg John and Hanna lived with John's parents. He worked in a garage and Hanna kept house and occasionally worked in a local store. After one year in the States a baby boy was born. The baby, Freddy, proved to be a sickly child. He was allergic to many foods and eventually developed an asthmatic condition. Often at night he had to struggle to breathe, and one of the parents had to continually keep him under observation. Whether it was from this form of strain or some other, John and Hanna's marriage began to head for the rocks. John started going out alone at night and returning very late. At first he ran around with fellows, but eventually he turned his attentions to other women. He became enamored with one Mrs. X, a local divorcee. Eventually John was spending more nights with Mrs. X than he was with Hanna and Freddy. Hanna's parents-in-law tried to reason with John to no avail. When he refused to pay the bills and left the household, Hanna appealed to welfare officials. She finally applied for a court order for support for herself and the baby, and considered the question of divorce as well. At this time investigation showed John to be living with Mrs. X some ten miles from Chambersburg. At the time of the writing of the case Hanna was pathetically considering various alternatives to her predicament.

The reader, not being able to see the flesh and blood people before him and observing behavior for himself, may find the problem doubly difficult, but on the basis of the materials presented, what appeared to be the causes of the marital difficulty? The following hypotheses, in one form or another, might be suggested as tentative explanations of the Clausens' difficulties. In each case brief comment will be made to indicate complications:

1. The marriage was religiously and culturally mixed although this did not necessarily mean that it had to result in marital difficulty. The cultural differences were not as extreme as one might first think because John's grandparents had originally come from Germany. Both parties apparently came from similar class levels. Since many of the people in Chambersburg are of German descent Hanna should not have had undue pressure put upon her because of her foreign and previous enemy status. The religious factor makes sense. Hanna remained a faithful Catholic and John was only a nominal Protestant after the war. The question is posed, however: Would the marital adjustment have been better had John been or become an active Protestant?

2. Both parties were immature and naive. Hanna at times seemed more like a bewildered, frightened girl than a woman old enough to have responsibility for a sick child and a philandering husband. It was especially disheartening and illuminating to some of the public officials to listen to her plea that "somebody should do something" to make her John see his responsibilities. Yet on the other hand Hanna stayed with her child faithfully, insisted that she would make an adaptation of some kind rather than return to her home in Germany, and in general retained personal stability. The author has observed a greater degree of personal disorganization in American-born women of refinement and culture when faced with relatively similar problems. John also seemed immature in many ways. By general community standards he acted more like a boy than a man in facing the responsibility of support for his wife and severely ailing child. Further, he repeatedly expressed bewilderment regarding the fact that his location in which he was living with Mrs. X could be found. He claimed at least to be unaware of his legal responsibility to provide for his wife and child. However, one local informant who knew John well made the following comment: "John C. is not an ignoramus. Like many of the fellows in the army abroad he fell for a girl. When she wouldn't 'shack up' with

him he reluctantly married her. He probably thought that she would never leave her father to come to America. What he has been trying to do over here is get her to go back home to her parents."

3. Sexual incompatibility was the problem. John complained to the investigator that his wife was cold and not interested in sexual activity after the birth of the baby. Hanna admitted that sex had little interest for her after the baby became ill. Her defense was that she feared another pregnancy. She felt that it would be difficult enough to rear one child under the circumstances, let alone two. She refused to use or allow the use of any method of birth control except the rhythm method. The investigator reported the impression that Hanna probably was not basically interested in sex, and the sick baby and fear of pregnancy were being used as excuses. It is difficult to separate cause and effect. More than one wife-mother has lost her sexual ardor when faced with illness in the family and the possible loss of the husband's support. Did the wife's lack of enthusiasm cause John to run around and to lose interest in supporting and caring for his wife and child, or was a reverse process at work? Furthermore many local people felt that John learned his "wild ways" in the army, and that his being drafted was the basic cause of the difficulty. To complicate the picture, the sexual adjustment during the early period of the marriage was reported to have been good.

4. The third party, Mrs. X, caused the marital difficulty. The investigator reported that Mrs. X seemed to have an uncanny ability to attract and manipulate John. She was reported to be a very sexy woman who knew how to make a man feel needed and wanted. She was able to have John pay more of her bills, and to keep him at her beck and call. At the time the case came to a head it appeared that Mrs. X was pregnant. She had been able to convince John of his responsibility and he reportedly told a number of local friends that he would "have to get a divorce from Hanna so he could marry Mrs. X and support her and a child." And most assuredly Hanna could have filed for divorce and named Mrs. X as the correspondent. One can easily visualize a headline in a yellow journal reading "Enraged Wife Accuses Hussy of Breaking Up Home." But did Mrs. X's aggressive entry into the picture cause the difficulty? Was this the event that precipitated the crisis or was the marital situation such that John was highly vulnerable to attraction? If John was open to attraction, was this because he had been in the army, had been brought up to permissively, was not religiously oriented, or what?

Many other causal hypotheses could be proposed on legitimate grounds. An analyst would wish to know much more about the childhood period of both parties, and would raise the question of neurotic drives being involved. The present author would like more data on the couple, including conceptions of roles held by the two parties and their basic personality patterns. Such information, however, is difficult to obtain. Hopefully the case material will demonstrate the complications and difficulties of any type of causal analysis. Often the best that can be done is to isolate certain factors that appear to be crucial in a case, and to focus upon them. These factors may be only indices of more basic factors which have not come to the surface. It is doubtful that we can ever completely understand all the aspects of the causal processes that lead to marital maladjustment and disorganization.

THE RESOLUTION OF MARRIAGE CONFLICT

The Harvard group has been doing some important work on the maintenance of functioning in marriage and family organization.[25] A position is taken that views family functioning in terms of equilibrium, disequilibrium, and reequilibration. The basis of equilibrium or its lack is primarily role complementation. In a smooth-functioning family the complementarity of roles is so high that the individuals go about their daily activities without much concern because each member feels that he knows what the other parties expect. Furthermore, roles complement each other, work has been allocated, and much behavior can take place with little thought given to it. However, strains may appear, giving rise to role conflict. Methods of dealing with this conflict typically fall into the following three patterns. First, *role induction* involves the attempt by one partner to get the spouse to change while he himself does not. Second, a traditional technique is developed whereby the one party takes the role of the other, to get his point of view. This is called *role reversal*. Third, reequilibration is achieved through a change in both partners. This is spoken of as *role modification*.

Role induction usually involves attempts to manipulate the partner. There are five methods or phases of this process. *Coercion* is the most typical process. It can vary from verbal assertions to the extreme of physical attack. It can vary in intensity from mild manipulation to outright torture. It is most often used in a culture that allows hostile-aggressive tendencies to be expressed. If it is successful it results in submission of the partner. Counterinduction may operate to make the method unsuccessful. Defiance is a specific neutralizing technique. *Coaxing* involves the manipulation of present and future rewards, including promising, pleading, tempting, and so on. It gives expression to a wish for gratification and triggers off the wish to respond. It can be neutralized by withholding or refusing, and can be countered by other induction techniques. *Evaluation* involves use of praise, blame, disapproval, or shame. By statements such as "stop acting like a spoiled child" a value is placed on the partner's behavior. He may accept the definition of the situation and desist, or he may counter the assertion. *Denial* is a neutralizer to this category. *Masking* is a more indirect approach. It involves use of censorship, evasion, distortion, and other such behavior. It is not necessarily unhealthy. In fact, "It is as significant to the functions of the social system, large or small, as is repression to the function of the personality as a system." The relevant neutralizing technique is *unmasking*. If masking has concealed some major discrepancy between the

[25] John Spiegel, "The Resolution of Role Conflict Within the Family," *Psychiatry*, Vol. 20 (1957), pp. 1–16.

partners and has served to prop up a shaky equilibrium, unmasking may release pent-up hostilities and result in an explosion. *Postponement* is a method of deferring potential conflict with the prospect of a change of mind. Many couples decide to "wait a few days" or "take time to think it over." By provoking behavior one partner may attempt to neutralize the postponement if he fears it or feels he has little to gain by it.

Role reversal, as an intermediate position, involves the use of the empathic abilities. It involves taking the role of the partner and trying to see and feel as he does. If one spouse proposes this and the partner responds by induction, then some type of maneuvering and countering will again take place. If the response is favorable it may lead to some form of more positive change.

There are also five phases of possible *role modification*. They follow, usually in order, after successful role reversal. *Joking* is an indication that modification is underway. This allows partners to remove from some of their involvement to a safer ground from which they can view their problems more objectively. The laughter helps drain off psychic energy which is made available with the partial solution of the conflict. By playfully considering some egregious solutions to their problem the partners may move toward more probable ones. Along with role reversal joking does not provide a sufficient basis for role modification. Either may be helpful in preparing for reequilibration, however. *Referral to third party* may be resorted to on the assumption that he will be more objective about the conflict or that he (or his organization) will have some skill to offer. The third party may, however, line up with one of the partners, especially if he is a family member or friend. If so, he may steer the process back to induction. A trained counselor may be able to avert this type of outcome by working with both partners or at least refusing to permit himself to be used to form a coalition. *Exploring* means a more serious trial of a new solution than was possible in the joking stage. Each partner is involved in the consideration of possible solutions. If a third party such as a counselor is involved he may be able to promote the process. Temporary retrogression may take place but the procedure usually perpetuates itself once it is underway. The partners show their willingness to adapt both by verbal discussion and overt behavior. *Compromise,* as used here, involves moving to something new and novel as a solution. The partners come to the realization that some modification of previous values or goals is necessary. Through mutual insight the couple move to a new type of complementation of roles. *Consolidation* is a very important last step. After compromising has enabled the couple to achieve a new working equilibrium they must work to achieve stability. The new roles must be carried for a time until they no longer seem strange. Each partner must learn to assume his obligations in the new role before he may reasonably receive its privileges. Eventually the new roles become normal and the problem subsides if the modification has been successful.

Role induction then, is essentially manipulative. One partner attempts to persuade the other to change. If he is successful equilibrium may be achieved for a time. Role modification, on the other hand, is nonmanipulative. Instead the couple move constructively toward a new marital balance within which each can feel free to live constructively.

FAMILY AND MARRIAGE COUNSELING

When conflict is underway one old method of attempting a solution is by a reference to a third party as has been shown. Ministers and priests, family members, and trusted members of the local community have often served as third parties to a marriage conflict. The general assumption made is that the third party will be more objective than either partner and therefore able to induce constructive processes of change.

With the increasing secularization and specialization of society new functionaries and agencies have emerged to give aid and counsel to those with family troubles. Important among these have been family social work agencies. These developed during the last century and they originally worked with family problems among the lower classes. Objective problems of neglect, drunkenness, desertion, child welfare, and the like were the primary concern. Over the years changes of organization and approach have been significant to the point that many programs bear little resemblance to those of past years. Very little direct relief or money is administered by family agencies, and they no longer wish to cater only to the poor. In most cases the programs are set up to handle various types of family problems or to refer them to appropriate agencies when they cannot meet the need.

One particular recent development in marriage counseling per se, is a more narrow and specific type of program. Many social agencies are now prepared to offer marriage counseling to couples who are in conflict. In some cases this is on a fee basis and the charges are graduated as they would be in a medical or mental health clinic. A major problem has been the public image of the family agency as an institution to serve the poor. Partly because of this public image and also because leadership in some cases has come from nonsocial-work sources, new developments of a parallel nature have taken place. Marriage counseling agencies or independent agencies have developed in certain areas. A pioneer in this movement was the Marriage Council of Philadelphia. Started in 1932 by a committee representing many professional interests, it has functioned under the leadership of Dr. Emily Mudd as an independent agency and in recent years as an adjunct of the Department of Psychiatry of the University of Pennsylvania. This organization has always engaged in both premarital and postmarital counseling. It operates on a fee basis and accepts clients from various levels of the community. Clients come via self- or professional referral.

While many of the counselors are social workers by training, other professions are also represented. The center serves as a training base for budding professionals from medicine, psychiatry, the ministry, counseling psychology, etc. Marriage counseling of a similar nature is done at the Merrill-Palmer Clinic in Detroit, the Menninger Clinic in Topeka, the Marriage Council of Baltimore, and elsewhere.

Further attention to marriage counseling will be given in Chapter 27. For illustrative purposes a case will be presented from the files of the Marriage Council of Philadelphia.[26]

Case Summary Identifying Information

Date   May 25, 1961

Names of Clients M   Mr. X   Case # 1359B, 1360D

              F   Mrs. X

Address (street)

    (city)

Telephone   CHILDREN

	Sex	Date of Birth
Date of Marriage July 30, 1949		
Date of Separation or Divorce	Female	9–17–52
Present Marital Status Married	Female	2–29–56

	Male	Female
Age	37 yrs.	30 yrs.
Nationality	U.S.	U.S.
Religion	Catholic	Protestant
Education	A.B., M.A.	High School
Occupation	Quality Control Supervisor	Housewife
Income	$5,700.	
Number of Interviews	22	22
Period Covered	From 9–19–60	From 9–19–60
	To present	To present
Fee Paid	$3.75	$3.75

[26] This is a typical marriage counseling case carried by a trainee at Marriage Council of Philadelphia according to Dr. Kenneth Appel, who presided at a local case conference when it was first presented. In his words, "It illustrates the dynamics of interaction between husband and wife, and between counselor and clients. While it came as an apparent problem of an interfaith marriage, as we got into the case more deeply, the basic problems came to be recognized as comparatively weak sex identification, and personal rigidities on the part of both spouses."

Mrs. X describes her mother as a compulsively neat housekeeper. Windows existed to be washed; floors to be swept; tables to be dusted. Mrs. X shared in the housekeeping chores. She was also baby sitter for her brothers.

Mrs. X describes her father as a peace-loving, placating person, with whom she had a close relationship. She used to play and work beside her father in his home workshop.

Mrs. X learned about sex from her family doctor and a high school nurse. Sex was not discussed in her home. When her younger brother was born, the client, then sixteen, was taking him for a ride in the carriage, when some of the teen-age boys teased that he was her baby. She was so embarrassed that she never again took him out for a ride.

In short, Mrs. X's background was strict and her sexual identification was more nearly masculine than feminine. Sex, from a woman's standpoint, was associated with depressions and emotional upsets prior to and at the time of menstruation, with illness and pain in childbirth.

Mrs. X says her older brother is very much like her mother, nervous, easily angered. She feels he needs psychiatric help.

Her younger brother is very quiet and retiring. Will sit and watch television by the hour; does not like to go out and play with the other children.

MARITAL INTERACTION (as the counselor sees it):
Mr. X describes himself as idealistic and perfectionistic. He places great emphasis upon principles, especially religious principles. At the beginning of counseling, he tended to see life in terms of absolutes.

Mr. X believes that a wife's place is in the home; that the husband is the head of the family, and should be the sole means of support. The husband should represent the final authority in any disagreement.

Mrs. X, whose mother forced her to assume considerable responsibility for housekeeping and care of her younger brothers, rebelled against the concept of a woman's role as that of housekeeping and child care. She would, therefore, sleep until ten or eleven in the morning, letting her husband get breakfast and get the older daughter off to school. The younger child would play upstairs until her mother got up.

Mrs. X was conflicted about and rejecting of sex. She felt that intercourse was unclean, and for years took a long hot shower after each experience, although she maintains that she enjoyed intercourse before the birth of her first child.

Her fear of sex was reinforced by the difficulties she had in successfully carrying her two children to full term, and by three miscarriages. With each pregnancy, she was forced to spend considerable time in bed.

Mr. X, for religious reasons, would not allow the use of any contraceptive measures. For almost a year before coming to Marriage Council, the X's had not had intercourse. During this period, Mr. X masturbated. This he would regularly confess to his priest.

Presenting Problems (as seen by clients):

Mrs. X: Husband domineering; husband's refusal to use contraceptive measures because of religious beliefs; fear of sexual intercourse and pregnancy.

Mr. X: Wife's refusal to have sexual intercourse; failure to give love to children; failure to get breakfast or to properly clean the house; general lack of affection for family.

Early History:

Mr. X: Mother died when he was two years old, several months after giving birth to a younger sister. Client was reared by father and paternal grandparents. Father remarried when client was nineteen. There were always several aunts, uncles, and cousins in the grandparent's home. Mr. X now feels that his father is a weak person, but this is an impression which he can substantiate only by the feeling that his stepmother now dominates his father.

Mr. X recognizes that he had a good deal of hostility as a child. When he was about three, a picture was taken which made him look like Shirley Temple. The women members of his family adored it, but in anger he knocked it over several times. He now recognizes that as a boy and a teen-ager he had to constantly prove that he was not a sissy. He got into numerous fights, and was put in a private military school for a year because of his family's belief that he needed more discipline. Later, in his teen years, he felt that he was the toughest kid on the block. When his shoulders began to broaden, he said they looked like those of a Greek god.

Mr. X had premarital sexual intercourse only one time, and that was with a prostitute while he was in the military service. She and another girl were "visiting" some friends of his when he returned from a date. They had intercourse. Afterwards as he lay in the bed, he worried about V.D. and at about three A.M. he sought out a "pro" station. Afterwards, he found a church, and had confession.

Early History:

Mrs. X: The client is the oldest of three children. One brother was born when she was ten, the other when she was sixteen. Mrs. X's mother had great difficulty during pregnancies, and had to stay in bed for varying lengths of time on each occasion. When her mother was pregnant with her older brother, Mrs. X, a child of 9–10, went home from school each day at recess to check on her condition. According to the client, her mother almost died when her younger brother was born. Her mother also had two miscarriages.

Mrs. X's mother suffered great premenstrual and menstrual tensions. On these "egg-shell" days, the entire family attempted to keep away from the mother, and, under penalty of punishment from father, the children were not to cross her or in any way disagree. During these periods, her mother would sometimes shake her or beat her on the head.

Mr. X, because of his feelings of inadequacies as a man felt the need to be superior and the final authority on all matters which affected the family. Mrs. X, because of her own hostilities, refused to be bossed. She expressed her hostility by withholding sex, and used sex as a form of control. Before they ceased having intercourse, she would use granting intercourse as a lever to getting out of the house, or to do things she wanted to.

Mr. X's feelings of inadequacy also affected his relationships with his superiors at work, and with those who worked with him. He was exacting, and somewhat hard to get along with, according to his statements.

Use Made of Counseling:
Mr. X: Since Mr. X's basic problem was his insecurity around his maleness, perhaps his greatest need was to identify with a male figure. This he did with the counselor.

In the beginning, Mr. X felt that the problems were altogether his wife's. He attempted, with considerable success for a time, to keep the focus away from himself by the use of his intellect. It was only as the counselor was able to get beneath the intellectual assertions to his feelings, anxieties, and fears, that progress was made.

As the client was helped to examine his feelings of anger at being thought a sissy, and his need to prove his manhood, the counselor was able to help him, step by step, recognize and name his feelings.

A real turning point came when Mr. X talked with a priest who told him it was not his responsibility if his wife used a diaphragm, and that he would not be culpable if he permitted its use.

Mrs. X: Mrs. X was helped to express deep feelings of hostility toward her mother which she had never previously recognized. As she recognized the inappropriateness of some of her mother's reactions, she began to see certain similarities between her own life and her mother's: her mother had had three children and two miscarriages; she has two children and had three miscarriages; her mother had "egg-shell days," she had "egg-shell days"; her mother had strong religious prejudices against Catholics; she, too, had some prejudices; her mother used to sleep until ten or eleven every morning, and so does Mrs. X; her mother screamed at her husband and children, and showed little affection, and so did she. Mrs. X also came to recognize that out of rebellion, she was neglecting the housekeeping chores which she intellectually accepted to be her responsibility.

The counselor sought to support Mrs. X, yet, at the same time, to help her recognize the inappropriateness of her reactions.

Present Interaction:
The X's can now talk about almost anything without losing control of themselves, or feeling that the other person is trying to make cutting remarks. Both say that they now enjoy sex relations. Mr. X is looking for a better paying job, more in keeping with his education and experience, although he says he is much happier now in his present job than he was previously.

While Mrs. X still has no desire to read Butterfield's book, *Sex Harmony in Marriage,* which the counselor gave her last December (at that time she read it, then kicked it out of the room), she does have a much more positive outlook on sex, and greater acceptance of the feminine role. As Mr. X has gained a more secure concept of his masculinity, he has found it easier to encourage his wife to share in decision-making. Each now feels more secure as a person, and more secure in his marriage.

SELECTED READINGS

Angell, Robert, *The Family Encounters the Depression* (New York, Scribner, 1936).

Bakke, E. W., *The Unemployed Worker* (New Haven, Yale, 1940).

Becker, Howard, and Hill, Reuben, *Family, Marriage, and Parenthood* (Boston, Heath, 1955), Part 5.

Bernard, Jessie, Buchanan, Helen, and Smith, William, *Dating, Mating, and Marriage* (Cleveland, Howard Allen, 1958), Chapter 11.

Cavan, Ruth, and Ranck, Katherine, *The Family and the Depression* (Chicago, The University of Chicago Press, 1938).

Elliot, Thomas, "The Bereaved Family," *The Annals of the American Academy of Political and Social Science,* Vol. 160 (March, 1932), pp. 1–7.

Farber, Bernard, *Effects of a Severely Mentally Retarded Child on Family Integration,* Monograph, Society for Research in Child Development, 1959, Vol. 24, No. 71.

Farber, Bernard, *Family Organization and Crisis,* Monograph, Society for Research in Child Development, 1960, Vol. 25, No. 75.

Foote, Nelson, and Cottrell, Leonard, *Identity and Interpersonal Competence* (Chicago, The University of Chicago Press, 1955).

Geismar, Ludwig, and Ayres, Beverly, *Patterns of Change in Problem Families* (St. Paul, Family Centered Project, 1959).

Goode, William, *After Divorce* (New York, Free Press, 1956).

Hill, Reuben, *Families Under Stress* (New York, Harper & Row, 1949).

Hill, Reuben, and Hansen, Donald, "The Family in Disaster," in G. Baker and D. Chapman (Eds.), *Man and Society in Disaster* (New York, Basic Books, 1962).

Komarovsky, Mirra, *The Unemployed Man and His Family* (New York, Holt, Rinehart and Winston, 1940).

Koos, Earl, *Families in Trouble* (New York, King's Crown, 1946).

Richardson, H. B., *Patients Have Families* (New York, Commonwealth Fund, 1945).

Schlesinger, B., *An Annotated Bibliography of the Multiproblem Family* (Toronto, University of Toronto Press, 1963).

Spiegel, John, and Kluckhohn, Florence, *Integration and Conflict in Family Behavior* (Topeka, Group for the Advancement of Psychiatry, 1954).

Vaughan, Elizabeth, *Communities Under Stress* (Princeton, Princeton University Press, 1949).

QUESTIONS AND EXERCISES

1. Why is it so difficult to isolate the causal process in the study of family problems and crises?

2. Devise an extended list of family crises, indicating a hierarchy of seriousness and anticipated disruptive effects upon family life at each level.

3. Discuss critically the contributions by the Harvard group to the study of conflict resolution in marriage.

4. Invite a marriage counselor to speak to your class. Have him comment on any theoretical or practical questions you might have in mind.

5. Organize a group to do a survey on marriage and family casework, counseling, and therapeutic facilities available in a given community. Include in each case an indication of the groups of people to whom the services are available.

6. Invite a representative of the Aid to Dependent Children program to speak to your group. Have him discuss some typical problems and crises faced by families where the father is absent.

7. If possible do a case study of a family which has undergone a crisis situation. Indicate some of the changes in roles and functions brought about by the crisis.

8. At what point do you think that marital maladjustment has reached the stage where it is impossible for the process to be reversed and a healthy marriage restored?

9. Write a paper indicating what the effect would be on yourself and your family if we were to experience a major stock market crash and depression.

10. Angell's concepts *adaptability* and *integration* grew out of his study of families who experienced an economic depression. Indicate whether or not these concepts can be applied to other family crises.

11. Analyze the following statement made by the casual observer of a marriage: "George and Mary's marriage failed because of sexual incompatibility."

12. What is the function of the newspaper syndicated advice columns regarding marriage and family problems, in your estimation?

26

Divorce

Marriage involves a status relationship between two people which is recognized by the state and the community. Under certain circumstances marital maladjustment replaces the expected marital adjustment to the point where divorce seems to be the only alternative. In other instances the couple, or one of them, simply wants to terminate the marriage for any of a myriad of personal reasons. It will be our purpose in this chapter to explain some of the typical aspects of divorce in America from the perspectives of society's expectations, the circumstances of particular couples, and some of the personal implications for those directly caught up in the process.

THE AMERICAN DIVORCE TRADITION

As is generally known, American law and procedure reflect the English background of the American colonies. Our divorce laws are therefore based on the traditional premise that marriages can be broken by divorce, but for just cause only. Marriage involves a special type of contract. The state has an interest in this basic relationship and will not allow the parties concerned to break it legally through mutual consent as would be true for most contracts.[1] Basic to the theory of marriage and divorce is the proposition that each party has certain minimum duties to perform. Divorce is provided as a form of redress to a spouse who has been injured by his partner's misconduct or failure to perform his duties. One party must be

[1] Sarah Knox, *The Family and the Law* (Chapel Hill, University of North Carolina Press, 1941), p. 26.

"innocent" and the other "guilty" for a divorce to be granted (a legal "fiction" from a realistic point of view).

Each state legislature has spelled out a series of grounds upon which divorce can be granted, upon clear and sufficient proof in the particular cases. These range from the one ground of adultery in New York to the fifteen or so grounds in Kentucky, which has the highest number. Below in Table 44 are listed the statutory grounds for the various states.

As can be seen, adultery is the most common ground allowed by statute in the various states. New York allows divorce for this reason only. Except for this unusual situation, desertion, cruelty, alcoholism, and conviction of a felony are also typical grounds. In actual practice cruelty and desertion are most often used by plaintiffs, although in states such as Ohio gross neglect of duty is a popular category.

Adultery is theoretically the most clear-cut of the grounds listed. In actual practice, however, the court can only operate on inference. In general, pictures of defendants in compromising situations, or sworn testimony of witnesses are taken as valid evidence. A grand jury investigation in New York recently uncovered what was common knowledge regarding the non-legitimacy of many adultery charges. Evidence indicated that many if not most adultery cases were open to the charges of connivance, collusion, and perjury.[2] What on its face seems to be fact may not be such and is not in many cases.

If the ground of adultery leaves something to be desired in regard to ease of measurement, cruelty, gross neglect, and others are even more difficult to handle. Vernier pointed out some years ago that "in the forty-three jurisdictions recognizing cruelty as a ground for absolute divorce it has been deemed necessary to define cruelty in twenty-seven different ways."[3] A perusal of the definitions of neglect used by the various states will indicate to even the most casual reader that the term is a grab bag into which much can be thrown.

It becomes clear, then, that the judge in a divorce court has wide discretion regarding the interpretation of the statutory grounds. What a judge says is cruelty is cruelty. What a presiding judge considers to be gross neglect of duty is gross neglect of duty. No clearly objective criteria exist at this time.

In the typical divorce case, then, Mary Doe sues John Doe for extreme cruelty or some ground authorized in their particular state. Mary indicates in detail John's shortcomings and guilt, meanwhile implying, or even asserting, that she is innocent of marital wrongdoing. After a waiting period the case is heard, with Mary repeating the charges in court under oath. John

[2] Morris Ploscowe, *The Truth About Divorce* (New York, Hawthorn, 1955), p. 101.

[3] Chester Vernier, *American Family Laws,* Vol. II (Palo Alto, Stanford University Press, 1931–1938), pp. 24–25.

TABLE 44

Divorce Laws as of July 1, 1963 *

State or other jurisdiction	Residence required before filing suit for divorce	Grounds for absolute divorce								
		Adultery	Mental and/or physical cruelty	Desertion	Alcoholism	Impotency	Non-support	Insanity	Pregnancy at marriage	Bigamy
Alabama	(a)	★	★	1 yr.	★	★	★(b)	5 yrs.	★	
Alaska	1 yr.	★	★	1 yr.	★	★	★	18 mos.		
Arizona	1 yr.	★	★	1 yr.	★	★	★		★	
Arkansas	2 mos.	★	★	1 yr.	★	★	★(h)	3 yrs.		★
California	1 yr.	★	★	1 yr.	★		★	3 yrs.		
Colorado	1 yr.(j)	★	★	1 yr.	★	★		3 yrs.		
Connecticut	3 yrs.(j)	★	★	3 yrs.	★		★	5 yrs.		
Delaware	2 yrs.(j)	★	★	2 yrs.	★			5 yrs.		★
Florida	6 mos.	★	★	1 yr.	★	★	★			★
Georgia	6 mos.	★	★	1 yr.	★	★		2 yrs.	★	
Hawaii	2 yrs.	★	★	6 mos.	★			3 yrs.		
Idaho	6 wks.	★	★	1 yr.	★	★	★★	3 yrs.		
Illinois	1 yr.(j)	★	★	1 yr.	★	★				★
Indiana	2 yrs.	★	★	2 yrs.	★	★	★	5 yrs.		
Iowa	1 yr.	★	★	2 yrs.	★				★(t)	

Table: State residency requirements (stars and time periods)

State										
Kansas	★	★★	5 yrs.	★	★★	★★	1 yr.	★★	★★★★	1 yr.(u)
Kentucky	★★	★★	5 yrs.		★★	★★(v)	1 yr.		★★★★	1 yr.
Louisiana						★			★★★	(y)
Maine			3 yrs.	★	★★	★	3 yrs.	★	★★★	6 mos.(j)
Maryland	★★			★★	★★★★	★	18 mos.			1 yr.(ab)
Massachusetts			5 yrs.	★★★★	★★★★★	★★★★	3 yrs.	★★★★★	★★★★★	5 yrs.(j)
Michigan			3 yrs.	★★★	★★★★★	★★★★	2 yrs.	★★★★★	★★★★	1 yr.(j)
Minnesota	★★	★★		★★	★★★	★★★	1 yr.	★★★	★★★★	1 yr.(j)
Mississippi			5 yrs.		★★	★★	1 yr.			1 yr.
Missouri			3 yrs.			★★	1 yr.			1 yr.(j)
Montana			5 yrs.	★★★★	★★★★★	★★★★	1 yr.	★★★★★	★★★★★	1 yr.
Nebraska			5 yrs.	★★★	★★★	★★★	2 yrs.	★★★	★★★	2 yrs.(j)
Nevada			2 yrs.	★	★★	★★	1 yr.	★★	★★★	6 wks.(j)
New Hampshire							2 yrs.			1 yr.(j)
New Jersey							2 yrs.			2 yrs.(j)
New Mexico		★	5 yrs.	★	★	★	★	★		1 yr. (ai)
New York	★	★								6 mos.
North Carolina	★	★	5 yrs.	★(h)	★★	★★		★★	★★★★	1 yr.(r)
North Dakota			5 yrs.	★★★	★★★★	★★	1 yr.	★★★★★	★★★	1 yr.
Ohio				★	★★	★★		★★	★★	1 yr.
Oklahoma	★	★	5 yrs.	★	★★★★	★★	1 yr.	★★★★★	★★★★	6 mos.(u)
Oregon	★	★	3 yrs.		★★★★	★★	1 yr.	★★	★★★★	1 yr.
Pennsylvania				★		★★	2 yrs.	★★★★	★★★★	1 yr.
Rhode Island							5 yrs.(am)			2 yrs.
South Carolina							1 yr.			1 yr.
South Dakota	★	★	5 yrs.	★★	★★	★★	1 yr.	★★	★★★★	1 yr.(j)
Tennessee	★	★	5 yrs.		★	★★	1 yr.		★★★★	1 yr.
Texas			5 yrs.	★★	★★	★	3 yrs.		★★★	12 mos.
Utah	★	★	★	★	★		1 yr.		★★	3 mos.
Vermont			5 yrs.	★★	★★		3 yrs.			6 mos.(as)

TABLE 44 (cont.)
Divorce Laws as of July 1, 1963 *

State or other jurisdiction	Residence required before filing suit for divorce	Adultery	Mental and/or physical cruelty	Desertion	Alcoholism	Impotency	Non-support	Insanity	Pregnancy at marriage	Bigamy
								Grounds for absolute divorce		
Virginia	1 yr.	★		1 yr.		★			★	
Washington	1 yr.	★	★	1 yr.	★	★	★	2 yrs.		
West Virginia	2 yrs.(j)	★	★	1 yr.	★		★★			
Wisconsin	2 yrs.	★	★	1 yr.	★	★				
Wyoming	60 days(j)	★	★	1 yr.	★		★	2 yrs.	★	
Dist. of Columbia	2 yrs.(j)	★		2 yrs.						

* Prepared by the Women's Bureau, United States Department of Labor.

★ Indicates ground for absolute divorce.

(a) No specific period required except 1 year when ground is desertion or defendant is non-resident, or 2 years if wife sues husband for non-support.

(b) To wife, living separate and apart from husband, as resident of the state for 2 years before suit, and without support from him during such time.

(c) May be enlarged into an absolute divorce after expiration of 4 years.

(d) Crime against nature.

(e) Court may forbid remarriage.

(f) Incompatibility.

(g) Crime before marriage.

(h) Also to husband in certain circumstances.

(i) Final decree is not entered until 1 year after interlocutory decree.

(j) Under certain circumstances a lesser period of time may be required.

(k) Female under 16, male under 18, complaining party under age of consent at time of marriage has not confirmed the marriage after reaching such age.

(l) In the discretion of the court.

(m) Habitual violent and ungovernable temper.

(n) Defendant obtained divorce from plaintiff in another state.

(o) Mental incapacity.

(p) Under decree of separate maintenance.

(q) Loathsome disease.

(r) Five years if on ground of insanity.

(s) Two years where service on defendant is only by publication.

(t) Unless at time of marriage husband had an illegitimate child living which fact was not known to wife.

(u) Five years if on ground of insanity and insane spouse is in out-of-state institution.

(v) If on part of the husband, accompanied by wasting of husband's estate to the detriment of the wife and children.

(w) Joining religious sect disbelieving in marriage.

(x) Unchaste behavior on part of wife after marriage.

(y) No statutory requirement for adultery or felony conviction; 2 years when ground is separation.

(z) Limited divorce may be enlarged into absolute divorce after 1 year for innocent spouse and after 1 year and 60 days for guilty spouse.

SOURCE: *Book of the States* (Chicago, The Council of State Governments, 1964).

Grounds for absolute divorce

Separation or absence	Felony conviction or imprisonment	Drug addiction	Fraud, force or duress	Infamous crime	Relationship within prohibited degrees	Prior decree of limited divorce	Other	Plaintiff	Defendant	State or other jurisdiction
	★	★				(c)	(d)	60 days(e)	60 days(e)	Alabama
5 yrs.	★	★					(f)	1 yr.	1 yr.	Alaska
3 yrs.	★			★			(g)			Arizona
	★			★						Arkansas
	★							(i)	(i)	California
3yrs.	★	★								Colorado
7 yrs.	★		★	★						Connecticut
3 yrs.	★	★	★				(k)	3 mos.(l)	3 mos.(l)	Delaware
					★		(m,n)			Florida
	★				★		(o)	(l)	(l)	Georgia
2 yrs.(p)	★	★								Hawaii
5yrs.	★						(q)	(s)		Idaho
	★			★						Illinois
				★						Indiana
								1 yr.(l)	1 yr.(l)	Iowa
	★		★				(q,w,x)	6 mos.	6 mos.	Kansas
5 yrs.	★		★							Kentucky
2 yrs.						(z)		wife, 10 mos.	wife, 10 mos. (aa)	Louisiana
										Maine
18 mos.	★	★					(ac)			Maryland

555

TABLE 44 (cont.)
Divorce Laws as of July 1, 1963 *

	Grounds for absolute divorce								Period before parties may remarry after final decree		State or other jurisdiction
Separation or absence	Felony conviction or imprisonment	Drug addiction	Fraud, force or duress	Infamous crime	Relationship within prohibited degrees	Prior decree of limited divorce	Other	Plaintiff	Defendant		
	★	★					(n)		2 yrs.		Massachusetts
2 yrs.(p)	★								(ad)		Michigan
	★	★		★	★	(ae)		6 mos.	6 mos.		Minnesota
	★						(o)				Mississippi
	★						(g,ag)		(af)		Missouri
3yrs.	★	★						6 mos.	6 mos.		Montana
2 yrs.	★			★				6 mos.	6 mos.		Nebraska
											Nevada
	★						(w,ah)				New Hampshire
								3 mos.(l)	3 mos.(l)		New Jersey
	★						(f)				New Mexico
2 yrs.									(aj)		New York
	★		★				(d)				North Carolina
	★		★			(c)		(l)			North Dakota
1 yr.			★				(n)	(ak)	(l)		Ohio
	★		★				(f,n)	6 mos.	6 mos.		Oklahoma
	★				★			6 mos.	6 mos.		Oregon
							(al)		(aa)		Pennsylvania
10 yrs.		★					(an,ao)	6 mos.	6 mos.		Rhode Island
		★									South Carolina
	★								(ap)		South Dakota

556

State	Residence					
Tennessee	2 yrs.(aq)	★		(aa)		(aa)
Texas	7 yrs.	★		(ar)		(ar)
Utah	3 yrs.(p)	★	(al)	3 mos.(l)		3 mos.(l)
Vermont	3 yrs.	★	★	(at)	6 mos.(l)	2 yrs.(l)
Virginia	3 yrs.	★		(d,av)	(aw)	(aw)
Washington	5 yrs.	★	★	(ax)	(au) 6 mos.	6 mos.
West Virginia		★			60 days	60 days(ay)
Wisconsin	5 yrs.	★		(g,ag)	(az) 1 yr.	1 yr.
Wyoming	2 yrs.	★	★			
Dist. of Columbia	5 yrs.	★		(ba)	6 mos.	6 mos.

(aa) When divorce is granted on ground of adultery, guilty party cannot marry the accomplice in adultery during lifetime of former spouse.

(ab) No specific period required except 1 year if cause occurred out of state, and 2 years if on ground of insanity.

(ac) Any cause which renders marriage null and void *ab initio*.

(ad) Not more than 2 years in court's discretion.

(ae) Limited divorce may be enlarged into absolute divorce after 5 years.

(af) When divorce is granted on ground of adultery, court may prohibit remarriage. After 1 year court may remove disability upon satisfactory evidence of reformation.

(ag) Husband a vagrant.

(ah) Wife's absence out of state for 10 years without husband's consent.

(ai) No time specified. Parties must be residents when offense committed; or married in state; or plaintiff resident when offense committed and action commenced; or offense committed in state and injured party resident when action commenced.

(aj) Defendant is prohibited from remarrying unless after 3 years court removes disability upon satisfactory evidence of reformation.

(ak) When husband is entitled to a divorce and alimony or child support from husband is granted, the decree may be delayed until security is entered for payment.

(al) Incapable of procreation.

(am) Or a lesser time in court's discretion.

(aa) Void or voidable marriage.

(ao) Gross misbehavior or wickedness.

(ap) When divorce is for adultery, guilty party cannot remarry except to the innocent person, until the death of the other.

(aq) To husband for wife's refusal to move with him to this state without reasonable cause, and willfully absenting herself from him for 2 years.

(ar) When divorce is granted on ground of cruelty, neither party may remarry for 12 months except each other.

(as) One year before final hearing, and 2 years if on ground of insanity.

(at) Intolerable severity.

(au) A limited divorce granted on the ground of cruelty or desertion may be merged with an absolute divorce after one year.

(av) Two years fugitive from justice; wife a prostitute prior to marriage.

(aw) When divorce is granted on ground of adultery, court may decree the guilty party cannot remarry. After 6 months the court may remove disability for good cause. Remarriage of either party forbidden pending appeal.

(ax) Want of legal age or sufficient understanding.

(ay) In court's discretion, guilty party may be prohibited from remarrying for a period not to exceed 1 year.

(az) Living entirely apart for 5 years pursuant to a judgment of legal separation.

(ba) Limited divorce may be enlarged into absolute divorce after 2 years.

557

may be represented by counsel at the hearing, but he usually does not himself appear. If children are involved Mary will probably be given custody of them, along with support payment and, less often, alimony.[4] A separation agreement dealing with property division and other matters is as a rule drawn up previous to the hearing by the respective counselors for the two parties, contingent upon favorable court action.[5] If not, the judge will settle such problems as he sees fit.

In these typical situations much is hidden under the surface. Often the case is fictional and involves fraud and collusion. Collusion in nontechnical language refers to the use of deceit, including agreement by the litigants. This may involve committing an offense through the use of force, the submission of false evidence, or the suppression of a valid defense.[6] Estimates of the amount of collusion involved in American divorce cases vary, but many judges and students of divorce suggest that 75 to 90 percent would be reasonable.[7] Strictly speaking, most litigants and their lawyers could be held accountable and charged with perjury. *In actual practice something approximating divorce by mutual consent has developed in many jurisdictions of the United States, although this is not officially recognized.* Especially does this statement hold for the great majority of cases in which the defendant does not make an appearance in court to defend himself. It also applies especially well in those states which allow "separation" for a specified period as a legal ground for divorce.[8]

THE MIGRATORY DIVORCE QUESTION

In cases such as that of the Nelson Rockefellers much publicity is given to migratory divorce. What is meant by this term? Briefly, it is more convenient to sue for divorce "away from home." In the Rockefeller case, for example, even if adultery were involved it would probably not be used as a ground. Since there was no indication of this, Mrs. Rockefeller had only to meet the requirements of another state in order to obtain a divorce.

---

[4] On the basis of his own limited experience in consultative and investigative work in divorce cases the author can clearly state that there is a tendency for the mother to be given custody of the child. In most circumstances the father must prove to the satisfaction of the judge that the mother is "unfit" to rear the child. Otherwise, she will tend to get it.

[5] In Morris Ernst and David Loth, *For Better or For Worse* (New York, Harper & Row, 1952), p. 130 it is claimed that the courts simply ratify separation agreements in 95 percent of the cases without inquiry as to their general desirability.

[6] See Fowler Harper, *Problems of the Family* (Indianapolis, Bobbs-Merrill, 1952), Section 2. See also Robert E. Lee, *North Carolina Family Law* (Winston Salem College Bookstore, Wake Forest College, 1955), p. 29.

[7] Ernst and Loth, *op. cit.,* Chapter 1.

[8] In North Carolina divorce may be granted if the litigants are separated for two years or more and if one or both parties has been a resident for six months or more.

In most similar situations the plaintiff temporarily moves to another jurisdiction in order to obtain the divorce.

Most of the so-called divorce meccas do not offer more grounds than does the average state. Instead, they have short waiting periods to establish legal residence. Certain states have been quite willing to cut the amount of time necessary to establish legal residence. At present Arkansas (60 days), Florida (90 days) and Nevada (45 days) are the best-known meccas, although Wyoming, Idaho and Alabama are giving indications of being interested in joining the market. The added factors of hot baths, exceptional sunshine, and wide-open gambling may make the competition extremely difficult!

In migratory divorce, then, the prospective divorcee typically leaves her home state, spends the necessary number of days in the new environment, and files for divorce at the end of this minimum period. The actual procedure thereafter is not different from that in other areas. The charges are heard and a decision is made. If the divorce is granted the litigants are free to go about their business in their own way.

Are migratory divorces valid? The full faith and credit clause of the constitution requires the states, in general, to recognize each other's legal decisions. The issue is jurisdiction. A court can issue a divorce only if it has jurisdiction over the parties concerned. In a number of instances in the past where migratory divorces were involved, courts in the "home" states of the litigants have permitted cases to be reopened on the charge that the state to which migration was made did not have actual jurisdiction over the parties involved.[9] Central to the matter is residence and domicile. Residence may be measured arbitrarily by a specified number of days. Domicile refers to intent and is highly subjective. It has the meaning of home in a basic sense. It is the place to which one intends to return. There can be no doubt that perjury is involved if strict domicile is required for a valid decree when the so-called migratory divorce is considered. Hundreds of people swear that they are bona fide residents of the particular state when actually their real home or domicile is elsewhere.[10] Can these cases be attacked and set aside? At present the answer given by legal writers is a qualified "no." The U.S. Supreme Court in four modern decisions has taken the position that the two litigants and interested third parties cannot contest the decrees if certain conditions are met.[11] They are as follows: (1) Both parties must

[9] As for example in the famous Williams case in North Carolina and Nevada. (See Williams v. North Carolina 317 U.S. 287, 1942).

[10] See the dissent by Justice Frankfurter in Sherrer v. Sherrer, 334 U.S. 343 (1947).

[11] See Sherrer v. Sherrer, ibid., and Coe v. Coe, U.S. 378 (1948).

The Supreme Court essentially took the .position that if a court raises the question of domicile, decides that it has it, and if the defendant has "had his day in court" the divorce must be recognized under the full faith and credit clause of the Constitution. This means that the home state cannot challenge the legality of a migratory divorce nor can the defendant. Having his day in court means that the defendant

be before the court, and (2) An opportunity must be granted to have the question of jurisdiction (or domicile) contested. In the first instance the defendant must be served and must appear or be represented at the hearing. In the second there must be a finding by the court that it has jurisdiction in the case. Specifically, it must find that the plaintiff is domiciled in the area over which the court has jurisdiction. If these requirements are met there is a strong chance that the divorce cannot be upset. In many cases, however, the defendant is not served or is not represented in court. Such cases are open to challenge at any time by one of the parties or a third party who has interests in the case. Furthermore, a new Supreme Court decision might at any time jeopardize all migratory cases in which the above-stated conditions are met. Clearly the migratory divorce situation is a muddled one and it will remain so in at least the immediate future.[12]

DIVORCE TRENDS

Whether the divorce rate in the United States is unduly high or not depends to a degree on the frame of reference from which it is viewed. The overall tendency has been upward. At the time of the Civil War slightly under 10,000 divorces were granted annually. Now the number runs around 400,000 per year. Making allowance for population and other changes, this still means that the divorce picture has changed considerably since the days of Johnny Reb and Billy Yank.

Divorce rates can be misleading, especially crude rates. In order to give some perspective we have chosen to indicate trends by using a number of measures or indices (see Table 45). Crude divorce rates are inadequate in that adults and children are lumped together to form the base for the rates. Further, rapid changes within the population are not adequately reflected in a crude rate. These might involve changes in age or sex composition of the populace, the rate of marriage, or other modifications in the social structure. The use of a rate based on the marriageable population of fifteen years of age and over is better in that children are omitted.

Some have preferred to compare divorces directly to marriages. This

---

was properly served and appeared in court himself or was represented by counsel. We are indebted to Professor Roddey Liyon, Institute of Government, University of North Carolina for aid on these and other points made in this chapter.

[12] Professor Herbert Baer has written authoritatively regarding the migratory divorce situation. See his "The Aftermath of Williams v. North Carolina," *North Carolina Law Review,* Vol. 28, 1949–50, p. 265; and "The Law of Divorce Fifteen Years after Williams v. North Carolina," *North Carolina Law Review,* Vol. 36, 1957–58, pp. 265–296. As he shows, the situation is still rather muddled regarding the chances that a particular migratory divorce will stand. Even though a litigant may not reopen a case if he appeared in court a home state might well attack a particular decision in one way or another. For example, it might charge one of the litigants with bigamy if a remarriage had taken place.

TABLE 45

Divorce Trends in the United States, Computed by Various Methods, 1890–1960

Year	Number of Divorces	Divorces per 1,000 Population	Divorces per 1,000 Married Females 15 Years of Age or Over	Divorces per 100 Marriages of the Same Year	Divorces per 100 Marriages (Based on Averages of Marriages) of Preceding 10 Years
1880	19,663	.4	—	4.3	4.9
1890	33,461	.5	—	5.8	6.5
1900	55,751	.7	4.0	7.9	8.8
1910	83,045	.9	4.7	8.8	9.7
1920	170,505	1.6	8.0	13.4	16.0
1930	195,961	1.6	7.5	17.4	16.5
1940	264,000	2.0	8.7	16.5	20.4
1946	610,000	4.3	17.8	26.8	37.7
1950	385,144	2.6	10.3	23.0	22.1
1960	393,000	2.2	9.2	25.8	25.7

SOURCE: Yearly Statistical Abstracts of the United States, U.S. Bureau of the Census, and Paul H. Jacobson, *American Marriage and Divorce* (New York, Holt, Rinehart and Winston, 1959).

enables one to quote probability ratios regarding the chances of divorce in forms easily understood. For example, referring to 1950 figures, one might say that the chances of a marriage ending in divorce were about 23 out of 100, or roughly one to four. This is, however, misleading. Marriages in 1940 would tend to end in divorce, if at all, during the decade 1941–1950. It has been suggested that a concept of "moving average" of marriages over a ten-year period will provide a good base to which divorces of a given year can be compared. A ten-year figure has the further advantage that any unusual years for the decade will be levelled out.

The reader may note a number of interesting items in Table 45. If all years were included it would be more clearly demonstrated that divorce rates go down during a depression or wartime period. As can be seen, however, a time of readjustment comes, as is demonstrated by the unusually high rate of the postwar year 1946.

Examination of the statistics will indicate that the overall divorce trend in the United States has been upward. There is a possibility that this will change. The divorce rate may become fairly stable. One special complication, however, is the increase in the number of teen-age marriages which are now taking place. This type of marriage has been highly vulnerable to divorce in times past. One can probably predict that many of these couples will keep the divorce courts and the divorce statisticians busy in the immediate future and that the divorce rate will continue slowly upward.

What are the chances, then, that a marriage will end in divorce? Taking all factors into account it is reasonable to suggest that a given marriage faces a one to four probability of divorce. This assumes a *U.S. marriage picked at random and under present conditions.* If a specific marriage has particular features about it to increase the expectation of solidarity the forecast would have to be modified. There is always the possibility that "conditions" may change to confuse the picture. Nevertheless, this rough probability ratio may be useful if used with proper caution.

THE SEARCH FOR CAUSES OF DIVORCE

The search for the causes of divorce is even more complicated than the search for the causes of marital discord. All of the causes involved in marital discord are involved in divorce, and more. We, therefore, refer the reader to Chapter 25 for a reminder that discord can stem from societal causes external to the couple, from causes involving the relationship of the couple, and from individual factors as well.

No absolute causal relationship exists between marital disintegration and divorce. Some cases of extreme disintegration do not end in divorce and divorce sometimes ensues when couples have a marriage which would rank as average or above in the community. What, then, is the relationship between marital maladjustment and divorce?

In any given community there is a range in marriage success from excellent to poor on the basis of any criterion we wish to use. No adequate study has yet been made where all the marriages in the community were subjected to careful scrutiny. On the basis of his own research, consultative work, and study of research and clinical findings of others, the author believes that in any typical community marriages fall into roughly equal quartiles, as follows:

Excellent	25%
Good	25%
Fair	25%
Poor	25%

Admittedly this must be taken as an approximate estimate. Used as a model, the relationship between these categories and chances of divorce can be considered. Other things being equal, the relationship between marital success and probability of divorce is an inverse one. The higher the marital success, the lower the risks of divorce. Statistically speaking, couples who fall into the lower categories of marital success are more vulnerable to divorce than those in the top two categories. Again the reader is reminded that the causes behind this are multiple and that attention was given to their discussion in the previous chapter. Other things must be equal for the relationship to hold. In actual practice modifying factors enter the picture, a number of which can be identified.

Social Status

In general the lower the social status of the individuals involved, the greater the risk of divorce.[13] This holds true for income, for occupations as they are typically ranked, and for educational level. Two closely related factors are also involved. Marriages involving those of the younger age categories and those of forced marriages are especially vulnerable to divorce. Financial and other types of pressures have a heavy impress on poorer families, as Koos and others have shown.[14] With less status to lose in the first place, family break-up through desertion or divorce does not have the same meaning that it has for people at the higher socioeconomic levels. This situation is, however, changing. Note the divorce of persons in public life who are well-known, such as Rockefeller, Douglass, Stevenson, and Salinger.

Religion

Religious groups in the United States accept divorce reluctantly, with Roman Catholics taking the most adamant position. The religiously identified tend to be more reluctant than the nonaffiliated to seek divorce, even with legally adequate provocation. Secularly oriented persons have the highest divorce rate.

Other Risk Factors

There are other categories of differential risks toward divorce. One of these is race. Negro families are more prone both to desertion and to divorce. In times past desertion was the most typical form of marital break-up among the poorer classes. Increasingly there is the tendency for what might have been only informal separations or desertions to become bona fide divorces.[15]

Besides social factors which affect divorce proneness, individual factors are also involved. In general there is an inverse relationship between mental health and the tendency to divorce, other things being equal. Again the reader is referred to the earlier discussions of individual factors involved in marital discord. These all operate as causes behind divorce too.

---

[13] William Goode, *After Divorce* (New York, Free Press, 1956), Chapter IV.

[14] Earl Koos, *Families in Trouble* (Rochester, N.Y., Kings Crown, 1946).

[15] Kephart believes that it is not legitimate to speak of desertion as the poor man's divorce. However, he does find in his Philadelphia studies that Negroes have higher desertion rates than chance would allow, comparatively speaking.

Individual predilections may move one person to seek redress from a bad marital situation by approaching the courts, whereas another person in relatively similar circumstances refrains from such action.

MOVING TOWARD DIVORCE

The foregoing discussion has dealt with the issue of differential risk of divorce. It may be worthwhile to move beyond this to the processes which seem to be involved in selecting out particular couples who divorce. Waller was among the first to attempt a delineation of the "alienation" process as he termed it.

1. Early in the process there is a disturbance in the sex life, and affectional response. Rapport is lost, with attempt to compensate for its lack in some cases.
2. The possibility of divorce is first mentioned. This tends to clarify the relationship somewhat with the initiator taking the lead and the partner remaining passive through the divorce cycle.
3. The appearance of solidarity is broken before the public. The fiction of solidarity is important as a face-saver. Once it is broken the marriage cannot be the same again.
4. The decision to divorce is made, usually after long discussion, although at times it is made without forethought.
5. A severe crisis of separation follows. Severing a meaningful relationship is a traumatic experience at best, even though it is felt to be the only alternative.
6. Final severance comes with the actual divorce. This may come after a long period of delay and separation. While it is usually thought of as closing the case, the actual legal procedure is necessary before the next stage of final adaption can begin.
7. A period of mental conflict and reconstruction closes the case. The former partners enter new social worlds and full estrangement takes place.[16]

It is suggested that the process has certain elements of the courtship process in reverse. As against greater and greater involvement the spiral of separation increases. One party makes a gesture of reconciliation which may or may not be well received. During the initial phases there is often a tendency to try periods of reconciliation. If basic differences are involved, these stopgap measures cannot stem the tide and the shallow dam again breaks to release a flood of bitterness and frustration. As the couple grows apart, reconciliation becomes more difficult.

Burgess, Locke and Mary Thomes have attempted graphically to illustrate the cumulative nature of divorce through the use of a case originally presented by Mowrer (see Figure 21 where it is reproduced). The concept

[16] From *The Family,* Revised, by Willard Waller and Reuben Hill, Copyright 1938, 1951 by Holt, Rinehart and Winston, Inc. Reprinted by permission of the publishers.

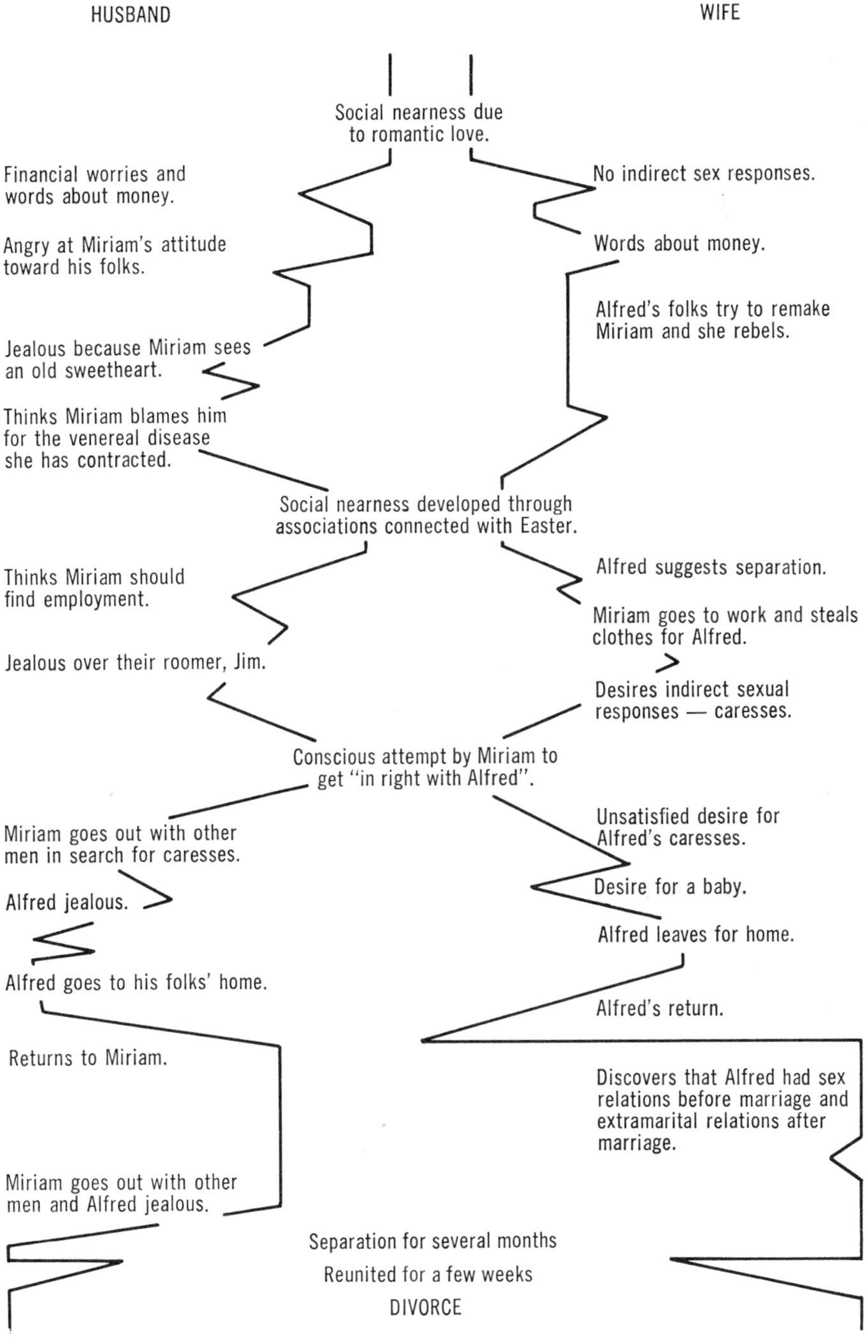

HUSBAND   WIFE

Social nearness due
to romantic love.

Financial worries and   No indirect sex responses.
words about money.

Angry at Miriam's attitude   Words about money.
toward his folks.

                                         Alfred's folks try to remake
                                         Miriam and she rebels.
Jealous because Miriam sees
an old sweetheart.

Thinks Miriam blames him
for the venereal disease
she has contracted.

Social nearness developed through
associations connected with Easter.

Thinks Miriam should   Alfred suggests separation.
find employment.
                                         Miriam goes to work and steals
                                         clothes for Alfred.
Jealous over their roomer, Jim.
                                         Desires indirect sexual
                                         responses — caresses.

Conscious attempt by Miriam to
get "in right with Alfred".

                                         Unsatisfied desire for
Miriam goes out with other   Alfred's caresses.
men in search for caresses.
                                         Desire for a baby.
Alfred jealous.
                                         Alfred leaves for home.

Alfred goes to his folks' home.
                                         Alfred's return.

Returns to Miriam.
                                         Discovers that Alfred had sex
                                         relations before marriage and
                                         extramarital relations after
                                         marriage.
Miriam goes out with other
men and Alfred jealous.

                    Separation for several months
                    Reunited for a few weeks
                    DIVORCE

FIGURE 21. *Development of Social Distance Between Alfred and Miriam Don-aven.* SOURCE: Ernest Burgess, Harvey Locke, and Mary Thomes, *The Family: From Institution to Companionship,* 3rd ed. (New York, American Book, 1963), p. 517.

of social nearness and distance is used to illustrate a developing estrangement.

It is our judgment that the Waller model of the alienation process is as sound as any yet proposed, but that there are many individual cases where it does not apply. Puzzling problems for all serious students of divorce revolve around the question of separating "drop outs" from those who carry through the completion of legal divorce. Many couples seem to be headed for divorce, only to reconcile and remain together. A relatively high proportion of divorce suits are dropped prior to a final hearing. Why do some couples persist in carrying through while others retreat to home and fireside or at least retreat from the divorce court? A number of particular factors probably operate in each case. In terms of the writer's experience the factors of pride, outside interference, and considerations of probable consequences seem to recur in cases of reconsideration of divorce. Personal pride is a very complicated motive and its overt manifestations are not predictable. One woman takes so much pride in the marital status that she will suffer humiliation rather than face the public disgrace of divorce. In another case, once she has spoken to a lawyer and revealed the intent to divorce to her friends, pride induces a woman to carry through to divorce, even though at times she is ready for reconciliation.

The behavior of third parties cannot be overlooked. More than one person, meaning to use a divorce threat as a weapon, is carried on to divorce by an eager attorney and helpful friends who insist that they too would never tolerate such behavior as that exhibited by the spouse. In past times neighbors and friends usually advised a discouraged spouse to bear the yoke in order to receive a reward in heaven later. Today a warring partner can usually find seconds who are quite willing to engage in any practice except the direct dueling itself. Seldom do relatives play a neutral, third-party role, although there are exceptions. In some cases, however, mutual friends encourage conciliation. Some recommend consultation with ministers and others for marriage counseling purposes.

When some rationality prevails, calculations of probabilities are made. Individually (and sometimes jointly) the situation is analyzed in terms of the potential rewards and costs of each status. A particular couple has a good community reputation, considerable tangible property, a moderate sex relationship, children to whom both are attached, but experience basic incompatibility regarding religion and general values. But cultural and value conflict makes it difficult to agree on child rearing, and slowly but surely the couple moves apart to the point that the sexual and affectional life also becomes unsatisfactory. For both spouses divorce will offer certain rewards but will require certain costs. For example, both may wonder whether the children will be better off under new circumstances than they are under conditions of hostility and frustration. The wife will have a strong chance of obtaining custody of the children and support for them. She will have the chance of remarriage and a possible better home environment for the children. On the negative side she faces the possibility that no suitable husband will step forward and that she will have full responsibility for the care and control of the children. This is just the beginning. For each partner dozens of considerations must be weighed in the balance. Unfortunately the level of wisdom attributed to Solomon is not always available to persons caught up in winds of marital discord.

Personality idiosyncracies are not to be overlooked. A neurotic partner can subtly but surely drive the spouse to the wall. Divorce may be something of a letdown to him in that he will have no one available for the time being to receive his barbs. Many a partner is willing to tolerate the neurotic partner, preferring the known difficulties of low-level marriage adjustment to the unknown contingencies of divorce.

POSTDIVORCE ADJUSTMENT

Waller long ago compared the shock of postdivorce life to bereavement following the death of the spouse. He showed that in certain cases the adjustment was more difficult than in the case of death.[17] In spite of the high divorce rate American society has not developed the supportive processes for the divorced person that it has for the person left alone by death. Economic, sexual, legal, emotional, and other difficulties often beset the divorcee. The process of breaking old habits and establishing a new life pattern is not a simple one. The judge may have "legally closed" the case, but this legal decree does not block off memories or solve personal problems. Especially difficult is the situation in which the couple once had a good marriage which lasted many years before it was finally broken. Readjustment is in such cases much more of an ordeal than in cases where the couple really had never developed a strong relationship.

More clinical work is needed to understand the process of emotional readaptation in postdivorce adjustment. It is known that previously stable individuals often act without typical restraint during the early postdivorce period. One person becomes sexually promiscuous, another becomes irresponsible in his spending of money. The loss of the controls of marriage plus the pressures of the loss of status induce many people to let down their defenses and allow irrational behavior to take over. Eventually more rational processes begin to reassert themselves as the individuals involved modify old roles and seek to establish new ones.

Social status, the number of children involved, and many other factors cannot be overlooked regarding the process of postdivorce adjustment. A young, attractive woman without children who divorces her alcoholic hus-

[17] Willard Waller, *The Old Love and the New* (New York, Liveright, 1930). See also Waller and Hill, *op. cit.,* Chapters 23 and 24.

band may find it relatively easy to remarry or to find employment, although education and training would complicate the latter type of adjustment. Over a period of years she may be able to achieve a higher status than she would have maintained by remaining with her husband. The middle-class woman of thirty-eight with four children may find it difficult to keep the same level of living to which she and the children were accustomed, even with high support and alimony payments. She may find also that husbands whom she considers eligible are not as plentiful as she had imagined they would be.

As far as men are concerned, those of wealth such as the late Thomas Manville seem to have no difficulty making new arrangements after a divorce, although some questions could be raised at times as to their adequacy. One recurring problem for the woman at the lower- and middle-class levels, on the other hand, is that of support and alimony payments by the husband when there are children involved. These days a divorced husband-father often remarries and has children by a second wife even though he is under court order to provide for a former spouse and children. Soon he is required to support two sets of children. That this can often induce financial strain goes without saying. Among the lower classes desertion by the father is a very typical reaction in such a situation.[18] If the husband is not found, the wife and children must usually turn to public services for support. If the husband is found and forced by law to assume his obligations or voluntarily does so, his double burden may be difficult indeed.

Remarriage of the Divorced

Regardless of the problems involved, divorces are sought and adaptations are made. A high percentage of the divorced group remarry. According to Glick, about two thirds of the women and three fourths of the men choose to remarry sometime during the postdivorce period.[19] This means that, age for age, divorcees are more vulnerable to marriage than single or widowed people. See Table 46. Further, there is a tendency to remarry rather quickly after the divorce has been granted. The modal category is the second and third year, which includes some 40 percent of those who remarry. One half remarry within five years. The divorced tend well above chance to choose mates who have also been divorced.[20]

Simple statistical rates may be boring to some, but serious consideration must be given to them. Surely remarriage rates in the United States indicate the great value placed on marriage by the major elements of our population. Other motivations, both general and specific, are no doubt involved.

[18] This has been demonstrated by various Aid to Dependent Children reports.
[19] Paul Glick, *American Families* (New York, Wiley, 1957), p. 142.
[20] Charles Bowerman, "Assortative Mating by Previous Marital Status: Seattle, 1939–1946," *American Sociological Review,* Vol. 18 (April, 1953), pp. 170–177.

TABLE 46

Marriage Rates by Previous Marital Status, for Bride and Groom, 1960 [a]

| | Previous Status | | | |
	Single	Divorced	Widowed	Not Reported
Bride	664,250	117,805	43,257	48,048
Groom	672,930	114,577	39,930	46,282

[a] Based on reports from 33 states.

SOURCE: U.S. Bureau of The Census, *Statistical Abstracts of the United States:* 1963, Washington, D.C.

It is logical to raise the question: How successful are remarriages of divorcees? Following Bergler and his "Divorce Won't Help" concept it would be expected that many inadequate personalities would simply show up again. Some do, and the divorce prone repeaters who appear in many a case history are no small category with which to reckon. On the other hand, in two studies of remarriage, adjustment for the parties concerned was reported to be much higher than common sense logic would have predicted.

The problem of judging the success in remarriage is a complicated one. In terms of studies which have been made results differ depending on whether the criterion used to measure success was divorce rate or marital adjustment. Monahan, focusing on divorce among reweds, has demonstrated rather conclusively that the chances of remarriages ending in divorce are greater than for first marriages.[21] On the other hand, both Goode [22] and Bernard [23] report that over 80 percent of the couples in their samples had second marriages which were satisfactory or better. Yet how can second marriages be both highly vulnerable to divorce statistically speaking and at the same time successful as a whole? Bernard suggests that remarriage acts as a highly selective force. Agreeing in part with psychiatrists she grants that the divorced group includes many people who are inadequate in personality. Remarriage selects the superior groups along with some who will be prone to second (and perhaps more) divorces. After the unstable categories drop out once more, a group of remarried people is left whose marriages are almost as successful as those who were never divorced.

Bernard points out that certain factors seem to be highly correlated with success in remarriage. Among them are class, education, attitudes

[21] Thomas Monahan, "How Stable are Remarriages?" *American Journal of Sociology,* Vol. 58 (November, 1952), pp. 280–288.

[22] Goode, *op. cit.,* Chapter 22.

[23] Jessie Bernard, *Remarriage* (New York, Holt, Rinehart and Winston, 1956), Chapter 4.

toward first marriage and spouse, and personality factors such as adaptability, resiliency, and will to succeed. In general, middle-class persons are more successful in remarriage than those of the lower class. Especially important is the "will to succeed" in the second marriage. Those with such a drive and those who have the maturity and adaptability are most inclined to be successful the second time around.[24]

On the basis of his studies Locke found that divorced women who have remarried reported adjustment which is about as good as women remaining in their first marriages.[25] Men who enter second marriages tend to be less well adjusted than their colleagues who have never been divorced, however.

A recent study by Earle found remarriages by divorced persons to be less successful than first marriages.[26] This is one of the few studies using marital adjustment as a criterion rather than divorce which suggests poorer adjustment for rewed couples.

Clearly more careful research is called for in this whole area. This will involve the use of matched groups and careful control of a number of variables, an imposing task indeed.

DIVORCE AND THE CHILDREN

Years ago it could be said that divorce often did not involve children. Statistically this was reasonably correct. As late as 1940 only 36 percent of the marriages ending in divorce involved children. Today the picture has changed considerably. Over one half of the divorces now involve children under eighteen years of age. As a matter of fact the number of children affected by divorce has risen sharply in the last two decades as can be seen in Table 47. From a rate of 36 percent in 1940 the rise in the proportion of decrees involving children has been sharp, reaching a height of 55 percent in 1958. The chances are that a levelling off will take place, at a relatively high point. In raw numbers the figures on the number of children and youth whose parents were once divorced is staggering. For the decade 1960 to 1970 somewhere in the neighborhood of 400,000 children per year will be affected by divorce or annulment.[27] Adding these children to those from

---

[24] *Ibid.,* Chapter 4.

[25] Harvey Locke and William Klausner, "Marital Adjustment of Divorced Persons in Subsequent Marriages," *Sociology and Social Research,* Vol. 33 (November–December, 1948), pp. 97–101.

[26] John Earle, *Parental Conflict in First Marriages and Remarriages as Reported by a Sample of Adolescents,* M.A. Thesis, University of North Carolina, 1961.

[27] Textbook writers are inclined to underestimate the number of children annually involved in divorce proceedings. For example, Simpson, *People in Families,* p. 369 states "In any very recent year approximately 300,000 children are affected by divorce." This book was copyrighted in 1960. Actually the report has been over 350,000 for each year since 1956 and the census people continually warn that these

the decade 1950 to 1960 there will be by 1970 a total of roughly seven million children, youth, or young adults in the United States who have felt the impact of divorce. It should be noted that this is a conservative estimate.

TABLE 47

Divorces and Annulments Involving Children, by Selected Years for the United States

Year	Percent of Divorces Involving Children	Average Number of Children per Divorce
1940	36.0	1.89
1950	43.1	1.83
1960	56.7	1.18

SOURCE: National Office of Vital Statistics, Special Reports and "Statistical Abstracts of the United States," U.S. Bureau of the Census, annual; and *Divorces,* Vital Statistics of the United States, Vol. III, 1961, pp. 3–12 to 3–14.

The impact of divorce on children is not easy to measure. Common sense tells us that children living in psychologically disturbed homes will be affected by the experience. Clinical observations and research findings sustain this logic to a degree. The basic question is this: Is a child worse off living with a divorced parent or with the one natural parent and a new parent in a new marriage than he would be if he were to remain in a disorganized home? This is a difficult problem to settle. We do know that children at the time of divorce procedure are often disturbed. As Despert and others have shown, the security of the children is immediately if not basically threatened.[28] Security is built on the predictability of surrounding environmental factors. Having an alcoholic mother regularly in the household, with all her faults, may seem preferable to life with father and a housekeeper (or a new mother) or life in the home of a relative or in a children's home. The folk saying to the effect that "we can handle devils that we know" is not inappropriate here.

The use of children as pawns in a marital cross fire is a potential corollary of the divorce process. It is doubtful that anyone who has observed custody battles would believe that the effect can be positive for the child. Astonishing occurrences are not unknown within the courtroom situation itself. In one case a four-year-old boy's parents had obtained a divorce and the paternal grandmother was able to obtain temporary control of the child. (She disapproved strongly of her new daughter-in-law.) The father obtained a hearing in order to regain custody of his son. In the words of the writer the following took place:

---

figures are probably underreported. As things now stand, there are probably more children involved in divorce in a given year than there are divorces.

[28] J. Louise Despert, *Children of Divorce* (New York, Doubleday, 1953), pp. 31–33.

At the first hearing the defendant appeared somewhat belligerent, but after strong representations by counsel and judge, she had agreed to produce the boy. At the time of the second hearing, the child was in the courtroom. At one point he was the object of a physical struggle between his father and grandmother. The child's own mother, who now lives in Nevada, also appeared in the courtroom and expressed a willingness to take the boy, as did the second wife of the child's father. Here the court adjourned the hearing and referred the case to the domestic relations investigator, who took the parties into the judge's chambers for interview. Later in the day her recommendation was accepted: legal custody to the father, right of visitation to the mother. The two younger women responded to the threat of the grandmother by working out an amicable agreement with reference to visitation.[29]

One can only conjecture some of the thoughts and feelings this four-year-old must have experienced both in and outside the courtroom. Fortunately custody conflicts involve only a very small proportion of divorce cases.

Especially difficult for the child is the experience of being required to choose between the parents regarding custody. Again, this is not a typical issue. One reaction by a girl in her early teens may be considered fairly typical of the minority:

What was I to do? There I was in the judge's chambers, with him asking me whether I wanted to go with my mother or father. What would you do? I really didn't know what I wanted. I resented, Dad's running around as much as mother did. But I've sometimes wondered, maybe Mom drove him to it. What if the one I go with remarries and I don't like the new step-parent? And what was the one I didn't choose going to think of me once the judge told them what I wanted? And what if the judge went against my wishes? Talk about the devil and the deep, blue sea.[30]

We must be wary of improper causal inferences here. Ordinarily there has been a history of considerable trouble over a period of time before parents finally appear in a courtroom asking that their relationship be severed. To suggest that the obtainment of a divorce decree by the parents is harmful to the child is to magnify only one portion of a causal chain.

Plant [31] and Despert [32] have warned that it may be more harmful to the child to keep him in an "impossible" home situation than to clarify the situation for him. Landis,[33] on the basis of research, suggests that the impact of divorce on the child depends to a great extent on his view of the home previous to the divorce action. If he has been unhappy the divorce may

---

[29] Maxine Virtue, *Family Cases in Court* (Durham, Duke University Press, 1956), pp. 23–24.

[30] It must be made clear that the judge is not required to follow the wishes of a child regarding custody. This is a matter of his discretion.

[31] James Plant, "The Psychiatrist Views Children of Divorced Parents," *Law and Contemporary Problems* (Summer, 1944), pp. 807–818.

[32] Despert, *op. cit.*, pp. 245–250.

[33] Judson Landis, "Trauma of Children When Parents Divorce," *Marriage and Family Living*, Vol. 22 (February, 1960), p. 7.

afford some relief. If on the other hand the divorce is unexpected the experience may come as something of a shock.[34] The same author finds that the degree of trauma depends to a certain extent on the age of the child. The younger the child, the less severe the trauma.

Nye compared the adjustment of children in broken homes to those residing in unhappy but complete homes.[35] In general the adjustment of the children in the broken homes was higher than that of the children in the unhappy, unbroken ones.

The research studies which have been made so far have been of great help in shattering prescientific ideas. Much more work must be done before we can, with confidence, answer many questions which recur.

CONCLUSION

Our discussion of divorce has not enabled us to examine many points which could be covered in a more extended study. Brief attention should be given to proposals for change in divorce practice.

Judge Paul Alexander of Toledo, Ohio was for years a leader in the legal fraternity interested in legal reforms affecting the family. He acted as the head of an Interprofessional Commission on Marriage and Divorce Laws which made a number of policy statements and engaged in several studies. In general, Judge Alexander favored the following program which is more or less espoused by the whole Interprofessional Commission:

1. The traditional concept that divorce is permissible only as relief to the innocent party in a marriage where the spouse has been guilty of a sin should be eliminated.
2. Regular adversary procedure in which a plaintiff sues a defendant, with customary cross-examination, etc. should be abandoned.
3. As a substitute a new concept such as "What are the Best Interests of the John Doe Family?" would be used as a criterion.
4. Therapeutic techniques would be used to diagnose the underlying causal factors involved as against the more superficial grounds.
5. Divorce would be granted only when reconciliation and reintegration of the marriage and family is impossible.
6. An integrated Family Court would be created in each community which

[34] Some persons doubt that a divorce can take place without the children's sensing that something is wrong. The author had a counselee who testified to the contrary, however. The counselee was a student who appeared during her senior year. It seems that her parents had difficulty when she was in the sixth and seventh grades of school. They finally agreed to remain together until the daughter was grown. In February of her senior year in college the petition for divorce was filed. The counselee was very disturbed for a period of about six weeks but achieved her equilibrium by graduation time.

[35] F. Ivan Nye, "Children in Broken and in Unhappy Unbroken Homes," *Marriage and Family Living,* Vol. 19 (November, 1957), pp. 356–361.

would have jurisdiction over marriage, divorce, and matters involving children. This court would administer the therapeutic program.

7. Uniform state laws would be passed to implement the therapeutic approach and minimize migratory action.[36]

In Toledo, Ohio Judge Alexander developed a program in which certain aspects of the therapeutic approach are carried out. The program cannot meet the ideal suggested above because of restrictions in the present law. This family court, along with certain others of a similar nature, stands as an example of the possible approach to divorce which may appear in the future. While certain problems immediately occur, the therapeutic idea is intriguing and deserves further investigation. The whole divorce picture is at this time a muddled one and while individuals disagree violently on remedial action, most are interested in some type of reform. This raises the whole question of planned change in the marriage and family area, which will be the central problem of our final chapter.

SELECTED READINGS

Abramson, Gilbert, "Grounds for Divorce," *Temple Law Quarterly* (Winter, 1959), pp. 219–230.

Alexander, Paul, "The Follies of Divorce: A Therapeutic Approach to the Problem," *American Bar Association Journal,* Vol. 36 (February, 1950), pp. 105–108, 168–172.

Association of American Law Schools, *Selected Essays on Family Law* (Brooklyn, 1950).

Baber, Ray, *Marriage and the Family* (New York, McGraw-Hill, 1953), Chapters 13 and 14.

Bernard, Jessie, *Remarriage: A Study of Marriage* (New York, Holt, Rinehart and Winston, 1956).

Davis, Kingsley, "Statistical Perspective on Marriage and Divorce," *The Annals of the American Academy of Political and Social Science,* Vol. 272 (November, 1950), pp. 9–21.

Despert, Louise, *Children of Divorce* (New York, Doubleday, 1953).

Ehrlich, Stanton, "What is a Divorce Lawyer," *Marriage and Family Living,* Vol. 21 (November, 1959), pp. 361–366.

Elliot, Mabel, "The Scope and Meaning of Divorce," in Howard Becker and Reuben Hill (Eds.), *Family, Marriage, and Parenthood* (Boston, Heath, 1955), pp. 669–707.

Ernest, Morris, and Loth, David, *For Better or For Worse* (New York, Harper & Row, 1952).

Glick, Paul, *American Families* (New York, Wiley, 1957), Chapters 6–8.

[36] Judge Alexander's position has been asserted in a number of published articles and dozens of speeches over the last fifteen years. See for example his "The Follies of Divorce: A Therapeutic Approach to the Problem," *American Bar Association Journal,* Vol. 36 (February, 1950), pp. 105–108, 168–172; see also his Introduction to Virtue, *Family Cases in Court, op. cit.,* pp. ix–xxxvii.

Goldstein, Joseph, and Katz, Jay, *The Family and the Law* (New York, Free Press, 1965).

Goode, William, *After Divorce* (New York, Free Press, 1956).

Goode, William, *World Revolution and Family Patterns* (New York, Free Press, 1963).

Harper, Fowler, *Problems of the Family* (Indianapolis, Bobbs-Merrill, 1952).

Jacobson, Paul, *American Marriage and Divorce* (New York, Holt, Rinehart and Winston, 1959).

"Migratory Divorce," *Law and Contemporary Problems* (June, 1935).

Monahan, Thomas, and Kephart, William, "Desertion and Divorce in Philadelphia," *American Sociological Review,* Vol. 17 (December, 1952), pp. 719–727.

Mudd, Emily H., "The Social Worker's Function in Divorce Proceedings," *Law and Contemporary Problems* (Winter, 1953), pp. 66–71.

Pilpel, Harriet, and Zavin, Theodora, *Your Marriage and the Law* (New York, Holt, Rinehart and Winston, 1952).

Ploscowe, Morris, *The Truth About Divorce* (Hawthorne, 1955).

Redmount, Robert, "Perception and Strategy in Divorce Counseling," *Connecticut Bar Journal Law Review* (September, 1960), pp. 249–269.

Rheinstein, M., "Our Dual Law of Divorce: The Law in Action Versus the Law of the Books," University of Chicago Law School, Conference Series No. 9, *Divorce,* 1952.

Steigman, Joseph, "The Deserted Family," *Social Casework,* Vol. 38 (April, 1957), pp. 1–4.

Vernier, Chester, *American Family Law* (Stanford, Stanford University Press, 1932), Vol. II.

Waller, Willard, and Hill, Reuben, *The Family* (New York, Holt, Rinehart and Winston, 1951), Chapters 23–24.

Waller, Willard, *The Old Love and the New* (New York, Liveright, 1930).

Zukerman, Jacob, "A Sociological Approach to Family Desertion," *Marriage and Family Living,* Vol. 12 (August, 1950), pp. 83–85.

QUESTIONS AND EXERCISES

1. Have an anthropologist speak to your class regarding divorces in preliterate societies.
2. Arrange a group project in which divorce trends in a local community will be studied. Compare the results with national statistics on a number of points.
3. Write a paper on children and divorce. Include case histories for illustrative purposes, if possible.
4. What is your general attitude toward divorce? Do you believe that divorced persons should be allowed to remarry? Discuss.
5. Write a paper discussing the strengths and weaknesses of present legal codes regarding divorce.
6. Set up a panel discussion which includes a minister who is known to be

liberal on matters relating to divorce and one who is considered to be conservative. Have each assert his general position and then ask each to allow questions from the audience.

7. Write a paper delineating carefully the essential legal basis for divorce in your state. Include both specific details and the general structure.

8. It has been suggested that basic incompatibility should be allowed as a ground for divorce. What advantages and what disadvantages can you see accruing if this were done in each of our states?

9. Arrange to have a judge from a court of domestic relations speak to your class on divorce as he sees it.

10. If possible, write case histories for a divorced couple. Include predivorce and postdivorce adjustment, legal grounds used, and the disposition of the children if there are any.

11. Write a paper analyzing the relationship between social class or occupational status and divorce.

12. Write a paper on migratory divorce in the United States. Include in summary form the major cases which have been involved in establishing precedents.

27

Programs for Improving Marriage and Family Life

The American family system is dynamic and we have recorded some of the changes which have taken place. Mate selection, husband-wife relationships, and parent-child interaction all have undergone change within the last two generations and they are still in flux. In spite of the trend toward conservatism in most institutional patterns, new methods of meeting problems are being used experimentally by individuals and families in our society.

People of all persuasions are dissatisfied with certain facets of the family system. Some would overhaul the system of mate selection, hoping that by a preventative approach marital problems would be lessened. Many point to outside forces with the suggestion that reforms in our economic and political system, or in such areas as housing would greatly strengthen family life. And as we saw in Chapter 3, certain theorists along with many institutional leaders feel that drastic changes in our whole family system are needed, if we are to escape continuous disorganization.

It seems desirable, then, in this final chapter, to analyze some of the proposed programs for family reform and reorganization which have been suggested and/or tried to a limited degree. In order to do this it may at times be necessary to express a preference for some value position. This the social scientist is hesitant to do. It is not within his role to tell society what it should do. He can, however, within the general framework of values and organization of a given society analyze systems, point out discrepancies and discontinuities as he sees them, and consider possible solutions to problems.

THE PROBLEM OF CONFLICTING VALUES

It is impossible to raise questions about the health of a family system and where it is heading without focusing on the total social system. How

577

strong is it? What are some persistent problems? We do not propose to attempt a full answer to such questions, but a few considerations may be raised. First, this is a heterogeneous, dynamic country, whatever else may be said for it. Old patterns are being challenged and new proposals are constantly being presented. American society is becoming increasingly urbanized and industrialized. Perennial cold war seems to be the order of our day, at least for the immediate future. Persistent problems appear in the realms of education, housing, full employment, as well as in certain other areas.

Clarification is needed regarding basic goals and the implementation of them. This should precede family reform. Once this is done, delineation of goals in the family area and means to implement them will be in order.

Problems appear both at the level of goals (or ends) and at the level of means (or procedures) to attain them. In a rapidly changing country there will probably always be a basic conflict between traditionalists and modernists. In general, argument at the abstract level centers on questions of freedom versus order, with traditionalists stressing the latter goal and modernists the former one. However, one should be wary of this categorization. A person might be conservative regarding divorce but oppose a national divorce law because he distrusts Washington, D.C. Some groups are wary of state control but propose rigid ecclesiastical control. Others are essentially the opposite. This diversity of viewpoint creates both theoretical and practical difficulties regarding proposed reform. However, in any large-scale society legal sanctions, educational programs, economic practices, political patterns, and even religious practices represent a compromise toward a working equilibrium. Perhaps this will always be so.

In spite of value conflicts and diversity of viewpoint a number of actions have been taken to improve marriage and family life in America. Some attention to these programs may be in order, after which consideration can be given to problems at the more general level.

THE MOVEMENT TOWARD REORGANIZATION

Marriage Counseling

One of the major approaches toward family efficiency is marriage and family counseling, discussed in Chapter 25. Informal counseling on marriage and family problems has been given by outsiders down through the years as long as there has been a family in existence. Neighbors, friends, and eventually ministers, lawyers, physicians, and other professionals offered advice. Even though the advice was sometimes given by professionally trained persons, we still think of this as nonprofessional or informal counseling because people were not trained to give family help.

More professional counseling has resulted from three sources: (1)

advances in the basic social and psychological sciences, (2) changes in orientation of social work and similar professions, and (3) an acknowledgement of need on the part of the public.

Skidmore *et al.* have suggested the term "marriage consulting" as an inclusive term to cover a broad range of counseling facilities.[1] The following might be included in this broad category:

I. Informal Marriage and Family Consultation
   A. Clergymen
   B. Lawyers
   C. Medical Practitioners
   D. Educators (Sociologists, Home Economists, Psychologists, Guidance Counselors, etc.)
II. Formal Marriage and Family Counseling
   A. Marriage Counseling
      1. Marriage Counseling Centers
      2. Private Marriage Counselors
      3. Family Court Marriage Counseling
   B. Social Work
      1. Private Family Agencies
      2. Public Welfare Agencies
III. Formal Counseling under Mental Health Auspices
   A. Mental Health or Guidance Centers
   B. Private Psychiatric Counseling
   C. Private Clinical Psychology

The use of the term "informal" is not meant to indicate unimportance. Instead it is a matter of primacy of the activity. Along with his other work the minister, lawyer, physician, or social scientist-educator may offer counsel regarding marriage and family. Many ministers now engage in a few sessions of counseling with engaged couples prior to marriage. Lawyers focus on matters pertaining to divorce and to problems with legal implications. Medical men consult on birth control, hereditary factors, and health problems pertaining to marriage. Family life educators often counsel along with their teaching in colleges and universities.

A number of problems arise in relation to informal counseling. Especially prominent are questions of training and referral. Marriage counseling requires careful training and experience. Competency in religion, theology, law, general medicine, or academic social science does not per se provide a man with the necessary background for marriage and family counseling. Too many well-meaning professional persons move freely into the marriage and family realm without hesitation. Cases which should be referred to other professionals are often not referred. However, in spite of this, informal marriage and family counseling forms the bulk of counseling done. Its

[1] Rex Skidmore, Hulda V. S. Garrett, and C. Jay Skidmore, *Marriage Consulting* (New York, Harper & Row, 1956).

value is presently great and it can become greater. In order for it to be improved, better methods of training will have to be provided and greater understanding of the referral process developed.[2]

Formal marriage counseling is still in its childhood. The major centers were all started within the last thirty years, and the essentials of modern procedure represent postwar developments. The American Association of Marriage Counselors was formed in 1942. This organization has attempted to set up standards for training and competency, and to serve as a general coordinating body. In 1948 a joint committee with representatives from this organization and the National Council on Family Relations issued a report on standards for acceptable and recognized training of adequate marriage counselors.

Marriage counseling is here regarded as a specialized field of family counseling which centers largely on the interpersonal relationship between husband and wife. It involves many disciplines and is interprofessional in character. Those who wish to enter this field, however, whether physicians, clergymen, psychiatrists, or social workers, must have a common body of scientific knowledge, techniques, and qualifications.

Standards for acceptable and recognized marriage counselors are herewith presented in terms of:

1. Academic training
2. Professional experience and qualifications
3. Personal qualifications

I. Academic Training
   A. Every marriage counselor shall have a graduate or professional degree from an approved institution as a minimum qualification. This degree shall be in one of the following fields:

Education	Psychology
Home Economics	Religion
Law	Social Anthropology
Medicine	Social Work
Nursing	Sociology

   B. Whatever the field of major emphasis, there shall be included accredited training in:
      Psychology of personality development
      Elements of psychiatry
      Human biology, including the fundamentals of sex anatomy, physiology, and genetics

---

[2] The British system of marriage counseling is quite different from our own; in that country greater stress is put on personality and aptitude than on formal background preceding counseling training. A screening committee interviews applicants, ordinarily married adults, who are then accepted or rejected. Those accepted are then given an intensive training which includes both course material and actual counseling under supervision. Our source for this information was the lecture by Mr. Joseph Brayshaw, of the National Marriage Guidance Council of Great Britain, which was given at the 1962 Groves Conference on Marriage and Family held in Baltimore, Maryland.

        Sociology of marriage and the family
        Counseling techniques

II. Professional Experience and Qualifications

  A. The candidate shall have had at least three years of recognized professional experience subsequent to obtaining his degree. In addition, he shall have had actual experience as a clinical assistant in marriage counseling under approved supervision.

  B. A candidate's qualifications shall include:

    1. Diagnostic skill in differentiating between the superficial and the deeper-level types of maladjustment, and the ability to recognize when the latter type requires referral to other specialists.

    2. A scientific attitude toward individual variation and deviation, especially in the field of human sex behavior, and the ability to discuss sexual problems objectively.

III. Personal Qualifications

  A. The candidate shall possess personal and professional integrity in accordance with accepted ethical standards.

  B. The candidate shall have an attitude of interest, warmth, and integration toward people, combined with a high degree of integration and emotional maturity.[3]

At present there are several hundred members of the American Association of Marriage Counselors in the various grade levels.

Fellow—a person who has had a minimum of five years in good standing as a member of the Association, and has in addition made a significant contribution to the field of marriage counseling.

Member—a person who has had recognized professional training and at least five years' experience in clinical marriage counseling, in accordance with acceptable ethical standards.

Associate—a person who has had recognized professional training and at least two years' experience in clinical marriage counseling, in accordance with acceptable ethical standards.

Affiliate—a professional person who, though not a clinical member of the Association, is judged to have made a significant contribution to the field of marriage, the family, or marriage counseling.

Associate in Training—a person who has met the necessary academic and professional requirements, and is, or has been within the past five years, under training in an approved clinical internship program in marriage counseling.[4]

Most regular members of the Association meet the above standards to a reasonable degree. Only a minority make their living by full-time mar-

[3] Based on the report entitled "Marriage Counseling," *Marriage and Family Living,* Vol. 11 (Winter, 1949), pp. 5–6, as slightly abridged by Skidmore, *et al., op. cit.,* pp. 190–192.

[4] Taken from the *Directory, American Association of Marriage Counselors, Inc.* (February, 1962).

riage counseling. Most of those who do practice in marriage counseling centers or in the family court agencies rather than in private practice.

Besides the nonsocial work group of marriage counselors, there is the social work professional body, many of whom are engaged in formal counseling dealing with marriage and the family. Certain private agencies have almost exclusively a family focus. These are organized under the Family Service Association. Between 250 and 300 local agencies operate in affiliation with this organization. Their counselors are trained in social casework. Besides this group there is the whole body of public welfare agencies. Most of our more than 3,000 counties in the United States have a public welfare department in which a variety of family problems are handled. The majority of the workers are not professionally trained, although there is an increasing disposition to hire those with social work training. Actually these agencies handle more problem cases by far than any of the other agencies or groups, although there is disagreement as to whether this should be called professional counseling if the individuals involved lack formal training.[5]

"Mental health" practice includes some emphasis on marriage and family problems. Focusing primarily on individual clients, counselors in mental health centers work with a wide range of problem cases. One special emphasis in some of the clinics is "child guidance." This often amounts to a team approach in which various family members are brought into the picture. Whether a team approach or an individual one is used in a center, or whether private counseling is done with individual clients, this approach is considered psychotherapy rather than marriage or family counseling.

Marriage counseling is defined as the process through which a professionally trained counselor assists two persons (the engaged or married partners) to develop abilities in resolving, to some workable degree, the problems that trouble them in their interpersonal relationships as they move into marriage, live with it, or (in a small number of instances) move out of it. The focus of the counselor's approach is the relationship between the two people in the marriage rather than, as in psychiatric therapy, the reorganization of the personality structure of the individual.[6]

Stroup and Glasser have attempted to delineate the orientation and focus of marriage counseling relative to the psychological and psychiatric professional emphasis in the following manner: [7]

[5] For a description of the development of the casework approach to marriage counseling see Frances Beatman, "Evolution of Treatment Methods in Casework Treatment of Marital Problems," in Victor Eisenstein (Ed.), *Neurotic Interaction in Marriage* (New York, Basic Books, 1956), p. 263.

[6] Emily H. Mudd, "Psychiatry and Marital Problems: Mental Health Implications," *Eugenics Quarterly* (June, 1955), p. 111.

[7] Atlee L. Stroup and Paul Glasser, "The Orientation and Focus of Marriage Counseling," *Marriage and Family Living,* Vol. 21 (February, 1959), p. 24.

TABLE 48

The Helping Professions in Relation to Each Other and Certain Specified Variables

Marriage Counselor	Family Caseworker	Clinical Psychologist	Psychiatrist	Medical or Lay Analyst
		Theoretical Framework		
A. Sociologically oriented 　1. Emphasis upon behavior or the problem 　2. Emphasis upon the situation 　3. Tends towards more inclusive levels		←————————→		A. Psychologically oriented 　1. Emphasis upon the individual, the behaver 　2. Emphasis on learning 　3. Tends towards less inclusive levels
B. Person in interaction; role relationships		←————————→		B. Individual personality and its functioning
		Content and Focus of Interview		
A. Marriage problems		←————————→		A. Personal problems
B. Educational resource, support, and clarification on the conscious level		←————————→		B. Depth therapy, often bringing unconscious material to the surface
C. Short-term contact		←————————→		C. Long-term contact
		Clients		
A. At least two in relation to one another		←————————→		A. Almost always one
B. Normal and neurotic		←————————→		B. Deeply neurotic and psychotic
C. Premarital and marital stages of development		←————————→		C. All stages of development
		Setting		
A. Any setting, after field has developed and public safeguards taken		←————————→		A. Any setting, with individual variations depending on field
		Major Goals		
A. Solution of marital or premarital problem		←————————→		A. Personality reorganization

SOURCE: Atlee L. Stroup and Paul Glasser, "The Orientation and Focus of Marriage Counseling," *Marriage and Family Living,* Vol. 21 (February, 1959), p. 24.

This approach has been criticized. Stokes makes the following comments:

My criticism concerns the proposition that marriage counseling should, because it is a relationship between two people, be approached from a predominantly sociological orientation. All my clinical experience leads me to reject this. I should prefer to state the matter thus: marriage counseling is a form of individual psychotherapy in which there is a special concern with the ways in which marriage partners interact with each other. It is inconceivable to me that I should counsel a marriage. I counsel the spouses as persons and help them evaluate their interactions with each other. This may lead to improvement in the marriage or to awareness of insurmountable incompatibilities and dissolution of the marriage. I have small concern with the preservation of the marriage as such. My primary focus is upon the dignity and satisfactions of the individual spouses and only secondarily upon the sociological values associated with the marriage. I cannot conceive of accomplishing enduringly successful marriage counseling upon any other terms.[8]

Ellis also has strongly suggested that most marriage counseling cases involve neurotic individuals and therefore some type of psychotherapy is needed with these cases.[9]

Probably in the immediate future the relationship between marriage counseling and mental health counseling will be somewhat confused. One can make a case for the proposition that marriage counseling is an important aspect of the family life movement, whereas guidance centers represent a major outcome of the mental health movement. The two are parallel and often overlap, but are not one and the same.

The Future

Marriage counseling is surely here to stay. How fast and in what direction it will develop is difficult to predict. A number of issues will remain in the immediate future. Among them are the following, some of which have been referred to previously:

1. Is marriage counseling psychotherapy?
2. Should marriage counseling involve a short-term, problem-focused approach, or should it have the basic goal of personality reorganization?
3. Should preventative marriage counseling be done as preventative medicine is handled by a physician?
4. What training should be required for persons who wish to engage in marriage counseling?
5. What should be the essential focus of marriage counseling?
6. How "directive" should the counselor be with the client?
7. Should both spouses be carried by the same counselor?
8. Should marriage counseling emerge as a separate profession?

[8] Walter Stokes' critique of Stroup and Glasser, *ibid.*, pp. 25–26.

[9] Skidmore, *et al., op. cit.,* footnote a number of references to controversies in the field of marriage counseling. Many of them are to be found in issues of *Marriage and Family Living* (Now called *Journal of Marriage and the Family*).

9. What is the ideal relationship of the counselor to social goals? How much stress should be put on the "saving" of a marriage?
10. Is marriage counseling primarily an art, or is it a science?
11. Should marriage counselors be licensed? If so, how rigid should the requirements be?

Family Life Education

Educational programs form a central portion of the family life movement. The more traditional approaches are a few generations old, but the more functional approach represents developments since World War I.

Within departments of sociology and anthropology in American colleges and universities courses on the family have been basic since the turn of the century. To a degree these courses have reflected the spirit of the times. If welfare and reform were a primary concern in these departments, courses would be focused on problems of family welfare. When interest in social origins was strong, considerable time was spent discussing the possible origin of the human family. As the modern scientific method emerged as an emphasis in social science, family study involved references to methodology in family sociology and findings of pertinence to students. In spite of these differences in orientation, courses known by the title "The Family" have been more or less institutional in character.

So-called functional courses eventually appeared. In many cases this reflected student demand. This was the case when the late Professor Groves introduced the first functional courses at Boston University and at the University of North Carolina. Implications for personal decision-making were the primary concern. *How* rather than *why* questions were often in the minds of students. How does one select a mate? How can a person tell when he is in love? What are the prerequisites for successful marriage? What is the best method of discipline to use with children? These and dozens of questions of a similar nature motivate students to seek out courses on marriage and family life.

The distinction between the institutional and the functional course is far from clear, however. Much depends upon the orientation and interest of the instructor. To be truly functional a course must have solid content. This means that often the teacher must lead the students away from the short-run immediate concerns to issues which are more fundamental and sometimes more abstract. How far students can be moved depends to a great degree on the type of students and the ingenuity of the teacher.

Not to be overlooked is the contribution of disciplines other than sociology. Home economics departments have for years offered a number of courses which bear on the family in one way or another. Besides the traditional concerns with clothing, textiles, nutrition, home management, and the like, courses in child development and family relationships have become prominent in the last twenty years or so. While the former have usually been elected by girls, the latter courses have a wider appeal and include some males on many campuses.

It appears that courses in marriage and the family are slowly enrolling a greater proportion of the student body. In a 1948–1949 study Bowman reported that out of some 1270 schools reporting, one half were making marriage and family courses available to the students.[10] At that time he estimated that 50,000 college students were enrolled in these courses. A study by Landis a decade later showed that about 80 percent of the colleges and universities reporting had offerings available for students.[11] Landis believes that most of our colleges and universities have or will have eventually some type of marriage and family offering in the curriculum. He believes that the total number of students taking such courses would run well over 100,000 as of 1959.

Some have voiced criticism of marriage and family courses for the college level, charging that they replace the more traditional subjects. The charge is probably true to a degree; a student's program has only a limited number of hours. The courses seem, however, to be here to stay. If taught properly, marriage and family studies can certainly raise questions which are important, if not profound. It is significant that Roman Catholic colleges and many Protestant denominational colleges are giving increasing attention to such courses, along with secular institutions. The former are no doubt more motivated by problems of family conservation. Nevertheless when denominational and secular schools can have a high degree of agreement on course content in an area where values are involved there would appear to be some fundamental rapport.

The Public Schools.   Colleges still cater to a limited portion of the population. For this reason some educators are advocating the addition of marriage and family courses in high school.[12] A number of problems are involved. First of all, the social sciences have not been as adequately handled at the high school level as have the natural sciences or the humanities. They have been unsystematically presented and have also been considered avenues for the indoctrination of the values prevailing in the more powerful segments of the community. Unfortunately, family life education at this level has meant only sex education to some. Consequently, if offered in the social studies division it has been assumed that indoctrination would be involved. Those opposed to birth control have had obvious fears. Those more liberal on such matters have worried lest their children be subjected

---

[10] Henry Bowman, "Collegiate Education for Marriage and Family Living," *The Annals of the American Academy of Political and Social Science,* Vol. 272 (November, 1950), pp. 148–155.

[11] Judson Landis, "The Teaching of Marriage and Family Courses in Colleges," *Marriage and Family Living,* Vol. 21 (February, 1959), pp. 26–40.

[12] See *Conference Proceedings, Golden Anniversary White House Conference on Children and Youth, Inc.* (1960), p. 213.

to values other than those prevailing in the home. When opposing forces are at odds school boards may simply ignore the subject.

A second problem is the crowded condition of the curriculum. The addition of the modern sciences to the traditional core of courses has meant that subjects without a strong group to back them have little chance of inclusion in the tight schedule. With college entrance becoming a grave concern to many, courses not required by the colleges will not have strong demand. Further in the immediate post-Sputnik era the trend was to stress whatever courses Soviet Russia happened to be emphasizing. Since the Soviets have not had an interest in bolstering the traditional family system it was hardly to be expected that they would have family life education in the public school curriculum. Providing trained teachers for the high school family life program would be a major task were this field to be developed fully. All would agree that capable teachers are presently in very short supply.

In spite of all the difficulties involved, many high schools have had family life content somewhere in the curriculum. This has often meant only a unit in a social studies, biology, or physical education course. For certain groups of girls, home economics programs have provided training. The idea that such education is for females only has not been a fortunate outcome. Certain schools, however, have outstanding programs: Tulsa, Oklahoma; Highland Park, Michigan; Wichita, Kansas; and Toms River, New Jersey. Most schools have not emphasized such courses.

Actually, one could make a strong case for the proposition that functional family life education should start in the lower school. The majority of young people will marry without the benefits of a college degree for some time to come. Sex pressures are great on teen-agers today. Calm, thoughtful presentation of technically reliable family materials should be of potential benefit. Many students will not receive them in the home or elsewhere. Family life education could be considered a preventative measure regarding future problems. Work at the premarital level might reduce the incidence and severity of problems which otherwise would come later.

The healthiest motive is probably positive rather than negative, however. If we wish to have strong families we ought to give at least minimum attention to family life in the public schools.[13] Parochial leaders are also beginning to recognize this. Roman Catholic, if not other parochial high schools, can be expected to put considerable stress on family life education in the future. Naturally it is easier for a subgroup, with a definitive ideology, to reach a higher degree of agreement on how to implement its basic goals than would be true of the more heterogeneous general community.

In spite of what this will involve financially and otherwise, realism

---

[13] See Gerald Leslie, "Personal Values, Professional Ideologies, and Family Specialists," *Marriage and Family Living,* Vol. 21 (February, 1959), p. 3, for a strong defense of marriage and family life education in the high school.

suggests that some training for marriage and family life should be carried on outside the home, probably in the schools.

Almost anyone may marry, may establish at least what passes for a home and becomes his castle even though he hates to live in it, and may, if he is biologically able, have children. Blindly, stupidly, or naively we assume that this "anyone" is prepared for these profound undertakings. How does he become prepared? Does he become prepared by reaching a certain age? By fulfilling the meager requirements of the law? By being subjected to a curriculum that includes little or nothing contributory to marriage and family life? By living in his own family, adequate or inadequate?

It is commonplace in discussing the family to mention its changing functions, to point out the shift from institutional functions to personality functions, and to say that some of the functions have been taken over by outside agencies. Does this suggest that others of the functions, therefore, must be taken over by outside agencies? Has the laboratory been stripped of part of its equipment? If the family no longer does what it used to do, may we still assume that it can educate its members for family life? To some extent, of course, it does and probably always will. But must we not conclude that this intrafamily education must be supplemented by that supplied by outside agencies? [14]

Legal Reform

Formal law has many implications for family life. Two major areas of reform can be distinguished. The first involves possible changes in the basic statutes. The second involves possible changes in procedures in the courts in relation to marriage and family problems. The two are, of course, not unrelated.

Marriage, Family, and Divorce Legislation.   One problem is the lack of uniformity in divorce laws. Why should a divorce be granted for a certain ground in one state and denied in another? Is it realistic to assume that couples in New York have more problems which lead to adultery than those of other states? These and other questions are raised regarding the desirability of retaining the great disparities which exist in this country regarding the legal groundwork for marriage and family life.

What about a Uniform Divorce Law? Agitation for this started back at the turn of the century. The American Bar Association, with the backing of President Theodore Roosevelt, organized a conference in 1906 to which most of the states sent representatives. A uniform model set was drawn up, after much discussion, to be presented to the various states. The delegates went back to their respective states and duly reported on the proceedings. Little has been heard regarding them since.

[14] Henry Bowman, "Education for Marriage and Family Life," *Marriage and Family Living,* Vol. 8 (Summer, 1946), pp. 63–64.

A decade or so ago persons considered to be liberal on marriage and divorce matters were reportedly much in favor of working toward uniformity of divorce law, either through the adoption of a suggested model by the various states or by a federal law which would require a constitutional amendment. Now the liberal groups are uneasy about such proposals. It is felt that a uniform law under present circumstances would represent an uneasy compromise, with the possibility being strong that the grounds for divorce in many states would be further restricted than they presently are.

Conservative groups (as far as the divorce issue is concerned) have also been uneasy about proposed legislation, fearing that the laws would become too liberal and that divorce would be made "too easy" to obtain. The practical consequence of this split has meant that little change has been proposed on the floors of most state legislatures for some time.[15]

Many persons in positions of leadership in this country fall into the middle range on marriage and divorce matters. They do not wish to promote divorce unduly, but they are concerned regarding the state of confusion which presently exists. They worry about the spread of disrespect for the law which may develop in situations where it is clear that hypocrisy is being practiced by those of high estate right down to those of the lowest levels of society. Numerous groups have passed resolutions suggesting that "something should be done" about the American divorce situation, but action tends to stop at that level.[16]

Again we must come back to the problem of freedom versus order. How much freedom should an unhappy couple have to seek relief? If they are denied relief, is general community stability necessarily enhanced? Similar questions can be raised ad infinitum. Given our heritage of freedom and heterogeneity, it is inevitable that divorce problems will be with us for some time to come.

Court and Legal Procedure.   Closely allied to the question of divorce law is the matter of procedures in divorce and related cases as handled by the courts. As was indicated in Chapter 26, men such as Judge Alexander have implemented the concept of family court. This type of court is modeled on the juvenile court in that broad discretionary powers are granted to the judge, adversary procedures are not allowed, and so on.[17]

Presently a small number of courts are operating along the lines of family courts. Included would be courts in San Francisco, Chicago, Indian-

[15] Judge Paul Alexander believes that it is useless to talk about legal reform unless it is granted that uniform standards will eventually emerge. See his introduction to Maxine Virtue, *Family Cases in Court* (Durham, Duke University Press, 1956).

[16] See *Conference Proceedings, Golden Anniversary White House Conference on Children and Youth, Inc.,* p. 362.

[17] See Paul Alexander, "What Is a Family Court, Anyway?" *Connecticut Bar Journal* (September, 1952), p. 270.

apolis, Milwaukee, Cincinnati, Toledo, Ann Arbor, and Detroit.[18] Cincinnati was one of the pioneers in this movement, starting the essentials of a family court organization at the beginning of World War I. The Toledo program is perhaps the best known. Proponents of the family court plan in Ohio have an advantage in that the legal underpinnings for such a court are stronger than in most states.

Actually, the family court ideal is still essentially little more than that. As Judge Alexander and others have pointed out on numerous occasions, our laws and procedures must be basically changed if we are to institutionalize a new court plan with a solid foundation. Among other things, this will mean that the judge represents the state as a third party with an interest in the general welfare of all families in trouble, at least of those which come to official attention. Nothing is to be decided under such a system until the case has been thoroughly investigated and until it is clear that reconciliation is impossible. Divorce petitions would not be heard until counseling had taken place.

Many problems arise at this point. How could we raise the money to support the investigating and counseling staffs needed to carry such a program? Does this mean that nonlegal personnel have too much authority in the courts? Is forced counseling legal? These and other questions are raised.[19] The problem of finances and support of personnel could be solved if communities really wished to use a therapeutic approach to divorce. Fundamental is the question of values and prerogatives. Presently divorce is essentially a suit of civil law. The problem boils down to this: How much of a right does an individual have to redress if he is in an unhappy marriage? Our present laws have as their basis relief to an innocent party. Would this individual right be violated if judges had broader discretionary powers? It is significant that certain men such as Tappan, trained in both law and sociology, have raised questions about the absence of adversary procedure even in the juvenile court.[20] Further, many lawyers feel that it is unfair to expect them to act as counselors of reconciliation. Their training instead has been in the direction of representation of the role of their individual client to his best advantage.

It is most difficult to assess the potentialities of the family court idea objectively. As Kephart points out, it represents basically a large-scale plan of sociolegal engineering.[21] If not done well and without vigorous and wholehearted backing such programs almost inevitably fail. Given the hand-

---

[18] See Virtue, *op. cit.*

[19] See *ibid.,* pp. 16–18 for a reference to a California court in which the judge expresses considerable disapproval of the use of investigators and consultants without a legal background.

[20] See Paul Tappan, *Juvenile Delinquency* (New York, McGraw-Hill, 1949), pp. 209–215. Many persons with a legal background argue in similar fashion against a family court. It is held that *individual* rights are violated if the court is given broad discretionary power based on concepts of general welfare.

[21] William Kephart, *The Family, Society, and the Individual* (Boston, Houghton Mifflin, 1961), Chapter 23.

icaps under which they presently operate, the family courts seem reasonably successful. Many counselors oppose the concept of counseling in a punitive atmosphere.[22] Is it possible to provide adequate counseling facilities in the community to which people may turn prior to divorce? Many members of the legal profession suggest that they would prefer this type of preventative approach to a change in court procedure. If used properly there would be advantages. The divorce court would be the place of last resort, which it should be. Given our present milieu it would appear that there is greater potential in the community approach in counseling than in legal reform which includes formal counseling.

MARRIAGE AND FAMILY RESEARCH

Definitive answers to abstract and practical questions are seldom easy to obtain. This is as true in the marriage and family field as it is in many others. The physical and social sciences have demonstrated, however, that consistent and persistent attention will bring results. If a problem can be attacked scientifically, a concerted onslaught will usually provide further knowledge if not a complete solution to the problem. In the human realm it is clear that some problems will defy solution in the foreseeable future while others have a more favorable prognosis.

A number of critiques of marriage and family research have been made within the last decade.[23] While there is not complete agreement among the critics, a number of points emerge. First, some coordination of marriage and family research activity is greatly needed. There is a tendency for individual researchers to go their own way with their own particular frames of reference. This results in a bevy of studies, the full meaning of which is at times dubious. Related to the lack of coordination are a number of other problems. Small-scale studies are usually made with limited samples. It is at times difficult to decide how widely any generalizations apply.

As Hill and Hansen, among others, have suggested, researchers need to operate from a more definitive theoretical base.[24] At present it is sometimes difficult to evaluate certain research efforts because they are not

---

[22] The whole Rogerian approach to counseling is based on the proposition that the client is free to accept or reject any suggestions made by the counselor. Further, the counselor is not to be punitive or authoritarian in his approach to the client. See Carl Rogers, *Counseling and Psychotherapy* (Boston, Houghton Mifflin, 1942).

[23] See for example Nelson Foote and Leonard Cottrell, *Identity and Interpersonal Competence* (Chicago, The University of Chicago Press, 1955), Chapters 1 and 6; Reuben Hill, "A Critique of Contemporary Marriage and Family Research," *Social Forces,* Vol. 33 (March, 1956), pp. 276–287, and William Kephart, "Some Knowns and Unknowns in Family Research: A Sociological Critique," *Marriage and Family Living,* Vol. 19 (February, 1957), pp. 7–15.

[24] Reuben Hill and Donald Hansen, "The Identification of Conceptual Frameworks Utilized in Family Study," *Marriage and Family Living,* Vol. 22 (November, 1960), p. 307.

related consistently to any given theoretical frame of reference. If there could be greater consistency at this point, research findings would become more meaningful. Further, glaring gaps or problem areas could then receive concerted attacks and breakthroughs might be reasonably expected.

Second, new ground must be broken. Research methodology is becoming more and more refined. This means new types of studies and new emphases. Longitudinal studies where families are followed over time, for example, offer great potential. A focus in which more than just the mother-child or husband-wife relationship is the center of attention is greatly needed. This means in effect a more dynamic research approach. It will be extremely difficult to handle because of the number of variables involved. No small problem is the matter of obtaining full access to homes or to respondents' true feelings and attitudes through the use of other than observational methods. These difficulties should serve as challenges rather than as insurmountable barriers, however.

We come back again to the question of emphasis. Talk is cheap, but research is expensive. Our society has not decided where it wishes to put its stress. "By their research emphasis ye shall know them" might be the modern equivalent of an old saying for a pragmatically oriented society. At present all the marriage and family researchers in the world represent a tiny band, although their number is growing. They need money and more adequate facilities. They also need to be challenged and encouraged to break new ground and to work toward the limits of their capacities.

OVERALL FAMILY POLICY

The foregoing material moves us toward some closing statements regarding marriage and family life in America. Time and again we have stressed that answers to problems cannot be given without reference to values. As a nation we are not sure what things are to be put first. If there could be more agreement on general values we could more easily relate marriage and family to our total schema. At the practical level, we are badly in need of a family policy.

What do we mean by a policy? It should be distinguished from a plan or specific program, which is concerned with more or less specified activities for a determinate time period and usually on an actual or estimated budget. We have innumerable programs, of private and governmental organizations, addressed to the family, but no underlying policy to give the programs much needed direction and articulation.

A policy is formulation of long-term goals and purposes and of the values and aspirations by which those goals and purposes are not only defined but are to be translated into activities and practices. Thus a policy is an affirmation, perhaps a reaffirmation, of what may be taken for granted or is implied, but what is frequently ignored or neglected or inadequately recognized in plans and programs and customary operations. Sometimes a policy serves to point out where these goals and purposes and these values are being blocked or sacrificed to various short-term ends or convenience.

A policy, therefore, might be likened to strategy, the broad, overall, long-term conception which gives direction and purpose to the tactics of immediately daily operations and decisions.[25]

A policy, then, not only indicates values or goals to be achieved but suggests certain means to be used to implement them. We often have individuals and groups working at cross-purposes partly because they agree on neither overall goals nor on implementation procedures.

An enunciated family policy would help clear the air and force many to take a stand on marriage and family matters. To have effect, such a proposal would require an official policy statement from Washington, D.C., with backing by the respective branches of government. It would be without real effect unless the general policy was backed by the churches, educators, welfare officials, medical people, business and labor, and so on.

If such an approach were to be considered seriously this would eventually mean that a ranking post in the government would be devoted to family life. To obtain the strongest impact this would entail cabinet rank, or at least important status in the Department of Health, Education, and Welfare.[26] At the state and community levels appropriate actions would be taken as well. It would be made clear that the officials in these posts would have the duty of assessing the potential impact of proposed legislation and administrative action on family life, either in general or in specific sectors.

As Baber points out, somehow it is always the family that is expected to make adaptations to new formulae and actions. It is supposed to absorb all pressures without being shattered. If such is the assumption why is not more attention given to this important institution? Hill speaks to the point:

This great national resource of recuperative capacities, America's families, has been intermittently and callously ignored and ruthlessly exploited by thoughtless vested interest. National morale depends upon the maintenance of adequate families equipped to provide the love-in-action which sends men back to their jobs morning after morning with some zest for work, and which speeds children on to school prepared to make something of the day's tasks. Our great oil and timber resources are tangible and visible, and the inches of top soil which produce our agricultural products may be dramatized by soil conservationists, but nations and communities are not strong because of their natural resources. They are measured by their effectiveness in using those natural resources in attaining the objectives of the good life. This effectiveness

[25] Lawrence K. Frank, "A National Policy for the Family," *Marriage and Family Living,* Vol. 10 (Winter, 1948), p. 1.

[26] One authority has recommended that a Federal Department of Family Security be formed. See Clifford Adams, "Factors Underlying Family Instability," *Marriage and Family Living,* Vol. 8 (1946), pp. 86–87.

is in turn directly related to the nation's families and their recuperative capacities. Through our families the basic satisfactions for which we toil are achieved and transmuted into good national morale and healthy personalities.[27]

At all levels, from the national down through the local community, the family is generally taken for granted or viewed with indifference. Congress will often appropriate more money than was asked for to a space agency. Family research, it seems, is a bit too expensive. Most people will agree that the opening up of space will be exciting and challenging to man. It may also have a tremendous impact on family life. Would it be unwise to prepare for this impact by some careful research into family dynamics? Many of our families are scarcely out of the horse and buggy age. How can they be projected into the space age with a minimum of strain? Both idealism and realism suggest the giving of serious attention to these and similar questions.

Moving Toward a Policy

One indication that the delineation of a family policy is not completely out of the question is provided by the actions of the 1960 White House Conference on Children and Youth. Called by President Eisenhower, the conference involved over 7,600 delegates from every State and Territory and from some foreign countries. Preceding the conference, some six million persons had engaged themselves in considering possible action which might be taken to meet the needs of children and youth within the general framework of American values and practices.

Out of the conference came a series of resolutions devoted to the family. These resolutions are significant enough to be given detailed consideration toward the development of an American Family Policy with recommendations for implementation.

THE FAMILY

In General

That it be recognized that—

the family as the basic unit of our society has primary responsibility for developing values, freedom, initiative, and self-discipline in children,

the development of the child's potential is vitally affected by the nature and quality of family relationships,

the individuality of each family and each member of the family must be acknowledged and preserved,

each family must ultimately determine solutions to its own problems in the light of its own goals and philosophy within the context of the community's goals and values,

[27] Reuben Hill, *Families Under Stress* (New York, Harper & Row, 1949), p. 356.

the absence of a strong sense of values in the individual, the home, and the community is a primary cause of many social problems that limit opportunities for children and youth; and that we must encourage the use of our resources to achieve long-term satisfactions, to build stability into family life, and to assure our children and youth of their full share of security and opportunities in the best American tradition.

Family Life Education

That it be recognized that—

in our complex society no family can be entirely responsible for its own destiny, and that marriage is a joint career requiring preparation to achieve success,

family life courses, including preparation for marriage and parenthood, be instituted as an integral and major part of public education from elementary school through high school; and that this formal education emphasize the primary importance of family life and particularly the child rearing role of the mother,

religious institutions and other community services, as well as the schools, strengthen their family life education programs, with materials suitable to each age level from the early years and marriage preparation courses at the Junior High level; and that these programs include counseling in personal relations, boy-girl relationships, problems, and the sacred nature of marriage, and methods of nurturing childrens' moral, spiritual, and ethical values,

trained social workers be added to school staffs to provide counseling and guidance to families,

existing facilities for parent education be expanded; and that family agency services include parent education beginning in the prenatal period and emphasized in well-baby clinics,

community planning councils collaborate with the medical profession to establish small discussion groups, to which expectant couples would be referred, preferably by physicians, for intensive study of the physical and psychological aspects of childbirth and child development and parent-child relationships,

schools take the initiative in broadening general educational opportunities for adults to enable them to help children and youth more effectively,

educational institutions and communities provide systematic training, with sound and practical materials, in the developmental changes and problems of early adolescence for all parents and future parents, as well as for physicians, teachers, and others who work with young people.

Counseling Services

That it be recognized that—

public and private marriage and family counseling services—such as those of social agencies, mental health clinics, clergymen, and physicians—be instituted or expanded,

counseling services for the solution of domestic relations problems be available in the courts and that hearings in such cases should be held in chambers.

Community Resources

That it be recognized that—

each community create a body representative of all professions, organizations, and agencies concerned with family life to—

coordinate programs and services

survey family needs

insure adequate education for marriage, parenthood, and family life, including counseling

insure that counseling and guidance are available to all without regard to economic or social status

stimulate professional growth and cooperation

develop a community atmosphere favorable to family life

all community resources for health, welfare, housing, and recreation focus on the family as a unit,

religious and community agencies give increasing emphasis to family recreation and study the role of recreation in developing moral and spiritual values in family life,

schools, religious institutions, youth-serving agencies, and all other community agencies cooperate to create a favorable atmosphere for understanding the dignity and sanctity of the role of sex in human relationships,

central reference services be set up so that families needing help in caring for children may be guided to the appropriate agency.

Problem Families

That it be recognized that—

one community agency be responsible for working with multiproblem families and for bringing to bear on their treatment the resources of churches, schools, employment, and vocational rehabilitation services; protective casework services, courts, mental health services, homemaker, day care and foster care services, home management counseling, premarriage and marriage counseling for early detection of problems; and that the services be expanded,

caseloads in public agencies be substantially reduced, to the point where effective work with problem families is possible,

the high costs involved in the rehabilitation of chronic problem families be recognized and interpreted to the public as an ultimate saving in human values.

Family Size

That it be recognized that—

planning for the size of families is desirable in order to relieve the deprivation of children, and that facilities and programs on a local, public, or private basis be available to married couples, providing medical advice and services for child spacing consistent with the creed and mores of the families being served,

[Minority reports ". . . the proposal would be acceptable if so worded as to be conditioned upon the necessity of first determining that planning the family size is desirable . . . by inserting the word 'when' in the opening phrase, so that it would read: '. . . that when planning . . .'

"Also that facilities and programs for family planning should be outside the province of public bodies and kept within the exclusive province of private agencies, particularly church groups."]

the function of the family is to carry out its responsibilities to children according to the primary obligation of marriage in accord with Divine and natural law; and that, therefore, the size of the family and the age at which people marry are in themselves not the fundamental factors in successful family life.

Family Economic Conditions

That it be recognized that—

the income tax exemption for child dependents be increased to enable families to provide more adequately for their children's total needs,

[Minority reports: ". . . the recommendation to increase the income tax exemption for children is unworthy of this Conference. It represents a narrow view of the total demands on our national budget and offers no assurance that the income thus remaining in the family would be used to the benefit of children and youth."]

a minimum annual wage be established for every worker as a means of strengthening family life,

the possibilities of undergirding family life economically through a system of family allowances be studied,

a program of children's allowances be developed to offset the inverse relationship between income and size of family,

[Minority reports: " . . . a child allowance system would drastically increase the involvement of government in family life with consequent threats to individual and family independence."]

Research

That it be recognized that—

appropriate government and/or voluntary agencies sponsor and conduct research in critical areas of family life; and that foundations, educational institutions, and government and private agencies develop better methods for interpreting, using, and coordinating the findings of completed research and make them readily available to the helping professions,

research be undertaken in the following areas:

the reasons for early marriage

family roles and relationships and their influence on members

the adequacy of one-parent families to rear children from infancy through teens

the effects on children of all ages of a mother working outside the home

multiproblem and hard-to-reach families (early identification, prevalence, causation, treatment)

curriculum consent of family life education
methods of teaching family life education and of training teachers

methods of helping more parents gain valid concepts of family living and child rearing

attitudes, concerns, and values of parents of various ethnic, social, economic, and religious groups—with assistance in research planning by qualified members of the groups studied

effective techniques and stimulating small group discussions of the neighborhood level to promote better relationships between preadolescent children and their parents.[28]

A perusal of these various resolutions will indicate that the goals could only be achieved with great difficulty, if at all. Any concerted attempt to put some of them into effect would arouse considerable controversy. Nevertheless, such a base forms the potential from which a family policy could emerge.

THE OUTLOOK FOR THE FUTURE

The American family is essentially a part of the total society and reflects the basic strengths and weaknesses of that society. It is heavily affected by the *zeitgeist* which prevails at any given period. If the perennial cold war becomes hot, families will be forced to absorb deprivation and

[28] Reprinted from the *Conference Proceedings* prepared for the *Golden Anniversary White House Conference on Children and Youth,* by permission of the National Committee for Children and Youth, copyright holders.

withstand dislocation, which are hard to envisage. In general, barring an outbreak of war, the material outlook is favorable.

Particular problems persist, however. There will be a tendency to apply machine technology to more and more areas. Technological unemployment resulting from automation will continue to be a problem. Machine approaches will sweep whole categories out of the working force overnight from time to time. The long-run effects of automation are presumed to be good. In the short run, many families are going to be hurt. Approaches combining counseling with retraining will be needed on a vast scale if these families are to withstand the setback of unemployment.

A major problem will be that of assimilating into the social structure families whose members lack education and marketable skills. We will have social dynamite on our hands unless some adaptive measures are taken which may have to be drastic. It is significant that about 70 percent of the young people aged eighteen to twenty-four whose mothers receive Aid to Dependent Children assistance do not finish high school.[29] Disorganization will be perpetuated in certain families for generations if we cannot break into the cycle and provide a catalyst to bring on constructive adaptation. These and other problems will require considerable attention if they are to be solved.

We must end on a mildly optimistic note, however. If this has not always been a land of milk and honey, it is a favored land. Great potentials lie in the multitudinous social atoms we call families. As Linton has suggested, if our world leadership somehow brings upon us the *Götterdämmerung* each man will search out his wife and children during the last hours. Barring this, the possibilities for the future, while they can be only dimly seen, are good.

SELECTED READINGS

Baber, Ray, *Marriage and the Family* (New York, McGraw-Hill, 1953).

Bee, Lawrence, *Marriage and Family Relations* (New York, Harper & Row, 1959), Chapter 18.

Bowman, Henry, "The Teacher as Counselor in Marriage Education," *Marriage and Family Living*, Vol. 9 (February, 1947), pp. 1–7.

Crist, John, "The Use of Literature in Marriage Counseling," *Journal of Counseling Psychology*, Vol. 3 (Spring, 1956), pp. 37–43.

Cuber, John F., *Marriage Counseling Practice* (New York, Appleton-Century-Crofts, 1948), Chapters 10–12.

Dyer, Dorothy, "A Comparative Study Relating Marital Happiness to University Courses Helpful in Marital Adjustment," *Marriage and Family Living*, Vol. 21 (August, 1959), pp. 230–234.

[29] This figure may be compared to the figure of about 38 percent of the young people of the same category whose mothers do not receive Aid to Dependent Children payment.

Fairchild, Roy, and Wynn, John Charles, *Families in the Church—A Protestant Survey* (New York, Association Press, 1961).

Foote, Nelson, and Cottrell, Leonard, *Identity and Interpersonal Competence* (Chicago, The University of Chicago Press, 1955), pp. 95–173.

Genné, Elizabeth Steel, and Genné, William Henry (Eds.), *Foundations for Christian Family Policy*, National Council of Churches of Christ in U.S.A., 1961.

Harper, Robert, and Hudson, John, "The Use of Recordings in Marriage Counseling," *Marriage and Family Living*, Vol. 14 (November, 1952), pp. 332–334.

Hill, Reuben, "Plans for Strengthening Family Life," in Howard Becker and Reuben Hill (Eds.), *Family, Marriage, and Parenthood* (Boston, Heath, 1955), Chapter 26.

Hill, Reuben, "A Critique of Contemporary Marriage and Family Research," *Social Forces*, Vol. 34 (March, 1956), pp. 276–287.

Hillman, Christine, "An Advice Column's Challenge for Family-life Education," *Marriage and Family Living*, Vol. 16 (February, 1954), pp. 51–54.

Johnson, Dean, *Marriage Counseling: Theory and Practice* (Englewood Cliffs, N.J., Prentice-Hall, 1961).

Karpf, Maurice, "Some Guiding Principles in Marriage Counseling," *Marriage and Family Living*, Vol. 13 (May, 1951), pp. 49–51.

Kephart, William, *The Family, Society, and the Individual* (Boston, Houghton Mifflin Company, 1961).

Kerckhoff, Richard, "The Profession of Marriage Counseling as Viewed by Members of Four Allied Professions: A Study in the Sociology of Occupations," *Marriage and Family Living*, Vol. 15 (November, 1953), p. 340.

Klemer, Richard, *A Man for Every Woman* (New York, Macmillan, 1959).

Laidlaw, Robert, "The Psychiatrist as Marriage Counselor," *American Journal of Psychiatry* (April, 1950), pp. 732–736.

Landis, Judson, "The Teaching of Marriage and Family Courses in Colleges," *Marriage and Family Living*, Vol. 21 (February, 1959), pp. 36–40.

Leslie, Gerald, "Personal Values, Professional Ideologies, and Family Specialists," *Marriage and Family Living*, Vol. 21 (February, 1959), pp. 3–12.

Morris, J. K., *Premarital Counseling—A Manual for Ministers* (New York, Scribner, 1960).

Mudd, Emily H., *The Practice of Marriage Counseling* (New York, Association Press, 1951).

Oates, Wayne, *Where to Go for Help* (Philadelphia, The Westminster Press, 1959).

Poffenberger, Thomas, "Family Life Education in a Scientific Age," *Marriage and Family Living*, Vol. 21 (May, 1959), pp. 150–154.

Rutledge, Aaron L., "The Future of Marriage Counseling," *The Merrill-Palmer Quarterly* (Summer, 1955), pp. 141–147.

Skidmore, Rex A., Garrett, Hulda Van Streeter, and Skidmore, C. Jay, *Marriage Consulting* (New York, Harper & Row, 1956).

Stewart, Charles William, *The Minister as a Marriage Counselor* (Nashville, Abingdon, 1961).

Stroup, Atlee L., and Glasser, Paul, "The Orientation and Focus of Marriage Counseling," *Marriage and Family Living,* Vol. 21 (February, 1959), pp. 20–24.

Virtue, Maxine Boord, *Family Cases in Court* (Durham, Duke University Press, 1956).

Wise, Carroll, *Pastoral Counseling* (New York, Harper & Row, 1951).

QUESTIONS AND EXERCISES

1. How do you explain the fact that marriage and family life reform has received only lukewarm public support?
2. Discuss from your point of view the potentialities and problems involved in the use of family life education programs in the public high school.
3. What to you would be the difficulties involved in developing a national family life policy for the United States?
4. Read some of the sociological literature on *social movements.* Write a paper in which you indicate whether or not you think the developing family life organization indicates the existence of a social movement.
5. From your point of view what are the possibilities of providing, during the next decade, adequate marriage and family counseling services in the average American community?
6. If you were sitting as a board member of a foundation which had decided to put its money into family life programs, what types of proposals would you encourage? Why?
7. Read the various articles in the literature by Judge Paul Alexander and others dealing with the family court movement. Write a critique of the proposed programs.
8. In your estimation what is the role of the private agency as against the public agency in furthering sound marriage and family relationships in the United States?
9. Discuss the pros and cons of uniform marriage and divorce legislation in the United States.
10. Arrange a panel composed of ministers, lawyers, social workers, and family life educators. Have these people discuss various methods of strengthening family life.
11. Do you predict a higher or lower state of family disorganization in America for the next two decades? Justify your answer.
12. Ideally what role should the Federal government play in promoting successful marriage and family living in the United States?

APPENDIX

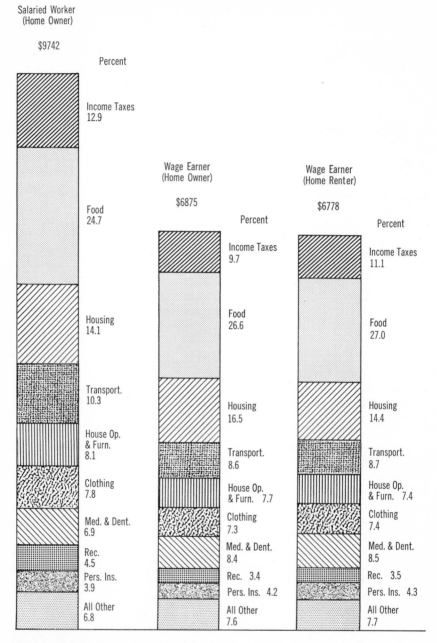

FIGURE 22. *Budgets for Salaried Worker and Wage Earner with Percents of Major Categories, September, 1961.* SOURCE: Reprinted from The Heller Committee, *Quantity and Cost Budgets for Two Income Levels* (Berkeley: The University of California, 1962) by permission of The Institute of Business and Economic Research.

Name Index

Subject Index